taken

room.

D1243340

ce

HANDBOOK OF
CONTEMPORARY CHINA

HANDBOOK OF CONTEMPORARY CHINA

edited by

William S Tay

Professor Emeritus
Hong Kong University of Science and Technology
and the University of California, San Diego

Alvin Y So

Chair Professor, Division of Social Science
Hong Kong University of Science and Technology

NEW JERSEY · LONDON · SINGAPORE · BEIJING · SHANGHAI · HONG KONG · TAIPEI · CHENNAI

Published by

World Scientific Publishing Co. Pte. Ltd.

5 Toh Tuck Link, Singapore 596224

USA office: 27 Warren Street, Suite 401-402, Hackensack, NJ 07601

UK office: 57 Shelton Street, Covent Garden, London WC2H 9HE

British Library Cataloguing-in-Publication Data
A catalogue record for this book is available from the British Library.

HANDBOOK OF CONTEMPORARY CHINA

ISBN-13 978-981-4350-08-2
ISBN-10 981-4350-08-7

Typeset by Stallion Press
Email: enquiries@stallionpress.com

Printed in Singapore by B & Jo Enterprise Pte Ltd

PREFACE

China launched its reform just over thirty years ago. No crystal ball then could have predicted its outcome. Titles of recent books such as *China Rules the World: The End of the Western World and the Birth of a New Global Order* and *The Beijing Consensus: How China's Authoritarian Model Will Dominate the Twenty-First Century* clearly confirm that China has finally arrived. Statistical projections from venerable institutions such as International Monetary Fund or Goldman Sachs appear to point toward a robust future: the former predicts that China's share of global GDP (in current prices) will pass the 10% mark in 2013; and the latter that China will surpass the US in terms of GDP in 2027.

There are, however, several well-known Chinese sayings which remind us about the truism that to know the past is to know the future. It is with this in mind that we accepted the invitation from Dr. Lim Tai-Wei on behalf of World Scientific to organize a handbook on China's reform for a professional and general readership interested in visiting or revisiting the travails of the last thirty years.

William S. Tay
Alvin Y. So

December, 2010

CONTENTS

1

DEVELOPMENT MODEL

Alvin Y. So

Hong Kong University of Science and Technology

Abstract

This chapter aims to provide a critical examination of the China Model of development. This chapter has three parts: first, a discussion what the major characteristics of the China Model are and why it is attractive to developing countries; second, an argument that researchers should not take the China Model for granted as its constituents are highly contested, and the term "Beijing Consensus" ironically belies the fact that there is no consensus on how to characterize China's developmental experience over the past thirty years; third, an analysis of the implications of the China Model for developing countries by examining the following three questions: (1) How can researchers move beyond the ideological fault line in the China field? (2) Why does the China Model work while other models such as neoliberalism and state socialism fail? (3) Can the China Model be copied?

Keywords: Economic development; export-led industrialization; poverty reduction; technological upgrading; neoliberalism; Maoism; socialism; post-socialist development; diaspora capitalism; local development; labor migration; Beijing consensus.

Since the turn of this century, the mass media have been buzzing regularly about China's remarkable development (*China Daily*, 2009; Wines, 2010; *Washington Post*, 2009):

- China became the largest producer of many key industrial and agricultural products by 2007, including rolled steel (566 million tons), coal

(2.5 billion tons), chemical fertilizers (58 tons) and personal computers (121 million, or 30% of the world's output).

- China surpassed the United States of America to become the world's largest automobile market — in units, if not in dollars. China also super-seded Germany as the biggest exporter of manufactured goods. In 2010, China — the world fifth-largest economy four years ago — overtook Japan as the second largest economy of the world (Barboza, 2010).
- China had a US$265 billion trade surplus with the US and held US$1.4 trillion in US Treasury in 2009.

Influenced by these promising economic indicators, both the mass media and policy circles have been using the *China Model* of development to discuss China's fast-speed economic development. The term, since 2004, has been upgraded to the *Beijing Consensus*, representing the alternative economic development model to the Washington Consensus, which is a US-led plan for reforming and developing the economics of small, third-world countries (Ramo, 2004). A Google Search on "Beijing Consensus" yields 110 results, showing that the term has gained popularity in the mass media.

It is reported that the China Model has begun to influence the developing countries in the South. *The Australia* (2010) stated that "after the Olympic Games, the success of China's model of development is increasingly apparent." The China Model was reported to be very well-received at the China-Africa Business Summit in Cape Town in 2009 and "is likely to inspire both Islamic countries and African countries to develop faster" (BBC, 2009a, 2009b).

However, despite the wide circulation of the term "China Model" since approximately 2004, not enough scholarly attention has been paid to China's developmental experience. Consequently, researchers are still not clear what exactly the China Model is. The aim of this chapter is to provide a critical examination of the China model of development. This chapter has three parts: first, a discussion of what are the major characteristics of the China Model and its attractiveness to the developing countries; second, an argument that researchers should not take the China Model for granted as its con-stituents are highly contested, and the term "Beijing Consensus" ironically belies the fact that there is no consensus on how to characterize China's developmental experience over the past thirty years; third, an analysis of the implications of the China Model for developing countries by specifically try-ing to answer the following three questions: (1) How can researchers move beyond the ideological fault line in the China field? (2) Why does the China Model work while other models such as neoliberalism and state socialism fail? (3) Can the China Model be copied?

Characteristics

Since the mass media and policy studies reports have not spelled out system-atically the nature of the China Model, this chapter takes the liberty to bring together key arguments in the literature for a reconstruction of the major characteristics of the China Model:

- *Fast-speed economic growth.* From 1978 to 2001, China's annual average growth rate was 8.1% and its annual rate of industrial growth was 11.5% (Kiely, 2008, p. 355). In a short span of 30 years, China has been trans-formed from a poor, backward third world country to an economic powerhouse of the world.

- *Export-led industrialization.* Since the turn of the century, China has become the global factory and the workshop of the world. China exports grew from US$18.1 billion in 1978 to US$266 billion in 2001, reflecting an annual average growth rate of 12%. By 2001, manufacturing exports accounted for 90% of total exports (Nolan, 2004, p. 910).

- *Innovation and technological upgrading.* Despite the assumption that China is trapped in labor-intensive, low-tech, sweatshop export produc-tion, China has modernized its educational system, upgraded its science and research capabilities, and participated in high-tech production. From the 1990s on, foreign corporations began to transfer a significant amount of their research and development activity into China. Microsoft, Oracle, Motorola, Siemens, IBM, and Intel have all set up research laboratories in China because of its "growing importance and sophistication as a market for technology" and "its large reservoir of skilled but inexperienced scientists, and its consumers, still relatively poor but growing richer and eager for new technology" (Buckley, 2004). In the first decade of the new century, China began to move up the value-added ladder of production and to compete with South Korea, Japan, Taiwan, and Singapore in spheres such as electronics and machine tools.

- *Poverty reduction.* China managed to reduce the share of the population liv-ing on less than US$1 per day from 64% in 1981 to 16% by 2006; effectively lifting 400 million people out of absolute poverty (UNDP, 2006). Thus, the China Model has worked more effectively than the IMF-designated Structural Adjustment Program in the Washington Consensus model for sub-Saharan Africa and the "shock therapy" for Russia (Zhang, 2006).

- *Independent and autonomous development.* According to Ramo (2004, p. 3–4), China shows "how to fit into the international order in such a way that allows [developing countries to be] truly independent, to protect their way of life and political choices in a world with a single powerful centre of gravity." As such, Beijing Consensus can be interpreted as "a theory of self-determination, one that stresses using leverage to move big, hegemonic powers that may be tempted to tread on your toes" (Dirlik, 2004, p. 3).

In short, the major characteristics of China Model are fast-speed economic growth, export-led industrialization, innovation and technological upgrading, poverty reduction, and independent and autonomous development.

Contestations and Interpretations

In recent years, as China has been making inroads in Africa, the Middle East, and Latin America for raw materials and minerals. As Chinese state enterprises are encouraged to extend their investments into other parts of the world, the China Model is put forward to provide an ideological foundation for the overseas adventures of the Chinese state and the Chinese transnationals. As Dirlik (2004, p. 2) remarks, the China Model "appears, more than anything, to be a sales gimmick — selling China to the world, while selling certain ideas of development to the Chinese leadership."

Developing and post-socialist countries are buying into this China model because they are highly dissatisfied with neo-liberalism's Washington Consensus, the shock therapy, and Structural Adjustment Program (Rodrik, 2006). The Brazilian leader Lula da Silva, for example, expressed his admiration for China and its ability to globalize without giving up its autonomy and sovereignty (Dirlik, 2004).

Developing countries certainly can learn from China's developmental experience, like export-led industrialization and poverty reduction. However, to portray the above features as the "China Model" becomes an exercise in ideological construction. Like other ideological models which articulate only half-truth, the China Model tends to accentuate, exaggerate, or idealize its positive features, while at the same time tries to hide, minimize, or define away its negative traits.

Once researchers start to *problematize* the characteristics of the China Model, they will find that the traits in the China Model are highly contested and the celebration of China Model is pre-mature, as seen in the following debates:

Problems of the Fast-speed Export-led Growth Model. Those who are on the left tend to take a critical stand on China's remarkable economic growth rate. Hung (2009, p. 25), for instance, argues that China's export-led growth model is "rooted in a developmental approach that bankrupts the countryside and prolongs the unlimited supply of low-cost migrant labor to coastal export industries. The resultant ever-increasing trade surplus may inflate China's global financial power, in the form of expanded holdings of the debt, but the long-term suppression of manufacturing wages restrains the growth of China's consumption power," makes it very difficult for China to re-orient its development model to achieve a balance between domestic consumption and exports. Thus, China can not free itself from dependence on the collapsing US consumer market and addiction to risky US debt.

Ching Pao-yu (n.d., pp. 39–40) also shares the observation that high-speed economic growth has not done China any good. Ching argues that "the development of the past thirty years has thrown tens of millions of workers out of the factories and has also ruined the foundation for long-term development of China's countryside. The capitalist development of the past thirty years has deprived a large portion of the Chinese population their basic necessities of life and has also ruined China's fragile environment. China has many environmental crises as a result and many more surely to come."

Technological Upgrading or Technological Dependence. Though the China Model highlights the commitment to technological innovation in China's developmental experience, Wang Yong (2008, p. 26) counters that "export-oriented growth model cultivates strong inertia, locking China in at the lower end of the value-added chain."

China's transformation into a world factory means that the Chinese firms have successfully hooked into global commodity chain and become assembly lines for foreign-brand transnationals, though the lion's share of the profits has gone to foreign investors. Kiely (2008) argues that this kind of linkage has *not* led to any significant technological upgrading and domestic linkages which have characterized the shift to developed country status, or indeed to the form of upgrading which characterized the first tier of East Asian newly industrializing countries.

China's Industrial Development Report also reports that transnationals have not exported their most current technology to China, and the technology they have exported to China is under strict controls to prevent dissemination (CASS, 2003, p. 28).

Autonomous Development or the Head Servant of the US. There is also a controversy regarding China's autonomous development. Ching (n.d., p. 38), for example, argues that "China has lost its autonomy in developing its economy just as other developing countries have. China is now dependent on the investment of multinational corporations and the foreign technology these corporations bring in. It is also dependent on the expansion of exports to the international market in order to maintain its high GDP growth."

How important are these transnationals to China's development? Roughly 2/3 of the increase in Chinese exports in the past 12 years can be attributed to non-Chinese-owned global companies and their joint ventures. Foreign-owned global corporations account for 60% of Chinese exports to the US. In 2004, retail giant Wal-Mart was China's 8th largest trading partner ahead of Russia, Australia, and Canada (Roach, 2006).

To Hung (2009, p. 16), China has little autonomy or independence. Instead, China is merely "the Head Servant" of the US and transnational corporations, "leading the others in providing cheap exports to the US and using its hard-earned savings to finance American purchase of those exports."

Poverty Reduction or Rising Social Inequality. Instead of the highly-celebrated poverty reduction in the China Model, researchers have pointed to the worsening income inequality in China. The Gini coefficient for household income in China, for example, rose from 0.33 in 1980, to 0.40 in 1994, and to 0.46 in 2000. The last figure surpasses the degree of inequality in Thailand, India, and Indonesia. In 2004, observers believed that China's Gini coefficient had exceeded 0.50, placing its income inequality near Brazilian and South African levels (Hart-Landsberg and Burkett, 2004, p. 59). Within a short span of 30 years, therefore, China has transformed itself from one of the most egalitarian to one of the most unequal societies in the world (Wang Feng, 2008).

Political Stability or Rising Social Conflict. The China Model portrays the Chinese communist party-state as fully in charge with the developmental process in China. The party-state also has widespread legitimacy, and unlike its communist counterparts in Soviet Union and Eastern Europe, the Chinese communist party-state is not under any threat of revolution. What the China Model fails to highlight, however, is that widening social inequality has caused social problems (such as rural bankruptcy, and labor unrests) which threaten social stability and the survival of the communist party-state.

In response to increasing social inequality and the cutting back of social benefits by the post-socialist party-state, the Chinese working class has become restless. *China Labour Bulletin* (2002, p. 1) reports that "almost every week in Hong Kong and mainland China, newspapers bring reports of some kind of labor action: a demonstration demanding pensions; a railway line being blocked by angry, unpaid workers; or collective legal action against illegal employer behavior such as body searches or forced overtime." According to the official statistics, in 1998 there were 6,767 collective actions (usually strikes or go-slows with a minimum of three people taking part) involving 251,268 people. This represents an increase in collective actions of 900% from the 1990s. In 2000, this figure jumped to 8,247 collective actions involving 259,445 workers (*China Labour Bulletin*, 2002, p. 2). Given such widespread labor protests, it is no wonder that the Chinese government has identified the labor problem as the biggest threat to social and political stability (So, 2007).

A Model or a Culprit to Pull Down Global Wage Rate. Though China is constructed as the model, many countries still see it as a competitor for foreign investments and jobs.

An *Economist* (2001) report noted the "alarm and despair" with which China's neighbors reacted to its rise: "Japan, South Korea and Taiwan fear a hollowing out of their industries, as factories move to low-cost China.... Southeast Asia worries about 'dislocation' in trade and investment flows [to China]." In addition, Global Labor Strategies (2008, p. 8) reported that "workers, communities, and countries throughout the world are confronting the challenges posed by China's growing role in the global economy. About 25% of the global work force is now Chinese. The 'China price' increasingly sets the global norm for wages and working standards at both the high and low ends of the production chain. As a result, the hard-won gains of workers in the global North are being rapidly undermined while the aspirations of workers in the developing world are being dashed as China becomes the wage setting country in many industries." Therefore, China as an export powerhouse only intensifies economic tensions and contradictions through the South, to the detriment of workers everywhere.

In sum, although the China Model and its derivative is labeled as "the Beijing Consensus," there is simply no consensus concerning the major ingredients of the China Model. While the proponents of the China Model want to highlight its positive features, such as its remarkable growth rate, export competitiveness and technological upgrading, poverty reduction, and independent development, critics of the China Model are quick to point out the harmful consequences of the China Model, such as rural bankruptcy, trapped in low-tech assembly line production, dependent on US consumer market, rising social inequality and social conflict, and the downward pull on global wage rate, etc. Moreover, since the reports of the China Model tend to be promoted by the policy circles and by the mass media, they fail to provide detailed documentation to support their arguments. As a result, the critics, especially those on the Left, tend to see the China Model as an exercise in ideology construction to justify the global reach of the Chinese party-state and transnational corporations.

What then is the implication of the China Model for the developing countries in the South? Critics have provided a great service by problematizing the China Model, pointing out China's path of developmental has many structural problems and many undesirable consequences. In short, the critics have been arguing that China could not and should not possibly be celebrated as a "model" for other developing countries to emulate.

Although this paper agrees with the critics that China is not without its developmental problems, the critics seem to have gone overboard by defining away the remarkable achievement of Chinese development over the past thirty years. This paper argues that if researchers want to make any advance in understanding the remarkable development of China, they need to perform the following three tasks: (1) move beyond the ideological lens to capture the complexity and ambiguity of China's development, (2) explain why China's development has worked while other packages like neoliberalism and state socialism have failed, and (3) explore the possibility whether the pattern of China's development can be copied by the countries in the South.

Beyond the Ideological Debate: The Ambiguity of China's Development

Studies of China's development are bound to be controversial because it defies any simple ideological labeling. Wallerstein (2010) articulates this issue well when he poses the question "How to think about China"? Wallerstein (2010) points out that people tend to debate the following three issues when they discuss China.

The first debate is whether to think of China as essentially as a socialist country or as essentially as a capitalist one. China of course still proclaims itself to be socialist; and China continues to be governed by the Communist Party. On the other hand, China seems to base the actual operations of its internal economic operations, and certainly its world trade, on market principles. On this capitalist-socialist divide, China seems to be neither purely capitalist nor socialist, but a hybrid of both capitalism and socialism, thus the Chinese communist party still insists that China belongs to "*market socialism*" (Szelenyi, 2010).

On the state-market divide, China is reported to be closely pursuing the path of neoliberalism, like liberating its market, downsizing its state bureaucracy, loosening its regulations, cutting back its social welfare commitment, privatizing its state economy, etc. On the other hand, despite these neoliberal policies, China still has a powerful state and a large state sector. The party-state is still in full control of the market, including the huge infrastructure of heavy industries, the promotion of industrial policy, the legacy of central planning, and corporatist control over the society (Baek, 2005, p. 487). To capture the above contradiction, So and Chu (forthcoming) prefers to label

China as "*state neoliberalist*" because China is neither purely statist nor neoliberalist, but a hybrid possessing both the characteristics of state developmentalism and neoclassical neoliberalism. According to So and Chu (forthcoming), state neoliberalism emerged when the party-state's survival was threatened by the growing number of labor protests in the cities and numerous peasant protests in the countryside at the turn of the 21st century. In order to preempt the intensification of class conflict, the party-state was induced to slow down, to stop, or to reverse the neoliberalism policy. Under the policy of "building a new socialist countryside" and a "harmonious society," the Hu/Wen regime has tried to move toward a more balanced direction between economic growth and social development. State neoliberalism policy has advocated a transfer of resources from the state to strengthen the fiscal foundation of the countryside. Besides abolishing the agricultural tax to help relieve the burden on farmers, the state increased its rural expenditure by 15% (to $15 billion) to bankroll guaranteed minimum living allowances for farmers, and an 87% hike (to $4 billion) for the health-care budget (Liu, 2007).

On the export-import divide, China is said to be having an extreme version of the export-growth model, as its trade dependence (measured by the total value of exports as a percentage of GDP) has been mounting continuously, reaching a level never attained in other East Asian economies (Hung, 2009). On the other hand, China has built up a strong import substitutive capital-intensive industry to capture the huge domestic Chinese market. China is able to have import-substitution and to produce for the global economy because imports and exports are performed by a dual economic structure of public and non-public sectors. On the one hand, small and medium-scale companies have propped up the export-oriented economy and investment in these companies have been supplied from the curb market rather than banks. On the other hand, large companies in the public sector have specialized in upstream sectors that had been developed by the import substitution industrialization. The finance of these large state enterprises has absolutely depended on state banks and they accomplished economy of scale by monopolies (Baek, 2005, p. 494). In China, the export sector and the import-substitution sector coexist side by side. Lee and Mattews (2009, p. 12) suggest that the export sector will provide competitive pressure to curb the potential for rent-seeking for the state enterprises, while the import sector can provide nurturing to domestic firms needed to bring the firms to the point where they could withstand the fierceful competition of the world market. After thirty years of development, China's corporation can produce commodity to meet the demands of the domestic market and to compete with those of the foreign corporation. In this respect, China's economy is neither purely export-led nor dominated by import substitution, but a hybrid economy walking on two legs to capture the dynamics of an export-led as well as an import-substituted economy.

On the core-periphery divide, the issue is whether China is still part of the South or has become part of the North. Thirty years ago, there was no doubt. China was a poor, third world country. China attended the Afro-Asian conference in Bandung in 1955, and China presented itself everywhere as a promoter of the interests of the South. But today China is classified as the strongest of the "emergent" nation and the second strongest economy in the world. The world press now speaks of the G-2 (the US and China), who in effect share world power. Again, China is neither a core nor a periphery, but a hybrid called "semi-periphery" which, in world-systems perspective, behaves like a periphery to the core, but behaves like a core to the periphery (like giving out aids and expanding its influence in Africa, Latin America, and the Middle East).

In short, researchers need to go beyond the dualism of capitalist vs. socialist, state vs. market, core vs. periphery in order to capture the complexity of China's development. If researchers can move beyond their ideological lens and obscurantism (Pan, 2007), they will find that China's developmental experience is highly ambiguous and it doesn't fit any conventional label in the literature. However, ambiguity aside, researchers still need to answer the question that critics of the China Model fail to raise, i.e., why is China able to transform itself from a poor, third world country to an economic powerhouse in thirty years?

Why the China Model Works?

In the China field, it is often stated that the communist experiment under Mao was a disaster. The Great Leap Forward in the late 1950s led to famine and the deaths of tens of millions of Chinese. The ten years of Cultural Revolution (1966–1976) turned the Chinese society upside down and resulted in political anarchy. In this scenario, China's march to modernization began only in 1978, after the rise of Deng Xiaoping, a pragmatist, who paid little attention to the revolutionary ideology of Mao. Hence, Deng became the hero of Chinese modernization, while Mao was held responsible for the economic backwardness and political turmoil in the first phase of the Chinese communist rule.

What is missing in the above account, however, is that China's remarkable economic growth over the past thirty years actually owes much to the historical heritage of the Maoist era. Despite many shortcomings, the Maoist legacy has provided China with a strong Leninist party-state, with all the powers concentrated in the communist party. Only political organizations (like peasants' associations and labor unions) formally sponsored by the party were allowed to operate; other organizations were either made ineffective or simply banned from operation. This Leninist party-state was all-powerful in the sense that it had extended both vertically and horizontally to every sphere in the Chinese society. Vertically, the Leninist party-state was the first Chinese state that was able to exert its political control all the way down to village, family, and individual levels. Horizontally, there was a great expansion of state functions. The Leninist party-state did not just collect taxes and keep social order, but also oversaw such functions as education, health care, marriage, culture, economic policy, and carried out the radical socialist policies of Land Reform, Collectivization, and the Cultural Revolution. After 1978, although the Chinese state was no longer interested in promoting revolutionary socialism, it still inherited a strong state machinery to carry out its developmental policy.

The critical issue, then, is how to explain the dramatic transformation of the revolutionary state in Maoist China to the developmental state in the reform era. This paper argues that the fading of the Cold War provided the pre-condition for China to re-enter the world-economy, and the success of the Asian NIEs (Newly Industrializing Economies) and their industrial relocation provided the incentives for the Chinese leaders to pursue developmental objectives, while the passing of the old generation and the occurrence of natural disasters provided the triggering events to overcome the inertia of the status quo.

The Fading of the Cold War. If the Cold War and the forced withdrawal from the world-economy prevented China from pursuing either export-oriented industrialization or import substitution in the 1950s and the 1960s, the fading of the Cold War since the late 1970s had provided the pre-condition for China to re-enter the world-economy to pursue developmental objectives.

The late 1970s was a period of declining American hegemony. Economically, the US faced the problems of inflation, low productivity, and recession. Its products were under strong competition with Japanese and German manufactures in the world market. Politically, the US was still plagued by its defeat in Vietnam and its failed attempt to fend off global Soviet expansionism. At this historical conjuncture, the US welcomed China back to the world-economy. China could be a new regional power to counterbalance Soviet military expansion and Japanese economic expansion in East Asia. Moreover, the vast Chinese market, the cheap Chinese labor, and the abundant Chinese raw materials and minerals could considerably increase the competitive power of American industry in the world economy.

East Asian Industrial Relocation. With US support in the 1950s and the 1960s, Japan, South Korea, Taiwan, and Hong Kong had become highly industrialized and their people enjoyed a much higher living standard than that in China. Thus, the Chinese state was motivated to follow the path of its successful East Asian neighbors to engage in export-oriented industrialization.

Furthermore, as Hong Kong, Taiwan, and South Korea were upgraded to the status of NIEs in the late 1970s, they gradually lost their geopolitical privileges with the US. They, too, had to face the trade restrictions (tariffs, quota, rising foreign currency value). Due to their economic success, there were also labor shortages, increasing labor disputes, escalating land prices, and the emergence of environmental protests — all of which served to raise the cost of production in the East Asian NIEs. As a result, the Asian NIEs felt the need of promoting an industrial relocation in order to secure a stable supply of cheap, docile labor force, and other resources in the 1980s.

Industrial relocation of the NIEs provided a strong incentive for the Chinese state to promote developmental objectives. From the Chinese perspective, China could be a favourable site for the NIEs' relocation because it has abundant cheap labor, land, and other resources. China is also close to Hong Kong, Taiwan, and South Korea, and they share a common Confucian cultural heritage with strong emphases on education, a diligent work ethic, and obedience to superiors (Gong and Jang, 1998). Consequently, China set up four special economic zones (SEZs) in 1979, opened fourteen coastal cities and Hainan Island in 1984 and three delta areas in 1985 for foreign investment, and pursued a coastal developmental strategy to enhance export industrialization in 1988.

Triggering Events. Although the fading of the Cold War and the NIEs' industrial relocation provided the precondition and an incentive for the Chinese state to transform itself into a developmental state, several triggering events were needed to overcome the inertia of the communist status quo.

Lin Yimin (2003) points out that the critical event that set in motion the efforts to reform the economic system was the passing of the old generation of revolutionary leaders. The death of Mao in 1976 was followed by the rise of a new coalition of political leaders who were leaning or receptive to some form of economic institutional change. Most of them were victims of the Cultural Revolution. Their return was accompanied by a national rehabilitation of lower level party-state functionaries. Most of these functionaries had prior experience in formulating and implementing economic policies.

Lin further explains that the shift in policy focus from socialist egalitarianism to economic development and the reshuffling of local leaders opened way for bottom-up institutional innovation. In provinces like Anhui, pro-reform leaders provided tolerance and even encouragement to certain attempts made by grassroots officials. This significantly changed the political risk perceived by the rank-and-file of the local state apparatus. Subsequently, when severe national disasters hit during 1977–1979, some local officials resorted to various forms of family production and justified their rule-breaking on the ground of coping with natural disasters. The good results of family farming in turn provided a ground of justification for the arrangement to be introduced to other provinces, which later led to decollectivization and the institutionalization of Household Responsibility system in the countryside. The great success of the economic reforms in the agricultural sector — as shown by the crop output growth from 2.5% during 1954–1978 to 5.9% during 1978–1984 — further empowered the Chinese state to develop various developmental strategies.

Developmental Strategies and Why They Worked: The Legacy of the Maoist Era. Once the Chinese state decided to pursue developmental objectives, it found itself blessed with many legacies of the Maoist era. To start with, the Maoist legacy of economic backwardness ironically worked to the advantage of economic reforms in the late 1970s. As Andrew Walder (1996, p. 9) points out, at the outset of the reforms, employment of China was 75% agriculture; in the Soviet Union 75% in industry. Since the Soviet Union was already an urbanized industrial society, Soviet economic reforms necessitated technological and organization innovations to boost industrial productivity in the urban sector. But since China was still mostly agricultural, the state could achieve rapid growth rates by simply taking labor out of agriculture and increasing its productivity by putting it to work in industry.

Second, the Maoist legacy of "self-reliance" resulted in a debt free economy for pre-reform China. Instead of relying on external support (such as Soviet aid, technology, and expertise), Mao focused on a "self-reliance" model of development, stressing national autonomy, the pride to be a poor country, mass mobilization, local development, and labor-intensive industries. As a result, China incurred almost no foreign debt when the state started its economic reforms in 1978. In stark contrast to many Eastern European states and Russia, China did not need to devote huge resources to servicing foreign debt, nor China need to resort to crushing bailout packages by the International Monetary Fund to shore up its economy.

Third, the Maoist legacy provided the much-needed rural infrastructure and local institutions to carry out the economic reforms. It was during the

Maoist era that reservoirs were constructed, irrigation system strengthened, and drainage network improved. During the Great Leap Forward, the state mobilized millions of peasants to construct dams, reservoirs, and large-scale irrigation systems for the communes. It was also during the Maoist era that rural industries and enterprises were set up in the communes; local officials accumulated managerial experience through running commune and brigade enterprises; and local governments were asked to promote development in the community. The Maoist commune model and its decentralization policy provided the medium to tap local resources, to train local leaders, and to arouse local initiatives. Without all these infrastructure and institutional foundations built in the Maoist era, it is doubtful whether agricultural productivity could increase so rapidly at the beginning of the reforms, and whether local village and township enterprises could play the leading role in China's industrialization in 1980s and 1990s.

With the Chinese party-state in full control of the development process, it carried out the following strategies of development: decentralization and local development, mobilizing diaspora capitalists, and controlled labor migration.

Decentralization and Local Development. Attracted by the policy of fiscal decentralization through which local governments could keep part of the tax revenue, local governments quickly engaged in market activities. The product was the formation of township and village enterprises (TVEs), which were not bound by the central plan and were free to seek out market opportunities. Kyung-Sup Chang (2003) remarks that for local cadres, running rural industries was no new experience since they had been in charge of rural industries since the Great Leap Forward in the late 1950s. Seizing the golden opportunity created by the policy of fiscal decentralization, many rural cadres have created a favorable political and administrative environment so the nascent businessmen did not have to be afraid of being condemned as "blood-sucking capitalists exploiting the workers." Once they received the signal that capital investment was tolerated by the "communist" party-state and after they were told that "to get rich is glorious," they began to initiate new industrial ventures, renovate or build factories, set up corporate organizations, mobilize villagers' economic resources, secure financial and technical cooperation from urban enterprises, and staff the management of rural industrial enterprises. Focusing on the South China case, George Lin (2003) points out that a new "bottom up" development mechanism has taken shape in which initiatives have been made primarily by local governments to solicit overseas Chinese and domestic capital, mobilize labor and land resources, and lead the local economy to enter the orbit of international division of labor and global competition. As a result, South China has experienced rural industrialization through which a great number of surplus rural laborers entered the TVEs without moving into the city. In the South Chinese countryside, it is common to find industrial and agricultural activities standing side by side. Lin stresses that the geographic outcome of intense rural-urban interaction in the countryside has been the formation of a dispersed pattern of spatial distribution that does not confirm to the classic definition of urban or rural but displays the characteristics of both types.

Mobilizing Chinese Diaspora Capitalism. In Eastern Europe, ethnic division is reinforced by religious conflicts and national conflicts, leading to ethnic violence and making ethnic separatism a highly explosive issue. It was the constant rebellions in ethnic minority regions that weakened the communist state, eventually led to its downfall and the breaking up of the Soviet Union.

However, in China, ethnic trait is generally a valuable asset for economic development, instead of being a source of political instability. Before 1978, Chinese diaspora capitalism thrived in Hong Kong, Taiwan, Singapore, and overseas Chinese communities. After the Chinese state adopted an open door policy for foreign investment in 1978, Hong Kong accounted for the bulk of China's foreign investment and foreign trade. By the early 1990s, Taiwan became the second largest trading partner and investor for Mainland China.

Focusing on Guangdong's Dongguan County as a case study, George Lin (2003) shows that the local government has sought every possible opportunity to cultivate kinship ties and interpersonal trust with the diaspora capitalists in Hong Kong in order to attract them to invest in Dongguan County. Special policies, including taxation concessions and preferential treatment regarding the import of necessary equipment and the handling of foreign currency, were announced to attract foreign investment. A special office was set up by the county government to serve Hong Kong investors with efficient personnel and simplified bureaucratic procedures. Economic cooperation between Dongguan and Hong Kong was arranged creatively and flexibly in a variety of forms, including joint ventures, cooperative ventures, export processing, and compensation trade. The general pattern is that designing and marketing are handled in Hong Kong, while labor intensive processes are performed in Dongguan. Access to cheap labor enables Hong Kong diaspora capitalists to compete effectively in the global market, and export processing has created jobs and income for Mainland China.

In discussing the case of Fujian province, Hsin-Huang Michael Hsiao (2003) also points out that Chinese diaspora capitalists have played an important role in the economic development of Fujian. In the 1980s, many

Southeast Asian Chinese business groups with Fujian origins, such as the Philippines' Tan Yu and Lucio C. Tan, Indonesia's Liem Sioe Liong, and Malaysia's Robert Kuok, made substantial investments in Fujian. By the early 1990s, Taiwan capital began to enter Fujian on a massive scale. By 1997, Fujian had attracted more than 4,900 Taiwanese enterprises, with the total realized investment exceeding US$6.9 billion. Taiwan capital has been highly diversified, ranging from small-scale labor-intensive manufacturing industries to capital-intensive heavy industries and high-tech industries.

Controlling Labor Migration. Before the reform era, the household registration (*hukou*) system had kept farmers in the countryside. In order to transfer resources from the rural to the urban sector, the Chinese state has loosened the household registration system since 1978, starting a trend of *non-hukou* migrant population from the countryside, reaching the size of about 100 million migrants in the late 1990s.

Kam Wing Chan (2003) contends that economic development in the reform era in China is intimately linked with migration. Migration is a redistribution of labor that helps balance China's regional supply and demand. The vast pools of rural migrants provide plentiful supply of cheap labor in sustaining China's urban economic boom. This labor force is also flexible, able, and willing to move quickly into new growth areas. In the cities, the full cost of hiring a migrant worker is only about one quarter of that of a local worker. Migrant workers are also willing to work not only for less and for long hours, but also often under unsafe conditions with minimal protection. The increasing supply of labor from outside has fostered the development of an urban labor market.

Kam Wing Chan also reveals the generally positive impact of migration for rural areas. Out-migration is an effective and cheap way to siphon off surplus rural labor and ease pressure on local land and resources. In addition, remittances have become a major contribution by migrant workers to their family back home. Chan estimates that remittances in the size of 180 billion yuan are sent back to rural areas every year, equivalent to 15% of China's agricultural sectors' GDP. Furthermore, working in the cities is an important opportunity for many farmers to learn about the modern world and skills. It is not uncommon for returnees to use their savings, skills, and business contacts they bring back to start up or invest in small businesses. And the remittances allow those working on the farm to purchase fertilizers and other needed modern inputs (such as better seeds) for farming.

Reform Sequence. Finally, the Chinese state benefited from carrying out reforms in the countryside before proposing any reform on urban economy. Rural reforms were much less complicated than urban reforms. In the late

1970s, the Chinese state increased procurement prices for agricultural products, encouraged peasants to engage in cash crop and rural industrial production, and allowed peasants to work in nearby market towns and faraway cities. With the success of the rural reforms, the Chinese state was more confident to work on the complicated urban reforms in the 1980s. Rising agricultural productivity, in turn, released surplus labor from the countryside, providing a large number of cheap laborers to urban factories.

In the Soviet Union, however, political reforms were carried out before economic reforms, with the hope that democratization would provide the communist party with the needed support to overcome bureaucratic resistance toward economic reforms. The Soviet Union also carried out reforms in urban areas first because of the deep-rooted problems in the countryside. But political reforms had unintentionally released new political forces that opposed the communist party, and urban unrest eventually led to the overthrow of the communist state in the Soviet Union.

In contrast, the Chinese state promoted economic reforms before carrying out major democratic reforms. In the late 1970s, communes were dismantled and peasants were asked to be responsible for their own living. In the early 1980s, the Chinese state tried to promote enterprise reforms to increase the power of the managers. In the mid 1980s, the Chinese state further opened fourteen coastal cities to attract foreign investment. Although in the reform period the Chinese state showed more tolerance toward dissent, granted more freedom toward the its citizens, and allowed local elections at the village level, the Chinese state was reluctant to promote any serious democratic reform to allow multi-party elections at the provincial and national level. As a result, the Chinese state could retain the Leninist structure. It did not have to share power with other political parties, and neither did it have to worry about the different critical voices in the civil society and the uncertainty of election outcomes. Without being distracted by democratic reforms, the Chinese state was able to concentrate on the economic front to promote its modernization programs.

Reform from above. Finally, China benefited from adopting the strategy of "reform from above." Even though China faced many serious developmental problems in the mid 1970s, the situation was not desperate. The Chinese state was not under the threat of foreign invasion, economic bankruptcy, or rebellion from below. As such, the party-state still had the autonomy and capacity to propose and implement various structural reforms under its control. The state could select certain types of reform, could vary the speed of reform, and, most importantly, had the freedom of making corrections of its mistakes.

Therefore, very different from the "shock therapy" approach in Eastern Europe, the reform in China has been a gradual, adaptive process without a clear blueprint. John McMillan and Barry Naughton (1992) remark that the reforms have proceeded by trial and error, with frequent mid-course corrections and reversals of policy. In other words, the economic reforms were not a complete project settled in the first stage, but an ongoing process with many adjustments. There was no rapid leap to free prices, currency convertibility, or cutting of state subsidies; nor were there massive privatization and the quick selling off of state enterprises. This gradualist approach practiced by the Chinese state was quite different to the "shock therapy" approach in Eastern Europe, which called for the dismantling of centrally planned economy as fast as possible. As Andrew Walder (1996, p. 10) correctly points out: "Where in Europe shock therapy and mass privatization are designed in part to dismantle Communism and strip former Communists of power and privilege, in China gradual reform is intended to allow the Party to survive as an instrument of economic development."

Can the China Model Be Copied?

What this paper has tried to show is that there is, in fact, no easily identifiable "model" which captures China's developmental experience over the past thirty years. The China Model is highly ambiguous in the sense that it is a hybrid and uneasy combination of contradictory elements, including capitalist vs. socialist, state vs. market, export-led vs. import substitution economy.

To the extent that a model can be described, it concerns process rather than blueprint or policy prescription. As Sarah Cook (2010) remarks, "the China Model is one of pragmatism, experimentation, and gradualism, looking for successes, keeping what works, and discarding what does not." This approach is reflected in widely-cited slogans of the Chinese communist party-state, such as "seeking truth from facts," "crossing the river by feeling the stones," and Deng Xiaoping's comment about the color of the cat being unimportant as long as it catches mice.

What is distinctive in China's developmental experience, therefore, is less an ideological set of policy prescriptions than a flexible process of adaptation to rapid changes within specific political and institutional contexts in a changing capitalist world-economy. As such, can the third-world developing countries copy China's *flexible process of adaptation*?

This flexible process of adaptation presupposes a strong state machinery which has the capacity not only to carry out its policies, but to make policy adjustments (speed up, slow down, or change course) in mid-course if it detects that the policies are not working. It also presupposes that the state has a high degree of autonomy in the sense that other social classes and political groups are too weak to capture the state for their own interests. For example, the capitalist class in China was simply too small, too weak, and too dependent on the party-state to become the agent of historical transformation in China. As the capitalist class was almost completely wiped out during the Cultural Revolution, the nascent capitalists emerged after the Cultural Revolution was politically impotent to capture the state. Facing growing labor unrest and popular struggle against such abuses as child labor in the coal mines, discrimination against immigrant workers and environmental degradation, the nascent capitalist class was powerless to stop the policies toward state neoliberalism (So and Chu, forthcoming).

In sum, unless the developing countries in the third world were able to come up with an apparatus as powerful and as autonomous as the Chinese communist party-state, reproducing the China Model would not be possible.

References

Baek, S. W. (2005) Does China follow the East Asian development model? *Journal of Contemporary Asia*, 35(4), 485–498.

Barboza, D. (2010) China passes Japan as second-largest economy. *New York Times*, August 15.

BBC Monitoring Asia Pacific (2009a) China-Africa business summit held in South Africa. *BBC Monitoring Asia Pacific*, October 24.

BBC Monitoring Asia Pacific (2009b) Singapore expert upbeat on China's economic development. *BBC Monitoring Asia Pacific*, August 27.

Buckley, C. (2004) Let a thousand ideas flower: China is a new hotbed of research. *New York Times*, September, 13. C1 and C4.

CASS (Chinese Academy of Social Sciences) (2003) *China's industrial development report*. 2003. Beijing: Economic Management Publisher. [In Chinese]

Chan, K. W. (2003) Migration in China in the reform era: Characteristics, consequences, and implications. In A. Y. So (Ed.), *China's developmental miracle: Origins, transformations, and challenges*, pp. 111–135. Armonk: M.E. Sharpe.

Chang, K. S. (2003) Politics of partial marketization: State and class relations in post-Mao China. In A. Y. So (Ed.), *China's developmental miracle: Origins, transformations, and challenges*, pp. 265–292. Armonk: M.E. Sharpe.

China Labour Bulletin (2002) *Hong Kong: Han Dongfang*, January 31. Retrieved from http://www.china-labour.org.hk/public/main

China Daily (2009) China's model creates economic miracle. *China Daily*, October 17.

Ching, Po-yu. n.d. China: Socialist development and capitalist restoration. Retrieved from http://www.bayan.ph/downloads/China%20Socialist%20Development%20and%20Capitalist%20Restoration.pdf

Gong, Y. and W. Jang (1998) Culture and development: Reassessing cultural explanation on Asian economic development. *Development and Society*, 27, 77–97.

Cook, S. (2010) China's development model. What is there to learn? Retrieved from http://www.iss.nl/DevISSues/Articles/China-s-development-model-What-is-there-to-learn

Dirlik, A. (2004) Beijing consensus: Beijing 'gongshi': Who recognizes whom and to what end?" Retrieved from http://www.en.chinaelections.org/uploadfile/200909/20090918025246335.pdf

Economist (2001) A panda breaks the formation. *Economist*, August 25, 2001.

Global Labor Strategies (2008) Why China matters: Labor rights in the era of globalization. Retrieved from http://laborstrategies.blogs.com/global_labor_strategies/files/why_china_matters_gls_report.pdf

Hart-Landsberg, M. and P. Burkett (2004) China and socialism: Market reforms and class struggle. *Monthly Review*, 56(3), 1–116.

Hsiao, H. M. Social transformations, civil society, and Taiwanese business in Fujian. In A. Y. So (Ed.), *China's developmental miracle: Origins, transformations, and challenges*, pp. 136–160. Armonk: M.E. Sharpe.

Hung, H. F. (2009) America's head servant? The PRC dilemma in the global crisis. *New Left Review*, 60, 5–25.

Kiely, R. (2008) Poverty's fall/China's rise: Global convergence or new forms of uneven development. *Journal of Contemporary Asia*, 38(3), 353–372.

Lee, K. and J. A. Mathews (2009) From Washington consensus to best consensus for world development. Paper presented to the Annual Convention of the Korean Economic Association at Seoul.

Liu, M. (2007) Beijing's new deal. *Newsweek*, March 26.

Lin, G. C. S. (2003) An emerging global city region? Economic and social integration between Hong Kong and the Pearl River Delta. In A. Y. So (Ed.), *China's developmental miracle*, pp. 79–110. Armonk: M.E. Sharpe.

Lin, Y. (2003) Economic institutional change in Post-Mao China: Reflections on the triggering, orienting, and sustaining mechanisms. In A. Y. So (Ed.), *China's developmental miracle*, pp. 29–57. Armonk: M.E. Sharpe.

McMillan, J. and B. Naughton (1992) How to reform a planned economy: Lessons from China. *Oxford Review of Economic Policy*, 8, 781–807.

Nolan, P. (2004) *China at the crossroads*. Cambridge: Polity.

Pan, W. (2007) The Chinese model of development. A talk given at the Foreign Policy Center. Retrieved from http://fpc.org.uk/fsblob/888.pdf

Petras, J. (2006) Past, present and future of China: From semi-colony to world power? *Journal of Contemporary Asia*, 36(4), 423–441.

Ramo, J. C. (2004) The Beijing Consensus. *The Foreign Policy Center*. Retrieved from http://219.143.73.108/bookscollection/reports/200909/P020090921 313163521955.pdf

Roach, Stephen S. (2006) Doha doesn't matter any more: Despite stiff resistance to the Doha agenda for five years, there have been powerful gains in world trade in the same period. *Business Times Singapore*, August 8, 2006.

Rodrik, D. (2006) Goodbye Washington consensus, hello Washington confusion? A review of the World Bank's economic growth in the 1990s: Learning from a decade of reform. *Journal of Economic Literature*, 44, 973–987.

So, A. Y. (2007) Beyond the logic of capital and the polarization model: The state, market reforms, and the plurality of class conflict in China. In H. Sharma (Ed.), *Critical perspectives on China's economic transformation*, pp. 99–116. Delhi: Daanish Books.

So, A. Y. and C. Chu (Forthcoming.) The transition from neoliberalism and state neoliberalism in China at the turn of the 21st century. In K.-S. Chang, S.-K. Kim and B. Fine (Eds.), *Developmental politics in the neoliberal era and beyond: Critical issues and comparative cases*. New York: Routledge.

Szelenyi, I. (2010) Capitalism in China? Comparative perspective. In Y.-W. Chu (Ed.), *Chinese capitalism: Historical emergence and political implications*, pp. 199–226. Hampshire, UK: Palgrave Macmillan.

UNDP (2006) UNDP China wins 2006 poverty eradication awards. Retrieved from http://www.undp.org/poverty/stories/pov-award06-China.htm

Walder, A. (1996) *China's transitional economy: Interpreting its significance*. London: Oxford University Press.

Wallerstein, I. (2010) How to think about China? *Commentary* No. 273, January 15, 2010. Retrieved from http://fbc.binghamton.edu/273en.htm

Wang, F. (2008) *Boundaries and categories: Rising inequality in post-socialist urban China*. Stanford: Stanford University Press.

Wang, Y. (2008) Domestic demand and continued reform: China's search for a new model. *Global Asia*, 3(4), 24–28.

Washington Post (2009) Unwrapping the enigmatic Chinese riddle. *Washington Post*, March 31.

Wines, M. (2010) As China rises, fear grow on whether boom can endure. *New York Times*, January 12.

Zhang, W. (2006) The allure of the Chinese model. *International Herald Tribune*, November 2.

2

POLITICS

Law Kam-yee

The Hong Kong Institute of Education

Abstract

This chapter aims to provide a concise review of reforms in different political institutions since China's reform and opening-up in 1978, and to analyze the progress, bounds, and agendas behind these reforms. We examine party-led reforms in the bureaucratic system, State Council, government agencies, legislature, judicial system, and rural politics, as well as changes and continuities in the Party elites' ideology of democratization and civil society–state relations. Along with political and economic reforms in the past three decades and as the process of state building gradually unfolds, the government has enacted more laws and regulations successfully. The Party has also transformed past administrative means into legal means with stronger leadership and governance. The Party's elites are gradually acknowledging the universality of democracy, although neither the adoption of Western context of freedom nor the establishment of liberal democracy in China is implied by such acknowledgement. The ultimate objective of the reforms is to drive the Party toward reclaiming its legitimacy. Currently, the paramount task is to strengthen party organizations and consolidate the Party's ruling capacity. This means that the Party may develop Singaporean-style authoritarianism and maintain its ruling position by laws and economic interests.*

Keywords: Authoritarianism; bureaucratic reform; civil society; democratization; governance; legitimacy; Party's leadership; political reform; rule by law; rural politics.

---

* The author's thanks go to Mr. Jeff Yu, who provided quality research assistance for the project.

I. Introduction

In August 2010, during his tour in Shenzhen to celebrate the 30th anniversary of the country's first special economic zone, Chinese Premier Wen Jiabao has argued that China should push forward not only economic restructuring but also political restructuring. Without political restructuring, China may lose what it has already achieved through economic restructuring, and the targets of its drive toward modernization may not be achieved. Wen advocates that the democratic and legitimate rights of the people be guaranteed. People should be mobilized and organized legally to participate in political, economic, social, and cultural affairs. The problem of over-concentration of power with ineffective supervision should be solved by improving institutions. He demands the creation of conditions to allow the people to criticize and supervise the government (Wang Guanqun, 2010). On one hand, Wen's assertion refutes the common sense criticism that China's reform has been partially avoiding political initiatives. On the other hand, it also implies the bounds of the political reforms planned by Chinese leaders — bounds that make China's case different from the Western experience of modernization. Such difference has become even more apparent with the hostile response of Beijing to Liu Xiaobo's receipt of the 2010 Nobel Peace Prize.

China has embarked on the road of reform and opening-up since the Communist Party of China's (CPC) Third Plenary Session of the 11th Central Committee in 1978. Apart from economic reforms, this session also proposed political reforms in light of the needs of the special circumstances at that time. In an interview during the 30th anniversary of the reform, Li Junru, Vice President of the Party School of the CPC, argued that China seeks to "combine reforms on the political system with those on the economic system and push them forward in the name of economic system reforms" (Xin Hua Wang, 2008). As we illustrate, this statement is not plain rhetoric. There are indeed various hidden agendas behind the political reforms initiated by the CPC. This chapter aims to make a concise review of reforms in different political institutions since China's reform and opening-up was launched in 1978, and to analyze the changes, boundaries, and agendas behind the reforms. It is believed that the CPC has been adjusting its governing institutions to make them compatible with economic development through decades of reform and, much more importantly, to reinforce the Party's leadership and legitimacy in the country.

Before going into the details of the reforms, a brief background of the reforms and the analytical framework is provided in the next section.

II. Background of the Reforms and Framework of Analysis

After the CPC had established the People's Republic of China (PRC) in 1949, China adopted a planned economy, with almost every production being centrally planned. Since the establishment of the collective production policy in the mid-1950s, peasants were organized and incorporated into the people's commune. Not only their production decisions but also their socio-political lives were directed by officials in charge of the communes. For instance, peasants were "encouraged" to have meals at designated dining areas established under the commune.

However, unlike in the Soviet Union, the macro-economic system in China was less rigid; localities still held some decision-making power. Decentralization was also more obvious during different political movements. For instance, during the Chinese Cultural Revolution, Mao Zedong — discontent with other top leaders and bureaucratism in the CPC — success-fully abolished the state apparatus and stopped the functioning of the central government. The localities, at that time, enjoyed unprecedented authority (Bu Weihua, 2008; MacFarquhar and Schoenhals, 2006). We should, how-ever, note that although power periodically descended downward within the hierarchy, CPC cadres still held the final power in all decision-making processes. A manager of a production plant, for example, had no autonomy in deciding on production and other matters.

Under the collective production policy and various waves of political movement before the opening-up, China's GNP kept growing. However, economic performance under the PRC was still disappointing. The average income of peasants was 73.3 yuan in 1957. In 1978, the amount increased to 133.57 yuan. In these 21 years, the gross increase was only 60.2 yuan, and there were 0.25 billion peasants suffering from food deficiency (Wu Jinglian, 2005). A strong sense of compensation and catching up was prevalent among leading cadres at that time. This sentiment became one of the main forces of reform (Xiao Donglian, 2008).

Putting economic considerations aside, and from a political perspective, since the CPC did not have a cadre retirement system before the reforms, veteran leaders from the revolutionary period still held high positions before the Cultural Revolution. After the Cultural Revolution, these old cadres resumed office, and the young cadres who originally substituted their older counterparts during the Cultural Revolution were ousted from power. Hence, the gap in the cadre team resulted in a lack of young and professional cadres. Not surprisingly, the average age of major leaders in about 30 ministries and committees in 1980 was 63; those above 66 years old comprised 40% of the total number. This discontinuity forced Deng Xiaoping and other leading cadres to consider rejuvenating the cadre team. Apart from this rejuvenating issue, survivors of the Cultural Revolution were plunged in turmoil. Deng Xiaoping and other top leaders were committed to reconstructing the socialist legal system and the decision-making mechanism within the CPC, to maintaining political stability and avoiding the resurrection of political chaos (Lee, 2010; Xiao Donglian, 2008). As Kou Jianwen (2005) explains from the same perspective, Deng Xiaoping had to initiate reforms because he found that "political life" inside the CPC was abnormal since the Cultural Revolution, and cadres lacked professional knowledge and were over-aged. At that time, political reforms were unavoidable.

To a certain extent, this quest for economic development and political stability is closely related to the building of legitimacy. Fewsmith (2010, p. 233) argues that because top leaders have given up their "solipsistic" claim to Marxism-Leninism after the Chinese Cultural Revolution, they were rewarded by "the opening up of the question of legitimacy, and the question of legitimacy has [become] a drive of China's political reform over the past thirty years… because performance legitimacy had become so important, the party had little choice but to reform itself" (p. 239). From a similar standpoint, Lee (2010) argues that the CPC leaders "intended to establish political stability directly and facilitate economic development indirectly under the goal of sustaining the political legitimacy of the CPC's rule of China" (p. 559). Zhao (2010), after reviewing how political reforms helped shape the "China Model," concludes that "[e]conomic growth has produced more wealth in society, steadily improved the living standards of the Chinese people, and therefore retained the performance legitimacy of the CPC regime." Although Zhao has reservations on the sustainability of the "China Model," he still recognizes the importance of political reforms to economic development and hence to the legitimacy of the CPC.

The relationship between economic growth and legitimacy is worth exploring. Along this line, we take note of Holbig and Gilley's insightful views (2010, p. 400):

> [e]conomic growth and material well-being are highly abstract notions… usually experienced by way of intertemporal, interpersonal, interregional, and international comparison. This is to say economic success is not *per se* a source of regime legitimacy; instead, it has to be framed in ways conducive to positive subjective perceptions of the regime, for example, as competent, efficient, fair, committed to the realization of the common interest while avoiding publicly manifest partiality or bias, capable of selectively embracing

the benefits of globalization while defending national interests on a complex international terrain, and so on.

From this light, an economic downturn does not necessarily lead to the decline in legitimacy. As Holbig and Gilley notes, "the Chinese elites' reaction toward the recent global financial and economic crisis is a striking example of the role of framing," which "earned the Chinese leadership praise from other developing and developed countries alike at the G20 summits in Washington and London as well as during other prominent gatherings" (2008, pp. 400–401).

We can therefore consider that economic development is associated with legitimacy, but not sufficiently. The CPC's governance capacity, or more precisely the perception of this capacity to solve social and political problems, is more closely related to its support and legitimacy. In terms of the CPC's attempts to reclaim legitimacy, some studies (e.g., Holbig and Gilley, 2008) find a clear shift in emphasis from an earlier economic-nationalistic approach to a more ideological-institutional approach, with the increasing importance of political institutionalization.

Although this paper focuses on institutional changes, we cannot neglect the ideological aspect of the new strategy. As Holbig (2006) argues, the theory of the "three represents" (the CPC represents demands for the development of advanced social productive forces, the direction of advanced culture, and the fundamental interests of the greatest majority) advocated by Jiang Zemin, former General Secretary of the CPC and President of the State, is important because it aims at "[re]defining the 'common interest' and mobilizing popular consent." Moreover, this theory justifies the recruitment of capitalists as party members. Although Holbig (2006, pp. 21–25) notes that there is strong resistance to Jiang's "three represents" and Hu Jintao, General Secretary of the CPC and the President of the State, later raised other terminologies to redefine the "three represents" and the CPC's main ideology, the "three represents" remains important because it explicitly marks a shift to the "ideological-institutional approach."

In the ideological-institutional approach, the redefinition of "common interest" widens the policy choices of the CPC, allowing it some time to adopt an "absorption strategy" as a reform policy. This widening of policy choices has a drastic impact on political reforms under our framework.

In the following sections, we review six areas of political reforms: (1) bureaucratic system, including the succession of leaders and the development of the civil service system; (2) State Council and other government agencies, with some discussion on the relationship between the central and local governments; (3) the legislative role of the National People's Congress (NPC), the judicial system, and the way their roles and status are reinforced; (4) NPC elections and the role of the Chinese People's Political Consultative Conference (CPPCC); (5) the zigzag experience in rural politics; and (6) the relationship between civil society and the state, with a concise discussion on how the state is facing the emergence of civil society alongside social and economic changes. After these reviews, we discuss the prospect of democratization in China, which is closely related to political reform as a whole.

Our review reveals that the effects of different policies are interlocking. Economic growth-related reforms increase economic and social complexities, which inevitably force the state apparatus to reform its role and attempt to strengthen its governance capacity to cope with the new environment. Therefore, through our analytical framework, we view the reform process as an institutional adaptation process, responding to the changing environment, in which different areas of reform influence one another. The objective of the adaptation process is not only to boost economic growth but also to enable the CPC to solve social and economic problems. The ultimate objective, then, is to help the CPC to reclaim its legitimacy. In addition, with this aim of reclaiming legitimacy, we argue that reform policies are bounded by perceived threats to the CPC. If the CPC leaders view a given reform as a threat to their monopoly of power, such reform is halted or retreated.

III. Leadership Succession and Bureaucratic Reforms

In response to the adverse consequences of the Cultural Revolution, reforming the bureaucratic system was prioritized in the political reform agenda. The focus was on leadership succession, developing the civil service, and improving the leadership's collective decision-making process.

In the late 1970s, Deng Xiaoping, Chen Yun, and other veteran leaders resumed their positions and set "four criteria" for cadre selection: revolutionary, young, knowledgeable, and professional. By adopting the strategy of gradual retirement and enhancing welfare packages for retired cadres, about 7,200 old cadres in the central government and state departments completed retirement formalities by the end of 1982, accounting for 81% of all should-be retired cadres (Xiao Donglian, 2008). The CPC also established the cadre retirement system, streamlined the structure of leading positions, and demanded improvements in the educational levels of cadres. In early 1982, the Central Committee and the State Council subsequently promulgated rules in which provincial-level leading cadres and deputy leading cadres should retire at the ages of 65 and 60 respectively. In the same year, the Central Committee clearly stipulated the staffing quota of provincial-level leader teams and improvements in the educational credentials of leader teams. Consequently, by the end of 1983, the number of ministers, deputy ministers, and directors under the State Council was reduced by 65%. The average age of new ministerial and committee leaders was reduced from 65.7 to 59.5 years, and the number of leaders with a minimum of junior college education was increased from the previous 38% to 50% (Kou Jianwen, 2005).

The 13th National Congress held in 1987 marked the climax of bureaucratic reforms during this period. Zhao Ziyang, then General Secretary of the CPC, proposed political system reforms and classified "state civil servants" into two types, "administrative" and "executive," similar to administrative officers and service officials in the West (Kou Jianwen, 2005). The report of the 13th National Congress also proposed to change the principle of "the Party governing cadres" (*Dang guan gan bu)* and disband party groups in the government (Burns, 1994; Li Suizhou, 2009). According to John Burns (1994), the plan proposed by Zhao Ziyang would loosen the Party Central's control on cadres, resulting in its control of only about 1% of high-ranking officials; other cadres would be managed by the Personnel Ministry. Unfortunately, Zhao was ousted amid the unrest that followed the "June 4th Massacre" in 1989. Hence, the reform proposed in the 13th National Congress met a sudden death and the process of reform was halted with Zhao's downfall.

Civil service reforms resumed in 1993 when the State Council promulgated the "State Civil Servants Provisional Regulations" (*Guo jia gong wu yuan zhan xing tiao li*) to set guidelines for the better management of civil servants. "The People's Republic of China Civil Servant Law" (*Zhong hua ren min gong he guo gong wu yuan fa*) was finally adopted in 2005. We should, however, note that the promulgation of the Civil Servant Law is regarded as a drawback by some scholars because the new law incorporated CPC's principle of "the Party governing cadres" into the legal framework, thus providing the principle a statutory foundation. Accordingly, the new law legitimates the role of the Organizational Department of the Central Committee in managing government officials, and the legal authority of the Party's Organizational Department is thus reinforced. Through the law, the CPC has strengthened its control on civil servants and promoted "re-politicization," reversing the "weakening politicization" proposed by the 13th National Congress (Chan and Li, 2007; Li Suizhou, 2009).

With regard to decision-making in the leadership, the CPC promulgated the "working rules" of the Political Bureau in early 1980s. More importantly, the meeting frequency of the NPC, the Political Bureau, and its Standing

Committee has been institutionalized since the 11th National Congress, signaling that the decision-making process has been stabilized and institutionalized. As more veteran party leaders passed away in succession in the 1990s, the duty of major state leaders has also been institutionalized, and the decision-making tier has emerged to have a clearer division of duties. For example, as Kou Jianwen (2005) explains, the positions of General Secretary, Premier, and Chairman of the NPC, among others, are now regularly filled by members of the Politburo Standing Committee. Prior to this, such regularity was not established.

Finally and most importantly, Zhao (2010, p. 426) further notes a recent attempt toward political institutionalization:

> In a move to institutionalize the decision-making system in the State Council, upon coming to office, Premier Wen Jiabao stopped making decisions at premier work meetings (*zongli bangong huiyi*), which did not have any legal status but were held regularly by his predecessors, Premier Li Peng and Premier Zhu Rongji, because it gave them a lot of discretionary power in the decision-making process. Instead, Wen has made decisions at the State Council Executive meetings (*guowuyuan changwu huiyi*) and State Council Plenary meetings (*guowuyuan quanti huiyi*) stipulated by the Constitution and State Council Organic Law.

This important change clearly indicates the CPC's attempt to institutionalize a decision-making mechanism.

To summarize briefly, we find that top leaders started political reforms in response to the turmoil brought by the Cultural Revolution. These reforms, with the aim of promoting economic development, also enhanced the government's capacity to initiate and direct economic reforms. The institutionalization of the Party's decision-making system by Zhao Ziyang can be regarded as an evolution to a rational-legal government, which occurred in response to the changing economic and social environment. We should, however, note that the retreat of reforms after the "June 4th Massacre" and the re-politicization of civil servants are logical outcomes in the light of our analytical framework. The "June 4th Massacre," being perceived by veteran leaders as an attempt to overthrow the CPC regime, has naturally driven reforms toward a conservative stance. The re-politicization of civil servants was an attempt to enhance the control of the CPC over the bureaucracy, which can arguably be viewed as a measure to enhance the monitoring of the state apparatus. Inevitably, this enhanced monitoring has increased the state's capacity to tackle problems as the tide of reforms continues.

IV. Reforms in the State Council and Power Decentralization in the Governmental Hierarchy

As mentioned earlier, a sense of compensation and catching up prevailed among high-tier cadres during the late stage of the Cultural Revolution. On one hand, the CPC intended to promote political stability and economic prosperity to reclaim its legitimacy. On the other hand, it was also eager to raise its capacity to cope with social changes. To achieve these goals, it adjusted the governmental system accordingly, and introduced reforms in the State Council, state-owned enterprises (SoEs), and the central-local government relations.

Since the launching of the reform and opening-up, the State Council has implemented six major reforms in 1982, 1988, 1993, 1998, 2003, and 2008. The Party's Central Committee and the State Council proposed streamlining the government's organizational setup and limiting the staffing quota of leader teams in 1982. Organizational streamlining was thereafter implemented at various extents. The reform in 1998 was the most far-reaching among all reforms; it sought to (1) change governmental functions, (2) adjust the division of duties between departments, and (3) streamline the organizational setup (Wang Lanming, 2009). In this set of reforms, the State Council re-divided over a hundred functions among its departments, and similar functions were merged and passed to the same department as much as possible. On the basis of the 1998 reforms, the 2003 reforms emphasized the followings: (1) deepening the reform of the management system of state assets and establishing the State Council's State-owned Assets Supervision and Administration Committee, which was authorized by the State Council to perform the duty of an investor on behalf of the state; (2) implementing the macro-regulatory system and restructuring the State Development Planning Commission into the State Development and Reform Commission; (3) implementing the financial supervision system and establishing the China Banking Regulatory Commission; and (4) pushing for systematic reforms and establishing the Ministry of Commerce to be in charge of trade and international economic cooperation. A "super-ministry system" (*Da bu zhi*) was proposed in 2008 with the aim of further integrating different departments.

Reforms in the State Council are obvious examples of institutional adaptations to the changing economic environment. Reforms in SoEs initiated during the early reform era, in contrast, has triggered the reforms in the State Council. Although the government hierarchy underwent power decentralization during the pre-reform era, localities enjoyed only little autonomy in production decisions, which ultimately resulted in low productivity. To solve this problem, Li Xiannian, Vice Premier of the State Council in the late 1970s, proposed for the first time that SoEs be given "independence" at the economic working meeting held by the State Council in 1978. Thereafter, the CPC's Central Committee pushed for the policy of "delegating power and relinquishing profits" (*Fang quan rang li*). Unlike those power decentralization policies in the pre-reform era, local officials and managers of SoEs enjoyed unprecedented autonomy, which boosted production efficiency and economic growth. Under the same philosophy, Deng Xiaoping and other leaders also proposed "eating from different ranges" (*Fen zao chi fan*) to change the financial relations between the central and local governments. For example, the policy allowed local governments to use freely their budget surplus, giving them more autonomy in and control over their financial and investment choices. Although the central government repeatedly adjusted the policy of "eating from different ranges" during the 1980s and the implementation of the policy varied in different provinces or municipalities, the central government was determined to implement the policy in the 1980s (Li, 1998). Apart from financial powers, the central government also delegated the power of investment execution. For example, in 1984 any local investment above RMB10 million should be approved by the central government, but in 1988 the amount for approval was increased to RMB50 million (Gong and Chen, 1994).

Scholars in China generally believe that the policy of power delegation described above was intended to push for administrative reforms and to enhance the efficiency of local governments and SoEs. However, this policy resulted in an overheating economy and a financial mess in the late 1980s. As some scholars argue, the delegation of power weakened state power and undermined the central government's ability to regulate the economy (Wang Shaoguang and Hu Angang, 1994; Wang Shaoguang, 1997). From the viewpoint of property rights, Wu Jinglian (2005) comments that this policy did not change the basic framework of the state in exercising its SoE ownership, which inevitably drove the reform into a dilemma, that is, the government practiced too much administrative interference or the enterprises lost their internal control.

Based on our analytical perspective, given that the basic framework of SoE governance was designed for the planned economy in the pre-reform era, this framework was destined to be incapable of adapting to the power delegation policy, as well as to the shift from a planned to a market economy. As Wu Jinglian further elaborates, ambiguity in the property rights of SoEs led to the loss of state assets, and the failure of government intervention as a result of power delegation caused inflation and widened income inequalities. Hence, after the Third

Plenary Session of the 14th Central Committee, the CPC no longer emphasized "delegating power and relinquishing profits." Instead, the CPC shifted its focus to the systematic innovation of enterprises, with "building the modern corporate system" as the new target of SoE reforms since the early 1990s.

Around the same period, apart from SoE reforms, the central government launched fiscal reforms in 1994 in the hope of regaining its financial strength. The new tax system officially and clearly divided revenues and obligations between the central and local governments, and increased the income of the central government. As to the transformation of SoEs, the Third Plenary Session of the 14th Central Committee of the CPC passed a resolution in 1993, clearly identifying the steps in building a modern corporate system and in transforming SoEs into modern enterprises with "clear property rights, definite responsibilities, separation of enterprises from administration, and scientific management." To experiment, the State Council has chosen 18 cities for the trial reform of "optimization of capital structure" since 1994. The State Council proposed the policy of "seizing the big and freeing the small" in 1995 and chose 300 key enterprises for reform. The policy revolved around building the corporate legal person system and modern corporate system by reforming the equity structure, building modern SoEs, and completing thorough reforms in the equity structure of SoEs (Gao Shangquan, 2008).

Apparently, institutional adaptations and innovations have been adopted in response to changing environments. Particularly, SoE reforms inevitably forced the State Council to review its role, leading to other waves of reform. In addition, with the accelerating growth of economic complexity, the frequency and extent of institutional adaptations and innovations have also increased as shown in reforms in the State Council. The evolution of SoEs and fiscal reforms clearly show that the impacts of different reforms are interlocking, if not path dependent. The power delegation policy initiated the first wave of reforms. When the reform went deeper, new problems emerged, and a second wave of reforms or institutional adaptations was adopted to solve emerging issues. As a whole, the political reform can be understood as the CPC's attempt to maintain its capacity to direct and regulate economic reforms and consequently guarantee political stability.

V. Reconfiguring the Legislative Role of the NPC and the "Rule-by-Law" Society

Although some people may still believe that the NPC is merely a rubber stamp in the legislative process, it has also undergone various reforms that enhanced its functions.

After the NPC resumed its operations in the early 1980s, it adopted several reforms to strengthen its legislative functions. The most important attempts were the establishment of specialty committees and the reinforcement of the role of the NPC Standing Committee. Since the first NPC, the NPC has established several specialty committees to assist in legislation. However, these committees stopped functioning during the Cultural Revolution. As already illustrated, the top leaders were eager to restore political order and the socialist legal system after the Cultural Revolution. Hence, the Fifth Session of the Fifth NPC endorsed the latest constitution in 1982, stipulating that seven committees (including the legislative committee) should be established in the Sixth NPC. Consequently, three additional committees were established in the Seventh, Eighth, and Ninth NPC respectively. Finally, the NPC established nine specialty committees. Moreover, the 1982 Consti-tution stipulates that the NPC's Standing Committee has the power of "enacting and revising laws other than those that shall be enacted by NPC." The NPC holds only one plenary session each year; hence, the NPC's Standing Committee plays the legislative role between sessions to avoid "vacuum periods" in legislation.

The legislative process has also been reformed. Since the 1990s, China has introduced the hearing system in administrative decision making and in legislative fields. The "Administrative Penalties Law" (*Xing zheng chu fa fa*) legislated in 1996 stipulated that before grave administrative penalties are enforced, parties involved have the right to ask for hearings. The "Legislation Law" (*Li fa fa*), adopted in 2000, introduced for the first time the hearing system in legislative procedures and stipulated that opinions from different channels, including workshops, demonstration meetings, and hearings, shall be heard during the review of bills listed in the agenda of the NPC's Standing Committee. The NPC held the first national hearing on individual income tax in 2005, which signified the introduction of the local hearing system into the central government (Zhao Jianmin and Zhang Chunxiang, 2007).

In contrast to legislative reforms, judicial reforms have lagged behind. For example, the "Judge Law" (*Fa guan fa*) and the "Lawyer Law" (*Lu shi fa*) were adopted in 1995 and 1996, respectively. The "People's Court Reform Outline" (*Ren min fa yuan gai ge gang yao*) was taken on board as late as in 1999, and newly recruited judges have been required to complete university education or higher. The NPC's Standing Committee also passed an amendment to the "Judge Law" in 2001, stipulating the National Uniform Judiciary Examination System for judges, procurators, and lawyers. Regarding court operation, the Supreme People's Court released the first "Five-Year Reform Outline" in 1999 and the second and third outlines in

2004 and 2008, respectively. Although the "Outline" includes mostly technical concerns, it proposes important reforms on the admission of evidence (Liebman, 2007). Apart from top–down reforms, as Liebman (2007) further notes, local judges have also attempted to initiate institutional innovation. The "Seed Case" in 2003 is an example. The decision rendered by the Luoyang Intermediate People's Court deviated from the past practice of avoiding the review of any conflict between low-level and upper-level laws.

Although certain reforms have been instituted, China still faces great difficulties in building a "rule-by-law" society. Apart from the issue of "judicial review" involved in the "Seed Case," the issue of the "judicialization of the constitution" sparked heated debates in recent years (Chen Hongyi, 2004). With regard to the role of judicial organs, the advocacy by Hu Jintao in 2007 even showed a drawback. During the National Legal and Administrative Working Meeting, Hu Jintao asked judges to observe "three priorities": "put the Party's career first, put people's interests first, and put the constitution and laws first." This raised doubts among academic circles on whether the emphasis on "put the Party's career first" may influence the building of a "rule-by-law" society. In relation to this, the Supreme People Court's Third Outline states clearly that judicial organs shall "hold high the great banner of socialism with Chinese characteristics," stick to Deng Xiaoping's theory and Jiang Zemin's theory of "three represents" as guide, implement Hu Jintao's theory of "scientific development perspective" in depth, and firmly instill the socialist concept of "rule-by-law." All of these are reflected in judicial reforms and their implementation is supervised by the ruling authority of the CPC.

Three estates of power in reforming China "cooperate" with one another, but such cooperation is far from the "checks and balances" found in the West. On one hand, NPC reforms show signs of progress, with the aim of enhancing the capacity of both the NPC and the CPC in legislative processes. On the other hand, the assertion of Hu and the Supreme People Court's Third Outline clearly show a drawback. This contradiction could be reconciled under our analytical framework. After all, different reforms are instituted to reclaim the legitimacy of the CPC. The boundary and limit of reforms must therefore be in line with "putting the Party's career first."

VI. NPC's Electoral Reforms and the Role of Democratic Parties

Apart from strengthening the functions of the NPC, there are other reforms in the NPC and the CPPCC. Reforms concerning the NPC's electoral system are the most important.

The first "Electoral Act" (*Xuan ju fa*) promulgated in 1953 clearly stipulated that each NPC member in the rural areas should represent eight times the population represented by that in the urban areas, that is, in accordance with the ratio of 8:1. Under this Act, urban areas have a larger proportion of representatives in the NPC. Since the reform era, the people's congress electoral method has been revised six times. Zhang Luhao (2010) and Han Dayuan (2010) carefully document different waves of reform and act amendments, and find that the reforms aim at equal representation. The reforms also attempt to institutionalize electoral processes. For instance, the 8:1 ratio was reduced to 4:1 in the congress of autonomous prefectures, counties, and autonomous counties in an amendment in 1979. The amendment in 2004 stipulated that the electoral committee could organize candidates to meet voters and answer their questions, thereby reinforcing the role of the electoral committee. The amendment in 2010 marked the end of "same vote but not the same right" by adding the rule that members of the people's congresses shall be elected by the same ratio for both rural and urban areas.

The amendment in 2010 signaled the CPC's determination to solve the issue of "same vote but not the same right" and revealed ideological changes behind it. As stated by Wang Zhaoguo, Deputy Chairman of the NPC's Standing Committee, when revising the Electoral Law in 2010, "the class and grassroots foundation for the people's democratic dictatorship led by the CPC has been reinforced and expanded gradually. The objective condition of electing congress members by the same ratio of population for urban and rural areas is mature" (*Xin Hua Wang*, 2010a).

Along with NPC reforms, congressional members have exercised greater autonomy and the right to veto and to address queries (Liu Jinsen, 2007; Tang Liang, 2004; Ye Changrong, 2009). According to data collected from mainland newspapers, 28 standing committees of the people's congresses at different levels said "no" to 46 bills; "not passed" peaks appeared in 2005 and 2006. In terms of categories, specialty reports of the government, courts, and procuratorates were the most vetoed, followed by official appointments and removal, but vetoes on law enactment and revision and plan enactment were relatively few (Yang Zhanghuai, 2009).

Although the Electoral Law has been improved continuously, there are still many problems. For example, the law does not specify the appointment of members of the electoral committees at county and town levels, as well as their specific functions, resulting in inadequate democracy, unclear qualifications, and low transparency of the committee (Zhu Yingping, 2010). As Zhu Hengshun (2009) argues, the Electoral Law also lacks a re-verification mechanism of voting, wider scope of direct elections, and perfection of the "candidates contest system" — the last one has even greater practical value than electing congress members by the same ratio of population for rural and urban areas. Moreover, we should note that, with regard to the qualification of congress members, the issue of "professionalization" has been highly controversial in recent years, demonstrating rooms for improvement in the current Electoral Law and in the role of congress members. Although it is claimed that there are more cases regarding congress' exercise of "right to veto and address queries," the number is not representative considering the high workloads of different levels of congress.

In contrast to NPC reforms, reforms on democratic parties and the CPPCC did not attract much attention, and the extent of reform was not as great as that of the NPC. The operation of democratic parties and the CPPCC was suspended during the Cultural Revolution. Deng Xiaoping reconfirmed the "consultative role" of democratic parties and the CPPCC after 1978, and the operation of democratic parties resumed. The CPC's 12th National Congress (1982) proposed that the CPC shall uphold the principle of long-term coexistence, mutual oversight, sincerity, and sharing of weal and woe with democratic parties to strengthen cooperation with democratic parties and non-partisan groups. The CPC promulgated the "Advice on Sticking to and Consummating the System of Multi-Party Cooperation and Political Consultations" (*Guan yu jian chi he wan shan zhong guo gong chan dang ling dao de duo dang he zuo he zheng zhi xie shang zhi du de yi jian*) in 1989 and identified the system of multi-party cooperation and political consultation as China's basic political system. The constitutional amendment passed by the Eighth NPC in 1993 further stipulated that the system of multi-party cooperation and political consultation led by the CPC will exist and develop for a long period. The Central Committee of the CPC promulgated the "Advice of the Central Committee of the CPC on Further Strengthening the System of Multi-Party Cooperation and Political Consultation led by CPC" (*Zhong gong zhong yang guan yu jin yi bu jia qiang zhong guo gong chan dang ling dao de duo dang he zuo he zheng zhi xie shang zhi du jian she de yi jian*) in 2005 and requested party organizations at all levels to include political consultation in their decision-making processes (Ye Changmao, 2009).

Members of the CPPCC and democratic parties have been introduced to the government to hold offices since the reform and opening up. Their representation in people's congresses at different levels has also increased, but both at a rather slow pace. In 2007, Wan Gang, Vice Chairman of the Chinese Party for Public Interests (*Zhong guo zhi gong dang*), was appointed Minister of Science and Technology. This made him the first ever minister — in 35 years — in the State Council to come from a democratic party. Wan's appointment signaled that breakthroughs in the participation of the CPPCC and democratic parties in the administration are difficult to achieve (*Zhong guo ping lun*, 2007).

Wang Zhaoguo's assertion is of foremost importance. Ideologically, it reflects the spirit of the "three represents," which redefines "common interest" and "mobilizing popular consent." Practically, the "expanded foundation" of the CPC allows it to reform its Electoral Law or even appoint democratic party members to key positions in the government. In fact, as we have discussed, the introduced hearing system is worth noting as another example of the new strategy, and leaders of the CPC now have wider policy choices and flexibility in initiating reforms.

VII. Rural Politics

Following the turmoil brought by the Cultural Revolution, the average income of peasants stagnated, and 0.25 billion peasants were caught in starvation. Rural reform was therefore the paramount agenda at the early stage of the reforms.

The people's commune was first abolished and "the household contract responsibility system" (*Jiating lianchan chengbao zerenzhi*) was established. Although this system included various forms of production, its core mission was to release control over peasants and promote peasant autonomy in deciding on production and retaining production revenues. As Xiao Donglian (2008) notes, after several debates, top leaders assigned high credit to the reform. In the summer of 1981, approximately 32% of the "production team" adopted the new system, constituting about 0.13 billion peasants. In 1993, the traditional people's commune system was basically abolished.

Another major reform in rural politics was the attempt to rebuild the autonomy of village committees after the collapse of the people's commune system. In 1983, the Central Committee of the CPC promulgated "the Notice on Separation of Party and Government and Establishment of Town Government," indicating the priority tasks of separating government administration from commune management, establishing town governments, and gradually building economic organizations based on production needs and the will of the people. This reform was intended to fill the political vacuum after the collapse of the people's commune and to empower villages. During its evolution, however, the village committee has inherited all the control rights of rural production teams on collective assets. Moreover, village committees were directly supervised by town governments. It was actually a return to the "integration of government administration with commune management" (*Zheng she he yi*), which was common in the pre-reform era, with government officials holding remarkable power over village affairs. This retreat not only held back peasants from voluntarily developing professional cooperative organizations, but also inhibited further innovations on the entire economic and social management system in rural areas (Chen Xiwen, 2009). To be more precise, this return resumed several problems, such as contradictions between village committees and party organizations, and expanded local governments. Specifically, the contradictions involved (1) the contradiction between village party branches, village committees and town party committees, (2) the contradiction between towns and villages, and (3) the contradiction between peasants and policies. Among these three, the contradiction between village party branches, village committees and town party committees is the most crucial (Guo Zhenglin, 2001).

In the middle-run, such regression in rural politics resulted in the failure of rural autonomy and the expansion of the rural cadre system that needs to be pampered by various rural taxes. The regression was finally attributable, although indirectly, to the "three rural issues" (*San nong wen ti*) (i.e., problems in villages, agriculture, and peasants) since the 1990s, with rural education and infrastructure development slowing down seriously.

Lately and with increasing difficulties, the CPC started focusing on rural areas. For instance, the agricultural tax was scrapped in 2006. It was reported that "in 2005, government departments at all levels were expected to allocate at least 200 billion yuan (US$24 billion) to benefit people living in rural areas, an average 222 yuan (US$27) for each of the 900 million rural residents in the country" (*The China Daily*, March 6, 2005). With the growing government capacity as a result of other reform areas (especially fiscal reforms that increased the central government's fiscal capacity), the central government started fostering further reforms in rural areas to resolve the "three rural issues" that have become accumulatively serious.

Economic subsidies aside, there are experiments on grassroots democracy in China to assist rural development, although the experiments have caused other problems. As Tang Liang (2004) notes, after the multiple-candidate electoral system for village committees had been strengthened during the 1990s, village committee members became replaceable by elections, but conflicts between village committees and party organizations also increased. To date, these tensions still exist.

Finally, despite the shortcoming of the "integration of government administration with commune management," there was an unintended consequence of the integration. As many studies on township and village enterprises (TVEs) show, the integration facilitated the development of TVEs. The town governments have imperative power over village development and their interests. For example, tax revenues are closely associated with village development. Town governments therefore provide great assistance in developing town enterprises and even assume the role of "managers" and "entrepreneurs." During the 1980s, the growth of food production declined due to the integration. However, peasants greatly increased their income by becoming workers in TVEs, and surplus laborers in villages were also successfully absorbed (Oi, 1996; Walder, 1995). Nonetheless, although TVEs significantly contributed to China's GDP in the 1980s, their importance declined after the market reforms in the 1990s.

VIII.   Relationship between the Civil Society and the State

Although the development of civil society does not lead directly to the reform of political institutions, the Party's response to changes and dynamics in civil society reveal the possibilities and bounds of China's political reform, as presumed by our analytical framework.

At the early stage of the reforms, intellectuals were managed by the Party's liberal attitude. The Party's top leaders not only tolerated, but sometimes even encouraged intellectual social actions that asked for democracy, such as the "Xidan Democracy Wall" (*xi dan min zhu qiang*) Movement in late 1970s. This toleration, however, stopped in 1981 when the leaders perceived that the growing civil society endangered their rule. Among those social groups formed during this period, the "Research Group on the Development of Chinese Village" (*Nongcun fazhan wenti yanjiuzu*) formed by a few young scholars was an exceptional case. It was officially recognized by the government and incorporated into the government decision-making mechanism. As Xiao Donglian (2008, p. 465) comments

> In some sense, as the progress of reform regarding Chinese peasants goes further and further, this increased the importance of the Research Group… young people in the Research Group were different from that of the Xidan Democracy Wall Movement. They consent with the economic modernization strategy of the CPC, agreeing that economic development and achieving economic modernization are the key roads to solve the problems faced by China.[1]

This comment reveals two significant insights: during this period, the CPC only tolerated those social groups that could help its rule, and the CPC adopted

---

[1] This English passage is translated from Chinese by the author.

the "absorption strategy," attempting to integrate social groups into the party-state apparatus. In fact, we can argue that the introduction of the hearing system in the legislative process evolved from this strategy, which was initially tried in the early 1980s.

After the suppression of the sprouting civil society in the early 1980s and the "June 4th Massacre" in 1989, until the mid-1990s, civil society development slowed down. The development, however, resurged recently, drawing much interest from China observers. With the development of civil society, spontaneous civic movements, such as "human rights movements" and "netizen movements," have all become active in the new millennium (Cai, 2010). These rapid changes have been reviewed and three significant findings appear. First, civil organizations increased their autonomy and legitimacy after the 1980s. Except for a few organizations that still receive state funds, most civil society organizations have no government involvement, and all civil non-corporate units do not get funds from the government. Second, most grassroots civil organizations are only nominally supervised by a certain party or government organization, and they actually enjoy greater autonomy. Third, leaders of most civil organizations are not party or government officials (e.g., Yu Keping, 2006a). Although the validity of these findings are questionable, to some scholars, rescue and reconstruction efforts after the Wenchuan earthquake in May 2008 showcase the unprecedented actions of civil organizations in China, including joint actions and cooperation with the government. These organizations have started to take root in districts (Chen Jianmin and Zhu Jiangang, 2009).

Spontaneous "human rights movements" in recent years have also started to receive extensive public response. Shanghai citizens initiated a "collective stroll" (*Ji ti san bu*) in 2008 to protest the passing of the Maglev train system through residential areas (*Xin Lang Wang*, 2010). Along with the development of the internet, online mobilization has started to exercise its influence, such as in the case of the "Safeguard Cantonese dialect" and "Cantonese speak Cantonese dialect" movements in Guangzhou. Benefiting from online mobilization, the movement has spread from the Mainland to Hong Kong in the summer of 2010. The recent "Deng Yujiao case" and other similar incidents have also been supported by online consensus to achieve the desired political effect — to challenge not only powerful and corrupted local cadres, but also the courts (*Zhong guo ping lun*, 2009). In 2010, about 600 villagers in Panyu and Dongguan, at Guangdong Province, initiated a "collective stroll" to protest the construction of incinerators (*Guang zhou ri bao*, 2010). This case reflects three significant features. First, a politically-concerned middle class has emerged. Second, the government has given up tough policies. Third, the media not only helps set up the issue, or expand and uplift its significance to the public, but also promotes action along the right course. New media, such as social networks, also play a critical role in terms of knowledge engine, collection of opinions, and transmission of messages (Zhu Jiangang, 2010).

Despite its efforts to crack down on human rights activists in recent years, the party-state does not completely exclude the development of civil society. For example, the Central Committee has focused on the development of social services in recent years, and local governments even bought social services provided by social groups (*Gong yi shi bao*, 2010). Under our framework, this acceptance is by no means strange. On one hand, with the "expanded foundation" proposed by the "three represents," the united front and flexibility choice of the CPC has increased. On the other hand, since strengthening the Party's capacity to solve social problems is one of the main strategies to reclaim legitimacy, cooperation among the CPC, social groups, and civil society is not strange. The Wenchuan earthquake, again, is a remarkable example of this collaboration. However, the campaign of human rights activists who were eager to hold corrupt local cadres responsible for severe casualties during the earthquake was brutally suppressed by the Party-manipulated legal apparatus.

IX. Democratization as an Ideological-Institutional Strategy

Although this chapter focuses on institutional reforms, democratization merits certain discussion because seemingly democratic attempts by the CPC resemble the logic of other political reforms under our analytical framework.

With regard to democratization in China, Western scholars have different forecasts. A number of scholars have an optimistic attitude toward the issue because they believe that political reforms in China, which have originated from higher authorities (especially the pro-reform faction in the Party) in recent years, reveal the development of democracy (Gilley, 2004; Fewsmith, 2007). There is also the prevalent pessimistic view that Chinese leaders will not accept Western liberal democracy as a universal value (Lynch, 2006). Even worse, Western liberal democracy encounters a big challenge in China as long as China's economy, which is being pushed forward by the CPC's authoritarian rule and use of nationalism, continues to be strong (Gat, 2007; Shirk, 2007). Looking back at the changing ideological position of think-tank elites in the CPC in recent years, the "universal nature" of democracy is gradually being acknowledged (Li, 2008), and some observers even argue that "democracy" may occur in China in the next ten years. However, this does not mean that the Western-form liberal democracy will be adopted in China.

An important question has been raised as to what kind of democracy will emerge if the CPC develops its "non-Western style democracy model" (Zhang Baohui, 2009, p. 117).

Putting the examination of foreign scholars aside, further questions as to the diverse meanings of democratization and democracy have been raised by Party's think-tank elites. The advocacy of Yu Keping, the well-known core advisor of President Hu Jintao in political reform affairs, that "democracy is a good thing" shows that his concept of "democracy" differs from the Western concept of liberal democracy. Yu does not only advocate "democratic politics with Chinese characteristics," but also clearly expresses his attitude against completely copying and imitating overseas political systems, claiming that (2006a, pp. 27–28):

> we should learn and borrow the advanced and reasonable things from abroad. [However], the learning and borrowing should comply with the actual conditions of our country and should be integrated with the actual conditions of our country in an organic manner. For instance, the system of people's congresses constitutes China's fundamental political system and is a democratic system with Chinese characteristics.[2]

The quote above may give readers the impression that, like the Chinese government, Yu Keping is anti-democratic. Yu Keping, however, in various circumstances, has repeatedly advocated "administration of the Party with laws," "establishment of equal election," and "increment democracy" (Yu Keping, 2006a,b, 2008, 2010). Among the top leaders, Hu Jintao has also repeatedly emphasized the development of intra-party democracy. In the 17th National Congress of the CPC and in various important speeches, Hu Jintao has stressed that the development of a socialist democracy is the consistent goal of the CPC. The development of an intra-party democracy and the promotion of "people's democracy" would complement each other and could effectively benefit the development of democracy (Liu Li, 2010).

The opinions of CPC elites on democracy seem contradictory. For instance, although Premier Wen Jiabao repeatedly expressed his positive views toward political and democratic reform during his Shenzhen tour in August and in the interview with CNN in September 2010, the *People's Daily* asserted in late October that while the government should continue political reforms, the country should neither directly copy the Western political model nor adopt a multi-party system nor the separation of powers

---

[2] This English passage is translated from Chinese by the author.

(*Xin Hua Wang*, 2010b). The *People's Daily*'s position clearly contradicts Wen's political advocacy.

Nevertheless, such kind of contradictions may not be as severe as they appear. As mentioned earlier, the CPC is taking a more "ideological-institutional approach" in reclaiming its legitimacy. Since the new millennium, CPC leaders have been attempting to reframe their ideology by proposing the "three represents" and other theoretical terminologies, portraying the CPC as a party that represents the interest of the whole society (Holbig, 2006). From this view, advocacies for democratic reforms by various leaders and elites may then be reinterpreted as a strategy to reclaim legitimacy. As Holbig and Gilley (2010, pp. 411–412) argue, various election experiments at the village level "[are] believed by the party to be a key source of legitimacy because it's a way to ensure that the CPC responds to growing social complexity and value shift." This function-oriented utilization of various democratic experiments is a good reflection of the overall CPC stance toward democracy.

No matter how minor they may be, there are indeed reforms in many areas: electoral law, NPC legislative process, and village-level elections, among others. These reforms could be understood as democratic progresses. However, if we consider Holbig's framework, we can argue that these progresses are function-oriented, and the process of democratization is bounded and limited by this orientation. All in all, although this paper aims to explore political institutional reforms, institutional reforms and the democratization process share the same logic, and reclaiming CPC legitimacy is their hidden and ultimate agenda.

X. Closing Remarks

This chapter argues that the economic backwardness and political instability caused by the Chinese Cultural Revolution and other pre-reform policies triggered China's reform and opening-up. At that time, reform was basically a question of survival to the CPC. Various reform policies, including political reforms, were then adopted. With the progress of reforms, social and political complexities increased, forcing the CPC to implement political institutional reforms. During this process, the CPC explored new ways, especially the ideological-institutional approach, to reclaim its legitimacy. This new strategy does not only rest on legitimacy by economic growth, but also on strengthening the CPC's governing capacity to tackle new complexities in the society. However, since the reforms are aimed at reclaiming CPC's legitimacy, the reform policies are bounded and limited by the interest of the Party. From this perspective, we can also explain the drawbacks of some of the reform policies.

As Elizabeth Perry argues (2007), the CPC's resort to an open-door-policy that welcomes even capitalists into the Party is a clear acknowledgement of its moribund condition. The leaders discover that advanced economic growth may indeed demand new arrangements that afford greater autonomy to legal institutions and civil society. Without a will on the part of its leadership to risk the impacts of such political transformations, the CPC could devolve into a run-of-the-mill authoritarianism that gives out with both the ideological and institutional features of its revolutionary past. A short thesis as it is, this chapter only touches on political changes in some areas since the reform and opening-up. However, we see that the political reforms since 1978 have several features: (1) The CPC proposed "four criteria", including "revolutionary", in reforming the bureaucratic system and in improving the efficiency of the state apparatus by enhancing the cadre quality; (2) The past practice of "the Party governing cadres" has been legalized by enacting the "Civil Servant Law," re-politicizing "civil servants," and strengthening cadre management; (3) Improvements in cadre quality are coordinated with economic development. Apart from streamlining the State Council's architecture, the CPC has established new organizations and management mechanisms. The CPC had also proposed "delegating power and relinquishing profits" as institutional reforms during the early period of reform, and it later decided to carry out SoE reforms to solve the issue of low enterprise efficiency and to develop a market economy; (4) The CPC has also strengthened the functions of the NPC in coordinating legislative needs. Different consultative mechanisms have been introduced, and different opinions are now heard during legislation; (5) Although the CPC claims that it is focused on the "rule-by-law," it has turned to emphasize "party leadership" and demanded to hold the power of control on court verdicts in recent years; (6) In contrast to reforms in other political fields, rural reforms were halted in the 1980s and the "three rural issues" have emerged. To maintain social stability, the CPC has resumed the "integration of government administration with commune management" in rural areas since 2000; (7) Finally, the CPC has also strengthened the management of civil society through various means, except for crackdowns, and has even resorted to asking help from civil society for its social governance.

In pointing out the insincerity of Tibet's exiled leader, the Dalai Lama, and Taiwan's former president Chen Shui-Bian on sovereignty disputes with China, Beijing authorities always remind international journalists an old Chinese preaching: "judge people by their deeds, not just by their words" (*ting qi yan guan qi xing*). In view of this, China observers may also find this motto useful when they judge the words and deeds of Chinese leaders presented to international journalists about China's political reforms. Premier Wen Jiabao's hope of

China's future political landscape expressed during his interviews with CNN in 2008 and 2010 have not changed too much: certain aspects of the political landscape will be in some way similar to the Western style. However, can observers confidently expect that China's thirty-year experience in political reforms is practically heading toward liberal democracy? After Jiang Zemin raised the theory of "three represents," the CPC has once encouraged the promotion of the Party's work in non-publicly owned economic organizations and the strengthening of party building (Xie Junchun, 2006). Hu Jintao, who advocated the development of grassroots party organizations in recent years, called on the Party to engage in in-depth learning and practice of scientific development, and concluded the campaign by reiterating that the key to reform and stable development is strengthening and improving the party's leadership (*Zhong yang zheng fu men hu wang zhan*, 2010). He further emphasized "reinforcing the state's role as the economic coordinator" from the "scientific development perspective" and "ruling the society by means of the Party and the law." Along with the reforms in the past three decades and as the state building has been implemented gradually, the government has successfully enacted more laws and regulations; the CPC could transform past administrative means into legal means for its administration. This means that the CPC has the possibility of developing a Singaporean-style authoritarianism and of maintaining its ruling position by laws and economic interests. As reviewed in this chapter, after all, reforms and democratic attempts are bound by the CPC's interests. The most sincere expression of Wen during those CNN interviews may be that he has never echoed the possibility of a multi-party competitive system in China's future political arena.

References

Bu, W. (2008) *"Zalan JiuShiJie": Wenhua da geming de dongluan yu haojie (1966–1968)*. Xiang gang: Zhong wen da xue chu ban she.

Burns, J. P. (1994) Strengthening central CCP control of leadership selection: The 1990 Nomenklatura. *The China Quarterly*, 138.

Cai, Y. (2010) *Collective resistance in China: Why popular protests succeed or fail*. Stanford: Stanford University Press.

Chan, H. S. and S. Z. Li, (2007) Civil service law in China: A return to cadre personnel management. *Public Administration Review*, 67(3).

Chen, H. (2004) Xiu xian yu zhong guo xian zheng qian jing. *Er shi yi shi ji*, 80. Xiang gang: Zhong wen da xue chu ban she.

Chen, J. and J. Zhu (2009) Kang zhen jiu zai: Zhong guo gong min she hui jue qi de qi ji? *Er shi yi shi ji*, 114, Xiang gang: Zhong wen da xue chu ban she.

Chen, X. (2009) Nong cun gai ge yu zhi du bian qian. In X. Meng (Ed.), *Zhong guo jing ji san shi nian: Jing dian hui wang (shang)*. Xiang gang: He ping tu shu you xian gong si.

China Daily (2005) *Agricultural tax to be scrapped from 2006. China Daily*, March 6, 2005. Retrieved from http://www.chinadaily.com.cn/english/doc/2005-03/06/content_422126.htm

Fewsmith, J. (2007) Democracy is a good thing. *China Leadership Monitor*, 22.

Fewsmith, J. (2010) Political creativity and political reform in China? In B. Womack, (Ed.), *China's rise in historical perspective*. New York: Rowman and Littlefield Publishers, Inc.

Gao, S. (2008) Zhong guo gai ge 30 nian: Cong gao du ji zhong de ji hua jing ji dao chong man huo li de she hui zhu yi shi chang jing ji. Gao Shangquan, *Gai ge li cheng: Xian gei gai ge kai fang 30 nian*. Beijing: Jing ji ke xue chu ban she.

Gat, A. (2007) The return of authoritarian great powers. *Foreign Affairs*, July/August.

Gilley, B. (2004) *China's democratic future*. New York: Columbia University Press.

Gong, T. and F. Chen (1994) Institutional reorganization and its impact on decentralization. In H. Jia and Z. Lin (Eds.), *Changing central-local relations in China: Reform and state capacity*. Boulder: Westview Press.

Gong yi shi bao (2010) Shou jie zhong guo she gong nian hui zhao kai ke xie zhong guo she gong nian lun. *Gong yi shi bao*, February 9, 2010. Retrieved from http://www.gongyishibao.com/news/newsshow.asp?id=2639

Guang zhou ri bao (2010) Dong guan 600 cun min bu man le se fen shao chang xuan zhi zai ci ji ti 'San bu.' *Guang zhou ri bao*, May 17, 2010. Cited in *Zhong guo xin wen wang*. Retrieved from http://www.chinanews.com.cn/sh/news/2010/05-17/2285138.shtml

Guo, Zhenglin (2001) Tan tan cun wei hui yu dang zhi bu de guan xi, Zhong guo xuan ju yu zhi li, *Zhong guo xuan ju Yu zhi li wang*, August 25, 2001. Retrieved from http://www.chinaelections.org/NewsInfo.asp?NewsID=54825

Han, Dayuan (2010) Cheng xiang 'Tong piao tong quan' de gui fan fen xi ji ying xiang, *Zhong guo xuan ju yu zhi li wang*, May 18, 2010. Cited in *Guo jia xing zheng xue yuan xue bao*. Retrieved from http://www.chinaelections.org/newsinfo.asp?newsid=177238

Holbig, H. (2006) Ideological reform and political legitimacy in China: Challenges in the post-Jiang era. *GIGA Working Papers: GIGA-WP-18/2006*. Retrieved from http://www.giga-hamburg.de/dl/download.php?d=/content/publikationen/pdf/wp18_holbig.pdf

Holbig, H. and B. Gilley (2010) Reclaiming legitimacy in China. *Politics and Policy*, 38(3), 395–422.

Kou, J. (2005) *Zhong gong jing ying zheng zhi de zhuan bian: Zhi du hua yu quan li zhuan yi 1978–2004.* Tai bei: Wu nan tu shu chu ban gu fen you xian gong si.

Lee, H. (2010) Political institutionalization as political development in China. *Journal of Contemporary China*, 19(65), 559–571.

Li, C. (Ed.) (2008) *China's changing political landscape: Prospect for democracy.* Washington, D.C.: Brookings Institution.

Li, C. L. (1998). *Centre and provinces — China 1978–1993: Power as non-zero-sum.* New York: Oxford University Press.

Li, S. (2009) Gong wu yuan zhi du: Dang zheng gan bu de bian ge. In J. Luo and Y. Zheng (Eds.), *Zhong guo gai ge kai fang san shi nian.* Xiang gang: Xiang gang cheng shi da xue chu ban she.

Liebman, B. (2007) China's court: Restricted reform. *The China Quarterly*, 191.

Liu, J. (2007) Cong ji jian you ying xiang de jian du shi jian shuo shuo ren da de jian du. *Ren da yan jiu*, January 5, 2007. Retrieved from http://www.rdyj.com.cn/inc/ShowArticle.asp?artid=1776&cat_id=12

Liu, L. (2010) Tui dong dang nei min zhu de ruo gan si kao. *Zhong guo xuan ju yu zhi li wang*, June 25, 2010. Cited in *Li lun yue kan*, No. 1 of 2010. Retrieved from http://www.chinaelections.org/newsinfo.asp?newsid=180300

MacFarquhar, R. and M. Schoenhals (2006) *Mao's last revolution.* Cambridge: Harvard University Press.

Oi, J. (1996) The role of the local state in China's transitional economy. In A. Walder (Ed.), *China's transitional economy.* New York: Oxford University Press.

Perry, E. (2007) Studying Chinese politics: Farewell to revolution. *The China Journal*, 57.

Shirk, S. (2007) *China: Fragile superpower.* New York: Oxford University Press.

Tang, L. (2004) *Jian jin. Min zhu: Bian ge zhong de zhong guo zheng zhi.* Xin jia po: Ba fang wen hua qi ye gong si.

Walder, A. G. (1995) Local government as industrial firm: An organizational analysis of China's transitional economy. *American Journal of Sociology*, 101.

Wang, G. (2010) Chinese premier calls for further reform, ideological emancipation. Retrieved from http://www.gov.cn/english/2010-08/21/content_1685351.htm. In *Chinese Government's Official Web Portal*, August 21, 2010.

Wang, L. (2009) Gai ge kai fang yi lai wo guo liu ci ji zhong de xing zheng guan li ti zhi gai ge de hui gu yu si kao. *Zhong yang ji gou bian zhi wei yuan hui ban gong shi wang*, cited in *Zhong guo xing zheng guan li*, December 26, 2009. Retrieved from http://www.scopsr.gov.cn/jgge/gwy/201003/t20100331_12380.htm

Wang, S. (1997) *Tiao zhan shi chang shen hua: Guo jia zai jing ji zhuan xing zhong de zuo yong.* Xiang gang: Niu jin da xue chu ban she.

Wang, S. and A. Hu (1994) *Zhong guo guo jia neng li bao gao.* Xiang gang: Niu jin da xue chu ban she.

Wu, J. (2005) *Dang dai zhong guo jing ji gai ge: Tan suo zhong guo jing ji shun li zhuan xing de mi mi.* Tai bei: Mei shang mai ge luo xi er gu fen you xian gong si.

Xiao, D. (2008) *Zhong hua ren min gong he guo ji (10): Li shi de zhuan zhe — Cong bo luan fan zheng dao gai ge kai fang (1979–1981).* Xiang gang: Zhong wen da xue chu ban she.

Xie, J. (2006) *Zhong guo gong chan dang de jie ji ji chu he qun zhong ji chu yan jiu.* Beijing: Zhong guo she hui ke xue chu ban she.

Xin, H.-W. (2010a) Wo guo xiu gai xuan ju fa ni qu xiao cheng xiang cha bie shi xian 'tong piao tong quan.' *Xin Hua Wang*, March 8, 2010. Retrieved from http://big5.xinhuanet.com/gate/big5/news.xinhuanet.com/politics/2010-03/08/content_13122538.htm

Xin, H.-W. (2010b) Renmin ribao: Yan zhe zheng que zheng zhi fang xiang ji ji wen tuo tui jin zheng zhi ti zhi gai ge. *Xin Hua Wang*, October 27, 2010. Retrieved from http://big5.xinhuanet.com/gate/big5/news.xinhuanet.com/observation/2010-10/27/c_12704461_3.htm

Xin, H.-W. (2008) Tan suo chuang xin de 30 nian: Zhong guo zheng zhi ti zhi gai ge de hui gu yu qian zhan, July 8, 2008. Cited in *Ren Min Wang*. Retrieved from http://news.xinhuanet.com/politics/2008-07/08/content_8510389.htm

Xin, L.-W. (2010) Hu hang ci xuan fu yan xian ju jian jue di zhi fan dui jian she. *Xin Lang Wang*, April 1, 2010. Cited in *Zhong guo xin wen zhou kan*. Retrieved from http://sh.sina.com.cn/news/s/2010–04–01/1402138853_3.html

Yang, Z. (2009) Wei tong guo an li pin xian, Tu xian min zhu jin bu. *Nan fang du shi bao*, October 12, 2009. Retrieved from http://gcontent.oeeee.com/b/15/b1563a78ec593375/Blog/ae9/912f6c.html

Ye, Z. (2009) *Zhi du zhuan gui de zheng zhi yi shu: Dang dai zhong guo jian jin shi zheng zhi fa zhan yan jiu.* Wu han: Wu han da xue chu ban she.

Yu, K. (2006a) *Min zhu yu tuo luo.* Beijing: Beijing da xue chu ban she.

Yu, K. (2006b) Guan yu 'Min zhu shi ge hao dong xi' de bian zheng. *Zhong guo xuan ju yu zhi li wang*, October 23, 2006. Cited in *Bei jing ri bao*. Retrieved from http://www.chinaelections.org/newsinfo.asp?newsid=97186

Yu, K. (2008) Yu ke ping tan 'Zhong guo mo shi' yu 'Pu shi jia zhi': Fang zhong yang bian yi ju fu ju zhang yu ke ping. *Zhong guo xuan ju yu zhi li wang*, November 18, 2008. Cited in *Shang hai dang shi dang jian*, No. 11 of 2008. Retrieved from http://www.chinaelections.org/newsinfo.asp?newsid=97186

Yu, K. (2010) Zhong hua ren min gong he guo liu shi nian zheng zhi fa zhan de luo ji. *Zhong guo xuan ju yu zhi li wang*, March 5, 2010. Cited in *Ma ke si zhu yi yu xian shi*, No. 1 of 2010. Retrieved from http://www.chinaelections.org/newsinfo.asp?Newsid=170720

Zhang, B. (2009) Min zhu hua. In J. Luo and Y. Zheng (Eds.), *Zhong guo gai ge kai fang san shi nian*. Xiang gang: Xiang gang cheng shi da xue chu ban she.

Zhang, L. (2010) Gui fan ren da dai biao xuan ju: 'Xuan ju fa' li ci xiu gai hui gu. *Zhong guo xuan ju yu zhi li wang*, March 8, 2010. Cited in *Zhong Guo Wang*. Retrieved from http://www.chinaelections.org/newsinfo.asp?newsid=171142

Zhao, J. and C. Zhang (2007) Cong qun zhong lu xian dao you xian duo yuan: Zhong guo da lu li fa ting zheng zhi du zhi fa zhan. *Zhong guo da lu yan jiu*, 50(4).

Zhong guo ping lun (2009) 'Deng yu jiao an' yuan he jiao dong zhong guo yu lun? *Zhong guo ping lun xin wen wang*, May 26, 2009. Retrieved from http://www.chinareviewnews.com/doc/1009/7/9/3/100979316.html?coluid=7&kindid=0&docid=100979316

Zhong guo ping lun (2007) Wan gang zhang ke ji bu: 35 nian lai min zhu dang pai ren shi shou ru ge. *Zhong guo ping lun xin wen wang*, April 27, 2007. Retrieved from http://www.chinareviewnews.com/doc/1003/5/7/0/100357099.html?coluid=7&kindid=0&docid=100357099

Zhong hua ren min gong he guo zhong yang ren min zheng fu men hu wang zhan (2010) Quan dang xue xi shi jian ke xue fa zhan guan zong jie da hui ju xing, Hu Jintao jiang hua. *Zhong hua ren min gong he guo zhong yang ren min zheng fu men hu wang zhan*. Cited in *Xin hua she*, April 6, 2010. Retrieved from http://big5.gov.cn/gate/big5/www.gov.cn/ldhd/2010–04/06/content_1573959.htm

Zhu, H. (2009) Xuan ju fa xiu gai: Yu shi ju jin tui dong min zhu zheng zhi fa zhan. *Ren da yan jiu*, December 5, 2009. Retrieved from http://www.rdyj.com.cn/inc/ShowArticle.asp?artid=2408&catid=10

Zhu, J. (2010) Gong min she hui zai she hui zhuan xing zhong jue qi. *Zhong guo xuan ju yu zhi li wang*, January 18, 2010. Cited in *Nan fang du shi bao: Shen ping*. Retrieved from http://www.chinaelections.org/newsinfo.asp?newsid=166694

Zhao, S. (2010) The China model: Can it replace the Western model of modernization? *Journal of Contemporary China*, 19(65), 419–436.

Zhu, Y. (2010) Wo guo ren da dai biao xuan ju wei yuan hui min zhu hua he gong zheng hua gou zao. *Ren da yan jiu*, May 5, 2010. Retrieved from http://www.rdyj.com.cn/inc/ShowArticle.asp?artid=2490&cat_id=11

3

SOCIAL CHANGE

Xiaogang Wu

The Hong Kong University of Science and Technology

Abstract

This chapter provides a sketchy description of three decades of social changes in China since 1978. The economic reform has re-configured the basic institutional make-ups of state socialist China: the household registration system (*hukou*), the work unit system (*danwei*), and the cadre-worker status distinction in the urban labor force. The changes of these intermediate institutions not only reflect social structural changes per se, but also serve as the keys to understanding the dynamic social life in China. Based on government statistics and other scholars' research, the paper highlights the impact of the changes and continuities of these institutions on individuals' life chances and social stratification in contemporary China.*

Keywords: China, economic reform; elite transformation; household registration; institutional transitions; labor markets; post-socialism; social inequality; social structure; work units.

Introduction

Few nations have undergone economic and social changes as dramatically as China has since the 1970s. According to the World Bank data, Chinese

---

* The author would like to thank the financial support from the Research Grants Council of Hong Kong to the research project "Social Mobility and Stratification Dynamics in China since Mid-1990s" (GRF 644208).

economy has performed consistently well for over three decades, with an annual growth rate of 10%. China's GDP has increased from only 148 billion US dollars (current price) in 1978 to 4.43 trillion US dollars in 2008 (World Bank, 2010), surpassing the United Kingdom, France, Germany, and Japan as the second largest economy on earth in 2010. The greatest beneficiaries of the growth and prosperity are Chinese people, whose living standards have improved significantly. For instance, the per-capita living floor space in both urban and rural areas have quadrupled within the same period, and the total household savings deposit, measured against the GDP, increased from 5.8% in 1978 to more than 71.9% in 2008 (National Bureau of Statistics, 2010). Ordinary Chinese citizens have enjoyed both a higher standard of living and new freedom to create a private life beyond the control of the state, despite the fact the Chinese Communist Party (CCP) continued to reject political reforms (Davis, 2000).

Accompanied with the rapid economic liberalization are accelerating social differentiation, growing inequality, and increasing disputes and social conflicts. In the course of social differentiation, new social forces have emerged with distinctive interests, competing with existing groups and consequently reshaping social order and power relations (Wu and Cheng, 2010). The party-state has retreated from the economic sphere and social life to a large extent. As a result, Chinese people now enjoy more autonomy and freedom than before (Goldman and MacFarquhar, 1999); on the other hand, they also need to be more responsible for their own with regards to employment, housing, and other well-being that used to be committed by the socialist state. The socialist social contract was gradually replaced by the market social contract (Tang and Parish, 2000).

From the very beginning, Chinese reformers have adopted an incremental approach to dismantle the socialist redistributive system, as manifested in Deng Xiaoping's famous phrase — "crossing the river by groping the stones." The social consequences of economic reforms reflect both the continuity and changes — the immense changes induced by the economic reform are also dependent on the past, which constitute the vibrant social landscapes of China today. As it is a daunting task to depict social changes in all respects in the thirty years, this chapter focuses on how economic reform has reconfigured the basic institutional make-ups of state socialist China: the household registration system (*hukou*), the work unit system (*danwei*), and the cadre-worker status distinction in the urban labor force. The changes of these intermediate institutions not only reflect social structural changes *per se*, but also serve as the keys to understanding the dynamic social and economic life in contemporary China.

Institutional Structures under Chinese Socialism

To examine social changes, we have to set up a benchmark for comparison. In the course of building up a socialist planned economy, Chinese government has gradually installed a set of intermediate institutions to facilitate the redistribution of resources and life chances by the state. The household registration that divided rural and urban China, the urban work unit system, and status distinction between cadres and workers within urban labor forces together characterized the social structure under Chinese state socialism before the reform.

1. *The Household Registration System (hukou)*

Key to the pre-reform social structure was the rural-urban divide, institutionalized by the household registration system (*hukou*). Under the registration system, all households had to be registered in the locale where they resided and also were categorized as either "agricultural" or "non-agricultural" (synonymously, "rural" or "urban") households (Chan and Zhang, 1999, pp. 821–822).

The installation and subsequent tightening of the *hukou* system reflected an effort on the part of the Chinese government to cope with demographic pressures created by its rapid socialist-style industrialization. After the civil war and two ensuing years of economic rehabilitation (1950–1952), millions of peasants were recruited by burgeoning state industrial enterprises established in urban areas as part of the first Five-Year Plan (1953–1957), and many more moved without restriction into cities to look for urban jobs (Meisner, 1999). To check this rapid influx into cities, the registration system made a distinction between agricultural and non-agricultural *hukou* that was used both to restrict further rural-to-urban migration and to return rural migrants to the countryside. This use was especially prevalent in the aftermath of the Great Leap Forward (1958–1960), which threw the newly established system into chaos. A dramatic increase in (nominal) industrial growth and urban inflow pushed China's urban population from 16.2% in 1958 to 19.7% in 1960, the all-time high in the pre-reform era (Wu and Treiman, 2004). The government soon realized that China's grain-production capacity was unable to sustain such a huge urban population, especially given the decline in agricultural production during the Great Leap Forward. Thus, beginning in 1959 the government expanded and rigorously enforced its use of the *hukou* system as a tool to control migration. About 18 million urban workers were sent back to their home villages between

1961 and 1963 (Chan, 1994, p. 39), and more than 20 million university and middle school students from urban areas were sent down to rural and border regions during the Cultural Revolution (1966–1976), to help reduce both urban unemployment and school crowding (Bernstein, 1977; Zhou and Hou, 1999).

The control on rural-to-urban migration via the *hukou* system was made possible by the people's commune system in rural areas, established after the agricultural collectivization, enabled local governments to bind peasants to the land. All adults had to participate in agricultural production to receive food rations for their households (Parish and Whyte, 1978) and migration was generally prohibited except with the permission of the village authority. The *hukou* system and restricted migration allowed the government to exploit the agricultural sector and sacrifice the interests of rural residents to those of urban residents. To ensure food grain needed for urban industrial growth, the government relied on a system of "unified purchase" (*tong gou*) to forcibly procure farm produce at low prices. At the same time, consumer products allocated free-of-charge or at low prices to urban residents as welfare benefits of their work units were sold at high prices in rural areas.

The government's discriminatory policy resulted in a substantial gap in income and living standards between rural and urban residents. Permanent urban residents also enjoyed many other welfare benefits delivered by the state, such as free or subsidized food grain, free or low-rent apartments, and retirement and medical insurance. The government also guaranteed every eligible urban resident a permanent job, but accepted no such responsibility for rural residents. Since the available resources are fairly limited given the level of economic development in China, with the *hukou* system the government was able to confine the majority of people in the bottom so as to make redistribution favorable to urban residents. As a result, *hukou* differentiates 70% of population in rural areas from 30% of population in urban areas, creating a fundamental structure of inequality in state socialist China. The rural-urban gap is usually likened to the distance between the earth and the heaven. Changing from rural *hukou* to urban *hukou* was very difficult (Wu and Treiman, 2004, 2007). According to the *hukou* regulations, even marriage to an urban resident did not entitle one to a permanent urban status (Whyte and Parish, 1984).

2. *The Work Unit System (Danwei)*

While peasants were confined to the rural collective sector, almost all urban workers were organized into *danwei* (work units), be it a factory, a store, a school, or a government office (Bian, 1994; Walder, 1986; Whyte and Parish, 1984). In Chinese official statistics, the work unit is defined as an independent accounting unit with three characteristics: (1) administratively, it is an independent organization; (2) fiscally, it has an independent budget and produces its own accounting tables of earnings and deficits; (3) financially, it has independent accounts in banks and has legal rights to sign contracts with government or business entities (Bian, 1994). In general, work units were classified into three categories based on their primary functions: (1) government or party agencies (*dangzheng jiguan*); (2) profit-making enterprises (*qiye danwei*), and (3) non-profit institutions (*shiye danwei*). Government or party agencies represented the state and assumed the central administrative role in Chinese society, while economic enterprises and nonprofit institutions were owned in varying degree by the state and were administrated directly or indirectly by the government.

As communist ideology proclaimed to eliminate private ownership over the means of production, after the economic recovery from the civil war, the government initiated the campaign called Socialist Transformation of the Capitalist Manufacturing and Commercial Industries in early 1950s, aiming to put vital private enterprises and institutions under state control. Other individual businesses and handicraft workers were organized into the collective sector, in which the properties of enterprises were literally owned by employees but operations were actually controlled by the government at the lower level. By 1956, the transformation was completed and the Chinese economy was dominated by state and collective enterprises, the two forms of public ownership (Bian, 1994, p. 24; Walder, 1986). Meanwhile, the rapid industrialization brought the birth of many new enterprises directly owned by the state. Furthermore, government administrative control also penetrated into non-profit institutions such as hospitals and schools, which were fully funded by government annual financial budget. The state work unit, supplemented by collective work units, has been major employers of the urban labor force until recent decades.

Due to the lack of autonomy, a work unit's goal was subordinate to that of the state. Work units not only worked towards their specific organizational goals but also carried out responsibilities of the state to its citizens. First, labor insurance and social security provisions were administrated through the work unit. Second, the work unit also directly supplied a range of state goods and services which, in market economies, would be supplied through markets or a variety of institutions and government agencies. In addition, the work unit performed a variety of sociopolitical services and therefore was the locus of a worker's social and political identity (Walder, 1986). In sum, the work unit was the basic cell of Chinese urban society and the crucial vehicle of social administration and social control (Li and Wang, 1992; Lu, 1989; Walder, 1986). The urban society has been organized as a hierarchy, in which each work organization functioned as a unit in the system dominated by the state.

In a typical redistribution process, the state first appropriated and mono-polized resources and opportunities and then allocated them to work units according to their positions in the redistributive hierarchy. Resources at a work unit's disposal were contingent upon its sector, ownership, and bureau-cratic rank in the redistributive hierarchy, among which the ownership dualism between the state and collective units probably was the most impor-tant (Bian, 1994; Liu, 2000; Walder, 1992). Urban workers and their families were largely dependent upon their affiliated work units for material resources and life chances (Walder, 1986, 1992). State workers, which accounted for 78% of the urban labor force by 1978 (National Bureau of Statistics, 2006), were provided with an "iron rice bowl" of permanent employment, as well as a variety of insurance, housing, and welfare benefits that were typically unavailable to collective workers. Once assigned to a work unit, workers could rarely change jobs in their lifetimes and mobility across different owner-ship sectors was even more difficult (Bian, 2002).

Beyond the urban context, the work unit system provided another insti-tutional basis for the effectiveness of the *hukou* system in restricting internal migration. Without a work unit, it was very difficult to survive in a city because housing, food, and other social services were unavailable through the market. Moreover, because employment quotas in all urban work units were tightly controlled by the government labor administration (Li and Wang, 1992; Walder, 1986), even rural residents willing to risk losing food rations by leaving their home villages would have little chance of getting a job in a city. This tight administrative control on both sides virtually eliminated unau-thorized rural-to-urban migration in the pre-reform era.

3. *Cadre-Worker Status Distinction*

Through the land reform in rural areas and the socialist transformation of capitalist economy in cities, landlords were wiped out since the mid-1950s. Because the class system based on property ownership was eliminated, the communist party claimed that socialist China was moving towards an egali-tarian society without the existence of exploiting classes. The occupational differentiation and social mobility seemed to be rarely observed in rural China, which was characterized as a de-stratified society, with most of its res-idents as farmers/peasants (Parish, 1984). In urban areas, the stratification based on work units rendered employees in state work units a privileged group. Within urban workplaces, employees were further distinguished into two status groups: cadres and workers.

State cadres (*guojia ganbu*) were a government-designated group, encompassing not only the administrative and professional elite but also the ordinary people in administrative or professional career tracks (about 20% of the urban labor force). State cadres were provided with better compensation packages and more career opportunities as they were kept in reserve for training and promotion into leadership positions (Bian, 2002). In contrast, those classified as "workers" most likely stayed in the group throughout their lifetime, and official promotion and change of status to state cadres (*ti gan*), if possible, would involve a very long bureaucratic procedure (Bian, 1994; Wu, 2001). Such a divide inside urban China's workplaces was similar to the line drawn between managerial staff and workers in western companies, although Mao's managers and professionals were fundamentally dependent upon the Communist party-state (Davis, 2000). In the countryside, the unsalaried village cadres exercised political and managerial authority over ordinary peasants but did not belong to the group of state cadres (Oi, 1989; Chan, Marsden and Unger, 1992).

Hence, notwithstanding the similarity to the line between white-collar and blue-collar jobs in western capitalist economies, the status distinction between state cadres and workers in Chinese workplaces was subordinate to the structural dualism between the rural and urban sectors and between the state and collective work units. Through the *hukou* institution, the majority of the national population was confined to rural areas, and socialist benefits such as permanent employment, housing, medical benefits and pensions were only available to urban residents. In the urban sector, privileges were rendered to employees in the state-owned work units (*danwei*). In the same work units, further distinction was made between cadres and workers. Such multi-layer differentials created a hierarchy of bounded social status groups: cadre, worker, or peasant. The labor markets for peasants, workers and cadres are explicitly segmented from one another, and the mobility from a lower status group to a higher status group is generally difficult, though changing jobs within the status group is relatively easier. Such a rigid status system has been associated with and intensified by institutional characteristics with respect to the *hukou* registration system and the work unit system, as described before (Bian, 2002; Wang, 2008; Wu, 2001).

To summarize, the genesis of the unique system probably is associated with demographic problems that the Chinese government needed to tackle and the economic development level when China attempted to install the state socialist regime. Chinese work organizations shared many similarities with their counterparts in the former Soviet Bloc; migration from rural to urban areas was also restricted in other state socialist countries. However, a key difference that contributed to the uniqueness of Chinese institutions was that it suffered from a massive oversupply of labor whereas a labor shortage was a major constraint on the Soviet industrial growth. While the Soviet Union had been predominantly urban society and already passed through demographic transition, China's population was still nearly 90% rural and still in the midst of this transition when state socialism was installed. Had the restrictive segmentation polices not been implemented under the redistributive system, the threat that rural migrants would inundate the cities and overtax housing supplies and municipal services might have made the system totally collapse. Therefore the Chinese government had to install unusually strict controls on labor mobility (via work units) and migration (via hukou) (Walder, 1986, pp. 28–30). The creation of a rigid pattern of status distinctions within the urban labor force could also be understood in this societal-historical context.

Rural Reform, *Hukou* and Labor Migration

1. *Growth in Rural Non-agricultural Sector*

China's economic miracles over the past three decades have been driven by two fundamental forces: economic industrialization and institutional reform. Economic reform started in rural areas since 1978 has first undermined the rigid hierarchy of social and economic controls. The commune system in rural areas was scraped, replaced by the household responsibility system as the major form of agricultural production. Peasants signed contract with the local government to deliver a fixed quota of grain in exchanging for farming on a household basis; as a result, they gained freedom to their labor and no longer need to report to the collective for daily work (Lin, Cai and Li, 1994). Such a reform has substantially relaxed the administrative control of population migration and labor mobility via the *hukou* system (Cheng and Selden, 1994; Chan and Zhang, 1999).

The release of surplus labor tied to the land helped create a rural labor market and drive the spectacular growth of rural non-agricultural sectors, largely constituted by local township and village-owned enterprises (TVEs) (Oi, 1990). From 1978 to the mid-1990s, TVEs were the most dynamic part of Chinese economy and fundamentally changed rural economy and society. As shown in Table 1, the non-agricultural employment in TVEs grew from 28 million in 1978 to 155 million in 2008, and the rural laborers involved in farm

Table 1. Share of year-end employment by different ownership types in rural areas, 1978–2008

Year	TVEs	Self-employed	Private	Farm	Total (Unit: 10,000 people)
1978	9.23	0.00	0.00	90.77	30638
1980	9.42	0.00	0.00	90.58	31836
1985	18.83	0.00	0.00	81.17	37065
1990	19.42	0.24	3.13	80.58	47708
1991	20.01	0.24	3.36	79.99	48026
1992	22.00	0.28	3.58	78.00	48291
1993	25.43	0.39	4.14	74.57	48546
1994	24.62	0.65	5.23	75.38	48802
1995	26.24	0.96	6.23	73.76	49025
1996	27.55	1.12	6.75	72.45	49028
1997	26.61	1.22	7.18	73.39	49039
1998	25.57	1.50	7.86	74.43	49021
1999	25.94	1.98	7.81	74.06	48982
2000	26.20	2.33	6.00	73.80	48934
2001	26.66	2.42	5.36	73.34	49085
2002	27.14	2.88	5.05	72.86	48960
2003	27.82	3.59	4.63	72.18	48793
2004	28.46	4.15	4.24	71.54	48724
2005	29.43	4.88	4.38	70.57	48494
2006	30.53	5.47	4.46	69.47	48090
2007	31.68	5.61	4.59	68.32	47640
2008	32.69	5.88	4.58	67.31	47270

Sources: National Bureau of statistics, *China statistical yearbook 2009*. Also available at http://www.stats.gov.cn/tjsj/ndsj/2009/indexee.htm

only decreased from 90.77% in 1978 to 67.31% in 2008. The share of TVEs value added increased from less than 6% in 1978 to 26% in 1996, despite the fact that GDP itself was growing rapidly during the period. Non-agricultural income not only raised peasants' living standards and contributed to the declining urban-rural gaps but also presented mounting competition for state-owned enterprises throughout the 1980s and early 1990s (Naughton, 2007, p. 274).

Most of TVEs employees were recruited from local peasants, who worked as both part-time wage earners and part-time farmers (Parish, Zhe and Li, 1995). From its inception, the rural non-farm employment has been truly market-oriented, wage determination in the rural public sector is found similar to that in the rural private sector, but quite different from that in the urban public sector (Peng, 1992). Unlike urban workers, peasant-workers are not entitled to job security and welfare benefits such as housing, pension and medicare plans, thus offer sufficient cheaper labor to rural industrialization. During economic recession, they can be easily let go and return to farm, regardless whether they are employed in the public or private sectors (De Brauw *et al.*, 2002). Local governments have no responsibility to create jobs for them. They are not even counted in government unemployment statistics (Solinger, 2001).

2. *Migration and Urbanization*

The initial development of urban labor markets in China was driven by laborers outside the urban formal employment system based on *danwei* (Wu and Xie, 2003). To enhance the development of the urban service sector, since 1983, the government had allowed peasants to enter cities and establish small urban businesses such as shoe-repair shops, barbershops, and restaurants (Li, 1993). Furthermore, millions of young peasants from rural areas were hired in the growing urban private sector. Even the state-owned enterprises preferred to hire rural workers either because they had no legal commitment to housing and other social benefits for these peasant-workers, or because the jobs were unattractive to urban workers (Cai, 2002).

As a result, the release of surplus rural laborers from the land in rural reform and the emergence of a free social space in urban reform have triggered a massive labor migration in China. Geographic mobility has been much easier than before. Since the late 1990s, out-migration to cities has prevailed over local employment in TVEs, when TVEs businesses encountered difficulties and were privatized (Cai, 2002). The government's bureaucratic control over population migration and labor mobility is waning rapidly (Liang, 2001; Liang and Ma, 2004).

Migration is also facilitated by China's economic globalization. In the 1990s, China's rapid rise as an international production force can be attributed to its low labor costs to a large extent. In labor-intensive manufacturing companies, typically in the Pearl River Delta of Guangdong province, majority of workers are rural migrants from in-land provinces such as Sichuan, Hunan, and Jiangxi, etc. The China's 2000 census data shows that there are over 11 million migrants in Guangdong province, nearly 70% residing in cities and towns. Migrant workers account for 1/3 of all urban labor forces in the province. In Shenzhen, the pioneer city of Chinese capitalist experiment, there are 5.7 millions migrants which account for 82.1% of the city's total residing population, and over 50% work in the manufacturing sector. In the nearby Dongguan city, migrants are 5.8 million in contrast to 1.7 million local residents (Wu, 2009a).

In the capitalist global production chains, *hukou*, the institutional legacy from the state socialist redistributive economy, has ironically been used as the main means to maintain a large pool of low-wage labor. Most migrant workers work for long hours without adequate compensations and protections. Many injured workers are simply dismissed and sent back to their home villages. These peasant-workers are not entitled to medical insurance and pension plan, despite the fact that they are stipulated by the labor laws. They can be laid off easily without much dispute rights (Pun, 2005). The official trade unions do not treat them as the eligible members. In the past twenty years, while the economy in the Pearl River Delta has grown exponentially, the monthly wages of migrant workers increased by only 68 RMB *yuan*. Migrant workers' wellbeing lagged far behind in China's economic prosperity.

It is also in the interest of local government authorities to implement the social exclusions and maintain a pool of flexible labor force. Chinese rural migrants in the urban economy serve a similar role as do those illegal immigrants in western developed countries (Roberts, 1997). First, the government does not have responsibilities to provide social service or public goods to rural migrants. When a labor dispute takes place, local governments are more aligned with employers' interests than with the protection of workers' rights, because local governments are competing with each other for Foreign Direct Investment (FDI) in order to boost local economic development, and serious implementation of labor law would drive the investors away. Second, a large pool of migrants not only contribute to the total GDP growth and generate extra revenues and surcharge fees for the local governments, but also help to increase the GDP per capita, since migrant workers usually are not included in the calculation on the per capita basis. Finally, the surging migrants are often blamed for the untidiness, crowdedness, traffic congestion, and rising crimes. Indeed, when the government would like to clean up the cities, these migrants are always affected. In particular, as the market reform proceeds further in urban China, many local workers have lost their jobs and privileges and become off-duty workers (*xiagang*), for whom the city government has responsibilities to provide employment opportunities. Local city governments issued laws and regulations stipulating that certain jobs have to hire those with local *hukou* and openly discriminate migrants.

Therefore, in the pre-reform era, rural and urban residents were spatially segregated by the *hukou* system under which majority of rural peasants lived in countryside and urban residents lived in cities. Social and spatial boundaries are largely consistent with each other. The surging migration in the reform era has brought visible social boundary into cities. Migrants are socially and spatially segregated in urban China. The *hukou* system is employed as the main basis for social exclusion. Hence, the large-scale migration from rural to urban areas in the reform-era has not dismantled the socialist segregation policy set by the household registration system. Instead, it has made the long-existing inequality and social injustice more visible.

The increasing geographic migration and persisting *hukou* system have led to a disparity between people's residence and registration place in the reform era. Table 2 presents the percentage distribution of national population by residence type and *hukou* status in China from 1982 to 2005. In 1982, when the economic reform just started, over 92% (=74.8/81.0) of rural *hukou* holders resided in rural areas, whereas about 77% (=14.6/19.0) of urban *hukou* holders indeed resided in cities. As of 2005, the *hukou* system has lost much of its effectiveness in restricting rural-urban migrations: only 71% (=52.5/73.9) of rural *hukou* holders still lived in villages whereas the rest 29% (=21.4/73.9) resided in urban areas and were often referred as "rural migrants" or "floating population." On

Table 2. Rural-urban residence and *Hukou* status in China, 1982–2005

Residence (*De Facto*)	*Hukou* Status (*De Jure*)		
	Agricultural	Non-agricultural	Total
1982			
Rural	74.8%	4.4%	79.2%
Urban	6.2	14.6	20.8
Total	81.0%	19.0%	100.0%
1990			
Rural	64.1%	2.5%	66.2%
Urban	15.5	18.3	33.7
Total	79.5%	20.5%	100.0%
2000			
Rural	60.2%	3.0%	63.2%
Urban	15.0	21.9	36.8
Total	75.2%	24.8%	100.0%
2005			
Rural	52.5%	1.9%	54.4%
Urban	21.4	24.2	45.6
Total	73.9%	26.1%	100.0%

Sources: Micro-data of China Population Censuses 1982, 1990, 2000 and Mini-census 2005.

the other hand, about 93% (=24.2/26.1) of urban *hukou* holders lived in cities and towns in 2005, although the percentage they account for the *de facto* urban population has declined from 70% (=14.6/20.8) in 1982 to 53% (=24.2/45.6) in 2005 because of increasing rural migration in urban areas (Liang and Ma, 2004).

On the other hand, despite the great ease in spatial migration, the *hukou* distinction creates an institutional hurdle for urbanization, which is typically associated with industrialization. Change from rural to urban status remains restrictive and selective. As Figure 1 shows, while the *de facto* urban population has increased from 20.8% in 1982 to 45.6% in 2005, the *de jure* urban population (with urban *hukou*) increased only slightly, from 19.0% in 1982 to 26.1% in 2005. The *hukou* continues to be used as the main criterion for social exclusion of rural *de jure* residents.

While the benefits associated with urban *hukou* have faded away as the urban reform proceeds (see next section, also Lin and Wu, 2009), the government still has to rely on the *hukou* distinction for administrative control and police monitors (Wang, 2004). Those migrants without stable jobs and residence places are often arrested as "vagrants," and sent to labor camps for several months to earn the fare the government would spend sending them home. This practice has been scolded not only by migrant workers themselves but also those educated urbanites. The public outrage culminated in an episode in 2003,

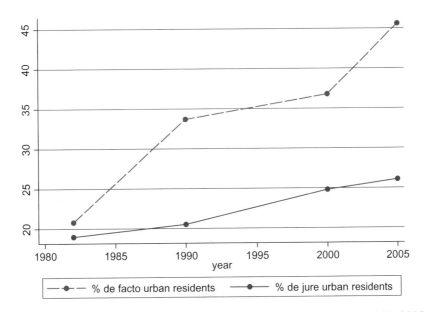

Figure 1. Percentage of *de facto* and *de jure* urban residents in China, 1982–2005

when Sun Zhigang, a college-educated migrant in Guangdong province (who supposedly held non-local urban registration status), was beaten to death in police custody after being detained on suspicion of vagrancy (he indeed held a white-collar job). Sun's death gave the impetus to the abolition of the Custody and Repatriation System (New York Times, 2005).

3. Recent Reforms on Hukou Regulations

As mentioned before, rural residents have temporarily benefited from the economic reform in the 1980s, but when the focus of reform was shifted to urban areas since the mid-1980s, development policies that neglected rural areas and agriculture, coupled with the rejection of citizenship to migrants, have created a huge gap in income, wealth, and life chances between rural and urban China in the 1990s, which may jeopardize the social stability and the country's long-term growth. In this context, the *hukou* regulations, after 20 years of reforms, began to adjust to accommodate the changes in labor markets in the beginning of the 21st century.

The elimination of the Custody and Repatriation System in 2003 had a significant impact on the *hukou* system, although it did not constitute a reform of the latter. For example, many provincial and municipal governments throughout China sped up their *hukou* reforms. The State Council's regulation ordered that migrant workers no longer be arrested for not possessing the right papers, and ordered police to provide urban residency documents to any migrant who can find a job.

Despite the regional variations, the qualifications required to obtain urban temporary registration tend to be similar and often consist of having fixed residence and stable employment (usually one year on the job) in an urban area. State regulations introduced in 2001 made the *hukou* reform more of a local government responsibility than a national government-based one. By the beginning of the twenty-first century, local governments had almost complete control over population administration within their jurisdictions. Municipal governments in several large cities did not immediately implement the reform policies introduced by the national government in 1998, and their refusal to do so was tolerated by the national authorities. The high fees associated with obtaining an urban *hukou* in large cities, such as Beijing, Shanghai, Guangzhou and Shenzhen, which are the most attractive to migrants, made access to these cities out of reach for most of peasants.

Nevertheless, several provinces and major cities began to speed up local *hukou* reforms in 2003 (South China Morning Post, 8 July 2003). Beijing, for example, introduced further reforms in the summer of 2003, by issuing a new type of *hukou* registration called the Beijing Employment and Residence Permit, which would give its holders "rights to housing, education, investment, social and medical insurance and a driver's license" (South China Morning Post, 8 July 2003). In order to be issued such a permit, however, a person must be residing in Beijing, be employed, have a bachelor's degree and two years of employment experience. This, according to the South China Morning Post, means that only "a selective few will qualify." In March 2004, it was reported that the province of Guangdong was taking measures to protect the legal rights of its 23 million migrant workers and their families, including the rights to education and medical insurance. These measures included setting up offices across the province, at the provincial and local levels, to offer better services to migrants. An article in the Shenzhen Daily on September 22, 2004 also discussed the reforms taking place in the city of Guangzhou, where rural *hukou* holders with regular jobs and fixed residences would become eligible for Guangzhou *hukou*. Another article on China Daily, December 28, 2004 discussed additional reforms planned by Guangdong province, which, according to an official at the Public Security Bureau, would lead to the total elimination of the agricultural *hukou* in the province in the years ahead.

Urban Work Units in Transitions

1. *The Work Unit and Changing Labor Relationship*

One of the most important policy changes since the reform was that the state has loosened its control over work units. They were granted more decision-making power and could now retain a larger share of the surpluses and distribute it to workers at their own discretion, either as direct bonuses, or as spending on shared living facilities (Walder, 1986). As a result, Chinese work organizations became less dependent on the state.

While the reformers' initial goal was to link the workers' material rewards closely to productivity, which would in turn improve a firm's economic performance, the loosened control over firms had both expected and unexpected consequences. First, it quickly became clear that firms' profitability depended on many external factors other than workers' productivity. Such external factors included technology, competition (i.e., whether a firm had a monopoly), and regional advantages (i.e., access to natural resources or foreign technology). Second, the patron-client relationship between managers and workers motivated firms to increase bonus payments to employees, often out-of-proportion to increases in productivity and profitability, only to be curtailed by policy measures such as setting a ceiling on bonuses in the late 1970s and levying bonus taxes on state firms in the 1980s. Third, while initially intended as a form of supplementary income, bonuses gradually became a main source of income, indeed constituting more than half of the total income on average in the late 1980s and early 1990s. While base salaries remained largely regulated by the government, the ability to generate bonus funds and to reward employees varied considerably from one firm to another. Therefore, variation in bonuses had become a main source of inter-firm income inequality in reform-era China. Finally, the incentive system that originated in the industrial sector began to be emulated by work units in all other sectors, even in those where profitability either cannot be meaningfully measured or is simply not meaningful, such as government branch offices, schools, hospitals, and research institutions.

When the state-mandated salaries became only a small proportion of workers' total compensations in the industrial sectors, workers in other sectors lagging behind pressured their *danwei* to generate extra revenues and to upgrade their living standards. Such institutional competitions had transformed all Chinese *danwei* to generate extra revenue via a subsidiary business so that it could pay bonuses/living stipends to their employees, and this payout was dependent more on membership in a *danwei* than on direct participation in revenue generation.

Danwei had two avenues to expanding their disposable resources — improve their efficiency and/or hide their discretionary revenues. A typical strategy was to establish new subsidiary firms (essentially with the state-owned assets) under legitimate excuses. Factories could lease empty offices for rent and could run shops, restaurants, and even hotels (commonly called tertiary industries or *sanchan*). The revenues from these sources were often unaccountable to supervising agencies and largely retained at the work units' discretion.

This practice of generating extra revenues for the financial benefit of employees extended to all types of *danwei* (including government agencies and non-profit institutions), in the form of collective moonlighting, that diverted themselves from their designated organizational functions. Many government bureaus abused their regulatory powers to benefit their own staff by imposing unauthorized surcharges and fines. Primary and middle schools began to charge students miscellaneous fees under different covers to generate extra funds to pay teachers. In short, all *danwei* tried to take advantage of their own structural positions and generate revenues for their employees, transformed from "rank-seeking" under the old redistributive system to "rent-seeking" in the socialist mixed economy.

Therefore, it has been argued that the importance of work units has increased, and the relationship between workers and their work units has been ironically strengthened since the late 1980s (Naughton, 1997). While the decentralization policy has allowed work units to retain more resources, and the labor market and the social security systems are not yet fully functional, workers naturally relied more on their work units to upgrade their living standards and gain access to life chances (Naughton, 1997). Consequently, earnings determination became more dependent on the organizational attributes of the employer than on the characteristics of individual employees. Earnings might vary significantly among people with the same level of education working at the same occupations solely because of their affiliations with organizations of different revenue-generating ability (Zhao, 1993; Zhao, 1994).

In the late 1990s, the Chinese economic reform began to change these conditions by weakening workers' organizational dependence on their work units. First, housing allocation has been marketized and privatized rapidly, starting in 1998. A nationwide policy to commercialize the urban housing sector was implemented, and most public housing units were sold to their current occupants at discounted prices. Direct allocation of new housing units by *danwei* ceased. Workers had to use their own savings and bank mortgages to purchase apartments (Zang, 1999). Meanwhile, the delivery of other in-kind benefits and services increasingly took the form of lump-sum cash payments, as the state further lifted its salary control on work units (Yang and Zhou, 1999).

Furthermore, for a long time since the Maoist era, the Chinese party-state had committed to providing urban citizens life-time employment and most social services via the unique work unit (*danwei*) system, to which over-staffing was almost an inherent problem (Wu, 2002). With the competition from the emerging market sector since the 1990s, Chinese state-owned enterprises (SOEs) have increasingly failed to make profits (Xie and Wu, 2008). To make the state-owned enterprises more efficient and sustainable, the government had to allow them to streamline superfluous laborers, though in a moderate way. The term *xiagang*, literally means step-down-from-the-post in Chinese, initially applied only to workers from bankrupted, merged, closed-down enterprises but gradually included those whose salary was cut or suspended (Lee, 2000). These off-duty workers continued to maintain their employment relationship with their original work units to receive living stipends and claim social security benefits (Lee, 2000). According to Chinese government statistics, there were 12.7 million laid-off (*xiagang*) workers at the end of 1997, 8.77 million at the end of 1998, 9.37 million at the end of

1999, and 9.11 million at the end of 2000. These figures include only those who were still looking for jobs at the end of the respective year; indeed, more workers have suffered from the experience of *xiagang* (Xie, 2006, p. 23).

While some *xiagang* workers may still be able to find a new job within the state sector, more tend to enter the market for survival, because the living stipends paid to *xiagang* workers would gradually fade away and the job opportunities in the state sector had been shrinking since the 1990s. Earlier studies have consistently reported that *xiagang* workers in the state sector tend to be less educated, in middle age, women, concentrated in certain industries and regions (Solinger, 2001; Xie, 2006). The state mass layoff thus had forced these workers to depart for the market sector in the end. In this sense, *xiagang* arrangement does not apply to employees in the private sector but instead serves as a transient step for the state work unit to streamline redundant work forces.

Finally, social security (pension and medical care) has now been success-fully detached from the work unit and unified at the provincial level, and the coverage has been further extended to the private sector. Both employers and employees are required to make contributions to the pension and medical care funds, with individuals maintaining separate accounts. When workers change jobs, the accounts remain the same. This reform has removed the hurdle for labor mobility, particularly into the private sector.

With the rapid growth of the private sector and foreign investment, com-peting against the state-owned enterprises, the Chinese government has increased its tolerance for unemployment, and enterprises and managers now are granted more power to lay off workers or cut payments and benefits (Wu, 2006). The massive layoff of state workers caused many workers to leave work units involuntarily, indicating that work units no longer served as patrons to protect workers' interests (Wu, 2010a). Management-labor relationships have worsened, and the patron-client relationship that once characterized the Chinese unique work unit institutions has been turned into what some schol-ars have called "managerial despotism" in the late reform era (Lee, 2000).

2. *The Growth of Self-Employment and Private Sectors*

The *danwei*-based system was further undermined by a newly expanding pri-vate sector as an alternative provider of resources and life chances outside the redistributive sector, though it does not mean the end of *danwei* as a persist-ent agent of stratification in Chinese society. Private economic activity in China takes two forms: individual/household businesses (*geti gongshang hu* or *geti hu*) and private enterprises (*siying qiye*) (Gregory *et al.*, 2000; Wu, 2006).

Unlike the radical privatization programs in post-1989 Eastern Europe and Russia, Chinese reformers have adopted an incremental approach to expanding the private sector without first closing down or privatizing state-owned enterprises (Qian, 2000). The government initially imposed various restrictions on the growth of the private economy. In the early 1980s, only individual family businesses (*geti hu*) were granted legal status, and a cap of eight was set on the number of employees a *geti hu* could hire. Private enterprises (*siying qiye*) on a larger scale, many of which evolved from individual family businesses, were not sanctioned until the mid-1980s. After a short period of setback between 1989 and 1991, the development of the private sector has gained new momentum when Deng Xiaoping called for further market-oriented reforms in his famous tour to southern China in 1992. Private ownership became fully legitimized and played an increasingly important role in China's economic growth.

To put the growth of the private sector in a historical context, domestic private enterprises barely existed by the end of the 1980s. In the mid-1990s, 8,220,000 employees worked for 655,000 private enterprises, which were owned by about 1,340,000 private entrepreneurs. By the end of 2004, the number of employees of private enterprises increased to 40,686,000, and the number of owners increased to 9,486,000 (Zhang, 2006, p. 345). These figures do not include the self-employed and small employers who hired fewer than eight employees (*geti hu*) and those working in share-holding companies and firms with investments coming from places outside China, including Hong Kong, Macau and Taiwan. According to the data from China's population mini-census in 2005 (authors' calculation), employment in non-state sectors accounted for 67.8% of the national non-agricultural labor force, of which 61.1% were wage employees, 6.6% were employers, and 32.3% were self-employed.

While self-employed workers were major players and economic winners in the early reform period, and individual/household businesses continued to outnumber private enterprises in quantity and employment size, their contributions to national economic growth seem to be diminishing, given the rise of private enterprises since the mid-1990s. As Table 3 shows, from 1989 to 2006, the contributions of private enterprises to national GDP and tax have increased drastically, whereas the contributions from self-employment (*geti hu*) sectors remained largely stagnant and even declined. Many self-employed workers were indeed migrant workers from rural areas and laidoff workers from state-owned enterprises, who were denied of access to jobs in formal employment sectors. It is no surprise that the involuntary self-employed workers no longer enjoyed earnings advantages over waged employees.

Table 3. Private enterprises and *Geti Hu's* contributions to national GDP and tax in China, 1989–2006

Year	Contribution to national GDP			Contribution to national tax		
	Private	Geti hu	Subtotal	Private	Geti hu	Subtotal
1989	0.57	3.29	3.86	0.04	4.39	4.43
1990	0.65	3.44	4.09	0.07	4.68	4.75
1991	0.67	3.59	4.26	0.11	5.04	5.15
1992	0.76	3.44	4.20	0.14	5.36	5.50
1993	1.19	3.93	5.12	0.25	7.40	7.65
1994	2.39	3.40	5.79	0.34	7.03	7.37
1995	3.78	4.59	8.37	0.59	6.65	7.24
1996	4.53	4.97	9.50	0.87	5.76	6.63
1997	4.97	5.77	10.74	1.10	5.59	6.69
1998	6.93	7.06	13.99	1.77	5.81	7.58
1999	8.57	7.88	16.45	2.39	5.39	7.78
2000	10.83	7.22	18.05	3.29	6.06	9.35
2001	11.45	6.68	18.13	4.32	6.00	10.32
2002	12.75	6.62	19.37	5.36	5.36	10.72
2003	14.79	6.44	21.23	6.94	5.23	12.17
2004	14.35	5.07	19.42	8.25	5.01	13.26
2005	14.98	5.36	20.34	9.44	4.82	14.26
2006	15.11	5.06	20.17	10.04	3.43	13.47

Data sources: Thirty years of China's non-public economy edited by Zhou Liqun and Xie Siquan, Chongqing University Press.

On the other hand, the exponential growth of private enterprises in the later 1990s can be attributed not only to policy shifts that grant more rooms for their development, but to the ownership re-structuring of small and medium-sized state and collective enterprises and the privatization of rural TVEs (Kung and Lin, 2007). This reform presented immense opportunities to incumbent managers to convert the public assets into their private properties (Walder, 2003).

Given the sizable growth of private entrepreneurs/capitalists in the past decade, the Communist Party and the Chinese government have cleared away both political and legal taboos for the development of a private economy. The private sector was elevated to a status equal to that of the state sector in the 15th National Congress of the Chinese Communist Party in 1997 and endorsed in the Constitution in 1999; protection of private property was incorporated into the Constitution by a recent amendment in 2003 (Zhang, 2006).

Perhaps the economic importance of private entrepreneurs as a newly emerging social force can be better appreciated by looking at the recent changes in the recruitment policies of the ruling Communist Party. In the Chinese authoritarian political system, to accommodate such fundamental changes in the economic sphere, the Communist Party started to recognize the political status of the new economic elite and intended to tame the competing social forces during China's economic transition. The former Chinese President and CCP General Secretary Jiang Zemin put forward a theory of "Three Represents", which aimed to incorporate the private entrepreneurs into the ruling party elite (Jia, 2004).

The private sector also provided more job opportunities for employees. Table 4 shows the percentage distribution of the urban employment rate by ownership type of the employer over time from 1978 to 2008. In 1978, almost 100% of people worked in the state or collective work units, whereas in 2008, more than 75% of urban laborers worked in the

Table 4. Number of employed persons at year-end in urban areas

Year	State	Collective	Self-employed	Private and others	Total (Unit: 10,000 people)
1978	78.32	21.53	0.16	0.00	9514
1980	76.19	23.04	0.77	0.00	10525
1985	70.19	25.95	3.51	0.34	12808
1990	60.71	20.83	3.60	14.86	17041
1991	61.06	20.77	3.96	14.21	17465
1992	60.97	20.27	4.14	14.62	17861
1993	59.80	18.58	5.09	16.53	18262
1994	60.12	17.61	6.57	15.70	18653
1995	59.14	16.53	8.19	16.13	19040
1996	56.44	15.14	8.58	19.84	19922
1997	53.14	13.87	9.23	23.75	20781
1998	41.90	9.08	10.45	38.56	21616
1999	38.25	7.64	10.77	43.34	22412
2000	35.00	6.48	9.23	49.30	23151
2001	31.91	5.39	8.90	53.79	23940
2002	28.91	4.53	9.16	57.41	24780
2003	26.82	3.90	9.27	60.01	25639
2004	25.34	3.39	9.52	61.75	26476
2005	23.74	2.96	10.16	63.13	27331
2006	22.71	2.70	10.64	63.95	28310
2007	21.89	2.45	11.28	64.39	29350
2008	21.34	2.19	11.95	64.52	30210

Sources: National Bureau of Statistics, *China statistical yearbook 2009*. Also available at http://www.stats.gov.cn/tjsj/ndsj/2009/indexee.htm

non-state sector. There was a significant structural shift in the late 1990s (Naughton, 2007). Hence, after 30 years of economic reforms, those who own and those who do not own the means of production have become increasingly divided (Bian, 2002). Scholars have also revived their interests in class issues (under the term "stratum" [*jie ceng*]), with the new middle class (including private entrepreneurs) being a focal point of research and interests (Lu, 2002). On the other hand, the formation of a new working class in the private sector has been attracting more and more scholarly attention (Pun, 2005).

3. *From Work Unit to Community Governance*

Urban China used to be characterized as a *danwei*-society, where all economic compensations, social services were delivered and political activities were organized through *danwei*, supplemented by neighborhood committees. The hierarchical *danwei* system also enables the party-state to manage and mobilize its citizens (Walder, 1986; Yang and Zhou, 1999). Given the fundamental structural changes described above, the work unit system is no longer able to exert its jurisdiction over the majority of urban residents by providing employment, fringe benefits and social service.

Foreseeing the weakening role of work units in social-political control and mass mobilization, the central government poured more resources to strengthen the organizations of street committees and neighborhood committees, under the name of "community construction." The idea of community construction was proposed initially by the Ministry of Civil Affairs in 1991. The primary motivation behind China's community construction project is to ease the social burdens on the state and enterprises (*danwei*), and to tackle social problems caused by economic reform. The community construction started with the launch of a policy of developing "community service" in urban China. Community service not only takes care of the well-being of those who are not covered by work units but also provides the livelihood for the unemployed, laid-off and under-employed workers in the community, who were forced out of the work units in the economic restructuring. The subsequent expansion of community services, coupled with a huge investment on infrastructure (community service centers), has strengthened the role of grassroots community as a new sector to replace certain functions that used to be performed by work units.

To be sure, the Chinese conception of community may not be understood in a western tradition, which very often ties the notion of community closely to that of the civil society and liberal democratic politics (Etzioni, 1993; Giddens, 1998). The community construction is largely a social engineering project to elaborate the current urban administrative system by repositioning and enhancing community — the modified neighborhood committees — as both a political surveillance and social control entity and a social service provider (Yan and Gao, 2007). To ensure the primacy of the CCP, then the Party General Secretary Jiang Zemin called for the establishment of a CCP branch in every community (Yan and Gao, 2007).

It is also possible, however, that residents' participation in community affairs may foster grassroots democracy and lead to a more open society in China. This process was facilitated by the housing reform and commercialization in urban China, especially since 1998. For most period of the People's Republic, the state directly controlled the production, allocation, operation, and pricing of urban housing, playing a dual role as both investor and developer, but without the concern of revenue or return. Under this system, the state collects an implicit income tax from workers through low wages and redistributes them back to urban dwellers in forms of housing, food, medical care, and the like. Housing provision was administered mainly through work units and homeownership and private property rights virtually vanished since the late 1950s. In the 1980s and early 1990s, work units had been granted autonomy to raise funds and construct housing for their own employees. It was not until 1998 when accelerating residential development and elevating urban homeownership were made as a top policy priority under then Premier Zhu Rongji's leadership. The explicit goal was to increase housing and related consumption, to improve economic efficiency, and to reduce the government's burden on maintaining and constructing urban housing. Work units no longer provide housing to new employees and old flats were sold to occupants with discount prices. Consequently, homeownership rate in urban China shot up sharply at the end of the 1990s, from about 30% in 1995 to more than 70% in 2000. Housing construction also reached a new record high (Yu, 2006).

The housing reform and commercialization of housing provision further detach urban residents from their work units and create an urban middle class of homeowners. These new home owners are more active in participating in community affairs and would not hesitate in defending their property rights, though in a moderate mode (Cai, 2005). Homeowners associations enjoy much larger autonomy compared to government-sponsored grassroots organizations such as neighborhood committees. They could be an important force to nurture burgeoning China's civil society and grassroots democracy (MacLeod, 2006).

Inequality, Education and Social Mobility

1. *Changing Inequality and Stratification*

The pattern of inequality and stratification in a society reflects how resources and life chances are distributed across different groups in the social structure, and the issue of distribution is always accompanied with economic growth. Not all Chinese people benefit equally from the economic miracles in the past three decades. The issue of who wins and who loses in the economic transition becomes a central concern among sociologists who study the social consequences of China's economic reforms.

The previous discussions on institutional arrangements under Chinese socialism suggest that pre-reform China was not as egalitarian as it was intended to be as the ideology claimed. For the first three decades of the People's Republic, while inequality based on property rights was largely eliminated, new forms of inequalities under socialism have been created by bureaucratic allocation of labor force through intermediate institutions on behalf of the state, such as the household registration (*hukou*), the work unit (*danwei*), and cadre-work status distinction. The unequal opportunity structure created by the socialist state itself can be counterbalanced only by the introduction of the market mechanism in the early reform period (Szelenyi, 1978). However, as the market continues to rise as the dominate mechanism in resource distributions, the government intervention is needed to curb the rising inequality by various social policies.

Indeed, the trajectory of changing inequality in China over the past three decades since reform has been consistent with the projections above. The change in income inequality presents a U-shaped pattern, first declining then increasing. As Table 5 shows, the Gini coefficient, a common measure of income inequality, declined from 0.317 in 1978 to 0.295 in 1980 and then increased to 0.449 in 2005 for the nation as a whole. Income inequality between urban and rural population, particularly prominent in China shows the similar pattern: the urban-rural ratio of income per capita declined slightly in the early 1980s, but has increased dramatically since then, from 2.5 in 1990 to 3.1 in 2000 and 3.2 in 2005. Urban-rural income inequality has contributed 43% to overall income inequality in China (Cai and Wan, 2006, p. 3).

Understanding the change of income inequality cannot simply rely on the determinants at individual levels. The institutions inherited from the socialist past continue to shape the path of China's development and mechanism of resource distributions, although they may have lost their original attributes in redistribution processes. For example, the bureaucratic rank of work unit may no longer matter in determining economic rewards (Wu and

Table 5. Trends in income inequality in China, 1978–2005

Year	Gini index	Urban-rural ratio of income per capita
1978	0.317	2.35
1980	0.295	2.75
1985	0.331	2.14
1990	0.357	2.51
1995	0.290	2.79
2000	0.390	3.10
2005	0.449	3.22

Data sources: Comprehensive statistical data and materials on 50 years of new China, China Statistics Publishing House, also available at http://www.stats.gov.cn/tjsj/ndsj/; World Income Inequality Database http://www.wider.unu.edu/wiid/wiid.htm

Guo, 2010), as suggested by Walder (1995), but the organizational profitability continues to play a prominent role in economic stratification. According to Wang Feng (2008), ownership type, industry, locale, and work organization have served as the basis of economic organization, social control, and benefits distribution under Chinese state socialism and also evolved into more permanent sources of economic inequality in the reform era. Urban inequality existed mainly across these categories, whereas equality within categories persisted to a large extent. Hence, the pattern of income distribution in urban China is characterized by the mixture of global inequality with local equality, which, to some extent, helps explain why the sharply rising inequality has not led to any clear sign of a revolution or social unrest in Chinese cities (Wu, 2009b; Whyte, 2010).

Status distinction between cadres and workers under state socialism becomes much more complicated than before. Based on occupational differentiation and the possession of organizational resources, economic resources, and cultural resources, according to a group of sociologists from the Chinese Academy of Social Sciences (CASS), Chinese people were classified into 10 social classes, including state/social administrators, managers, private enterprise owners, routine non-manual workers, self-employed, service workers, manufacturing workers, farmers, and the jobless/ unemployed/semi-employed (Lu, 2002). Although these categories were called "social strata" (*shehui jieceng*), they are essentially nominal classes.

How is changing inequality related to the transformation of class structure in China? Lin and Wu's analysis (2009) revealed that, while education and party membership are important predictors of income in China, class is the most important predictor of inequality and it was more important in 2005 than in 1988. Between-group comparisons of income show that private owners and cadres' income advantages have increased over the decades. They are the main winners in the economic transitions, whereas peasants, workers in the private sector, and even the self-employed are the losers. China's momentum of changes in inequality is associated with the shifting effect of *hukou*, *danwei*, skill/authority in the workplace, and means of production. The development of labor markets and the privatization since the mid-1990s seem to have enhanced the role of the ownership of authority/skills and economic capital in generating inequalities in the course of China's market transition.

The emergence and growth of middle classes in China have increasingly received attention among both scholars and policy makers since the 1990s. The new middle class, often referred to as "the new social strata" in Chinese (*xin shehui jieceng*), are comprised of professionals and managers who work in privately-owned high-tech firms and foreign-invested companies, the self-employed and private business owners, and others who are employed in non-public sectors. Many of them have relatively higher education and also higher income. According to estimation, this group, about 50 million in size, manages or controls about 10,000 billion RMB of capital, owns over half of the technology patents and contributes to one third of the national tax (Ye and Ji, 2007).

Scholars have long speculated on how the new middle class differs from other social groups in terms of their political attitudes and social values and the implications for China's path to democracy and rule of laws (Cai, 2005; Dickson, 2003; Zhang, 2008). The middle classes, growing out of the private sector and prospering in the capitalist competitions, not only are more aware of their civil and property rights but also have more viable means (cultural and economic resources) to protect their rights in case of violation. Empirical analyses on the legal choice of dispute resolutions suggest that, as Weberian theorists predicted, the new middle class is more affined to rationality and the law. The emergence and the growth of the middle classes would have positive contributions to the legal development in China. However, the regime's ruling elites hold even more favorable attitude towards the law. The elites, in alliance with the new middle class (new economic elites), are the major actors from above in the promotion of the rule of law in China. The rule of law would not necessarily threaten the regime's stability (Wu and Cheng, 2010).

The Chinese policy makers have come to recognize the importance and potential threat of the new social strata to the regime. Under the leadership of Jiang Zemin, the ruling Communist Party revised its membership recruit-ment policies by inviting the new economic elites to join the Party in an attempt to tame the rivaling social forces (Jia, 2004; Jiang, 2002). A sizable middle class is also seen as the pillar stone for maintaining social stability and reducing social conflicts.

2. *Educational Expansion and Persisting Inequality*

Accompanied with China's rapid economic development is the question of how to restructure the educational system and provide more access to educa-tional opportunities, as sustainable economic growth demands skilled labor (Hannum, Park and Cheng, 2007). Indeed, the commencement of the reform era was marked by the completely dismantling of the educational poli-cies adopted during the Cultural Revolution, which severely condemned the system of evaluating student performance by examinations (Tsui, 1997; Wang, 2002). On the other hand, economic growth afforded more resources for educational development and school expansion. In 1980, the Chinese government set the target of universalizing primary education by the end of the 1980s and the implementation of nine-year compulsory education in the 1990s (Tsui, 1997). In 1985, *the Decision on the Reform of the Education Structure* was launched, followed by the 1986 *Compulsory Education Law*. With the increase in educational resources, these goals were largely achieved by the mid-1990s.

As Table 6 shows, the school enrollment rate (age 6–15) had already reached over 98% in the mid-1990s. The rate of transition to junior high school, given the completion of primary school education, after an initial decline in the mid-1980s, also reached over 90% by 1995, and 99.5% in 2008. In contrast, the expansion of senior high school education beyond the com-pulsory levels was quite slow until recently. The rate of transition to senior high school experienced an initial drop until the late 1980s and remained lower than 30% before 2000. Even the recent expansion of senior high school education was not at a pace comparable to the expansion of higher education. More strikingly, starting from the late 1990s, the rate of transition to college increased dramatically (Liu, 2004; Min, 2007).

In the 1990s when China proceeded deeply into marketization, to accom-modate the increasing number of enrollments and increasing educational costs, high schools and colleges have been allowed to charge tuitions and other fees (Min, 2007). Educational affordability has also become one of the great-est public concerns and economic considerations that significantly affect the decision to continue schooling (Kahn and Yardley, 2004). Connelly and

Table 6.   Educational expansion in China, 1978–2008

	Enrollment rate of school-age children %	Transition rate to junior high school %	Transition rate to senior high school %	Transition rate to tertiary school %
1978	95.5	87.7	40.9	—
1979	93.0	82.8	40.0	—
1980	93.9	75.9	45.9	—
1981	93.0	68.3	31.5	—
1982	93.2	66.2	32.3	—
1983	94.0	67.3	35.5	—
1984	95.3	66.2	38.4	—
1985	96.0	68.4	41.7	—
1986	96.4	69.5	40.6	—
1987	97.2	69.1	39.1	—
1988	97.2	70.4	38.0	—
1989	97.4	71.5	38.3	—
1990	97.8	74.6	40.6	27.3
1991	97.8	75.7	42.6	28.7
1992	97.2	79.7	43.4	34.9
1993	97.7	81.8	44.1	43.3
1994	98.4	86.6	46.4	46.7
1995	98.5	90.8	48.3	49.9
1996	98.8	92.6	48.8	51.0
1997	98.9	93.7	44.3	48.6
1998	98.9	94.3	50.7	46.1
1999	99.1	94.4	50.0	63.8
2000	99.1	94.9	51.1	73.2
2001	98.3	95.5	52.9	78.8
2002	98.6	97.0	58.3	83.5
2003	98.7	97.9	60.2	83.4
2004	98.9	98.1	62.9	82.5
2005	99.2	98.4	69.7	76.3
2006	99.3	100.0	75.7	75.1
2007	99.5	99.9	79.3	71.8
2008	99.5	99.7	83.4	72.7

Sources: National Bureau of Statistics, *China statistical yearbook 2009*. Also available at http://www.stats.gov.cn/tjsj/ndsj/2009/indexee.htm

Zheng's analysis (2007) suggests a growing rural-urban gap in attending senior high school or vocational school, due to the improvement in urban areas outpacing those in rural areas. Wu's (2010b) multivariate analysis confirms that the rural-urban (*hukou*) gap in the likelihood of transition to senior high school level enlarged, and the effect of their father's socioeconomic status increased — even after taking into account of regional variations in economic development. There are some anecdotal reports on the decline in the number of student enrollments from disadvantaged family backgrounds at several elite universities (Liu, 2004; Min, 2007; Yang, 2006). Children of managers and professionals are more likely than their counterparts from other backgrounds to get into college now than before (Li, 2006). The expanding opportunities in higher education are increasingly taken by women, students from urban areas, particularly from large cities (Wu and Zhang, 2010).

Since education plays an increasingly important role in attaining a better job and receiving more economic benefits in a modern society, the question of "who gets educated" assumes a central place in stratification research. To understand the change of stratification outcomes in a society that is undergoing dramatic transformation in the mechanism of resource distribution, it is necessary to investigate how the transformation has altered the allocation of educational opportunities among different social strata, which may have a long-term impact on the change in social structure.

3. *Social Mobility*

China's tremendous social and economic changes since 1978 were driven by two fundamental processes simultaneously: economic industrialization and institutional transitions. Economic industrialization has transformed economic structures so to create more occupational opportunities for social mobility (Treiman, 1970). Yet this was largely not the case under the socialist-style industrialization program since the early 1950s. As described before, since the Chinese government installed a unique *hukou* system to control inflow of peasants into cities and create a structural barrier for moving out of agriculture, the state-led industrialization (typically focusing on heavy industry) may not have created non-agricultural occupational opportunities as many as those countries under different development paths. Indeed, the rural-urban institutional divide, according to Wu and Treiman (2007), has contributed to high immobility (in agriculture) on the one hand, and unusual "openness" in the urban population among which individuals from rural origins are highly selective based on the criteria imposed by the government.

The market-oriented economic reform since 1978 has led to a spontaneous industrialization and population migration which is different from the state-dominated industrialization but much similar to that experienced by other developing countries. Despite the *hukou* system is still in place and rural migrants were discriminated, they were offered more opportunities in industrial and service sectors and likely to achieve socioeconomic mobility, which were unavailable in the pre-reform period when the migration and employment were strictly controlled by the government rather than the market, and the priority was given to the development of heavy industry. As shown in Table 7, during the socialist industrialization period, from 1952 to 1975, while the share of GDP output from the secondary and tertiary sectors combined increased from 49.5% in 1952 to 71.8% in 1975, the employment in non-agricultural sectors only increased from 16.5% to 22.8% in the same period. Since the reform, the employment growth in non-agriculture sector (particularly in the tertiary industry/service sector) seems to catch up: increasing from 29.5% in 1978 to 60.4% in 2008 (from 12.2% to 33.2% in service sector, where good jobs are located).

Hence, rapid changes in economic and occupational structures imply that there are more opportunities for intergenerational mobility and career mobility. According to the research by the CASS, the intergenerational mobility rates increased from 41.4% (32.4% upward) prior to 1980 to 54.4% (40.9% upward) after 1980. The overall job mobility rates was only 12.3% prior to 1979, but increased to 30.3% between 1980 and 1989, and 54.2% between 1990 and 2001. The upward mobility from the first job to the current job was only 7.4% prior to 1979, but increased to 18.2% in the 1980s, and further to 30.5% in the 1990s (Lu, 2004, p. 13). On the other hand, in terms of relative mobility, the increase in income inequality and the emergence of propertied class may suggest that the market transition may increase the intergenerational transmission of class status previously reduced by the state intervention, as Gerber and Hout (2004) found in post-Soviet Russia.

Economic reforms in former state socialist countries have led to the emergence of a market sector in the redistributive economy, which has offered "a new window of opportunity" and an alternative avenue for social mobility, thus also yielded important implications for changes in social stratification (Nee, 1989). In the dual opportunity structure, "one could climb the rank order of the bureaucratic hierarchy, or one could try the market" (Szelényi, 1988, p. 65). To a great extent, the question under debate — who wins and who loses in the course of market transition — is contingent upon who stays in the hierarchy and who switches to the market sector at different stages of reform (Szelényi and Kostello, 1996).

In the early stages of economic reforms when participation in the market was highly risky and required little skill, entrants into the market sector tended to be those in the low tiers of the social hierarchy, who were not at risk of losing privileges like those enjoyed by workers in the state sector. However, as marketization proceeded and the risks in the market were further

Table 7. Changes in economic structure and employment structure by sectors, 1952–2008

Year	GDP share by industry			Employment share by industry		
	Primary	Secondary	Tertiary	Primary	Secondary	Tertiary
1952	50.5	20.9	28.6	83.5	7.4	9.1
1957	40.3	29.7	30.1	81.2	9.0	9.8
1962	39.4	31.3	29.3	82.1	8.0	9.9
1965	37.9	35.1	27.0	81.6	8.4	10.0
1970	35.2	40.5	24.3	80.8	10.2	9.0
1975	32.4	45.7	21.9	77.2	13.5	9.3
1978	28.2	47.9	23.9	70.5	17.3	12.2
1979	31.3	47.1	21.6	69.8	17.6	12.6
1980	30.2	48.2	21.6	68.7	18.2	13.1
1981	31.9	46.1	22.0	68.1	18.3	13.6
1982	33.4	44.8	21.8	68.1	18.4	13.5
1983	33.2	44.4	22.4	67.1	18.7	14.2
1984	32.1	43.1	24.8	64.0	19.9	16.1
1985	28.4	42.9	28.7	62.4	20.8	16.8
1986	27.2	43.7	29.1	60.9	21.9	17.2
1987	26.8	43.6	29.6	60.0	22.2	17.8
1988	25.7	43.8	30.5	59.3	22.4	18.3
1989	25.1	42.8	32.1	60.1	21.6	18.3
1990	27.1	41.3	31.6	60.1	21.4	18.5
1991	24.5	41.8	33.7	59.7	21.4	18.9
1992	21.8	43.4	34.8	58.5	21.7	19.8
1993	19.7	46.6	33.7	56.4	22.4	21.2
1994	19.8	46.6	33.6	54.3	22.7	23.0
1995	19.9	47.2	32.9	52.2	23.0	24.8
1996	19.7	47.5	32.8	50.5	23.5	26.0
1997	18.3	47.5	34.2	49.9	23.7	26.4
1998	17.6	46.2	36.2	49.8	23.5	26.7
1999	16.5	45.8	37.7	50.1	23.0	26.9
2000	15.1	45.9	39.0	50.0	22.5	27.5
2001	14.4	45.1	40.5	50.0	22.3	27.7
2002	13.7	44.8	41.5	50.0	21.4	28.6
2003	12.8	46.0	41.2	49.1	21.6	29.3
2004	13.4	46.2	40.4	46.9	22.5	30.6
2005	12.2	47.7	40.1	44.8	23.8	31.4
2006	11.3	48.7	40.0	42.6	25.2	32.2
2007	11.1	48.5	40.4	40.8	26.8	32.4
2008	11.3	48.6	40.1	39.6	27.2	33.2

Data sources: *Comprehensive statistical data and materials on 50 years of new China,* China Statistics Publishing House, also available at http://www.stats.gov.cn/tjsj/ndsj/

reduced, workers with more marketable skills started to seek the new opportunities available in the market. Communist cadres also learned to embrace the market to cash in on their political and social capital (Wu, 2006). In the face of competition from these groups, "with more to lose but also more to gain," the early market pioneers were marginalized under certain circumstances (Wu and Xie, 2003).

Market transitions have brought not only new opportunities for people to take advantage of, but also job losses and downward mobility for those who suffer from, particularly in the late reform period. Since the mid-1990s, the growth of the private economy in China has gained a new momentum, which, on one hand, attracted talented workers from the state sector, but on the other hand, pushed some state-owned enterprises into bankruptcy because of market competition. Many workers were pushed into the market for a living (Cai, 2002; Lee, 2000; Solinger, 2002). Among the recent market entrants, those who were forced to leave the state sector might possess less human and political capital or other unobserved characteristics negatively associated with potential earnings, whereas those who were self-selected into the market sector might possess certain observable or unobservable characteristics that are positively associated with potential earnings. The workers, who entered the market through these two mechanisms, fared differently, and contributed to the sharply rising labor market inequality in contemporary China.

Summary and Conclusions

While three decades is almost a snapshot in China's thousands of years of long history, it is a significant moment and critical step for China to re-emerge as a global power in the world. Unlike the transformation in the 1950s, in which the state power played a dominant role in economic and social engineering, massive social changes since the 1980s were induced by economic liberalization and the retreat of the state power to some extent. The economic reform has re-configured the basic institutional make-ups of state socialist China: the household registration system (*hukou*), the work unit system (*danwei*), and the cadre-worker status distinction in the urban labor force, and affected people's life chances. The changes of these intermediate institutions not only reflect social structural changes per se, but also serve as the keys to understanding the dynamic social life in Chinese society.

Key to the success of China's economic transition is the incremental approach that reformers adopted. The socialist redistributive system was not dismantled over night. Instead, they persisted and evolved with the changes in economic spheres. In other words, they are not only affected by but also contribute to the success of the economic reform. The vibrant social landscapes in China today show both the continuity and changes. It might be the continuity that can help us understand why China can sustain such a long-term economic growth and carry out fundamental reforms while maintaining social and political stability.

To be certain, many social and political problems arise during the social and economic transitions. Exacerbating inequality, official corruption and malpractices, ambiguous and unjust property rights, and environmental pollutions have fuelled social discontent. Public protests have escalated dramatically over the decades, growing from 8,700 in 1993 to 32,000 in 1999, almost by fourfold, and concurrently to 87,000 in 2005 by tenfold (Chen, 2008). The increasing popular discontent and mass protests suggest a new set of state-society relations that appear to challenge the social stability and thus push for the regime transformation.

Recently, development priorities have gradually shifted from over-emphasis on efficiency and growth to social justice and harmony, guided by the Scientific Development Concept, the new socio-economic ideology of the Communist Party under the leadership of Hu Jintao and Wen Jiabao. The Scientific Development Concept intends to incorporate sustainable development, social welfare, a people-centered society, increased democracy, and, ultimately, the creation of a harmonious society. According to Chinese President and the CCP General Secretary Hu Jintao, such a society would be the one in which "all the people can work to their fullest abilities, be paid according to their hard-work and get on well with each other." To achieve the goal, a social justice guarantee system based on "equal rights, equal opportunities, fair rules and fair distribution" is thus called for (Hu, 2007). The concept reflects a trend within the Party under the Hu-Wen Administration to subscribe to more populist policies and guidelines on social development after decades of high rate of economic growth. How these specific social policies lead to social changes and progresses yet remains to be seen.

References

Bernstein, T. P. (1977) *Up to the mountains and down to the villages: The transfer of youth from urban to rural China*. New Haven: Yale University Press.

Bian, Y. (1994) *Work and inequality in urban China*. Albany: State University of New York Press.

Bian, Y. (2002) Chinese social stratification and social mobility. *Annual Review of Sociology*, 28, 91–116.

Cai, F. (2002) *Employment in rural and urban China: Issues and options.* Beijing, China: Social Science Academic Press [in Chinese].

Cai, F. and G. Wan (2006) Studies on income inequality and poverty in transition China: What do we know and what we should know? In F. Cai and G. Wan (Eds.), *Income inequality and poverty in transition China*, pp. 1–22. Beijing: Social Science Academic Press.

Cai, Y. (2002) The resistance of Chinese laid-off workers in the reform period. *The China Quarterly*, 170, 327–344.

Cai, Y. (2005) China's moderate middle class: The case of homeowners' resistance. *Asian Survey*, 5, 777–799.

Chan, A., R. Marsden and J. Unger (1992) *Chen village under Mao and Deng.* Hong Kong: Oxford University Press [in Chinese].

Chan, K. W. (1994) *Cities with invisible walls.* Hong Kong: Oxford University Press.

Chan, K. W. and L. Zhang (1999) The *hukou* system and rural urban migration in China: Processes and changes. *The China Quarterly,* 160, 818–855.

Chen, C. J. (2008) Growing social unrest in China: Rising social discontents and popular protests. In G. Wu and H. Lansdowne (Eds.), *Socialist China, capitalist China: Social tension and political adaptation under economic globalization.* pp. 10–28. London, UK: Routledge.

Cheng, T. and M. Selden (1994) The origins and social consequences of China's *hukou* system. *The China Quarterly*, 139, 644–668.

Connelly, R. and Z. Zhen (2007) Enrollment and graduation patterns as China's reforms deepen, 1990–2000. In E. Hannum and A. Park (Eds.), *Education and Reform in China*, pp. 81–92. London, UK: Routledge.

Davis, D. (2000) *The consumer revolution in urban China.* Berkeley, CA: University of California Press.

De Brauw, A., J. Huang, S. Rozelle, L. Zhang and Y. Zhang (2002) The evolution of China's rural labor markets during the reforms. *Journal of Comparative Economics*, 30, 329–353.

Dickson, B. (2003) *Red capitalists in China: The party, private entrepreneurs, and prospects for political change.* Cambridge, UK: Cambridge University Press.

Etzioni, A. (1993) *The spirits of community: Rights, responsibilities and the communitarian agenda.* New York: Crown Publisher.

Gerber, T. P. and M. Hout (2004) Tightening up: Declining class mobility during Russia's market transition. *American Sociological Review*, 69, 677–703.

Giddens, A. (1998) *The third way: The renewal of social democracy.* Cambridge: Polity.

Goldman, M. and R. MacFarguhar (1999) Dynamic economy, declining party-state. In *The paradox of China's post-Mao reforms*, pp. 3–36. Cambridge, MA: Harvard University Press.

Gregory, N., S. Tenev and D. Wagle (2000). *China's emerging private enterprises.* Washington, DC: International Finance Corporation.

Hannum, E., A. Park and K.M. Cheng (2007) Introduction: Market reform and educational opportunity in China. In E. Hannum and A. Park (Eds.), *Education and Reform in China*, pp. 1–23. London, UK: Routledge.

Hu, J. (2007) Report to the seventeenth national congress of the communist party of China on October 15, 2007. Retrieved from http://www.china.org.cn/english/congress/229611.htm

Jia, H. (2004) The three represents campaign: Reform the party or indoctrinate the capitalists. *Cato Journal*, 24(3), 261–275.

Jiang, Z. (2002) Speech at the 16th communist party of China's congress. Retrieved from http://www.idcpc.org.cn/english/policy/3represents.html

Kahn, J. and J. Yardley (2004) Amid China's boom, no help hand for young Qingming. *The New York Times*, August 1, 2004.

Kung, J. and Y. Lin (2007) The decline of township-and-village enterprises in China's economic transition. *World Development*, 35(4), 569–584.

Lee, H. Y. (2000) *Xiagang*, the Chinese style of laying off workers. *Asian Survey*, 40(6), 917–937.

Li, L. and F. Wang (1992) *Dangdai zhongguo xiandaihua jingcheng zhong de shehui jiegou jiqi bianqian* (Social structure and its transformation in the course of contemporary Chinese modernization). Hangzhou: Zhejiang Renmin Publishing House [in Chinese].

Li, Q (1993) *Dangdai zhongguo de shehui fenceng yu liudong* (Social stratification and mobility in contemporary China). Beijing: China Economy Press [in Chinese].

Li, Y. (2006) Institutional change and educational inequality: Mechanisms in educational stratification in urban China (1966–2003). *Zhongguo Shehui Kexue*, 2006(4), 97–207 [in Chinese].

Liang, Z. (2001) Tha age of migration in China. *Population and Development Review*, 27, 499–524.

Liang, Z. and Z. Ma (2004) China's floating population: New evidence from the 2000 census. *Population and Development Review*, 30(3), 467–488.

Lin, J. Y. F., F. Cai and Z. Li (1994) *Zhongguo de qiji: Fazhan zhanlue yu jingjin gaige* (China's miracle: Development strategy and economic reform). Shanghai: Sanlian Press.

Lin, T.-H. and X. Wu (2009) The transformation of the Chinese class structure, 1978–2005. *Social Transformations in Chinese Societies*, 5, 81–116.

Liu, J. (2000) *Danwei China*. Tianjin: Tianjin Renmin Press [in Chinese].

Liu, J. (2004) *Education in transitional Chinese society*. Liaoning Renmin Press [in Chinese].

Lu, F. (1989) The work unit: A special form of social organization. *Zhongguo Shehui Kexue*, 55, 71–83 [in Chinese].

Lu, X. (Ed.) (2002) *Research report on social stratification in contemporary China*. Beijing: Social Science Academic Press [in Chinese].

Lu, X. (Ed.) (2004) *Social mobility in contemporary China*. Beijing: Social Science Academic Press [in Chinese].

MacLeod, C. (2006) China's homeowners get small taste of democracy. *USA Today*. Retrieved from http://www.usatoday.com/news/world/2006-04-17-china-homeowners-cover_x.htm

Meisner, M. J. (1999) *Mao's China and after: A history of the People's Republic*. New York: The Free Press.

Min, W. (Ed.) (2007) *China education and human resource development report 2005–2006*. Beijing: Peking University Press [in Chinese].

National Bureau of Statistics (2010) *China statistical yearbook 2009*. Beijing: China Statistics Publishing House.

Naughton, B. (1997) The economic foundation of a unique institution. In L. Xiaobo and J. P. Elizabeth (Eds.), *Danwei: The changing Chinese workplace in historical and comparative perspective*, pp. 169–194. Armonk, NY: M. E. Sharp.

Naughton, B. (2007) *Chinese economy: Transition and growth*. Cambridge, MA: The MIT Press.

Nee, V. (1989) A theory of market transition: From redistribution to markets in state socialism. *American Sociological Review*, 54, 663–681.

New York Times. (2005) China to drop urbanite-peasant legal difference. November 2, 2005.

Oi, J. (1989) *State and peasant in contemporary China: The political economy of village government*. Berkeley: University of California Press.

Oi, J. (1990) The fate of the collective after the commune. In D. Davis and F. V. Ezra (Eds.), *Chinese society on the eve of Tiananmen: The impact of reform*, Cambridge: The Council of East Asian Studies, Harvard University.

Parish, W. L. (1984) De-stratification in China. In J. Watson (Ed.), *Class and social stratification in post-revolution China*, pp. 84–120. New York: Cambridge University Press.

Parish, W. L., and M. K. Whyte (1978) Collective agricultural organization. In *Village and family in contemporary China*. Chicago: University of Chicago Press.

Parish, W. L., X. Zhe and F. Li (1995) Non-farm work and marketization of Chinese countryside. *The China Quarterly*, 143, 697–730.

Peng, Y. (1992) Wage determination in rural and urban China: A comparison of public and private industrial sectors. *American Sociological Review*, 57, 198–213.

Pun, N. (2005) *Made in China: Subject, power and resistance in a global workplace*. Durham, NC: Duke University Press.

Qian, Y. (2000) The process of China's market transition (1978–1998): The evolutionary, historical, and comparative perspectives. *Journal of Institutional and Theoretical Economics*, 156, 151–171.

Roberts, K. D. (1997) China's 'tidal wave' of migrant labor: What can we learn from Mexican undocumented migration to the United States? *International Migration Review*, 31, 249–293.

Shirk, S. L. (1993) *The political logic of economic reform in China*. Berkeley, CA: University of California Press.

Solinger, D. J. (2001) Why we cannot count the 'unemployed'. *The China Quarterly*, 160, 671–688.

Solinger, D. J. (2002) Labor market reform and plight of the laid-off proletariat. *The China Quarterly*, 170, 304–326.

South China Morning Post (2003) Permit reform in capital offers migrants first-class benefits, July 8, 2003.

Szelenyi, I. (1978) Social inequalities in state socialist redistributive economies. *International Journal of Comparative Sociology*, 19, 63–87.

Szelenyi, I. (1988) *Socialist entrepreneurs*. Madison: University of Wisconsin Press.

Szelenyi, I. and E. Kostello (1996) The market transition debate: Toward a synthesis. *American Journal of Sociology*, 101, 1082–1096.

Tang, W. and W. Parish (2000) *Chinese urban life under reform: The changing social contract*. Cambridge, MA: Cambridge University Press.

Treiman, D. J. (1970) Industrialization and social stratification. In O. L. Edward (Ed.), *Social stratification: Research and theory for the 1970s*, pp. 207–234. Indianapolis: Bobbs-Merrill.

Tsui, K. (1997) Economic reform and attainment in basic education in China. *The China Quarterly*, 149, 104–127.

Walder, A. G. (1986) *Communist neo-traditionalism: Work and authority in Chinese industry*. Berkeley and Los Angeles: University of California Press.

Walder, A. G. (1992) Property rights and stratification in socialist redistributive economies. *American Sociological Review*, 57, 524–539.

Walder, A. G. (1995) Local governments as industrial firms: An organizational analysis of China's transitional economy. *American Journal of Sociology*, 101, 263–301.

Walder, A. G. (2003) Elite opportunity in transitional economies. *American Sociological Review*, 68, 899–916.

Wang, J. C. F. (2002) *Contemporary Chinese politics: An introduction*. New Jersey: Prentice-Hall.

Wang, F. (2004) Reformed migration control and new targeted people: China's *Hukou* reform in the 2000s. *The China Quarterly*, 115–132.

Wang, F. (2008) *Boundaries and categories: Rising inequality in post-socialist urban China*. Stanford, CA: Stanford University Press.

Whyte, M. K. and W. Parish (1984) *Urban life in contemporary China*. Chicago: University of Chicago Press.

Whyte, M. (2010) *Myth of the social volcano: Perception of inequality and distributive injustice in contemporary China*. Palo Alto, CA: Stanford University Press.

World Bank, World Development Indicators — Last updated July 27, 2010. Retrieved from http://www.stats.gov.cn/tjsj/ndsj/2009/html/J0935E.HTM

Wu, X. (2001) *Institutional structures and social mobility in China: 1949–1996*. Unpublished Ph.D. Dissertation, Department of Sociology, University of California at Los Angeles.

Wu, X. (2002) Work units and income inequality: The effect of market transition in urban China. *Social Forces*, 80(3), 1069–1099.

Wu, X. (2006) Communist cadres and market opportunities: Entry into self-employment in urban and rural China. *Social Forces*, 85, 389–411.

Wu, X. (2009a) Household registration, social exclusion, and rural migrants in Chinese cities. In G. Wu and H. Lansdowne (Eds.), *Socialist China, capitalist China: Social-political conflicts under globalization*, pp. 29–54. London, UK: Routledge.

Wu, X. (2009b) Income inequality and distributive justice: A comparative analysis of mainland China and Hong Kong. *The China Quarterly*, 200, 1033–1052.

Wu, X. (2010a) Voluntary and involuntary job mobility and earnings inequality in urban China, 1993–2000. *Social Science Research*, 39, 382–395.

Wu, X. (2010b) Economic transition, school expansion and educational inequality in China, 1990–2000. *Research in Social Stratification and Mobility*, 28, 91–108.

Wu, X. and D. J. Treiman (2004) The household registration system and social stratification in China, 1955–1996. *Demography*, 41(2), 363–384.

Wu, X. and D. J. Treiman (2007) Inequality and equality under Chinese socialism: The Hukou system and intergenerational occupational mobility. *American Journal of Sociology*, 113(2), 415–445.

Wu, X. and J. Cheng (2010) New middle class and the rule of law in China. Paper presented in the Inaugural East Asian Law and Society Conference, University of Hong Kong, Feb 5–6, 2010.

Wu, X. and M. Guo (2010) Workplace and life chances: Organization-based stratification in urban China. Working paper, Center for Applied Social and Economic Research, Hong Kong University of Science and Technology.

Wu, X. and Y. Xie (2003) Does the market pay off? Earnings returns to education in urban China. *American Sociological Review*, 68, 425–442.

Wu, X. and Z. Zhang (2010) Changes in educational inequality in China, 1990–2005: Evidence from the population census data. *Research in Sociology of Education*, 17, 123–152.

Xie, G. (2006) Market transition and laid-off workers. *Shehuixue Yanjiu*, 121(1), 22–58 [in Chinese].

Xie, Y. and X. Wu (2008) *Danwei* profitability and earnings inequality in urban China. *The China Quarterly*, 195, 558–581.

Yan, M. C. and J. Gao (2007) Social engineering of community building: Examination of policy process and characteristics of community construction in China. *Community Development Journal*, 42(2), 222–236.

Yang, D. (2006) Access to higher education: Widening social class disparities. *Tsinghua Journal of Education*, 27(1), 19–26 [in Chinese].

Yang, X. and Y. Zhou (1999) *The Chinese work-unit system*. Beijing: China Economy Press [in Chinese].

Ye, X. and Y. Ji (2007) Eight characteristics of the new middle strata. *People's Daily*, June 11, 2007. Retrieved from http://politics.people.com.cn/GB/1026/5845372.html

Yu, Z. (2006) Heterogeneity and dynamics in China's emerging urban housing market: Two sides of a success story from the late 1990s. *Habitat International*, 30(2), 277–304.

Zang, X. (1999) Urban housing reforms in China. In X. Zang (Ed.), *China in the Reform Era*, pp. 49–79. Commack, NY: Nova Science Publishers.

Zhang, H. (2006) New stages of private entrepreneurs' growth. In *Society of China: Analysis and forecast* (Zhongguo shehui xingshi fenxi yu yuce). Beijing: Social Science Academic Press [in Chinese].

Zhang, Y. (2008) China's middle class current political attitudes. *Social Science in China* 2.

Zhao, R. (1993) Three features of the distribution of income during the transition to reform. In K. Griffin and R. Zhao (Eds.), *The distribution of income in China*, pp. 74–94. New York: St Martin's Press.

Zhao, Z. (1994) On several issues of inequality in social distribution. *Shehui Kexue Zhanxian*, 1, 112–121 [in Chinese].

Zhou, X. and L. Hou (1999) Children of the cultural revolution: The state and the life course in the People's Republic of China. *American Sociological Review*, 64, 12–36.

4

LAW

Bin Liang

Oklahoma State University

Abstract

This article provides a brief survey of significant changes to China's legal system since its reform era (1979-present). In the last three decades, China's legal system has gained tremendous development through a process of systemization, professionalization and bureaucratization, and played increasing roles in both national affairs and people's private lives. This survey follows these developments and contrasts China's legal system in the pre-reform era (1949–1978) with the reform era. Important scholarly studies of China's legal system are also traced in this survey, and special attention is paid to key theories proposed in this field. Next, this survey goes over China's policing, courts, and corrections, and analyzes unique features in their daily operations. A special case is also given to China's accession to the World Trade Organization and how the world system transforms China's legal system domestically. Finally, this survey discusses increasing public participation in China's legal system and how such participation may play a critical role in transforming China's legal system in the future.

Keywords: Chinese legal system; legal reform; policing; courts; corrections; WTO impact; public participation.

1. Introduction

To Western audience, studying China's legal system has always been a very intriguing and challenging job, given China's unique history, culture, and politics. Many still hold the belief that contemporary China does *not* have a formal legal system, and political leaders and official cadres are able to rule the country at will. This view ignores dramatic changes already happened to China in the last three decades and their long-lasting impact to the future of China (see e.g., Liang, 2008). If China's economic reform and growth have been eye-catching since 1979, China's transformations in other domains, including its legal system, are equally enlightening.

This chapter provides a brief survey of significant changes to China's legal system since its reform era (1979–present). First, to help the audience gain a better understanding of dramatic changes in the reform era, a discussion of China's legal system and its (dys)function in the pre-reform era (1949–1978) was given. During these decades, the Chinese Communist Party (CCP) reduced the function of the legal system to a tool for class struggle, and this era was labeled by many as an era of "rule of man." Second, only after the economic reform did the CCP start to rebuild China's legal system. Responding to economic reforms, substantive changes have been made to the structure of the legal system through a process of systemization and bureaucratization. This review focuses on the professionalization process in particular.

Third, this survey systematically traces important scholarly studies of China's legal system in the last three decades, especially on key theories proposed to understand China's legal reform. Fourth, this survey briefly goes over three key branches of China's legal system, including policing, courts, and corrections, and analyzes their unique features. Fifth, a special case is given to China's accession to the World Trade Organization (WTO), and how the world system transforms China's legal system domestically. Sixth and finally, this chapter highlights how increasing public participation via new means (e.g., the Internet) plays a critical role in transforming China's legal system and its potential impact in the future.

2. Pre-Reform Era (1949–1978)

1949 is a turning point in Chinese history. It not only indicated the founding of a new China (the People's Republic of China, PRC), but also represented a dramatic social change in which China turned into a socialist country. Economically, the first Constitution of PRC (1954) provided that non-public economic forms should be restricted and transformed gradually into either state-owned or collective-owned economic entities subject to the socialist planned economy (Gong *et al.*, 1999; Xin, 1999). Corresponding to the planned economy, the CCP wanted a static society governed by state plans politically and socially. Administrative organizations were set up nationwide, from ministries at the central government to neighborhood committees in local communities, to help the governance of the central government. Ideologically, Chairman Mao Zedong classified all contradictions (*maodun* in Chinese) during this period into two kinds and made clear distinctions between the "antagonistic" (people vs. enemy) and the "non-antagonistic" (people vs. people) contradictions. High-pressure dictatorship (e.g., through criminal punishment) should be adopted only against the enemies (see e.g., Clark and Feinerman, 1996). As a consequence, one's political classification (*chengfen*) became a means for political control, critical to one's life and career.

In 1958, the Standing Committee of the first National People's Congress (NPC), the highest legislative body, passed the *Regulations of the PRC on Residence Registration*. This household registration (*hukuo*) system drew a distinction between the rural and the urban, bound people (especially peasants) to their native places (e.g., lands), and made migration and social transition very difficult, if not impossible. It worked as a means of political administration as well as an effective means of social (status) control (see studies on the *Hukou* system by Solinger, 1999; Whyte and Parish, 1984).

In urban cities, the workplace (*danwei*) exercised tight control over its workers. Its functions went beyond supervision over one's work performance and extended to govern one's political performance, one's after-work life (e.g., mass entertainment organized by *danwei*), and even one's private life (e.g., marriage matches). *Danwei* became another important means of social control (Walder, 1986). Combined with other control mechanisms such as one's personal files (*dang'an*) and class labels, the household registration and *danwei* all had a great impact on people's lives in this historical period. Within such a system, the function of law and the legal system was reduced to be a governmental tool.

Based on orthodox Marxism, the CCP repudiated Western democracy and rejected the idea of an autonomous legal system and its functions (e.g., separation of power and checks and balances). Instead, law was believed to be associated with the nature of the state and by no means impartial. It is a tool for the maintenance of state domination. Rather, class struggle had been viewed as an effective means to push forward society evolution. In a series of social movements (e.g., the "Anti-Rightists" campaign, the "Great Leap Forward" movement, the "Cultural Revolution"), law and the legal system were utilized as tools for class struggle, and their existence and functions were subject to politicians' discretions. In 1959, for instance, the Ministry of Justice (MOJ) and the Bureau of the Legislative Affairs (under the State Council) were both closed, followed by abolishment of justice bureaus in provinces, autonomous regions, and municipalities (Xin, 1999).

In addition, a mass-line policy was adopted in the whole country to motivate people to participate in class struggles. The mass-line policy called for popular justice at the community level and encouraged greater involvement and mobilization of the masses to manage their own affairs, to resolve their own conflicts, and to achieve self-policing and discipline as well as mutual policing (Tao, 1997). These movements further weakened the function of China's nascent and brittle legal system. In the heyday of class struggle during the Cultural Revolution period (1966–1976), state legal systems were severely paralyzed. For example, in this 10-year period, the third session of the NPC could *not* hold its regular meetings (even though required by the national Constitution) and passed only one law. The revised Constitution in 1975 contained merely 30 articles, a sharp reduction from a total of 106 articles in the 1954 Constitution. The people's procuratorates were completely abolished and regrouped into public security organizations (Xin, 1999). It was not unusual that key legal branches such as the police, procuracy and courts were smashed by extremely feverous youths, the Red Guards, in social movements (Bracey, 1988; Gold, 1991). This period of time is later described by scholars as lawlessness or a period of the "rule of man."

As summarized by Chen (1999), the characteristics of the justice and legal system during this period were evident in three aspects. First, the Marxist concept of law was used as a tool to remold the society, to suppress class enemies, and to enforce party policies rather than to protect individual rights. Second, justice was both politicized and popularized. Social and legal distinctions were made based on one's (political) class membership and the implementation of the mass line policy led to mass trials for ideological indoctrination. Third and finally, extra-judicial organizations, procedures, and measures were often utilized to impose sanctions and settle disputes. These three features exactly represented *natures*, *forms*, and *operations* of the legal system during this historical period.

3. Reform Era (1978–Present)

(1) *Rebuilding of the Legal System*

After 1978, realizing the mistake of the "rule of man" and its disastrous consequences, the Chinese government started its legal reform. The first step was to reinterpret the function of law and the legal system. To answer the calls of economic reforms, the function of law as a tool for class struggle was de-emphasized, and the material character of law was emphasized. As a result, it demanded law be used to support and facilitate the economic development

(Wang and Zhang, 1992). In addition, it was pointed out that legal means should be used to solve not only contradictions between the people and the enemy, but also contradictions *among people*. Once the importance of legalization was recognized theoretically, legal practice quickly expanded. In 1999, for the first time, the national Constitution was revised to guarantee that "the People's Republic China practices ruling the country in accordance with the law and building a socialist country of law" (Article 5).

The first task of China's legalization in the reform era was to rebuild the legal system. In staggering speed, new laws, regulations and rules (both at the central governmental and local levels) were enacted, and many important ones (e.g., the Constitution, the *Criminal Law*, the *Criminal Procedure Law*) were amended several times, catering to the needs of the new era. From 1978 to August 2002, for instance, the NPC and its Standing Committee passed 301 laws, 7 law interpretations, and 122 decisions regarding laws. It was officially announced that China had accomplished its task of building a *preliminary* legal system (the *People's Daily*, September 26, 2002).[1] The lawmaking process also became more systematic, and there has been evidence that the NPC and its Standing Committee gained more power and became less subject to the Party's control (e.g., Tanner, 1999). In July 2000, the Standing Committee of the NPC passed the *Legislative Law of the PRC* (*lifa fa*) and formalized the lawmaking procedure.

Second, the functions of basic legal branches such as the police, procuracy and courts were quickly restored and greatly expanded. Take the judicial system for example, in 1978, the total number of cases accepted by all courts was 447,755; the number skyrocketed to more than 5 million after 1996, and reached 5.5 million by 2007. In addition, the nature of court cases changed dramatically: in 1978, criminal cases represented more than 30% of all cases; its share steadily decreased, and by the end of the 20th century, criminal cases represented only about 10% of the total cases (it was 13% in 2007). In contrast, civil litigations outgrew criminal cases after the reform. Civil litigations represented about 60% of the total cases over the years after economic dispute litigations were separately reported; at the same time, economic cases increased quickly to more than 20% in the mid 1980s and stabilized around 25% by the end of the 20th century (data from *China statistical yearbooks*).

---

[1] The preliminary system covered seven major legal areas (including Constitution law, civil and commercial law, administrative law, economic law, social law, criminal law, major procedural law) and three tiers of laws, rules and regulations (including laws, administrative regulations, and local regulations).

In 1982, the *Civil Procedural Law* (CPL) took effect, and for the first time Chinese citizens could sue the government or its officials for administrative misconduct. In 1990, the new *Administrative Litigation Law* (ALL) further guaranteed citizens' administrative litigation rights. The total number of (accepted) administrative litigation cases increased from 5,240 in 1987 to 108,398 in 2008 (about 1.8% of the total cases). However, data consistently show that a significant number (an average of 40%) of all accepted cases were withdrawn (reasons unspecified), and citizens managed to win only in less than 15% of total cases (data from *China Statistical Yearbooks*).

In similar fashions, other key legal branches were restored and expanded. By 2008, the total number of the people's procuratorates at all levels reached 3,634, and the number of people working in the system increased to 227,453 (data from *China Statistical Yearbooks*). In 1994, the MOJ proposed to establish a legal aid (*falü yuanzhu*) system nationwide, aiming to provide high-quality, free legal assistance for all who need it. By the end of 1996, merely three legal aid organizations existed at the provincial level (in Sichuan, Guangdong, and Beijing). But it has expanded very quickly since then. In 2001, Tibet established its legal aid center, and as a result the China's legal aid system covered all provinces. In July 2003, the *Regulations on Legal Aid* was passed by the State Council, and it became effective in September. By the end of 2008, there were 3,268 legal aid organizations nationwide with 12,778 official workers (the *People's Daily*, January 26, 2007). In 1999, the legal aid system provided assistance in 91,726 cases, and the number jumped to 546,859 in 2008; financial support for the legal aid system was also increased from 27.8 million yuan in 1999 to 683 million yuan in 2006 (data from *China Statistical Yearbooks*). Despite such development, problems such as insufficient funding and staffing and uneven regional development still plague the practice nationwide.

Before the legal reform, lawyers had never played a significant role in the legal system. In 1979, a little more than 2,000 lawyers worked in less than seven hundred law firms in the whole nation. With the quick development of the legal system, law became a popular profession. The number of law firms as well as the number of lawyers quickly increased. By 2007, China had 13,593 law firms with a total 143,967 lawyers (both full-time and part-time).[2] Moreover, the organization of law firms has been changing. In the 1980s, all law firms were state-owned firms, consistent with the nature of China's economic structure. By the end of 1980s, cooperative law firm,

---

[2] By comparison, China's lawyers accounted for a mere 0.0001% of the population, while lawyers accounted for 0.32% of the population in the US and 0.09% in West Germany (Peerenboom, 2002b, p. 130).

another form of organization, was allowed to exist, and it developed quickly over the years. Since the mid 1990s, the number of partner-type law firms grew as most cooperative law firms changed their organizations into partnerships. By early 2005, 70% of all law firms existed in various forms of partnerships in China (the *People's Daily*, February 16, 2005). At the same time, foreign law firms also landed and opened their offices in China. In 1992, five foreign law firms became the first group of foreign law firms to open offices in Beijing and Shanghai, and another seven law firms from Hong Kong kicked off their operations in mainland China. The momentum kept going, and by April, 2004, a total of 129 foreign law firms and 42 Hong Kong law firms had opened their branches in a number of major cities in China (the *Legal Daily*, April 13, 2004).

(2) *Professionalization*

In the process of building a legal system, a new term, "legal professionalism," was proposed. Special efforts were made (i) to designate the legal profession as a unique profession with its own rules and practices; (ii) to professionalize different players working within the legal profession; and (iii) to elevate the legal system to a higher level and grant it a relatively autonomous status.

First, Chinese scholars and the government recognized a long-time problem, i.e., law and the legal system were not granted an independent status, and its practice was always subject to influences of administrative policies and controls. In order to change this nature, an autonomous effective legal system was set as one goal of the legal reform. Specific rules (e.g., the *Civil Procedural Law*) were adopted to provide that all courts are to "exercise judicial power independently and are not subject to interference by administrative organizations, public organizations or individuals" (Potter, 1995, p. 74).

One measure to make the legal profession distinctive was to change the equipment and outfit of its major players. In May 2001, both judges and procurators' official uniforms were changed. The new uniform abandoned the old military style and was designed in a dark-color, suit-style consistent with international standards (the *People's Daily*, June 29, 2001). In 2002, the All-China Lawyers' Association enacted uniform dressing codes for lawyers who show up in courts, and the new dressing codes took effect in 2003 (the *Beijing Evening News*, October 12, 2002). With the new attires, players in the courtroom can be easily identified, and they appear more formal and part of a unique profession. In addition, many other trials (e.g., use of gavels, adoption of witness oath-taking system) were introduced into the courtroom to formalize the procedure and practice. Those changes may have looked minuscule, but they all served the same purpose to formalize the court procedure and grant more power and authority (at least symbolically) to judges.

Second, the low education level of legal practitioners in general was always a deep concern for the advance of legal professionalism in China. In 1995, both the *Judges Law* and the *Procurators Law* went into effect, and one specific function of both laws was to raise the professional level of judges and procurators. For example, the *Judges Law* required that new judges must have either a law degree or a university degree with special legal knowledge. For acting judges who were army retirees without formal education, the new law required them to receive various training within a limited time.

In addition, internal exams were held within the judicial and the procuratorial systems after 1995 to control the quality of judges and procurators. From 1995 to 1999, over 90,000 judges and 59,000 procurators took their exams. In January 2002, the *Judges Law* and the *Procurators Law* were revised, and the professional bars were again raised for new judges or procurators. In the same year, the MOJ, the Supreme People's Court (SPC), and the Supreme People's Procuratorate (SPP) decided to combine exams for judges, procurators, and lawyers into one national judicial qualification exam. All who want to practice law have to pass the unified national exam. In 2002, the first national law exam was held. More than 360,000 people took the exam, but less than 8% of them passed the minimum score requirement. In the next four years, the passing rate was kept below 15% each year and only in 2007 and 2008 was it raised to over 20%. From 2002 to 2008, over 1.7 million people (including repeats) took the exam but only 271,477 managed to pass it (data from *China Statistical Yearbooks*). Once exams became the standardized method of selection, they were adopted in other domains within the legal system, such as the prison system and the enterprise legal consulting service (the *People's Daily*, April 11 and July 31, 2002).

Even with such great efforts, the education level of legal practitioners in China is still not promising. By July 2002, official statistics reported that only 47% of lawyers, 29.9% of procurators, 24.9% of judges, and 22% of public notaries held university degrees (the *People's Daily*, July 24, 2002).[3] These low percentages showed how serious the obstacle is. It will take many years for China to reach the goal set by both the *Judges Law* and the *Procurators Law*.

---

[3] A report in the *People's Daily* on July 17, 2005 raised the percentage of judges who hold a college degree to 51%. Note the situation is definitely uneven in the whole nation and it is considerably worse in western, poor provinces. For instance, while the percentage reached 77% in Guangdong province in 2001, some local people's courts in Shanxi province did not even have one single judge who held a college degree by the end of 2003 (the *Legal Daily*, April 26, 2005).

Third, another step in the process of professionalization was to enact internal rules and regulations to govern practitioners. For instance, in 2000, both the SPC and the SPP adopted regulations to prohibit spouses and children of high officials in the judicial and procuratorial systems from providing paid legal services and conducting relevant businesses (the *People's Daily*, November 23 and 25, 2000). In 2001, regulations on judges' and procurators' withdrawals from trials (e.g., due to conflicts of interest) were enacted and implemented. The scope of this regulation went even beyond one's official term, and it provides that judges and procurators cannot represent clients in trials within two years after their official retirement/termination (the *People's Daily*, March 23, 2001). Further, the SPC published the *Professional Ethical Rules for Judges*, and introduced a practice of resignation at fault in the same year. Reportedly, a total of 2,512 judicial workers were punished due to violations of these regulations in 1998; the number increased to 1,450 in 1999, 1,338 in 2000, and then decreased to 1,080 in 2001 (the *People's Daily*, October 9, 2002). In 2006, the SPC also announced the establishment of a formal press release system for national people's courts and asked lower level courts to follow suit. This is another move to centralize courts' control (the *People's Daily*, September 13, 2006).

4. Studies of China's Legal System

(1) *Progress of Studies*[4]

Study of the Chinese legal system has its own history along with the development and growth of China. Before 1980, there were very few studies on the Chinese legal system. Works done by scholars such as Jerome Cohen (1968, 1970) and Victor Li (1978) gave a good description of the communist legal system under the leadership of the CCP. These comparative works emphasized the differences between communist practices and Western legal practices.

Entering the 1980s, scholars expanded their research on the Chinese legal system. Several trends were observable in this period. First, as a continuation of the efforts in the 1970s, scholars noticed the initial development of the legal system after the reform. Studies on the criminal justice system in general, on crime punishment and on police administrative power and control in particular all showed new signs of legal changes besides heavy reliance on analyses of

---

[4] Due to length limit, full citations are not provided in the section below. For a detailed review with full citations, see Liang (2008).

the communist practices. Second, a group of scholars started examining China's low crime rate and recidivism rate. Their comparative works such as studies on the correctional system were written as introductions to the Western audience of how the Chinese legal system was able to maintain such effective crime control. Some other scholars turned their focus to Chinese culture and legal traditions for potential answers. Third, in an effort to explain the Chinese legal system to audiences from other legal and cultural backgrounds, some scholars applied concepts used in the study of the Western legal and social systems, such as "social control," in their studies of the Chinese legal system. To some extent, there is an opposing focus between the last two groups: on the one hand, an emphasis on the uniqueness of the Chinese culture and its legal traditions may lead to the argument of culture determinism; on the other hand, the application of Western generated value-laden concepts, such as social control, in the Chinese society tends to ignore social and cultural differences, and leads to problems associated with cultural imperialism.

The study of the Chinese legal system blossomed after 1990 and in the new century. Studies have been expanded in several directions. First, many studies focused on new laws in China on foreign trade, investment, and other business-related activities. These studies served a clear purpose for foreign businessmen and investors in China. Second, studies of crime, crime control, and punishment in China have been deepened and expanded into many sub-fields, such as juvenile delinquency, death penalty, gang and organized crime, workplace theft and official offense, sexual offenses, official corruption, money laundering, prison system and prisoners, criminal defendants' confession and legal representation, anti-crime campaigns, new public order crimes, and recidivism and crime prevention. Third, studies on policing and police power in China clearly traced new changes after the reform and showed the different roles played by the police, people's new conceptions about the police work, and adjusted relationships between the police and the community. Fourth, given changes in the legal system in China, more scholars started working on analyses of the legal reforms and transitions. This was the time that the term "legal reform" first appeared in scholars' works. Uncertain about the nature of the new reform, some scholars questioned the effect of China's legalization and pointed out limitations of the Chinese legal reform compared with the Western model of the rule of law. Fifth, legal scholars with Chinese backgrounds have started publishing works from their perspectives, with a mixed expectation of both introducing the emerging legal system to the Western audience (a going-out approach) and analyzing issues in the Chinese legal system based on Western models and lessons (a bringing-in approach). Sixth, the study of the Chinese legal tradition has been expanded in two directions. On the one hand, studies traced backwards to ancient Chinese legal traditions and tried to show the continuity of those traditions. For this group, the emphasis was on the legal traditions in the past. On the other hand, some scholars focused on the most recent development of the Chinese legal system and tried to show the impact of legal traditions on the current legal reforms. For this group, the focus was on the present. In any event, studies in both directions made significant contributions to a deeper under-standing of what Chinese legal traditions are and how they impact the current legal reform. Finally, some scholars began to pay special attention to the growing court system in China. This is consistent with the changes of the legal system in the new era when the court is gaining more and more power.

(2) *Major Theories on China's Legal Reform*

"Rule of law" vs. "rule by law": one most noticeable theory is the contrast between 'rule of man' and 'rule of law,' and the Chinese 'rule by law' as pro-posed by scholars. As discussed above, from the beginning of its legal reform, the Chinese government tried to build a legal system based on law in order to avoid the same mistake of the 'rule of man' during the Cultural Revolution period. As a matter of fact, early discussions among Chinese domestic scholars focused primarily on the confrontation between the rule of law and the rule of man. The general agreement seemed to target exces-sive influence by powerful individuals, and to replace the rule of man with the rule of law (e.g., Wang and Zhang, 1992). Over the years, the process of legal systemization and bureaucratization seemed to support the fact that China was moving towards its goals.

Scholars studying Chinese political and legal systems abroad, however, raised doubts on China's practice of the rule of law. They proposed that China is practicing instead the 'rule by law' (Epstein, 1992; Keith, 1994; for efforts to reconcile such conceptual differences, see Peerenboom, 2002a, 2004; Zheng, 1998). For example, as Chen (1999) argued, the Western notion of the rule of law embraces a series of important concepts, such as supremacy of law, judicial independence, equality before the law, separation of powers, checks and balances, a parliamentary system, and protection of human rights. All those key concepts are still very inadequately developed in China. Keith (1994) pointed out that the Chinese 'judicial independence' (*shenpan duli*) refers to the elimination of the Communist Party's political influence in actual judicial decisions rather than the total elimination of the Party's influence over the general policy direction of the judicial process. In essence, China's judicial independence did not originate from the concept of separation of powers. Potter (1995, 1998) concluded in his study that the Chinese government's approach to law is fundamentally instrumentalist, and laws and regulations are enacted explicitly to achieve immediate policy objectives of the regime. Rather than a limit on the state power, law is a mechanism to exercise state power in China.

The Chinese government indeed made no intention to hide the guidance (as one form of control) of the CCP over the building of the legal system. The official definition of "ruling the country in accordance with the law" (*yifa zhiguo*) was codified as follows: "under *the lead of the Communist Party* and based on the Constitution and laws, the populace administer national affairs, economic, cultural, and social affairs via various means. It is to guarantee all national affairs to be done according to laws, and to realize the systemization and legalization of the socialist democracy. The basic system and law will not be changed with changes of national leaders or changes of those leaders' personal opinions" (the *People's Daily*, June 20, 2001; November 1, 2002). Apparently, the focus was on restraint of individuals' excessive powers, not the lead of the Party in general, despite of the confusion. In January 2001, President Jiang Zemin proposed one more term "building the country based on moral education" (*yide zhiguo*), and called for a combination of both the "moral education" and the rule of law. It was argued that moral value is another important component of the superstructure in addition to the legal system (based on the Marxian doctrine), and both moral education and the legal system are necessary for the advance of Chinese socialism (see, e.g., the *People's Daily*, February 1 and 22, April 7 and 29, 2001). The term "building the country based on moral education" was defined as follows: "*guided by Marxism, Leninism, Mao's thought and Deng's theory,* (it is) to build socialist moral-value system consistent with the development of the socialist market economy; to make the morality model automatically accepted by the populace" (the *People's Daily*, November 1, 2002; March 2, 2003). The definition once again specified the guidance of the Party (in)directly in the process of moral education.

Decentralization vs. centralization: another constructive argument among scholars is on the application of the decentralization theory in China's legal reform. The decentralization theory was first proposed to explain China's economic development after the reform. With the decline of the planned economy, the central government placed increased reliance on the market and material incentives and granted more substantive decision-making power to local governments and individuals. Once the economic decentralization theory gained its popularity, efforts were made to expand it into legal domains. For example, Tanner (1999) pointed out an increasing acquisition of power and influence by various political organizations (e.g., the NPC) in the law-making process, and argued that a further *decentralization of (policy-making) power* among "elite, bureaucratic, institutional and social groups" is necessary for a more open, consultative and democratic legal and political system in the future. Another famous scholar, Zhu shuli (1989) noticed that when local governments increased their economic bargaining power, they also gained some leeway to substantiate general policies and laws from the central government. As a result, Zhu argued that the systematization of law was helped and enhanced by the *decentralization of legislative power* with the development of the economic reform. This argument of decentralization of legislative power (e.g., law-making) was later echoed by some other scholars as well (e.g., Lu and Miethe, 2007).

In contrast, Liang (2008) asked for caution with the expansion of the decentralization theory, both theoretically and empirically. Indeed, the term decentralization has rarely been carefully defined. Overemphasis of decentralization misinterpreted the power relationship between the central government and the local, ignored the macro level control by the government, and blurred important distinctions among economic, administrative, and legal controls. Conceptually, it would be more helpful to look at the issue as a continuum, rather than a dichotomy (decentralization v. centralization), so that scholars, researchers, and practitioners can focus on specific measures adopted (e.g., which one is more salient and dominating) at different stages (pre-, inchoate or advanced reform period) in different fields (economic, administrative, or legal). Liang further argued that the process of legalization should be explored within a broader scope as part of China's ongoing political reform. The Chinese government has adopted legal reform as a new means of legitimizing and maintaining its political control through the *centralization of power* in the new era. Only in such a way could the audience gain a better understanding of the necessity of China's legal reform and its corresponding political implications.

5. Contemporary Criminal Justice System

(1) *Police and Policing*

The promulgation of the *Police Law* in 1995 is considered a milestone in Chinese policing as an effort to create a more professional and modern police force. Contrary to many people's misunderstanding, the police system in China is not a centralized system. Rather, based on the new law, it consists of many different forces such as public security organization, state security organization, police working in courts and corrections, and specialized armed police. Recent data showed that the total number of police officers in China reached 1.7 million in 2007; but the police-population ratio is only 13 officers per 10,000 citizens, one of the lowest in the world (e.g., Tanner and Green, 2008).

In contrast to many other nations, one dominant feature of the Chinese police is its unique organization philosophy, the "Party line, mass line, and prevention line" philosophy. First, the Party line requires that the police be under the control of the CCP and follow directives and policies of the Party. Second, the mass line requires that the police maintain close contact with the public to better serve the interests of the people. Third, the prevention line requires that the police utilize various social mechanisms in crime control and prevention (Dai, 2008). Indeed, local public securities often work closely with neighborhood committees to carry out their daily functions, and many argue that these neighborhood committees could hardly be labeled "informal" in China due to their close connections with formal systems. Though their nature and importance have been changing and declining after the reform, these neighborhood committees still have significant influence over public life, especially on crime control and prevention.

Based on Chinese laws (e.g., *Administrative Penalties for Public Security*), Chinese police enjoy great authority and power to impose a wide range of administrative sanctions (including short-term detention) without court approval in cases of minor offenses and public order violations. Potential abuse of power and lack of judicial supervision has long been criticized by international civil rights organizations. In 1997, one most criticized measure, shelter and investigation (*shourong shencha*) was abolished, but others are still kept alive and the Chinese police often rely upon these administrative penalties in their daily operations.

In the pre-reform era, China had enjoyed a very low crime rate, and its successful crime control and low recidivism rate often amazed the Western audience. After the economic reform, however, China's crime rate has been steadily climbing. Official data showed that the rate of criminal cases per 100,000 people was around 70 in the late 1970s, but it jumped to 200 in 1990, broke the 300 marker in 2001, and reached an all-time high of 363 cases per 100,000 people in 2004. To fight worsening crimes, the Chinese authority adopted two specific policing strategies. First, a series of anti-crime campaigns, the so-called severe strike campaigns (*yanda*), have been launched (Liang, 2005). In these campaigns, criminals were punished more severely and criminal punishments usually were rendered faster. Take death sentence and execution for example, data compiled by the *Amnesty International* over the years showed that in both 1996 and 2001 when severe strike campaigns were carried out, the number of death sentences and executions increased significantly (e.g., doubled or tripled) compared with other years, a clear result of harsh crackdowns. Based on both *Criminal Law* and *Criminal Procedure Law*, all death sentences had to be reviewed by the SPC. To cooperate with the official crackdown in these campaigns, however, the final review power was granted to lower level courts. Only until 2007 did the SPC take back such review power. Given the lessened and speedy review and approval, cases were finalized at a much faster pace, even at the expense of formal legal requirements. For instance, during the 1996 anti-crime campaign, three men in Jilin province were arrested for robbery on May 21 and executed on May 31. Their trial and sentencing by the trial court, review, and approval of death sentences as well as the appeal hearing by the appellant court all took place in five days between May 24 and 28 (reported by the *Amnesty International*)! Though the long-term crime control effect of such campaigns is very questionable, such campaign-style policing has served other functions (e.g., political showoff, gaining public support) and it has become an indispensable part of China's contemporary policing.

Second, after the reform, the old community-workplace centered control approach started losing its effect, giving way to a more individual-based control approach. Facing increasing crime rates, a *comprehensive management* (*zonghe zhili*) strategy was implemented to improve the community-workplace centered approach with the individual-based control strategy. This approach, initially proposed in the last 1970s and early 1980s, called to mobilize and coordinate all political, legal, economic, administrative, and educational efforts, and it is viewed as an effective long-term crime control and prevention strategy. In fact, the Chinese government has realized that pure crackdown (e.g., campaigns) could not stop crimes, and it has to come up with new measures to revamp the comprehensive management. A recent move in 2006 by the public security organizations was to set up police offices in neighborhoods to improve community policing. By the end of 2006, over 133,000 such neighborhood offices were established and over 220,000 police stationed in communities as a result (the *Legal Daily*, February 5, 2007).

(2) *Courts*

In sharp contrast to its minimum roles in the pre-reform era, China's court system has been growing tremendously along with China's legalization in the reform era. In fact, compared with the procuratorate and the policing systems, the court system has been the most active player in recent years, especially since the second half of the 1990s. Court reform has become a popular slogan and many new regulations have been put forward to answer new calls. In 1999, for instance, the SPC published *An Outline of the Reform of the People's Courts in the Next Five Years* (*renmin fayuan wunian gaige gangyao*), and new guidelines have been enacted every five years since then.

Though Chinese courts have been taking on increasing roles in the new era, the overall structure of the court system stayed the same over the years: in addition to the national Supreme People's Court and specialized courts (such as maritime courts), the general court system in each province consists of three-tiers, including the High People's Court (i.e., the provincial supreme court), the Intermediate People's Courts, and the Basic People's Courts. In addition, the Basic People's Courts often set up people's tribunals as mini-branches of the courts located in remote areas to help people who have difficulty traveling. Within each court, specialized divisions (e.g., criminal division, civil division, juveniles division) are set up to handle different types of cases. By 2004, there were 222,000 judges working in some 3,500 courts nationwide. The judge-population ratio, one judge per 6,000 citizens, is well below those of developed nations (Cabestan, 2005).

Traditionally, the Chinese judicial system belongs to the civil law system and follows the inquisitorial trial model. As a result, no precedents can be directly cited by judges as sources of ruling (a common practice in the common law system), and judges have great power and discretion in trial proceedings. In recent years, however, the Chinese court system has been incorporating new elements from other nations' legal systems. For example, in criminal cases, more measures have been adopted to honor and protect criminal defendants' rights. The 1996 revised *Criminal Procedural Law* provides that "no one is guilty of a crime without a people's court rendering a judgment according to law" (Article 12). It ended officially the notorious practice of convicting people with analogy (when no specific laws existed regulating the alleged wrong behavior). However, as many (e.g., Luo, 2000) pointed out, such a progress has not yet reached the level of the presumed innocence as known in Western nations. Some local authorities in China even adopted a 'zero confession' policy as a way to protect defendant's right to remain silent. It is again not clear to what extent such new practices will make a substantial impact in real practice. In contrast, civil cases are often much less controversial and more open to new reform measures. In 1998, the SPC published regulations to change the traditional inquisitorial trial model to the adversarial model in civil cases. Now, it is the parties (and their attorneys), rather than the judge, who are responsible in case investigation and evidence presentation at trials. The direct confrontation by parties in a civil suit therefore looks more familiar to the Western audience.

A number of unique features of the Chinese court system stand out in comparison to that of the Western system. First, less stringent rules of evidence are utilized in the Chinese system. Except for a few evidential rules specified in civil, criminal procedures, and administrative litigation laws, a unified rule of evidence is still under construction in China. Problems such as hearsay evidence, character evidence, and lack of witness testimony plague proper trial proceedings, especially in criminal cases. Second, a mixture of formality and informality is often witnessed in court, and Chinese judges have multiple roles to play (e.g., as adjudicator, mediator, moral educator). Mediation is indeed built into civil cases, and a peaceful outcome through mediation is viewed as the preferred result. Third, the traditional notion of 'substantive justice' still dominates over the trial proceeding, and the court is willing to ignore or bend the rules of procedure requirements in order to achieve such a goal. For instance, in many criminal cases, guilt is predetermined even before the trial begins and the whole purpose of the trial is to condemn vice and punish criminals. Fourth, the court system itself still struggles from lack of complete judicial independence. Internal review (e.g., by the adjudication committee of the court rather than the sitting judges) and external review systems (e.g., approval by higher level courts or even non-judicial personnel) still have a role to play in some rulings (especially when it is judged that these rulings will have a great social impact).

(3) *Corrections*

There is a visible divide between two ideological groups among studies on China's correctional systems. On the one hand, dissident critics (e.g., Wu, 1992) of the Chinese system exposed the 'dark side' of the system, and sometimes compared it to the Soviet Gulag or the Nazi concentration camps. On the other hand, some scholars (mainly Chinese domestic scholars) held a positive view on the Chinese correctional system (e.g., Du, 2004). They often criticize the Western standards, point out how the Chinese practice is rooted in its unique culture and tradition, and praise significant achievements of the Chinese practice such as moral education effect and low recidivism rate. Such confrontation is by any means likely to continue given the strong ideological connotations.

Similar to other branches, the Chinese corrections have experienced dramatic changes in the last three decades after the reform. In addition to *ad hoc* piecemeal measures (e.g., anti-crime campaigns, shelter and investigation centers), a new *Prison Law* was enacted in 1994, with a goal of integrating Chinese orientations (e.g., moral education and rehabilitation) with Western modern concepts of scientific classification, control of official discretion, and prisoners' rights. The new law greatly softened revolutionary wordings of the old laws, and put a strong emphasis on scientific management (e.g., through diagnostics and classifications). Males, females, and juveniles are now given separate detention, and prison education is also based upon classification. The new law further codified a number of prisoners' rights such as visitation rights, rights to send and receive mail, personal and habitation rights, and protection against humiliation. Though viewed as a positive move, the effectiveness of the new law in reality is hard to test empirically due to the secrecy of prisoners' lives behind the walls.

Most reliable research (e.g., Seymour and Anderson, 1998) estimated that the overall prison population in China is just around 2 million, among which 1.5 million are inmates of labor-reform camps (*laogai*) and reeducation-through-labor camps (*laojiao*), and the rest are in jail. The actual rate of the prison population to the general population is indeed in the same general range as the world average. The proportion of political prisoners (a practice heavily criticized by Western civil rights organizations) has been continuously declining and the majority of prisoners are incarcerated for committing crimes in the new era.

Another hotly debated feature of the Chinese corrections is the use of prison labors. Though criticized as inhuman and forced labor by Western civil rights groups, the Chinese government has been consistently enforcing such a policy. Comparative scholars (e.g., Shaw, 1998) noticed that such a practice was indeed borrowed from the Western practice of work disciplines and religious education in prisons. The Chinese system tries to integrate both laboring and thought reform and believes that productive labor is designed as a vehicle through which thought reform can be effectively carried out. In this process, education, consisting of various forms (such as curriculum education, vocational training, cultural education, political study, and moral reform) constitutes a main part of inmates' lives. Such a practice is rooted in the Chinese history, philosophy, culture and social milieu. Most recent research (e.g., Seymour, 2006) debunked the myth of the high profitability of the prison industry. Despite virtually free inmate labor, prison industry in China ran into both qualitative and quantitative problems (e.g., low skills, lack of resources, capital investment and production incentive) in the reform era. Evidence suggests that even the most high-performing provincial prison system (e.g., in Qinghai) continued to be a financial drain. The hostile international environment (e.g., opposition to prison exports) did not help either with the image and the operation of the prison industry.

China's low recidivism rate has caught the eyes of Western scholars for a long time. The national overall recidivism rate reported by the majority of scholars was limited to a single digit (under 10%), and only a few reported one as high as 15%. Similarly, the recidivism rate of juvenile delinquents hardly exceeded 10%. Despite the overall low range, these numbers were not without variations. Besides the differences between adult offenders and juveniles, regional variations (e.g., some regions such as in Xinjiang reported double-digit numbers even as high as 60%) and variations among different crimes (e.g., higher recidivism rates for crimes such as prostitution and particularly drug use) were noticed and reported. In any event, the overall data supported this amazingly low recidivism rate especially given the size of China, and the Chinese government is not shy at bragging its achievement.

6. Accession to WTO and Its Impact

China's accession to the WTO in 2001 is another milestone in China's contemporary history. Its economy impact is profound. First, formal entry into the WTO requires China further open its door to foreign trade. Take China's import tariff rate for example. In 1982, China's average import tariff was 55.6%, and it was still as high as 35.9% in 1994; it was quickly lowered to 23% in 1996 and then to 17% in 1997. After the accession, it was further lowered in the new century and fell below 10% in 2005. Second, as a new member of the WTO, China is committed to opening its domestic market and applying nondiscriminatory policies to foreign investors and enterprises. By the end of 2005, governmental reports showed that 470 of the top 500 transnational enterprises had already opened direct operations in China. Third, as a new member, China is obligated to follow game rules in the global system. Anti-dumping cases are such an example. Because of its production of primarily low-cost, labor-intensive products, China has quickly become a main target in anti-dumping cases after its reform. WTO (anti-dumping) data showed that from 1995 to 2009 China was the number one target in anti-dumping cases, leading in both the number of investigations and the number of measures imposed by other nations against China. As a result, China has been learning how to defend itself and at the same time to utilize the same rules in its own interest. In 1997, the State Council promulgated the *Anti-dumping and Countervailing Regulation of the PRC* (which was replaced by new regulations in 2001). From 1997 to the summer of 2005, Chinese enterprises initiated 39 anti-dumping investigations against other nations with a total value over 6 billion (US) dollars (the *People's Daily*, August 10, 2005).

Although China's accession to the WTO is primarily a result of its economic needs, the impact of such accession on China's domestic legal system has been equally important. First, entry into the WTO has already brought a round of legal changes domestically. In preparation and as a requirement for being a WTO member, China has revised more than 3,000 domestic laws, administrative regulations, and orders that were in conflict with WTO agreements and stipulations (Xue and Jin, 2009). At the same time, protection for intellectual properties (often a deep concern for foreign investors) was strengthened after China's accession. From 2000 to 2004, the public security organizations cleared 5,305 intellectual property cases, and the procuratorates filed charges against 2,566 people (the *People's Daily*, April 22, 2005). From 2002 to 2006, people's courts accepted 54,321 intellectual property civil litigations, more than doubled the number of cases in the preceding five years (from 1997 to 2001) before China's entry of the WTO (the *People's Daily*, January 10, 2007).

Second, as China's economy further integrates into the global system, its legal system becomes more open to other nations' legal practices and international standards. On the one hand, more laws are enacted to deal with foreign-related affairs and protect investors' interests. In August 2002, for instance, the SPC handled down decisions on issues related to international trade administrative litigations. For the first time, foreigners and organizations may bring up administrative litigations in the Chinese courts to counter wrongful governmental decisions. On the other hand, increasing legal communications between China and other nations have led to significant changes in China's domestic legal practices. For example, facing international pressure, the Chinese government has taken some measures to tighten its death penalty practice. In 2006, the SPC ordered that all death penalty cases adopt open trials in their *appeals* (*er'shen*) after July 1, 2006, and the SPC further enacted detailed rules (e.g., witness testimony) with regard to such open trials. In 2007, the SPC finally took back the power to review and ratify all death penalty cases, ending a 26-year practice of allowing lower high courts to use such power. Due to such efforts, it was reported that the number of death sentences meted out by the courts in 2006, though not revealed, hit a record low in more than a decade (which is confirmed by the *Amnesty International* data).

Third, the entry into the WTO has a potential impact on China's political-legal reforms. It is acknowledged that the entry of and continued membership in the WTO requires a change of the Chinese government's role in the management of the national economy. A closed, authoritarian polity should be gradually changed to a polity built upon a more transparent, rational legal system. The abolition of 'administrative review and approval' (ARA) (*xingzheng shenpi*) is such a relevant example. For many years, ARA was used as an effective means to control key industrial and commercial projects; however, it does not meet the requirements of the market economy within the global economic system. The rescission of ARA took place first on foreign trade and banking system as part of China's compliance with the WTO rules before it spread into other areas. From December 2002 to May 2004, the State Council reviewed over 1,795 projects and abolished ARA in over 1,600 of these projects (the *People's Daily*, May 25, 2004).

In sum, China's entry into the global system has a great impact on its domestic changes, including its legal system. Granted, more changes and reforms took place at the economic level rather than the political-legal level, and China's participation in various domains is highly selective, catering to its interests (see e.g., Potter, 2004). Nevertheless, simply following WTO rules (e.g., due process, transparency, nondiscrimination, and judicial review) could have a long-term impact in changing China's legal system (Lam, 2009; Qin, 2008).

7. Public Participation and Its Impact

Chinese people's participation in the legal system in the reform era is a dramatic contrast to their participation in the mass-line movements and class struggles in the pre-reform era. In the new era, public participation shows an increasing diversity, involving different players, representing different interests, and for different reasons. Three most important forms of participation are briefly highlighted below.

First, given increased legal consciousness and awareness of one's rights, an increasing number of citizens have begun consciously utilizing China's legal system, especially the court system (as evidenced by the dramatic increase of court cases over the years), in their daily lives to safeguard their own interests. 'Legal talk' is no long uncommon among the masses despite of China's cultural tradition of disliking and avoiding lawsuits. Law is expected to play a more important role in the new century, and even political leaders need to legitimize their actions within the legal boundary.

Second, though the main players of the legal system (e.g., judges, lawyers, prosecutors, police officers) have become increasing professionalized, there is still a strong call for lay persons' participation in the system. Take the people's assessor system (*renmin peishenyuan*) for example. As part of the civil law tradition, China utilizes an assessor system, rather than a jury system. In practice, people's assessors form a judge panel along with professional judges in trial, and they enjoy the same amount of power in decision-making based on law. Though the assessor system encounters numerous problems (e.g., lack of training, assessors rarely exercising independent opinions), the government heavily supports and favors the continuation and expansion of lay participation in the formal system.

Third, the general public has showed increasing interests in voicing their own opinions through various means (e.g., media). Such public opinion plays a role of indirect supervision and has already forced significant changes in the government's actions. In recent years, the use of the Internet has greatly facilitated such public participation. Though China did not start its Internet service until the mid-1990s, its Internet users have grown exponentially. Annual survey data by the Chinese Internet Network Information Center showed that Internet users in China reached 2 million in 1998, surpassed 100 million in 2005, and reached 420 million by June, 2010. China has already replaced the United States as the largest Internet user of the world.

Though Chinese Internet users mainly use the Internet for nonpolitical reasons, they do not shun away completely from political issues. Rather, their participation shows in a unique form (often event driven) at critical moments (sometimes unexpected), and their online response, reaction, and participation have already created an unexpected amplification of public engagement in some key events (e.g., Zheng, 2008). Take the 2009 "hiding from the cat" event for example. In February, 2009, Li Qiaoming, an inmate at the Jinning (county) jail in Yunan province, was mysteriously injured and died. The local authority announced that Li got injured when he was playing a game called "hiding from the cat" (*duo maomao*) with his jailmates. What was unexpected after the official announcement was the strong criticism and questioning by Internet users, and suddenly "hiding from the cat" became a new online bomb. Under the pressure, the Chinese Communist Party Propaganda Department in Yunan recruited five Internet users to form a special investigation committee, traveled to Jinning jail and conducted its investigation. Due to lack of access to key evidence, the committee could not reach a conclusion but posted its investigation online. Later, the authority announced the result of its official investigation. The new investigation revealed that Li was bullied by his jailmates even before the incident, and he was blindfolded and beaten on the incident day. As a result, his head was hit and bumped into the wall, which eventually caused his death. Li's jailmates made up the story of playing the game to cover the truth. The investigation also uncovered numerous violations of prison management by prison guards. One director of the procuratorate in Jinning was deposed, and three jailmates were charged with assaults and sentenced in August along with two prison guards who were found negligent. The "hiding from the cat" event finally came to an end, but the term becomes a new symbol among Chinese Internet users. It is true that public engagement in major events such as the "hiding from the cat" is non-systematic, spontaneous, and unpredictable. These events, however, do carry a great potential to shake political-legal reforms to some extent in China in the future.

8. Conclusion

In three decades after the reform, China has been changing dramatically in almost every aspect including its legal system, and such changes will be likely to continue in the 21st century. To gain an up-to-date and proper under-standing of those changes that China has gone through is crucial to analyzing China's contemporary reforms, its roles in the global system, and its future plans. In contrast to the pre-reform era, China's legal system has gained tremendous development and played increasing roles in both national affairs and people's private lives. There is ample evidence that China's legal system has become more professionalized, adopted more international standards, and played more similar roles as that of many other nations. At the same time, however, China's system still hangs on to many unique Chinese characteris-tics due to its history, culture and polity. These characteristics in many aspects influence the daily practices and operations of the legal system, from the lack of independence of the court system, campaign-style policing, to thought reform and prison laboring in the correctional system. It is not true that all such characteristics carry a negative effect: for instance, the practice of medi-ation as a tradition is deeply rooted in China's history and culture, and it may well be a valid reason for China's low crime rates. The ability to see through changes happened to the Chinese system and how and why these unique characteristics continue to play a role in contemporary Chinese society is crit-ical to one's understanding of the changing Chinese legal system.

References

Bracey, D. H. (1988) Like a doctor to a patient, like a parent to a child — Corrections in the People's Republic of China. *The Prison Journal,* 68(1), 24–33.

Cabestan, J. P. (2005) The political and practical obstacles to the reform of the judi-ciary and the establishment of a rule of law in China. *Journal of Chinese Political Science,* 10(1), 43–64.

Chen, J. (1999). *Chinese law: Towards an understanding of Chinese law, its nature and development.* The Hague, Boston: Kluwer Law International.

Clark, D. and J. Feinerman (1996) Antagonistic contradictions: Criminal law and human rights in China. In S. Lubman (Ed.), *China's legal reforms*, pp. 135–154. Oxford, New York: Oxford University Press.

Cohen, J. A. (1968) *The criminal process in the People's Republic of China, 1949–1964: An introduction.* Cambridge, MA: Harvard University Press.

Cohen, J. A. (Ed.) (1970) *Contemporary Chinese law: Research problems and perspectives.* Cambridge, MA: Harvard University Press.

Dai, M. (2008) Policing in the People's Republic of China: A review of recent literature. *Crime, Law, and Social Change*, 50, 211–227.

Du, J. J. (2004) *Punishment and reform: An introduction to the reform-through-labor system in the People's Republic of China.* Hong Kong: Lo Tat Cultural Publishing Co.

Epstein, E. J. (1992) A matter of justice. *China Review*, 5.1–5.37. Hong Kong: Chinese University Press.

Gold, T. B. (1991) Youth and the state. *China Quarterly*, 127, 594–612.

Gong, P., J. Xia and W. Liu (Eds.) (1999) *Dangdai zhongguo de falü geming* [Chinese law revolution at the contemporary era]. Falü Chubanshe [China: Law Press].

Keith, R. C. (1994) *China's struggle for the rule of law.* Houndmills, Basingstoke, Hampshire: St. Martin's Press.

Lam, E. (2009) *China and the WTO: A long march towards the rule of law.* Wolters Kluwer.

Li, V. H. (1978) *Law without lawyers: A comparative view of law in China and the United States.* Boulder, Colorado: Westview Press.

Liang, B. (2008) *The changing Chinese legal system, 1978–present: Centralization of power and rationalization of the legal system.* New York: Routledge.

Liang, B. (2005) Severe strike campaign in transitional China. *Journal of Criminal Justice*, 33, 387–399.

Lu, H. and Miethe, T. D. (2007) Provincial laws on the protection of women in China: A partial test of Black's theory. *International Journal of Offender Therapy and Comparative Criminology*, 51(1), 25–39.

Luo, W. (2000) *The amended criminal procedure law and the criminal court rules of the People's Republic of China: With English translation, introduction, and annotation.* Buffalo, NY: William S. Hein & Co., Inc.

Peerenboom, R. (2002a) *China's long march toward rule of law.* Cambridge, MA: Cambridge University Press.

Peerenboom, R. (2002b) Law enforcement and the legal profession in China. In J. Chen, Y. Li and J. M. Otto (Eds.), *Implementation of law in the People's Republic of China*, pp. 125–147. The Hague, Boston: Kluwer Law International.

Peerenboom, R. (Ed.) (2004) *Asian discourses of rule of law: Theories and implementation of rule of law in twelve Asian countries, France, and the US*. London, New York: Routledge.

Potter, P. B. (1995) *Foreign business law in China: Past progress and future challenges*. South San Francisco, CA: The 1990 Institute.

Potter, P. B. (1998) The Chinese legal reform: Continuing tensions over norms and enforcement. *China Review*, 25–60. Hong Kong: Chinese University Press.

Potter, P. B. (2004) Legal reform in China: Institutions, culture, and selective adaptation. *Law and Social Inquiry*, 29(2), 465–495.

Qin, J. Y. (2008) Trade, investment and beyond: The impact of WTO accession on China's legal system. In D. C. Clarke (Ed.), *China's legal system: New developments, new challenges*, pp. 166–187. New York: Cambridge University Press.

Seymour, J. D. (2006) Profit and loss in China's contemporary prison system. In P. F. Williams and Y. Wu (Eds.), *Remolding and resistance among writers of the Chinese prison camp: Disciplined and published*. New York: Routledge.

Seymour, J. D. and R. Anderson (1998) *New ghosts, old ghosts: Prisons and labor reform camps in China*. Armonk, NY: M.E. Sharpe.

Shaw, V. N. (1998) Productive labor and though reform in Chinese corrections: A historical and comparative analysis. *Prison Journal*, 78(2), 186–212.

Solinger, D. J. (1999) *Contesting citizenship in urban China: Peasant migrants, the state, and the logic of the market*. Berkeley, CA: University of California Press.

Tao, L. (1997) Politics and law enforcement in China. In T. V. Lee (Ed.), *Law, the state, and society in China*, pp. 99–142. New York: Garland Publishing, Inc.

Tanner, M. S. (1999) *The politics of lawmaking in post-Mao China: Institutions, processes and democratic prospects*. Oxford: Clarendon Press.

Tanner, M. S. and E. Green (2008) Principals and secret agents: central versus local control over policing and obstacles to "rule of law" in China. In D. C. Clarke (Ed.), *China's legal system: New developments, new challenges*, pp. 90–121. New York: Cambridge University Press.

Walder, A. G. (1986) *Communist neo-traditionalism: Work and authority in Chinese industry*. Berkeley, CA: University of California Press.

Wang, Y. and G. Zhang (Eds.) (1992) *Zhongguo falixue zongshu yu pingjia* [The summary and evaluation of Chinese legal theory study]. Zhongguo Zhengfa Daxue Chubanshe [University of Political Sciences and Law Press].

Whyte, M. K. and W. L. Parish (1984) *Urban life in contemporary China*. Chicago, IL: The University of Chicago Press.

Wu, H. (1992) *Laogai — The Chinese gulag*. Boulder, Colorado: Westview Press.

Xin, C. (1999) *Zhongguo de falü zhidu jiqi gaige* [The Chinese legal system and current legal reform]. Falü Chubanshe [Law Press, China].

Xue, H. and Q. Jin (2009) International treaties in the Chinese domestic legal system. *Chinese Journal of International Law*, 8(2), 299–322.

Zheng, Y. (1998) *From rule by law to rule of law? A realistic view of China's legal development*. East Asian Institute, National University of Singapore.

Zheng, Y. (2008) *Technological empowerment: The internet, state, and society in China*. Stanford, CA: Stanford University Press.

Zhu, S. (1989) *The change of law and its characteristics in the People's Republic of China: 1978 to present*. Unpublished master's thesis, Arizona State University, Arizona.

5

POPULATION

Zhongdong Ma

Hong Kong University of Science and Technology

Abstract

Population study is a fundamental unit in social science. Demography concerns itself with the dynamics of population behavior, primarily with respect to the size and structure, as well as movement. China is the largest country in the world, with an immense population of more than 1.3 billion people today, which constitutes almost one-fifth of the world's total. China has a huge population, but a poor foundation with relatively inadequate and unevenly distributed natural resources. These are China's basic national conditions. Population changes may have profound consequences for a wide range of areas in sociology, demography, social policy and others. Insight into these changes is of great value for many purposes, and will benefit researchers and policy makers in different fields. This chapter deals mainly with questions of Chinese population, in particular, the size, characteristics, growth, and the factors affecting the changes in population.

Keywords: Urbanization; census; fertility; mortality; floating population; population; migrants; sex ratio.

1. The Chinese Population: Size, Growth and Composition

(1) *Huge Population Size and Growth*

China has been the largest country in the world in terms of its huge population, currently estimated at 1.34 billion people in the Chinese mainland. In all, six censuses were conducted in 60 years since 1949 during which three baby booms were recorded in the 1950s, the 1960s and the late 1980s. Data in Figure 1 shows

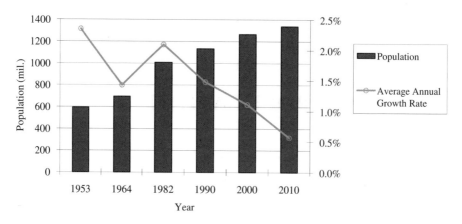

Figure 1.   Population growth, China, 1953–2010

Data sources: National Bureau of Statistics of China.

a rapid population growth since the founding of the People's Republic of China in 1949. China's population was 594.35 million in 1953 according to its first census. It increased rapidly in the 1950s, 1960s and 1970s, broke the mark of 1 billion in 1982 (the third census), doubled the size of 1953 in 1990 (the fourth census), and reached the size of 1.34 billion in the early 2010s. In close to 57 years from 1953 to 2010, population in China more than doubled and increased by 745 million, with an annual growth rate averaged slightly above 1.4%.

The first baby boom was in the 1950s after the civil war and land reform, evidenced in the 100 million difference in population size between the second census in 1964 (695 million) and first census in 1953 (594 million). In the 11-year period, the annual growth rate was 1.4%, despite the negative or very slow growth between 1960 and 1963 because of the widespread famine following Great Leap Forward and natural disasters. The total population reported in the third census in 1982 was 1.0 billion, an increment of 313 million over 1964, with an average annual growth rate of 2.1%. The second baby boom hit China in the period between 1963 and 1970, forcing China to initialize family planning programs in the 1970s which led to a one-child policy since 1979. As the second baby boomers entered into marriageable ages, they produced the third baby boom in the late 1980s. According to the fourth census in 1990, the total population increased to 1.13 billion, and the annual growth rate was still as high as 1.5%. As of 2000, the fifth census reported that the total population in mainland China reached nearly 1.27 billion and the average annual growth rate declined to 1.11%. Since then, the growth rate has gone down quickly to a low level less than 1%. As a result, population grew slowly in the 2000s. In November 2010, China conducted its sixth

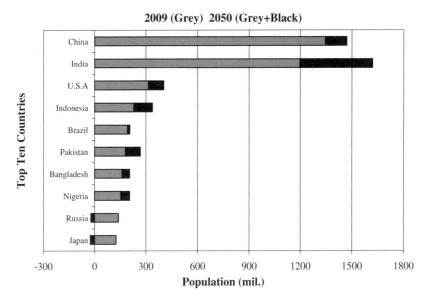

Figure 2. The ten countries' population in the World (2009) and projection for 2050

Data sources: Population Reference Bureau, 2009.

population census, total population in the Chinese mainland was 1.34 billion, and the average annual growth rate reaches its lowest level (0.57%), indicating that the ages of rapid population growth is over in the country.

In Figure 2, we compared the top ten most populous countries in the world in 2009. From the table, we can find that China remains No. 1 in the ten countries with the largest population in the world and accounts for nearly 20% of total world population. However, in less than 15 years, India is expected to take over China as the world largest population, given that the current growth rate in India is considerably higher than that in China. China's population is projected to be at its peak around 2040 at about 1.5 billion before a slow decline.

(2) *Highly Uneven Population Distribution*

Distribution of population in China has been highly uneven. The normal geographic division of the East and the West is done by drawing a line between Tengchong County in Yunan province and Heihe County in Heilongjiang province. The East accounts for 42% of land and 90% of population, whereas the West accounts for 58% of land but only 10% of population. The sparsely populated West is main due to the harsh environment including rigid climate in Qinghai-Xizang plateau (elevation >4000 m) as well as arid or semi-arid climate in Xinjiang, Neimeng and Loess plateau in Northwest (elevation 1000–2000 m).

Table 1.   Population distribution by region, China, 2005

Region	% Population	% of Area	Population density (person/sq. km)
Eastern	41.3%	11.2%	511.5
Midst	31.7%	17.5%	251.5
Western	27.0%	71.3%	52.6

Data sources: National Bureau of Statistics of China.

By contrast, conditions in the East are more favorable for living and production than the West by having (1) small hills and plains with fertile soil (elevation < 1000 m); (2) temperate climate with plenty of precipitation in the summer; (3) higher levels of development in agriculture, transportation, and education than the West; and (4) the economies of agglomeration. Apart from the environmental factors, differences in fertility, mortality and interregional migration can also affect the distribution. For example, the higher fertility level in the Western Region helps to increase the share of population in the Western region, whereas increasing migration to the most developed regions in the Eastern Region reduce such a share.

Based on the level of development, China can be further divided into three regions[1]: the Eastern, Central and Western Regions. Table 1 shows the regional differences in the distribution of China's population. The Eastern Region accounts for the least portion of land (11.2%) but largest share of population nearly 42%, whereas the Western Region accounts for the largest portion of land (71.3%) but the least share of population (27%). In between is the Central Region which accounts for 17.5% of land and one-third of the population. Such an uneven distribution results in much difference in population density measured by number of persons per square kilometers. The density in the East Region (511.1) almost doubles that in the Central Region (251.3), which in turn is almost five times as high as that in the West Regions (52.6).

(3) *Rapid Urbanization*

Urban-rural distribution has been changing drastically since the early 1950s. The urban share of population has nearly quadrupled from around 13% in 1953

---

[1] The eastern region consists of 11 provinces, municipalities, and autonomous regions: Beijing, Tianjin, Hebei, Liaoning, Shanghai, Jiangsu, Zhejiang, Fujian, Shandong, Guangdong, and Hainan; the central region includes eight provinces and autonomous regions: Shanxi, Jilin, Heilongjiang, Anhui, Jiangxi, Henan, Hubei, and Hunan; the western region covers 12 provinces and autonomous regions: Sichuan, Chongqing, Guizhou, Yunnan, Tibet, Shaanxi, Gansu, Qinghai, Xinjiang, Inner Mongolia, and Guangxi.

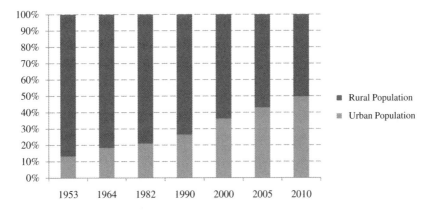

Figure 3. Rural-urban population composition, China, 1953–2005

Data sources: National Bureau of Statistics of China.

to 50% in 2010. Since the 1950s, the growth of urban population has gone through different stages. Figure 3 shows increasing importance of the urban population in the past six decades. Rapid industrialization in the 1950s brought up the urban share from 13.0% in 1953 to 18.3% in 1964, with an average annual growth rate of 0.5%. During the period of Cultural Revolution (1965–1976), the economy was stagnant and so was the urbanization. Mao even sent his Red Guard to the countryside for "re-education" by the peasants. The urban share only rose slightly in the early 1980s to 20.9% in 1982, with an average annual growth rate of less than 0.2%. Urbanization finds its impetus from economic reforms and urban share picked up in the 1980s from 21% in 1982 to 26% in 1990s and increased rapidly after 1990 to 36.2% in 2000, 43% in 2005, and 50% in 2010. The speed of urbanization, which is measured by the annual increased share of urban population, has also been increasing since the economic reform, from 0.7% in the years in the 1980s, to 1.0% in the 1990s, and further to 1.4% in the early 2000s.

As we will show soon, massive rural-urban labor migration contributes significantly to the rapid urbanization since 1990. However, a vast majority of migrants from the rural areas find it difficult to settle in the urban destinations, partly due to the control of the household registration system (*hukou*) which prevents them to be an urban resident, partly due to the rising living costs in housing and children's education. Migrants often leave their dependants behind in rural villages. The highly floating nature of labor migration and its huge volume exceeding 100 million make the urbanization in China a painful, unstable, and incomplete process. With development

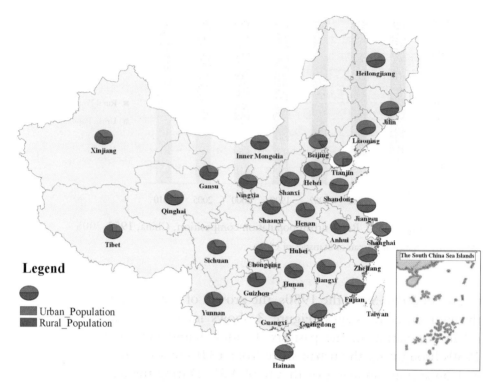

Figure 4.   Urban/Rural share of population by region, China, 2005

Data sources: National Bureau of Statistics of China.

proceeding, gradual removal of the household registration system helps to speed up and improve the process urbanization.

Figure 4 (Map) shows that the urban share of population is jointly determined by the level of development and that of industrialization. In 2005, urban population accounted for 45% or more in all provinces in the Eastern Region and four designated cites (Beijing, Shanghai, Tianjin and Chongqing), but much less in the Central or Western Regions, mostly between one-quarter to forty percent, with the exception of Neimeng, Jilin and Heilongjiang which are rich in industrial resources.

(4) *Nationalities*

China is a unified multi-national county with 56 nationalities. According to the sixth population census in 2010, minority people totaled 113.8 million or 8.5% of the total, indicating an increase of 7.4 million or 6.9% over that in 2000 based on the fifth census, which was higher than the growth rate of the Han People (5.7%).

2. Population Structure: Composition by Sex and Age

Population age-sex structure is a dynamic result of its past fertility, mortality, and migration, it is also a fundamental reality with demographic, social, and economic consequences.

The best way to show population structure is to depict a population pyramid by sex and five-year age group. The 2010 census data indicates children ages 0–14 were only 18.3% of the total population, in contrast to adult people ages 15–64 and older people ages 65 and over, which constituted 74.5% and 8.9% respectively of the total population. China's 2005 population pyramid in Figure 5 shows a sunken area in the age structure especially at ages 20–24 and also in ages 25–29. The recent term "Population Dividend" states the presence of a vast majority in the labor force ages. The low dependent ratio with it indicates a golden era for economic growth.

In 2005, the median age was 35.4 for the total population. The difference in median age was minor geographically among three big regions and hierarchically among three urban/rural settlement types (city, town and rural areas). The share of young dependents was greater in the rural areas (20.8%) than the urban areas (15.5%) whereas the share of old dependents was also slightly larger in the rural areas (8.8%) than the urban areas (7.5%). Massive labor migration of rural adults helps to explain the surprisingly reversed order of the share of old dependents, whereas the considerable rural/urban

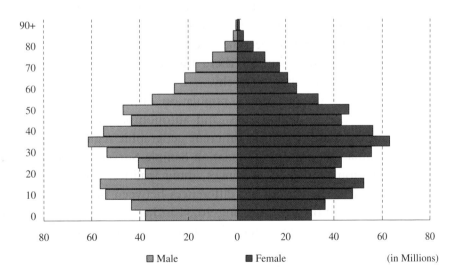

Figure 5. Age-sex distribution of China's population, 2005

Data sources: National Bureau of Statistics of China.

gap in the share of young dependents can be explained by joint effects of labor migration and the rural/urban differential in fertility.

As a result of downward transition in its mortality, the sex ratio of total population declined and the decline was in the sex ratio from younger age categories to older ones. Data from the 2005 China One Percent Population Sample Survey shows that, the sex ratio for the childhood was very high for the youngest age group younger than 5 (123), high for those aged 5 to 14 (116), but relatively normal at 105 through young and adulthood ages (15–64). The sex ratio for the elderly ages 65–84 was 94. For the oldest-old aged 85 or over, the sex ratio declined to 52.

The extremely high-sex ratio at birth since the early 1990s is mainly a result of strict fertility control in a son-preference society. The widespread ultrasound technology since the early 1990s in China provides cheap and easy tools to identify the gender of the fetus. In a majority of the rural areas, a couple is allowed to have a second child several years after giving birth to a girl. For those families with strong son-preference, they need to make "full" use of this right to make the second birth a son. The process is through the new technology to identify the gender of the fetus and do selective abortion if needed until the birth of a son.

Due to the high sex ratio at birth, some scholars estimate the cumulated shortage of females in the coming decades amounts to forty millions or more. The shocking impact of such sex imbalance can be observed once these cohorts enter into labor and marriageable ages, reflected by recent shortages of young female labor migrants in the Pearl River Delta and shortages of nannies in Beijing. In a few years time when the 1990s' cohorts are marriageable, the "marriage squeeze" would become a serious problem in the rural areas and small towns as young females there migrate to cities and resort to marriage to move up the urban hierarchy.

The sex composition of China's population differs to varying degree between the provinces, municipalities, and autonomous regions. Figure 6 presents the differential sex ratio in different geographic regions. According to the 2005 China One Percent Population Sample Survey, the sex ratio of the total population of the 31 provinces, municipalities, and autonomous regions was 102.19. There were big differences between the highest, being 110.46 in Hainan, and the lowest, being 96.34 in Jiangsu. Hainan, Guangxi, Yunnan, and Guizhou provinces had the highest sex ratio, and all of them were over 106. As a comparison, Shandong, Sichuan, Tibet, and Jiangsu provinces had the lowest sex ratio, and all of them were below 100.

Population aging in China has been propelled by both the dramatic reduction in fertility to well below the replacement level and the gradual

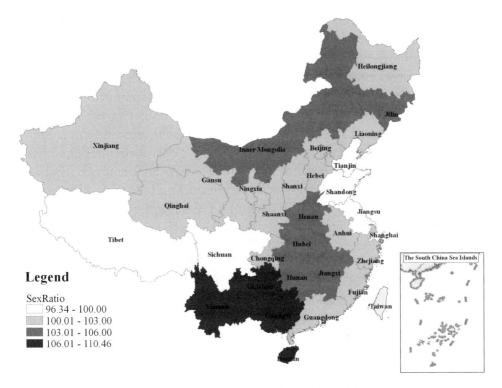

Figure 6. Sex ratio by region, China, 2005

Data sources: National Bureau of Statistics of China.

extension of average life span to over seventy years. Figure 7 shows the proportion of the old people aged 65 and over in the past years. As both fertility and mortality were much higher in the 1960s than now, the proportion of the population age 65 and older was only 3.6% in 1964. The rapid reduction in mortality that started in the 1960s and the sharp decline in fertility during the 1970s sharply changed the population structure. Elderly share increased steadily in the last three decades from 4.9% in 1982 to close to 9% in 2010, which indicates that the elderly population has surpassed the mark of one hundred million. What is amazing about more aging in China are its great speed and large volume as the first baby boomers are fast approaching old age in five years, to be followed closely by the second baby boomers in slightly more than fifteen years. The elderly share is expected to reach double digits soon and catch up quickly with that in developed countries.

The dependency ratio indicates the number of people in the dependent ages (aged below 15 or over 65) per 100 people in the working ages (aged

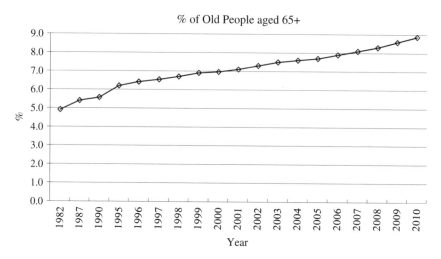

Figure 7.   The proportion of the elderly aged 65 or over, China, 1982–2010

Data sources: National Bureau of Statistics of China.

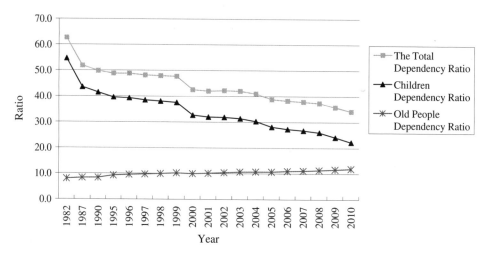

Figure 8.   Dependency ratio, China, 1982–2010

Data sources: National Bureau of Statistics of China.

15 through 64). The dependency ratio has been decreasing since the early 1980s. Figure 8 shows the dependency ratios from 1982 to 2010. In 1982, the total dependency ratio was 62.6, but the figure declined to a much lower level of about 35% in 2010. With a sharp fertility decline and rapid population aging, there has been a dependency shift from young to old people which should be accompanied by a shift of funds from education of children to

medical care of the elderly. Traditional family supports for the elderly are not enough, given a much larger number of old parents relative to their adult children and outward migration of adult children particularly in the rural areas. There are urgent needs for the government to set up practical programs of social services to cope with the increasing demand in the future by a vast number of the elderly.

3. Fertility and Mortality

Demographically speaking, three factors — fertility, mortality, and migration — jointly determine the growth of population. The major part of population growth over the past few decades has been due to the change in fertility and mortality rates.

(1) *Fertility*

1) *Fertility trends in China*

To measure the fertility level, one can divide the number of births in a year by the total population and obtain a *crude birth rate* (CBR). CBR is not a good measure of fertility level because it can be affected by population structure. For example, in the absence of fertility/birth changes, the entry of boomers into marriageable ages can increase CBR significantly. The total fertility rate (TFR) is the sum total of the age-specific fertility rate of women, and it can be looked upon as the number of births a woman would have during her childbearing age if she follows the current birth rates. Unlike CBR, TFR is not affected by the population structure and is often used for comparison of fertility level from time to time or among different places.

During the past several decades, China's population has experienced a dramatic change from high to very low fertility. Figure 1 shows China's remarkable decline in the total fertility rate over the period 1970–2000. Since the early 1970s, China has experienced a pronounced and rapid decline in its fertility. In the 1970s, the total fertility rate (TFR) consistently and dramatically declined from 5.81 in 1970 to 2.75 in 1979. In the 1980s, fertility continued declining until 1986, when it rebounded to 2.59 in 1987. Fertility in 1990–1992 remained slightly above the replacement level. The sharp decline happened in the period between 1992 and 1995 to 1.5 or 1.6 and since then remains at remarkably low levels well below the replacement level.

The dramatic decline in China's TFR in the past four decades can be largely attributed to a strong birth control policy. The strictness of the policy has gone through "U" curve, getting stricter from the 1970s to 1990s and relaxing slightly in the late 2000s which is possibly relaxed further in the 2010s. In the 1970s the Chinese government promoted three reproductive norms as the basic guidelines for family planning program. These three norms are "Late, Sparse, and Few," where "Late" refers to the postponement of marriage, "Sparse" refers to spacing of a subsequent birth for at least four years, and "Few" refers to a small number of children, respectively. Before 1978, the government suggested the number of children in a family be "One not Enough, Two just Right, but Three too Many." In 1978 this was changed to "One Is the Best, Two at Most." In 1979, the Chinese government launched its one-child policy.

The total fertility rate is still regarded as the most common period fertility measure in the analysis and interpretation of fertility trends. However, they relate to the childbearing experience of a hypothetic birth cohort rather than any real individual or group. Most importantly, the influence of the changes in fertility timing (tempo) may cause misinterpretation of TFR. To illustrate the postponement effects of fertility, it is important to consider the fertility age pattern.

Figure 9 shows a comparison between the age pattern of childbearing of Chinese women in 1964, 1989 and 2005. There was a substantial reduction in the age-specific fertility rates throughout the childbearing ages between 1964 and 2005. The drop in TFR during late 1960s and 1980s was the result of falls in fertility at almost all age groups. The pattern for 1964–1989 is characterized by a large fertility decline between 30% and 90% for each age group, with the most significant decreases in 30–39 years of age. However, in the

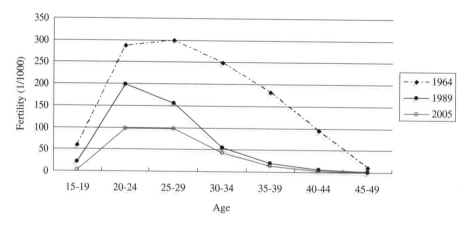

Figure 9.   Age-specific fertility rates, China, 1984–2005

Data sources: Data in 1964 and 1989 are from Yao and Yin (1994); data in 2005 is from the 2005 China One Percent Population Sample Survey.

period 1989–2005, the fertility rates declines in the older age groups were not significant while rates at the young age groups kept declining.

2) *Fertility by parity in 1990s*

The sharp and continuous decline in fertility in China is associated with postponement of low-order births and curtailment of high-order births.

In China, differences in income, educational attainment and population policy between rural and urban area, appear to be significantly correlated with differential fertility. Fertility rate varies between the urban and rural areas. Over the past years, the total fertility rate of the urban population has always been lower than that of the rural population.

The fertility decline was initially caused by the strict fertility control. As development proceeds, increase in income fails to keep up with that of prices for housing, education and others. The opportunity costs of having two or multiple births increase sharply even in the rural areas as millions of young females migrate to cities for wage jobs, to gain both financial and decision power in the family as well as learn the urban experience of concentrating limited resources on the education of a few children. Interestingly, as young couple in the large cities become extremely insecure and vulnerable, the DINK (Double Income No Kids) families are emerging especially in large cities where such young couples account for even ten percent of their cohorts.

As fertility declines to a low level, there are risks and consequences. There is a risk that fertility may decline further to the lowest level (TFR < 1.3). Persistently low fertility also has serious consequences on population structure, which in turn causes negative impact on China's socio-economic development by breaking the sex balance, speeding up population aging, leveling off or even reversing labor growth. There has been a call for the end of "one-child" policy. In the urban areas, the policy has been revised to allow a second child if both the husband and wife have the only child status. Clearly, the impact of this policy is limited given that a vast majority of current marriages cannot satisfy this condition. More relaxation aiming at two-child policy is needed to avoid the further decline of fertility to the lowest low level.

(2) *Mortality*

1) *Mortality trends*

Mortality can be measured in several ways. We can simply divide the number of deaths in a year by the total population to obtain a Crude Death Rate (CDR).

We can also divide the total number of deaths of infants less than one year old by total number of live births that year to obtain an Infant Mortality Rate (IMR). During the last few decades since the founding of the New China, the mortality level of the Chinese population has undergone a profound transformation. The death rate of China's population has dropped, but there were fluctuations. Figure 10 presents the changes of death rate in the period of 1949–2008.

Before 1949, mortality was very high in China. CDR was estimated around 20 per thousand persons and IMR at more than 100 per thousand infants. In the 1950s, the patriotic public health campaigns advocated by the government and epidemic-control arrangements reduced the level of disease-carrying channels. Land reform reduced inequality in the rural areas. As results of land reform and rudimentary universal health care, socialist China made significant progress in the reduction of mortality during the 1950s, cutting down CDR by half to slightly above 10 per thousand (Figure 10). It rebounded in the period the Great Leap Forward and subsequent famine from 1958 to 1962. CDR reached its highest level in 1960 to 25 per thousand per year because of widespread famine that killed millions people. In fact, 1960 was the only year that China experienced a negative population growth. Economic recovery led by Liu Shaoqi and Deng Xiaoping brought down the death rate again in 1961–1962. CDR had since 1962 decreased gradually until the mid-1970s before leveling off at around seven percent from the late 1970s onward. As development proceeds, CDR actually increases mainly because of the share of elderly increase. Like CBR, CDR is

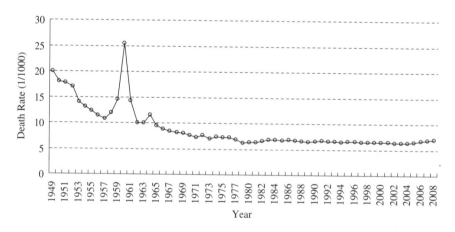

Figure 10.   The crude death rates, China, 1949–2008

Sources: Data in 1953–1964 and in 1964–1982 are from Coale (1984); data in 1990 and 2000 are from National Bureau of Statistics of China.

affected by population structure and hence is not a good measure for the comparison of mortality levels from time to time or from country to country. One example is that the CDR for a developed country such as Sweden is possibly higher than that for a developing country whose population is much younger than that of Sweden.

By summation of risks of dying at each age, Life Expectancy at birth (e_0) calculated from a life table is a good measure of mortality level. The life expectancy at birth for males and females in China for 1953–2000 is given in Figure 11. The life expectancy at birth increased in all periods for both sexes, although not to the same extent. e_0 increased by 19.6 years (1.29% per year) for males and by 17.6 years (1.17% per year) for females from period 1953–1964 to 1964–1982, an increased by 5.2 years (0.31% per year) for males and by 7.3 years (0.43% per year) for females from the period 1964–1982 to the year 1990. In the decade from 1990 to 2000, e_0 increased by 2.8 years (0.28% per year) for males and by 2.9 years (0.29% per year) for females. Mortality decline in China has slowed down after 1970s. In 2000, e_0 for females was 3.7 years longer than that for males, whereas the difference is 3.4 years in the period 1953–1964. Thus, although mortality for both sexes continued to decline during the past several decades, the expected number of years to be lived for females on the average increased more rapidly than that for males.

Life expectancy can be used for international comparison because it is not affected by age structure. There has been a strong and positive relationship between income per capita and life expectancy. This has true in China over the years of development (Figure 11). International comparison show that China has done well in this field with a relatively high expectancy currently

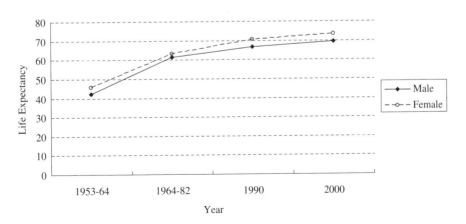

Figure 11.   The life expectancy at birth by sex, China, 1953–2000

Data sources: National Bureau of Statistics of China.

estimated at 73 years (71 for male and 75 for female), which is comparable to that in many middle-income countries including Malaysia (74.6) and Brazil (72.4) and hence outstanding in the list of developing countries, ahead of that in Thailand (70.6) and Indonesia (70), which are in turn much higher than that in India (64).

2) Age patterns of Mortality

Changes in life expectancy at birth are the result of changes in mortality for different age groups. Figure 12 shows the comparison of age specific mortality rates for males and females in the period 1953–1964 and in year 1995.

There were substantial improvements to mortality for both males and females in the past several decades of 1953–1995. In most age groups, the decline in male mortality was greater than that in female mortality. Although all age groups in China show decreasing trends, the decreasing extents vary among different age groups. Among all age groups, decline in infant mortality (m_0) were the most substantial improvement for both sexes in the past several decades. Infant mortality was higher for females than males in past years, and m_0 for males declined faster than females over time. Mortality improvements in childhood, adulthood and early-older age groups were gradual during this period. The old age groups had more substantial improvements compared with adulthood. In the period 1953–1995, infant mortality declined by 84.2% for males and 79.6% for females. The decline was almost 80% for all ages of childhood period below 14 for both sexes. For the

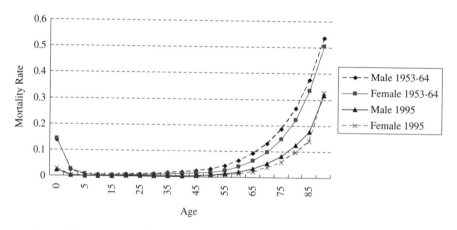

Figure 12. Age specific mortality rates by sex, China, 1953–1964 and 1995.

Sources: Data in 1953–1964 is from Coale (1984); data in 1995 is from National Bureau of Statistics of China.

adulthood age groups 15–49, the decline was more than 70% for both sexes, and for late adulthood period 50–64, the decline was around 70% for both sexes. The five-year age group mortality rates for both sexes decreased by 35 to 63% in old age at 65 and over.

The sharp mortality decline in China can be explained by the theory of epidemiological transition, that the major causes of deaths shift from infectious diseases to degenerative and man-made diseases such as vascular disease and cancer. Transplantation of medical technology from the West to combine with the Chinese Medicine and the rudimentary universal health care system, including the use of "barefoot" doctors are the key to understand the relatively low mortality in China. With the socio-economic development and recent reform in medical system, further mortality decline is expected.

4. Floating Population

Before 1980s, the migration took place in little, mainly because that China restricted internal movement in various ways. Since the 1950s, China has had a household registration (*hukou*) system to control geographic mobility and, in particular, to limit rural-to-urban migration. In the later 1970s, China implemented economic reforms. One of the major consequences of the economic reforms has been the relaxation of household registration system, and resulted a dramatic rise in population mobility, especially moving from inland rural area in the underdeveloped central and western regions to the costal more developed cities, searching for work. The conventional term for internal migrants in China is "floating population," a phrase that describes the large and increasing number of migrants without local household registration status. The growth of this population group reflects fundamental social and demographic changes in Chinese society since the economic reforms.

(1) *Trends of the Inter-County Floating Population*

Figure 13 shows the growth of the inter-county floating population from 1982 to 2005. In 1982, four years after the introduction of economic reforms in 1978, the inter-county floating population of around 7 million accounted for about 0.7% of the total population. By 1990, it was nearly 22 million and accounted for about 1.9% of the total. During this period, the inter-county floating population increased 7 million, averaging an increase of 1.9 millions. The size then doubled in the five years from 1990 to 1995, reached 44 millions, which accounted for about 3.6% of the total population. In 2000, the inter-county floating population increased to 79 million, which accounted for about

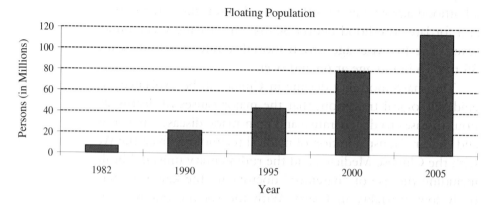

Figure 13.   Inter-county floating population, China, 1982–2005

Data sources: Data in 1982–2000 are from Liang and Ma (2004); data in 2005 is from the 2005 China One Percent Population Sample Survey.

6.1% of the total. The floating population increased at a faster speed after 2000. During the period from 2000 to 2005, the inter-county floating population increased from 79 million to 115 million (accounting for around 8.8% of the total population in 2005), averaging an increase of 7.2 million a year, or an average annual growth rate of 7.8%.

(2) *Inter-Provincial Temporary Migrants*

Inter-provincial temporary migrants are defined as migrants who move to other provinces (municipalities or autonomous regions) outside his or her household registration residence for a period of more than six months. Table 2 shows the size and the distribution of the inter-provincial temporary migrants by region and province in 2005. Data from the 2005 China One Percent Population Sample Survey shows, inter-provincial floating population were found in every province of China, and the size of inter-provincial temporary migrants were around 61.5 million in 2005. In the eastern regions, the number of inter-provincial temporary migrants was 51.8 millions, which accounted for around 10% of the total population in the eastern region; in the central region, it was 3.5 millions, which accounted for around 1% of the total population; and in the western region, the figure was 6.2 millions, accounted for 1.8% of the total population. The above results illustrate the close relationship between the socio-economic development level and population mobility, and reflect a strong magnet force of the growth poles. The province with the largest number of inter-provincial temporary migrants was Guangdong with 19.5 millions, accounting for 19.9% of total population in

Table 2. Inter-provincial temporary migrants by regions, 2005

	Number (in Millions)	% of the total population
Eastern	51,824	10.0
Beijing	4,090	26.1
Tianjin	1,411	13.2
Hebei	994	1.5
Liaoning	1,319	3.1
Shanghai	5,768	30.0
Jiangsu	4,926	6.5
Zhejiang	7,839	15.0
Fujian	3,885	10.6
Shangdong	1,638	1.8
Guangdong	19,546	19.9
Hainan	409	4.8
Central	3,451	0.9
Shanxi	580	1.7
Jilin	435	1.7
Heilongjiang	420	1.2
Anhui	345	0.6
Jiangxi	271	0.7
Henan	382	0.4
Hubei	596	1.1
Hunan	422	0.7
Western	6,209	1.8
Inter Mogolia	585	2.5
Guangxi	396	0.9
Chongqing	471	1.6
Sichuan	644	0.8
Guizhou	514	1.4
Yunnan	1,029	2.4
Tibet	65	2.4
Shaanxi	567	1.6
Gansu	210	0.8
Qinghai	160	3.1
Ningxia	146	2.4
Xinjiang	1,422	6.8

Data sources: The 2005 China One Percent Population Sample Survey.

Guangdong. Zhejiang (7.8 millions) and Shanghai (5.8 millions) rank second and third respectively. Inter-provincial temporary migrants accounted for more than 30% of total population in Shanghai, given the relatively small size of Shanghai's total population. In Jiangsu, Beijing, and

Fujian, the size of inter-provincial temporary migrants was all over 3 millions, and in Shangdong, Xinjiang, Tianjin, Liaoning, and Yunnan, the size was also more than 1 million.

Inter-provincial migrants in Guangdong mainly came from Hunan, Guangxi, Sichuan, and Hubei; migrants in Zhejiang mainly came from Anhui, Sichuan, Jiangxi, and Guizhou; more than 30% of Shanghai's migrants came from Anhui, and another 20% came from Jiangsu. In Jiangsu, more than 40% of inter-provincial migrants came from Anhui; in Beijing, they mainly came from Hebei, Henan, and Anhui. The results depict a pattern that more developed regions attract inter-provincial migrants from less developed adjacent areas.

5. Conclusion

Over time, China has experienced considerable population change, characterized by a rapid fertility and mortality decline as well as a huge floating population in recent two decades. On the other hand, China is facing serious problem of its population structure including growing gender imbalance and rapid population aging. Population aging is caused primarily by fertility decline. An issue of growing concern to China's policy makers is the effect of one-child policy on the size of the elderly population. Because of its uneven, low levels of social and economic development, China is not yet ready to deal with the social security burdens that a rapid increase in the elderly would impose. The continuing growth of China's floating population raises the problem of major cities' over-expansion, and poses challenges to the social development. Although alarmed by the potential problems for the future, the government and the society have yet to find a way to cope.

References

Coale, A. J. (1984) *Rapid population change in China, 1952–1982.* Washington D.C.: National Academy Press.

Liang, Z. and Z. Ma (2004) China's floating population: New evidence from the 2000 census. *Population and Development Review*, 30(3), 467–488.

Yao, X. and Y. Hu (1994) *Basic data of China's population.* Beijing: China Population Publishing House.

6

ETHNICITY

Barry Sautman

Hong Kong University of Science and Technology

Abstract

Ethnicity presents one of contemporary China's major social cleavages. The topic is often described in ethnological terms that speak to folkways, but this essay focuses instead on the aspect of ethnicity in China most discussed globally, politics, especially state policies and their consequences for inter-ethnic and minority/state relations. After detailing the geography, demography, political economy and history of China's ethnic groups, it addresses the government's main ethnic policies: official recognition of ethnic groups, ethnic regional autonomy and affirmative action, but also policies on religion, discrimination and separatism. It is argued that state policies have produced mixed results for China's ethnic minorities: whether viewed from the standpoint of minorities or placed in historical and comparative perspective, the policies have both notable achievements and deficiencies. The prospects for preserving and extending positive aspects of ethnic policies are weighed in light of the changing nature of the Chinese economy and society.

Keywords: Chinese ethnic groups; ethnic politics; ethnic policies; autonomy; affirmative action; discrimination; separatism.

I. Introduction

Ethnicity in China is a topic that has overwhelmingly focused on the roughly one-tenth of the population classified as belonging to one or another of ethnic minority group (*shaoshu minzu*). China's ethnic minority peoples vary

137

greatly in terms of the population size of the 55 officially-recognized groups, from several thousand to many millions. There are wide disparities in their levels of geographical dispersion, from living mainly in a single county; for example, the Dulong (*dulong zu*), to being present in almost all of China's 1,467 counties (the "Muslim Chinese", *hui zu*). There are large variations in income and educational level among minorities. For example, the Manchu (*man zu*) and Koreans (*chao xian zu*), mostly concentrated in northeast China, are highly educated and prosperous, while the Lahu (*lahu zu*) and Pumi (*pumi zu*), who are based in the southwest, have much lower education and income levels. In part, such differences are related to the degree to which groups live inter-mixed with the Han (*han zu*) majority population. The degree of minority group distinctiveness from the majority population and from other minorities is also highly variable. For example, among minority people as a whole, 60% speak their own languages, but almost no Manchu speaks the Man language. In contrast, over 90% of Tibetans speak Tibetan and do so overwhelmingly as their mother tongue (State Council Information Office, 2009; Johnson, 2009; Zhongguo Shehui Kexue Yuan Minzu Yanjiusuo [ZSKYMY], 1994, pp. 750–753).

The nine-tenths of China's population that is officially classified as Han have been of secondary interest in discussions of ethnicity in China. When Han are represented in media, it is as normative, patriotic and invisible, while minorities may be seen as more distinctive, possibly separatist, and visible (Zhao and Postiglione, 2010, pp. 1–18). In academic circles, however, Han studies are now blossoming (Mullaney, 2009; Leibold *et al.*, forthcoming). In very recent years, more attention has been paid to how Han think of themselves in relation to ethnic minorities among whom they live. That is largely due to events in Tibet and Xinjiang, large areas of western China where ethnic tensions have been strongest, as a result of both grievances and political interventions by separatist diasporic forces. Overall and like minorities in other countries, e.g., Hispanic- and African-Americans, China's minorities have less identity with the state and are less likely to identify themselves as part of its nationality (Chinese) than are Han (Shan, 2010, pp. 13–22).

Ethnicity can be considered from many perspectives, but the most common ones in China are ethnological/ethnographic approaches that seek to understand the distinctly ethnic aspects of the quotidian existence of minorities. The knowledge these approaches provide is basic to comprehending cultures and social structures of ethnic groups, as well as aspects of group relations. Much of what ethnology tell us about folkways does not however directly address the constructed perceptions about the place of ethnicity in Chinese society. Outside China, these perceptions have largely been shaped by external actors, are more political than classically anthropological, and mainly concern inter-ethnic and minority/state relations.

Because inter-ethnic relations and relations between minority groups and the state are the basis for much of the global interest in ethnicity in China, this essay focuses on ethnic politics in China, particularly ethnic policies. There has been a substantial degree of stability in ethnic policies in China during the last several decades, but as a result of protests and riots in Tibet and Xinjiang in 2008 and 2009, policies are debated more (Xie, 2010) and are more of a focus of international attention (Grunfeld, 2006, pp. 35–60; Clarke, 2010, pp. 213–229). Accordingly, after an introduction to ethnic minorities in China, we will consider the main policies that affect ethnicity in China, followed by a brief conclusion about how they might evolve in a rights-expanding direction, to create a higher degree of inter-ethnic equality and less conflicted minority/Han and minority/state relations.

II. Ethnicity in a Chinese Context

A. *Territory and Demography*

Chinese often describe their country as having a large territory, a numerous population, and a long history (*dida renduo lishi chang*). The territory is large due to China's extensive ethnic minority areas; the population is huge mainly because of 1.2 billion Han. China is the same size as the United States, but only a tiny part of the US is comprised by the only officially-designated minority areas, those of Native Americans, native Alaskans and native Hawaiians, while most of China's territory is "ethnic minority autonomous areas" (*shaoshu minzu diqu*), the best known of which are associated with Tibetans, Uyghurs and Mongols and are mostly located in western China.

The Tibetan areas are all on the Qinghai-Tibet Plateau (*qingzang gaoyuan*) of western China. The western and central part of the Plateau is a provincial-level Tibet Autonomous Region (TAR, *xizang zizhiqu*), which covers territory formerly ruled by Dalai Lamas. In the eastern Plateau, there are ten Tibetan autonomous prefectures (*zangzu minzu zizhizhou*) and two Tibetan autonomous counties (*zangzu minzu zizhixian*), in four provinces (Qinghai, Sichuan, Gansu and Yunnan) that encompass areas that mostly had not been ruled by Dalai Lamas during one to two centuries before the proclamation of the People's Republic of China (PRC) in 1949.

Tibetan areas make up a fourth of China and their ethnic composition does not fit the common conception outside China of Tibetans having been reduced to a minority of Tibet's population. China's fifth national (2000) census was an enumeration that Western demographers regard as conforming to international standards (Kennedy, 2001). It counted as residents all civilians who had lived in an area for the preceding six months or more. The census showed that ethnic Tibetans and other minority peoples made up four-fifths of the population of the Tibetan areas, with Han the remaining fifth. Contrary to what Tibetan exiles had claimed, the census indicated that the percentage of Han had diminished somewhat from the time of the 1990 census. (Fischer, 2008, pp. 631–662; Congressional-Executive Commission on China, 2005). The sixth national census (2010) found that in the TAR, where half of China's Tibetans live, ethnic Tibetans are 90.5% and Han are 8.2% of the population (XH, 2011).

The Xinjiang Uyghur Autonomous Regions (XUAR) is a predominantly Turkic Muslim area where Uyghurs are the largest ethnic group, 46% at the 2000 census. Han are 40% of the population, a number that has been more or less stable for several decades, because Han migration into Xinjiang has been counter-balanced by higher non-Han birthrates and by substantial Han outflows, both to places of origin and to thriving locales mainly on China's eastern seaboard. Other, mainly Muslim, ethnic minorities are about 13% of residents of Xinjiang, which constitutes one-sixth of China's territory.

The Inner Mongolian Autonomous Region (IMAR) constitutes one-eighth of China's territory. Mongols are only about 20% of the region's population, although Inner Mongolia was already mainly Han well before 1949. Inner Mongolia is more industrialized than Xinjiang, which is in turn more industrialized than Tibetan areas. The most important IMAR urban areas are also closer to the rest of China than is Tibet and Xinjiang. Thus, unlike those other regions, there are ethnic problems, but a much lower level of ethnic conflict, in the IMAR (State Statistical Bureau, 2001).

Tibet, Xinjiang and Inner Mongolia together make up more than half of China. There are two other provincial-level autonomous regions (*zizhiqu*). Guangxi, in the southwest, is the region of the Zhuang, China's largest ethnic minority, 18 million at the 2005 mini-census, compared to 11.2 million Uyghurs, 5.4 million Tibetans and 5.8 million Mongols. Ningxia, in central-west China is the largest autonomous area of the 10 million-strong Hui minority, who are not merely Han people who practice Islam, but have a distinct culture (State Statistical Bureau, 2005; Gillette, 2000).

Below the autonomous regions in the territorial hierarchy are multi-county ethnic autonomous prefectures (*minzu zizhizhou*) and ethnic autonomous counties (*minzu zizhixian*). When all ethnic autonomous areas are taken into account, they amount to close to two-thirds of China's territory. In these areas and in non-autonomous jurisdictions as well, there are also 1,173 still-lower ethnic minority entities, called ethnic townships (*minzu xiang*) and ethnic villages (*minzu cun*). In these, the leadership is expected to be drawn from local minorities, but there is no autonomous law-making power (State Statistical Bureau, 2005).

Minorities were 8.49% of the 1.37 billion Mainland Chinese enumerated in the 2010 census, i.e., almost 114 people, a population close to Japan's 128 million. The minority population had grown by almost 7% in 2000–2010, while the Han population grew by 5.75% (China Daily, April 29, 2011). About 71% of China's minority people live in autonomous areas, which thus contain over 90 million minority people (State Council Information Office, 2009). In 2005, 103 million or 8.7% of China's then 1.187 billion Han lived in ethnic autonomous areas. Although Han were 53% of the autonomous areas' population, they were a majority in only 43 of the country's 155 autonomous areas: 3 of 5 regions; 10 of 30 prefectures; 30 of 120 counties. (National Bureau of Statistics [NBS], 2006; Zhou, 2009, pp. 329–348).[1]

The rate of population increase among minorities has in the past couple decades undergone the demographic transition to lower growth expected with increased education and income. The total fertility rate of minorities varies greatly, but on the whole is greater than that of Han Chinese. Ethnic minority people were put by the 2000 census at 8.4% of China's population, but the 2005 mini-census announced that they were 9.4% (Liu, 2006). The 1% sample size in 2005 and re-classifications of Han to ethnic minority status account for some of the difference, but much of it is due to a higher rate of natural growth among minorities than Han.

B. *History*

Minorities have played a large role in Chinese history. In the fifteen and a quarter centuries from the start of the Northern Wei Dynasty (*beiwei chao*) in 386 AD until the downfall in 1911 of China's last emperor, minorities formed ruling dynasties during 837 years or just over half the period. (Su, 1984, pp. 51–71).[2] Despite the cyberspace presence of "a small but increasingly vocal" group of Han supremacists (Leibold, 2010), the prestige of the last dynasty, the Qing (*Qing chao,* 1644–1911), whose rulers were ethnic Manchu from northeast China, has in recent years recovered from what it was when it was overthrown a century ago, during China's "century of humiliation" at the

---

[1] Because many autonomous areas have several minorities, *eponymous* minorities are less than half the population in 70% of autonomous areas. Zhou, 2009, 341.

[2] For a chronology of ethnic minority Chinese dynasties see Su Meng-fen (1984). On cataloging and classifying Chinese history. *Cataloging and Classification* 4(2), 51–71.

hands of foreign powers. Many Chinese now regard the greatest emperors to have included not only several each from the much earlier Han Dynasty (*han-chao*, 206 BC–220 AD) and Tang Dynasty (*tangchao*, 618–907 AD), but also the Qing emperors Kangxi and Qianlong.

Although China's major ethnic group is called "Han" (*han zu*), that category only became a self-identifier for most of China's population in the 19th Century. Indeed, the concept of an "ethnic group" (*minzu*, or, more properly, *zuqun*) only came to China in the late 19th century, via Germany and Japan. The term Han was derived from the name of a dynasty that Chinese regard as especially glorious and was used more narrowly before the 19th century than now.

For hundreds of years, from at least the Northern Song Dynasty (*bei song chao* 960–1127), the term "Han" was used to distinguish indigenous people of northern China from "tribal" conquerors who came from still further north, such as the Jurchen (*nv zhen*) and Mongols (*menggu zu*). It did not apply to people in other parts of China. Many southern Chinese, especially those of Guangdong province and their diaspora, referred to people we now call Han as Tang people (*tang ren*), again employing the name of an especially glorious dynasty. It was only during the Qing that the term Han was used to differentiate most of China's population from the ruling Manchu people, who had themselves been "tribal" conquerors of lands to the south of their historic homeland. For example, one of the non-Manchu components of the Qing military forces (*ba qi zhi*, the "eight banner system" of Manchu, Han and Mongol soldiers) was called the Han Army (*hanjun*). Its soldiers were Han in the sense that they represented themselves as descendants of the subjects of Han Dynasty, whose territory had been much smaller than that of the Qing and did not include many of the lands now associated with China's minority peoples, including the Manchu homeland in the northeast. The Manchu of northeast China origin represented themselves as directly descended from the Jurchens, the non-Han people who had ruled north China during the Jin Dynasty (*jin chao*, 1122–1234 AD). After the overthrow of the Qing however, the new Republic of China (ROC, *zhonghua minguo*, 1911–1949) considered all bannermen, regardless of their claimed ethnic origins, to be Manchu (Elliot, 2001).

Before the late 19th century then, there was less of a sense than there is today of a Han people with a common culture. Han Chinese did have overlapping cultural elements: a language with many mutually unintelligible dialects, but a mutually-intelligible writing system; a notion of common descent, generally from Han or Tang dynasty subjects; a philosophical and religious heritage of indigenous Confucianism and Daoism (*rujia, rujiao*;

daojia, daojiao); and holidays, such as Spring Festival (*chun jie*) and mid-Autumn Festival (*zhongqiu jie*). In other respects however, their cultures were far from wholly congruent.

Just as there was no sense of a fully coherent Han people before the 19th century, the Chinese state was not conceived in the European-derived way that it is today. The present name for China, originally referred, during the Zhou Dynasty (*zhou chao*, late 9th century BC-256 BC), to only several small kingdoms in what is now west-central China. It did not refer to a single, immense "Middle Kingdom," nor was it necessarily perceived by Chinese as "center of the world," as non-Chinese often imagine. These small kingdoms were first united during the Qin Dynasty (*qin chao*, 221–207 BC). Since then, there have been many configurations among dominant polities in what is now China's territory. There was at least one kingdom, group of kingdoms, or empire that was thereafter known as China (*zhongguo*) and also a larger geographical entity known as China. Like the geographical entities that were Germany and Italy before their political unifications in the 19th century, China as a geographical concept often contained within it kingdoms and principalities that were, in different ways, subordinate to a more encompassing dynasty.

During imperial times, Emperors ruled not only places where what is now called Han culture prevailed. Each also counted among his subjects the ancestors or ethnic precursors of many peoples who are now termed minorities. Their elites publicly recognized that they were imperial subjects, for example when paying obeisance at the court. Every emperor regarded himself as the "Son of Heaven" (*tian zi*). His legitimacy was based on the "Mandate of Heaven" (*tian ming*). "All under Heaven" (*Tianxia*) thus had an actual or potential relationship to the imperial realm. In terms of governance, *Tianxia* was not the whole world, but core spaces associated with what is now called China (Zhang, 2006, pp. 124–157). Especially during the Qing Dynasty and its immediate predecessor the Han-led Ming Dynasty (*ming chao*, 1368–1644) terms unmistakably associated with the notion of China (*zhongguo, hua, xia, zhongxia, zhonghua*) were used as the equivalents of *Tianxia*.

Under the Qing especially, there was a complex system of what Europeans called provinces, vassalages, and tributaries. The Qing clearly identified the non-Han areas that were not provinces, but where people were imperial subjects, such as Tibet and Xinjiang. Territories not part of the empire itself, but having a tribute-bearing relationship with the imperial court were treated differently from those where the people were imperial subjects. The former, unlike the latter, were not governed by imperial offices and were not garrisoned by imperial armies.

From the mid-18th Century onward and largely for political reasons, some Westerners, as well as those Han who regarded the Qing rulers as derived from a marginal and subordinate people, excluded frontier minority areas from what they considered to be China (Ishikawa, 2003, pp. 7–26). Westerners came up with the term "China Proper," to be used for the contiguous provinces with overwhelmingly Han populations. Some Westerners and ethnic separatists continue to equate Chinese with only Han or at least not with Tibetans or Uyghurs, even though they would not, for example, exclude those who are not white from the category of Americans or British. Most Chinese elites however have not thought in such terms and have regarded Han, minority and mixed areas as parts of China (*zhongguo*) and the emperors, whether of Han or ethnic minority extraction, as rulers of China and perforce as Chinese (*zhongguoren*). That changed temporarily, during the last few decades of the Qing, when some Han elites were discontented with the dynasty because of China's humiliations and provoked anti-Qing political mobilization by representing the Qing emperors as "foreign" and thus unworthy to rule China. The claim that Qing rulers were not Chinese, but only Manchu, continues as a leitmotif of those in the West who sympathize with Tibetan separatism (Sperling, 2010).

The mid-Qing was an era of great expansion of the imperial realm. It doubled in size in the 18th century, taking in many non-Han peoples. Imperial rule was oppressive, as millions died during suppressions of rebellions, especially in minority areas of western China, although mainly those to the east of the Tibetan and Uygur areas. In some places and times moreover, the Qing imposed alien political systems and cultural practices on conquered peoples.

The Chinese conquest empire was different however from Western and Japanese colonial systems. Colonialism typically featured complete political subordination to the colonizing country in law and fact and *de jure* racial discrimination, including slavery, during much of the colonial era. Colonialism often involved the de-industrializing or impoverishing exploitation of colonized regions. The Qing, however, allowed for a substantial autonomy in most minority areas, based on imperial edicts of 1791 and 1854 and other arrangements. Local rulers in some regions, such as the Dalai Lamas in Tibet and Muslim rulers of Xinjiang (*begs* or commanders), continued to retain significant local power and most employed systems of governance different from those used elsewhere in China. The Qing emperors did however confirm the positions of high civil and religious officials in many minority regions. They had a military presence in and conducted foreign relations for these regions as well. That is why no foreign state regarded Tibet or Xinjiang as independent, sovereign entities, although foreign states did understand that at most times these regions enjoyed considerable autonomy.

The system of Manchu overlordship applied in "Inner China" was less evident in border areas, where most ethnic minorities lived. Imperial elites may have been convinced that most minorities were cultural inferiors — and one stream of thought held that they were inherently so — but there was not the pervasive subordination of peoples that existed in Western and Japanese colonies. The distinction in the degree of state repression in Han and minority areas was much less than between European metropoles and colonies. For example, the widespread Taiping Heavenly Kingdom (*taiping tianguo*, 1850–1864) rebellion mainly involved Han, yet more than 20 million people died in its suppression.

Minorities in late imperial China exercised political power, participated in the local economy at all levels, and maintained cultural institutions without much state interference. Han migration to some border regions, especially Inner Mongolia and Yunnan provinces, did literally marginalize some minorities. Their land was often seized and their members pushed into remote areas. Generally however, rather than colonial-style monopoly over economic activity and systematic exploitation, there was nominal tribute from minority elites, to whom substantial imperial gifts were made, including funds for infrastructure building. Preferential policies existed for minority merchants, students and scholars who came to "inner China" (*nei di*).

Unlike the European colonialists then, imperial China did not generally implement policies to grow wealthy at the expense of distant peoples. The emperors lost money on their empire, but gained territorial buffers against foreign encroachment. Most minority areas, far from being exploited by the center, were subsidized by it. Today, the central government owns China's natural resources and extracts them in minority areas, inevitably so, as these areas are two-thirds of PRC territory; yet because many minority areas are remote or mountainous, extraction is often not profitable. The subsidies provided to most minority areas far outweigh profits from these areas.

By the late Qing dynasty, prominent Han revolutionaries and reformers were highly influenced by Western Social Darwinism. Some opponents of the dynasty, such as the young scholar Zou Rong and the then-revolutionary, but later Japanese puppet leader, Wang Jingwei, adopted anti-Manchu racism to mobilize against the Qing (Ishikawa, 2003).[3] After the dynasty was overthrown

---

[3] Ishikawa, 2003, Anti-Manchu: 18. Japanese militarists who tried to separate China's northeast ("Manchuria") adopted the view of earlier anti-Manchu revolutionaries that the historic Manchu homeland in the northeast had never belonged to the Ming Dynasty. Ibid.

in 1911, there were extensive pogroms against the Manchu population in which tens of thousands were killed (Struve, 2004, pp. 5–13). Although it never controlled the bulk of China's territory, the subsequent republican regime generally favored assimilating ethnic minorities, who they saw as members of an overarching Chinese ethnic group or Chinese nation (*zhonghua minzu*). The republic's authoritarian leader from 1927–1949, Jiang Jieshi (Chiang Kai-shek), argued there were no real differences between Han and other peoples in China and thus no reason to grant recognition to minorities. In contrast, the Chinese Communist Party (CCP), from the late-1930s, when it was still very marginal, gave mainly cultural and economic autonomy to minority areas in the small territories they controlled in the northwest. The system they adopted was taken, with much modification, from arrangements for minorities in the then-extant Soviet Union.

The first ethnic autonomous region was established in Inner Mongolia, two years before the proclamation of the PRC. Since then, many Chinese accounts of ethnicity in China have begun with the same sentence: "China is a multi-ethnic, unified state" (*zhongguo shi yige duominzu tongyi de guo-jia*). The "multi-ethnic" part of the slogan indicates that China officially recognizes the existence of its ethnic groups. The characterization of China as "unified" emphasizes national integrity (all peoples in China are part of the Chinese nation); territorial integrity (all parts of China are inalienable); and political integrity (all parts of China, except Taiwan, Hong Kong and Macau, are under CCP leadership). Ethnic politics in China essentially revolves around interpretations of and challenges to the concepts reflected in this slogan. Its starting point is the state's ethnic policies.

III. China's Major Ethnic Policies

A. *Official Recognition of Ethnic Minorities*

The Republic of China (ROC, 1911–1949) only grudgingly recognized minorities. In order to argue that China was basically mono-ethnic and thus a nation-state like the world's leading powers of the time, ROC founder (Sun Yat-sen) said in the early 1920s that minority people numbered only 10 million or 2.5% of China's then-population. Statistical yearbooks of the time indicated there were then at least 26 million minority people in China. (Attané and Courbage, 2000, pp. 257–280) Jiang Jieshi, who succeeded Sun both as head of the Guomindang (*Guomindang*, "Nationalist Party") and ROC leader, held that China's ethnic groups were no more than clans (*zongzu*) of a single "race" (*zhongzu*) (Chiang, 1947, pp. 12–13; Leibold, 2003, pp. 103–124).[4]

After the PRC was founded in 1949, however, the CCP encouraged ethnic groups to seek official recognition. From 1949 to 1979, about 400 groups applied and 56 were eventually recognized (Gladney, 2004, p. 9). Some minority people had little sense of being part of their officially-designated group; for example, the three separate language groups that were classified as Yi; the Amdowas and Khambas of eastern Tibet, who saw themselves as Tibetan Buddhists, but not as Tibetans (*bodpa*, who were then conceived as only constituting people living in the region around Lhasa); and the part of the Turkic-speaking, oasis-identifying Muslims of Xinjiang who, only after the Soviets and the CCP revived and applied to them an ethnonym dormant for five centuries, came to regard themselves as Uyghurs (Harrell, 1989, pp. 179–197; Rudelson, 1997, p. 5; Petersen, 2006, pp. 63–73; Tsering, 2009).[5] State recognition nonetheless created group consciousness where it had not existed, because it signified official ethnic equality and was a pre-condition for minority rights, such as ethnic regional autonomy (*minzu quyu zizhi*) and preferential policies (*youhui zhengce*).

B. *Ethnic Regional Autonomy: The Centerpiece of China's Ethnic Policies*

1. *Structures and Politics of the Ethnic Regional Autonomy System*

The CCP practice of ethnic regional autonomy dates back to the late-1930s (Lai, 2010, pp. 62–85; Xia, 2007, pp. 399–424). It first emerged in Chinese law in 1949 and is now based on the 1984 Law on Ethnic Regional Autonomy (LERA *minzu quyu zizhifa*) and its 2001 amendments (Tibet Information Network, 2001).[6] In 1997, President Jiang Zemin declared ethnic regional autonomy as one of China's three fundamental political institutions along with the National People's Congress (NPC) and multi-party cooperation.

---

[4] The Guomindang nevertheless had to provide much the same autonomy the Qing had given to minorities (Leibold, 2003).

[5] "The whole of Amdo and major portions of Kham only looked towards faraway and remote Lhasa as a very important site for pilgrimage, a spiritual Mecca of sort. The kings and chieftains of these regions entertained their own ambitions, and their political allegiance more often than not swung toward Beijing." (Tsering, 2009).

[6] On the 2001 amendments, see Tibet Information Network, 2001. www.tew.org/development/autonomy.law.html.

President Hu Jintao stated in 2003 that ethnic regional autonomy is one part of "three insists" (*sange jianchi*), along with adherence to socialism and CCP leadership (Lai, 2009, pp. 5–13). The avowed purpose of ethnic autonomy is to allow minorities "to have an institutional guarantee to exercise their rights to make their own decision on affairs related to their group identity." Its design however does not permit minorities *by themselves* to make final decisions on their internal affairs or other matters that impinge on their interests (Zhou, 2009, pp. 338–347).

The eponymous ethnic group, for example, Uyghurs in the XUAR, is the "leading" one within an autonomous area. Its members take up the highest *government* posts in that jurisdiction, because the LERA and local autonomy laws require that most such positions in autonomous areas be filled by titular minorities. They also provide for language and cultural rights. Minorities do not, however, typically fill the highest CCP post in autonomous areas, that of party secretary; yet that post is the most powerful one within every political jurisdiction of China.

Minorities have not achieved proportional participation in politics either, in part due to ethnic educational disparities. They were underrepresented at 6.6% of the CCP's 80 million members in 2011 (China Daily, June 25, 2011). The CCP recruits its member mainly from among urban, better educated and prosperous people, while many minority groups tend to be more rural, less educated, and poorer than the Han population as a whole. For example, in 2009, 32.4% of CCP members had a higher education, while such graduates were no more than 8% of China's adult population and a lower percentage among minorities. (New York Times, 2010; Wang, 2007, pp. 149–163). Minorities are poorly represented at the CCP's highest level. Only one of the 25 Politburo members is a minority, although at the next level down, the Central Committee, minorities (especially Tibetans and Uyghurs) are over-represented (Li, 2008, pp. 1–13).

Autonomy is circumscribed in the political realm and the Chinese government makes no claim that minorities enjoy a high degree of autonomy, in contrast with what it says about Hong Kong and Macau, where local elites rule special administrative regions (SARs). Their "high degree of autonomy" (*gaodu zizhi*), symbolized in slogans of "one country, two systems" (*yiguo liangzhi*) and "Hong Kong people rule Hong Kong" (*gangren zhigang*), is possible because the population is overwhelmingly Han and no separatist movements exist.

The ethnic regional autonomy system is a complex hierarchy of intersecting territories. The largest autonomous areas are the five autonomous regions, with each a provincial-level jurisdiction that has one eponymous or titular minority for whose benefit the region was ostensibly created. Below the autonomous regions in the hierarchy, there are autonomous prefectures. Prefectures in China, whether autonomous or not, are sub-provincial jurisdictions that each contain two or more counties. Each autonomous prefecture lies within an ordinary province or within one of the autonomous regions and has one or two eponymous minorities. Autonomous prefectures are, in most respects, subordinate to the province or autonomous region in which they are found. Examples include Yushu Tibetan Autonomous Prefecture (*yushu zangzu zizhizhou*) in Qinghai Province and the Boertala Mongolian Autonomous Prefecture (*boertala menggu zizhizhou*) in the XUAR.

At the base of the ethnic regional autonomy system, there are 120 autonomous counties, almost all of which have titular minorities; for example, the Xinbin Manzu Autonomous County (*xinbin manzu zizhixian*) in Liaoning Province. Three autonomous counties are designated as "multi-ethnic" (*duominzu*) and have four or more substantial minorities, none of which is eponymous. Some autonomous counties lie within and are subordinate to an ordinary province, some are within an autonomous region, and some are within an autonomous prefecture that is, in turn, in a province or autonomous region. Examples include the Sunan Yugur Autonomous County (*sunan yuguzu zizhixian*), within Gansu province, the Bama Yao Autonomous County (*bama yaozu zizhixian*) within the Guangxi Zhuang Autonomous Region, and the Muli Tibetan Autonomous County (*muli zangzu zizhixian*) within the Liangshan Yi Autonomous Prefecture (*liangshan yizu zizhizhou*), which is in turn within Sichuan Province.

Some minorities have multiple autonomies: Tibetans have the TAR, ten Tibetan autonomous prefectures and two Tibetan autonomous counties, with these autonomous prefectures and counties all within four provinces. Some autonomous areas (43 of the 155) have two or three titular minorities; instead of the typical one eponymous minority or the four or more minorities that characterize the "multi-ethnic" counties. Examples include Hubei province's Enshi Tujia/Miao Autonomous Prefecture (*enshi tujiazu miaozu zizhizhou*) or Guizhou province's Weining Yi, Hui and Miao Autonomous County (*weining yizu huizu miaozu zizhixian*).

Some ethnic groups' larger-scale autonomies have within them several other ethnic groups' smaller-scale autonomies: the XUAR has one Kighiz, one Hui, one Kazakh, and two Mongol autonomous prefectures. There are six autonomous counties within Xinjiang that each have an eponymous ethnic group that is not the titular ethnic group of either the autonomous prefecture in which it is found or in the XUAR. For example, the Qapqal Xibe

Autonomous County (*chabu chaer xibo zizhixian*) is within the Ili Kazhakh Autonomous Prefecture (*yili hasake zizhizhou*), which is within the XUAR. The Taxkorgan Tajik Autonomous County (*tashikuergan tajike zizhixian*) is not within any other ethnic group's autonomous prefecture, but it is in the XUAR and thus within the autonomous region of another group, the Uyghurs.[7]

All large and medium-sized minority groups, and most small ones, have titular territories, but due to the hierarchical and intersecting nature of the ethnic regional autonomy system, a single ethnic minority cannot, in most cases, dominate the government within an autonomous area. Moreover, in autonomous areas where the government perceives a significant separatist threat, i.e., in Tibetan areas and Xinjiang, autonomy is the most underdeveloped. For example, Xinjiang prefecture-level and county-level party secretaries are all Han and, unlike elsewhere, none of Xinjiang's twelve autonomous areas, at the regional, prefecture and county levels, have yet promulgated its own autonomy regulation (*zizhi tiaoli*) (Becquelin, 2004, pp. 358–378; Lundberg and Zhou, 2009, pp. 269–327). The low level of autonomy in these regions is thus both a cause for complaint by diasporic separatists and, in large measure, a product of their own activities.

While the state does not grant a high level of politico-legal autonomy for any minority area, these areas do have limited administrative autonomy (Lai, 2010, p. 63). There is a modification power (*biantong quan*) that allows autonomous areas to diverge from the laws and regulations made at higher levels. An autonomous region can make its own selected laws or regulations diverge from the laws or regulations of the central government. An autonomous area can modify, within its own territory, the laws or regulations of the province or autonomous region within which it lies. An autonomous county can do likewise to laws or regulations of the prefecture, province or region within which it is subsumed.

The exercise of modification power, however, requires the permission of the next-higher political jurisdiction. It has been little used at the system's top level, the five autonomous regions, which have generally not asked the central government for permission to modify central laws according to their regional needs. The regions have, however, passed general local legislation, such as language laws, that do not require higher-level approval. The vast

---

[7] See List of Autonomous Areas by Country, http://www.statemaster.com/encyclopedia/List-of-autonomous-areas-by-country. The existence of smaller autonomies within larger ones was highly developed in the ex-Soviet Union and known as "matrioshka-type federalism," after the Russian dolls-within-dolls.

majority of prefecture and county-level autonomous areas have also enacted autonomy regulations that spell out their powers, as well as many ordinary laws and regulations that diverge from those of jurisdictions above these prefectures and counties (Ghai and Woodman, 2009, pp. 29–46). By late 2008, there were 135 autonomous regulations (*zizhi tiaoli*), 474 separately-enacted regulations (*danxing tiaoli*), and 70 alteration or supplementary decisions (*biantong he buchong guiding*).

The assertion that ethnic regional autonomy in China is "fake" is thus inaccurate. Autonomy exists, but at a low level and mainly in the cultural sphere. Autonomous areas have disregarded or modified some laws enacted by higher-level political entities, albeit with the approval of the next highest level entity. For example, the TAR has modified a few politically non-sensitive national laws, such as those on family planning, the minimum age of marriage and retirement, holidays, the languages of government and instruction, etc. In 2005, the State Council (SC *guowuyuan*) also promulgated decisions on implementing the LERA. It specified fields for taking measures to strengthen implementation and called for more detailed policies by departments of the SC and local governments. As a result, about seven ministries or departments under the SC adopted or drafted relevant policies and about 12 provinces adopted regulations on the implementation of LERA (Lundberg and Zhou, 2009, p. 321).

Besides the cultural aspect of autonomy, which allows for official use of minority languages and celebrations of minority holidays, it is also social, in building minority cadre forces and middle classes (Lundberg and Zhou, 2009, pp. 308–321). For example, the Kazakh head of the Xinjiang Chinese People's Political Consultative Conference (CPPCC *zhongguo renmin zhengzhi xieshang huiyi*) has stated, "I was born in a peasant family in Yining City in northern Xinjiang. Without such good [autonomy] policies, I would never have been the chairman of the regional CPPCC Committee" (Xinhua News Agency [XH], 2009, July 20). Han cadres, by contrast, are more likely to attribute Han upward mobility to national policies. For example, a Shanxi official has put it that "[i]f it had not been for [the reform policies of] Deng Xiaoping, I would be behind an ox in a field right now" (Fallows, 2009). Minority language use and cadre participation in decision-making are the essence of the "ethnicalization" (*minzuhua*) of autonomous areas (Zhou, 2009, p. 343). Ethnic regional autonomy is also economic, in providing special poverty alleviation and infrastructure funds to autonomous areas (Zhao, 2004, p. 196).[8]

---

[8] The state also supports the "ethnic economy" (*minzu jingji*) used by minorities, such as the production of handicrafts and food. See Ethnic Affairs Commission of Jinlin Province (2005).

Chinese law generally entitles minorities to ethnic autonomy, while international law does not grant the same privilege (Heintze, 2009, pp. 389–407; Suksi, 1998, pp. 151–171; Welhengama, 2000, p. 133).[9] China's ethnic autonomous areas relate to the central government much like autonomies in other parts of the world, in that autonomies and central governments typically have the same political system. (Wang and Sha, 2002). Electoral democracies with autonomous areas, such as Italy with Sud Tyrol, have electoral democratic autonomies. Illiberal states have illiberal autonomous areas, such as Iraq's Kurdistan autonomous government that represses minorities and tries to subsume their identities into that of Kurds (Human Rights Watch, 2009).[10] The autonomous areas of authoritarian states have authoritarian governance, such as pre-2011 Southern Sudan (Ashworth, 2009).

China's minority people seem to value their areas being designated as autonomous because such areas often receive greater state subsidies than non-autonomous ones (Guo, 2008). In 2008, the government of a Shaanxi county that had been an historic home of the Qiang minority (*qiangzu*) urged its residents to register as Qiang if they could prove a blood relationship. It hoped to reach the 30% minimum needed for the county to apply for designation as a Qiang autonomous county. Thousands of the 120,000 residents registered, knowing that they would then become eligible for individual preferences and that if its application were approved, the county would receive preferential treatment in development (Li, 2008).

While top CCP leaders in many minority areas are Han and top party leaders can always trump state leaders if need be, the two leaderships are so intertwined that trumping must be rarely necessary. The party secretary of the autonomous region, prefecture, or county may be a Han, but the number

---

[9] The Chinese government has said that Tibetans have a right to autonomy under Chinese law (see XH, 2004, May 23). On the absence of a right to autonomy for minorities under international law, "There is no general rule in international law to grant autonomy to any groups, perhaps with the exception of indigenous peoples" (See Heintze, 2009, pp. 389–407 [392]); "There is undoubtedly no right to autonomy at the level of general international law" (See Suksi, 1998, pp. 151–171 [151]); "Autonomy does not have a strong basis in international law. Internal domestic arrangements such as autonomies fall within the sphere of constitutional law, which are normally beyond the control of general international law"(See Welhengama, 2000, p. 133).

[10] Human Rights Watch (2009): calling on regional government to recognize Shabaks and Yazidis as distinct ethnic groups, instead of imposing Kurdish identity on them and ensure they can participate in public affairs.

two party position (often an executive deputy party secretary (*changwu fushuji*), is typically filled by a minority who is also the highest state official in the jurisdiction. There are prefecture-level minority Party secretaries in some autonomous areas; for example, in Liangshan Yi Autonomous Prefecture. (Bovingdon, 2004, p. 29; Harrell, 2000).[11] In 2000, half the TAR prefecture-level Party secretaries were Tibetans and in the late 1980s, Tibetans were Party secretaries in sixty-three of the seventy-five TAR counties (Wang, 2002, pp. 79–111; Sautman and Eng, 2001, pp. 20–74).

In some autonomous areas, minorities are well-represented in the bureaucracy, in other areas they are underrepresented, despite preferential policies in hiring minority officials. In part, under-representation occurs because, in many minority areas, the levels of minorities' education and experience are lower than that of Han (Zhang and Verhoeven, 2010, pp. 290–306). In part, it also reflects stereotypes about competencies that are common both among Han and minorities; for example, that Han are particularly competent in areas like finance, because of a greater flare for quantitative reasoning.

The long history of Han-minority conflict has not been ended through the device of ethnic regional autonomy, but the level of such conflict should be considered. It has overwhelmingly involved Tibetans and Uyghurs, who together are one-eighth of the minority population. The 2008 protests and riots in Tibetan areas and 2009 anti-Han pogrom in Urumqi, Xinjiang did not only reflect grievances, but were likely intended to embarrass the Chinese government and rally support for separatism in the run-ups to the Beijing Olympics and celebration of the 60th anniversary of the PRC. The degree of violence arising from inter-ethnic and minority/state conflict, even after these incidents, cannot however be compared to that in many other parts of the world. For example, China's neighbor India is wracked by ethnic conflict through much of the northern part of the country, especially in Kashmir and the Northeast states. The conflict in Kashmir alone has cost tens of thousands — perhaps as many as 70,000 — dead. There said to be 700,000 Indian army and paramilitary personnel and 70,000 civilian spies present in Kashmir, a territory of some 10 million inhabitants (Wax, 2010; Bedi, 2010; Bamzai, 2010).

Inter-minority conflict is common in many countries (Alekseev, 2008; Cheung, 2005, pp. 3–40). In China, for example, Tibetans have had armed clashes with Hui and Mongolians. (Associated Press, 2003). There is no

---

[11] Harrell (2000) "[A]lmost all county party secretaries are Yi, and a majority of prefectural secretaries have been Yi, though some have been Han."

evidence however that autonomy has lead to inter-minority oppression in China. As the leading scholar of ethnicity in China, the Beijing University sociologist Ma Rong has attested:

> The great majority of 'minority group regions' or 'ethnic regions' are in fact multi-ethnic regions par excellence; ethnic regional autonomy. . . takes into account the interests of both the autonomous ethnic groups within the ethnic region and all other non-autonomous ethnic groups within the autonomous region (Ma and Zhou, 1999, p. 458).

C. *Preferential Policies: Subsidies for Areas; Affirmative Action for People*

There are two categories of preferential policies in China. The central state and subordinate jurisdictions subsidize most ethnic autonomous areas and virtually all impoverished minority areas. Preferential economic policies for minorities have included, for example, the absence of regional taxes in Tibet and the provision of part of the revenues from state oil production in Xinjiang to the region's government, albeit an inadequate proportion until changes were made in 2010. Government entities and some private firms also apply affirmative action to individual ethnic minority people, by virtue of their ethnic group membership, but the scope of affirmative action varies according to the ethnicity of individuals. Examples include liberal family planning measures, admission to schools with lower exam scores, quotas in hiring cadres, and economic preferences, particularly in providing anti-poverty grants and low-cost bank loans to minorities who start businesses (Zhou and Hill, 2009; Wang, 2007, pp. 149–163; Clothey, 2001).[12]

The most important preferential policy affecting minorities in China may well be the state subsidies provided many autonomous areas. A scholar has noted, "whenever the issue of fiscal transfers comes up, the central government never tires of emphasizing that ethnic regions deserve preferential treatment" (Wang, 2004, pp. 101–136). Official figures indicate that the central government, together with sister provinces and municipalities, supplied 93% of the 2008 TAR budget and 53% of Xinjiang's 2004 budget (Wang, 2009). In general, the poorer and more potentially unstable a minority area

---

[12] The literature from outside China on preferential policies for minorities in China is overwhelmingly concentrated on education. See, e.g., Zhou and Hill, 2009; Wang, 2007, pp. 149–163; Clothey, 2001.

is, the more the central government provides subsidies. That allows, for example, wages of staff and workers in Tibet, including ethnic Tibetans, to be second only to those in Beijing (Asian Labour News, 2005).

China's preferential policies were designed when the state sector was extensive and they still exist mainly in areas of state activity. However, the state sector is now shrinking. In 2007, state-owned enterprises (SOEs) employed only 22% of the urban workforce (Schucher, 2009, pp. 121–144). SOEs in state-monopolized industries with the best jobs — finance, telecommunications, public utilities, tobacco, petroleum, and electricity — employed less than 8% of China's urban workers in 2005. Although these SOEs still provide the most lucrative industrial employment, paying out 55% of China's total wages in 2007, that is a significant decline compared to the almost 100% of total wages that they paid three decades earlier (Huang, 2009).

Only a few preferential policies directly affect the private sector, such as state bank loans to ethnic minorities to start businesses (Sautman, 1998, pp. 86–118) and state programs that sponsor Uyghurs for work outside Xinjiang (Ma, 2008).[13] As the state sector has shrunk, discriminatory hiring and layoffs have affected some minority groups, such as Uyghur men (Maurer-Fazio, 2007, pp. 159–197). Privatization makes it harder to apply ethnic preferences (Zang and Li, 2001, pp. 34–48). Private sector employers can operate outside the control of or with the collusion of officials, who often are business people as well or receive bribes from business people to implement policies benefitting them. Local officials have also become more powerful as a result of the decentralization that has accompanied privatization (Weimer, 2004, pp. 163–189). A Han who grew up in Xinjiang explains:

> In the free market economy local officials are more powerful and have much more leeway over the implementation of policies set by the central government and frequently they carry out policies that benefit themselves, which means they may distort or ignore the central government's preferential policies toward ethnic minorities (Weston, 2008).

Indeed, the CCP in Xinjiang has recognized that growing market forces lessen government powers of intervention, increase employment difficulties for minority workers, especially in farm and non-state industrial work, and make

---

[13] In 2007, after Guangdong firms were encouraged to hire Uighurs, 900,000 Xinjiang people, many of them Uighur women, were said to be working outside Xinjiang as export laborers. Most returned to Xinjiang within a year. Opposition by Uighur men to Uighur women working outside is widespread (Zhai, 2009).

it harder to implement equal opportunities, let alone preferential policies, for minorities. (XUAR CCP Organizational Department, 2001, pp. 34–38).

D. *Other Ethnic Policies*

Apart from ethnic regional autonomy and preferential policies, there are three other ethnic policies present in China: the suppression of separatism, state actions (or the lack thereof) related to discrimination, and what are regionally based, but ethnically impacting policies on religion. These policies are as important as ethnic regional autonomy and preferential policies in terms of vindicating minority rights and are substantial topics in debates about China's ethnic policies.

The suppression of separatism is allowed as a deterrent under international law, if it is carried out lawfully (Hsiao, 1998, p. 727). As it stands in China, however, such suppression is marked by the beatings and torture typically meted out by police (Subcommittee on International Operations and Human Rights, 1997; U. N. Social Council, Commission on Human Rights, 2006), not just to separatists, but to many others who come into their grip. The suppression of separatism is presently a net cast too wide, as evidenced by the repression of public displays of religious respect for the Dalai Lama in the TAR.[14] But it is also a net cast too narrowly, as demonstrated by the Chinese government's frequent failure to confront foreign governments that attempt to leverage separatism against China in order to counteract it as a purported strategic competitor. (Sautman, 2009; Sautman, 2005, pp. 87–118; Press TV, 2008; Mah, 2008).[15]

The existence of ethnic discrimination has been denied by Chinese government officials (XH, 2007; XH, 2007).[16] It is however present in employment. Minorities' earnings in the years since the mid-1990s have fluctuated around 90% of those of Han earnings, not because minorities are subjected to wage bias, but largely because minorities are 5–10% less likely

---

[14] Only one portrait of the Dalai Lama is publicly displayed in Lhasa, at the Norbulinka palace. (*Sunday Tasmanian*, 2008) His pictures are in monasteries in Qinghai and other provinces. (WP, 2010).

[15] The US and Indian governments particularly support separatist groups. Advisory and financial links between the World Uygur Congress and US National Endowment for Democracy (NED) are well-developed (Rupee News, 2009).

[16] Government media have acknowledged the existence of employment discrimination against disabled persons and migrants, as well those who are HIV positive or Hepatitis B carriers. (XH, 2007).

than similarly qualified Han to hold a job (Ding and Myers, 2010, p. 6; Hasmath *et al.*, 2009, p. 12). Discrimination is more prevalent in the private sector, but not absent from the public sector (Congressional-Executive Commission, 2009; Hu, 2009) and is found as well in access to hotel rooms, the Internet, taxis, and other amenities (Saimaiti, 2009; Kaltman, 2007).[17]

Top officials decry discrimination and stress that policies should benefit minorities. Thus, in a 2005 speech, Hu Jintao called for more freedom of religion, strengthened ethnic regional autonomy, requiring Han officials to learn minority languages, greater quotas for hiring minority cadres, and more recognition of their contributions (Hu, 2005). Discrimination against minorities is thus not justified by cadres or academics, but is sometimes excused. For example, a scholar at the China Institute of Contemporary International Relations, a state think-tank, has written:

> Though it is unfair, it is understandable if a business owner is more willing to hire an employee who is more fluent in Mandarin Chinese, shares the same work ethics as the employer and is better at establishing the social networks so critical to business success in East Asian societies (Wei, 2009).

Brian Kaltman's 2004–2005 survey of Uyghurs and Han in Urumqi, Shanghai, and Beijing found that "Han generally held discriminatory views about the Uighur, and the Uighur, in turn, expressed racist views about the Han" (Kaltman, 2007). Herbert Yee's 2000 and 2001 surveys of Uyghurs and Han in Xinjiang cities showed that both groups express prejudices against each other (Yee, 2005, pp. 35–50; Yee, 2003, pp. 431–452). So too did Ji Ping and Gao Bingzhong's 1987 survey (Ji and Gao, 1994). More recently, Reza Hasmath found that although ethnic minority people in Beijing — mainly Man, Hui, and Koreans — generally have higher educational levels than Han, most minority interviewees were convinced that they are discriminated against with regard to high-wage, education-intensive jobs. They attribute this ethnic penalty to stereotyping by employers, even though most interviewees grew up in Beijing, speak fluent Mandarin (*putonghua*), and are assimilated into Han culture (Hasmath, 2009; Kaltman, 2007; China Law

---

[17] Saimaiti (2009) attributies hotel and internet discrimination to local police regulations that do not bar Uyghurs from using services, but create administrative problems for businesses that provide them. Han and Hui taxi drivers assert they pass up Uyghurs because they refuse to pay the full fare (Kaltman, 2007, pp. 115–116).

and Government, 2006).[18] The ethnic penalty is apt to be still greater in ethnic minority areas, where language and cultural differences may be stark and serve as an excuse for discrimination.[19]

China's anti-discrimination policies lack an effective enforcement mechanism (Liu, 2009). The Employment Promotion Law of 2008, Article 62, allows discriminated workers to sue, but because courts operate under direction of local officials who have ties to business and who are ideologically opposed to actions that may inhibit economic growth, enforcing judgments is problematic (Peerenboom, 2009; Zeng, 2007, pp. 991–1024). Laws that forbid hate-speech are also not enforced. (Leibold, 2010). Yet discrimination, together with ethnic inequalities, Han migration, and restrictive religious policies, is presumably a major factor in reinforcing separatism, which the state has long argued is in turn a significant barrier to growth (Xizang Ribao, 1995).

Regionally-based, but ethnically-impacting policies on religion include restrictions on religious practice and control of religious institutions, mostly in Tibetan areas (especially the TAR) and Xinjiang. There, Party members, university students, state workers, and children are barred from engaging in public religious activities. There are limitations on the number of Tibetan Buddhist monks and frequent denials of building permits for new mosques in Xinjiang, (US State Department, 2009) where beards and head scarves are not permitted in schools and civil servants can be fired for praying during working hours (Ng, 2010). State discourses on religion also have political consequences. In Tibetan areas, there is official criticism of popular financial support for religious activities (Propaganda Committee of the Ganzi, 1990) and *ad hominem* attacks on the Dalai Lama, including denials that he is a religious leader (Zhao, s.d.). In Xinjiang, officials counter-pose development and religious devotion, citing this supposed contradiction as a reason for prohibiting students and government workers from participating in fasting in the Muslim month of Ramadan (Wong, 2008; Germain, 2009).

---

[18] Only 16% of Beijing Uyghurs that Kaltman interviewed felt Han discriminated against Uighurs in jobs, but unlike elsewhere, "Beijing's Uighurs tend to retain legitimate employment." (Kaltman, 2007, p. 29). Discrimination by Han against other Han, for example against Henan natives in Beijing, is also pervasive (China Law and Government, 2006).

[19] For Han, minority, and Western reports of employment and other discrimination against Tibetans and Uighurs, see Posting of Kai Pan to CNReviews.com (2009); Posting of Ilham Tothi to Xinjiang jingji fazhan yu minzu guanxi, (2006) and Fallows (2009). Reports of exclusion of ethnic minorities from certain jobs in Xinjiang go back years. See Bruce Gilley, 2001, p. 26.

The situation with respect to controls over religion is however quite different outside Xinjiang and the Tibetan areas. A Belgian scholar's examination of policies in highly multi-ethnic Yunnan province concluded:

> [E]thnic minorities in this region enjoy a relatively high level of religious freedom, not in opposition to the party-state but with its full blessing. . . . Where the suspicious gaze from the central government and party is limited or even absent, the picture of religious freedom for minority nationalities becomes markedly more nuanced. It might be argued that in several instances minority nationalities have greater freedom in practicing religion than their Han Chinese neighbors. Practices such as ancestor worship, divination or cults dedicated to local deities are more likely to be tolerated by the authorities in areas with minority nationalities (Wellens, 2009, pp. 433–435; see also Economist, 2007).

IV. Multi-Ethnicity/Multi-Culturalism

Ethnic regional autonomy and preferential policies represent official multi-ethnicity in the realm of political economy. The record is mixed. Autonomy is circumscribed by CCP control, but nevertheless offers some features valued by minorities, as indicated by efforts by minority elites to have their localities declared ethnic autonomous areas. Preferential policies are even more sought after by minorities. Yet, preferential policies are now being eroded by the growth of private sector employment, which generally provides a lowered standard of living compared to state employment and has contributed to the creation of a very unequal society throughout China.

There have been discussions among officials and scholars about protecting minority rights and cultures by changing from a model of economic growth to one of human development. A shift in state development strategy to the "Great Opening of the West" (*xibu dakaifa*) in 1999 was supposed to represent a change, but the growth of a private economy less amenable to preferential policies has overwhelmed such efforts. It has lead to a growing Han-minority income gap in some parts of China, while in other places, studies show there is little or no gap and discrimination plays no role where a gap exists.[20]

---

[20] Gustafsson and Ding (2009, p. 604) show that the main factor determining income differences is that rural ethnic minorities generally do not live in the same places as rural Han. Li and Ding (2009) found that Hui in urban Ningxia are not discriminated against and benefit from affirmative action.

Multi-ethnicity in the cultural realm — multiculturalism — is not something new to China. Many dynasties fostered cultural multi-ethnicity, especially the Tang, Northern Song, Yuan and Qing. Foreign guests were impressed by the imperial capital and courts' cultural diversity. Multiculturalism is virtually mandatory in all official representations of Chinese culture today; for example, in official New Year television extravaganzas, there are many performances by minorities (McCarthy, 2009).

Chineseness represented as inclusive of minority contributions to the development of an overarching Chinese nation (*zhonghua minzu*) is now widely accepted, including among most minorities, although some minority intellectuals do not think along those lines. There is also something of a cultural "ethnic fever" (*minzu re*) among young, urban Han and especially a Tibet fever (*xizang re*). That is one reason why five million Chinese tourists visited Tibet in the fight eight months of 2010, almost two tourists for every TAR Tibetan (XH, 2010). "Ethnic fever" is connected to a burgeoning cultural production of minority groups, especially Tibetans, that belies exile claims of "cultural genocide" (Sautman, 2009). It is also connected to the desire of some Han to escape the crass materialism of contemporary capitalism, through absorbing the spirituality or naturalness that they believe is common among some minorities.

A. *China's Multi-ethnicity in Comparative Perspective*

The situation of China's ethnic groups can be compared to those in other states, such as Canada, that see themselves as models of multiculturalism. Canada's 2006 census showed 16% of its people were "visible," i.e., non-white, minorities, over a fourth of them ethnic Chinese. Indigenous peoples ("First Nations") are an additional 4% of Canada's population. Thus, Canada's minority proportion is twice that of China. Minorities in China are also 20–30% more likely to be farmers than are Han, but Canada's visible minorities are overwhelmingly urban. In 2006, some 43 % and 42% of Toronto and Vancouver's populations were visible minorities, because four-fifth of immigrants to Canada are non-white and three-fourths of them settle in Toronto, Vancouver or Montreal (Statistics Canada, 2008). Toronto has the highest proportion of foreign-born residents (44%) of any city in the world, while it was reckoned around 2009 that foreigners made up only 0.6% of Beijing's 18 million people (Experiencing China, s.d., 2009) and the 2010 census found only about 600,000 foreigners in China, i.e., less than one twentieth of one percent of the country's population (Shan Juan 2011).

Greater diversity advantages Canada, but does not signify that it has done better than China in achieving an equitable multiculturalism. Canada's business and political elites are still disproportionately white

(Matheson, 2006).[21] Although it is predicted that discrimination will diminish as visible minorities reach majority levels in several key Canadian cities, it is still common enough for 20% of visible minorities to have reported that they had experienced discrimination sometimes or often in the past five years (SC, 2003).

Multiculturalism was adopted as Canada's national policy in 1971. The idea was to reject the previous British/French melting pot idea and affirm contributions made to Canada by other Europeans, mainly through financing ethnic cultural activities. Canada's immigration policies had been fundamentally altered in 1967, however. The composition of new immigrants shifted radically from Europe to Asia, the Caribbean and the Middle East. The meaning of multiculturalism shifted too, because immigrants from these countries were not concerned about history and culture, as much as they were about discrimination and participation in Canada's politics, economy and society. The Multiculturalism Act of 1988 focused on combating prejudice and discrimination and promoting equal participation of minorities. Federal multicultural programs are now mostly about these objectives, although only about a dollar a year from each Canadian supports such programs. Official multiculturalism in Canada has not brought an ethnically egalitarian society and *ceteris paribus,* visible minorities earn substantially less than whites on account of their "race" alone (Li, 2008; Reza, 2006).

Canada has anti-employment discrimination machinery, which China lacks. It has had a federal employment equity law since 1984 and provincial preferential policy laws in Quebec and British Columbia. Yet such laws only apply to government and large corporations, which do not have to meet quotas. "Market forces" discrimination thus exists in Canada as in China. "Sticky floors" and "glass ceilings" operate. In the last decade, the 11% minority-white income gap created by discrimination alone has grown to 15–18%. Public sector ethnic wage parity exists alongside significant private sector disparities, although even in the public sector, Canada's visible minorities have only had a percentage of jobs that is half their proportion in the total population (Hou and Coulombe, 2010, pp. 29–43; Block and Glabuzi, 2011).

As in Canada, China's private sector is generally not compelled to adopt preferential policies for minorities, although in some places, there are incentives to do so. The Xinjiang government has since September, 2009, required businesses operating in the region to hire at least half their new employees from among local residents (Global Insight, 2009; Guardian, 2009).[22] The

---

[21] As of 2006, visible minorities were 7.8% of Canada's members of parliament (Matheson, 2006).
[22] UK Councils have schemes that offer jobs to locals who get university degrees and these end up with a large number of ethnic-minorities (Guardian, 2009). There is however no language issue involved in the United Kingdom.

order applies to all Xinjiang-registered firms and to those that have undertaken projects in the region. Businesses are also urged to recruit more minority employees. The policy includes subsidies for newly recruited locals that amount to half their pension contributions for the first three years, college graduates who commit to work in the countryside and other communities, and service workers (XH, 2009). The new policy remains inadequate, however, as it does not *require* hiring minorities.

V. Conclusion: China's Multi-ethnic Future

It is likely that only a radical expansion of preferential policies can obviate Han-minority educational and other differences. Studies indicate that increasing education increases the probability of access to off-farm employment by rural minorities and to higher status jobs generally (Campos and Petrick, 2009; Hannum and Xie, 1998, pp. 323–333). A great boost in financing minority education is particularly needed. That cannot happen however without minorities themselves being able to spearhead the demand for changes. Yet China's leaders fear organization of social movements that might be influenced by separatists, who come with external backing.

For China to achieve an equitable multi-ethnic society, minorities also need the power of self-representation — the right to articulate their own critiques of ethnic inequality and their own understandings of their history and culture. These critiques would include understandings that contradict the current hegemonic and sometimes Han chauvinist discourse. Self-representation of ethnic minorities cannot happen however without both a rejection of separatism by minorities and the state's recognition that overcoming ethnic inequality is an urgent political task.

China's transformation from the world's most egalitarian society to the one of the most unequal does not bode well for China's multi-ethnic future. The more societies are unequal overall, the more they tend to be ethnically unequal. China's leaders recognize that this presents a problem of regime legitimacy and have taken steps to mitigate it. The spread of a neo-liberal economy to minority areas however is offsetting this effort, as neo-liberalism sharply erodes state participation in economic affairs and seeks privatization as well as curbs on public spending. While some argue that international human rights norms can create an equitable multi-ethnicity in China, these norms are presently tied to the spread of neo-liberalist capitalism. Improved inter-ethnic relations are more likely through redistribution in all spheres. The goal would be to achieve the equality-in-fact (*shishi shang de pingdeng*) promised by top leaders. For example, Hu Qili stated in 1985 that:

> The general principle in the work of the Party toward the nationalities is to unswervingly show concern for and assist the minority nationalities to develop their economy and culture, build the social material and spiritual civilizations and gradually achieve de facto equality for the various nationalities (Hu, 1985).

De facto equality would presumably put an end to all aspects of ethnic subordination. Only then would China's ethnic relations be based on an equitable multi-ethnicity.

References

Alekseev, M. (2008) Inter-minority xenophobia in the Russian federations: Ethnic, religious and status differentials. *National Council for Eurasian and European Studies.* Retrieved from http://www.ucis.pitt.edu/nceeer/2008_822–01g_Alexseev.pdf

Ashworth, J. (2009, September 2) The state of Sudan's comprehensive peace agreement. *IKV PAX CHRISTI.* Retrieved from www.ikvpaxchristi.nl/files/Documenten/AF%20Sudan/CPA%20%20ALERT.pdf

Asian Labour News (2005, February 21) High TAR wages benefit the privileged. Retrieved from http://www.hartford-hwp.com/archives/55/783.html.

Associated Press (2003, February 23) Clash between Tibetans and Chinese Muslims injures hundreds.

Attané, I. and Y. Courbage (2000) Transitional stages and identity boundaries: The case of ethnic minorities in China. *Population and Environment,* 21(3), 257–280.

Bamzai, K. (2010, September 13) Arrested development. *India Today.*

Becquelin, N. (2004) Staged development in Xinjiang. *China Quarterly,* 178, 358–378.

Bedi, R. (2010, June 30) Unrest in Kashmir escalates as curfew is extended. *Irish Times.*

Block, S. and G. E. Galabuzi (2011) Canada's colour-coded labour market: The gap for racialized workers. Canadian Centre for Policy Alternatives. Retrieved from http://www.policyalternatives.ca/sites/default/files/uploads/publications/National%20office/20/03/colour%20coded%20labour%20market.pdf

Bovingdon, G. (2004) Autonomy in Xinjiang: Han nationalist imperatives and Uyghur discontent. *Policy Studies,* (11), 29. East-West Center.

Campos, B. C. and M. Petrick (2009) Ethnic minorities and rural occupation outcomes in Southern China. (Paper for EAAE PhD Workshop). Giessen, Germany. Retrieved from http://www.iamo.de/fileadmin/fg-china/wiki/WebsiteProjAbstracts/CASTRO_PETRICK_2009a.pdf

Canwest News (editorial) (2008, April 2) Majority of Canada's visible minorities live in just two cities.

Cha, A. (2009, July 15) China unrest can be traced to program that sends Uighurs across country to work. *Washington Post*.

Cheung, K. K. (2005) (Mis)interpretations and (in) justice: The 1992 Los Angeles "riots" and "Black-Korean conflict". *MELUS* (30), 3–40.

Chiang, K. S. (1947) *China's destiny*. London: Dennis Dobson.

China Daily (April 29, 2011) China 2010 population census.

China Daily (June 25, 2011) More than 80 million are Party member.

China Law and Government (editorial) (2006) Voices against discrimination: An update of recent cases and development. *China Law and Government*, (3), 9–14.

China Today.com. s.d. (2009) *The Communist Party of China*. Retrieved from http://www.chinatoday.com/org/cpc/.

Chinese People's Political Consultative Conference. (1949) Common program of the Chinese People's Political Consultative Conference, art. 50 (September 29, 1949). In A. Blaustein (Ed.), *Fundamental legal documents of communist China* (1962), 34–53. New Jersey: Fred B. Rothman & Co.

Clarke, M. (2010) China, Xinjiang and the globalisation of the Uyghur issue. *Global Change, Peace and Security*, 22(2), 213–229.

Clothey, R. (2001) China's minorities and state preferential policies: Expanding opportunities? *Annual meeting comparative and international education society*. Eric Document No. 453139. Retrieved from http://www.eric.ed.gov/ERICDocs/data/ericdocs2sql/content_storage_01/0000019b/80/17/0c/05.pdf

Congressional-Executive Commission on China (2005) *2005 annual report: VI. Tibet*. Retrieved from http://www.cecc.gov/pages/annualRpt/annualRpt05/2005_6_tibet.php.

Congressional-Executive Commission on China (2009) *Governments in Xinjiang continue to sponsor, sanction job recruitment that discriminates against ethnic minorities* (newsletter no. 2). Retrieved from http://www.cecc.gov/pages/virtualAcad/newsletterListing.phpd?NLdate=20090227&show=EMR.

Ding, S. and S. Myers (2010) Inter-temporal changes in ethnic urban earnings inequality in China. Retrieved from http://www.ccer.pku.edu.cn/download/11034–1.pdf

Economist (editorial) (2007) When opium can be benign.

Elliot, M. (2001) *The Manchu way: The Eight Banners and ethnic identity in late imperial China*. Stanford: Stanford University Press.

Ethnic Affairs Commission of Jinlin Province (2005) "Shaoshu minzu texu yongpin gaishu" (Summary of ethnic minority special products). Retrieved from http://218.62.26.208:82/gate/big5/mw.jl.gov.cn/jlmz/mzjj/mmzc/200512/t20051225_107519.htm

Experiencing China, s.d. (2009) How many foreigners are there in Beijing? Retrieved from http://www.aihong.li/index.php/life-in-beijing/travel-in-china/59-about-china/130-how-many-foreigners-are-there-in-beijing.

Fallows, J. (2009) China's way forward. *The Atlantic.* Retrieved from http://www.theatlantic.com/doc/200904/chinese-innovation/2

Fallows, J. (2009, July 10) No Uighurs need apply. *The Atlantic.* Retrieved from http://www.theatlantic.com/science/archive/2009/07/-no-uighurs-need-apply/21071

Fischer, A. (2008) "Population invasion" versus urban exclusion in the Tibetan areas of Western China. *Population and Development Review,* 34(4), 631–662.

Germain, E. (2009, October 28) Where a picnic is against the law. *Global Post.* Retrieved from http://www.globalpost.com/dispatch/morocco/091020/where-picnic-against-the-law.

Gilley, B. (2001) Uighurs need not apply. *Far Eastern Economic Review,* 164, 26.

Ghai, Y. and S. Woodman (2009) Unused powers: Contestation over autonomy legislation in the PRC. *Pacific Affairs,* 82(1), 29–46.

Gillette, M. (2000) *Between Beijing and Mecca: Modernization and consumption among urban Chinese Muslims.* Stanford: Stanford University Press.

Gladney, D. (2004) *Dislocating China: Muslims, minorities and other subaltern subjects.* London: C. Hurst.

Global Insight (editorial) (2009, September 24) Local businesses in Xinjiang asked to hire more locals as government tries to stem ethnic tension.

Grunfeld, T. (2006) The advantages and perils of globalization: The case of Tibet. In S. Weigelin-Schwiedrzik, *et al.* (Eds.), *As China meets the world: China's changing position in the international community* (35–60). Vienna:Verlag der Osterreichischen Akademie der Wissenschaften.

Guo, X. L. (2008) *State and ethnicity in China's Southwest.* Leiden: Brill.

Guardian (U.K.) (editorial) (2009, June 17) Local councillors put faith in graduates. Retrieved from http://www.guardian.co.uk/society/2009/jun/17/local-councils-graduates.

Gustafsson, B. and S. Ding (2009) Temporary and persistent poverty among ethnic minorities and the majority in rural China. *Review of Income and Wealth,* 55, 588–606.

Hannum, E. and Y. Xie (1998) Ethnic stratification in Northwest China: Occupational differences between Han Chinese and national minorities in Xinjiang, 1982–1990. *Demography,* 35(3), 323–333.

Harrell, S. (1989) Ethnicity and kin terms among two kinds of Yi. In C. Chien and N. Tapp (Eds.), *Ethnicity and ethnic groups in China* (179–197). Hong Kong: New Asia College, Chinese University.

Harrell, S. (2000) Legitimacy in the eyes of the few: The contemporary Chinese state and its minority citizens. Retrieved from http://faculty.washington.edu/stevehar/berkeley.html

Hasmath, R. (2009) Developing minority nationalities in contemporary urban China. In R. Hasmath and J. Hsu (Eds.), *China in the era of transition: Understanding contemporary state and society actors.* New York: Palgrave Macmillan.

Hasmath, R. (2009) Ethnic minority disadvantage in China's labor market. (working paper), *s.d.* Retrieved from http://www.class.uh.edu/econ/faculty/emliu/ASR%20Paper%20(13%20July%2009).pdf.

Heintze, H. J. (2009) Evolution of autonomy and federalism. In J. Oliveira and P. Cardinale (Eds.), *One country, two systems, three legal orders: Perspectives of evolution: Essays on Macau's autonomy after the resumption of sovereignty by China.* Berlin: Springer.

Hou, F. and S. Coulombe (2010) Earnings gaps for Canadian-born visible minorities in the public and private sectors. *Canadian Public Policy*, 36(1), 29–43.

Hsiao, A. (1998) Is China's policy to use force against Taiwan a violation of the principle of non-use of force under international law. *New England Law Review* 32, 715–742.

Hu, J. T. (2005, November 3) Speech to the central ethnic affairs work conference. May 27, 2005. Retrieved from http://politics.people.com.cn/GB/1024/3423605.html.

Hu, P. (2009, November 3). Tantan da Hanzu zhuyi (Speaking of Han chauvinism). *Free More News.* Retrieved from http://freemorenews.com/2009/09/03/hu-to-talk-about-hanchauvinism/.

Hu, Q. L. (1985) Speech at the Tibet Cadres Meeting Marking the 20th Anniversary of the Tibet Autonomous Region (August 31, 1985). In Q. L. Hu, *In Tibet: Importance of equality, unity and the 'Religious Issue'*, XH, Aug. 31.

Huang, C. (2009) Going backwards ever faster. *South China Morning Post*, August 2.

Human Rights Watch (2009) On vulnerable ground: Violence against minority communities in Nineveh province's disputed territories. Retrieved from http://www.hrw.org/en/node/86357.

Ishikawa, Y. (2003) Anti-Manchu racism and the rise of anthropology in early twentieth century China. *Sino-Japanese Studies*, 15, 18, 7–26.

Ji, P. and B. Z. Gao (1994) Xinjiang weihan minzu jiaorong zhuyinsu de lianghua fenxi (A quantitative analysis of the main factors affecting Uygur-Han mingling in Xinjiang). In N. G. Pan and R. Ma (Eds.), *Zhongguo Bianyuandiqu kaifang yanjiu* (Studies of the opening up of China's border regions). Hong Kong: Oxford University Press.

Johnson, I. (2009, October 3) In China, the forgotten Manchu seek to rekindle their glory. *Wall Street Journal.*

Kaltman, B. (2007) *Under the heel of the Han: Islam, racism, crime and the Uighur in China.* Athens: Ohio University Press.

Kennedy, B. (2001) Dissecting China's 2000 census. *Population Reference Bureau.* Retrieved from http://www.prb.org/Articles/2001/DissectingChinas2000Census.aspx.

Lai, H. Y. (2009) China's ethnic policies and challenges. *East Asian Policy*, 1(2), 5–13.

Lai, H. Y. (2010) Ethnic autonomous regions: A formula for a unitary multi-ethnic and state. In H. C. Jae and T. C. Lam (Eds.), *China's local administration: Traditions and changes in the sub-national hierarchy*, pp. 62–85. London: Routledge.

Law of the People's Republic of China on regional national autonomy (1984) Retrieved from http://www.novexcn.com/regional_nation_autonomy.html.

Leibold, J. (2003) Rethinking Guomindang national minority policy and the case of inner Mongolia. In C. Chu and R. Mak (Eds.), *China reconstructs*. Lanham: University Press of America.

Leibold, J. (2010) More than a category: Han supremacism on the Chinese internet. *China Quarterly*, (203), (forthcoming).

Leibold, J. (2010) Sheep in wolves' clothing? The book the Han nationalists love to loath. *The China Beat*, January 7. Retrieved from http://www.thchinabeat.org/?p.=1301.

Leibold, J. (eds.). *Critical Han studies: Understanding the largest ethnic group on earth*. Berkeley: University of California Press (forthcoming).

Li, C. (2008) Ethnic minority elites in China's party state leadership: An empirical assessment. *China Leadership Monitor*, 25 1–13.

Li, P. S. (2008) The market value and social value of race. In M. A. Wallis and S. M. Kwok (Eds.), *Daily struggles: The deepening of racialization and feminiization of poverty in Canada*. Toronto: Canadian Scholars' Press.

Li, S. and S. Ding (2009) An empirical analysis of income inequality between a minority and a majority in urban China: The case of Ningxia Hui autonomous region. *Hitotsubashi University, Global COE Hi-Stat Discussion Paper Series (No. 022)*, 17. Retrieved from http://hermes-ir.lib.hit-u.ac.jp/rs/bitstream/10086/16463/1/gd08–022.pdf

Li, X. R. (2008) Join a minority, says government. *Shanghai Daily*, December 23. Retrieved from http://www.shanghaidaily.com/sp/article/2008/200812/20081223/article_385551.htm

Liu, J. (2009) Employment discrimination in China: The current situation and Principal challenges. *Hamline Law Review*, 32, 133–189.

Liu, Y. L. (2006) China releases latest census results. *Worldwatch Institute*, March 21, Retrieved from http://www.worldwatch.org/node/3899.

Lundberg, M. and Y. Zhou (2009) Regional national autonomy under challenge: Law, practice and recommendation. *International Journal of Minority and Group Rights*, 16(3), 269–327.

Ma, R. (2008) Nan Jiang Weiwuerzu nongmin gongzuo xiang yanhai chengshi-Xinjiang Kashi diqu Shufu xian laowu shu diaocha. (Investigation of Southern Xinjiang Uighur peasant export laborers' migration to coastal cities from Kashgar region's Shufu county). *Shehuixue renleixue zhongguowang*, Dec. 26. Retrieved from http://www.sachina.edu.cn/Htmldata/article/2008/12/1689.html

Ma, R. and X. Zhou (1999) *Zhonghua minzu: Ningjuli xingcheng yu fazhan* (The Chinese ethno-nation: Cohesion, viability and development). Beijing: Beijing University Press.

Mah, B. (2008) U.S. Funding for the Tibetan exiles: Past and present. *China Study Group* (April 10). Retrieved from http://chinastudygroup.net/2008/04/us-funding-for-the-tibetan-exiles-past-and-present/

Maurer-Fazio, M. (2007) An ocean formed from one hundred rivers: The effects of ethnicity, gender, marriage, and location on labor force participation in urban China. *Feminist Economics*, 13(3–4), 159–197.

Matheson, A. (2006) Seeking inclusion: South Asian political representation in suburban Canada. *Electoral Insight*, December 2006. Retrieved from http://www.elections.ca/res/eim/article_search/article.asp?id=146&lang=e&frmPageSize

McCarthy, S. (2009) *Communist multiculturalism: Ethnic revival in Southwest China*. Seattle: University of Washington.

Mullaney, T. (2009) Introducing critical Han studies. *China Heritage Quarterly*, (19).

National autonomy law revised to support Western development policy. (2001) Retrieved from http://www.tew.org/development/autonomy.law.html.

National Bureau of Statistics (NBS) (2006) 2005 One percent population survey statistics. National Bureau of Statistics (NBS).

National Endowment for Democracy. s.d. National Endowment for Democracy's list of spending in China (Xinjiang). Retrieved from http://www.ned.org/where-we-work/asia/china-xinjiang.

National People's Congress (1984) Law of the People's Republic of China on regional national autonomy Retrieved from http://www.novexcn.com/regional_nation_autonomy.html.

New York Times (editorial) (2010, March 7) Educated and fearing the future in China. Retrieved from http://roomfordebate.blogs.nytimes.com/2010/03/07/educated-and-fearing-the-future-in-china/

Tze-wei, Ng. (2010) Bloodshed and tears. *South China Morning Post*. Retrieved from http://china.hrw.org/timeline/2004/trials_of_a_tibetan_monk/appendix_vii_ganzi_tibetan_autonomous_prefecture_religious_po.

Peerenboom, R. (Ed.) (2009) *Judicial independence in China: Lessons for global rule of law promotion*. Cambridge: Cambridge University Press.

Pendakur, K. (s.d. 2006) Visible minorities in Canada's workplaces: A perspective on the 2017 problem. Retrieved from http://www.sfu.ca/~pendakur/pendakur_2017.doc

Petersen, K. (2006) Usurping the nation: Cyber-leadership in the Uighur nationalist movement. *Journal of Muslim Minority Affairs*, 26(1), 63–73.

Posting of Ilham Tothi to Xinjiang jingji fazhan yu minzu guanxi (Xinjiang's economic development and ethnic relations). Retrieved from http://www.uighurbiz.net/bbs/viewthread.php?tid=487&extra=%20page1 (February 22, 2006, 15:18).

Posting of Kai Pan to CNReviews.com (2009, September 1) Stories of Han discrimination and prejudice in Tibet and Xinjiang. Retrieved from http://cnreviews.com/life/society-culture/stories-han-discrimination-prejudice-tibet-xinjiang_20090910.html

Press TV (2008, May 1). Hayden: China to be main US adversary. Retrieved from http://www.presstv.com/Detail.aspx?id=53869&sectionid=3510203

Propaganda Committee of the Ganzi Tibetan Autonomous Prefecture Committee of the CCP. (1990) Ganzi Tibetan autonomous prefecture religious policy. In

Human Rights Watch (Ed.), *Trials of a Tibetan monk: The case of Tenzin Delek,* (Appendix VII), 100.

Reza, N. (2006). A comparison of the earnings of Canadian native born and immigrants (2001). *Canadian Ethnic Studies Journal*, 38(2), 19–46.

Rudelson, J. (1997) *Oasis identities: Uighur nationalism along China's silk road.* New York: Columbia University Press.

Rupee News (editorial) (2009, August 12) National Endowment for Democracy and Carl Gershman Support Rebiya Kadeer Uygur Separatists. Retrieved from http://rupeenews.com/2009/08/12/national-endowment-for-democracy-carl-gershman-support-rebiya-kadeer-uygur-separatist/

Saimaiti, K. (2009, October 11) Sorry your ethnic group can't use the internet. *Asian Pacific Reader.* In *Black and White Cat.* Retrieved from www.blackand-whitecat.org/2009/10/12/sorry-your-ethnic-group-cant-use-the-internet.

Sautman, B. (1998) Preferential policies for ethnic minorities in China: The case of Xinjiang. *Nationalism and Ethnic Politics*, 4(1–2), 86–118.

Sautman, B. (2005) China's vulnerability to ethnic minority separatism in Tibet. *Asian Affairs: An American Review*, 32(2), 87–118.

Sautman, B. (2009) *All that glitters is not gold: Tibet as a pseudo-state* (Maryland Series in Contemporary Asian Studies, no. 198: 3). Maryland: University of Maryland.

Sautman, B. (2009) Tibet and the (mis-) representation of cultural genocide. In B. Sautman (Ed.), *Cultural genocide and Asian state peripheries.* New York: Palgrave Macmillan.

Sautman, B. and I. Eng (2001) Tibet: Development for whom? *China Information,* 15(2), 20–74.

Schucher, G. (2009) China's employment crisis: A stimulus for policy change? *Journal of Current Chinese Affairs*, 38(2), 121–144.

Shan, J. (2011) Almost 600,000 foreigners counted in China. China Daily, April 30.

Shan, W. (2010) Comparing ethnic minorities and Han Chinese in China: Life satisfaction, economic well being and political attitudes. *East Asian Policy*, 2(2), 13–22.

Sperling, E. (2010) The history boy. *Rangzen Alliance* (2010). Retrieved from http://www.rangzen.net/2010/06/24/the-history-boy.

State Council Information Office (SCIO) (2005) Regional autonomy of ethnic minorities in China. Retrieved from http://www.china.org.cn/e-white/20050301/index.htm

State Council Information Office (SCIO) (2009, September 27) China's ethnic policy and common prosperity and development of all ethnic groups. Retrieved from http://www.china.org.cn/government/whitepaper/node_7078073.htm

State Council Information Office (SCIO) (2009) China's ethnic policy and common prosperity and development of all ethnic groups. China Daily, September 27. Beijing: China Daily.

State Statistical Bureau (2001) *2000nian renkou pucha zhongguo minzu renkou ziliao (Tabulation of ethnic groups in the 2000 population census of China).* Beijing: SSB.

State Statistical Bureau (2005) *2005nian quanguo 1%renkou chouyang diaocha zhuyao shuju gongbao* (*Bulletin of important statistics from the 1% sampling of the 2005 national census*). Beijing: SSB.

Statistics Canada (SC) (2003) Ethnic diversity survey: A portrait of a multicultural society. Ottawa: Statistics Canada.

Statistics Canada (SC) (2008) Aboriginal peoples. Retrieved from http://www12. statcan.ca/census-recensement/2006/rt-td/ap-pa-eng.cfm

Statistics Canada (SC) (2008) Ethnic origin and visible minorities. Retrieved from http://www12.statcan.ca/census-recensement/2006/as-sa/97–562/index-eng. cfm?CFID=3516137&CFTOKEN=26807816

Struve, L. (2004) A brief historical introduction. *History and Memory*, 16(2), 5–13.

Su, M. F. (1984) On cataloging and classifying Chinese history. *Cataloging and Classification*, 4(2), 51–71.

Subcommittee on International Operations and Human Rights (US) (1997) Hearing on Human Rights in China before the Subcommittee on International Operations and Human Rights of the Human International Relations Commission (FDCH Political Transcripts).

Suksi, M. (1998) On the entrenchment of autonomy. In M. Suksi (Ed.), *Autonomy: Applications and implications*. Dordrecht: Kluwer.

Sunday Tasmanian (Australia) (editorial) (2008, April 6) Lhasa has changed.

Tibet Information Network (1999, June 21) Nomads killed in pasture fights.

Tsering, D. (2009, October 21) Tibetan democracy. *Phayul*. Retrieved from_www. phayul.com/news/article.aspx?id=25774

U.N. Economic and Social Council, Commission on Human Rights (2006) Report of the Special Rapporteur on Torture and Other Cruel, Inhuman or Degrading Treatment or Punishment. 2, U.N. Doc.E/CN.4/2006/6/Add.6 (prepared by Manfred Nowak). Retrieved from http://www.universalhumanrightsindex. org/documents/844/813/document/en/pdf/text.pdf.

U.S. State Department (2006) International religious freedom report (2006). Retrieved from http://beijing.usembassy-china.org.cn/rel_freedom2006.html.

U.S. State Department. (2009) International religious freedom report (2009). Retrieved from http://hongkong.usconsulate.gov/uscn_hr_2009102601.html

Wang, L. Q. (2009) Jianding bu yidi zai Zhongguo Gongchangdang lingdao xia puxie Xinjiang ge minzu gongtong fanrong fazhan de guanghui pianzhong (Unswervingly writing a brilliant new chapter in the common prosperity and development of all ethnic groups in Xinjiang under the leadership of the Chinese Communist Party). *Qiushi*, October 1.

Wang, L. X. (2002) Reflections on Tibet. *New Left Review*, 14, 79–111.

Wang, S. G. (2004) The political logic of fiscal transfers in China. In D. Lu and W. Neilson (Eds.), *China's West region development: Domestic strategies and global implications*. Singapore: World Scientific.

Wang, T. Z. (2007) Preferential policies for ethnic minority students in China's college/university admissions. *Asian Ethnicity*, 8(2), 149–163.

Wang, T. Z. and B. L. Sha (Eds.) (2002) *Guoji shiye zhong de minzu quyu zizhi* (Ethnic regional autonomy in international perspective. Beijing: Minzu Chubanshe.

Washington Post (editorial) (2010, Septmber 8) Tibetans Hopes Hinge on Dalai Lama.

Wax, E. (2010, July 17) A message in a hail of stones. *Washington Post.*

Wei, D. (2009, August 17) What are root causes of unrest in China? *Korea Herald.*

Weimer, C. (2004) The economy of Xinjiang. In S. F. Starr (Ed.), *Xinjiang: China's Muslim borderland.* Armonk: ME Sharpe.

Welhengama, G. (2000) *Minorities' claims from autonomy to secession: International law and state practice.* Aldershot: Ashgate.

Wellens, K. (2009) Negotiable rights? China's ethnic minorities and the right to freedom of religion. *International Journal of Minority and Group Rights* 16(3), 433–435.

Weston, T. (2008) Growing up Han: Reflections on a Xinjiang childhood. *The China Beat*, Apr. 27. Retrieved from http://www.thechinabeat.org/?p=94.

Wong, E. (2008, October 19) Wary of Islam, China tightens a vise of rules. *New York Times.*

Xia, C. L. (2007) From discourse politics to rule of law: A constructivist framework for understanding regional ethnic autonomy in China. *International Journal of Minority and Group Rights*, 14(4) 399–424.

Xie, L. Z. (ed.) (2010) *Lijie minzu guanxi de xin silu: shaoshu zuqun wenti de qu zhengzhihua* (New perspectives for understanding ethnic relations: The depoliticization of ethnic minority group problems). Beijing: Shehui kexue wenxian chubanshe.

Xinhua News Agency (2004, May 23) China safeguards Tibetan people's full right to autonomy.

Xinhua News Agency (2007, March 29) China has no racial discrimination claims official. (by Dainzhub Ongboin, Vice Director, State Ethnic Affairs Commission).

Xinhua News Agency (2009, March 25) Chinese scholar rebuffs Western criticism over China's Tibet policy.

Xinhua News Agency (2009, July 20) Official: Ethnic unity most important for regional development.

Xinhua News Agency (2009, September 23) China's Xinjiang orders businesses to recruit more locals.

Xinhua News Agency (2010, September 8) Tibet receives five min tourists in eight months, up 24.5 percent.

Xinhua News Agency (2011, May 4) Tibet's population tops 3 million; 90 percent are Tibetan.

Xinjiang Uighur Autonomous Region CCP Organizational Department. (2001). Guanyu zhengque renshi he chuli xingshi xia Xinjiang minzu wenti de diaocha baogao" (Investigation report regarding the correct understanding and handling of Xinjiang ethnic problems under the new situation). *Makesizhuyi yu Xianshi*, 13(2), 34–38.

Xizang Ribao (Tibet) (editorial) (1995, January 14) Tibet holds economic conference. In *BBC Summary of World Broadcasts* (1995, February 6).

Yee, H. S. (2003) Ethnic relations in Xinjiang: A survey of Uighur-Han relations in Urumqi. *Journal of Contemporary China*, 12(36), 431–452.

Yee, H. S. (2005) Ethnic consciousness and identity: A research report on Uighur-Han relations in Xinjiang. *Asian Ethnicity*, 6(1), 35–50.

Zang, X. W. and L. L. Li (2001) Ethnicity and earnings determinations in urban China. *New Zealand Journal of Asian Studies*, 3(1), 34–48.

Zeng, X. (2007) Enforcing equal employment opportunities in China. *University of Pennsylvania Journal of Labor and Employment Law*, 9, 991–1024.

Zhai, I. (2009, September 19) Reconciling Han and Uighurs is no easy task: But it must be done. *South China Morning Post*.

Zhang, J. X. and J. C. Verhoeven (2010) Access to higher education of 25 ethnic minorities in Yunnan province, Southwestern China. *Frontiers of Education in China*, 5(2), 290–306.

Zhang, S. M. (2006) A historical and jurisprudential analysis of Suzerain-Vassal state relationships in the Qing dynasty. *Frontier History of China*, 1(1), 124–157.

Zhao, Q. Z. (s.d.). Chinese media should switch on for half a year covering the 2010 Shanghai Expo. Retrieved from http://english.eastday.com/e/ICS/u1a4382586.html

Zhao, S. S. (2004) *A nation by construction: Dynamics of modern Chinese nationalism.* Stanford: Stanford University Press.

Zhao, Z. Z. and G. Postiglione (2010) Representations of ethnic minorities in China's university media. *Discourse: Studies in the Cultural Politics of Education*, 31(4), 1–18.

Zhongguo Shehui Kexue Yuan Minzu Yanjiusuo (ZSKYMY). (1994) *Zhongguo shaoshu minzu yuyan shiyong qingkuang (The situation of Chinese ethnic minority language use).* Beijing: ZSKYMY.

Zhou, M. L. and M. H. Ann (Eds.) (2009) *Affirmative action in China and the US: A dialogue on inequality and minority education.* New York: Palgrave Macmillan.

Zhou, Y. (2009) Legal predicament of combining "regional" and "national" autonomy: A group rights perspective. *International Journal of Minority and Group Rights*, 16(3), 329–348.

7

FOREIGN POLICY

Simon Shen

The Hong Kong Institute of Education

Abstract

China in the 21st century faces a mixture of old and new challenges. The traditional study of foreign policy is often conducted on a linear scale: the making of foreign policy is the exclusive responsibility of the government; and national interests of the state and the policy making process are handled by elites only. Such a top-down approach has inevitably neglected the fact that the discipline of international relations is increasingly multidimensional in nature contemporarily. In the case of China, the country has undergone subtle but revolutionary changes in foreign relations, emerging from a socialist state which was revisionist in nature from the perspectives of the status quo to a rising power which aspires to become a contemporary status quo defender. This chapter provides a brief description of contemporary Chinese foreign policy and is presented in five sections. First, it reviews the development of Chinese foreign policy in contemporary history since the reform era begun in 1978; second, it identifies the key differences between the contemporary Hu era policies and what went before; third, it discusses the formal and informal processes which impact the foreign policy decision making process; fourth, it examines various bilateral relations and dynamics between China and other major actors in the world; and finally, new and non-traditional agendas and challenges which confront China in this increasingly globalized world order are discussed.[1]

Keywords: China; foreign policy; international relations; post-Cold War world order.

Part I: Evolution of Chinese Foreign Policy Since 1949

In the early days of the People's Republic of China, the outlook and philosophy of Mao Zedong paved the way for a nominally radical and practically nationalist foreign policy stance. Guiding principles such as self-reliance, building a united front with the developing world and anti-hegemonism are indispensable in the analysis of Chinese foreign policy before 1978. While some principles proposed in the 1950s, like the Five Principles of Peaceful Coexistence — territorial integrity, non-aggression, non-intervention in domestic affairs, reciprocity and peaceful coexistence — remain today cornerstones of Chinese foreign policy, the Maoist revolutionary principles are obviously no longer practical.

The Deng Xiaoping Era

De-radicalization of Maoist foreign policy occurred when the Chinese leadership recognized a two-pronged state of affairs: when revolutionary methods no longer guaranteed Beijing's diplomatic success in all fronts, and when the Beijing leaders found defining China as a status quo defender more appropriate for their regime's long-term sustainability. These became the new guiding principles for Deng Xiaoping by which to formulate China's foreign policy in the reform era, when between 1978 and 1989 China enjoyed the first period of normalization with most powers in the world.

The Tiananmen Incident in 1989 shattered this progress completely and initiated a new era in contemporary Chinese foreign policy, which is, to some

---

[1] Various previous works of the author have been consulted for parts of this chapter's materials, including *Multi-dimensional Diplomacy of Contemporary China* (with Jean-Marc Blanchard) 2010; *Online Chinese Nationalism and China's Bilateral Relations* (with Shaun Breslin) 2010; *Redefining Nationalism in Modern China: Sino-American Relations and the Emergence of Chinese Public Opinions in the 21st Century* 2007; *Chinese Response to Anti-terrorism* 2007, among others. The author acknowledges research assistants Mr. Francis Lam, Mr. Lester Lee and Miss Jenny Lau for their assistance in preparing the chapter.

extents, still shaping Chinese diplomacy today. Facing international isolation, Deng offered the following recipe for China in the post-Cold War world order:

Lengjing guancha (making cool observations);
Shouzhu zhendi (securing its position);
Chenzhuo yingfu (calmly coping with issues);
Taoguang yanghui (concealing its capacities and biding its time);
Shanyu shouzhuo (good at maintaining a low profile); and
Juebu dangtou (never claiming leadership) (Li, 1998).

This — particularly *taoguang yanghui* — became China's prescription throughout the 1990s. Practitioners of Deng's strategy can be said to prefer promoting national grandeur in the international arena by maximizing national security in a cooperative (or even concessive), isolationist and self-strengthening manner. This is, again to some extent, comparable to US isolationism before WWII, when the conservatives stressed the lack of importance of engaging in international affairs even though they believed the US would achieve greatness in this way.

However, as the leading offensive realist intellectual Yan Xuetong in China told his nation, "since 1994, the utility of this strategy to maintain national interests has been ever-decreasing, whereas the Chinese threat theory is increasingly popular [in the West]" (Yan, 2004). The real challenge to this strategy did not come about until 1999, when the flaws in dealing with the US after the Belgrade Embassy Bombing were fully exposed.

The Jiang Zemin Era

Jiang Zemin officially led China from 1989, but in reality only took over the country after Deng's death in 1997. When he handled the Belgrade embassy bombing in 1999, and later the spy plane collision incident in South China Sea in 2001, based on Deng's principles, a series of weaknesses in the principles were exposed. These included its lack of a time frame for ending China's projection of itself as a weaker nation; its lack of a mechanism for guaranteeing any foreign concessions even when China acts in a concessive manner; its isolationist tendency, which contradicted the globalized trend; its implication of a long-term challenge to the US hegemony as long as it harbored the China threat theory; its lack of a direct communications mechanism to eliminate unnecessary misunderstanding when accidents occurred, among others. After 9/11, when the US actively sought China's assistance in the global anti-terror coalition, these areas of weakness in Deng's principles which had led China into a more defensive position than its national capability could have afforded were further identified. Indeed, the need to isolate after the Tiananmen Incident was something that was imposed rather than being an intentional strategy.

The most important change Jiang made for Chinese foreign policy after 2001 was to abandon isolationism. The abandonment was partly a response to intellectuals and ordinary citizens, who had pressed for more engagement with the world as a means of facilitating China's long-term competition with the West. Whereas Deng had used 24 characters to summarize his strategy, Jiang used a more concise 16 to conceptualize his ideas:

> *Lengjing guancha* (making cool observations);
> *Chenzhuo yingdui* (dealing with the situations calmly);
> *Bawo jiyu* (grasping opportunities);
> *Yinshi lidao* (making best use of the situation) (*People's Daily*, 2001, December 17).

Whereas *taoguang yanghui* had been the central thesis of Deng's recipe, *yinshi lidao* was the key to Jiangism. It taught people to take advantage of a situation created by others instead of creating the situation directly. Both continuity with and changes from Dengism can be observed in Jiang's revisionism. Regarding continuity, the risk aversion against direct confrontation with the West remained unchanged; and the issues of a time frame and the lack of a mechanism for forcing the West to make concessions remained unresolved. But other problems, such as the lack of a direct communications mechanism and the isolationist nature of China in the globalized system, were redressed. In a marked change from the Chinese aloofness to most global engagement in the 1990s, Beijing took a leading role in implementing the trilateral cooperation after 9–11 (Vladimir, 2004). *Newsweek's* Fareed Zakaria even regarded China as the "greatest beneficiary" after 9–11 (Zakaria, 2002).

In the views of the West, Jiang's strategy can be seen as multidimensional, "all-round" diplomacy (*quanfangwei waijiao*) or great power strategy (*daiguo zhanlue*) to promote the further engagement of China in the world (*People's Daily*, 2002, January 28). As part of its strategy to establish links to reduce the likelihood of confronting a broad coalition united by its hostility towards China, Beijing intensified its efforts to build partnerships with other actors it considered likely great powers in a future multipolar world. Instead of passively living in global isolation, Jiang took a more aggressive approach based on mutual benefit using the idea of great power strategy. To understand this we may refer to China's Academy of Social Sciences, which laid down four core concepts in Jiang's diplomatic strategies:

(1) a drive for great-power status in world affairs;
(2) a need for a stable international environment for Chinese economic development;
(3) a restraint on the part of Chinese leaders in world politics in order to avoid onerous obligations and commitments that would hamper China's growth and development; and
(4) a recognition by post-Deng Xiaoping leaders that China's success at home and abroad depends on ever-closer interaction with world affairs, which requires China to take up more international responsibilities than in the past (Tang and Zhang, 2005).

China's new multidirectional diplomacy has sparked differing reactions. Optimists like David Shambaugh see that "bilaterally and multilaterally, Beijing's diplomacy has been remarkably adept and nuanced, earning praise around the region. As a result, most nations in the region now see China as a good neighbor, a constructive partner, a careful listener, and a non-threatening regional power" (Shambaugh, 2004). Shambaugh added that the rise of China will create a certain new order and replace American influence in the region (Shambaugh, 2004; Kang, 2004). However, scholars other than optimists like Aaron Friedberg have identified six schools of thought about China's foreign policy after 9/11, most of which contain obvious elements of skepticism:

(1) Liberal optimists argue that China further engages itself in the international system and reduces conflicts against the US, which is seen as the primary status quo defender.
(2) Realist pessimists argue that the ultimate aim of multidimensional diplomacy is to assist China's rise and to challenge the United States' leadership in the economic, political and cultural spheres and will result in the "tragedy of great power politics."
(3) Realist optimists argue that the construction of the Beijing Consensus may shift the multipolar world of the post-Cold War back to its previous bipolar nature, which is arguably the most stable international security structure.
(4) Liberal pessimists argue that the illiberal and non-democratic nature of China may fundamentally violate the "peaceful union" and result in

severe conflict between the non-democratic camp, led by China, and the democratic camp, led by the US.

(5) Constructivist optimists argue that people-to-people diplomacy and the increasing conformity of international norms will make China socialized under the democratic international structure, which in turn will shape its foreign policy behavior to lean more to Western ideals.

(6) Constructivist pessimists argue that multidimensional diplomacy, which increases the interaction between China and the world, may reinforce the authoritarian identity and the rise of primordial nationalism. The assertiveness of such nationalism will be harmful to the world order as well as Sino-American relations (Friedberg, 2005).

The Hu Jintao Era

In partial response to such skepticism, Hu Jintao has since taking over China's leadership made new efforts to cast aside the shadow of Jiang's magnanimity. In December 2003, when China's Premier Wen Jiabao made his first official visit to the US, peaceful rise (*heping jueqi*) officially became the new mandate of Chinese foreign policy (*People's Daily*, 2003, December 10). When Hu attended the Boao Forum for Asia in June 2004, the theory was renamed as "peaceful development" (*heping fazhan*) but the former name remains a more popular choice in everyday usage. The thesis not only continued the legitimacy of Jiang's multidimensional diplomacy, but also borrowed the concept of making China a "responsible state" framed by Western constructivists in the hope of dismissing further China threat theories. Since then, the continuous engagement of China in the world is designed so the country is "engaged," "respected" and "tolerated" in an active manner without harming the "different social systems and cultural traditions" (*People's Daily*, 2004, June 25).

Constructivism emphasizes the role of constructed images and self-image imposed on other nations, instead of absolute interests. According to leading constructivist Alexander Wendt, "anarchy is what states make of it," because "there is no 'logic' of anarchy apart from the practices that create and instantiate one structure of identities and interests rather than another; structure has no existence or causal powers apart from process" (Wendt, 1995, p. 135). Politicians could well apply constructivism to explain the mechanism of international relations as a strategy: a strategy designed to construct an image of reality. When a nation wishes to advance its national interests through constructing a desired national image to be taken up by the international system, it may intentionally use constructivist techniques — such as reconstructing reality — to create a more appealing national image. This is the background of Chinese academic Qin Yaqing's initiative of constructing China as a responsible state and the peaceful rise connotation of Zheng Bijian, who first proposed the term of Hu Jintao.

As a result, Hu has introduced the active and responsible role for China of "world peace patrol" and a "common development promoter" (*People's Daily*, 2004, June 25). When Hu made his keynote speech in the United Nations, the responsibility of China — to "actively participate in international affairs and fulfill its international obligations, and work with other countries to build a new international political and economic order that is fair and rational" — became as high-sounding as that of the US (*People's Daily*, 2005, September 16). As argued by British international relations scholar Rosemary Foot, even if the definition of a "responsible state" includes normative values like the embracing of democracy, Beijing might still wish to risk the influx of democratic ideas and assume the role of a responsible state in order to repudiate its previous label as a challenger of the status quo (Rosemary, 2001).

Such responsibility is also consistent with China's domestic policies under Hu's "harmonious society" (*hexie shehui*), which is described as a "scientific development concept" that shifts China's primary focus from a purely economic growth model to a more balanced, Confucian-style approach aimed at maintaining growth while addressing daunting social issues such as the wide gap between rich and poor, widespread environmental degradation, and government and corporate corruption (Geis II and Holt, 2009). In 2004, after the 16th Politburo meeting, the CCP formally introduced the idea of a "harmonious society" through recognizing the importance of "democracy and rule of law, justice and fairness, courtesy and friendship, stability and the harmony between humans and the environment" (*People's Daily*, 2006, October 18). Although the main target of a harmonious society is internal reform, the idea has also been mirrored in China's foreign policy, paraphrased as "harmonious international order" (Yahuda, 2007). Michael Yahuda points out that "the emphasis on harmony implied that the Chinese leaders believed that a new stage had been reached in the development of patriotism... which means as far as foreign policy was concerned that the country would build on its new great power status to follow its national interest" (Yahuda, 2007, p. 344). It is not surprising that many observers suggest that China is more like a status quo-oriented power since then, "in other words, the wish to be richer and more powerful has not transcended into concerted military effort to replace the US as the predominant state regionally or globally" (Iain, 2003, p. 56).

Part II: Identifying the Changes in the Hu Era and Beyond

In discussing Chinese foreign policy trends that have evolved since Mao, it is valuable to identify what other major changes have taken place in the pre-Hu period. Three more macro trends of developments can be observed as follows.

From Great Power Bandwagon to Cross-Regional Diplomacy

First, as Thomas Christensen rightly argues, after the end of Cold War, the CCP officially repositioned the regime from a champion of the communist cause to the representative of national interest (Christensen, 1996). At the same time, Hu has taken a more balanced approach to a range of partners, especially those outside China's immediate neighborhood. The idea of the "theory of opportunities in China" (*zhongguo jiyulun*) was proposed by Hu and used to expand the "good-neighboring" policy beyond the boundaries of Asia. For instance, regional cooperation between China and Europe was established at various levels, such as the Asia-Europe Summit, the Galileo Programme, and the negotiation of the Partnership and Cooperation Agreement. African states, which had been called a "Third World Buddy" by Mao, are now referred to as "a new type of strategic partnership" following the 2006 Forum (MOF, 2006). China has helped several African nations, such as Tanzania, Uganda and Zambia, set up Special Economic Zones echoing those established on China's periphery in the 1980s; the Forum on China-African Cooperation (FOCAC) held in 2006 arrived at an action plan encompassing a wide range of activities from economic cooperation to health care and education. China has also actively engaged with the Latin Americas in the US's backyard, best symbolized by Hu's much celebrated regional tour of the continent's leaders: Argentina, Brazil, Chile and Cuba. Compared with Jiang's use of great power diplomacy, Hu has helped China reach out beyond its immediate Asian neighbors to other regions.

Apart from the main regional powers like the EU, or potential partners in Africa and Latin America, smaller partners and so-called US enemies have not been overlooked. Hu concluded his eight-African-country visit in February 2007 by visiting the Republic of the Seychelles, an archipelago nation of 115 islands in the Indian Ocean. During his trip, Hu pledged to develop deeper ties with the Republic of the Seychelles, through cooperation in economics, administration and financial assistance (*China Daily*, 2007, February 10). Apart from oft-neglected countries like the Seychelles, China has also engaged with countries considered US enemies. China has explicit diplomatic links with the Bush Administration's so-called "axis of evil" — Iran, Iraq and North Korea — and "rogue states" — like Zimbabwe, Sudan, Myanmar and even Pakistan. For example, it is accused of supporting the Myanmar junta in return for natural resources, and engaging with Darfur despite the pressure applied during the 2008 Beijing Olympic Games. Instead of the bandwagon focusing only on the big powers, Hu has set out to build a more balanced international environment for China's development. Last but definitely not least, Beijing's traditional friendship with Pyongyang makes it literally the only power that can wield any influence over this hermit communist regime. This endows China with an irreplaceable value in the world.

From Bilateral Arrangement to Multilateral Engagement

In addition to having new targets, Hu departed from traditional Chinese foreign policy in the sense of having a new model of engagement. In the past, state-to-state bilateral negotiations dominated Chinese diplomacy. Before the era of Jiang and Hu, the CCP believed that the multilateral institutions, most of them implicitly dominated by the US, were used to constrain the will of China in the global arena (Medeiros and Fravel, 2003). Recent years, however, have witnessed a change in Beijing's understanding of multilateralism and/or multipolarity. The idea of multipolarity was first introduced by Mao's three worlds theory and was reframed by Deng. In his *Selected Works*, Deng claims that "no matter how many poles there might be in the world, three poles, four poles, or even five poles… for the so-called multipolarity, China should be counted as one of the poles" (Deng Xiaoping, 1990).

After the end of the Cold War, the idea of multipolarity began to be reinterpreted as a means of constraining hegemonic power (i.e., the US) so as to protect Chinese national interests: "It helps weaken and curb hegemonism and power politics, serves to bring about a just and equitable order and contributes to world peace and development" (Jing, 2007, pp. 30–31). In its formal definition of multipolarity, the Chinese Foreign Ministry describes it as a fair and just international system: "Our efforts to promote the development of the world towards multipolarization are not targeted at any particular country, nor are they aimed at re-staging the old play of contention for hegemony in history. Rather, these efforts are made to boost the democratization of international relations" (MoFA, 2003). Analyzing the speech of Deng and other domestic discourses from China, scholars such as Christopher Hughes and Alastair Johnston have argued that regional multilateralism between China and regions like Southeast Asia has gradually replaced traditional bilateral alliances and alignments as the new way to safeguard China (Hughes, 2005;

Iain, 2003). Multilateralism is also seen by Chinese scholars as a relatively peaceful way for China to reduce the bilateral friction with the US (Yan, 1999).

As a consequence, China has actively participated in different multilateral negotiations and has changed its attitude in multilateral affairs. For example, China voted for Resolution 1441 on weapons inspections in Iraq in 2002 and supported UN Resolution 1769 in 2007 to send peacekeeping troops to intervene in the humanitarian crisis in Sudan's Darfur, which is considered to be a key Chinese ally in Africa. Such moves deviate sharply from China's Five Principles of Peaceful Coexistence proposed by Zhou Enlai during the Cold War, where non-interference in domestic affairs of other countries became a rule to which Beijing rigidly adhered. China's establishment of the Shanghai Cooperation Organization (SCO) and the Bo'ao Forum and entry into the World Trade Organization were also historic steps which visibly demonstrated the country's new active multilateralism.

Besides these formal mechanisms, China has initiated various informal multilateral dialogues over the last decade. For instance, China has worked with Vietnam and the Philippines to solve the South China Sea oil disputes by temporarily shelving the issue of sovereignty. The Six-party Talks to solve the North Korean nuclear crisis in Northeast Asia is seen as a great achievement for Beijing in constructing this multilateral platform from the UN framework (Yahuda, 2007, p. 346). These moves echo Beijing's claim to be a responsible power, moves which tie in with its identity construction process as will now be discussed.

From Classical Neo-realist to Realist-constructivist Identity Construction

Most scholars see Chinese foreign policy after Mao as no longer defined by "ideologies and the social systems of other countries," but conducted "entirely on the basis of the merits of the matters themselves" (Zhao, 2004). Perceiving the world as structured by "poles," which are able to exert influence on international affairs, China puts great emphasis on the neo-realist principles of sovereignty, balance of power and strategic alliances, etc. (Zhao, p. 141). David Lampton, one of today's most prominent sinologists, has summarized the realist domination of China's foreign policy principles, structure and mechanism as follows:

(1) Dealing with foreign policy pragmatically, without strong ideological and other biases.

(2) More cooperative toward prevailing international conditions and attentive to international affairs, and expanding Chinese interests through unsentimental interchange based on China's relative strength.
(3) Increased institutionalization, professionalism and regularized decision making processes, so as to avoid unnecessary but costly mistakes and insure broad support for foreign action.
(4) The increasingly professional PLA influences much of the policy areas including Taiwan, United States, Japan and North Korea, resulting in a more nationalistic concern over defending sovereignty and Chinese security (Lampton, 2001).

However, realist principles could be potentially dangerous for Beijing. Scholars like Susan Shirk have warned that as the Chinese economy continues to flourish, a highly nationalistic public may push the political elite towards the edge of taking risky and irresponsible action if a counter-ideology is not provided (Shirk, 2007). Hu's diplomacy is indeed a response, which is no longer seen in a pure realist setting but leans towards a hybrid form of "realism as the *Ti* (basis), rationalism as the *Yong* (usage)" as suggested by Daniel Lynch — or, more simply, a mixture of interests and ideology (Lynch, 2009).

New concepts have, therefore, been featured. In an interview with a Shanghai television station, Zheng Bijian, one of Hu's mentors in the foreign policy arena, explained that the goal of China's peaceful rise was to enhance its "discursive power" (*huayuquan*) in the contemporary world order: in other words, the official advisor suggested that it is useful for the CCP to speak about peacefulness as a tactic to gain the normative (discursive) right and power to advance its realist interests in the international system (Lynch, p. 88). Being seen as a responsible power therefore becomes a key means for China to enhance its discursive rights. For instance, determined to show itself as capable of responsibility during "SARS diplomacy" in 2003, Beijing gave full cooperation to international investigations after its initial ineffectiveness in reporting and controlling the epidemic, and linked this change to China's international reputation (Shen, 2004). China's campaign for the World Health Organization's Director-General's post in 2006 also showed commitment toward the international norms and orders. The choice of Margaret Chan was a deliberate construction of the new China image: impartiality and professionalism, and a willingness to contribute to international organizations, through the borrowing of Margaret Chan's Hong Kong identity (Shen, 2008). During the campaign, China repeatedly rejected claims of an interventionist approach towards Chan's bid as well as in her future work: Beijing "would not put pressure on Chan or intervene in her job" (*Oriental Daily*, 2006, September 7).

Apart from leaning towards international norms, as part of its constructivist campaign to enhance its discursive power, China wishes to offer developing countries an alternative development model — the so called "Beijing Consensus," a term coined by the investment banker Joshua Ramo — to the Washington Consensus model: China believes that "China at the moment is not only a model for China, but has begun to remake the whole landscape of international development, economics, society and, by extension, politics" (Ramo, 2004, p. 3). Former UN Secretary-General Kofi Annan also argued that the Chinese model and the rapid economic growth of China were beneficial to other developing countries (*People's Daily*, 2004, June 16). Although China does not acknowledge whether it has intentionally built up the Beijing Consensus, promoting and propagandizing China's soft power is a goal firmly entrenched in current Chinese foreign policy (*Zhongguo Xinwenshe*, 2004, June 10). Other rising economic powers in the BRIC bloc are more or less modeling themselves on China's success. As David J. Rothkopf suggests in *Foreign Policy*, "China is the muscle of the group and the Chinese know it... we should see the emergence of the BRIC bloc for what it is at its heart, a major amplifier of the influence of the country at its heart, China" (Rothkopf, 2009). After the global financial crisis hit in 2008, Hu assumed the role of the leader of the developing countries in that year's G20 Summit (*The China Review News*, 2009, March 24).

Part III: The Chinese Foreign Policy Making Process

Having understood how the guiding principles of Chinese foreign policy have evolved, we should briefly look at the actual decision making process. Although China is today more engaged with the rest of world, the country's foreign policy making process still differs greatly from the Western model. As a unitary state run by the Chinese Communist Party, the division of labor between various departments and party branches is not always as clear as it might be made to look on paper.

The Formal Party-State Apparatus

The foreign policy decision making process in the PRC is essentially a top-down process, as one of the characteristics of the Chinese political system is the high concentration of political power in the CCP (Lu, 2000, p. 8). In the past, when Mao and Deng were in command, the paramount leaders were often referred to as the apex of the party-state system, possessing the defining power in influencing the direction of foreign policy. Since the death of Deng, exclusivity at the top is no longer maintained; instead, a collective decision making process has become more entrenched under Jiang's and Hu's leadership and various departmental interests must be taken into consideration when foreign policies are made.

Under the formal structure of the process, the National People's Congress (NPC) of the PRC is the highest organ of state power and is responsible for decisions on questions of peace and war (NPC, 2010a). The NPC meets for about a week every year to determine policy; when the NPC is not in session, the NPC Standing Committee exercises the power of the highest state organ but under the supervision of the full congress of the NPC, and is responsible to and reports its work to the full congress of the NPC (NPC, 2010b). Lanteigne correctly notes that "a majority of the true governing power in China has shifted to three bodies, the Secretariat, the Politburo and at the very top the CCP Standing Committee" (Lanteigne, 2009, p. 25). In daily operations, the central foreign affairs bureaucracy is made up of several departments: the Ministry of Foreign Affairs (MoFA) and the Ministry of Commerce (MoC) — combining the domestic commerce functions and the Ministry of Foreign Trade and Economic Cooperation (MoFTEC) from 1982 to 2003 — under the State Council, the International Liaison Department of the CCP Central Committee, the General Staff Department under the Central Military Affairs Commission (CMC) of both the CCP and the PRC (that share the same membership), among many others (Lu, 2000, p. 25).

The State Council has set up a "foreign affairs small group" (*waishi xiaozu/waishikou*) to facilitate internal coordination which is made up of representatives from MoFA, MoC and specific State Councillors in charge of foreign relations. The MoFA is China's leading foreign policy and diplomatic body. Its major responsibility is to "implement the state's diplomatic principles and policies and related laws and regulations; safeguard national sovereignty, security and interests on behalf of the state; run diplomatic affairs on behalf of the state and the government; and handle diplomatic activities between leaders of the CPC and the state with foreign leaders" (MoFA, 2010). Likewise, the MoC is mainly responsible for economic-oriented diplomatic activities. However, at times the decision making power remains at the upper level of the central CCP leadership, and MoFA's role is limited to overseeing more routine and relatively low-level decision making. But since MoFA's power extends to concluding bilateral and multilateral treaties and handling international judicial cooperation, its role in influencing decision making in the globalized world has been enhanced in recent years.

The role of the CMC, as representing the People's Liberal Army (PLA) in the party-state, is less obvious to the outside world. Officially the CMC is the highest state military organ and is responsible for commanding the entire armed forces in the country. But in reality, their roles include more. As Lieberthal notes, "the communists' armed struggle for power lasted more than twenty years and created an almost unique, symbiotic relationship between the party and the military" (Lieberthal, 2004, p. 229). The importance of the CMC was further demonstrated by the controversy aroused when Jiang stepped down from all other positions for Hu but remained head of the military for a few more years, and still retained substantial influence in the military afterwards. Traditionally, despite the potentially diverse interests shared by all these different units, Chinese foreign policy appears to the outside world as having a strong unitary stance. In recent years, however, the military has increasingly demonstrated slightly differing opinions from the State Council in handling foreign relations as proven by the repeated publication of more offensive realist-oriented books and articles by PLA generals, such as the *Great Power Dream* by Liu Mingfu, on their theoretical personal capacities (Liu, 2010). Whether this trend suggests that any future tendency towards more obvious divergent viewpoints among Chinese foreign policy decision makers will be made public will be interesting to see.

Public Opinion, the Rise of Nationalism and Online Activism

Despite the fact that foreign policy remains as vital and sensitive as it was in the past, the decision making power is no longer completely concentrated in the hands of the few paramount leaders. With the dawn of the 21st century, the role of public opinion in China has contributed a notable part to the official foreign policy making process. Chinese leaders repeatedly stress how they study public sentiment about foreign policy from discussion forums, letters to the editor and even *shangfang* (appealing to the highest authority). In international negotiations, public opinion is frequently cited as being a concern when populist pressure is beneficial to that particular negotiation, such as about re-evaluation of the RMB or territorial unity. Yet the extent of the impact of public opinion remains difficult to assess in China, because on the one hand there are no legitimate ways of doing so in this unitary state when taboos are all too obvious, while on the other, there are no formal mechanisms in place to ensure sufficient official attention is being paid to such opinion.

Nationalism plays a particularly crucial role in shaping public opinion in Chinese foreign policy. To many scholars, "nationalism is one of the key enduring driving forces which have shaped Chinese foreign over the period" (Chen, 2005, p. 35). While contemporary Chinese nationalism originates from China's desire to redeem the humiliations of the past, "Chinese nationalism today... comprises an inter-stitching of state inculcated patriotic political appeals, Han ethnic identification, and culturalist pride, a confusion of aspiration for national greatness alongside growing sub-national assertions of regional identity, open-minded optimism and anti-foreign resentment" (Unger, 1996, p. xvii). In this context, popular nationalism can be defined as the "assertion of national pride and confidence as China gears up for economic growth and international recognition" that the general public expresses in a bottom-up manner (Xu, 2007, p. 101). With the frequent outbursts of anti-American and anti-Japanese sentiment since the 1990s, the official foreign policy makers are subject to increasing domestic pressure against taking seemingly weak positions over world issues, despite the fact that the party-state had an obvious role in the start of contemporary Chinese nationalism. In fact, Chinese nationalism can be regarded as a double-edged sword for the party-state where foreign policy is concerned: on the one hand, it is a convenient tool for the party-state to mobilize public support at the negotiating table; on the other, it constrains the party-state's flexibility when dealing with foreign powers.

In recent years, the growth of the internet — which harbors strong nationalist sentiments in China — facilitates public opinion to play a more robust role in the foreign policy making process. As argued by Fewsmith and Rosen, online opinions are already assimilated into China's top-level elites' decision-making process (Fewsmith and Rosen, 2006). For further evaluation of the role of the internet in facilitating civil society, we could consult Jürgen Habermas and his concept of a "public sphere" as a necessary means for democratic communication (Habermas, 1992). Built upon Habermas' ideal in the West, the influence of the online public in Chinese foreign policy is best summarized in terms of its ability to change the authority's mindset; inject online opinions into the decision-making process; and shape foreign policy directly by launching actual movements (Hong, 2009; Geise, 2005; Lagerkvist, 2005).

Part IV: Bilateral Relations

Despite China's increasing presence on various multilateral platforms, bilateral relations remain the core component of Chinese foreign policy. In addition to its complicated relations with the US, China has also developed a "long-term comprehensive partnership" with France; a "comprehensive cooperative partnership" with Britain; a "trustworthy partnership" with Germany; a "long-term stable and constructive partnership" with the EU; and a "friendly and cooperative partnership" with Japan, to name a few. Its contemporary bilateral relations with the major areas of the world can be described as follows.

Sino-US Relations

Since the end of the Cold War, Sino-US relations have become a defining feature of global stability. Leaders from both countries generally agree that their bilateral relations can never be too good or too bad: the biggest concern is whether it is plausible to build up a stable Sino-US "constructive strategic partnership," first articulated by Clinton, by identifying common interests. According to Clinton, Washington applied a "comprehensive engagement" policy with China which involved the establishment of strategic dialogues between the US and high level Chinese officials while frequently challenging domestic Chinese policy on human rights and democracy (Shambaugh, 2000). This direction has been generally followed by his successors, especially after 9–11 when the two countries' bilateral relations improved greatly, even though offensive realist scholars from both sides, such as Yan Xuetong and John Mearsheimer, often see the two as inevitably direct rivals (Jia, 2003). Conflicts between the two countries remain highly visible on almost every single front, especially that of Taiwan, Tibet, human rights, trade imbalance, RMB re-evaluation, regional security and new security issues ranging from health to climate change. How decision makers interpret these differences and pick up specific topics will directly shape future Sino-US relations and even global security. In any sense, comprehensively positive or negative Sino-US relations are both impossible to be achieved. For instance, after the inauguration of Barack Obama, the US found itself relying on China during the global financial crisis, while at the same time, China's encirclement by US allies in the Asia-Pacific region has been seen by Beijing as rearmament, and Washington's pressure for RMB's re-evaluation has been seen as provocation.

Sino-Japanese Relations

Sino-Japanese relations are dominated by historic narratives which date back to WWII, and since 1989 China has used anti-Japanese sentiment as a key element to promote patriotism. The rightist movement in Japan, aimed at establishing Japan as a "normalized power" via constitutional amendment which would allow the development of unconstrained military capabilities, also began to rise at the same time. With both countries aiming to exert more influence over the Asia-Pacific region in the 21st century, as Sutter argues, "future stability in East Asia depends heavily on the relationship between the region's main power, Japan and China" (Sutter, 2002). Over the past decade, despite ongoing Sino-Japanese trade development, bilateral relations have generally deteriorated for a number of reasons, and this has happened along-side the fact that China has replaced Japan as the second largest economic entity in the world. First, China sensed increasing threats from the Japanese military, especially after the passing of the Anti-Terrorism Bill by Tokyo in 2001 which permitted the Japanese Self Defence Forces to take part in the War in Afghanistan. This was interpreted by Beijing as the beginning of a plan to dispatch Japanese troops overseas and set up a comprehensive military intervention system (Friedberg, 2002). Territorial disputes over the sover-eignty of the Diaoyutai/Senkaku Islands and other resource bases in the East China Sea have further triggered regular nationalist reactions from both sides. The visit to the Yasuuni Shine by various Japanese prime ministers, most notably Junichiro Koizumi between 2001 and 2006, provided a recurring irritation for Beijing. Intermittent large-scale anti-Japanese demonstrations have broken out, as in 2005, after Japan announced its bid for permanent membership of the United Nations Security Council and planned to approve a new edition of a history textbook, and as in 2010, when Japan detained a Chinese fisherman in the Diaoyutai region (Roy, 2005). We should however note that attempts to improve Sino-Japanese relations are often made, but are invariably ineffectual in changing the bigger picture. For instance, in 2009, then — Prime Minister Yukio Hatoyama of Japan vowed to shift Japan's US-centric foreign policy to a more Asia-focused one, leading to a short-lived Sino-Japanese honeymoon which ended after his untimely fall.

Sino-Russian Relations

After decades of Sino-Soviet tension dating back to the late 1950s, there was a rapprochement in 1989, but the break-up of the Soviet Union that shortly followed meant Sino-Russian relations had to be developed anew from zero. Western countries always worry about a potential Sino-Russian alliance built upon their common values: preservation of territorial integrity, opposition to extreme religious movements, an inclination towards authoritarianism despite Russia's nominal democracy, strategic attempts to balance themselves against the West, and similar economic patterns in the BRIC bloc, among others. The establishment of the Shanghai Cooperation Organization (SCO), domi-nated by China and Russia, is sometimes seen as a potential Eastern NATO should a new Cold War break out in the future. But there are also structural problems hindering the likelihood of such an alliance taking place. For instance, the two would be in direct competition where regional energy resources are concerned, which was rightly pointed out by Norling over the Siberian pipeline struggle in 2003 (Norling, 2007, p. 33). A trade imbalance always exists, which leads Moscow to protest with various measures from time to time. Anti-Chinese sentiment is present in some of the heavily Chinese-populated border regions of Russia, such as the former Chinese territory of Vladivostok. The end result is a lack of comprehensive trust between China and Russia and this constrains their cooperation at the practical level.

Sino-European Union Relations

A new chapter in relations between China and Europe was started in 1975 when formal diplomatic relations were established between China and the European Community (Taube, 2002). Since then, despite the continued existence of bilateral relations between China and major individual European powers, such as France, Germany and Britain, relations are gradually being included in the macro Sino-European relations framework, which is largely economic-oriented. The creation of a single European market has benefited an expanding China by accelerating trade and capital flow. Since 2004, China has become the European Union (EU)'s second most important trading partner, leading a European Commission policy paper on trade and investment to state that "China is the single most important challenge for EU trade policy" (Commission of the European Communities, 2006). In addition, China and the EU are both eager to improve their relations to the level of a strategic partnership in order to off-set US influence: in 2005, both sides claimed "to look ahead to the future, developing the strategic relationship through concrete actions" (Council of The European Union, 2005). However, it should not be overlooked that China's relations with the EU are not as clear as are portrayed, as national interests often override EU central policy and it has thus been difficult to generalize a clear Sino-European interactive pattern (Song, 2009, p. 125). The roles France and Germany adopt towards China, for example, are rarely consistent (Weske, 2007). When a particular government in the EU develops a strong interest in its own bilateral relations with China over sensitive areas such as human rights and trade balance, as was the case during the early years of Germany's Angela Merkel and when France's Nicolas Sarkozy displayed reservations about the Beijing Olympics, it tends to have a knock-on effect on Sino-EU relations as a whole.

Sino-Indian Relations

In November 2006, China and India signed a joint declaration of mutual friendship, which was intended to serve as the groundwork for a future Sino-Indian strategic partnership. To some Chinese scholars, the declaration would solve some of the existing bilateral problems by identifying the West as their common opponent (Zhong, 2009). However, the reality remains different: India is seen by many Chinese observers as one of the least friendly countries towards China and one which could pose potential challenges in the future. Despite India's economic boom, mainstream Chinese scholars do not hold India's economy in sufficiently high esteem to justify serious discussion on a "Chindia" economic integration, but many of them think highly of India's military potential by focusing on its regional nuclear deterrence strategy and a sea power capable of challenging China (Wang, 2009). This attention among Chinese academia is made partly to alert fellow Chinese to the potential that India might one day take revenge for its military defeat by China in the 1962 border war, and partly to exert a sense of urgency among the nationalists (Zhan, 2009). Moreover, while China remains the most important ally of Pakistan and their alliance is viewed by the Indians as an attempt to encircle their nation, India reacts with a counter-encirclement campaign against China. This view is strongly held by Chinese academia particularly when US-Indian friendship is taken into consideration (Wei, 2007). As unification, sovereignty and irredentism are topics which constantly catch Chinese attention, the Chinese border area with India is seen as particularly fragile because of the hosting of the Dalai Lama in Dharamsala. Beijing therefore is overwhelmingly alert to any role India may have in supporting separatism in China (Chen, 2006). The increasing Sino-Indian economic exchange is seriously overshadowed by all the above, leaving their bilateral relations to be one of the least positive ones in contemporary Chinese foreign policy.

Sino-ASEAN Relations

The Association of Southeast Asian Nations (ASEAN) functions differently from the EU, with its supranational structure, by having an intergovernmental mechanism among its member states which sees trade and development as the most important issues within the bloc while ideological issues are always sidelined. The same rationale dominates Sino-ASEAN relations as well: immediately after the end of the Cold War, bilateral trade between China and the ASEAN bloc rose in 1992 to be 15 times higher than in 1975. The financial crisis in 1997 and China's fixed exchange rate currency encouraged

ASEAN to rely further on China. The expansion of China's economy inevitably led to its competition with ASEAN for foreign direct investment in the region, but, as Ravenhill argues, ASEAN still benefits from building closer economic ties with China as its constituent members adjust to becoming component suppliers to the world's factory (Ravenhill, 2006). However, bilateral relations between China and individual ASEAN members reveal political issues to be thornier: the growing influence of ethnic Chinese in Southeast Asia, territorial disputes and the existence of close ties with the US among most ASEAN members are the major fault lines. As argued by Womack, the relationship between ASEAN and China is not relative, since ASEAN countries did not seek to hold a balance of power as they decreased their military budgets when China increased its in 1997 (Womack, 2003). In particular, the unsolved sovereignty issue of the Nansha/Spratly Islands in the South China Sea led to fierce conflicts between China and Vietnam, the Philippines and Malaysia and reached a military level in 1988 and 1995, leaving most ASEAN members worried by the China threat theory. This was temporarily eased after 1997 when China showed moderation and flexibility in employing a "new security concept" in an ASEAN meeting, paving the way to future ASEAN Plus Three and East Asian Community integration.

Sino-Middle East and Central Asian Relations

China used to rely heavily on the Middle East for oil, the area accounting for 40–50% of China's total oil imports in the past, making energy security the prime concern of China's bilateral relations with the region. For this reason, China has traditionally given strong ideological and anti-Israeli support to Islamic countries in the Middle East and enjoyed much popularity in return. However, the rise of Islamic terrorism has casted doubts over Sino-Middle East relations as the alleged link between Xinjiang separatists in China and Al-Qaeda and other religious extremists in the Middle East — and also Turkey — raises new concerns for Beijing in the region. As a result, the former Soviet republics in Central Asia, which are largely dominated by the US, have become a new chessboard for China in its quest to find a replacement source of energy outside the Middle East. In contrast with the strategies of Washington and Moscow, one of the major attractions Beijing is offering in its competition in the region is access to multilateral networks which offer economic opportunities to Beijing. As Chien-peng Chung soberly noted, one of China's ulterior motives in engaging itself in regional organizations like the SCO is to safeguard its energy interests in Central Asia (Chung, 2004). In return, authoritarian regimes in Central Asia such as Kazakhstan and

Turkmenistan are receiving moral support from China to sustain their own regional security.

Sino-African Relations

China's multidimensional diplomacy of the past decade has extended to third world countries in Africa and Latin America as new arenas of Chinese attention. Indeed, there was a time when China's support of her African comrades against imperialism (best symbolized by the huge investment in, but poor outcome of, the Tanzam Railway) was a key cornerstone of Chinese diplomacy. Sino-African relations started to wane after 1976, but when China's economic reform produced its early successes in the late 1990s, rapprochement was achieved. The milestone marking China's re-entry into Africa was May 1996 when Jiang Zemin visited Africa and presented a Five-point Proposal for Sino-African relations, namely "reliable friendship, sovereign equality, non-intervention, mutually beneficial development and international cooperation," replacing the ideological motor with the concept of mutual benefit (Alden, 2005). Since 2000, China and Africa have organized a regular Forum on China-Africa Cooperation (FOCAC) as a multilateral platform for China and all African countries which have established diplomatic relations with Beijing. There are a plethora of reasons for China now to consider Africa seriously: the rich energy resources in Africa, the existence of a potentially huge market for Chinese products, strategic calculations against the West, shrinking of Taiwan's international vacuum, and the export of China's soft power and the China model of development are all rational options for Beijing. China always claims that it has a lot in common with Africa, as both have been victims of imperialism, have shared the developing nations' sense of humiliation in the contemporary international arena and the urge to restore dignity, and have a determination to take control of their own destiny (Muekalia, 2004). At the same time, the repeated emphasis by Beijing that the aid it gives to Africa has no strings attached, in sharp contrast to that offered by the West-dominated World Bank or International Monetary Fund, appears to be an attractive alternative to Africa's leaders. Recent Sino-African cooperation has already invited much skepticism from the West, and China's role in humanitarian tragedies in Africa — Sudan's Darfur in particular — has been a focal point of Western attack. The potential competition posed by cheap Chinese imports for domestic African goods as well as suspicion about China's "neo-imperialism" in Africa have also led to anti-Chinese sentiment in several African countries, especially those with stronger democratic traditions such as Zambia. However, given the aforementioned complimentary nature of Sino-African relations, it is likely that relations will be further developed in the future.

Sino-Latin American Relations

Until the turn of the century, competition with Taipei to establish diplomatic ties in Latin America was Beijing's prime concern in the region, but this is now no longer the case. In November 2008, Beijing launched its first ever policy paper on South America and the Caribbean in a move largely seen as a watershed for China's declared program of increasing involvement in the Latin American continent (Jiang, 2008). Although Sino-Latin American relations had been even more neglected than Sino-African relations, they have witnessed tremendous growth in recent years, such that China is now the second largest trading partner with many Latin American countries. Establishing increasing links between China's state-owned enterprises and Brazil's energy giant Petrobras in 2008 was a representative milestone that has further enabled China to cooperate with the Latin Americans. From Beijing's perspective, there are six means of promoting economic relations by investing in Latin America's infrastructure: ports and docks, railway lines, transportation, roads and agricultural production (Yuan, 2006). In noting that most South American countries have lost a significant market share to China since 2001 and that this trend is likely to continue, especially in the manufactured goods markets, many Western scholars have reservations about China's popularity in South America, but to date anti-Chinese sentiment in the region has been negligible (Jenkins and Peters, 2008). Since the Latin American countries which are currently governed by left or centre-left governments tend to follow Beijing's development model rather than the neo-liberal Washington Consensus, the presence of China in the region also has profound implications for the US's continued dominance over its backyard. Perhaps the positive view about the prospects for building a "Latin America-China-USA triangle" that would benefit all three parties is that it would temporarily ease US suspicion, but the longer term prospect of such remains uncertain (Cheng, 2006).

Part V: Untraditional Challenges for Chinese Foreign Policy in the New Era

Since the end of the Cold War, China has had to face — besides the traditional state-oriented foreign policy topics — a wide range of new issues which feature various non-state actors. These include the challenges of globalization, human rights, terrorism, climate change, health, soft power, among others.

Globalization

Since China's entry into the world market various external factors have begun to affect its foreign policy making process. Globalization of the market economy and China's participation in global governance have inevitably meant that economic considerations as well as the interests of other states have influenced some of its decision making, while the rapid development of the internet has created a public sphere which is likely to continue its strong sway on foreign policy decision making. Engagement in regional and global governance, such as joining the World Trade Organization (WTO), already renders Chinese foreign policy making subject to multilateral considerations. The phenomenon crucially reflects the shifting focus of the Chinese security concept. While on one hand, the "China Model," showcasing China's economic success and its ability to survive the global financial crises, attracts attention from the rest of world, "a transfer of economic sovereignty quickens as China embraces international norms and regimes. The shift not only occurs from national to international organizations, but more alarmingly, it also moves from the state to localities and firms" (Wu, 2001, p. 280).

Human Rights

Beijing is strongly opposed to any idea that suggests human rights should be placed above sovereignty — a trend that has been promoted by the West since the end of the Cold War. The "Blair Doctrine," which strongly supports human rights, calls for just that and was the guiding principle behind the Kosovo war, which in turn led to the bombing of the Chinese embassy in Belgrade in 1999. Before China joined the WTO, human rights had been listed by the US as a condition for China's most-favored nation status to be renewed. In recent years, Beijing has become slightly more flexible in handling human rights where Chinese foreign policy is concerned. Since the War in Iraq, the merit of multilateral negotiations on the domestic affairs of third-party nations has been added to the Chinese emphasis on sovereignty; the importance of negative liberty in Iraq had been acknowledged as the regime was failing to provide its people with a minimal level of positive liberty. Since then, China has at times supported conditional humanitarian intervention in Sudan, implying that the values of sovereignty and human rights are no longer mutually exclusive from Beijing's perspective. These values could be framed as "authoritarian liberalism" or "statism with a human face," as borrowed from the US neo-conservative jargon "conservatism with a human face" (Chen and Churchill, 2007). However, if violation of human rights in China were to be cited as a reason for foreign intervention, Beijing would still immediately see this as a violation of China's sovereignty. As a result, any moral support given by the West to Chinese dissidents is always viewed with extreme suspicion.

Terrorism

Since the 1990s, China has been working assiduously with its neighbors to deter and reduce terrorism, ethnic separatism and religious extremism. Beijing calls this triumvirate "the Three Evil Forces" and has used this code-phrase to promote cooperation for security purposes both for its own good and for the sake of global stability. With the establishment of the SCO, China and the other member countries have strengthened and deepened political trust and pragmatic cooperation in various fields and greatly contribute to regional stability. In particular, in setting up the Regional Anti-Terrorists Organization (RATS) in 2004, with its headquarter in the Uzbek capital of Tashkent and a "database of terrorist-affiliated persons and can cross-check lists of terrorists groups," the SCO "paved the way for its member states to enhance cooperation and jointly deal with the economic crisis and other challenges" (*Xinhua*, 2010, June 9). However, the effectiveness of China's anti-terrorism contribution remains uncertain as its experience of dealing with non-state-oriented terrorists is still limited. When a group of terrorists cannot be controlled by external powers, China's own existing multilateral anti-terrorist mechanism is unlikely to be any more effective.

Climate Change

Climate change is a crisis that recognizes no borders. China would like to demonstrate to the world that it leads developing countries in paying the most attention to the issue. In June 2007, China's National Development and Reform Commission constructed a 62-page climate plan, referred to as its National Climate Change Programme (CNCCP), saying that it has a key responsibility in combating climate change (NDRC, 2007). According to official sources, China aims to produce more of its energy from non-fossil fuels (renewable/alternative energy and nuclear power); plant more trees, increasing forest areas; resonance global civil society's calling to encourage recycling and tap the potential of climate-friendly technologies; and adhere to its promise at the Copenhagen Conference of cutting at least 40% of its emissions. The rationale is that if a developing country like China can step up and take concrete measures to balance sustainable economic growth and environmental preservation, developed countries will have less excuse not to address climate change and be pressured into taking greater action. However, the measures China has taken are regarded as insufficient by the West, especially as the very status of China as a developing state is disputed. While the West thinks that the sheer economic size of present-day China renders it ineligible for any privileges and that it should follow the same Western practice in environmentalism, continuing arguments can be guaranteed.

Health

Infectious disease is identified as another unconventional security threat in contemporary international relations. As stated by the World Health Organization, "pandemic influenza and other emerging epidemic diseases present a major threat to life, economies and security in an increasingly globalized world" (WHO, 2006). Since the launch of the International Health Regulations in 2007, the global information exchange, coordination and crisis management systems have been greatly improved (Jacobs, 2010). In keeping with this, public health in China is seen as a global health issue. As previously mentioned, China's handling of the SARS and H1N1 crises was seen as gradually showing transparency and credibility. However, Beijing still has reservations about its level of compliance to the global health standard, especially as reports of undisclosed AIDS epidemics in China remain a sensitive issue. The combination of China's under-controlled health system and its vast population remains a potential threat to the world, and future conflicts between stability and transparency in the name of global security are almost certain to continue.

Soft Power

One of China's key areas of concern is improvement of soft power after the term's popularization by Joseph Nye (Kurlantzick, 2006, p. 3). For example, Beijing is establishing Confucius Institutes and increasing the provision of Chinese language teachers to the world. The Chinese film industry has enjoyed a following and plaudits from Hollywood fans and professional judges, and Chinese movies are now beginning to provide cultural discovery for Western audiences. The Beijing Olympic Games in 2008 were considered an unreserved success, not only for their opening and closing ceremonies, but also for the economic and psychological investments made. The administration of and security provided for the Games were much applauded. Since 2010, China's state news agency Xinhua has launched a 24-hour global news channel in English. However, all these achievements have their respective limitations and are mostly viewed by the West as state-led missions. How these attainments can metamorphose at a more civil level without risking loss of orthodoxy is a challenge Beijing faces as it vows to make its foreign policy people-oriented in the 21st century.

Final Words

After reviewing contemporary Chinese foreign policy in different key aspects, we must bear in mind that there are many more areas that cannot be fully covered in this short chapter, and the changes in contemporary Chinese foreign policy are always accompanied with continuity. After all, China's construction as a "responsible state" and rising power remains constrained by the necessity to preserve core national interests. Any elaborated version of the responsible state connotation would be viewed in suspicion. For example, Beijing has been very cautious about the impact of the democratic side of the idea of "responsible stakeholders" suggested by Robert Zoellick, who explicitly made a link between the stability of the international system and the democratization of China, as he sees domestic problems in China as threatening the whole world (Zoellick, 2005; Blumenthal, 2007). Not surprisingly, the Chinese criticized this statement as camouflage of the US's attempt to contain a rising power, and that their bottom-line has been to check against the influx of Western liberal values into China (*Liaowang*, 2007, October 9). As Michael Yahuda has noted, despite China's participation in multilateral platforms, contemporary Chinese foreign policy does not plan to build upon the liberal ideals which founded the UN or WTO (Yahuda, 2007, p. 340). On less ideological fronts, Hu has also rejected the extended idea of the theory of "great developing power's responsibility" (*fazhanzhong daguo zerenlun*), which asked China to share the responsibility for the surge in global food prices (*Wenweipo*, 2008, August 7). All these happened when China expresses its incentive to serve as a status quo defender under the peaceful development and harmonious state principles. Although China has started to depart from the principles of Maoism and classical realism in the Cold War, protecting national interests, as with most nations, is still its most fundamental principle when foreign policy is concerned.

References

Alden, C. (2005) China in Africa. *Survival*, 47(3), 147–164.

Baylis, J. and S. Smith (2005) *The globalization of world politics: An introduction to international relations*. New York: Oxford University Press.

Blumenthal, D. (2007) Is China at present (or will China become) a responsible stakeholder in the international community? *Reframing China Policy: The Carnegie Debates*, June 11.

China Daily. (2007, February 10) Chinese, Seychelles Presidents Pledge Cooperation. Retrieved from <http://www0.chinadaily.com.cn/china/2007-02/10/content_806451.htm>

Chen, K. X. (2006) Chinese countermeasures for solving the Tibet matter. *Yinshan Xuekan*, 19(3), 93–97.

Chen, Z. (2005) Nationalism, internationalism and Chinese foreign policy. *Journal of Contemporary China*, 14(42), 35–53.

Chen, T. C. and D. Churchill (2007) Neo-liberal civilization, the war on terrorism, and the case of China. In S. Simon (Ed.), *Chinese response to anti-terrorism* pp. 41–64. New York: Nova Science Publishing, 2007.

Cheng, J. Y. S. (2006) Latin America in China's contemporary foreign policy. *Journal of Contemporary Asia*, 36(4), 500–528.

Christensen, T. (1996) Chinese realpolitik: Reading Beijing's world view. *Foreign Affairs*, 75, 37–52.

Chung, C. P. (2004) The Shanghai cooperation organisation: China's changing influence in central Asia. *The China Quarterly*, 180, 989–1009.

Council of The European Union (2005) Joint statement of the eighth China-EU summit, 5 September. Retrieved from http://www.consilium.europa.eu/uedocs/cms_Data/docs/pressdata/en/er/86119.pdf

Commission of the European Communities (2006) Closer partners, growing responsibilities: A policy paper on EU-China trade and investment. Brussels, COM(2006) 632 final.

Deng Xiaoping (1990) Guoji xingxi he jingji wenti (The international situation and economic problem), in *Deng Xiaoping Wenxuan* (*Selected Works of Deng Xiaoping*), 3, 353–356.

Fewsmith, J. and S. Rosen (2006) The domestic context of Chinese foreign policy: Does public opinion matter? In D. Lampton (Ed.), *The making of Chinese foreign and security policy in the era of reform, 1978–2000*, pp. 151–187. Stanford: Stanford University Press.

Friedberg, A. (2002) 11 September and the future of Sino-American relations. *Survival*, 44(1), 33–50.

Friedberg, A. (2005) The future of U.S.-China relations: Is conflict inevitable? *International Security*, 30(2), 7–45.

Geis II, J. P. and B. Holt (2009) 'Harmonious society', rise of the new China. *Strategic Studies Quarterly*, Winter Issue, 75–94.

Geise, K. (2005) Surfing the virtual minefield: Doing ethnographic research on the Chinese internet. *Berliner China-Hefte*, 28, 20–43.

Habermas, J. (1992) Further reflections on the public sphere. In C. Calhoun (Ed.), *Habermas and the public sphere*, pp. 421–461. Cambridge, MA: MIT Press.

Hong, J. (2009) China's cyber forums and their influence on foreign policymaking. In H. Reza and H. Jennifer (Eds.), *China in an era of transition: Understanding contemporary state and society actors*, pp. 209–228. New York: Palgrave Macmillan.

Hughes, C. R. (2005) Nationalism and multilateralism in Chinese foreign policy. *The Pacific Review*, 18(1), 119–135.

Iain, A. J. (2003) Is China a status quo power? *International Security*, 27(4), 5–56.

Jenkins, R. and E. D. Peters (2008) The impact of China on Latin America and the Caribbean. *World Development*, 36(2), 235–253.

Jia, Q. (2003) The impact of 9–11 on Sino-US relations: A preliminary assessment. *International Relations of the Asian Pacific*, 3, 159–177.

Jiang, S. X. (2008) The long view, China's first South American policy paper is a road map for future relations. *Beijing Review*, 51(48). Retrieved from <http://www.bjreview.com.cn/world/txt/2008-11/25/content_166481.htm>.

Jing, M. (2007) Changing ideology in China and its impact on Chinese foreign policy. In G. Sujian and H. Shiping (Eds.), *New dimensions of chinese foreign policy*, pp. 7–39. New York: Rowman & Littlefield Publishers.

Jacobs, L. (2010) China's capacity to respond to the H1N1 pandemic alert and future global public health crises, Centre of International Relations, University of British Columbia, Working Paper No. 12.

Kang, D. (2004) Getting Asia wrong: The need for a new analytical framework. *International Security*, 27(4), 57–85.

Kurlantzick, J. (2006) China's charm: Implications of Chinese soft power. *Policy Brief*, 47, 1–8.

Lagerkvist, J. (2005) The rise of public opinion in the PRC. *China: An International Journal*, 3(1), 119–130.

Lampton, D. (2001) China's foreign and national security policy-making process: Is it changing and does it matter? In D. Lampton (Ed.), *The making of Chinese foreign and security policy in the era of reform, 1978–2000*, pp. 1–38. Stanford: Stanford University Press.

Lanteigne, M. (2009) *Chinese foreign policy: An introduction*. New York: Routledge.

Li, Q. F. (1998) *Jiayu guoji fengyun de kangbiao: Deng Xiaoping waijiao zhanlue six-iang (The compass of international challenge: The diplomatic strategic thoughts of Deng Xiaoping)*. Beijing: Lantian chu ban she.

Liaowang. (2007) Daguo zeren de tiaozhan (The challenge of great power responsibility). Retrieved from <http://lw.xinhuanet.com/htm/content_1380.htm>.

Lieberthal, K. (2004) *Governing China: From revolution through reform*. New York: W.W. Norton.

Liu, M. F. (2010) *Daguomeng (Great power dream)*. Hong Kong: Chung Hua Publishing.

Lu, N. (2000) *The dynamics of foreign-policy decision-making in China*, 2nd Ed. Boulder, Colo.: Westview Press.

Lynch, D. (2009) Chinese thinking on the future of international relations: Realism as the *Ti*, rationalism as the *Yong*? *The China Quarterly*, 197, 87–107.

Medeiros, E. S. and M. T. Fravel (2003) China's new diplomacy, *Foreign Affairs*, 82(6), 22–35.

Ministry of Foreign Affairs of PRC, MoFA (2003) China's views on the development of multipolarization. August 18. Retrieved from <http://www.fmprc.gov.cn/eng/wjdt/wjzc/t24880.htm>.

Ministry of Foreign Affairs of PRC, MoFA (2006) Declaration of the Beijing summit of the forum on China-African cooperation (Draft). November 16. Retrieved from <http://www.fmprc.gov.cn/eng/wjdt/zyjh/t279852.htm>.

Ministry of Foreign Affairs of PRC, MoFA (2010) Main responsibilities of the ministry of foreign affairs of the people's republic of China. Retrieved from http://www.fmprc.gov.cn/eng/wjb/zyzz/t558670.htm

Muekalia, D. J. (2004) African and China's strategic partnership. *African Security Review*, 13(1), 5.

National People's Congress of PRC, NPC (2010a) Major functions and rights of the NPC. Retrieved from http://www.npc.gov.cn.

National People's Congress of PRC, NPC (2010b) The standing committee. Retrieved from http://www.npc.gov.cn/englishnpc/Organization/node_2847.htm

National Development and Reform Commission of the PRC, NDRC (2007) China's national climate change programme, June. Retrieved from <http://www.ccchina.gov.cn/WebSite/CCChina/UpFile/File188.pdf>.

Norling, K. (2007) China and Russia: Partners with tension. *Policy Perspective*, 4(1), 33–48.

Oriental Daily (2006, Sept. 7) Shiwei Xuanqing Zhuanli (WHO election become competitive). September 7. Retrieved from <http://orientaldaily.on.cc/archive/20060907/new/new_a65cnt.html>.

People's Daily (2001) Talk freely about world situation, speak glowingly of China's diplomacy. December 17. Retrieved from <http://english.peopledaily.com.cn/200112/17eng20011217_86880.shtml>.

People's Daily (2002) China's diplomacy steaming hot in a cold season. January 28. Retrieved from <http://english.peopledaily.com.cn/200201/28/eng20020128_89450.shtml>.

People's Daily (2003) Full text of speech by premier Wen Jiabao at a dinner. December 10. Xinhua News Agency. Retrieved from <http://www.china.org.cn/english/features/82092.htm>.

People's Daily (2004) Annan Zanyang Zhongguo Fazhan Moshi (Annan praised the China development model). June 16, p. 7.

People's Daily (2004) Hu: China's strategy of development and its contribution to Asia. April 24. Retrieved from <http://english.peopledaily.com.cn/200404/24/print20040424_141416.shtml>.

People's Daily (2005) China to keep to road of peaceful development, Hu. December 22. Retrieved from <http://english.peopledaily.com.cn/200512/22/eng20051222_230059.html>.

People's Daily (2006) Zhonggong zhongyang guanyu goujian shehui zhuyi hexie shehui ruogan zhongda wenti de jueding (CCP Central Committee's Decision on Many Important Problems for Constructing Socialist Harmonious Society). October 11.

Ramo, J. C. (2004) *The Beijing consensus.* London: The Foreign Policy Centre.

Ravenhill, J. (2006) Is China an economic threat to Southeast Asia? *Asian Survey,* 46(5), 653–674.

Rosemary, F. (2001) Chinese power and the idea of a responsible state. *The China Journal,* 45, 1–19.

Rothkopf, D. J. (2009) The BRICs and what the BRICs would be without China.... *Foreign Policy,* June 15.

Roy, D. (2005) The sources and limits of Sino-Japanese tensions. *Survival,* 47(2), 191–214.

Shambaugh, D. (2000) Sino-American strategic relations: From partners to competitors. *Survival,* 42(1), 97–115.

Shambaugh, D. (2004) China engages Asia: Reshaping the regional order. *International Security,* 29(3), 64–99.

Shen, X. H. S. (2004) SARS diplomacy of China and Taiwan. *Asian Perspective,* 28(1), 45–66.

Shen, X. H. S. (2008) Borrowing the Hong Kong identity for Chinese diplomacy: Implications of margaret chan's world health organization election campaign. *Pacific Affairs,* 81(3), 361–382.

Shirk, S. (2007) *China: The fragile superpower.* New York: Oxford University Press.

Song, X. N. (2009) *The European Union and China: Partnership with competition.* The University Press of Kentucky.

Sutter, R. (2002) China and Japan: Trouble ahead? *The Washington Quarterly*, 25(4), 37–49.

Tang, S. P. and Y. L. Zhang (2005) China's regional strategy. In D. Shambaugh (Ed.), *Power Shift: China and Asia's New Dynamics.* Berkeley: University of California Press.

Taube, M. (2002) Economic relations between PRC and states of Europe. *The China Quarterly*, 169, 78–107.

The China Review News. (2009) Waijiao bu jiu Hu Jintao chuxi G20 fenghui deng Dawen quanwen (The Full Transcript of Question and Answers Section from the Ministry of Foreign Affairs on Hu Jintao attending the G20 Summit). March 24. Retrieved from <http://www.chinareviewnews.com/crn-webapp/doc/docDetailCNML.jsp?coluid=7&kindid=0&docid=100922653>.

Unger, J. (Ed.). (1996). *Chinese nationalism.* Armonk, New York: M.E. Sharpe.

Vladimir, M. (2004) Global developments after the war in Iraq and possibilities for interaction among Russia, China and India. *China Report*, 40(2), 131–138.

Wang, Y. D. (2009) India is ferocious. *Dongbeizhichuang*, 6, 62–63.

Wei, L. (2007) Analyzing the American-Indian relationship and its implication for China. *Jiaoxue Yu Yanjiu*, 5, 67–72.

Wendt, A. (1995) Anarchy is what states make of it: The social construction of power politics. In J. D. Derian (Ed.), *International theory: Critical investigations.* New York: New York University.

Wenweipo (2008) Hu Jintao bochi 'fazhanzhong daguo zerenlun' (Hu Jintao rejects 'the theory of great development country's responsibility). July 8. Retrieved from <http://trans.wenwepo.com/gb/news.wenweipo.com/2008/07/08/IN0807-080078.htm>.

Weske, S. (2007) The role of France and Germany in EU China relations. EU China European Studies Centre Programme. Working Paper. Retrieved from <http://www.cap.lmu.de/download/2007/2007_eu-china_weske.pdf>.

Womack, B. (2003) China and Southeast Asia: Asymmetry, leadership and normalcy. *Pacific Affairs*, 76(4), 529–548.

World Health Organization (2006) Threat of pandemic influenza and emerging diseases. Retrieved from http://www.who.int/mediacentre/events/2006/g8 summit/influenza/en/index.html

Wu, B. (2001) The Chinese security concept and its historical evolution. *Journal of Contemporary China*, 10(27), 282–292.

Xinhua. (2010, June 9) SCO aims to develop through regional stability. June 9. Retrieved from <http://news.xinhuanet.com/english2010/indepth/2010-06/09/c_13341224.htm>.

Xu, B. (2007) Official and nonofficial nationalism in China at the turn of the century. *Issues and Studies*, 43(2), 93–128.

Yan, X. T. (1999) Guoji huanjing ji waijiao siako (Consideration on the international environment and foreign policy). *Contemporary International Relations*, 8, 7–11.

Yan, X. T. (2004) Heping jueqi de fengqi, yiyi ji celiu (The disagreement, significance and tactics of peaceful rise). *Zhongguo Shehui Kexue (China Social Science)*, November.

Yahuda, M. (2007) China's foreign policy comes of age. *The International Spectator*, 42(3), 337–350.

Yuan, X. (2006) How to promote China's economic integration with Argentina. *Journal of Latin America Studies*, 32(3), 3–7.

Zhan, D. X. (2009) Treat the Indian complex attitude rationally. *Shishi Baogao*, 7, 49–52.

Zakaria, F. (2002) The big story everyone missed. *Newsweek*, 141(1), 52.

Zhao, S. S. (2004) Beijing's perception of the international system and foreign policy adjustment after the tiananmen incident. In S. Zhao (Ed.), *Chinese foreign policy: Pragmatism and strategic behaviour*, pp. 140–150. London: M.E. Sharpe, Inc.

Zhong, S. W. (2009) Cooperation and balance: Chinese strategic choice towards India. *Chongqing Keji Xueyuan Xuebao*, 3, 48–49.

Zhongguo Xinwenshe. (2004) 'Beijing gongshi' shoudao kending zhongguo jiasu tuijin ruanshili jianshe (The Beijing consensus received positive feedback, China has speeded up its development of soft power).

Zoellick, R. B. (2005, September 21) Whither China: From membership to responsibility? *Remark to National Committee on U.S.-China relations.*

8

ENVIRONMENT

Yok-shiu F. Lee

The University of Hong Kong

Carlos Wing-hung Lo

Hong Kong Polytechnic University

Anna Ka-yin Lee

The University of Hong Kong

Abstract

From the beginning of the reform and open door policy period, in 1978, to the present moment, China has consistently subordinated the importance of environmental protection to the pursuit of rapid economic growth in the name of constructing a socialist modernized state. Remarkable achievements in economic development have been made in the last three decades, and people's living standards, in material terms, have been vastly improved, but China has paid a very heavy price, in environmental terms, for such gains. Confronted with a widening spectrum of problems manifesting rapid environmental deterioration, major initiatives and measures have been repeatedly undertaken by the Central government to improve the efficacy of the country's environment protection apparatus. This chapter reviews the challenges encountered, and progress made, in the field of environmental protection, tracing the impacts of rapid industrial and urban growth on the country's environmental contours and ecological landscape. We argue that, despite of the pro-environment actions undertaken by the Central government, the prospect for a quick reversal of the current trends of environmental degradation remains slim because such efforts have always been resisted or even negated by local governments bent on pursuing economic growth at the cost of environmental protection. Unless China's political culture is reformed to allow a greater degree of transparency in local governance matters and that the implementation of environmental policies and programs is effectively and vastly strengthened, the country will be hard pressed to achieve even its modest environmental targets in the foreseeable future.

Keywords: Acid rain; air pollution; carrying capacity; circular economy; cleaner production; climate change; emission caps; emission reduction credits; emission standards; energy efficiency; enforcement, of environmental regulations; environmental degradation; environmental enforcement; environmental impact assessment; environmental NGOs; environmental protection; environmental protection bureaus; environmental risk; environmental tax; environmental technology industry; environmental watchdog; forest coverage; greenhouse gases; industrial emissions; international agreements; international cooperation; Kyoto protocol; logging; noise pollution; overgrazing; pollutant discharge fees; pollution; pollution accidents; public health; public participation; public environmental awareness; renewable energy; sustainable development; three synchronizations; water pollution; water quality; willingness to pay.

Confronted with a widening spectrum of problems manifesting rapid environmental deterioration, the Chinese government began to undertake organized efforts, since the 1980s, to strengthen its environmental governance regime. These included the establishment of an environmental protection structure that extends to the grass-root level, the formulation of a comprehensive set of environmental protection policies and programs, the institution of an environmental legal system through an active environmental legislation exercise, and the most important of all, the elevation of environmental protection to a national-level concern.

In the past two decades, major initiatives and measures have been repeatedly undertaken by the Central government to improve the efficacy of the country's environment protection apparatus. First, "sustainable development" was officially adopted in 1992 as the country's long-term national development strategy for socialist modernization, confirming the nation's commitment to environmental protection. Secondly, criminal penalties were extended to punishing the culprits of serious environmental violations in the 1996 revision of the Criminal Law, which gave enforcement agencies a big stick to combat and deter environmentally damaging activities. Thirdly, the State Environmental Protection Administration (SEPA) was upgraded to become the Ministry of

Environment in 2008, ten years after its Chief was accorded ministerial rank in 1998. The elevated administrative status has helped lift its bureaucratic clout and strengthen its administrative capacity. Fourthly, Government spending on environmental protection has steadily increased since 1990, growing from 0.73% of the GDP (130 billion *yuan*) in the Eighth Five-Year Plan (FYP) to 0.93% (360 billion *yuan*) in the Ninth FYP, and then up to 1.30% (839 billion *yuan*) in the Tenth FYP.

Fifthly, the enforcement of pollution control regulations was tremendously tightened up in 1996, when the regime uncharacteristically issued an ultimatum to polluters who posed serious threats to the nation's water resources. This led to the closure of 84,000 heavily polluting enterprises, particularly small but significant industrial sewage generators such as paper mills, electroplating plants, and dyeing factories. Subsequently, the SEPA's "Measures on Administrative Sanctions for Environmental Protection" was substantially revised in 1999 to facilitate more stringent regulatory enforcement. Sixthly, government control over non-governmental environmental organizations has been relaxed as a result of an official acknowledgement of their positive contributions to sustainable development. This decision has encouraged the rapid increase in the number of green associations all over the country. Seventhly, the regime has become an active participant in global cooperation in the field of environmental protection. Since the early 1990s, China has entered into a number of international and regional environmental conventions and agreements, including the Kyoto Protocol. It has also taken concrete actions to fulfill its obligations, under such agreements, to control the trans-boundary movement of hazardous waste and to reduce the production of ozone-depleting substances, for instance.

This chapter reviews the challenges encountered, and progress made, in the field of environmental protection in China, tracing the impacts of rapid industrial and urban growth — unleashed by the post-Mao leadership's reform agenda to lift the nation from poverty — on the country's environmental contours and ecological landscape. We argue that, despite of the pro-environment actions undertaken by the Central government, the prospect for a quick reversal of the current trends of environmental degradation remains slim because such efforts have always been resisted or even negated by local governments bent on prioritizing economic growth over environmental protection. Unless China's political culture is reformed to allow a greater degree of transparency in local governance matters and that the implementation of environmental policies and programs is effectively and vastly strengthened, the country will be hard pressed to achieve even its modest environmental targets in the foreseeable future.

1. Deteriorating Environmental Conditions

Water pollution has remained a prevalent issue and there is no sign of abating. One of the major pollution sources is untreated industrial and domestic sewage (Table 1). According to the *2008 Report on China's Environment,* water quality of the seven major river systems and their tributaries were moderately contaminated (Ministry of Environmental Protection, 2009). Overall, the water quality found along 45.0% of the length of these rivers were classified as grades IV, V, and worse-than-grade V. Haihe River was the most heavily polluted. Huanghe River, Huanhe River, and Liaohe River were moderately polluted whereas the Pearl River and Changjiang River were deemed as clean.

In addition, largely as a consequence of excessive contamination by nitrogen and phosphorus, the water quality measured in major lakes and reservoirs was found to be unsatisfactory. In particular, the water quality in Taihu Lake, Zhenchi Lake, Baiyang Lake, and Dalai Lake was worse-than-grade V because it was subject to a high degree of eutrophication. In the same vein, ten key national large reservoirs suffered from nitrogen pollution and widespread eutrophication. In 2008, only Miyun Reservoir and Shimen Reservoir reported grade II water quality whilst Dongpu Reservoir's water quality belonged to grade III. The water quality recorded in the following five reservoirs was classified either as grade V (Dahuafang Reservoir, Yuqiao Reservoir and Songhua Lake) or worse-than-grade V (Menlou Reservoir and Laoshan Reservoir) (Ministry of Environmental Protection, 2009).

The quality of seawater in offshore water bodies was only modestly satisfactory because of a prevalence of inorganic nitrogen and phosphate pollution. In the 1990s, the occurrence of algae blooms in offshore areas was becoming more frequent and their scale increasingly larger. Data collected in the 2000s, however, showed a reversing trend: In 2008, the number of algae bloom incidents was 68, 14 lower than that reported for 2007 (Ministry of Environmental Protection, 2009). The total area affected by algae blooms declined from 15,000 square kilometers in 2000 to 13,738 square kilometers in 2008. The East China Sea, where 69.1% of algae blooms were found, recorded the worst seawater quality (Ministry of Environmental Protection, 2009).

Surging air pollution has become a highly noticeable problem in many parts of China in the past two decades. In 2008, out of 519 cities regularly monitored for their air quality, 23.2% reported poor air quality (grade III or worse-than-grade III). Only 4.0% of the cities attained grade I air quality. Major air pollutants that have long been baffling the cities included PM10, sulfur dioxide and nitrogen dioxide. Cities in northern China were exposed to more polluted air than their southern counterparts. In recent years, the

Table 1. Indicators on industrial and domestic sewage discharge

Indicator	Unit	1998	2000	2001	2002	2005	2006	2007	2008
Sewage discharged	100 million tons	395.3	415.2	433.0	439.5	524.5	536.8	556.8	571.7
Industrial sewage discharged	100 million tons	200.5	194.2	202.7	207.2	243.1	240.2	246.6	241.7
Domestic sewage discharged	100 million tons	194.8	220.9	230.3	232.3	281.4	296.6	310.2	330.0
Proportion of industrial sewage meeting discharge standards	%	61.5	76.9	85.2	88.3	91.2	90.7	91.7	92.4
Proportion of domestic sewage meeting discharge standards	%	—	14.5	18.5	22.3	37.4	—	—	—
COD discharge	10,000 tons	1499.0	1445.0	1404.8	1366.9	1414.2	1428.2	1381.8	1320.7
Industrial COD discharge	10,000 tons	806.0	704.5	607.5	584.0	554.7	541.5	511.1	457.6
Domestic COD discharge	10,000 tons	693.0	740.5	797.3	782.9	859.4	886.7	870.8	863.1

Source: National Bureau of Statistics, and Ministry of Environmental Protection. *China Statistical Yearbook on Environment 2009.* Beijing: China Statistics Press, 2010.

concentration levels of the major pollutants have started to decline, but only modestly. However, acid rain attacks have become increasingly frequent and they have spread all over China. In 2008, 252 cities, out of a total of 477 cities monitored for acid rain occurrence, were found to be affected by acidic precipitations to varying degrees. Of the 252 cities suffering from acid rain, 34.4% reported an occurrence rate of 25% per annum. The number of cities that suffered from severe acid rain with pH values below 5.0 was 115. Most of the acid rain attacks were concentrated in areas situated to the south of Changjiang River inside Sichuan Province, and to the east of Yunnan Province, including Zhejiang, Fujian, Jiangxi, Hunan, and Chongqing.

Although industrial, commercial as well as residential zones were subject to various degrees of noise nuisance, noise pollution has not been considered a serious environmental issue. In 2009, out of 354 cities monitored for noise pollution, 24.3% reportedly suffered from a low level of noise pollution, and only 1.1% of the cities were exposed to moderate levels of noise nuisance (Ministry of Environmental Protection, 2010). Compared with the figures recorded in 2008, the improvement in noise pollution abatement was almost negligent: the number of cities without any noise nuisance impact increased by 1.3%, and those suffering from moderate levels of nuisance went up by 0.1% (Ministry of Environmental Protection, 2010). Overall speaking, in the past three decades, an increasing number of complaints has been filed by the public against this nuisance, and noise pollution's detrimental impact on public health has become increasingly recognized as a problem.

Pollution has increasingly worsened in both industrial zones and rural areas populated with industrial enterprises in the past three decades. Industry-induced environmental degradation in rural areas was at its worst in 1995 and since then pollution control efforts were stepped up to reverse the situation. Table 2 shows that during the 11th Five-Year Plan period of 2001–2005, the amount of major industrial pollutants declined markedly: particulates, COD and solid waste dropped by 8.0%, 8.7%, and 42.8% respectively. However, industrial SO_2 and smoke/dust emission control were ineffectively managed and they jumped by a hefty 38.4% and 11.4% respectively in the same period. Industrial emissions have thus remained a major source of air pollution. Subsequently, this problem has remained at the top of the nation's environmental policy agenda.

The pace of the degradation of the ecological environment has started to slow down in recent years. Yet, the size of the affected areas has continued to expand and they were subject to intensified environmental impacts. Forest coverage has remained at a low level of 18.2%. The central government responded to this problem by increasing the number of nature reserves from

Table 2.   Amount of major pollutants in industrial sewage discharged

Indicator	Unit	1998	2000	2001	2002	2005	2006	2007	2008
COD	Million tons	8.0	7.0	6.1	5.8	5.5	5.4	5.1	4.6
Arsenic	Tons	844.1	578.7	463.4	369.1	453.2	245.2	187.4	214.9
Cyanide	Tons	1768.8	923.8	899.5	772.9	573.8	457.1	381.5	256.1
Volatile hydroxyl-benzene	Tons	13359.3	4077.8	2445.7	2132.4	4166.1	3453.1	2926.3	1916.1
Petroleum	Tons	50996.0	34243.9	28734.2	25261.9	23471.6	19152.7	16899.8	13315.1
Mercury	Tons	12.2	10.1	5.6	4.8	2.7	2.6	1.2	1.4
Cadmium	Tons	158.2	138.5	118.1	105.6	62.1	49.4	39.2	39.5
Hexavalent chrome	Tons	234.0	119.7	121.4	111.1	105.6	96.4	69.0	75.3
Lead	Tons	1063.8	655.2	533.9	484.8	378.3	339.1	319.7	240.9

Sources: National Bureau of Statistics, and State Environmental Protection Administration. *China Statistical Yearbook Environment 2007.* Beijing: China Statistics Press, 2008.

National Bureau of Statistics, and Ministry of Environmental Protection. *China Statistical Yearbook on Environment 2008.* Beijing: China Statistics Press, 2008.

National Bureau of Statistics, and Ministry of Environmental Protection. *China Statistical Yearbook on Environment 2009.* Beijing: China Statistics Press, 2010.

2,395 in 2006 to 2,538 in 2008 (National Bureau of Statistics and Ministry of Environmental Protection, 2008). In addition, recent afforestation efforts have continued to outstrip the rate of tree felling. In 2006, for instance, the net annual tree growth was 497 million cubic meter while the annual logging figure was 365 million cubic meter. In 2008, afforestation projects expanded the forest areas by 1.31 million hectares (Ministry of Environmental Protection, 2009).

Despite the implementation of the cropland-to-grassland conversion program since 2003, the scale of cattle ranching still exceeded the pasture areas' carrying capacity. For instance, the carrying capacity of Inner Mongolia, Qinghai, Gansu, Xinjiang Autonomous Region, Sichuan, and Tibet was exceeded by 20.0%, 38.0%, 38.0%, 39.0%, 39.0%, and 40.0% respectively (State Environmental Protection Administration, 2008). Overgrazing has posed a threat to land resources, leading to an increasing rate of occurrence and the scale of severe dust storms. Dust storm attacks were the most severe in spring 2006, with 18 episodes recorded in northern China (State Environmental Protection Administration, 2008). Still short of an effective solution, environmental managers believe that the chance of controlling and reversing ecological degradations in the near future remains slim.

2. China's Changing Perspective on Environmental Protection

The Chinese government's perspective on environmental protection has undergone three major shifts in the post-reform era, marking four distinctive views on the importance of the environment in relation to the country's overall development strategy: (i) pollution first, clean-up afterwards; (ii) sustainable development; (iii) cleaner production; and (iv) low-carbon economy.

At the beginning of the reform years, China was dominated by an obsession with economic modernization. The primary objective of the economic reform program was the pursuit of rapid economic growth through large-scale industrialization and accelerated urbanization. The perspective on environmental protection shaped by this pro-growth development paradigm was "pollution first, clean-up afterwards." This attitude of giving a higher priority to economic development than environmental protection was attributed to a perception that the Western model of economic development since the Industrial Revolution was a success. Top government officials believed that polluting and damaging the natural environment was an inevitable side-effect in achieving an economic leap. Only after the national economy had taken off, their logic reasoned, could a solid material basis be built for managing and protecting the environment. Therefore, the ecological and natural environment was given very little due regard and was severely damaged for a prolonged period.

An immediate consequence of the "pollution first, clean-up afterwards" development strategy was a rapid and large-scale destruction of the environment. By the late 1980s, even though industrial pollution was already getting out of control, the planners kept to their major clean-up tactic — "pollution control as the core, supplemented by prevention measures." Even though attention was drawn to the need to contain and prevent industrial effluents, economic development was still a priority national policy goal.

In 1992, in response to the "UN Declaration of Environment and Development" promulgated at the Rio Earth Summit, China openly embraced the concept of sustainable development because its overall connotation was considered consistent with her own national policy objective of seeking a balance between economic growth and environmental protection in the pursuit of socialist modernization. However, faced with the challenges imposed by a huge population, limited natural endowment, an underdeveloped economy, China's interpretation of sustainable development was tainted with a deep concern for economic growth. Lifting the nation out of poverty was still China's top national priority, and this green path to development promoted by the international community was reformulated by the government as "sustainable development with Chinese characteristics" (Zhang, 1997).

Despite its limited green content, as some critics might argue, this conceptual re-formulation nevertheless represented an environmental awakening on the part of the Chinese political elites. It signified a shift from a heavily economically-biased development paradigm to an environmentally sensitive one. It also signified, as far as the country's overall approach to environmental management was concerned, a fundamental shift away from a remedial mode to a proactive manner. For the first time, environmental protection was formally recognized by the Chinese leaders as "the key to sustain economic development" and was given a national-level commitment in the 9th Five-Year Plan, also referred to as China's first-ever green plan of development (Zhang, 1997).

China has taken on, right into the 21st Century, a more progressive interpretation of the sustainable development concept than its own earlier disposition. It began to stress the importance of pursuing "quality" economic growth ("Tenth Five-Year Plan of China on economic and societal development," 2001). The reasons for the planners' willingness to adopt a heightened level of green commitment at that time were four-fold. First, the target of 7%+ annual growth had been effectively met under the first green development plan, showing that achieving material well-being and pursuing sustainability may not be incompatible goals. Secondly, the inability to reverse the overall trend of environmental deterioration despite greater efforts in pollution control and natural environment protection has indicated the limits of piecemeal solutions. Thirdly, gains from enhancing industrial performance have reached their limits under the traditional development approach, and an environmentally friendly approach based on technological innovation appeared to be the only viable alternative for another productivity leap in the third stage of the modernization drive. Fourthly, China has made many green promises in exchange for international support for hosting the 2008 Olympic Games and joining the WTO.

The regime's belief in the urgency and feasibility of integrating environmental performance with economic prosperity was manifested in the country's 10th Five-Year Plan (2001–2005), which was marked by a commitment to reducing the environmental cost of economic progress and was underpinned by a "new thinking" of socialist modernization. According to this new mode of orientation, further industrial productivity gains should result from improving the industrial sector's environmental performance. The major means to achieving such gains would include the use of energy-saving technology, the replacement of highly polluting factories with clean technology users, the development of high-tech industry, and the marketization of the industrial sector to eliminate environmentally less competitive and inefficient enterprises (Zhu, 2001). Although the conception of sustainable development was still dominated by a utilitarian view, China has adopted yet a more proactive mode of environmental management than the earlier period.

Despite of a heightened awareness of the importance of environmental protection and the adoption of a proactive version of the sustainable development paradigm at the top of China's bureaucracy, the implementation of the 10th Five-Year Plan at the local level in regard to pollution control targets was considered a failure. As a consequence, in formulating the 11th Five-Year Plan, the central government extended, and gave added emphasis to, the idea of pursuing "quality" economic growth. Environmental protection efforts were intensified, and the prevention of pollution at source was given a high priority. Specifically, the central planners introduced the broad objective of building a "resource-saving and environmentally-friendly society." To propagate this newly-minted idea, they characterized such a society as a sustainable production and consumption system that called for "low-input (of raw materials), high-output (of material goods), low consumption (of energy), low emissions (of pollutants), and the recycling of wastes into productive materials" (*People's Daily*, 2001). Alternatively dubbed the "circular economy," this development strategy signified the beginning of the loss of appeal of the model of unbridled pursuit of GDP growth. The intense interests generated by a heightened commitment to environmental protection under the 11th Five-Year Plan thus helped crystallize the third major perspective on environmental protection — cleaner production. Underscored by the action agenda of "saving energy and reducing emissions," this broad programmatic theme was finally formally codified in Premier Wen's 2008 Government Report (Wen, 2008).

The catalyst triggering China's latest paradigm shift on environmental protection — from cleaner production to low-carbon economy — was the international community's debate over how to structure a post-Kyoto regime to tackle climate change. Eager to show a determination to assume environmental responsibility at the international level, in part to fend off international pressure to commit to an absolute carbon reduction target and in part to respond to the constraints of domestic resource bottlenecks, China's political leaders have thus decided to globalize their environmental perspective and embrace the notion of building a low-carbon economy. Evidence pointing to this shift included a public statement made by Premier Wan at the 2009 Asia-Pacific Economic Cooperation Forum, confirming the strategic goal of nurturing a low-carbon economy as China's operational blueprint for attaining sustainable development. The publication of the *2009 China Human Development Report*, entitled "China and a Sustainable Future: Toward a Low Carbon Economy and Society," was a crucial step taken by the central planners in translating this idea into policy actions. Current deliberations connected to the formulation of China's 12th Five-Year Plan (2011–2015) have reinforced the centrality of "low-carbon economy" as a strategic instrument to counter the dual challenges of climate change and environmental degradation.

3. Ineffective Environmental Management

The promulgation of "Environmental Protection Law of the People's Republic of China (Provisional)" in 1979 signaled the emergence of environmental protection as one of the major policy concerns of Chinese government in the post-Mao era (Lo, 1992). After more than three decades of institutional and legal reform, China has basically established a highly institutionalized environmental administrative framework stretching from the central to the basic level and provided it with a set of environmental laws and regulations for regulatory control. Major measures adopted for preventing pollution included environmental impact assessment, "three syndronizations," and the pollutant discharge fees program (Sinkule and

Ortolano, 1995). In addition, public environmental awareness has been actively promoted through green education and propagation programs organized by local environmental agencies (Jie, 1997). In fact, China's commendable effort in the building of an administrative legal regime and administrative system for environmental protection within such a short period of time has been praised and endorsed by the World Bank and many scholars. Despite all these remarkable institutional build-ups, government performance in pollution control and environmental protection in all major aspects was on the whole far from satisfactory. Most of the measures have achieved limited results in pollution control and in the prevention of the environment from further degradation.

Although it is unfair to say that most government efforts in pollution control have been merely cosmetic measures, it was a fact that an excessive emphasis on economic development has overwhelmed the concerns for environmental protection. Environmental agencies at all levels have found it difficult to obtain active support and cooperation from other bureaucratic authorities in charge of economic development to take a tough stand on tackling environmental problems. Strong and influential government agencies such as planning commissions, economic commissions, construction commissions, and industrial and commercial bureaux are known to be reluctant to endorse and enforce stringent environmental measures for fear that such measures might slow down economic growth (Edmonds, 1994; Jahiel, 1997, 1998; Ross, 1988; Sinkule and Ortolano, 1995; Smil, 1993). With a strong pro-growth orientation, both central and local governments have usually sided with these economic bureaux and have subordinated environmental protection to economic interests when the two come into conflict. Under a nation-wide passion for economic growth, aggravated by the environmental agencies' lack of sufficient resource support, most environmental measures have not been fully implemented and many pollution control regulations have not been stringently enforced.

One major initiative undertaken by the central government to temper local governments' over-enthusiast pursuit of economic growth without due regard to environmental protection was the introduction of an environmental quality administrative leadership responsibility system at all levels of government. Under this new leadership responsibility system, provincial governors, city mayors, and township heads — not their subordinates in the environmental protection departments — are held responsible for the overall environmental quality of their jurisdictions. All government jurisdictions must incorporate specific environmental objectives and measures into their jurisdiction's overall economic and social planning. Under this responsibility system, key officials are evaluated annually by a higher-level government, which has the authority to appoint, reappoint, and remove the officials in question, according to a set of explicit performance indicators. If a local leader failed to meet the targets for three consecutive years, that individual will not be eligible for promotion consideration in the following five years. Overall, the environmental quality administrative leadership responsibility system has had positive impacts by heightening local leaders' concern for environmental protection as a part of the locality's social and economic planning exercise. Yet the overall effect of the system should not be overstated as environmental quality is, after all, only one of the many criteria for evaluating a local leader, who has to balance environmental protection against many competing priorities such as economic growth, health care, and social stability.

Environmental Impact Assessment

The adoption of "Environmental Impact Assessment Law of the People's Republic of China" in 2000 underlined a critical change in China's environmental management approach — its core focus was shifted from remedial pollution clean-up to proactive prevention. Environmental impact assessment (EIA) is the major policy instrument adopted by the Chinese government for active prevention of pollution. According to the national environmental protection law and the regulation on the environmental protection of construction projects, all major development projects, regardless whether they are new or extended, are legally required to conduct an EIA. Development projects that fail to meet environmental requirements are rejected through this control mechanism. In this way adverse environmental consequences of development can be minimized. It is required by regulations that the EIA of a development project should be prepared by a licensed EIA agent and the report must specify the proper measures to assure that environmental facilities and the principal parts of the project to be designed, constructed and put into operation in a synchronized manner to fulfill the legal requirements of "three synchronizations." A development project is not allowed to commence its construction work before its EIA report is approved by the local environmental protection bureau. Individual municipalities like Shanghai and Guangzhou have taken a further step to require all development projects, regardless of scale, to go through the EIA scrutiny process.

In reality, it is difficult for the EIA system to realize its full potential. Since leading government officials and bureaucratic authorities responsible for economic and construction at all levels have consistently regarded economic benefits and urban growth as priority concerns in considering the applications of development projects, it was rarely the case that projects with substantial pollution impact have been rejected by local environmental protection bureaus. This is particularly the case when the projects were supported or sponsored by senior government officials or other powerful government units. As a result, the EIA requirement was reduced to formality and environmental protection bureaus were forced to become rubber-stamps. Most notably was the practice of approving sites by municipal leaders for economic development projects prior to the initiation of the EIA process. Once the project site was approved, it would be very difficult for a local EPB to insist on the project's cancellation or relocation even if major adverse environmental effects were identified in the subsequent environmental impact statement. The best it can do, in most cases, is to require the project to adjust its design and to adopt mitigation measures.

In addition, many consultant agents providing EIA services to development projects for a fee are closely linked with local EPBs. For example, in Guangzhou, the Guangzhou Research Institute for Environmental Protection Sciences (GRIEPS) and the Yidi Environmental Company are two major EIA agents. The former is the research institute of Guangzhou's EPB while the latter is its subsidiary. The situation in Shanghai is similar. The Shanghai Academy of Environmental Science (SAES), being the research institution of city's EPB, is developers' preferred EIA agent, even though all agents are required by law to follow the same fee schedule. It is therefore not surprising that the EPB-related agents have monopolized EIA services within their respective localities. Although these research institutes and subsidiaries are administratively and financially independent from the bureaus, their involvement in preparing EIA reports gives rise to potential conflicts of interest, given the close working relationship between the staff of these subsidiaries and those working in the bureaus. Although it is difficult to identify precisely the effect of such potential conflicts of interest in the EIA process, it is a fact that none of the EIA reports prepared by the GRIEPS and SAES has been rejected by their respective EPBs.

Furthermore, most local EPBs cannot strictly enforce the "three syndronizations" requirement because their administrative capacity is constrained by limited budgetary and personnel resources. During the construction phase, it is a common phenomenon that contractors fail to take appropriate abatement measures to prevent excessive noise and dust, or to put up the necessary pollution control facilities to treat waste water and connect the sewage to the drainage system. For example, in both Guangzhou and Shanghai, the shortage of manpower has prevented EPBs and their local agents from any vigorous enforcement, rendering frequent and regular site inspections out of the question. Limited enforcement of environmental regulations is also frequently detected in project completion approval. Many projects are allowed to operate without the installation of proper pollution control facilities. Some projects have been able to delay such installations for many years after their start-up. As a result, some production plants have failed to meet emission standards due to incomplete pollution treatment facilities, and in some cases, such problems have persisted for years after the project's inauguration (Lo, Tang and Chan, 1997). A lack of active compliance has occurred in the operation of the projects. Most project developers have not followed the project design to set up an environmental unit to monitor or improve the performance of pollution facilities. The practice of not operating pollution control facilities is very common in China, due to the fact that the cost of operations and management is much higher than the payment of pollution discharge fees and fines (He, 1997; Jahiel, 1998; Sinkule and Ortolano, 1995).

Finally, the EIA system in China was not open for public participation. The system was dominated by local EPBs without any formal channels for public consultation and citizen participation. All EIA regulations and decisions are conducted by the EPB in the absence of any public consultation and supervision. The regulatory process is operated more or less in a "black box" manner without any transparency. No open consultation is conducted for people to express their opinions, nor for those affected to register their grievances even in cases where the projects have profound impacts on members of the public. In addition, there is no public access to EIA documents. The lack of genuine public scrutiny has greatly reduced the accountability effect of the EIA system. As a whole, public interests have been constantly neglected in favor of bureaucratic and business interests. While this facilitates administrative convenience and helps to prevent any delay cost arising from public consultation, the environmental agencies easily succumb to polluting interests. In recent years, some local EPBs have indicated that some forms of public participation are desirable to improve EIA enforcement. Increasingly, citizens are encouraged to report cases of non-compliance and to lodge their complaints against pollution to the municipal governments and their environmental agencies. However, the practice of placing environmental governance institutions under popular supervision is still foreign to China's bureaucratic tradition and there is strong bureaucratic resistance to involving the public in the EIA process (Tang, Tang and Lo, 2005).

The Pollution Discharge Fee System

The pollution discharge fee system, which is based on the principle of "polluter pays," is the major environmental protection program that China has introduced to tackle increasingly serious water and air pollution problems, with the objective of reducing the emission of industrial effluences and air pollutants through a financial incentive structure. The Chinese government has enacted legal regulations relating to the levy of pollution discharge fee from industrial enterprises in the early 1980s. Under this scheme, the maximum amount and concentrations of major water and air pollutants that each polluting unit was allowed to emit were prescribed in the form of an emission permit. Based on local regulations and emission standards, EPBs at all levels were charged with the responsibility of imposing and levying fees or fines on polluting enterprises that have exceeded the official limits in discharging pollutants. The amount to be levied was decided according to the fee and fine schedule set up by the national government. Since the regulatory standards and fee schedules are relatively well-defined, local EPBs can determine the amount of fines or fees payable by a polluting enterprise in a rather straightforward and non-controversial manner.

However, China's pollution discharge fee system has failed to provide industrial enterprises with sufficient financial incentive to induce them to reduce pollutant emission. Many environmental officials and scholars have pointed out that the level of both fees and fines in the national schedule were set too low without much flexibility. Local governments were not allowed to adjust the level of fees and fines according to local conditions. Thus in richer localities such as Guangzhou and Shanghai, the pollution fees and fines imposed on certain factories were actually well below the operations and management costs of pollution treatment facilities. A paper factory in Guangzhou, for example, was paying RMB 4.4 million in water pollution fees in early 1990. If the factory were to deal with the pollution problem itself, it was estimated that it needed to invest RMB 100 million in capital equipment and incur an annual operating expense of RMB 14.4 million, based on the price level at that time (He, 1997). Thus it was quite a widespread phenomenon that factories stopped operating their pollutant treatment facilities and decided instead to pay discharge fees or fines.

Another institutional pitfall of this system was that water and air pollution control at the local level was directly financed by the pollution discharge fees and fines collected. Accordingly to national and local regulations, at the discretion of the environmental protection bureaus, 80% of the fees and fines collected were used to help the polluting units upgrade their pollution-reduction technologies and facilities in the form of either a loan or direct financial assistance. The remaining 20% would become a part of the income of the environmental protection bureaus. Such an arrangement has created strong incentives for officials to enforce pollution standards. It has also substantially augmented the operating budgets of local EPBs. For example, environmental agencies in Guangzhou collected a total of RMB 45 million from pollution fees and fines in 1990, compared with several million yuan collected each year prior to 1984 (Guangzhou Environmental Protection Office, 1991). With a direct financial interest connected to enforcement, local environmental protection agencies actually have a perverse interest in welcoming factories to continue to emit pollutants so that the agencies could continue to collect the discharge fees (Lo and Tang, 1994).

Recognizing the adverse impact of the unreasonable fee structure of the levy scheme and the problematic use of the fees collected, the central planners started to reform the pollution discharge fee system by the end of 1990s. Implemented in 2003, the revised version was different from the earlier model in the following four aspects. First, the method of calculation was changed from measuring the quantity of pollutants discharged by an enterprise exceeding emission standards to measuring the quantity of all pollutants discharged. Secondly, the base unit for assessing the fee was changed from the concentration of pollutants to that of the total quantity of pollutants (National Development and Reform Commission, 2007a). Thirdly, the basic unit of assessment was changed from the number of times of exceeding the maximum pollution concentration level to that of a pollution equivalent (PE). Fourthly, instead of calculating the fee on the basis of the one pollutant which has recorded the highest degree of exceeding the maximum emission limit, the levels of all the pollutants would be counted. A total of 100 pollutants are now listed in the new charging scheme. Accordingly, all the pollution that an enterprise discharges is required to be converted to units of pollution equivalents (PEs) and the total amount of discharge fee is calculated on the basis of the total number of PEs and the unit price of each PE. All these changes have enabled the new charging scheme to make enterprises more accountable for their pollution operations.

Another major change introduced to the discharge fee system was the implementation of "two separate lines of revenues and expenses" in the collection and the use of pollutant fees to replace the former arrangement of using pollution fee to directly subsidize environmental protection agencies. Under the new system, all pollution fees and fines collected now go directly to the local finance bureau, becoming a part of the local government's revenue and is set aside as a special fund for environmental protection. The consequence of the reform was that local EPBs were no longer guaranteed a portion of the fees collected; similarly, enterprises were no longer guaranteed a partial refund of the pollution discharge fees that they have paid.

However, the new pollution discharge fee system has not fundamentally rectified the problem of a generally low level of pollution fees. The story has thus remained the same: in the case of a paper mill, it would prefer to pay RMB 0.6

as the pollution fee for one tonne of waste water discharged, instead of paying the much higher treatment cost of RMB 3.0. In other words, there was a lack of financial incentive for enterprises to reduce their pollution. At the same time, a sound information management system to collect and handle enterprises' pollution data was not available and the implementation of the pollution fee system was always undermined by informal politics. As such, due to design flaws and various institutional constraints, the potential of using the pollution discharge fee system to reduce industrial pollution has not been fully obtained.

Recently, there was discussion on the possible introduction of environmental tax to replace the practice of collecting the pollution discharge fee. Influenced by the positive experience of Western countries in instituting a comprehensive environmental taxation system for improving environmental governance, top officials in the Ministry of Environmental Protection have openly expressed the urgent need of introducing environmental tax to improve the effectiveness of environmental administration in China (International Energy Conservation Environmental Protection Association, 2010). Although the issue of environmental tax has been included in the agendas of the Ministry of Finance, Tax Bureau, and the Ministry of Environmental Protection, no decision has yet been made (Xinhua, 2010).

Lax Enforcement by Environmental Agencies

Through a series of environmental legislations, China has built quite a complete environmental legal regime. All major types of environmental pollution problems have been put under a regulatory control system. However, despite the steady progress made in environmental law-making, environmental pollution has not been brought under control. Under the prescriptions of environmental laws and pollution control regulations, a large number of highly polluting enterprises should have shut down their production facilities, suspended their production, converted their production lines to manufacturing cleaner products, or relocated their plants to other industrial areas. However, they have not been forced to follow through such actions because governments at all levels have accorded a higher priority to local economic interests. In the absence of active support from local governments and cooperation from other bureaucratic agencies, it was difficult for local EPB to take a tough stand against polluting plants. The core of the problem was thus resistance from local government leaders and other bureaucratic authorities to allow EPBs' to stringently enforce environmental regulations.

This regulatory stalemate persisted until 1996, when the central government started to show determination to curb rampant industrial pollution.

Instruction was issued by the State Council to order governments all levels to take a hard line in the enforcement of pollution control regulations and to set deadlines for enterprises and factories with serious pollution to close down or stop their production activities. Notable outcomes were achieved in the cleaning up of the Suzhou Creek (Liu, 1998). The water of Suzhou Creek, the largest tributary of Huangpu River, was deadly polluted with hardly any living organisms. The clean-up effort to recapture the beautiful scenery of Suzhou creek was organized by the Shanghai municipal government in 1997, with the objective of total elimination of all sources of pollution in three years' time (Ye, 1997). Thus all enterprises along the river were required to install their own wastewater treatment facilities. Because of these tough measures, the water quality of Suzhou Creek was greatly improved.

However, the outcome of these clean-up efforts depended very much on whether local EPBs could consistently and strictly enforce environmental rules and regulations in the long run, whether they could secure active support from local governments, whether they could obtain adequate enforcement power and resources, and whether they could sternly penalize enterprises and factories for unlawful pollution acts. The control of water pollution in the Huai River provided a notorious example of the failure of regulatory enforcement in China, where years of organized effort to control and reduce industrial pollution have been to no avail. Huai River was probably the most polluted river in China, and clean-up efforts were started in September 1995 under the leadership of State Councillor Song Jian, who was also the Chairman of the Environmental Protection Committee of the State Council. A total of 5,000 small polluting factories were shut down in 1996, while another 1,500 with heavy emissions were ordered to be closed within a short period of time when they failed to meet the emission standards prescribed by the new environmental laws (Liu, 1998). Despite of all these efforts, the water quality of Huai River has remained very poor (Economy 2004).

4. Growing Public Environmental Awareness

For decades, the issue of environmental protection was never a matter of great concern in the mind of the public nor figured prominently in government's political agenda. For a long time, people regarded pollution and environmental degradation as inevitable by-products of economic development. Beginning in the late 1980s and early 1990s, sparked by a marked increase in news media coverage of environmental issues such as lax law enforcement, public environmental consciousness inside China started to grow. Heightened environmental consciousness was also facilitated by an increasing concern for global environmental problems expressed by the world community (especially since the 1992 Rio Earth Summit) (Lee, 2005). Consequently, by the mind 1990s, the Chinese government began to admit the seriousness of the nation's environmental problems and introduced an increasing number of environmental education programmes and environmental campaigns at the central, provincial and local levels (Wong, 2010).

Surveys on public environmental attitudes, both local and national, have been carried out since the mid 1990s. However, the survey results were not fully comparable across time and space due to diverse methodologies and the lack of sufficient longitudinal data (Lee, 2005). The first comprehensive study of public environmental awareness, which appeared in 1998, was conducted by the Contemporary China Research Center of Peking University. Another major public environmental attitudes survey was conducted in December 2007. Sponsored by the China Environmental Awareness Programme, it aimed at promoting environmental education, raising the environmental awareness of the whole nation, and offering scientific data to support decision-making (Wong, 2010). Data generated from these two surveys — undertaken nine years apart — were quite sufficient to help delineate the Chinese people's awareness, knowledge, attitudes, and degree of commitment to environmental protection during a period of rapid economic development.

While the findings of the above two surveys have revealed a surge in environmental awareness among the general public in recent years, they have also helped highlight some gaps between the public's environmental awareness, knowledge, attitudes, and practices (Wong, 2010). People's awareness of environmental issues has yet to be translated into actual environmental behavioral change, for instance. Most respondents in the 1998 survey were not willing to pay extra for goods and services in the interest of protecting the environment (Wong, 2010). The 2007 survey found that people's attitudes in this regard had not changed that much: the public's willingness to pay extra for an environmentally friendly lifestyle remained at a low level. Even though many professed that they were willing to act to protect the environment, the most common actions favored by the respondents included saving water, electricity and gas, using environmentally friendly products, promoting resource saving and recycling programmes, and consuming organic or other environmentally sound products (Wong, 2010). That is, the public would undertake environmentally friendly actions only if these actions do not incur additional expenses or result in too many personal inconveniences.

Observations made by some researchers, both domestic and foreign, strongly suggest that public opinion on the environment has not been a major force in shaping China's environmental policies (Lee, 2005; Yuan, 1999). The basic understanding of the nature of many issues on the part of the public has been mostly shaped by state policies propagated by the media (Lee, 2005). In addition, constrained by China's non-democratic institutions and structure, public interests have not always been fully represented in state policies. In regard to the environmental policy arena, this limitation is furthered compounded by the fact that the public generally expects other actors, particularly the government, to take charge of the environmental protection agenda (Wong, 2010).

While very low regard was given by many local government officials to public environmental attitudes, national-level government agencies have begun to recognize citizen engagement as a legitimate and powerful tool in driving the overall effort to enhance the country's environmental quality (Wong, 2010). For example, the State Council, as early as 1996, issued a "Decision concerning Environmental Protection Issues" that welcomed the engagement of both the media and citizens in exposing illegal actions that degraded the environment. In 2006, in launching the China Environmental Awareness Program in partnership with the United Nations Development Programme, the Chinese government formally recognized the important function of raising public environmental awareness to reinforce the efficacy of environmental initiatives. These central government-sponsored initiatives have also helped contribute to the growth of environmental NGOs in China.

5. Impacts and Limitations of Environmental NGOs

In response to an increasing number and severity of environmental woes, and in accepting the fact of their limited capacity to regulate the rapidly growing industrial economy, government officials at both central and local levels have started, since the 1990s, to explore alternative approaches, such as enlisting the help of local environmental NGOs (ENGOs hereafter), to tackle environmental ills. This strategy has helped achieve some notable environmental policy successes, such as keeping the growth rate of total emissions below that of the growth rate of industry (Stalley and Yang, 2006; Tang and Zhan, 2008).

The past two decades (1990–2010) have witnessed a rapid growth of ENGOs in China. However, due to difficulties in definition and data collection, the exact number of ENGOs in China has remained elusive — informed estimates have ranged from several thousand to several hundred thousand (Cooper, 2006). Yet there is no denying that these organizations have grown in size and capacity. In particular, some of them often receive international assistance, some enjoy the support of local news media organizations and universities, and a smaller number have cooperated with government officials who share their views (Lu, 2007; Turner and Zhi, 2006). With strengthened capacity, the ENGO sector has appeared to have begun to make an impact on some environmental policies and the decision-making processes concerning the environment (Lu, 2007). This is a major departure from the 1990s period, when most ENGOs adopted a "non-confrontational stance" and their activities focused mostly on environmental education and non-political activities, designed primarily to raise the level of public environmental awareness (Ho, 2001).

In the past ten years, ENGOs have begun to play a more active and prominent role in China's public media and internet space. Their elevated profile has lent them a platform to broaden their appeal to a larger public and add strength to their voice in shaping the outcome of major environmental policy debates (Yang, 2005). Two important events have marked the watershed of the development of China's ENGOs in terms of their strength and degree of sophistication. The first was the campaign to save Nujiang, which proved that China's ENGOs had the capacity to quickly organize an effective national campaign that was able to trigger a pro-environment decision on the part of the government (Turner and Zhi, 2006). Another case in point was an official ban imposed by the then State Environmental Protection Agency (SEPA) on 30 large development projects that had failed to comply with the environmental impact assessment requirement. This incident, which was sparked off by a statement collectively issued by 56 civic ENGOs, was unprecedented in China's short history of environmental enforcement (Tang and Zhan, 2008). Similar events recorded in the past decade strongly suggest that ENGOs have become the most dynamic civil society organizations in China. Compared to NGOs working in the other sectors, they have demonstrated a higher level of capacity in mobilizing public support for collective actions and policy campaigns (Lu, 2007).

The mission, structure, and the degree of autonomy and influence of the ENGOs have been largely determined by China's overall political climate and regulatory processes. In general, China's ENGOs have been classified into three major types — student environmental groups, government-organized NGOs (GONGOs), and civic ENGOs (Tang and Zhan, 2008). Student groups are usually affiliated with, and monitored by, university administrations. They rarely participate in policy-making processes and have a weak working relationship with local EPBs (Tang and Zhan, 2008). The second group, GONGOs, was mostly created by higher-level authorities to lend support to implementing national environmental protection programs at the local level and to help keep powerful local governments and industries in check (Turner and Zhi, 2006). Many were established with the explicit purpose of receiving funding from international organizations and foundations (Tang and Zhan, 2008). They are usually partnered with international ENGOs so as to prove themselves to be a reliable force in implementing projects and influencing policies (Turner and Zhi, 2006). In contrast to the student groups and GONGOs, civic ENGOs are founded and run entirely by private citizens; many of them are therefore more independent and grass-roots-oriented than the former (Tang and Zhan, 2008). The civic ENGOs have provided a viable forum for cultivating voluntary civic engagement (Tang and Zhan, 2008). Most civic ENGOs, however, have been careful in dealing with local governments — they avoid undertaking activities that contain sustained confrontational elements that are commonly associated with environmental movements in other parts of the world (Stalley and Yang, 2006). Instead, they tend to organize activities that pertain primarily to environmental education, which is considered politically neutral and therefore palatable to the authorities. This strategy has proven viable and it has allowed most civic ENGOs to survive and grow (Tang and Zhan, 2008).

The development of the ENGO sector has been structured by the following two regulations: the "Regulations for the Registration and Management of Non-Government and Non-Commercial Enterprises (1998)" and the "Regulations for the Registration and Management of Social Organizations (1998)." These two regulations have provided China's ENGOs with a pathway to legality and effectiveness (Cooper, 2006; Turner and Zhi, 2006). In addition to these two regulations, a number of new laws have also been promulgated to give ENGOs and the public a strong legal standing to participate in the policy decision-making processes. In 2000, for instance, the National People's Congress passed the Legislation Law, which specified that public hearing and other consultative mechanisms should become as an integral part of the lawmaking processes (Tang and Zhan, 2008). The revised EIA law also formally stated the requirement for public participation in the EIA process (Tang and Zhan, 2008). In March 2004, the State Council issued a new set of Guidelines for the Full Implementation of the EIA Law, which allowed the public to get access to most government information that was previously not specified as open or public under the Law of State Secrets (Turner and Zhi, 2006). All of these requirements have helped trigger more demand for ENGOs to assist in the EIA process as well as other environmental campaigns because they tend to have better grass-root contacts than government agencies (Tang and Zhan, 2008). All in all, the issuance of these regulations clearly signaled the Chinese leaders' acknowledgement of the legitimacy of alternative forms of association in the public sphere in formulating government policies to contribute to environmental protection (Tang and Zhan, 2008).

In addition to the formal regulations that have facilitated ENGOs' participation in environmental policy-making, many ENGO leaders have used their personal connections with the party-state to exert their influence or express their voice. Indeed, a few ENGOs are famous for their connections with the government. Leading examples include the All China Environment Federation, the China Environmental Protection Foundation, Friends of Nature, Global Village Beijing, the Global Environmental Institute Beijing. The leaders of these ENGOs have established their personal connections with government officials at either the central or the local level (Tang and Zhan, 2008).

While the ENGOs are enjoying more support now than previously, a number of challenges have remained. First, China's ENGOs generally lack technical capacity (Lu, 2007). Many civic ENGOs and student groups do not have a strong legal and technical capacity due to a lack of human resources. They are thus unable to actively engage in either public policy debates or participate in detailed technical discussion on certain environmental issues such as energy and biodiversity. This limitation has thus weakened their ability to challenge local governments and industries when handling complex EIAs (Turner and Zhi, 2006). Secondly, most players in the ENGO sector suffer from a lack of collaboration among themselves and hence they are not able to muster sufficient leverage to deal with the government (Shi, 2009; Tang and Zhan, 2008). This problem is compounded by the fact that ENGOs operating in the same city may not be fully aware of each other's activities and therefore do not engage in frequent contact with each other (Lu, 2007). The competition for limited external funding has been a key factor constraining the extent of cooperation between the ENGOs.

Thirdly, while some ENGOs have begun to forge a closer networking and coordination relationship among themselves, major differences between the leading organizations — in terms of ideology, competency, and style — have remained and they have impeded a high degree of collaboration to emerge in this sector. For instance, ENGOs which choose to avoid confrontation with the government tend to stay away from those organizations which they perceive as too "radical." The "radical" ENGOs, in turn, are often disdainful of their "timid" counterparts. ENGOs that are technically sophisticated tend to look down upon organizations that they consider as "amateurs."

Lastly, many ENGOs in China have difficulties securing sufficient and sustainable funding. International organizations and foundations have played a rather prominent role as major funders for ENGOs in China. However, this type of funding often goes directly to government agencies; and the ENGO sector has only received a meager amount from this source of funding (Tang and Zhan, 2008). The ENGOs' financial independence is further crippled by the fact that domestic funding has never been stable because it has been coming from a handful of dedicated but not necessarily philanthropic individuals, making it very hard to sustain the organizations (Cooper, 2006; Tang and Zhan, 2008). In recent years, there have been signs that a few domestic foundations, such as the Society for Entrepreneurs and Ecology, have been providing an increasing amount of funding to ENGOs in China. Yet, overall speaking, the reach and influence of ENGOs in China are still limited by their financial resources. This limitation has also placed significant constraints on their capacity building agendas and organizational development plans.

The receipt of international funding has been one of the major controversial issues debated amongst the ENGO sector in China because critics argue that it has unduly influenced the focus of the environmental campaigns conducted by China's ENGOs. Up until the turn of the century, many ENGOs in China did not focus their campaigns on issues that have galvanized international environmental groups, such as climate change and international trade on illegal logging (Lu, 2007). They have, instead, focused primarily on localized and immediate issues such as air and water pollution problems. However, as the ENGO sector has started to become increasingly dependent on international funding, it is likely that they will face increasing pressure from foreign donors to tackle globally relevant issues (Lu, 2007). Many ENGOs, however, have admitted that global-level topics such as climate change were complicated subject matters that extended beyond their immediate concerns. They had difficulties, for instance, understanding the importance of climate change as they have yet to see an extreme example of its impacts (Shi, 2009). The ENGO sector as a whole has instead been urged by critics to focus more on the domestic agenda than global concerns (Shi, 2009). As such, looking into the near future, ENGOs in China will need to strike a balance between two sets of contrasting demands ensuing, respectively, from international donors and domestic interests, in addition to overcoming such operational constraints as the lack of resources and limited technical capacity.

6. International Cooperation on Environmental Protection

China's involvement in global-scale environmental protection activities from the early 1990s onward was characterized by passive compliance, as illustrated by its ready commitment to an array of international protocols and conventions, such as measures designed to control the trans-boundary transfer of hazardous waste, reduce ozone-inducing pollutants, and conserve biodiversity (CCICED, 2006). Since the endorsement of the Sustainable Development Declaration at the 1st Earth Summit in July 1992, China has cooperated with other nations as well as international organizations in facilitating regional and global environmental management projects. In that same year, China's Council for International Cooperation on Environment and Development (CCICED) was established, setting an important milestone for China in internationalizing its national environmental protection strategy. Partnered with the UNEP and 22 international council member nations, this Council is an essential institutional platform for China to seek advice from other countries on how to improve its own environmental practices. China has also engaged in regional and global environmental protection projects through its membership in the UN's Division for Sustainable Development.

China's acquiescence to international agreements on environmental protection stems from several practical considerations. First, environmental cooperation projects at the international level help compensate for its own deficiencies in environmental know-how and technology. For instance, China has reached an agreement with the United States in securing advanced technology in power generation to help her minimize carbon dioxide emissions. China has also received ample assistance from the World Bank and the west in developing and introducing cleaner methods to burn coal efficiently (CCICED, 2006). Secondly, foreign aid constitutes a major source of funding for China's environmental management projects — the country has received billions of US dollars in the form of loans and subsidies for environmental improvements projects in the past two decades. In 2002, for instance, Japan and South Korea offered financial assistance to China to help combat the problem of sandstorm hazards, which has turned into an international, cross-boundary, environmental ill affecting the ambient air quality over a wide region in North-east Asia. China's enthusiasm in support of the ratification of the Kyoto Protocol was driven in a large part by the financial benefits it has received — under the framework of Clean Development Mechanism — in the form of substantial amount of emissions reduction credits sold to industries in the west. Thirdly, China embraces international cooperation in environmental protection because it has helped open up business opportunities for the country's fledging environmental technology industry. This is particularly true for the clean energy and technology sector. For instance, China has become a leading global producer and a major exporter of solar panels since the mid 2000's.

Since China was conferred the title of the "world's factory" at the turn of the century, the country's development model was increasingly scrutinized and branded as unsustainable by critics. In addition, after China became the world's largest emitter of greenhouse gases in 2006, it faced escalating pressure from the west to commit itself fully to the global climate protection agenda and to agree to an absolute carbon reduction target. Confronted by such international demands, China's earlier position of passive compliance with international agreements has been gradually replaced, in the second half of the 2000's, by an assertive activist stance in the global arena. This assertive posture is the most prominent in regard to the global debate on how to share the responsibilities for climate protection between developed and developing countries.

China's assertive and active mode of exchange with the west, in relation to the international carbon agenda, was driven by its perceived unfairness in how the country has been criticized for its increased emissions of greenhouse gases. The rebuttal put forward by the Chinese government runs along the following arguments. First, the increased carbon emissions recorded on China's territory ensue mostly from industrial production transplanted from the west to China. This relocation of manufacturing industry constitutes, in effect, an export of a large portion of the west's carbon footprint to the People's Republic (Ang, 2007). Western countries are therefore hypocritical in criticizing China for increased emissions when they are investing in industrial production in China and, at the same time, reaping the benefits of such industrial investment in the form of low-cost manufactured imports.

Secondly, while total emissions in China have gone up, they were still less than one-quarter of those of the United States on a per capita basis. China, with a population of 1.3 billion people, released 4,760 kg of carbon dioxide on a per capita basis in 2007. Compared to the United State's per capita emission figure of 19,280 kg, Chinese officials have thus argued that the country's per capita emission was still relatively low (Chang, 2007). Thirdly, China should not be asked to impose a cap on its carbon dioxide emissions because it was, under the 1997 Kyoto Protocol, considered a developing country and was therefore exempted from emission reduction. She has, instead, committed to the principle of "common but differentiated responsibilities" in mitigating climate change (PBL Netherlands Environmental Assessment Agency, 2007). Fourthly, an objective assessment of China's overall GHG emissions, as some Chinese government officials have claimed, should take into consideration such broader parameters as historical contribution to current carbon concentration. International comparisons of total cumulative carbon emissions have shown that, measured on a historical per-capita basis, China is ranked at the 78th place in the world, not the first (Watts, 2009).

Resisting the call to enforce mandatory emission caps on its greenhouse gases, China's clearly articulated position on the global carbon debate therefore conveys a new-found sense of confidence in international negotiations over environmental governance matters. Asserting that the international community should respect the developing countries' "right to develop," Chinese government officials have repeatedly argued that the burden for protecting climate should rest with the rich industrialized countries (BBC News, 2007). Specifically, China wanted developed nations to commit to more ambitious reduction targets, to share low-carbon technology with developing countries, and to set up a UN fund that would help finance the purchasing cost of related intellectual property rights for use across the globe (Watts, 2009).

In 2007, China officials, in unveiling the country's first national program to combat climate change, claimed that China was taking a "positive and earnest" attitude toward this global concern (Chang, 2007). Devoid of specific targets for absolute reduction of GHG emissions though, China's broad climate protection strategy entailed energy conservation measures, programs to extend forest coverage and family planning policies to slow down population growth. The principal thrust of the strategy was energy-oriented: low-carbon energy sources — such as renewable energy and nuclear energy — were promoted, and improving energy efficiency — in both industrial and agricultural sectors — was emphasized (National Development and Reform Commission, 2007b.

In preparation for intensive international negotiations over climate change at the 2009 Copenhagen Conference, China then announced its decision to reduce the intensity of carbon dioxide emissions per unit of GDP in 2020 by 40–45% compared with 2005 levels. However, it has continued to oppose the imposition of any legally binding emission reduction targets on the developing countries. Given China's insistence that it needs to be granted reasonable carbon emission quotas to allow its economy to continue to grow, in pace with the twin processes of rapid industrialization and urbanization, and given that the "high carbon" character inherent in China's energy structure would not be fundamentally altered in the short term, the carbon question will in all likelihood remain a highly contentious international environmental governance issue between China and the west in the years to come.

7. Conclusion

China's overall environmental conditions have continued to deteriorate despite the promulgation of plenty of environmental laws and regulations, the setting up of ambitious environmental targets and the commitment of an ever increasing amount of financial resources earmarked for environmental protection. The failure to produce tangible improvements, despite of decades of efforts to arrest environmental decline, stems primarily from the problems of ineffectual implementation at the local level. Very often, the effectiveness of many well-intentioned and well-structured environmental projects was vastly reduced by local governments' passive resistance. The collapse of the "Green GDP" campaign, launched by SEPA in 2005, was a vivid example of how local officials, driven solely by their own self-interests, torpedoed a central government-sponsored environmental initiative.

Public health, in recent years, has been subject to an increasingly higher level of environmental risk because of a rising number of cases of pollution accidents. For instance, 131 environmental accidents were officially recorded in the first eight months of 2010, far exceeding the total number of such cases in 2009. A great number of industrial enterprises were highly vulnerable to environmental accidents because they were, to begin with, poorly equipped in pollution control, their pollution treatment facilities were mostly left in idle, and their management capacity to deal with pollution accidents was limited. But this high risk situation was aggravated by the lax enforcement of pollution control and industrial safety regulations. Many major pollution accidents were usually administratively handled, greatly undermining the deterrent effect of environmental regulations and associated criminal provisions. Consequently, non-compliance in the industrial sector has been widespread — and this was the major cause of the frequent occurrence of environmental accidents.

Taken together, weak implementation and lax enforcement tell us that the key problem lies with local officials, who have not been given the right kinds of incentives to place a higher priority on environmental protection. Many of them invariably turn a blind eye to serious environmental pollution problems out of self-interest and siphon off environmental protection funds to unrelated, illegitimate projects that do not benefit the environment. The crucial step that needs to be taken to improve China's environment therefore goes beyond acquiring the state-of-the-art pollution-control technologies, for instance; it should, instead, entail a fundamental reform of the political and bureaucratic culture to allow a reformulated incentive structure to entice local officials to pay equal — if not more — attention to environmental protection, vis-à-vis economic growth. In this regard, the government must loosen the restrictions it has placed on the most potent force for environmental change — the budding environmental NGO sector and its allies in the media — and allow them to play an increasingly active role as environmental watchdog at the local level.

References

Ang, A. (2007) China tops US in carbon emissions: Researchers cite industrial growth. *The Boston Globe.*

BBC News (2007) China unveils climate change plan. *BBC News.* Retrieved from http://news.bbc.co.uk/2/hi/6717671.stm

CCICED (2006) Report of study team on a review of China's environment and development. Retrieved from http://www.cciced.org/2008-02/26/content_10729090.htm

Chang, A. (2007) China: Rich nations wrong to criticize its CO_2 emissions while buying its products. *Insurance Journal*. Retrieved from http://www.insurance-journal.com/news/international/2007/06/22/81037.htm

Cooper, C. M. (2006) 'This is our way in': The civil NGOs in South-West China. *Government and Opposition*, 41(1), 109–136.

Economy, E. (2004) *The river runs black: The environmental challenge to China's future*. Ithaca, NY: Cornell University Press.

Edmonds, R. L. (1994) *Patterns of China's lost harmony*. London: Routledge.

Guangzhou Environmental Protection Office (1991) *Integrated environmental management in Guangzhou*. Guangzhou: Guangzhou Environmental Protection Office. In Chinese.

Harris, P. G. (2006) Environmental perspectives and behavior in China: Synopsis and bibliography. *Environment and Behavior*, 38(1), 5–21.

He, Z. (1997) Discussion on discharge fee system. In C. W. H. Lo and Z. Q. Wu (Eds.), *Occasional paper series on environmental law and environmental management in Guangzhou, Hong Kong, and Macau*, pp. 117–126. Beijing: China Environmental Science Press.

Ho, P. (2001) Greening without conflict? Environmentalism, NGOs and civil society in China. *Development and Change*, 32, 893–921.

International Energy Conservation Environmental Protection Association (2010). Suming, Deputy Director of Research Institute for Fiscal Science: Formulate financial policy to facilitate energy conservation and environmental protection. Retrieved from http://www.ieepa.net/news/html/20100810170617.html [in Chinese].

Jahiel, A. R. (1997) The contradictory impact of reform on environmental protection in China. *The China Quarterly*, 149, 81–103.

Jahiel, A. R. (1998) The organization of environmental protection in China. *The China Quarterly*, 156, 757–787.

Jie, Z. H. (1997) Publicity and education are the basic tasks of environmental protection. *Environmental Protection*, 2, 2–4 [in Chinese].

Lee, Y. S. F. (2005) Public environmental consciousness in China: Early empirical evidence. In K. A. Day (Ed.), *China's environment and the challenge of sustainable development*, pp. 35–65. New York: M. E. Sharpe.

Liu, M. S. (1998) State councillor song on harness of Huaihe river. *Beijing Review*, 41(1), 15.

Lo, C. W. H. (1992) Law and administration in Deng's China: Legalization of the administration of environmental protection. *Review of Central and East European Law*, 18(6), 453–473.

Lo, C. W. H. and S. Y. Tang (1994) Institutional contexts of environmental management: Water pollution control in Guangzhou. *Public Administration and Development*, 14(1), 53–64.

Lo, C. W. H., S. Y. Tang and S. K. Chan (1997) The political economy of EIA in Guangzhou. *Environmental Impact Assessment Review,* 17, 371–382.

Lu, Y. Y. (2007) Environmental civil society and governance in China. *International Journal of Environmental Studies,* 64(1), 59–69.

Ministry of Environmental Protection (2009). 2008 Report on China's environmental status. Retrieved from http://jcs.mep.gov.cn/hjzl/zkgb/2008zkgb/200906/t20090609_152536.htm [in Chinese].

Ministry of Environmental Protection (2010) 2009 report on China's environmental status. Retrieved from http://jcs.mep.gov.cn/hjzl/zkgb/2009hjzkgb/201006/t20100603_190428.htm [in Chinese].

National Bureau of Statistics, & Ministry of Environmental Protection (2008) *China Statistical yearbook on environment 2008.* Beijing: China Statistics Press.

National Development and Reform Commission (2007a) Pollution discharge fee system in China. Retrieved from http://www.sdpc.gov.cn/jggl/jgqk/t20070404_126543.htm [in Chinese].

National Development and Reform Commission (2007b) China's national climate change programme. Retrieved from http://www.ccchina.gov.cn/WebSite/CCChina/UpFile/File189.pdf [in Chinese].

PBL Netherlands Environmental Assessment Agency (2007) Chinese CO_2 emissions in perspective. Retrieved from http://www.pbl.nl/en/news/pressreleases/2007/20070622ChineseCO2emissionsinperspective.html.

People's Daily (2001) Report on the tenth five-year Plan of China. Retrieved from http://www.people.com.cn/GB/historic/0315/5920.html [in Chinese].

Ross, L. (1988) *Environmental policy in China.* Bloomington and Indianapolis: Indiana University Press.

Shi, J. T. (2009) Carbon debate creates climate for China's civil society to grow. *South China Morning Post.*

Sinkule, B. J. and L. Ortolano (1995). *Implementing environmental policy in China.* London: Praeger.

Smil, V. (1993) *China's Environmental Crisis: an Inquiry into the Limits of National Development.* Armonk: M. E. Sharpe.

Stalley, P. and D. N. Yang (2006) An emerging environmental movement in China? *The China Quarterly* (186), 333–356.

State Environmental Protection Administration (2008) 2008 Report on China' environmental status. Retrieved from http://jcs.mep.gov.cn/hjzl/zkgb/2008zkgb/200906/t20090609_152536.htm [in Chinese].

Tang, S. Y., C. P. Tang and C. W. H. Lo (2005). Public participation and environmental impact assessment in Mainland China, Taiwan: Political foundations of environmental management. *The Journal of Development Studies,* 41(1), 1–32.

Tang, S. Y. and X. Y. Zhan (2008) Civic environmental NGOs, civil society, and democratisation in China. *Journal of Development Studies*, 44(3), 425–448.

Tenth five-year plan of China on economic and societal development (2001). *Hubei Politics*, 5, 6–19 [in Chinese].

Turner, J. L. and L. Zhi (2006) Building a green civil society in China. In L. Starke (Ed.), *State of the world 2006: A worldwatch institute report on progress toward a sustainable society*, pp. 152–170. New York and London: W.W. Norton & Company.

Watts, J. (2009) China ready for post-Kyoto deal on climate change. *Guardian*. Retrieved from http://www.guardian.co.uk/environment/2009/may/06/china-seeks-climate-change-deal

Wen, J. B. (2008) Progress report on the Chinese government, Retrieved from http://www.gov.cn/gongbao/content/2006/content_268766.htm. In Chinese.

Wong, K. K. (2010) Environmental awareness, governance and public participation: public perception perspectives. *International Journal of Environmental Studies*, 67(2), 169–181.

Xinhua (2010) Interpretation of NPC report 2010. Retrieved from http://www.gov.cn/2010lh/content_1550071.htm [in Chinese].

Yang, G. B. (2005) Environmental NGOs and institutional dynamics in China. *The China Quarterly*, 181(46–66).

Ye, L. (1997) Shanghai restores Suzhou River. *Beijing Review*, 40(35), 22–23.

Yuan, F. (1999) A survey on Chinese residents' environmental consciousness in Beijing and Shanghai. In X. L. Xi and Q. H. Xu (Eds.), *A survey on China's public environmental consciousness*, pp. 109–130. Beijing: China Environmental Science Press.

Zhang, K. M. (1997) Sustainable development and China. *China Environmental Management*, 2, 4–7 [in Chinese].

Zhu, R. J. (2001) Report on the tenth five-year Plan of China. *China Politics*, 4(27–28) [in Chinese].

* The research for this chapter is partially funded by the project "Changes in the Enforcement of Environmental Regulations in China: A Longitudinal Study of Environmental Enforcement Officials in Three Cities" of The Research Grants Council of the Hong Kong Special Administrative Region (RGC No.: Poly U 5469/10H).

9

URBANIZATION

Fulong Wu*

Cardiff University

Abstract

This paper examines urban development in China through the perspective of economic restructuring. First a review of the establishment of an export-oriented economy and its institutional foundation *vis-à-vis* fiscal and land policies. Then an examination of the basic characteristics of the world's factory model and how it defines the process of urbanization and urban development. Comparisons of contrasting spatial forms of upper market commodity housing estates and migrants' villages point toward a hybrid urban form that essentially reflects the contradiction of the world's factory regime. Finally some speculations about the transition of the world's factory regime and the impact of recent global economic crisis on China's urban development.

Keywords: The Chinese city; economic development; economic restructuring; housing development; land development; the impact of global economic crisis.

The process of Chinese urbanization had been slow, driven by state-led industrialization until 1979 when the economic reform started. The slow urbanization process is a deliberate strategy to "economize urbanization" (Chan, 1994), namely to achieve industrialization without urbanization because consumption under the specific state industrial development regime was regarded as wasteful and unproductive (Wu, 1997). This resulted in a phenomenon of "under-urbanization," similar to the one seen in other

* The author would like to acknowledge the support from ESRC/DFID research grant (RES-167-25-0448).

Table 1.   The speed of urbanization in China

Periods	Annual increase of urban and town population (million)	Percentage point added to the urbanization level (% point) per year
1981–1985	11.91	0.86
1986–1990	10.20	0.54
1991–1995	9.96	0.53
1996–2000	21.46	1.44
2001–2005	20.61	1.35
2006–2009	14.94	0.90

Source: CNSB, various years; Wei (2010, p. 3).

Central and Eastern European countries. Before 1979 the ratio of urban population to the total population was maintained below 19%. Since 1996, Chinese urbanization has entered a fast growth period, averaging at 1.25% point per year, raising the ratio of urban population to 46.6% in 2009 (Wei, 2010) (Table 1), although the exact rate and speed of urbanization in China is a complicated issue that depends on the spatial definition of urban and rural areas (see Zhou and Ma, 2003; Chan, 2010a).

The post-reform urbanization process is characterized by increasing dominance of large cities in the urban system. This is attributed to some basic features of Chinese urbanization (Chan, 2010a). First, China operates a hierarchical top-down policy control, despite significant devolution of economic decision making to lower government. The higher the position in the hierarchy is, the more powerful the ability to capture mobile resources. Second, the appointment of local officials is made by the upper levels of government. Because of this top-down control and the switch of the evaluation to economic performance in the process of cadre appointment, local officials strive to fulfil economic targets, expand the economic scales of their localities, and elevate their localities in the hierarchy of the administrative system. By doing so, local officials can accumulate political capital to get promoted. There is then a very strong growth mentality. We will further argue that such a growth mentality is more deeply rooted in an exported-oriented approach to urban and economic development.

The End of Constrained Urbanization

China's economic reform originated from the rural sector. The land contract system released a significant amount of redundant agricultural laborers and started the wave of rural urbanization in the 1980s. Such an urbanization process, referred to as "urbanization from below" (Ma and Fan, 1994), is different from the one driven by state-led industrialization in the planned economy. Essentially, rural urbanization is driven by the process of the development of non-agricultural activities in the rural area. The release of agricultural labor force was absorbed through *in situ* rural manufacturing development, creating a phenomenon of "leaving the land but not the village." Behind rural urbanization is the development of township and village enterprises (TVEs). In the Yangtze River Delta (especially southern Jiangsu), TVEs formed the base of the rural collective economy, while in Zhejiang province (particularly in southern area near Wenzhou), privately owned small enterprises were behind rural industrialization (thus known as the "Wenzhou model"), and in the Pearl River Delta, overseas investment from Hong Kong promoted so-called "exo-urbanization" (Sit and Yang, 1997). The development of rural small towns created the dual-track urbanization in China (Shen *et al.*, 2006): on the one hand, there has been a tendency of dominance of large cities under the formal urbanization process combined with state project and foreign capital (Lin, 2002); on the other hand, dispersed urbanization process created many small towns and special market towns. Since 2005, the new wave of constructing the "new countryside" began to extend infrastructure to the rural area, with the attempt to consolidate and merge scattered villages into designated towns.

Such a rural urbanization process came to an end when massive privatization of rural collectives occurred. Privatization picked up momentum since the mid-1990s, and fundamentally changed the nature of the earlier "Sunan model" which ceased to exist (Shen and Ma, 2005). The TVEs virtually collapsed after pervasive ownership transformation (*zhuan zhi*). Replacing this endogenous urbanization is large-scale land development driven by foreign investment. Industrial parks are developed to serve foreign and overseas investors. Accompanying the collapse of rural collectives is the demise of village level governance and up-scaling of control to the central towns and cities. The low efficiency of scattered rural industrialization, namely "leaving the land but not the village," was recognized. The newly established system of land leasing consolidated the power of municipalities and counties to forge large-scale development based on industrial zones. Since the late 1990s, there have been waves to establish industrial and export zones (Cartier, 2001), leading to large-scale land development (Hsing, 2006).

The Establishment of World's Factory and Dynamics of Urban Development

China's joining WTO symbolizes the establishment of the world's factory regime, which heavily depends upon foreign investment and export as the driver for economic growth. The export-oriented development has been remarkably effective, capitalizing China's comparative advantages of cheaper and abundant labor force and overcoming the constraints of capital and market. By achieving a status of world's factory, China has significantly expanded its production capacities. At the core of this world's factory regime are entrepreneurial local governments who play the role of development organizer. Through institutional devolution, they are becoming independent and self-motivated developers. The tax-sharing system effectively enforces local governments to expand their own tax revenue through "discretionary" land development, although land development is now increasingly subject to the central control through land quotas.

The dependence upon land revenue results in the so-called "fiscal regime based on land development" (*tudi caizheng*). Inter-city competition and incentive of land revenue dissolves possible local resistance, which is known as NIMBYism in Western developed economies. The legacy of strong state land control allows the local government to become the *de facto* land owner and developer who monopolizes the land supply. Using the instrument of cheaper land, entrepreneurial local governments strive to attract foreign and overseas investors. More precisely, in order to attract foreign capital in manufacturing sectors, the local government offers significant concession in land leasing premium. In the early 1990s, some cities even leased land at "zero value." In the densely developed area such as the Yangtze River Delta, competition for industrial investment has been particularly fierce (Zhang and Wu, 2006), leading to the net loss of value in land leasing because the actual cost of development exceeds the leasing fee. There are two explanations for this aggressive land leasing behavior. First, attracting foreign investment can ensure the increase in GDP, very much desired by local political leaders, because the promotion of local cadres is based on their performance in economic development (Chien, 2008). Second, the local government, while not getting a full land value from leasing of industrial land, can get the value-added tax and cooperate tax from manufacturing industries. This effectively converts once-for-all land leasing premium into a long-term source of revenue. However, under the current tax-sharing arrangement, the local government can only retain 25% of value-added tax and corporate tax (Tao *et al.*, 2009). Land leasing through the "spill-over effect," i.e., the development of industries promoting urban development, increases the retail sale tax and commercial and residential land value, while the retail sale tax and the premium of land leasing stay local entirely. The inflated commercial and residential land values can greatly expand the local revenue which is now heavily dependent upon the land leasing fee.

Thus the local government operates very much like a land development corporation. The land development business includes the following steps:

1. use cheap and subsidized land to attract investment in manufacturing industries;
2. expand the overall GDP volume and in turn raise the land value of the city through industrial development;
3. lease the serviced land to commercial and residential markets through auction or biding so as to capture the differentiate rent between leased land and rural land;
4. use the land revenue to invest in infrastructure while filling the local tax gap;
5. acquire rural land through compulsory purchase at a lower value and convert the required rural land into serviced land so as to raise the land value and attract investment, leading to a premium price for commercial and residential development.

To complete the above circle of development, the local government needs the labor force for industrial development. Under the urban-rural duality, the cost of rural labor is suppressed, because the rural labor is confined to the traditional agricultural sector, and the supply of migrant labor is relatively abundant. The arrival of capital in the locality means that the migrant labor force is almost automatically made available and brought into the production process without much difficulty until recent migrant labor shortage. Migrants are not entitled to the welfare provided in the urban area and depend on the market for basic needs such as housing, education, and healthcare. The operation of world's factory means local governments are business-oriented, targeting the GDP growth rate and land revenue generation, while using sustained fast growth to ensure job creation and in turn maintaining social stability.

The migrant labor force, while physically working in the world's factory, is invisible in two ways: first, low incomes make them ineffective consumers. They are not, for example, the customers of commodity housing beyond their means. Most migrants live in private rental housing in so-called "urban villages," developed informally by local farmers based on their assigned plots for farmers' housing. Second, they are not active citizens and have no voting rights. Because cheaper land supply is used as an instrument to attract investment and promote growth, the result is inevitably over-consumption of agricultural land, leading to scattered and sprawled growth patterns. Rather than developing a compact city as the Chinese city was in the past, new urban development is characterized by massive expansion of the built-up areas. In rapidly industrializing areas, urban development literally takes the form of factory building with large parcels and wide grid roads. To justify the speed of growth, often exceeding the national standard of city planning, local governments organize and prepare non-statutory plans such as urban conceptual or strategic development, which often propose the development of new towns or new districts. Through administrative annexation, the municipality strives to expand its control over the rest of its city-region, forming so-called "urban clusters" or the system of cities.

The dynamics of urban development rely on the land development as the driver. Figure 1 shows the total land leased on the market from 1995–2009. It can be seen that since 2001 the amount of land leased has increased steadily, despite the tightening policy in 2004, which reduced the total amount of land leasing in that year and 2005. However, in 2006, the land leasing area increased significantly. Despite a dip in 2008 in the midst of financial crisis, land leasing started to increase again under the demand for land under the stimulus package. All these account only for the formal land market. In fact, despite the control of the central government over land leasing and establishment of development zones, local governments attempt to develop various "new district" or "reform experiment zones." The illegal land conversion has been widespread.

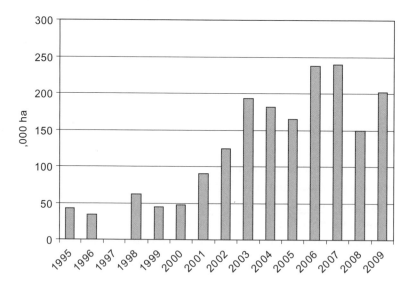

Figure 1. The total amount of land leasing in China, 1995–2009

Source: China State Land Administration Bureau (1996–1997); China Ministry of Land and Resources (1999–2005), China Ministry of Land and Resources (2010).

Fragmented Spatial Form

Contemporary urban transformation in the Western developed economies has produced a fragmented spatial form. According to Dear and Flusty (1998), the classic concentric zones model of Chicago School can no longer describe the spatial form of post-industrial cities like Los Angeles. They describe this new spatial form as the pattern of "postmodern urbanism," characterized by sharp contrasts between different residential forms such as "gated communities" and "ethnoburb" with concentrated transnational immigrants. Greater diversity and fragmentation are major features of postmodern urbanism because new developments are "occurring on a quasi-random field of opportunities" (p. 66), brought about by flexible accumulation rather than a Fordist approach of large-scale industrial development. While this characterization of contemporary urban space is still subject to debate, there is a general consensus that the new urban form sees higher heterogeneity and spatial juxtaposition and division, described by concepts such as "quartered city" or "layered city" (Marcuse, 1997).

The spatial form of Chinese cities under the world's factory regime shares some similarity with fragmented postmodern urbanism in the West. But the underlying logic might be different (Ma and Wu, 2005), because the Chinese cities continue to be affected by path-dependent processes left behind from state socialism. Still, they see crowded streets and migrant settlements commonly found in the developing world. On the other hand, elitist consumption space represented by luxurious and often western-looking villas, glittering shopping malls, supermarkets, office buildings, and new economic space of high-tech and financial clusters are built, transforming the skyline of contemporary Chinese cities. Thus, the Chinese cities see both the elements of the "First World" and the "Third World" mixed in a short spatial distance. For example, in suburbs, the most luxurious gated communities can be juxtaposed next to the poorest "urban villages" with concentrated migrants (Huang, 2005). In the central area elite consumption and entertainment districts such as Xintiandi in Shanghai contrasts sharply with dilapidated and shanty areas inherited from the pre-1949 era which perhaps experienced little changes in the last six decades despite rapid urban transformation. Figure 2 shows such juxtaposed spaces in Shanghai, China's most globalized city. These landscapes could not be labeled by any singular category.

The strategy of establishing the world's factory effectively turns the rural-urban dualism under state socialism into a new dualism within the city, namely between urban households having permanent urban registration

Figure 2. Juxtaposed spaces in Shanghai

status and migrant workers who are not entitled to the "right to the city" but reside in urban areas. According to the National Statistical Bureau which organized a major survey at the end of 2008 (www.gov.cn, 29 March 2009), there were a total of 225.42 million rural migrant workers, among whom 140.41 million worked outside the local township and towns, accounting for 62.3% of the total. In the narrow sense, these 140.41 million rural migrants are truly migrant population outside their local places and most likely live in the large cities. The capacity to govern a huge migrant population without granting their equal entitlements, while maintaining a relatively stable social order, is much attributed to the authoritarian past as well as enhanced efforts of "community construction" which rebuilt grass root (neighborhood) governance (Friedmann, 2007). Such a new dualism is physically manifested as startlingly different neighborhoods.

Chinese Informal Settlement: Urban Villages (*chengzhongcun*)

Chinese cities may not have a problem of prevalent slums in South Asia or *favela* in Latin America. However, the migrant population apparently concentrates in the peri-urban area (Wu, 2006). They are accommodated in the rural villages encroached by the urban built-up areas. These villages are known as "urban villages" (*chengzhongcun*), which is the Chinese version of informal settlements, because villagers built their own houses in a spontaneous way, which is quite different from commodity housing development because the land of village development is not acquired by state ownership. The housing developed by villagers either individually or collectively could not be sold in the market, because it is not legally recognized, and thus the deed for the property could not be obtained from the land register. In this sense, the housing developed in urban villages is "informal," mainly for private rental, and in most cases a formal contract between the landlord and tenant is not deemed necessary. The construction is often possible because of the lax development control in the rural area where the formal management of city planning has not been strong.

What defines "urban villages" is not the concentration of migrants but the unique form of land ownership. In China, there are two basic forms of land ownership. In the city, land is owned by the state, while the land use right can be leased through the payment of land premium to the municipality (Yeh and Wu, 1996). In the rural area, land is collectively owned, while the plot of housing site is assigned to the farmer household. Only those who bear the status of rural household registration can have an entitlement to a housing plot known as *zhaijidi*. Rapid urban expansion engulfed former rural villages. To save the cost of compensation, village land was left out, while the farmland was acquired in the process of land requisition. As a result, urban development encircled the sites of village (typically used by farmers as their housing plots), forming an island of collective ownership land in the state land. Urban villages are characterized by chaotic land uses and extremely high building coverage (Zhang *et al.*, 2003). Individual households extend their buildings up to the boundaries of land plot because they want to maximize the use of space. Migrant workers are excluded from the mainstream public housing provision. Since they are unable to afford formally built commodity housing, they usually live in urban villages. Private rental housing in urban villages provide affordable accommodation to migrants. Renting housing to migrants brings about a steady income to local farmers. However, public facilities lack proper investment and maintenance as urban villages are essentially a place under "private governance" (Webster, 2002), although there is no gate or access restriction. These villages are not maintained and serviced by the municipal government. They are generally over-built in terms of building coverage, resulting in narrow alleys, unpaved and often filthy streets. The poor conditions of some urban villages, especially their infrastructure, may resemble that of slums or *favela* in Latin America. However, one important difference is that dwellers in the Chinese urban villages are job active, and often work in the formal sector of the global economy (Wu, 2009). They may have a low educational attainment but are the basic labor force for the labor-intensive export industry.

The current practice of urban village redevelopment is to demolish the whole village to give way to real estate investment. There have been some differences in the redevelopment approach: for example, Zhuhai in southern China adopted a more proactive model to allow villagers to share land revenue, whereas Guangzhou controlled redevelopment through government-led reconstruction (Tian, 2008). But redevelopment practices are more and more following Guangdong way of so-called "redevelopment of three olds" (*san jiu gaizhao*), namely the redevelopment of "old villages, old factories and old urban areas." The main motivation of the redevelopment approach is to speed up the process of redevelopment through compensating villagers with the property in the redeveloped village area, namely villagers can receive *in situ* property of equivalent space of demolished housing, and the village retains the newly developed commercial space as the collective asset. The initiative of redevelopment is now decentralized to individual villages which are allowed to set up their own development companies. They could either cooperate with real estate developers or redevelop the area by themselves. Part of the redeveloped area is thus converted into state land on which commodity housing and commercial buildings can be built, with which buyers can receive their deeds. While part of the space retains collective ownership, through the repayment to the land leasing premium at a discount price later, villagers are allowed to convert their properties into commodity housing. The consequence of this policy is that it removes the resistance of villagers to redevelopment, which has been widespread because the municipal government monopolizes the supply in the primary land market and captures the differential rent between collectively-owned rural land and the price of leased land. Through this scheme of redevelopment, investment in the redeveloped site helps to develop relocated housing on the site and villagers are allowed to retain the revenue generated from village redevelopment. The policy effectively expands the land supply, because in the Pearl River Delta, the protection of agricultural land and excessive construction of urban areas in the past have led to the shortage of land for the new round of development. The government may also use this policy to upgrade the economic structure, since village redevelopment gradually erases the affordable housing for low-level migrants, making the city less attractive to the labor-intensive industries.

Packaged Suburbia and Gated Communities

In contrast to the spontaneously self-built urban villages, Chinese new suburbs present an orderly and designed environment. The majority are commodity housing estates, following the concept of residential "micro-district" (*xiaoqu*). However, different from the preset technical norms in the socialist period, the design standards become more differentiated to suit different consumer groups (Wang and Murie, 2000). In a highly competitive market for commodity housing, developers try to invent various packaging and design tactics to boast that their products are unique and tailor-made for their customers, using "modern" (read "Western") design techniques. To attract upwardly mobile middle class who are more likely buying the commodity apartment or house as the second property in addition to their inner city apartment, often allocated by their workplaces, developers attempt to distinguish their products from the product of mass and collective consumption. This is particularly apparent in some upper market villa projects.

In the designed suburb, some developers adopt the idea of "new urbanism" in the US, specifically the neo-traditionalist urban design which emphasizes the cosy and compact residential environment of American small towns. What is selectively adopted in the Chinese version of "new urbanism" is not the compact form and small town atmosphere, but rather an elitist style of design, even to the extent of ostentatious, decorative "western"-style built forms (Wu, 2010). To be precise, these western styles are not in their authentic forms, but often a mixture and package of different styles (Wu, 2010). Many are built in gated communities and include club houses. Some even include amenities such as golf courses (Giroir, 2007).

Typically for upper-market villa compounds but also seen in commodity housing estates, developers use various tactics to beautify and package their projects (Wu, 2010). For example, they may create magnificent gates, even in a neoclassical and monumental style. These gates are not just for security, as they do in the gated communities of the US. Disproportionate in size and often over-designed, these gates serve as a label for their products, very much similar to the package of commodities. For many projects, they also use foreign architectural styles, often mimicking European houses to present a chic outlook. The most popular is so-called "continental European" style (*oulu shi*). In extreme cases, the whole residential area could be packaged into a particular style. For example, in Songjiang new town, about 40 minutes by metro to the city proper of Shanghai, a micro residential district, literally a master-planned community called "Thames Town," is constructed in an English style. Similarly, using foreign or exotic names is another tactic to signify otherwise nameless greenfield where these projects are usually built. We then have a collection of strange names for these residential places such as Napa Valley, McAllen, Fontainebleau, Yosemite, Orange County, and Rivera. While these places have their "foreign names," they usually have their translated Chinese versions. Often, the Chinese names do not bear any resemblance to the foreign places, but the purpose is to use complex and unusual place names, to project a sense of sophistication and taste.

Ironically, while the property-led development dismantles traditional neighborhoods, developers sell the vision of "community life" to property-buyers. Following the discourse of "new urbanism," the developers claim that there is a vibrant community behind the gate. They attempt to depict suburbia as a home within communities. In reality, these places have been built for a very limited time and are not "memorable places" (Tomba, 2005, p. 939). Social network and interaction have not been fully formed. A major obstacle to the community building is that many homeowners are actually not living in these places. Many are the buyers of second or third property. In an interview in Shanghai's Songjiang new town in July 2010, we were told that most buyers are in the range of owning the third and fourth property in Thames Town. No wonder the place is quiet and used by art studios for wedding photos. However, there is a common interest bonding homebuyers — homeownership and property value. Initially encouraged by the government, homeowners associations are set up because these gated communities are under "private governance" (Webster, 2002; Webster *et al.*, 2005), managed by property management companies rather than municipal utility services department.

The emergence of homeowners association transforms neighborhood governance which was traditionally dominated by residents' committees (Read, 2003). In the process of rebuilding territorial communities, the role of residents' committees has been strengthened. Now, the homeowners association opens up a new self-governed space for residents. In upper market estates, we witness a waning role of traditional governance approach by quasi-government residents' committees. In the recent dispute of green space preservation and environmental protection in some gated communities, the homeowners association plays a vital role to resist the decision by the developer. Because of this rising role of self-governed organization, the attitude of government about the homeowners association became ambiguous; Out of concern over the power of homeowners' association, the government tries to define the role of homeowners association strictly in the sphere of property management rather than social management or mobilization. On the other hand, to cope with rising social mobility, the government strengthens community management through professional social workers and cadres. Small residents' committees are consolidated and merged into larger *shequ* (community) committees, and the appointment of carders is formalized. As a result, for residential management, we see a shift from governance composed of the volunteers from retired people and housewives living locally to formally appointed and professional cadres forming a formal tier of governance with an allocated administrative budget.

As a general trend, the Chinese city sees greater diversity in terms of landscapes and heterogeneity in terms of social composition and governance. The startling difference between organic and chaotic urban villages and designed and packaged suburban gated communities reflect the underlying mechanism of the world's factory regime and social inequalities. Such a regime utilizes low-cost migrant workers to forge production capacities, while giving a mean-tested wage to the labor force and forcing them to live under a cost-minimizing livelihood. At the same time, this approach generates trade surplus and foreign exchange reserve. With the expectation of inflation and currency appreciation, surplus capital flows into real estate, boosting land values. The upwardly mobile middle class, despite the pressure of house price inflation, benefits from the development of world's factory and property value appreciation, and are eager to pursue a good life. Such a passion for private car and designed homes suits the local government well in its entrepreneurial endeavor to improve the image of the city and raise land revenue from property development.

Uprooted Urban Society

The Chinese society has been remarkably stable. Fei Xiaotong, a renowned Chinese sociologist, attributes this stability to its social structure. He describes rural China as an "earth-bounded" society (Fei, 1992), because people are related with each other through close but "differentiated associations" ranging from the inner circle of the family, to outer circle of extended family, further to the ring of villagers. The dense social networks knits Chinese peasants into a self-governance web. Such a feature has been inherited and preserved even in the socialist period, through state work-units which organize collective consumption. These work-units, including enterprises and public institutions, are more than production units or workplaces. They are "total social entities" carrying out social provision, housing development and distribution, political mobilization and social management (Whyte and Paris, 1984). The result is the so-called "communist neo-traditionalism" (Walder, 1986), or the "totalitarian society" (Sun, 2004) in which the "state controls the economy and monopolizes all social resources; and politics, society and ideology are highly overlapped with each other" (Sun, 2004, p. 31). In the cities, this feature of totalitarianism was strengthened by state housing provision combined with state-led industrialization.

The development of work-unit compounds combining workplace and living place was common practices, resulting under-differentiated social spaces in urban China. Residential differentiation was more based on occupations (Yeh *et al.*, 1995) rather than social classes. Only after the housing reform, tenure inequalities began to shape residential differentiation based on housing tenures (Li and Wu, 2008).

This self-contained pattern of urban development is broken in the process of transformation from state-led industrialization to establishing a world's factory regime. Large-scale rural to urban migration not only allows peasants to abandon agricultural activities but also forces them to leave the rural society and become "sojourners" in the cities. Such a process is "incomplete urbanization" (Chan, 2010a), because traditional rural population has not been completely urbanized and many migrants are in the status of "temporary" migration without urban welfare and other benefits in the cities. Because of the costs of childcare, education and housing, many migrants live in the dormitory and leave their families behind. Because of family separation and absence of normal family life, migrants often experience anxiety and loneliness. The outflow of younger labor force has left behind older and weaker rural population as well as women and children. The gender imbalance results in unstable family and social relations, eroding the feature of "earth-bounded society."

In terms of residential mobility, migrants mainly live in private rental housing and follow the available job. When they return to the countryside during the Spring Festival, they do not normally keep their rented room, because they have few possessions and uncertainty in jobs, and it is always possible to find alternative rental housing. The informal rental market plus job instability mean that their residence cannot be permanent. Although migrants tend to cluster on the basis of their place of origin (Zhang, 2001; Ma and Xiang, 1998), these villages are different from an established rural villages bounded by long-term social relations. Although the rural village is integrated through family ties or "differentiated associations" as described by Fei (1992), the "urban villages" are divided between original villagers and new arrivals. While original villagers belong to the proprietor class and are entitled to the village share-hold company which controls village collective assets, migrants are excluded from any claim to benefits from village development. The situation is the same for other places such as old urban areas and workplace compounds where new migrants have no membership or entitlement. This institutional exclusion led to the rootless status of migrants. No matter how long they have been living in the community, they are still sojourners. This enforced nature of "sojourner," on the other hand, hinders migrant population from developing social capital. Rather, they adopt a cost-saving approach and try to reduce the living costs and maximize savings. They willingly tolerate poor living conditions and send remittances back to the countryside.

Massive urban redevelopment also transformed traditional urban neighborhoods. In the socialist period, as an inferior type of public housing belonging to the municipality rather than state owned enterprises, traditional neighborhoods had limited resource to maintain their services and over time saw deterioration of housing conditions and service facilities. Through the formal channels such as job recruitment and university education, residents with better human capital were absorbed by the state sector. Since housing reform, a new channel appeared through the housing market. Richer residents moved out from these neighborhoods by purchasing commodity housing and relocated to suburbs. Accompanying this spontaneous relocation is enforced demolition and relocation. Property and infrastructure development razed many traditional neighborhoods into garish high-rise office buildings, shopping malls, hotels and luxury apartments (Friedmann, 2007). But long before large-scale real estate development, the development of larger modern residential districts already transformed close neighboring of residents in the old city. The design of compartmentalized units reduces physical interaction between neighbors, compared with the ample shared space in traditional courtyard housing such as *hutong*. With the demolition of old housing and the development of new apartments, the Chinese cities are experiencing important changes in social characteristics. The traditional method of social control, namely *hukou* registration, becomes less effective. Thousands of residents who moved to the new suburb still maintain their place of registration in the matured urban areas because the services such as schooling are better there, creating a unique phenomenon of discrepancy between the registered place and actual place of living (known as the "people and *hukou* separation," *renhu fenli*). The social complexity eventually leads to the breakdown of traditional society and the urban society is now being uprooted.

Constraints to the World's Factory and Post-crisis Urban Development

The Chinese growth regime relies on three critical elements: the overseas market guaranteed under WTO, the state's capacity to govern, and the abundant low-cost labor force. The global economic crisis has significantly changed the first element. There has been a slowing down of Western consumer markets. In the meantime, trade protectionism increases. Accompanying the protectionism is the pressure on China to reduce greenhouse gas emission. China has announced that by 2020 it will cut down the carbon dioxide emission intensity by 40 to 45% per GDP unit. To achieve the target requires some serious adjustment of economic structure and the change of the development approach. Now the target of achieving emission reduction is becoming a measurement of local government performance, in addition to the GDP growth rate, according to the local government officials we interviewed (June 2010).

As for the third element it is obvious that, the cheaper labor force may not be unlimited. The growth of labor force will end in 2017, according to Cai (2007), who argues that China is now witnessing the Lewis Turning Point. According to Lewis (1954), the developing economy is divided into traditional and modern sectors. Because of the dualism, the supply of surplus labor is almost unlimited, thus maintaining the labor cost to a stagnant level, until all surplus laborers are absorbed into the modern sector. After this point, the dual sectors are integrated into the modern economy in which labor costs increase along with economic growth. The evidence of labor cost increase might indicate the turning point of this economic integration. As early as 2004, the Pearl River Delta began to see migrant shortage, which spread over other places. The evidence of rising migrant workers' cost in 2009, according to Cai (2007), suggests that the agricultural sector could no longer release surplus labor for industrial development in the cities without incurring additional labor costs. However, whether there is a demographic change that renders a turning point to the Chinese economy is still subject to debate. In the post-crisis era, global trade imbalance, rising trade protectionism, the pressure to reduce greenhouse gas emission, and possible reduction in labor force mean that the growth regime of world's factory reaches serious constraints; and it is not possible to continue the current urban development approach. In the remainder of this chapter, three possible major trends that might bring challenges to existing urban development will be discussed.

Urban Development under the Pressure of Real Estate Boom

Prior to the global financial crisis, the Chinese economy had experienced a hyper capital liquidity problem. To control the excessive liquidity, the Chinese central bank raised the bank deposit requirement and baseline interest rates. A related move was the tightening of land management since 2004. The macroeconomic policies, while intended to address some structural problems of Chinese world's factory, namely redundant production capacities and low value-added growth, actually made the manufactory sector more difficult to cope with falling profit rates. Export-oriented industries were confronted with appreciation of renminbi currency and improved Labor Contract Law which allowed migrant workers to receive better compensation. In addition to the abolishment of agricultural tax in 2006, the incentive for migrant labors to work in the city had been reduced, resulting in so-called "migrant shortage," especially in the heartland of export industries in the Pearl River Delta. Before that, Chinese manufacturing industries tried to reduce labor cost while benefiting from various tax concession and preferential treatment made by the local government. The "worsening" production condition from rising interest rate, labor cost, and tightening land policy compelled some manufacturing industries to abandon production and shift the capital into the stock and real estate market. With the expectation of renminbi appreciation, international "hot money" found their ways into China and made indirect investments in the property markets. All these led to a highly volatile real estate market, which had experienced a property boom. Just prior to the global financial crisis in 2008, there was a real estate boom. Consequently, the government adopted economic tightening policies to prick the bubble. But the global financial crisis, started suddenly in mid-2008, interrupted the tightening policy. The fiscal policy turned from being tight to positive. The positive fiscal policy was intended to save the export-oriented manufacturing industries that were hit hard by the global downturn; the shift helped real estate developers to get out their strained capital chain.

Similar to the days after Asian financial crisis, housing development became a major economic driver in late 2008. The central government aimed to boost domestic demand. But instead of raising consumption capacity which has a highly distorted income distribution structure, the chosen measure was to expand investment in public works and infrastructure. A 4 trillion yuan ($586 billion) stimulus package boosted investment, but at the same time created a further imbalance between investment and consumption. The stimulus package made capital available before the recovery of the real economy. With injected capital liquidity, large state-owned enterprises began to aggressively bid for land, with the expectation of land appreciation. The involvement of large state-owned enterprises suddenly turned the sluggish property market into a V-shaped recovery. The property price experienced dramatic inflation in 2009. In the primary land leasing market, the price broke historical record in land sales, creating so-called premium land plots (*di wang*). With the constrained overseas market, capital shifted toward the built environment. In 2009, the total land premium reached 1.5 trillion Yuan ($224.8 billion). Hangzhou and Shanghai each leased more

Table 2. The land revenue and its percentage to budgetary local revenue in selected cities (2009)

City	Land revenue	Budgetary local revenue	The percentage of land revenue to the local revenue
Hangzhou	105.4	101.9	103.39
Shanghai	104.3	254.0	41.06
Beijing	92.8	202.7	45.79
Tianjin	73.2	n.a.	n.a.
Guangzhou	48.9	265.6	18.41
Ningbo	48.8	96.6	50.51
Chongqing	44.0	68.2	64.53
Wuhan	36.1	100.5	35.92
Chengdu	32.4	84.6	38.30
Xiamen	30.3	45.1	67.12

Source: Yuan, 2010: p.159; Xinhua News (www.xinhua.com: 10 Jan 2010).

than 100 billion Yuan, while Beijing and Tianjin leased 92.8 and 73.2 billion Yuan (Xinhua news, 10 Jan 2010; Yuan, 2010, p. 159). For 70 major large and medium cities, in 2009, 1,083 billion Yuan land premium were collected, a 140% increase than 2008.

Table 2 shows the land leasing revenue and the ratio of land leasing revenue to the budgetary revenue. For many cities, land revenue exceeds half of regular budgetary revenue, and land leasing and development become a major driver of local economic growth. The difficulty of maintaining overseas trade market, means that capital diversion to the real estate market will continue. It is very likely that urban development will be driven by real estate expansion in the post-crisis era, and not so much by foreign investment in manufacturing before the crisis.

From Urban Rural Dualism to Structured Social Exclusion

Migrant population, as the "industrial reserve army," shoulders the cost in times of crisis to a disproportionate extent (Chan, 2010b). Chinese urban development is built upon this indispensable component of low-cost labor. Under the world's factory regime, cheap labor is the basis for the "China price." In the post-crisis era, the government aims to boost domestic household consumption. However, the root cause of insufficient domestic demand is the under-consumption of the majority, especially the rural population and migrant labor (Chan, 2010b). In reality, the policies to boost domestic consumption actually target the rising middle class instead of migrant population. For example, affordable housing schemes are not designed for migrant population; and the rapidly expanding private car market is beyond their affordability. To promote domestic consumption as a driving force for the economy, the government may likely encourage the development of niche market for the urban upper- and middle class, because they are vocal and could possibly be promoted to generate new demand (such as private cars). The demand imperative of boosting consumption may override the concern over social equality, as the development of market is regarded as a priority. History tells the same story: the market development approach was adopted in the aftermath of the Asian financial crisis. In order to raise the incentive of homeownership, the government radically abolished in-kind housing allocation and pushed the urban residents into the commodity housing market.

In addition, we may see a new dynamism of structured social exclusion which has been so far absent in China but exists widely in more advanced market economies (Wacquant, 2008). Chinese migrant population in the cities, although occupying a low social status, are job-active and closely participate in the global commodity production. In a sense, they are not marginal, but are at the core of the mainstream economy in terms of their economic position (Wu and Webster, 2010). With the shift of development in the post-crisis period, we may see a new process of "de-industrialization," in which the excessive production capacities have to be removed. Economic restructuring, the pursuing of innovation and capital intensive development, may lead to limited capacity of job creation. For migrants who are already in the city, especially the second generation of migrants, it becomes increasingly unrealistic for them to return to the countryside when there is an economic downturn. According to Chan (2010b: 667), among 14 million migrants who returned to the countryside and stayed there, only 2 million found work. Out of 56 million migrants who came back to the city after the Spring Festival, 45 million found work. Assuming that all migrants staying in the city found work, the total unemployed migrant labor amounted to 23 million in early 2009, resulting in a 16.4% unemployment rate. For the second generation migrants who were either born in the cities or came to the cities right after primary school, they have little experience of farming. The question for post-crisis urban development in urban China is whether there would be a future "underclass" (Solinger, 2002) separated from the mainstream economy and society. If this were the case, we would see a very different dynamic from the past, because a large pool of workforce may fall out from the production process and lose the means to earn a living through the job market, while existing state-organized welfare program could not cover them. The state welfare system is not ready to expand without serious financial implications. So far the Chinese city has been largely able to avoid homeless and consequent squatters. Will the Chinese city see the development of slums and squatters? And will the constraint of production capacities create "urban outcasts" like those in the advanced western economies (Wacquant, 2008)? If so, the Chinese city would see a wholly different social spatial form, changing from spatially juxtaposed to segregated social spaces.

Economic Restructuring, Innovation, and Low-Carbon Eco-City

Priori to the global financial crisis, the Chinese economy was under the pressure to change its growth approach. The process was driven by rising production costs and currency appreciation. The process of restructuring can be typically seen in southern Jiangsu. After the collapse of collective rural economy (characterized by TVEs), the new Sunnan model is characterized by large-scale land development and foreign capital in manufacturing industries. In the municipality of Suzhou, for example, clusters of electronic manufacturing industries are formed. Within the municipality of Suzhou there is a county-level city, the city of Kunshan. In 2007, there were 1,100 ICT companies located in Kunshan alone, with $14 billion investment. The assembly and production of notebooks accounted for 40% of the total world production. But even before 2008, labor intensive enterprises began to close down and were relocated to Vietnam and other Southeast Asia countries and Chinese inland region. The Chinese government also encourages economic restructuring, moving away from low productivity and low innovative capacity to more innovative and higher value-added industries. The global financial crisis accelerates this process. In southern China like Guangdong, an explicit policy to "free the cage and change the bird" (*tenglong huaniao*) has been adopted to promote the upgrading of industrial structures.

An important policy agenda for urban development is to encourage the "indigenous innovation capacities." Economic development zones have been an approach to attract foreign investment. But in the new environment, they are increasingly used as an incubation space to foster innovation. The establishment of various development zones has significantly expanded the built-up area of the cities, which is often used by local government to capture mobile resources and enhance the administrative status of locality. The central government initiated several crack-down movements to eliminate over-use of land and illegal development of development zones. This zone fever has been extensively documented in the literature of Chinese urban development (e.g., Hsing, 2006). Now development zones are consolidated. There are two major types of development zones: national economic and technological development zones (ETDZs), and national high and new technological industrial development zone (HNTIDZs). In total, the central government approved 49 national ETDZ and 5 equivalent industrial parks, 56 national HNTIDZs, or in fact "high-tech parks." These zones facilitate the clustering of high-tech industries and innovation in new technologies.

The government now encourages the transition from a purely investment oriented zone to a new functional area of key industries and industrial agglomeration. The development of these zones benefit from entrepreneurial land development. In fact, many zones have a development corporation status. Now many of these development zones are no longer isolated from the city but are part of municipal functional area. To enhance the economic competitiveness, the municipality provides various policy supports. For example, the Shanghai municipal government adopts a so-called "focusing on Zhangjiang" policy to concentrate the resources of the city of Shanghai to build Zhangjiang High-Tech Park, including relocating some medical university and research institutions in the park. Other high-tech parks include Zhongguancun Science Park in Beijing and Shenzhen High-tech Park. The Zhongguancun Science Park, based on ICT industries, is becoming a major base for R&D. Now, Zhongguancun is no longer a geographically bounded area like a development zone, but rather a collection of zones which include the Haidian zone as the core, an extended Haidian zone further towards the northwest suburbs, Fengtai zone, Jiuxianqiao electronics city, Changping zone, and Yizhuang zone. The multiple parks help to stimulate the link of R&D inside the zone with the rest of the city. It is foreseeable that innovation will continue to be the major theme of post-crisis urban development in China.

The second trend in post-crisis urban development is the enthusiasm for so-called "eco-cities" and "low-carbon cities." In response to climate change and international pressure on the reduction of greenhouse gas emission, the Chinese government announced some measurable indicators. It was announced that in the 11th five-year period (2005–2010) the per unit GDP energy consumption should be reduced by 20% of the same figure in 2005. The target is not an easy one. To achieve the target, it has been disaggregated to the local governments. However, China is in the midst of rapid industrialization and urbanization. With the increase of living standard, there will be rising demand for energy; for example, the wider use of private cars and the separation between job and residence will lead to longer commutes. With the pressure to cut emission, various local governments seize the new opportunities to develop "low-carbon" or "eco-cities." For example, Dongtan in Shanghai has once claimed to be the world's first eco-city. But with the problem of land acquisition and land development quotas, the project is now halted. But in other places such as Tianjin, Caofeidian, Suzhou, and Shenzhen, through international collaboration, new eco-cities are under development. To save the land, Sino-Singapore Tianjin Eco-city is situated on non-arable land, including one-third saltpan, one-third deserted beach, and one-third wastewater area. Caifeidian eco-city is developed through land reclamation. Besides these major developments, there are more cities to join the fever of eco-cities and low-carbon cities, indicating a move away from traditional export-oriented approach. However, many so-called low-carbon cities have not fully recognized the difficulty in achieving the target of zero emission or carbon neutral, but are simply using the title to capture new development opportunities. Some rush into alternative energy developments such as solar and wind programs. The development of new energy may lead to over capacity without overcoming some technical challenges.

Conclusion

From the economic reform in 1979 to joining the WTO in 2001, China developed a new approach to economic growth and capital accumulation, which is a departure from self-contained and indigenous industrialization. The "open-door" policy that allows the large-scale inflow of foreign and overseas investment and conscious efforts to insert Chinese production activities into the global production chain eventually transform China into the world's factory. Through economic devolution, fiscal reform, and local land revenue generation, local governments become entrepreneurial agents in organizing land and urban development. Urban and rural dualism maintains a low-cost labor supply, and state monopoly of land requisition allows local governments to capitalize the differential rent to fund infrastructure development. Spatially this kind of urban development leads to a fragmented form, with the sharp contrast between packaged gated communities and spontaneous urban villages inside the city. Socially, the increasing social complexity erodes so-called "communist neo-traditionalism" and turns an earth-bounded rural society into an uprooted urban society. In terms of governance, Chinese cities witness unprecedented mobility: for rural migrants, they live in the city while retaining their rural household registration in the countryside; for urban residents, many have moved to the suburbs while keeping their registered places inside inner areas, causing so-called "people and *hukou* separation." Both impose a great challenge to urban governance, with the state initiating various programs to rebuild the community, results of which remains to be seen.

The global financial crisis has profound implications for Chinese urban development because it undermines the structural coherence of the regime. The pressure to cut greenhouse gas emission, the accelerated trade protectionism, the rising labor costs, and a dwindling rural sector means that advantages are fading and constraints increasing. Three tendencies in urban China in the post-crisis era can be identified: a real estate boom, structured social exclusion, and the tendency towards economic restructuring with emerging form of urbanism that includes high-tech parks and eco-cities. To achieve sustainable urban development, the future task for the government is to manage these tendencies, to minimize financial fallout from unrestrained property boom, to avoid the formation of an "under-class" while boosting the middle class/domestic demand, and to prevent the overconsumption of resources under the name of eco-development. All these would be new challenges to the Chinese state. In order to re-establish the structural coherence, an institutional change is required.

References

Cai, F. (2007) The turning point confronting the Chinese economy and its challenge for development and reform. *Chinese Social Sciences (Zhongguo shehui kexue)* 3, 4–12.

Cartier, C. (2001) 'Zone fever', the arable land debate, and real estate speculation: China's evolving land use regime and its geographical contradictions. *Journal of Contemporary China*, 10(28), 445–469.

Chan, K. W. (1994) *Cities with invisible walls*. Hong Kong: Oxford University Press.

——— (2010a) Fundamentals of China's urbanization and policy. *The China Review*, 10(1), 63–94.

——— (2010b) The global financial crisis and migrant workers in China: 'There is no future as a labourer; returning to the village has no meaning.' *International Journal of Urban and Regional Research*, 34(3), 659–677.

Chien, S.-S. (2008) The isomorphism of local development policy: A case study of the formation and transformation of national development zones in post-Mao Jiangsu, China. *Urban Studies*, 45(2), 273–294.

China National Statistical Bureau (various years). *China statistical year books*. Beijing: China Statistical Press.

China Ministry of Land and Resources (1999–2005) *Almanac of China's land and resources.* Beijing: China Land Press [in Chinese].

China State Land Administration Bureau (1996–1997) *China land yearbook.* Beijing: Peoples' Press [in Chinese].

Dear, M. and S. Flusty (1998) Postmodern urbanism. *Annals of the Association of American Geographers,* 88(1), 50–72.

Fei, X. (1992) *From the soil: The foundations of Chinese Society (A translation of Fei Xiaotong's Xiangtu Zhongguo, by Gary G Hamilton and Wang Zhen).* Berkeley, CA: California University Press.

Friedmann, J. (2007) Reflection on place and place-making in the cities of China. *International Journal of Urban and Regional Research* 31(2), 257–279.

Giroir, G. (2007) Spaces of leisure: Gated golf communities in China. In F. Wu (Ed.), *China's emerging cities: The making of new urbanism,* pp. 234–255. Abingdon, Oxon: Routledge.

Hsing, Y.-T. (2006) Land and territorial politics in urban China. *China Quarterly,* 187, 1–18.

Huang, Y. (2005) From work-unit compounds to gated communities: Housing inequality and residential segregation in transitional Beijing. In L. J. C. Ma and F. Wu (Eds.), *Restructuring the Chinese City: Changing Society, Economy and Space,* pp. 192–221. London: Routledge.

Li, Z. and F. Wu. (2008) Tenure-based residential segregation in post-reform Chinese cities: A case study of Shanghai. *Transactions of the Institute of British Geographers,* 33(3), 404–419.

Lin, G. C. S. (2002) The growth and structural change of Chinese cities: A contextual and geographic analysis. *Cities,* 19(5), 299–316.

Ma, L. J. C. and M. Fan (1994) Urbanisation from below: The growth of towns in Jiangsu, China. *Urban Studies,* 31(10), 1625–1645.

Ma, L. J. C. and F. Wu, (Eds.) (2005) *Restructuring the Chinese city: Changing society, economy and space.* London: Routledge.

Ma, L. J. C. and B. Xiang (1998) Native place, migration and the emergence of peasant enclaves in Beijing. *The China Quarterly,* 155, 546–581.

Marcuse, P. (1997) The enclave, the citadel, and the ghetto: What has changed in the post-fordist US city. *Urban Affairs Review,* 33(2), 228–264.

Read, B. L. (2003) Democratizing the neighbourhood? new private housing and home-owner self-organization in urban China. *The China Journal,* 49(1), 31–59.

Shen, J., Z. Feng and K.-Y. Wong (2006) Dual-track urbanization in a transitional economy: The case of Pearl River Delta in South China. *Habitat International,* 30, 690–705.

Shen, X. and L. J. C. Ma (2005) Privatization of rural industry and de facto urbanization from below in southern Jiangsu, China. *Geoforum,* 36, 761–777.

Sit, V. F. S. and C. Yang (1997) Foreign-investment-induced exo-urbanisation in the Pearl River Delta, China. *Urban Studies*, 34, 647–677.

Solinger, D. J. (2002) Labour market reform and the plight of the laid-off proletariat. *The China Quarterly*, 170, 304–326.

Sun, L. (2004) *Transformation and division: Changing social structure since economic reform.* Beijing: Tsinghua University Press [in Chinese].

Tao, R., X. Lu, F. Su and H. Wang (2009). Chinese transition under the regional competition: Fiscal incentive and rethinking on development models. *Economic Research (Jinji Yanjiu)* 7, 21–34 [in Chinese].

Tian, L. (2008). The Chengzhongcun land market in China: Boon or bane? — A perspective on property rights. *International Journal of Urban and Regional Research*, 32(2), 282–304.

Tomba, L. (2005) Residential space and collective interest formation in Beijing's housing disputes. *The China Quarterly*, 184, 934–951.

Wacquant, L. (2008) *Urban outcasts: A comparative sociology of advanced marginality.* Cambridge: Polity Press.

Walder, A. G. (1986) *Communist neo-traditionalism: Work and authority in Chinese industry.* Berkeley, CA: University of California Press.

Wang, Y. P. and A. Murie (2000). Social and spatial implications of housing reform in China. *International Journal of Urban and Regional Research*, 24(2), 397–417.

Webster, C. (2002) Property rights and the public realm: Gates, green belts, and Gemeinschaft. *Environment and Planning B*, 29(3), 397–412.

Webster, C., F. Wu and Y. Zhao (2005) China's modern gated cities. In G. Glasze, C. Webster and K. Frantz (Eds.), *Private Neighbourhoods: Global and Local Perspectives*, pp. 153–169. London: Routledge.

Wei, H. (2010) Chinese urbanization and urban development in the midst of rapid transition. In J. Pan and H. Wei (Eds.), *Chinese urban development report no. 3*, pp. 1–35. Beijing: Social Sciences Academic Press [in Chinese].

Whyte, M. K. and W. L. Parish (1984) *Urban life in contemporary China.* Chicago, IL: University of Chicago Press.

Wu, F. (1997) Urban restructuring in China's emerging market economy: Towards a framework for analysis. *International Journal of Urban and Regional Research*, 21, 640–663.

———. (2009) The state and marginality: Reflections on urban outcasts from China's urban transition. *International Journal of Urban and Regional Research*, 33(3), 841–847.

———. (2010) Gated and packaged suburbia: Packaging and branding Chinese suburban residential development. *Cities*, 27(5), 385–396.

Wu, W. (2006) Migrant intra-urban residential mobility in urban China. *Housing Studies*, 21(5), 745–765.

Wu, F. and C. Webster (Eds.) (2010) *Marginalization in urban China: Comparative perspectives.* Basingstoke: Palgrave Macmillan.

Yeh, A. G. O. and F. Wu (1996) The new land development process and urban development in Chinese cities. *International Journal of Urban and Regional Research,* 20(2), 330–353.

Yeh, A. G. O., X. Q. Xu and H. Y. Hu (1995) The social space of Guangzhou city, China. *Urban Geography,* 16(7), 595–621.

Yuan, X. (2010) The progress in urban real estate development and the direction for adjustment. In J. Pan and H. Wei (Eds.), *Chinese urban development report no. 3,* pp. 152–167. Beijing: Social Sciences Academic Press [in Chinese].

Zhang, J. X. and F. Wu (2006) China's changing economic governance: Administrative annexation and the reorganization of local governments in the Yangtze River Delta. *Regional Studies,* 40(1), 3–21.

Zhang, L. (2001) *Strangers in the city: Reconfiguration of space, power, and social networks within China's floating population.* Stanford: Stanford University Press.

Zhang, L., S. X. B. Zhao and J. P. Tian (2003) Self-help in housing and Chengzhongcun in China's urbanization. *International Journal of Urban and Regional Research,* 27(4), 912–937.

Zhou, Y. and L. J. C. Ma (2003) China's urbanization levels: Reconstructing a baseline from the fifth population census. *The China Quarterly,* 173, 176–196.

10

HIGHER EDUCATION

Ka-ho Mok

The Hong Kong Institute of Education and Zhejiang University

Li Wang

Zhejiang University

Abstract

In the last few decades, the Chinese government has tried to adopt ideas and practices along the line of neo-liberalism to reform the social service delivery mode and social policy provision. It is against this wider context that major social policy areas like health, education and housing have been going through the processes of marketization and privatization. As a result, people have to bear heavy financial burden for meeting these welfare and social policy needs. After privatizing and marketizing education for a few decades, the Chinese government was recently confronted with criticisms for its failure in tackling the problems related to "new three mountains phenomenon" (namely heavy financial burdens for meeting health, education and housing needs). Based upon a case study of Beijing, together with the analysis of secondary data, this chapter focuses on how higher education is privatized and marketized and also covers the consequences. It examines how the government has tried to revert the tide of privatization. This chapter will critically discuss the policy implications throughout the processes of transformations that have taken place in higher education in mainland China.

Keywords: Privatization and marketization of higher education; the quest for social harmony; deprivatization of education; changing state-market relations; educational inequality.

Introduction: Privatization of Higher Education in China

In its narrowest definition, privatization refers to the transfer of shares or assets from government to the private sector, usually by means of sale. It is also known as denationalization. In its broader definition, however, denationalization is only one type of privatization. Broadly speaking, privatization covers all at tempts to increase participation of the private sector and strengthen market in national socio-economic setting, including diminishing public participation, encouraging public-private partnership and creating opportunities for markets (Starr, 1998; Belfield and Levin, 2002; The Privatization Org, 2007). Bennett (1997) suggests three major forms of privatization. They are: (1) divestment, which echoes with the narrow definition, (2) delegation, to hand over the managerial autonomy and responsibilities to other agents while retain the state ownership, and (3) displacement, by displacing the government by the private sector in certain areas gradually and passively (Savas, 1992). Privatization, as a process instead of a state, can be elaborated by a continuum, of which one extreme is pure private and another pure public. Any movements in the spectrum away from the public extreme to the private extreme can be regarded as privatization. In this process, one point deserves special attention is that although absolute increase of the private sector and strengthen of market are definitely the main themes no matter what approaches privatization employs, it does not necessarily lead to the overall shrink of the public sector. In contrast, privatization could be achieved theoretically by increasing the private/public ratio in the national economy whereas the government remain robust and the public sector without shrinking. In this chapter, privatization is interpreted in the broadest sense, by which it means either less "publicness", or more "privateness."[1] The reason for

---

[1] Adopting the broad definition, this paper will not distinguish privatization from its synonyms, such as marketization and deregulation. However, this does not mean these terms have the same meaning. Instead, each of them has different focus. Marketization emphasizes the involvement of market and the adoption of market principles, while deregulation often refers to simplify regulations or remove restrictions on certain areas. Nevertheless, they are all related to the process of more private involvement and/or less public intervention. Therefore, in this chapter, marketization or deregulation are viewed as specific strategies of privatization.

adopting a broad definition is because it allows us to explore diverse strategies of the privatization and the dynamics of the implementation in the Chinese context which will be examined in detail below.

The following chapter is set out against the above theoretical framework to critically examine how higher education in Mainland China has experienced/transformed in lines with privatization strategies in the last two decades, while most recently, the Chinese government has tried to bring back the "publicness" to higher education when confronting the problems generated from the privatization of higher education. The chapter is divided into several parts: part one reviews major policy change in higher education (higher education) since the 1970s when higher education resumed development after the Cultural Revolution. After examining key concepts related to privatization and marketization of education, the second part of the chapter critically examines how higher education has been privatized/marketized. The third part of the chapter examines the Chinese government response of to the criticisms of intensified educational inequality resulted from privatizing/marketizing higher education by making attempts to "bring the state back in" by revitalizing the role of the state in education.

Understanding Privatization of HE in China

A Brief Policy Background and Methodology

Since the adoption of the open-door policy in the late 1970s, China has transformed itself from a highly centralized planned economy into a more dynamic and market-oriented economy to achieve more flexibility, creativity and vitality in mobilizing and allocating resources, and ultimately to facilitate economic growth and improve people's livelihood. In terms of public sector management, decentralization and marketization strategies have been introduced to improve the efficiency and effectiveness of delivery of public services. In order to avoid over-centralization and stringent rules that would kill the initiatives and enthusiasm of local educational institutions, the Chinese government initiated reforms in its bureaucracy to streamline administration, to devolve power to units at lower levels and to offer them more flexibility to run education since the 1980s. In addition, because of limited state financial resources in support of higher education development to satisfy the pressing demand for education, diversified funding resources, proliferating providers and marketized higher education are becoming increasingly popular in mainland China (Mok, 2006).

In the post-Mao era, the Chinese government has begun to review its education systems. Various kinds of reforms have been introduced to make the education systems more responsive to the changing needs and expectations of the society. The first comprehensive reform in Chinese education was the promulgation of the *Decision of the Central Committee of the Communist Party of China on the Reform of Educational Structure* by the Chinese Communist Party (CCP) Central Committee in 1985. The major objective of this reform was related to eliminate excessive government control over schools and higher education institutions (higher education institutions). In 1993, the *Mission Outline of the Reform and Development of China's Education* was issued to further reduce over-centralization in bureaucratic control and to allow local governments to determine their educational developments, especially encouraging the local governments to search for non-state resources to finance education (CCCCP and the State Council 1993). According to Article 25 of the *Education Law* issued in 1995, the state gave full support to enterprises, social institutions, local communities and individuals to establish private (*minban* or people-run) schools under the legal framework of the government (State Education Commission, 1995). All democratic parties, social organizations, retired cadres and intellectuals, collective economic organizations, and individuals are thus encouraged to actively contribute to developing education by various means and methods (Wei and Zhang, 1995).

Due to the diversified university revenues, funding for education has no longer come solely from the state but from other sources such as social donations, tuition fees, and capital investment from enterprises. Education consumption has become a mix of private and public (Cheng, 1995; Hayhoe, 1996; Mok, 2006). What makes education funding sources more diversified is the implementation of the *Law of the People's Republic of China on Promotion of Privately-Run Schools* in 2002 and the *Regulations of the People's Republic of China on Chinese-Foreign Cooperation in Running Schools* in 2003. These two particular legal documents further provided a framework conducive to the rise of *minban* (or private) schools. Realizing that depending on the state funding alone would not easily meet the pressing demands for education, the central government has allowed non-state sectors (including the market) to engage in education provision, the legal documents mentioned above did give a green light to *minban* schools' owners to make profit through provision of *minban* education and provided incentives for more investors to get into this business (Mok, 2008).

In addition, the privateness of higher education has become more prominent especially after China was admitted into the World Trade Organization (WTO). According to the WTO and the General Agreement on Trade in Services (GATS), higher education is regarded as a private good

(Mok, 2009). In recent years, transnational higher education and private international schools are mushrooming in Mainland China. While before the mid-1980s transnational higher education was prohibited, by 1999, more than 70 local higher education institutions qualified to offer transnational higher education programs in cooperation with foreign partners (Huang, 2003, pp. 232–233). Attracting more international resources to China is one of the Chinese government's strategies to upgrade the overall quality of higher education to meet the goal of internationalization. In recent years, the government's allowance for establishment of foreign-local joint universities has reaffirmed this strategy and at the same time marked a new phase of transnational higher education in China (Mok and Chan, 2011).

Thanks to the proliferation of *minban* schools and programs, together with the privatization and marketization of education, students and parents have enjoyed more choices and opportunities in education. But the privatization process also suggested that the state has reduced its responsibility in education provision and financing, shifting the financial burden of education to individuals and families. It is against this context that while the opening up of education in China is well-received by some, a growing number of critics have pointed to the problems it has brought and raised concerns related to the intensified educational inequality and excessive financial burden on families to support their children's education (Mok, Wong and Zhang, 2009). Therefore, people in the mainland criticize the government for failing to remove the three new mountains which symbolizes heavy financial burdens shouldered by the people in financing education, housing and healthcare (Mok *et al.*, 2010).

In response to these criticisms and out of the fear of potential of social unrest resulting from people's dissatisfaction of the government's inability in addressing social inequality, the present government has pledged to adopt a new governance approach, of which the central plank are the "harmonious society" and "people-centered development." In response to the pressing demand of education, coupled with the need to reduce educational inequality, the Chinese government has tried to adopt reform agendas recently by broadening and strengthening compulsory basic education, offering assistance to students in poor regions, and eradicating the institutional and financial barriers for migrant children to study in urban public schools. The latest effort is the introduction of "National Outline for Medium and Long Term Educational Reform and Development" (hereafter "The Outline") (State Council 2010), which will be the blueprint for education reform for the period of 2010–2020. A draft version was issued by the government in early 2010 for public consultation, inviting suggestions and feedbacks from different stakeholders to develop a comprehensive package for education reforms. The document clearly shows that the government does recognize the urgent need to alleviate the overwhelming financial burden of individual families, as it is stated in The Outline that a primary goal of national education policies is to assure equality. The Outline has significant implications for the development of education in China, in the coming decade at least, in that it demonstrates the state's intention to bring back welfare and strengthen the public nature of education.

This chapter is partially based upon the fieldwork data collected by the authors in Beijing, China in 2008, through policy and documentary analysis and secondary data analysis. In 2008, a small scale survey was conducted in six public universities and one private college by random sampling. Three hundred and fifty three copies of valid questionnaires were collected, with a response rate of 73.75%. In addition, field visits were conducted whereby 12 academics at the sampled institutions and one government officials at educational authorities were interviewed for examining their perception and evaluations of changes in higher education governance in Beijing. Given the size and diversity of the higher education sector in China, the chapter does not intend to make generalization out of the interviews and survey data collected from this case study. Nonetheless, the data and observations to be reported and discussed in this chapter would provide concrete evidence related to the motives behind the practices of marketization and privatization of higher education in Mainland China, the analysis of which would hopefully contribute to an in-depth understanding of policy making and policy implementation of the privatization in higher education. Apart from making use of the empirical data generated from the case study, this chapter also draws on national statistics and policy/document analysis when discussing the privatization/marketization processes that has taken place in Chinese higher education sector.

Privatization of HE in Practice

1) Proliferation of private colleges

Divestment was adopted in several public universities in China to reform the operation of the institutions. Known as *zhuan zhi* (tansformed) institutions, they were privatized to be operated on a cost-recovery basis, enjoying greater autonomy and observing market rules. However, these higher education institutions are still owned by the state, since the ownership is separated from management of the institutions and only the latter privatized (Mok, 2005).

The *zhuan zhi* institutions merely constitute a tiny minority of the private higher education, whereas the majority are start up private colleges. The private higher education sector has developed quickly since the establishment of the first private higher education institutions, China Social University (*zhong guo she hui da xue*), in 1982. There are two types of private higher education institutions, namely, *minban* higher education institutions and independent colleges. The former, also known as people-run higher education institutions, are operated by social societies, individuals or other non-public organizations. Funding for *minban* higher education institutions usually comes from non-fiscal sources, such as donations and money raised by the founders (Standing Committee of National People's Congress [SCNPC] 2002). Similar to *minban* higher education institutions, the financial input for independent colleges is also from non-fiscal funding. But this type of higher education institutions must be run by both public universities and non-public partners, according to the *Measures for Establishment and Management of Independent Colleges* (*du li xue yuan she zhi yu guan li ban fa*) (MOE, 2008). To assure the education quality of independent colleges, the public university eligible to run independent colleges are normally good universities with national reputation for quality teaching and research. Although the private higher education has developed quickly, it only constitutes a small part of the whole higher education system compared with their public counterparts. In 2007, there were 1,908 public higher education institutions in China, of which only 906 were private colleges across the country (Figure 1) (NBSC, 2008). Moreover, compared to public universities, private higher education institutions are of low quality. For example, they mainly focus on education at lower levels. Some of them are accredited to award the bachelor's degree, but many are limited to provide vocational training or diploma courses only.

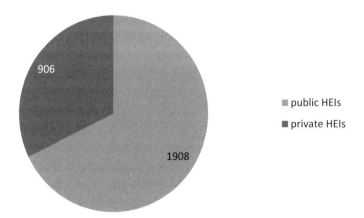

Figure 1. Number of public and private HEIs in China in 2007

Source: NBSC 2008.

2) Delegation in HE governance

The Chinese higher education system was built by copying the Soviet model. In the Mao's era, Marxism and Leninism were the dominating government philosophy, as a result of which, the CCP and the government had absolute power over every aspect of social life. As part of the supportive mechanism of a planned economy, higher education at that time was inevitably under direct and entire control of the party and the state. Fundamental changes have taken place in the state university relationship since the economic reforms in the late 1970's. A set of decentralization policies have been issued, allowing the higher education sector in China a certain degree of autonomy. The style, strategy and location of university governance were different from Mao's time due to the reforms and restructure of the whole public sector.

The *Decision of the Central Committee of the Communist Party of China on the Reform of Educational Structure* is the first policy that clearly granted a certain degree of institutional and academic autonomy to higher education in China (CCCPC, 1985). As mentioned above, the policy document initiated fundamental changes in university governance in many aspects, including academic autonomy and administrative flexibility. First, higher education institutions were allowed to enrol commissioned and self-funded students outside the state plan. Second, universities were able to adjust the contents of a major, decide teaching plans and choose textbooks. Third, universities were allowed to be commissioned to train students in collaboration with other organizations. Fourth, it was permitted that the institution can nominate its vice presidents, appoint and dismiss other managers below that rank. Fifth, higher education institutions can decide how to use the budgetary appropriation on capital expenditure. And finally, higher education institutions can use funding raised by institutions on international academic activities (Long and Liu, 2006). Although the granted autonomy on academic related issues, administration and personnel management was very limited, the "decision" marked the first attempt of devolution in higher education. Then in 1992, more autonomy was granted to higher education with the promulgation of Opinions about deepening reform and expanding autonomous rights for universities affiliated with the Commission of education (Commission of education, 1992). Among these changes, institutions were allowed to propose tuition levels (subject to approval of the Commission of Education). The *Programme for Educational Reform and Development in China* promulgated in 1993 jointly by the State Council and the Central Committee of CCP further promoted decentralization practices in higher education governance. It was specified in Article 18 that through decentralization, the governance and funding responsibility should be partly devolved from the central to the provincial governments. Practices such as joint-development and merger were also encouraged to reform the governing structure of higher education. Apart from decentralization of university governance, this policy was committed to give greater autonomy to higher education in enrolment, establishment of new majors, personnel management, distribution of funding and international exchange programs. It was also stated in the policy that incorporation of higher education institutions, which is crucial for a fundamental change in the governing structure as well as for empowering the higher education sector, was supported by the state (CCCCP and State council, 1993).

Following the guideline policy, a series of regulations regarding university autonomy were issued successively to implement the principles. What marked a watershed in the history of university of autonomy in China is the promulgation of the *Higher Education Act* in 1999 (Standing Committee of the National Peoples Congress, 1999). According the act, higher education institutions in China are independent organizations legally recognized since their establishment. In addition, university autonomy, including academic decisions and administrative flexibility, proposed in previous rules and guidelines, is legitimated through the act. In the same year, the MOE issued another policy document, known as *Opinions from MOE about deepening reform on personnel and distribution system in higher education*, to specify the autonomy and responsibility of universities on personnel management (Ministry of Education, 1999). As a result of the policies and regulative rules, higher education was granted greater autonomy compared with three decades ago. At the same time, more responsibilities, particular in financing, were also devolved to higher education institutions.

3) *Displacement of public funding in HE*

Higher education was solely funded and provided by the state in Mao's China. After the adoption of privatization, however, financing of higher education has become much diversified and heavily privatized. Resources from the private sector have been successfully mobilized to fund higher education. For example, the tuition fee constituted a large proportion of university income, soaring from 15.1% of the total amount in 1996 to 31.5% a decade later (National bureau of statistics of China, 1996, 2005). Investment in private colleges also increased significantly, given the quick development of private higher education as noted above. In absolute terms, both private and public funding increased steadily every year. But if we look at the public/private split, it is clear that the higher education sector in China has become

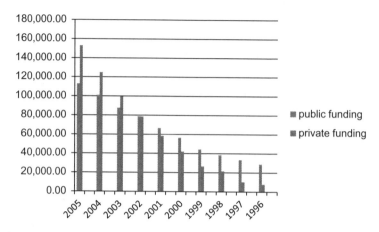

Figure 2.   Public/private funding on HE (1996–2005) Unit: million yuan
Source: NBSC 1996–2005.

increasingly reliant on private sources. Figure 2 shows the changing share between public and private funding in the last decade. In the 1990s, most of the university revenue came from public funding, especially budgetary appreciation from local and central governments. But the share of public financing was shrinking year by year, falling from over three quarters in 1996 to less than half in the new millennium. At the same time, the percentage of private funding increased significantly. It soared from less than one quarter to over half of the total revenue within a decade (National Bureau of Statistics of China, 1996–2005).

4) *Emerging transnational HE*

Since China's admission to the WTO in 2001, one significant progress of Chinese higher education related to privatization has been the rise of transnational higher education. In China, transnational higher education provision previously took the form of joint programs, twinning programs and online and distance learning which was usually conducted at faculty and departmental levels in local higher education institutions. The demand for such kinds of education has increased in the past few decades. As China has ceaselessly attempted to open up its higher education to the world in order to increase educational supply and bring in international quality resources, in the past few years three foreign higher education institutions have been approved by the Ministry of Education to establish joint universities with local institutions, they are the University of Nottingham Ningbo, China, the Xi'an Jiaotong-Liverpool University, and the United International College (UIC).

Their experiences in provision, financing and governance would provide lessons for us to reflect upon the prospects and challenges of transnational higher education in China. Founded by the University of Nottingham from Britain and the Zhejiang Wanli Education Group-University in 2004, the University of Nottingham Ningbo, China is the first Sino-Foreign University in China. Nottingham possesses a 37.5% share of the joint university; the Wanli Education Group invested about £14 million for the infrastructure (Time Higher Education Supplement, 2007). Private higher education institutions are usually seen as second tier colleges in China, targeting at local students unqualified for public universities, but the University of Nottingham Ningbo, China is an exception. In 2009, it got the approval of the Ministry of Education of China to recruit students from Hong Kong, Taiwan and Macau (*Wenweipo*, February 23 2009). In the same year, it started to cooperate with the University of Nottingham in Britain in recruiting 20–50 PhD students per year in the fields of cultural studies, English studies, commerce, computer science, international communication, sustainable development and engineering, etc. (*Wenweipo*, January 19, 2009). These achievements in extending and enhancing the quality of student pool make the university well-received in the community.

The Xi'an Jiaotong-Liverpool University is another joint university founded in 2006 by a British higher education institution and a local one — the University of Liverpool and the Xi'an Jiaotong University. Residing in the Suzhou Industrial Park in the city of Suzhou of the Jiangsu Province, the university specializes in teaching and research in the fields of science, engineering and management. The University of Liverpool has a 30% share of the joint university. But differing from the University of Nottingham Ningbo, China, the financial source for the share comes not from the foreign mother school but from a US higher education company, Laureate Education, which currently owns more than 50 accredited institutions in 21 countries and serves more than 550,000 students. The University of Liverpool was given by Laureate Education a UK£1 million bond for operation in China (Ball, forthcoming). This case reveals that higher education in China is now regarded as a business and investment by overseas companies, and on this ground Chinese higher education is increasingly connected to the global market of transnational higher education.

The United International College in Zhuhai, Guangdong Province, co-founded by the Beijing Normal University and the Hong Kong Baptist University marks a milestone in Hong Kong higher education, as it is the first joint university in China established by a Hong Kong university. UIC now has about 4,000 students; its teaching staffs are coming from more than 20 countries and regions. Its significance is bolstered recently after the Hong Kong government has declared that higher education industry will become one of the pillars of Hong Kong economy. As Executive Vice-President Professor Kwok Siu Tong said, "exporting education" was the guiding principle that UIC adhered to and should also be the norm that other Hong Kong institutions had to take notice of when they decided to expand their educational services in China. Kwok explained that the idea "refers not only for Hong Kong institutions to offer a single course or to set up a Sci-tech research base in China, but to export a whole set of educational system, including curriculum design, teaching management, and governance model, etc." (*Hong Kong Economic Journal*, April 16, 2009). Taking quality assurance as example, the quality assurance system of UIC is mainly operated and maintained by the Hong Kong Baptist University: UIC has borrowed the model from Hong Kong Baptist University to set up an Academic Assurance Committee to "monitor closely the academic planning and development of the college." Besides, Hong Kong Baptist University has set up an Academic Consultation Panel which visits UIC from time to time to conduct assessment of UIC's academic standards. Institutional Reviews were also conducted to "evaluate the teaching, academic research and management at UIC." In this light, the UIC can be seen as an experiment of implanting the higher education system of Hong Kong in China's soil.

Privatization of HE: Issues and Challenges

Privatization of the higher education system in China is largely a top-down process initiated by the state following the regulations and policies examined earlier. It is thus important to refer to opinions of stake holders — students and staff towards implementation of privatization. The section below combines empirical data collected in Beijing in 2008 in the attempt to probe into implementation of privatization and its influence on higher education provision, control and finance.

1) Private HE and quality issues

The proliferation of the private higher education institutions has contributed greatly to the expansion of the Chinese higher education system. However, compared to public universities, private colleges are generally considered to be of worse quality. As mentioned earlier, private higher education institutions mainly focus on courses at lower level. In addition, the admission requirements are also low. In the survey conducted in Beijing, students were asked to rate the admission requirements on a five-point Likert scale:

"Was it difficult to be admitted into this institution?"
Means: public higher education institutions 2.80; private
higher education institutions 3.80
(1 = very difficult, 2 = difficult, 3 = fair, 4 = easy, 5 = very easy)

Obviously, it is much easier to be enrolled by a private college compared with a public one. Focusing on lower level educational courses, coupled with lower admission standards, private higher education institutions mainly attract students who are not good enough to go to public universities. Nevertheless, survey date indicated that students in private colleges were happy about the courses provided which were thought to be practical and useful. Correspondents in public and private institutions were asked to evaluate if the courses they learnt were useful:

"How would you rate the practicality of the courses?"
Means: public higher education institutions 3.01; private
higher education institutions 2.72
(1 = very useful, 2 = useful, 3 = fair, 4 = useless, 5 = very useless)

"Are the courses useful for future jobs?"
Means: public higher education institutions 2.74; private
higher education institutions 2.70
(1 = very useful, 2 = useful, 3 = fair, 4 = useless, 5 = very useless)

The means of data from private students are slightly lower than those from public universities on both items. In other words, students in private colleges may be a bit happier about the course design because what they learnt was practical and useful for future career. Guided by market principles, private higher education institutions are supposed to offer courses which are career oriented. The survey data agreed with this assumption. But when it came to teaching quality in general terms, it was agreed that teaching in public universities was better. As shown in the survey,

"How do you think about the quality of teaching in your institution?"
Means: public higher education institutions 2.58; private
higher education institutions 2.81
(1 = very high, 2 = high, 3 = fair, 4 = low, 5 = very low)

Table 1.   Academic qualification of teachers in private and public HEIs

Unit: person

	Doctoral degree		Master's degree		Bachelor's degree		Diploma & below		Total	
	number	%	number	%	number	%	number	%	number	%
Private										
Full time	652	3.0	2896	13.3	14941	68.6	3287	15.1	21776	100
Part time	1855	7.1	6796	25.9	16335	62.3	1221	4.7	26207	100
Total	2507	5.2	9692	20.1	31276	65.2	4508	9.4	47983	100
Public										
Total	134587	10.1	395654	29.6	765681	57.4	38587	2.9	1334509	100

Source: MOE, 2006.

The mean of teaching quality in private colleges was 2.81, close to "fair," while the figure of public institutions was 2.58, closer to high. This suggests the teaching quality in private higher education institutions is worse than in public universities. The less satisfying teaching quality is closely related to the less qualified academic staff members in private colleges, most of whom were junior teachers worked part time with lower educational credentials. In 2006, 80.6% of the teaching staff in public universities worked full time, while only 19.4% worked part time. In contrast, part-time staff constituted 54.6% of all 47,983 teachers employed by private higher education institutions (MOE, 2006). Among the full-time staff in private colleges, only 3% had a doctorate, compared to 10% of the full-time staff in public universities. If the education credentials are positively related to teaching performance, the teaching quality in private higher education sector is worrying as the majority of the teacher only had bachelor's degrees and a large number of teaching staff even had yet receive any university education (Table 1).

2) *State university relationship: Centralized decentralization*

Figures (3–12) below indicate that the sampled higher education institutions enjoyed much academic autonomy. Most of the academic related decisions were made at institutional level. Over half of the correspondents agreed their universities can define campus mission and objectives, nearly two-thirds thought their institutions can decide to open or eliminate courses, and all of them agreed that institutions could decide course content and objectives.

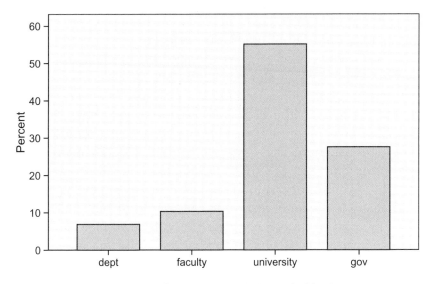

Figure 3.   Defining campus mission and objectives

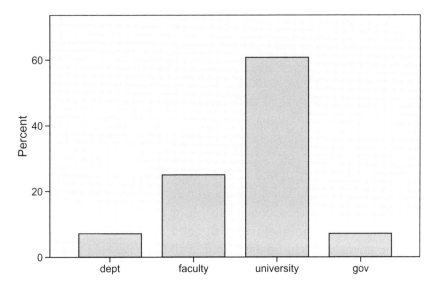

Figure 4.   Opening or eliminating courses

Other issues that most of the correspondents thought their institutions could make a final decision are determining student-faculty ratios, setting degree requirements, establishing new undergraduate programs, reviewing existing undergraduate programs, eliminating existing undergraduate programs, adding or discontinuing existing academic department or division, and offering full-fee-paying courses or programs (Figures 3–12). However, in-depth

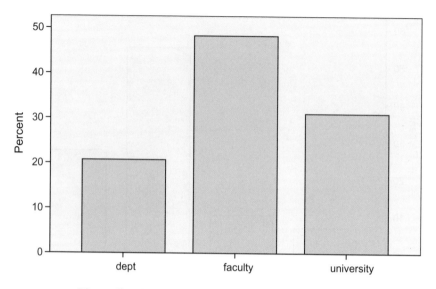

Figure 5.   Determining course content and objectives

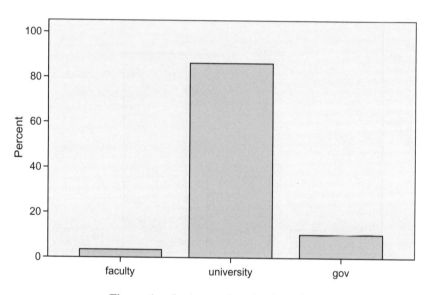

Figure 6.   Setting student-faculty ratios

interviews revealed that although in most occasions universities can determine the above academic related issues, the state still retained control over them by means of giving institutions conditioned autonomy. For example, several interviewees, one from a university affiliated MOE, one from a university affiliated with Beijing municipal government, and two from private

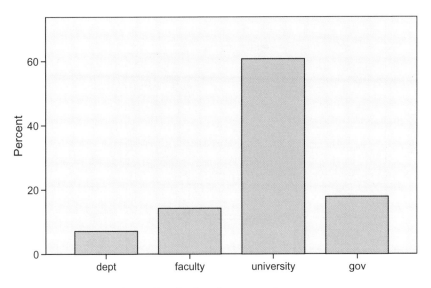

Figure 7. Setting degree requirements

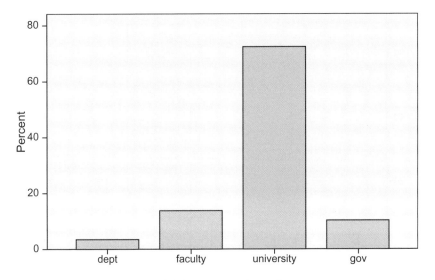

Figure 8. Establishing new undergraduate programs

colleges, pointed out that the autonomy in setting campus missions and objectives was very limited in that it was the state that decided what kind of institution it would be (F, MOEU, BJ, AP; I, LU, BJ, L; K&L, MC, BJ, L). Key aspects determining university ranking are determined by the government, such as the sequence in enrolment, the level of courses provided, and

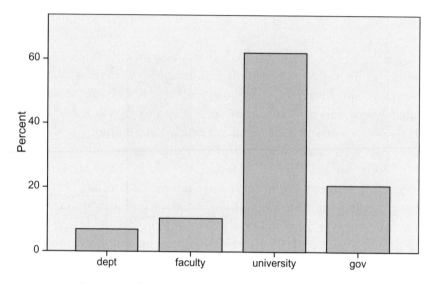

Figure 9.   Reviewing existing undergraduate programs

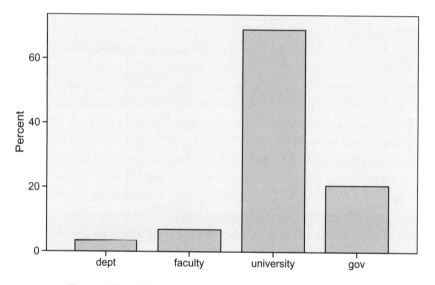

Figure 10.   Eliminating existing undergraduate programs

positioning as a teaching or research university. In other words, the basic goal of an institution has already been defined since its establishment. Therefore, what the institution is allowed to do is to specify it. In fact, an interviewee revealed that the state had withdrawn the autonomy that was granted to individual university on enrolment.

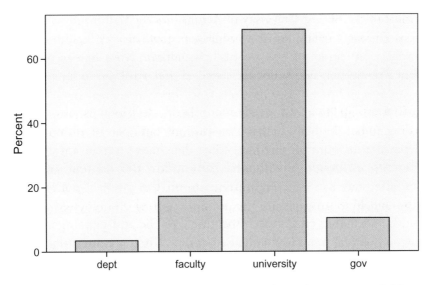

Figure 11. Adding or discontinuing existing academic department or division

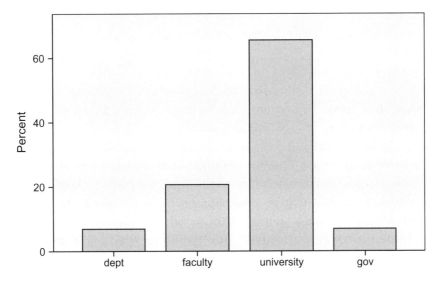

Figure 12. Offer full-fee-paying courses or programs

"Universities used to enjoy more autonomy on enrolment for a period when there were a small amount of extra places that could be decided by universities in addition to the state quota. Soon it was reported some universities were abusing the autonomy in enrolment. After the notorious corruption scandal of the Beijing University of Aeronautics and Astronautics, a prestigious university selling the extra admission quota at very high prices, the flexibility on enrolment was eventually withdrawn. Now the size of enrolment is completely decided by the state." (I, LU, BJ, L)

Autonomy in the rest academic related decisions is also restricted. According to law, higher education institutions can open or eliminate courses and departments, but they need to report the change to relevant government departments. Although institutions can decide the content of academic courses, the state has strict requirements on the political courses such as Marxism and Maoism to assure the political control on higher education and the youth. All higher education institutions, public and private, are required to provide political training for their students. When it comes to student-faculty ratios, individual institutions can adjust the ratio according to the guideline rate of 14:1 specified by *opinions from MOE about deepening reform on personnel and distribution system in higher education* (MOE, 1999). Universities are allowed to set specific degree requirements, but there is a government department, known as Academic Degrees Committee of the State Council, in charge of the all kinds of issues related to academic degrees. As an interviewee who was the vice president said,

"Institutions are accredited by the commission of academic degrees in degree awarding. As a prerequisite for setting up a new institution, the institution must obey Regulations of the People's Republic of China on Academic Degrees." (O, IC, ZH, VP)

As to opening or eliminating undergraduate programs or departments, the location of the decision depends on the type of programs. Universities can make decision on non-degree programs on their own but any change in degree-related programs is subject to the government's approval. A representative from universities affiliated with the municipal government added that permit from the municipal government was necessary for establishing any fee-charging programs in her institution (H, LU, BJ, AD). It is interesting to note that such structural changes are not always initiated by universities; instead, sometimes the government asks public higher education institutions to open or eliminate a department or major according to the national plan, as revealed by an interviewee from a university affiliated with MOE (A, MOEU, BJ, A). As to the tuition fees, under the accumulated pressure from the public on the rocketing tuition fees, the government now has strict control on the tuition charged by public universities. The tuition level is set by the MOE, the

State Development and Reform Commission, and the Bureau of Commodity Price (National development and reform commission, 2007). As an interviewee from the finance office in a public university said,

> "Even though we are allowed to propose the tuition fee, we have no control on it. The higher education tuition fees was no longer an economic issue, rather, it became a political and social focus that need to be handled carefully." (A, MOEU, BJ, A)

Apart from the retained control over key aspects of university management, the dual organizational control — the Party-State system, is also effective in assuring the leadership of the ruling party and smooth implementation of state decisions. For example, the university president and the secretary of the CCP branch in a university, two senior university leaders, are appointed by the state and the ruling party. Moreover, the dual system is also embedded in institutional structures, forming a kind of "soft power" that the government can get the higher education institutions do what it wants without forcing it to do so (Nye Jr., 2004). As an interviewee revealed,

> "It is a common practice that some old carders come to work in universities after retiring from the government. Those former officials then become university leaders. In doing so, the connection between the state and higher education is strengthened." (D, MOEU, BJ, CD)

In short, interviewees were frustrated by excessive state control on their institutions and expect more academic and administrative freedom. One interview painted a dream picture of the state university relationship:

> "Ideally, the relationship between the state and the higher education sector should be a kind of partnership. The major role of government in university governance should be financial support and policy guidance. Unfortunately, there is still a long way to go to achieve this." (F, MOEU, BJ, AP)

3)   *Privatizing HE financing: Intensified inequality*

As shown earlier, the state shifted its role from a sole funding agency of higher education to one of the supporters. Accordingly, privatization has been used to mobilize resources from the private sector. Most of the correspondents (72.4%) agreed that privatization was to mobilize all possible resources from the society to develop the higher education sector in China. An interviewee who was a senior official in the MOE stressed,

"The public appropriation is not enough. The higher education sector needs extra resources. So privatization is adopted to mobilize resources from the society." (J, MOE, BJ SO)

Privatization is proved to be very successful in mobilizing private resources. Indeed, private funding accounts for a larger proportion in China now than in many OECD countries. Nevertheless, encouragement on multi-methods and multi-channel of provision and funding strategies has inevitably led to the increase of the tuition fees (Mok, 1997). Our above discussion related to transnational higher education has clearly shown high tuition fees being charged by these programmes. While the tuition fee of ordinary university is a few thousands Chinese *yuan* per year, the tuition fee of the Xi'an Jiaotong-Liverpool University is about 50,000 *yuan* per year. Such a huge gap of tuition fees between ordinary higher education institutions and joint universities reveals the fact the latter targets at the rich, at least the middle class, as former Vice President Professor Hongcai Wu straightforwardly said that, "people have no money cannot study here." The reason for high tuition fees is partly due to high salary of teachers, as Wu admitted that some quality teachers in UIC could get a yearly salary of over one million dollars (*Wenweipo*, October 16, 2008). Higher tuition fee is essential to the improvement and maintenance of quality education of private education in some cases, but in others it is to cover the financial cost. With no state support and limited donation from the community, ULC has been running on a deficit of HK$5 to 6 million dollars every year since its founding. In order to cover the financial burden, the school has raised the tuition fee, its major source of income, several times in the past few years, from about HK$38,000 in 2005/06 to HK$41,000 in 2007/08 and to HK$50,000 in 2009/10, sparking a controversy among students in the campus (*Mingpao*, September 28, 2009). In fact, financing problem aside, joint universities may also have to ensure and strike for autonomy in enrolling students, more recognition of the degrees conferred, etc.

The growing prominence of "privateness" since the adoption of open-door policy and market economy has generated the tension between the merit-based selection mechanism and financial criteria within the context of commodification of education. China Youth and Children Research Centre reported that tuition fees in public universities had increased by 25 times from 200 *yuan* in 1989 to over 5,000 *yuan* in 2007, while during the same period of time, inhabitant income for urban and rural residents increase only by 9 and 6 times respectively (NBSC, 2008). Moreover, a report by National Development and Reform Commission recently estimated that in the last decade, each student needed to spend over 10,000 *yuan*, including tuition fees and accommodation cost for their undergraduate study in public universities every year, and much more in private institutions (National Development and Reform Commission, 2007).

In contrast, income of urban households (per capita annual disposable) and income of rural households (per capita annual net) in 2005 were 10,493 *yuan* and 3,254.9 *yuan* respectively (NBSC, 2006). This means that higher education has become unaffordable to many low and even middle income families in China (Wang, 2008; Zhou, 2008). This is echoed by a survey conducted by 21st Century Education Development College, indicating that about 80% of the correspondents think the tuition fee is unreasonably high. The soaring cost of higher education has become an important cause for educational inequality in China. As a result, students are deprived the opportunity to receive tertiary education if they cannot afford the high cost of going to college even if they are qualified.

Bringing the "Public Back In" Education

In face of the prosperous development of higher education after the reforms, it is easy to overshadow some issues that deserve attention. For example, while the introduction of market principles did not fix problems associated with the bureaucratic system like inefficiency, it brought market failures to the higher education sector. The private sector and market mechanisms are over emphasized and educational inequalities deteriorated rapidly in the privatization process. In this regard, "bringing the public back" is one of the most frequently heard demands from critics to address the problems of privatization and marketization of public service delivery. As discussed above, one of the most hotly disputed issues associated with privatization of higher education is the rocketing tuition fee, which has posed serious challenges to equal access to higher education. To address the problem, free higher education has been provided in selected normal universities in China since 2006. More recently, the central government decided to allocate 80% of the quotas of free higher education to underdeveloped regions in central and west China, as a further response to inequity issues resulted from privatization (MOE, 2009). In addition, in the latest blueprint for national development — the 11th five-year plan (2006–2010), the state vowed to increase the public expenditure on higher education to a level that its average growth rate outgrows the rate of overall public revenue (Xinhuanet, 2009).

In fact, since the adoption of "scientific approach to development" (*kexue fazhanguan*), "people-centered development" and "harmonious society" as guiding principles of governance, it is undeniable that the Central government has increased its role in public service, yet questions remain on in what areas and in what ways the government will step in, as the Central government does not attempt to regain control in every aspect of the higher education sector. Taking the latest "National Outline for Medium and Long Term Educational Reform and Development" as example, we can find that there are two areas — administration and financing — in higher education in which the government deploys two different governance approaches (General Office of the State Council, 2010). The Outline seems to signal that the government intends to reduce its direct participation and control in the former, while it will be the other way round in the latter. For administration of higher education, the government pledges in the Outline that it will promote autonomy and self-management of higher education institutions, by means of granting more flexibility in, for example, teaching and learning activities, conducting scientific research, technology exploration, and human resources management. Democratic checkup and social participation will also be encouraged to monitor and assist the management of the schools (Chapter 13). Moreover, the Outline calls for further opening up of Chinese higher education to the world, and highlights the need to bring in more international quality resources, such as attracting foreign prestigious higher education institutions to offer educational services in China (Chapter 16). This pragmatic approach demonstrates that for the sake of enhancing the quality of higher education, the Chinese government is willing to step a little bit back and to bring in more stakeholders as long as they are contributing to higher education and not attempting to challenge the ultimate authority of the government.

However, in regard to educational financing, the government has decided to step in instead of stepping back. Although the Outline still sticks to the principle that higher education should be mainly sustained by the inputs from the owners and investors, and by donations from the community, and tuition fees (Chapter 18), it also indicate the state's commitment to share more of the financing responsibility. As proposed in the Outline, the Central government will set up special fund for supporting higher education of local regions, especially the Western and Central regions. The responsibility of helping the underdeveloped provinces is also shared with higher education institutions in the eastern area, which are encouraged to enroll students from the western region (Chapter 7). In fact, this proposed strategy is not entirely new but echoing to the Premier Wen Jiabao's working report 2010 (BBC

Chinese, 2010). To sum up, the Outline reiterates the state's leading role in education provision, coordination and regulation on the one hand, and encourages participation of non-state actor in educational provision on the other (Chapter 14 and 15). Thus, it suggests that privatization and decentralization of higher education will not be halted despite the problems mentioned above. In this regard, it is expected that the future education development in China will continue to depend on a combination of state and market effects (Mok, 2008a).

Conclusion

In conclusion, instead of suggesting a sharp return to a socialist welfare model, the recent attempts to reinsert the "publicness" into higher education is best described as "less a matter of reversal-cum-reconstruction… but more an exercise in "damage control" by which private and para-state organizations… are subject to new forms of regulation and some direct measures of subsidy are introduced to address the plight of the very poor" (Painter and Mok, 2008, pp. 147–148). That means, while retaining the good elements of market force in mobilizing resources and increasing provision, the government has spotted and decided to eradicate certain bad elements, namely the skyrocketing financial burden and growing inequalities of education, that are critical to the maintenance of social harmony. Therefore, the recent efforts seemingly increase the "publicness" of higher education could be better translated into an aspiration for good governance that complements the market economy rather than a retreat of the process of marketization and privatization.

References

Ball, S. (forthcoming) Global education, heterarchies, and hybrid organizations. In K. H. Mok (Ed.), *The search for new governance of higher education in Asia*. New York: Palgrave.

BBC Chinese (2010) *Text transcript: Summary of Wen Jiabo's government working report*. Retrieved from http://www.bbc.co.uk/zhongwen/trad/china/2010/03/100305_china_congress.shtml

Belfield, C. R. and H. M. Levin (2002) *Education privatization: Causes, consequences and planning implications*. Paris, UNESCO.

Bennett, A. (1997) The measurement of privatization and related issues. In A. Bennett (Ed.), *How does privatization work: Essays on privatization in honour of professor V.V. Ramanadham*. London: Routledge.

Central Committee of the Chinese Communist Party (CCCCP) (1985) *Decision of the CCP central committee on the reform of the educational structure.* CCP. Beijing, Foreign languages express.

Central Committee of the Chinese Communist Party (CCCCP) and State Council (1993) *Mission outline of the reform and development of China's education (zhong guo jiao yu gai ge he fa zhan gang yao).* Central Committee of CCP and State council.

Cheng, K. M. (1995) Education — Decentralization and the market. In L. Wong, and S. MacPherson (Eds.), *Social change and social policy in contemporary China.* Aldershot: Avebury.

Commission of education (1992) *Opinions about deepening reform and expanding autonomous rights for universities affiliated with the commission of education.* Beijing.

General Office of the State Council (2010) *The State Council passed 'national outline for medium and long term educational reform and development.'* www.gov.cn: Beijing.

Hayhoe, R. (1996) *China's universities 1895–1995: A century of cultural conflict.* New York and London: Garland Press.

Hong Kong Economic Journal (2009) Exemplifying the 'education paragon,' Hong Kong schools are going to China to co-found schools. April 16.

Huang, F. (2003) Policy and practice of the internationalization of higher education in China. *Journal of Studies in International Education*, 7(3), 225–240.

Long, X. Z. and Z. G. Liu (2006) Policy analysis and implications on institutional autonomy since the market reform (gai ge kai fang yi lai wo guo da xue ban xue zi zhu quan de zheng ce wen ben fen xi ji qi shi). *Heilongjiang Researches on Higher Education*, 150(10).

Mingpao (2009) *The Hong Kong Baptist University's UIC receives complaints for an increase of tuition fees to 50,000 per year*, September 28.

Ministry of Education (1999) *Opinions from MOE About Deepening Reform on Personnel and Distribution System in Higher Education (jiao yu bu guan yu dang qian shen hua gao deng xue xiao ren shi fen pei zhi du gai ge de ruo gan yi jian).* Beijing: Ministry of Education.

Ministry of Education (2006) *Number of full-time teachers by field of study in non-state/private HEIs.* Retrieved from http://www.moe.edu.cn/edoas/website18/38/info33638.htm

Ministry of Education (2008) *Establishment and management methods for independent colleges (du li xue yuan she zhi yu guan li ban fa).* Beijing: Ministry of Education.

Ministry of Education (2009) *Six changes in higher education enrolment this year.* Retrieved from http://www.edu.cn/09gaozhao_8100/2009-0603/t20090603_381716.shtml

Mok, K. H. (1997) Privatization or marketization: Educational development in post-Mao China. *International Review of Education*, 43(5), 547–567.

Mok, K. H. (2005) Globalization and educational restructuring: University merging and changing governance in China. *Higher Education*, 50, 57–88.

Mok, K. H. (2006) China's response to globalization: Educational decentralization and marketization in post-Mao China. In K. H. Mok (Ed.), *Education reform and education policy in East Asia*. London: Routledge.

Mok, K. H. (2008) When socialism meets market capitalism: Challenges for privatizing and marketizing education in China and Vietnam. *Policy Futures in Education*, 6(5), 601–615.

Mok, K. H. (2008a) When neo-liberalism colonizes higher education in Asia: Bringing the 'public' back in the contemporary university? In D. Rhoten (Ed.), *Globalization, massification and commercialization of contemporary universities*. New York: Columbia University Press.

Mok, K. H. (2009) The growing importance of the privateness in education: Challenges for higher education governance in China. *Compare*, 39(1), 35–49.

Mok, K. H. and Y. W. Lo (2007) The impacts of neo-liberalism on China's higher education. *Journal of Critical Education Policy Studies*, 5(1).

Mok, K. H., Y. C. Wong and X. Zhang (2009) When marketization and privatization clashes with socialist ideals: Educational inequality in urban China. *International Journal of Educational Development*, 29(5), 505–512.

National Bureau of Statistics of China [NBSC] (1996–2008) *China statistic yearbook*. Beijing. China statistics press.

National Development and Reform Commission (2007) *Notice on tuition standard for HEIs Affiliated with Ministries (guan yu gong bu zhong yang bu shu gao xiao xue fei biao zhun de tong zhi)*. Retrieved from http://www.ndrc.gov.cn/zcfb/zcfbtz/2007tongzhi/t20070706_146668.htm

Nye, J. S. Jr. (2004) *Soft power*. New York: PublicAffairs.

Painter, M. and K. H. Mok (2008) Reasserting the public service delivery: The de-privatization and de-marketization of education in China. *Policy and Society*, 27(2), 137–150.

Shanghai Education and Research Centre (2002) Review of expansion of higher education in China in the past three years. *Education Development Research*, (9).

Standing Committee of the National Peoples Congress (1999) *The act of higher education*. Standing Committee of the National Peoples Congress.

Starr, P. (1989) The meaning of privatization. In S. B. Kamerman and A. J. Kahn (Eds.), *Privatization and the welfare state*. Princeton, NJ: Princeton University Press.

State Council, the People's Republic of China (2010) *National outline for medium and long term educational reform and development*. State Council.

State Education Commission (SEC) (1995) *Education law.* Beijing: State Education Commission.

Savas, E. S. (1992) Privatization in post-socialist countries. *Public Administration Review*, 52(6), 573–581.

The Privatization Org (2007) *Types and Techniques of Privatization.* Retrieved from http://www.privatization.org/database/whatisprivatization/privatization_techniques.html

Times Higher Education Supplement (2007) Nottingham university: Reaping 'A phenomenal return on a £40 million investment,' September 21. London: *Times Higher Education Supplement.* Retrieved from http://www.timeshighereducation.co.uk/story.asp?storyCode=310522&sectioncode=26

Wang, L. (2008) Social exclusion and educational inequality in China. Paper presented at *Policy and Politics International Conference.* Bristol, UK.

Wei, Y. T. and G. C. Zhang (1995) A historical perspective on non-governmental higher education in China. Paper presented at the *International Conference on Private Education in Asia and the Pacific Region*, University of Xiamen, Xiamen China.

Wenweipo (2008) *Suzhou industrial park is transforming into a modern new city, which will be a housing, shopping and tourism spot*, October 16.

Wenweipo (2009) *The university Nottingham Ningbo is approved to enroll Hong Kong students*, February 23.

Xinhuanet (2009) *The 11th five year plan.* (*115 gui hua gang yao*). Retrieved from http://news.xinhuanet.com/ziliao/2006–01/16/content_4057926.htm

Zhou, Z. W. (2008) On the industrialization of China's education industry lost in direction. *Theoretical Observation*, 50(2), 94–97.

Appendix: Interview Details

Interviewee	Type of affiliation	Location	Position
1. A	University affiliated with MOE	Beijing	Administrator (financial office)
2. B	University affiliated with MOE	Beijing	Administrator
3. C	University affiliated with MOE	Beijing	Center director (professor)
4. D	University affiliated with MOE	Beijing	Center director (professor)
5. E	University affiliated with MOE	Beijing	Administrator
6. F	University affiliated with MOE	Beijing	Associate professor
7. G	University affiliated with MOE	Beijing	Professor
8. H	University affiliate with the municipal government	Beijing	Associate dean (professor)
9. I	University affiliate with the municipal government	Beijing	Lecturer (used to be an administrator)
10. J	MOE	Beijing	Senior official
11. K	Minban college	Beijing	Lecturer
12. L	Minban college	Beijing	Lecturer
13. M	Minban college	Beijing	Panel chair (Lecturer)

11

RELIGION

David A. Palmer

The University of Hong Kong

Abstract

In the three decades since the end of the Maoist era, all forms of religion in China have been undergoing restoration, innovation and expansion. Belying Marxist and secularist predictions of religion's inevitable demise, most forms of religion, whether new or traditional, indigenous or foreign, official or illegal, ethnic or universal, communal or individual, and all combinations thereof, have enjoyed increasing popularity. This chapter begins with a discussion of what counts as "religion" in the Chinese context and how it can be measured, and present a brief outline of the historical factors underlying the current situation. It then provides an overview of the PRC's policy toward religion, which constitutes the framework within which (or, more often, outside of which) Chinese religious life is organized. It finally presents the basic evolution since 1979 of Chinese communal religion, the *qigong* movement, the Confucian revival, Buddhism and Daoism, Islam, and Christianity.

Keywords: Buddhism; Catholicism; Confucianism; Daoism; Islam; Protestantism; *qigong*; religion.

Introduction

In the three decades since the end of the Maoist era, all forms of religion in China have been undergoing restoration, innovation and expansion. The phenomenon has had significant impacts on the People's Republic's international relations and internal politics; a growing influence on Chinese civil

293

society, intellectual discourse and grassroots social organization; and, in various contexts, intriguing connections between economic life and religious beliefs and networks. The growth of religion in China has occurred in the wake of humanity's most thorough and sustained experiment in creating a society without any religion at all, during the Cultural Revolution years (1966–1976) when all forms of religious activity and organization were banned for a decade. Belying Marxist and secularist predictions of religion's inevitable demise, most forms of religion, whether new or traditional, indigenous or foreign, official or illegal, ethnic or universal, communal or individual, and all combinations thereof, have enjoyed increasing popularity. These changes have put pressure on the state's regulatory framework for religion, which remains essentially unchanged since the 1950's, while the future role of religion in Chinese society remains an open question. This chapter will begin with a discussion of what counts as "religion" in the Chinese context and how it can be measured, and present a brief outline of the historical factors underlying the current situation. It will then provide an overview of the PRC's policy toward religion, which constitutes the framework within which (or, more often, outside of which) Chinese religious life is organized. It will finally present the basic evolution since 1979 of Chinese communal religion, the *qigong* movement, the Confucian revival, Buddhism and Daoism, Islam, and Christianity.

Counting Religious Believers in China

According to official statistics, there are 100 million religious believers in Mainland China, amounting to approx. 8% of the population. Most scholars, however, consider this figure to be a serious underestimation. In 2007, some Chinese researchers, operating independently, released a survey which raised the figure to 300 million (Vermander, 2009, p. 6); while in 2010, a joint Chinese-American survey was announced which claimed that over 85% of the adult population have some sort of religious belief or practice (Yang *et al.*, 2010; Yang, 2010).

The reason for these discrepancies — besides the fact that local religious affairs officials have a career incentive to under-report the extent of religious activity in their jurisdiction — can be attributed to the complex organizational structure and patterns of identification in Chinese religious culture. In primarily Christian and Muslim societies, most people explicitly identify with a single, exclusive religion, each of which has its own institutions which aim to structure all aspects of a member's religious life, from life-cycle rituals (weddings, funerals) to theology, individual spirituality, moral teachings, congregational activity and social engagement. All of these aspects of spiritual and religious life are widespread in Chinese culture, but they are not organized into a single institution; they are not always clearly distinguished from secular life, and they are usually not the subjects of a conscious identification by individuals. Thus, it is likely that, if asked what religion she believes in, a Chinese person is likely to respond "none," even though she may well have a small shrine to Guanyin, the goddess of mercy, in her home, and goes to burn incense at a temple at special occasions. Furthermore, people may engage in acts of worship of gods without themselves being clear about how much they actually "believe" in what they are doing. As a result, surveys and statistics can be a misleading tool for taking the pulse of religious life, unless survey designers and users have a clear understanding of how religious practices and beliefs fit into Chinese culture and society. More recent studies have refined their methodology, by trying to measure not only religious affiliation, but also the extent to which people actually engage in religious practices such as burning incense at a temple, attending a church, wearing a charm, or following fengshui rules, or believe in notions such as heaven, hell, reincarnation or supernatural forces. A survey directed by Fenggang Yang and a Chinese research firm, using a sample of 7021 cases conducted in 2007, thus incorporated such types of elements into his questionnaire, yielding the following data, among others:

— In the previous 12 months, up to 754 million had practiced some form of ancestor worship.
— around 362 million had practiced some form of divination (including fortune-telling, face-reading, etc).
— around 141 million believed in the god of wealth (*caishen*), and a similar number practiced fengshui restrictions or had consulted a fengshui master.

In terms of religious affiliations, the survey estimates that around 185 million self-identify as Buddhists (around 18% of the adult population); 33 million self-identify as Christian (3.2% of the adult population, including 30 million Protestants and 3 million Catholics); and 12 million self-identify as Daoists (1.2%). Only around 15% can be counted as true atheists, having neither supernatural belief nor participated in any religious practices (Yang *et al.*, 2010; Yang, 2010).

There are many reasons for the low levels of explicit religious affiliation of Chinese people, in spite of relatively high levels of religious beliefs and practice. One common explanation, held throughout most of the 20th century by

Chinese intellectuals and most Western scholars, is that Chinese beliefs are unorganized and incoherent motley of superstitions, which hardly deserve to be called "religion." Recent historical, anthropological and sociological scholarship, however, has questioned this view and established that it is itself a product of China's modern intellectual and political history, in which the adoption of Western and Christian categories has led to Chinese religious culture being ignored, denigrated, or vigorously repressed by both the Republican (1912–1949) and Communist (1949–present) political regimes (Goossaert and Palmer, 2011).

Historical Background

In order to understand the complex diversity of religious affiliations and organizations in contemporary China, as well as the difficulties and contradictions of the Chinese state's current policy toward religion, it is essential to review this historical process. In the late imperial era (the Ming and Qing dynasties, 1363–1911), China was a religious state, with the Emperor acting as the supreme religious authority in his capacity as "Son of Heaven," who derived his legitimacy from the "Mandate of Heaven." Government was conducted by ritual as much as by law and administrative procedure, and the Confucian ideology upheld by the bureaucratic class was not only a moral philosophy, but essentially a ritual system derived from classics such as the *Liji* (the *Book of Rites*), which prescribe how to conduct sacrifices to the spirits of Heaven, Earth, of the four cardinal directions, the main agricultural crops, and so on. Magistrates and administrators were the priests of this ritual system in the provincial capitals and county seats. The imperial cult overlaid millions of autonomous popular deity cults and temples, most of which were the main organizational form of social groups, ranging from territorial communities (villages, irrigation alliances, neighborhoods and cities) to professional guilds (for carpenters, boatmen, merchants, etc.) and charities, and even sworn brotherhoods and underworld societies. Through the ancestor cult of families, lineages and clans — which was also the organizational foundation of the large landholding estates and corporations of South China — domestic units and kinship networks were also integrated into the empire's Confucian orthodoxy. A religious dimension was integral to most forms of social organization, the culture was steeped in a common cosmology, and so, generally speaking, there was no distinct religious identity or affiliation. Buddhism and Daoism existed as organized "teachings," but, with the exception of a small number of lay devotees who had "taken refuge" in Buddhism or become a disciple of a Daoist master, these religions existed primarily as esoteric traditions, with specialized monks and priests offering ritual and spiritual services to the population at large and to temple communities, which hired them as needed, most often without claiming any formal affiliation to one or the other set of teachings. These functions could also be played by the priests and masters of myriads of local ritual traditions as well as by lay devotional associations and salvationist movements, some of which preached millenialist and apocalyptic doctrines. These movements, often led by charismatic preachers and healers, did recruit large numbers of self-identified followers. The Ming state, fearful of sectarian rebellions, banned the latter groups as "heretical doctrines (*xiejiao*). It also restricted the number of Buddhist and Daoist monks, and attempted to co-opt popular divinity cults by canonizing them, with the Emperor giving gods official ranks and honoring them with promotions in the hierarchy of the pantheon. Through these measures, the state attempted to impose itself as the final and supreme authority in religious matters. Although it restricted or banned organized religious groups and unlicensed temples, the state did so in the name of orthodoxy as a religious institution itself, based on essentially the same cosmology as the religion of the people (Yang, 1960; Lagerwey, 2010; Goossaert, 2011).

The introduction of Christianity and Western influence challenged the traditional Chinese religious system. From the 16th to 18th centuries, Catholic Jesuit missionaries had adopted a strategy of integrating Christianity and Chinese civilization. This involved downplaying the religious elements of Chinese culture, depicting elite Confucianism as a rational moral philosophy compatible with Christian religion, and dismissing the rest as superstition. Later, in the 19th century, a more aggressive missionizing approach was more exclusive and denigrating of Chinese religion. By the early 20th century, with China humiliated by the Western powers and Japan, modernizing intellectuals sought to understand the keys to Western power, and concluded that it derived from its science and/or its religion — neither of which China possessed. Christianity became the model for a new concept of "religion" (*zongjiao*) — understood as a unified system of belief, theology and ethical principles, with a scriptural canon, an educated clergy, exclusive congregational membership and worship, and highly organized national institutions. This model became the norm for the religious policy and regulations of all Chinese states, from the Chinese revolution of 1911 until the present. When Chinese constitutions stipulated the freedom of religious belief, and regulations provided for the recognition and registration of religious organizations, they have (with a few short-lived exceptions) applied only to the "religions" fitting the Christian model, i.e., Christianity itself (usually understood in

China as two separate religions, Catholicism and Protestantism), Islam, Buddhism and, more problematically, Daoism. All the rest — including most of the religious system outlined above — was delegitimized as superstition, and became the target of anti-superstition campaigns and movements to confiscate popular temples and convert them into schools, government offices, barracks, granaries and other uses, throughout the first half of the 20th century (Nedostup, 2009; Goossaert and Palmer, 2011).

PRC Religious Policy

After the PRC was established in 1949, the new regime based its religious policy on the same categories. Official, state-controlled religious associations were established for the Buddhists (1953), Protestants (1954), Muslims (1954), Catholics (1957) and Daoists (1957), which, combined, had only 11.4 million declared followers. Redemptive societies such as Yiguandao, which had more followers than any of the recognized religious institutions, were ruthlessly exterminated as "reactionary sects and secret societies." And ancestor worship, communal religion, and temple cults, which were practiced by almost all Chinese people, were banned as "feudal superstition" (Laliberté, 2011; Yang, 2006, p. 103; Palmer, 2008, 2011).

The religious policy of the PRC built on the ideology and experience of the Chinese Communist Party (CCP) as elaborated during the Chinese civil war and in "liberated areas" prior to 1949. Ideologically, the CCP followed the Marxist dictum that religion was the "opiate of the masses," an instrument of domination by the ruling classes and an illusionary otherworldly hope for people who had no chance to improve their lives in this world. In theory, this meant that religion would naturally disappear once the class-based social structure was eliminated and the peoples' hopes and desires attained through communism. There was thus no need to directly attack religion; it was its class foundations which had to be destroyed. In practice, however, the CCP developed a more pro-active and two-pronged approach to religion, in the context of its United Front policy of building friendly ties with potential non-communist allies, in a common struggle against the enemy. Those religious individuals and groups which were identified as actively collaborating with the CCP's enemies (depending on the time and context, this meant Japanese invaders, the Kuomintang, the feudal landlords, capitalists, colonialists, or imperialists) were to be targeted and ruthlessly eliminated, while those who shared the CCP's ideals and were willing to cooperate with the Party, were to be nurtured and strengthened with government assistance, so that they could use their social influence and religious legitimacy to support the regime.

Geopolitical considerations were crucial in drawing the battle-lines of the United Front. Christianity was tainted by its close organizational association with foreign churches, Western imperialism and anti-communism; both Protestants and Catholics were torn by struggles between pro-CCP "patriotic" believers, who ran the official associations, and those who did not rally to the new regime, who were struggled against and driven underground, planting the seeds of the underground Catholic church, loyal to the Vatican, and the Protestant "house churches." Buddhism and Islam, on the other hand, were the religions of the ethnic minorities of the vast Western border-lands including Tibet and Xinjiang, which needed to be placated to ensure their allegiance to the Peoples' Republic; these religions were also used to build diplomatic bridges with Asian and Third World nations. Buddhism and Islam thus became important instruments in the PRC's ethnic and foreign policies (Welch, 1972; Goossaert and Palmer, 2011).

But by the end of the 1950's, leftist radicalism undermined the alliances of the United Front; a short respite in the early 1960's was followed by the total suppression of all forms of religion during the Cultural Revolution. Even the official religious associations were banned, as well as the State Council's Bureau of Religious Affairs and the Party's United Front Department itself. Tibetan Buddhists were the first to be alienated and the 14th Dalai Lama (Tenzin Gyatsob, 1935), who had held positions as Deputy Chairman of the Standing Committee of the National Peoples' Congress, took exile in India with his court in 1959; the more pro-Beijing 10th Panchen Lama (1938–1989) was himself imprisoned from 1964 to 1977. All temples, monasteries and churches were closed. Muslims suffered greatly, in some areas being forced to eat pork. Christians could only worship in secret. The shrines, statues, and manuscripts of communal cults were destroyed. Celibate monks were forced to marry, and many priests and pastors were sent to re-education camps. Little visible religion of any kind remained.

Following Deng Xiaoping's accession to power and the launch of the new policy of reform and opening up, the PRC government began a process of undoing the excesses of the Cultural Revolution. Religious leaders were reha-bilitated and a small number of temples, monasteries, churches and mosques were re-opened. The Religious Affairs Bureau was re-established in 1979 and the United Front policy was renewed. The 1982 constitution guaranteed the freedom of individual religious belief, although it placed restrictions on many aspects of religious organization and activity.

The policy framework was outlined in more detail in "Document no. 19," also issued in 1982. This document stressed the importance of individual religious freedom and the counterproductive results of forcing people away from religion, calling for a more gradual approach — but it reiterated the ultimate goal of marginalizing and ultimately eliminating religion, and called for a more vigorous promotion of atheist education and propaganda. At the same time, the document called for a better implementation of religious freedom through the re-establishment of the official religious associations, the opening of more designated places of worship, the training of clergy, and the development of international religious exchanges — all of which were limited to the clergy, places of worship, and activities of the five officially-recognized religious associations. Document 19 legitimized the restoration of legal religious life, while inscribing it into a clear regulatory framework compatible with Marxist eschatology (MacInnis, 1989).

The 1980's saw the beginnings of a religious revival, as worshippers reclaimed and rebuilt confiscated or destroyed temples, churches and mosques. In Tibet and in the Muslim areas of the West, religious fervor bloomed, pent up for well over a decade. By the early 1990's, following the Tiananmen student movement of 1989, the CCP leadership became aware that religion continued to be an important social force. Prior to the Tiananmen events, riots had occurred in Tibet in February and March 1989, and Muslims, in the "Chinese Salman Rushdie Affair," had also demonstrated in several provinces to protest the publication of derogatory stories about Islam in Chinese books. Outside China, the Polish Catholic Church had played a role in triggering the chain of events leading to the collapse of the Soviet Bloc, and Islam was a potential political factor in the several newly-independent central Asian states along China's borders with Xinjiang. The CCP leadership became concerned with how to more effectively control religion, and, through a series of high-level meetings of the State Council and with religious leaders, elaborated the doctrine of the "mutual adaptation of religion and socialist society" (in which it was primarily the former that was expected to adapt to the latter). A new policy ordinance issued in December 1990, "Document no. 6," followed by other regulations in 1994, called for the closer monitoring of religious activity, places of worship and personnel.

These policy orientations led to a gradual expansion and strengthening, through the 1990s, of the institutional structure of religious management in the PRC. The basic foundations of this structure had been laid in the 1950's, but after its abolition in the mid 1960s and its restoration in the 1980s, efforts now turned to its more systematic implementation at the provincial and local levels (Madsen and Tong, 2000; Chan and Carlson, 2005). The system of religious management involves three major types of organization: the United Front Work Department, which is an arm of the CCP; the Bureau of Religious Affairs (renamed State Administration of Religious

Affairs — SARA — in 1996), which is an agency of the government under the State Council at the national level; and the official Associations of the five recognized religions (Buddhism, Daoism, Islam, Protestantism and Catholicism), which are, in theory, democratic associations of believers. The United Front department is charged with developing close personal relations with the friendly leaders of non-communist organizations including minor political parties, commercial enterprises, overseas Chinese, ethnic minorities, and religious leaders. The United Front helps to arrange the appointment of respected religious leaders on political bodies such as the Peoples' Political Consultative Conferences, turning religious vocations into political careers, symbolically drawing clerics into the political process. The SARA oversees the implementation of religious policy, including the registration of places of worship and clergy, mediating disputes between religious communities and other segments of society, and the negotiation of the return to religious communities of properties confiscated by other government departments during the Cultural Revolution (a process which is still ongoing, over 35 years later). Different divisions within SARA are assigned to each of the five recognized religions. An additional division, established in 2004, is charged with research and policy recommendations, including issues in relation to religious communities "other" than the five officially recognized ones, including Chinese popular religion, the Russian Orthodox Church, and "new religions," notably the Bahá'í Faith and the Mormons. By the mid 2000s, these "other" forms of religion were increasingly viewed by SARA as a legitimate reality and tolerated in practice — although the government, at the time of writing, is afraid of opening a Pandora's box by providing an avenue for formally registering any of them. In some provinces, the temples of popular religion can obtain legal status by registering as Daoist or, in rarer cases, as Buddhist.

The official religious associations are responsible for each religion's places of worship, and are the formal employer of the clergy. They also run seminaries and institutes for the training of clergy, which combine religious knowledge with secular and political education. Although their staff wear religious robes, these associations operate in a manner similar to other state-run socialist work units (*danwei*). Though autonomous in theory, the associations are embedded in a wider hierarchy in which they ultimately report to SARA. The latter, as well as United Front officials, play a role in the "election" of association leaders, trying to ensure that the individuals chosen to head the religion will enjoy both the respect and legitimacy of the religious believers, and the political approval of the government, so as to be able to effectively handle the relations between the state and the religious community (Palmer, 2009).

This institutional structure exists at the national, provincial, and municipal or county levels. Other organs also play a role in the formulation and implementation of religious policy. Academic institutions, notably the China Academy of Social Sciences and its provincial counterparts, as well as certain universities, engage in academic research on religion. By treating religion as a form of "culture" worthy of serious inquiry, their research, conferences and publications help to legitimize religious life, while they also act as think-tanks, conducting surveys and offering policy recommendations to the authorities (Overmeyer, 2001; Dunch, 2008). The police (Public Security Bureau) and other specialized agencies, on the other hand, are entrusted with repressing illegal forms of religion, especially the groups designated as "evil cults" (*xiejiao*), notably Falun Gong and some Christian sects (Tong, 2009; Dunn, 2009).

"Minority nationality customs" are an important legitimizing category for the religious practices of ethnic minorities. Indeed, while official and intellectual discourse does not consider religion to be a component of Han ethnic identity, religion (or "exotic customs" which are in fact religious) is considered to be an integral component of ethnic minority culture, and the defining aspect for some nationalities such as the Muslim Hui. Official policy toward ethnic minorities, which seeks to preserve the outward markers of ethnic diversity and identity (while promoting their substantive assimilation), thus tends to be far more open toward religion among the minority nationalities than for the Han (except when religion is suspected of fomenting separatism, as discussed below). In the 10 minority nationalities designated as Muslim, all members of the ethnic group are automatically considered to be Muslim believers.

From the mid 1990s and until today, government discourse on religion has become increasingly positive. The crackdown on Falun Gong in 1999 (see below) caused a brief chill for many forms of religious activity, but it also generated an elaborate official discourse on socially-destructive "evil cults," contrasted to the true "religions" which, it was stressed, make positive contributions to social stability and development (Palmer, 2008). That a group such as Falun Gong could seemingly appear out of nowhere and quickly recruit millions of followers, led many officials to conclude that peoples' spiritual needs were being neglected, and that more orthodox forms of religion should be given more space in order to avoid the spread of sectarian movements. Nowadays, the doctrine of religion as an "opiate" is rarely mentioned, and speeches by senior leaders have admitted that religion still has a long life ahead of it. The positive contributions of religion to society are recognized, and its potential contributions to economic development, culture, and charity and philanthropy, are now explicitly praised and encouraged. At the same time, the authorities still fear the influence and legitimacy such contributions could bring to religious organizations, and so there are still many obstacles for religious communities to engage in charitable projects (Laliberté, Palmer and Wu, 2011). Overall, although the legitimate space for religion has steadily expanded over the past decades, the basic framework for China's religious policy remains essentially unchanged since the 1950s.

Most of religious life in China, however, from Chinese communal religion to new religious movements, as well as unregistered Protestant house churches, Catholic communities loyal to Rome, and other informal groups, either does not fit under the official category of "religion" or has not been integrated into the official associations and thus, paradoxically, escapes from state management under the religious policy. It exists in a vast and growing grey area, often tolerated but with ambiguous legal status. Many temples, rituals and practices have secured legitimation by presenting themselves as something other than religion — as forms of Chinese traditional medicine, sports and science (in the case of *qigong* in the 1980s and 1990s — see Palmer, 2007); as state-supported "intangible cultural heritage" according to UNESCO norms (in the case of many deity cults, temples and ritual traditions); as tourist resources; as environmental or educational programmes; or as platforms for building economic and political ties with Chinese worshippers from Taiwan, Hong Kong, Macau, and Southeast Asia (Chau, 2005b; Yang, 2006; Yang, 2004).

Revivals of Communal Religion in Rural China

Chinese "communal religion" refers to an integrated whole including a sacred local geography, temples and their organizing committees, cyclical festivals, ritual specialists, life-cycle rituals, and the ancestor cult. The sacred geography is expressed in popular lore about the *fengshui* energetic qualities of features of the landscape including mountains, rivers, stones, trees, tombs, and temples, and in relation to which villages and homes are positioned and oriented. Temples and shrines are the centers of communal worship of local gods and saints; they are the embodiments of local mythology and history, and are built and managed by lay committees of community members with moral authority (chosen in various ways including as representatives of each family or lineage in the village, selected by lot, etc.). Many temples host annual fairs which, especially in North China, are carnival-like events drawing crowds in the tens of thousands over several days, who come to worship, watch opera performances, shop at makeshift market stalls, and enjoy the noisy crowds. In the South, cyclical *jiao* rituals (held at intervals of five or so years) and other festivals are also common, and often feature processions in which deity statues are paraded through the community's territory. While lay committees do most of the organizing, ritual specialists — who may be non-monastic Daoist or Buddhist priests (especially in the South), masters of salvationist traditions of the Unborn Mother cults, lay scripture-recitation groups, or others — are hired or invited to provide the liturgy, often with the assistance of amateur musicians. These ritual specialists also officiate at life-cycle rituals, notably births and funerals, and conduct healing rites. The cult of ancestors is conducted at an altar containing tablets for the deceased of recent generations, located in the central room of traditional peasant homes, and at their tombs, notably during the annual grave-sweeping festival (Qingming). While official policy, in order to eliminate the unproductive use of land by sprawling tombs, calls for the replacement of burials by cremation, cremation rates actually dropped in some areas in the post-Mao years, and remain low until today outside the cities (Goossaert and Palmer, 2011, pp. 231–232). In South China, lineage halls are also common, federating through periodic rites the descendants of a common ancestor in the same village or region. In single-surname villages, the lineage hall is often the main community organization. In the past, lineages often owned large land estates and managed their resources, running schools and charities for their members. Today, lineages no longer directly own land, but they remain powerful sources of identity and play an important role in local politics.

The revival of Chinese communal religion has been uneven in different regions, depending on a range of factors. The level of tolerance and support of local authorities is an important concern, and can vary based on personal and kinship ties between cadres and temple activists, as well as the incentives provided by the use of popular religion to build ties with potential investors from overseas Chinese communities, or to secure government funding for heritage protection. Another factor is the appearance of capable activists with deep local ties and political skills, such as retired Party cadres, to take the lead and organize religious activities and rituals. And finally, the transmission of local religious memory is crucial. In some villages, priests and old people with good memories (even though liturgical manuals were destroyed during Maoist campaigns, they had them committed to memory and copied them down in the 1980s) have been able to reconstruct their traditions, which, sometimes, were only interrupted for a few years during the heat of the Cultural Revolution. But in other places, the interruption of transmission has been longer, and elder authorities are weak or forgetful, leading to the nearly complete disappearance of the local system of worship — or the younger generations are not interested in learning their skills (DuBois, 2005; Jones, 2011).

Earlier scholarly research seemed to indicate that the revival of communal religion was stronger in the coastal areas of South China, notably in Zhejiang, Fujian and parts of Guangdong (Dean, 1992; Tam, 2011; Yang, 2000). This could be explained by the government's more open policy in these provinces in the early period of post-Maoist reforms, greater material affluence (Chinese temples and rituals are expensive to build and stage), and ties with overseas Chinese eager to go on pilgrimage to return to the source of their ancestral cults (such as Mazu for many Taiwanese, and the Patriarch of the Clear Stream for Singaporeans: see Yang, 2004; Kuah, 2000). But more recent research has shown that, although it was perhaps slower to take off, popular religion is also undergoing a significant revival in the poorer, landlocked provinces of North China (Chau, 2005b; DuBois, 2005; Jones, 2010; Johnson, 2010).

The weak penetration of the state, and the low level of legitimacy of local cadres, has enabled popular temples in some rural areas to act as the main form of public organization and as a "second level of government," collecting funds from residents and building schools, roads, bridges and other facilities (Dean, 2001). Some studies suggest that strong temple associations (or lineage halls in single-surname villages) contribute to a higher level of responsibility and accountability of local officials by creating social solidarity and enforcing common moral norms (Tsai, 2007). In recent years, county and local governments have become more tolerant of popular religion, and in increasing numbers have become its active promoters, under policies promoting heritage, tourism and local identity. At the same time, however, structural changes may have a profound impact on the forms of popular religion. Massive temporary migration of laborers to the cities has left many villages inhabited mostly by their children and elderly parents. In such places, rituals and festivals are poorly attended, except for the Chinese New Year, when most migrant workers return home. In the cities, the migrant laborers are disconnected from their local traditions; if they participate in religion, it is more likely to be Christianity, which they may then bring back to their native villages. Furthermore, the government's drive to create a "new socialist countryside" starting in 2006, which has been expanding the reach of the state into rural areas and, in many places, involves destroying old villages to rebuild them in modern buildings near major transportation arteries, will undoubtedly have a deep impact on traditional religious culture, which is so closely tied to local memories of place and longstanding community relationships.

Post-Mao Urban Religious Culture and the *Qigong* Movement

While religious policy has attempted to identify, categorize and administer fixed and monolithic religious institutions, the social reality of religion has been one of rapid change, innovation and diversification. Much of the discussion of the "revival" of religion in post-Mao China has understood this revival in terms of a return to tradition, after decades of revolutionary campaigns which had cut the Chinese people off from their cultural and spiritual roots. However, owing to the profound ruptures in the transmission of tradition over the 20th century, coupled with the historical weakness of Chinese religious institutions and the contemporary reality of massive urbanization and commodification of culture, the reality is that most "returns" to tradition are, to a greater or lesser degree, innovations and reinventions which recombine elements of traditional culture to construct a spirituality or religiosity adapted to modern life.

This has been notably the case in urban China. The rural-urban divide is profound, but a product of the 20th century. In traditional China, local diversity flourished among the cities, towns and villages, but they all shared a common framework of culture, cosmology, and religious practices. In the modernizing projects of the Republican era (1912–1949), large cities became showcases of social experimentation, urban planning, rationalization, and hygiene, consciously in contrast to the "backward," "superstitious" countryside. The socialist regime further entrenched this distinction by concentrating resources and investments into urban development, and through the *hukou* household registration system which created distinct categories of citizenship for rural and urban dwellers. This division is reflected in China's religious landscape, in which the rural areas are the repositories of tradition, both looked down on by modern urbanites, and the subject of their nostalgic yearnings.

The objective conditions for traditional communal religion, based on ascriptive ties to kinship and territorial groups, hardly exist in urban China, where, for almost 50 years until the late 1990s, the primary social unit was nuclear families living and working in the compounds of state-run work units. Ancestor worship, lineages, and neighborhood temples and shrines all but disappeared, and only in rare exceptions did they resurface in the post-Mao era: many traditional neighborhood communities had been dispersed by urban planning and assignment to residence in work units. For several decades, most urban Chinese had little or no direct contact with traditional forms of worship; religious practice could be said to have almost completely disappeared.

And yet, religious culture suddenly resurfaced in the post-Mao urban China, most visibly expressed through what came to be called "*qigong* fever," the most widespread form of urban religiosity in the 1980s and 90s, in which one or two hundred million persons participated in some way or another. This was a craze for traditional breathing, meditation, gymnastics, and healing methods, often steeped in Buddhist or Daoist symbolism, which drew millions of adepts, and turned into mass movements led by charismatic masters. The phenomenon was spurred by the confluence of many trends, including the official promotion of *qigong* as a simple form of physical exercise derived from Chinese medicine and which could be practiced by the masses; a fascination among some leading scientists, military leaders, and media for paranormal phenomena under the guise of scientific research; and the booming popularity of Hong Kong and mainland kung fu films, TV series, and novels steeped in religious lore, ranging from *Shaolin Temple* to *Journey to the West*, which popularized Chinese cosmology and featured the magical feats of martial artists based on the same techniques of mind and body control as those of *qigong*.

Qigong had emerged as a new category in the early 1950's, when the PRC's new health authorities, in the process of creating new, modern institutions of traditional Chinese medicine, engaged in a programme of revamping traditional healing practices, expurgating any "superstitious" content and reinterpreting the cosmology in materialist terms. *Qigong* was designated as one of the disciplines of Chinese medicine, alongside the materia medica, acupuncture, and massage, and state-run *qigong* clinics and sanatoria established in several cities. The goal had been to secularize the rich traditions of breath, mind, and body training which had been taught for centuries but often in a religious context. That religious imprint could not be completely washed away, however, and *qigong* was banned as "feudal superstition" during the Cultural Revolution.

Qigong resurfaced in the 1970s, and was officially rehabilitated in 1979. Hundreds of masters quickly emerged, each teaching his own set of *qigong* exercises to groups of practitioners who gathered in parks and other public spaces. These groups expanded and formed national networks of practitioners of the same method. *Qigong* became an important component in the culture of early-morning mass exercises in urban spaces.

But in the late 1970s and early 1980s, the *qigong* category also came to have associations going far beyond its original modern meaning as a set of health exercises. Some scientists conducted laboratory experiments on *qigong* masters who were said to be able to mentally emit *qi* (vital energy) to heal patients without bodily contact, and claimed to have discovered the material basis of this "external *qi*." At the same time, the print media were caught up in a craze of reports about children with paranormal powers such as reading with their ears or moving objects from a distance. When *qigong* masters were discovered who purportedly had the same powers, the claim was made that *qigong* was a body of knowledge which could systematically train and develop the "extraordinary powers" latent in every human being, opening the tantalizing prospect of a new scientific revolution. China's most politically influential scientist, Qian Xuesen (1911–2009), the architect of China's nuclear bomb and the Chairman of the National Association for Science and Technology, became an enthusiastic promoter of what he called "somatic science" (*renti kexue*) which would combine Chinese medicine, *qigong*, and paranormal studies. This enthusiasm spread to the National Defense research institutions, which saw much potential in the military applications of paranormal abilities, opened special research units, and kept *qigong* masters on its payroll for conducting experiments and to offer healing treatments to the aging leaders of the CCP's Long March generation.

Among the practitioners in the parks, some *qigong* methods induced trance states, glossolalia, and visions of popular gods, while many masters became charismatic cult figures. Yan Xin, the most popular master, filled entire sports stadiums for his mass healing lectures, during which he emitted *qi*, the sick claimed they were healed, and paraplegics stood up from their wheelchairs. *Qigong* became a booming subculture with its own official associations sponsored by the health, sports, and science authorities, several mass-circulation popular *qigong* magazines, a growing market for books and manuals on *qigong* masters and techniques, and thousands of masters, many of whom began to build highly integrated organizations of trainers and practitioners. One of the largest of these, Zhong Gong, led by master Zhang Hongbao, which claimed 30 million practitioners, built a sprawling commercial corporation based on the sale of a progressive series of training workshops, and which also included health products, universities, and real estate investment (Palmer, 2007).

Falun Gong, which was launched in 1992 by Li Hongzhi, began as one of thousands of *qigong* methods, but it quickly grew in popularity. In contrast to most other *qigong* forms, the focus of Falun Gong went beyond exercises and healing to emphasize moral cultivation. Li Hongzhi described a supernatural cosmology replete with demons, Buddhas, spirits and aliens, and an apocalyptic worldview in which salvation could only be attained through exclusive commitment to himself and his method, and abandonment of all worldly attachments, including to emotional feelings and affections for other people, to other forms of healing or medicine, and to other religious practices or teachings.

Li Hongzhi moved to the United States around 1995, but Falun Gong continued to grow in China, attracting millions of practitioners in all the cities, and it was criticized in the press. Mass actions in response to criticisms, such as letter-writing campaigns and sit-ins, became a core dimension of spiritual cultivation. On April 25, 1999, over 10,000 practitioners quietly surrounded Zhongnangai, the central Beijing compound of the CCP leadership, for the whole day.

The demonstration, the largest of its kind since the Tiananmen student movement a decade earlier, shocked the CCP leaders, who saw it as an existential threat. President Jiang Zemin resolved to exterminate the movement, now designated an "evil cult," through a ruthless repression campaign launched in July 1999. The suppression led to the end of the *qigong* movement as a mass phenomenon. Yoga grew in popularity and replaced *qigong* as a popular form of meditation and health practice. By 2000, Falun Gong had disappeared as a public movement in Mainland China, but an underground network of diehard followers continued to subsist. Now based overseas, Falun Gong became a global cyber-network linking followers around the world through a cluster of websites, a digital TV station, and a newspaper, the *Epoch Times*, published simultaneously in several languages. This network was mobilised to publicise China's human rights abuses of Falun Gong practitioners in China, and, starting in 2004, to spearhead a campaign to discredit and topple the CCP as an "evil Party" (Palmer, 2007; Ownby, 2008; Penny, forthcoming).

The Confucian Revival

In the aftermath of the *qigong* movement's collapse, the first decade of the 21st century saw a new wave of cultural revivalism, this time around Confucianism. Similar to *qigong*, Confucianism does not fall under the official category of religion in the PRC; but instead of restricting its development, this indeterminate status has allowed it to expand under a great variety of forms and guises. The collapse of the imperial state in 1911 had implied the dissolution of the ritual order, the examination system based on the Confucian classics, and the traditional bureaucracy which had formed the institutional structure of "Confucianism." In Republican China, the Confucian heritage had been carried and recast into in a wide range of forms: (1) popular syncretistic salvational movements and redemptive societies such as the Universal Morality Society (Wanguo daodehui), the Fellowship United in Goodness (Tongshanshe) and the Way of Pervasive Unity (Yiguandao); (2) an independent "religion," the Kongjiao, imitating the organizational forms and in competition with Christian churches (and aspiring to be declared China's state religion); (3) an ethical tradition compatible with Christian faith and the ideological foundation of the New Life Movement; and (4) a secular system of thought according to the norms of Western philosophy. With the establishment of the PRC in 1949, Confucianism became the very emblem of the old feudal order: the redemptive societies, which had more members than the five officially recognized religions among the Han Chinese, were ruthlessly suppressed as "reactionary sects and secret societies" (*fandong huidaomen*), while Confucian philosophy became a taboo topic even among academics (Goossaert and Palmer, 2011).

In the 1980s and into the 90s, Confucianism began to reappear as a topic of discussion and debate, but mostly confined to academics, as part of a broader trend in the post-revolutionary period to explore and rediscover China's traditional culture and thought, to debate its relevance to the contemporary period, and to re-examine whether it was the source of, or a solution to, China's ills and even its political dysfunctions. Numerous conferences were held, and restoration works and ceremonies were undertaken at the ancestral temple of Confucius at Qufu (Shandong), with tourism promotion as one of the main motivations. This occurred in the broader context of the economic rise of the four "Asian Dragons" (South Korea, Taiwan, Hong Kong and Singapore), which stimulated much discussion on whether their economic growth was related to their "Confucian" culture of academic success, hard work and strong family ties — a notion promoted by Singapore president Lee Kuan-yew through his theory of "Asian values." Meanwhile, overseas academics, such as Tu Wei-ming of Harvard, were working on contemporary reformulations of Confucian ethics and spirituality, and re-introducing them into curricula and academic discourses in Singapore and China. During this period, then, although interest in Confucius was increasing on the mainland, a sharp contrast remained between the mainland, which was seen as "cut off" from its Confucian traditions and largely ignorant of is heritage, while an organic connection with the past supposedly existed in Taiwan, Hong Kong, Singapore, and among overseas Chinese. Various groups and individuals from these areas were actively promoting the dissemination of Confucian ideas in the mainland, and Confucius became a useful symbol for the PRC government in building patriotic ties with Chinese from Taiwan and overseas (Billioud and Thoraval, 2007; Billioud and Thoraval, 2008; Makeham, 2008).

In the 2000s, however, Confucianism became much more of a mass phenomenon in mainland China, as well as the subject of a more focused involvement and instrumentalization on the part of the state. A multitude of popular initiatives took inspiration from the Confucian heritage. Most wide-spread was the classics recitation movement (*dujing yundong*), which encouraged children and adults to nurture the habit of reading, memorizing and reciting the classics. This could take the form of small groups of children being taught by an amateur retired teacher, programmes introduced into the formal curriculum of schools, or early-morning gatherings of students and retirees in campuses, parks and public spaces to read and comment the texts. Many enthusiasts established "academies" as places for the collective study and intellectual discussion on the Confucian teachings, as venues for providing more formal classes, or as centers for recruiting and deploying volunteers to teach the classics or do other acts of social service. Most of these academies were fragile non-profit affairs, but some were businesses, offering workshops for a growing market of business entrepreneurs in search of moral purpose and cultural capital. Similar continuing-education programmes in "national studies" were also launched by a growing number of universities, catering to the same market.

Most of these initiatives do not consider themselves "religious," and contain little or no element of worship. But some groups learn and strive to practice ritual, and the cult of Confucius is popular in these circles. Some explicitly call for Confucianism to be declared as China's national religion, a position shared by some high-profile academics. Others are Buddhist groups which promote Confucian virtues and textual study as part of a wider range of religious activities (Billioud and Thoraval, 2009; Ownby, 2009; Dutournier and Ji, 2009).

Meanwhile, while the state's stance toward Confucianism remains ambivalent, it has allowed for a much wider discursive space for its officially-sanctioned promotion. Though Hu Jintao's principle of "harmonious society" does not itself make explicit reference to Confucius, it seems to signal a shift in the official ideology which can be involked to legitimate all manner of initiatives inspired by Chinese traditional thought. And the establishment of a worldwide network of "Confucius Institutes" as an emblem for the international projection of Chinese "soft power," while still devoid of much content, symbolically elevates the Sage into a global symbol of socialist China.

Daoist and Buddhist Temples, Clergy and Lay Networks

In the 1950s, only a few dozen large Buddhist and Daoist temples had been preserved in the cities, as well as the main mountain monastic centres, and it is these officially-designated temples and monasteries which were re-opened after the Cultural Revolution — a few temples in each of China's large cities, and the sacred mountains and monastic complexes of Emei, Huashan, Putuoshan, etc. This represented only a tiny fraction of China's historically Daoist and Buddhist temples. Thousands had been destroyed, both during the Republican and Maoist revolutions; many others were still standing, but were occupied by the Cultural Relics authorities or by other units, none of which were willing to turn this valuable real estate over to religious communities. The Daoist and Buddhist associations in several cities tried to claim former temples, but the negotiations, usually conducted by the Religious Affairs Bureau, were difficult. Only if a strong case could be made to identify the temple as Daoist or Buddhist could the process begin, which was not always easy owing to the traditionally communal management of most temples. Even then, protracted negotiations and government support were required, which was unlikely; but it did occur, such as for the City God temples of Shanghai and Xi'an, which were restored and reopened under the municipal Daoist associations (Goossaert and Fang, 2009).

Since the 1950s, the large urban temples had been cut off from their traditional ties with networks of local temples and communities, and from their economic base of providing ritual services for the communities in which they were embedded. Instead, they obtained a meager revenue from the government and from the sale of entrance tickets. But since the 1990s, as part of a general trend to push state-owned work units to become financially self-sufficient, urban temples have been required to find new sources of income. Tourism is one trend, with Buddhist and Daoist monasteries and sacred sites becoming tourist showcases charging high entrance fees. Another option has been for temples to offer healing, meditation, and health-cultivation programmes, summer camps and workshops, sometimes similar to *qigong* activities of a decade earlier. And many temples have become more active providers in the market for ritual services (including funerals and rites for healing and blessings), previously dominated by householder ritualists, as described below (D.R. Yang, 2005). All of these trends imply a deeper participation in the market economy, which has led to much criticism of Buddhism and Daoism becoming excessively commercialized. Temples and monastic complexes require substantial funds to build and manage; but they can also become lucrative income streams. Many local governments have enthusiastically promoted the construction of grandiose temples and giant Buddha statues, in the hopes of stimulating tourist development, even in places where there are no historical sacred sites. The Shaolin temple has become an extreme example of a Buddhist monastery, of which almost nothing remained in the early 1980s, becoming a multinational kungfu-themed tourism, media and entertainment conglomerate (Ji, 2011). Some real estate developers have seen temples as an attractive addition to the standard investment portfolios of shopping malls and residential estates (Chan and Lang, 2011). In the summer of 2010, a Daoist priest in Chongqing, who had developed a successful model of turning his monastery into a retreat centre for healing and meditation workshops for well-heeled business elites and pop stars, was the subject of a media campaign to discredit him as a quack and swindler. The high profits from successful temples and religious tourist attractions lead to frequent conflicts between religious communities and tourism authorities and investors over the management and distribution of revenues.

Most of the monasteries are staffed by resident monks from Buddhist and Daoist (Quanzhen) monastic orders, which, as self-contained religious institutions ostensibly devoted exclusively to spiritual cultivation, are the closest match to the state policy's framing of religion. Monastic identity is defined by the norm of celibacy, "leaving the family" (*chujia*) to enter the religious community, although it is not observed very strictly in practice, especially among the Daoists. Monks still practice the tradition of moving from one monastery to another around China in search of masters, creating national networks of circulating clerics, which connect with local networks of temples and their branches and offshoots. And these networks are overlaid by the state's hierarchies of local, provincial and national Buddhist and Daoist Associations and Religious Affairs bureaus (Herrou, 2011).

In the Daoist case, however, the vast majority of priests are not monastics but the so-called "householder" Daoists who live at their own homes with their families, are not affiliated to a single temple, and operate as independent ritual specialists providing life-cycle and healing rituals to individuals and families, and communal rituals for local temples. In some areas, they practice the Zhengyi liturgical tradition, while in other regions local traditions such as Lüshan, Meishan, and vernacular Buddhist ritual forms predominate. Until recently these "superstition specialist households" could not operate legally (Chau, 2006), but local Religious Affairs authorities and Daoist associations have begun a process of registering and licensing some of them, particularly if they are affiliated to the more orthodox Zhengyi tradition (Lai, 2003).

Many communal temples, which originally had only a tenuous connection with a recognized religion, are claiming a Daoist (or sometimes Buddhist) identity in order to secure their legality through affiliation to the local Daoist or Buddhist Association. "Daoistication" (*daojiaohua*) is an option considered by the religious affairs authorities, and experimented with in some regions, for registering and monitoring communal temples. But this normalization, whether it involves householder priests or communal temples, also involves engaging with a process of religious standardization emanating from the official institutions. This can involve posting Buddhist or Quanzhen Daoist monks at communal temples, attending political meetings, and undergoing formal academic-style training which substitutes secular discursive knowledge on religious history and philosophy for traditional master-disciple apprenticeship (Yang, 2011).

Meanwhile, Chinese Buddhism and Daoism are becoming integrated into transnational religious networks. In the Daoist case, temples in Hong Kong, Taiwan, Singapore and Malaysia have played a significant role in financing the reconstruction and expansion of temples on the mainland, and even in reintroducing or legitimating ritual traditions (Dean, 2011). And with the growing popularity of Daoist health and self-cultivation traditions in Europe and North America, Western Daoist organizations and enterprises are bringing groups of practitioners on "energy tours" to China, where they visit sacred mountains and interact with Chinese monks. Some monks have even been invited to give lectures and workshops in Western retreat centers. Daoism is thus gradually becoming connected to global circuits, interlinking and transcending its traditional embeddedness in local society and national identity (Siegler, 2006; Siegler and Palmer, forthcoming).

In the case of Han Buddhism, transnational flows have contributed to the growth of lay Buddhist movements. The Republican era had seen the emergence of reformist tendencies, often called "engaged" or "humanistic" Buddhism (*renjian fojiao*) which afforded a greater role to the laity and advocated greater participation in contemporary social life and issues; but after 1949, though the modernizing rhetoric of reformist Buddhism was retained, there was little room for concrete innovations, and in the 1980s and into the 90s, there was little capacity within the mainland Buddhist institutions to engage with society or develop lay movements. During this period, however, since the late 1960s, Taiwan had become a world centre of reformist Buddhism and the base of several globalizing new Buddhist movements, such as Dharma Drum Mountain (Foguangshan) or the Compassionate Relief Foundation (Ciji gongdehui), which developed new forms of Buddhist lifestyle and identity (Madsen, 2007; Huang, 2008). These have had a direct and indirect impact on the mainland, contributing to a vibrant lay Buddhist culture. The first decade of the new century has seen the sprouting and flourishing of myriads of loosely-organized popular Buddhist networks, ranging from groups of devotees who print, compose, distribute and preach about morality books in temple courtyards, to gatherings of white collar professionals in vegetarian restaurants and business entrepreneurs who invite monks to give Dharma talks and initiations to themselves and their friends (Fisher, 2011; Fan and Whitehead, 2011).

Often it is lamas of Tibetan Buddhism who are patronized by these entrepreneurs, a sign of the growing popularity of their tradition among the Han. While the mystery and spiritual traditions of Tibet have long been a source of fascination for the Han, as in the West, they have become more widely publicized and accessible with the development of tourism. Beyond the flood of documentaries, exhibitions, glossy magazine features, backpacker guides, package tours and adventure expeditions to Tibetan areas, which are gaining in popularity among culturally sophisticated Chinese urbanites, a growing trickle of Han spiritual seekers are sojourning in Tibetan monasteries and spiritual camps located in the remote highlands of Gansu, Sichuan and Tibet.

Tibetan Buddhism has become a multifaceted, transnational and multiethnic religious movement in the post-Mao era. A conservative theocracy isolated and almost virtually cut off from the outside world in the first half of the 20th century, Tibet had been suddenly thrust into revolutionary politics with its full integration into the PRC state in the 1950s. The Dalai Lama's flight to India in 1959 along with thousands of other monks, set the stage for an unprecedented globalization of Tibetan Buddhism, especially after many of these lamas ended up migrating to Western countries, and the Dalai Lama became an internationally revered spiritual leader and bestselling author. Like all religions in China, Tibetan Buddhism suffered from harsh persecution during the Cultural Revolution, but owing to the ethnic and political factor, the revolutionary campaigns have reinforced deep grievances and resentment between Tibetans and Han Chinese, and a deep religious faith has become a key vehicle for the expression of ethnic identity and aspirations vis-à-vis the Chinese state. Following the Cultural Revolution, both the PRC government and the Dalai Lama made attempts to initiate reconciliation, but this failed in the 1980s. For some time the authorities tolerated Tibetans' veneration of the Dalai Lama, but by the end of the 1990s, he was being demonized as a splittist, and later as a terrorist. Monks and common people have had to reconcile, but increasingly have to choose, between their religious loyalties and the requirements of survival and development within the socialist system. (Goldstein and Kapstein, 1998; Makley, 2007)

Islam

Hui Muslims had been active within China's nationalist movement during the Republican period, and the CCP had developed strong ties with Muslim communities in the northwest during the Yan'an period in the 1930s and 40s. Under the PRC after 1949, Islam, though recognized as a religion, has been largely subsumed as a "minority nationalities" issue: all members of 10 out of

China's 56 ethnic groups are considered to be Muslim by birth — the Hui, Uyghur, Kazakh, Dongxiang, Kyrghyz, Salar, Tajik, Uzbeks, Baonan, and Tatar. Many special accommodations were made for their religious and ethnic customs, and two Muslim-majority autonomous regions — Xinjiang and Ningxia — were established (Gladney, 1996).

After the Cultural Revolution, the 1980's witnessed the re-establishment of official Islamic institutions and the revival and expansion of infrastructures. Mosques were restored and rebuilt, until, by some accounts, there were now more mosques than before 1949. Pilgrimages to Mecca were resumed, with believers traveling to Saudi Arabia through both official and unofficial channels in rapidly increasing numbers. Publishing operations, both official and informal, were re-activated. Affirmative action programmes such as a more relaxed birth control policy and lower entrance standards for university, enjoyed by all minority nationalities, encouraged Han people to marry into or otherwise seek to join these nationalities, so that, between 1982 and 1990, the Hui population grew by 19% in eight years.

As in the 1950's, the official China Islamic Association is dominated by members of the Ikhwan movement, an anti-sufi reformist tradition which had been active as Chinese nationalists in the Republican period. Most of the mosques rebuilt with state funds after the Cultural Revolution are affiliated to the Ikhwan, while the sufi and traditional Islam (known as "old teachings," or *gedimu*) continue to predominate in rural Hui villages. Having been so effectively co-opted by the state, however, the Ikhwan have lost some of their legitimacy in the eyes of many Muslims. Disaffection with the Ikhwan seems to have stimulated the growth of the Salafiyya movement, introduced to China in the 1930's, which advocates political quietism and an uncompromising adherence to scripture, rejecting the Ikhwan drift toward secularism, Marxism, and political co-optation (Gladney, 1999).

Just as, in the 1950's, the CCP had adroitly played its Muslim card as part of its diplomatic strategy, the same approach was used in the post-Mao period, as trade and economic links have boomed between China and Muslim countries in Southeast Asia and the Middle East — the latter being crucial suppliers of oil and important clients for Chinese-sponsored infrastructure development projects. Many of these collaborations involve Hui as leaders, interpreters, or cultural consultants, while the increased links also facilitate religious exchanges: hundreds of Chinese Muslims have obtained scholarships to pursue Islamic studies in Muslim countries, while foreign Islamic foundations fund the construction of mosques and Islamic schools in China.

The increased links with other Muslim countries, especially of the Middle East, have had a certain impact on the practice and values of the Hui. Arabia, as the root of Islam, is often seen as the standard for Islamic authenticity, and as the source of an alternative civilizing discourse to the Han-centred hegemony emanating from the Chinese state. Countering Han-centred stereotypes of Hui backwardness, many stress the higher principles of purity, truth, and hygiene contained in Islamic civilization, and identify with the prosperity and material advancement of the Arabian states — producing a trend of "Arabisation" among the Hui, including the adoption of Arabic architectural styles for mosques (replacing the Chinese temple style of older mosques with domes), enrolling in Arabic language lessons, watching Middle-Eastern videos, and adopting Arabic "Muslim" dress codes (such as blandly coloured womens' headdresses and *hijab*) (Gillette, 2000).

If geopolitical considerations have been a factor in an exceptionally lenient treatment of the religious practices of the Hui, it has been just the opposite for the Uighurs and other Muslim peoples of the far West. Here, in the face of violent acts of resistance by Uighurs, the Chinese state successfully lobbied both the neighboring central Asian states, which were ethnically and historically close to the Uighurs, and the United States, otherwise keen to take up the cause of human rights in China, to obtain cover for a brutal suppression of any expression of perceived Uighur nationalism, in a campaign whose targets included any expressions of Islam outside of narrow, officially-sanctioned confines.

Sporadic anti-Han protests and incidents occurred throughout the 1980's. Some Uighur resistance groups took inspiration from the Mujahideen victory against the Soviets in Afghanistan in 1989. It was the Baren rebellion, launched near Kashgar with calls to *jihad* in April 1990 — in which dozens of rioters were killed by the army — which marked a turning point in the state's approach to the Uighurs and Islam in Xinjiang. From then on, the CCP resolved to crush any signs of dissent and to strictly control religious life. This occurred only months after the Tiananmen student movement, and just as the Soviet bloc was collapsing, with several new Muslim-majority republics attaining independence on the Western borders of Xinjiang. China's leaders feared the breaking away of Xinjiang, leading by domino effect to the disintegration of China and the end of the CCP regime. Tensions were aggravated by a series of bomb blasts in Urumqi and even in Beijing in the mid 1990's, and again by riots in July 2009. The "strike hard" campaign launched to fight crime throughout China in 1996, was, in Xinjiang, primarily directed at any suspected "separatist" activity, including much of the religious life. Unregistered mosques were closed, loudspeakers for the call to prayer were removed from minarets, in some instances certain prayers were banned, children were punished at school for showing signs of

Islamic practice, and teachers and employees at state-run units were deliberately offered meals during the fast of Ramadan. Religious regulations, which were only loosely enforced among the Hui elsewhere in China, such as limiting to two the number of students under each imam, were strictly applied (Kung, 2006, p. 385).

Due to the dearth of in-depth research, it is impossible to accurately gauge how deeply Islam is associated with Uighur nationalism, with some scholars stressing that the Islamic dimension is but a minor element. Clearly, however, Islam is being driven underground, and it seems likely that, in the absence of any other source of international support, and with possibilities for employment and material advancement increasingly blocked by Han immigrants, coupled with the stress on Uighur culture, Islam may become possibly the only remaining cultural and spiritual resource to which the Uighurs can turn (Castets, 2003; Fuller and Lipman, 2004).

Christianity

The Cultural Revolution had a defining impact on the evolution of Chinese Christianity. Owing to their direct association with foreign imperialists and a sometimes explicitly and actively anti-communist orientation, the persecution of Christians had been intense and systematic throughout the Mao years. And yet, the Christian community survived, and even expanded, through the worst years of oppression. Already, the failure of the state-controlled patriotic Catholic and Protestant associations to rally most of the faithful in the 1950's, had driven many to meet in small groups in their homes — the beginning of the "house church" movement — and led to the emergence of underground Protestant and Catholic networks. The imprisonment, torture and execution of many priests, ministers and lay leaders only steeled the resolve of communities which developed narratives of martyrdom and of bearing the Cross for their faith. Christians gave a spiritual meaning to their sufferings, endowing them with a force with which they could bear the abuse and emerge with an even stronger faith. It was such people who, once released, returned to minister to their flocks in caves, in fields, in private homes at night, or even to missionize to other villages. Hundreds if not thousands of new house churches were thus founded in the 1970s. These underground churches were definitively cut off from Western influence, were strongly rooted in the local contexts of believers' lives, and became far more "self-governing, self-financing and self-expanding" than the official "Three-self" churches could ever have hoped to become. These were communities in which the frequent absence of the clergy due to repeated arrests and imprisonment, led to the laity coming to play a strong role in the organ-ization of liturgical and community life — a situation that continued into the 21st century, when all churches faced an acute shortage of clergy which could not keep up with the growing numbers of believers (Hunter and Chan, 1993; Madsen, 1998; Vala, 2009).

By the late 1970's and early 1980's, the seeds, which had been planted during the Cultural Revolution, began to come to fruition, as both Catholic and Protestant religious activity came back into the open. On the one hand, religious activity was more tolerated, many churches and cathedrals were re-opened or rebuilt, some church property was returned, and it was no longer necessary to meet secretly to worship. On the other hand, the Religious Affairs Bureau and the state-sponsored Patriotic Associations were re-established; these once again attempted to establish their leadership over the believers, leading to renewed conflicts over legitimacy and authority, and to the division of Christian communities into the state-sponsored churches and unofficial, autonomous groups which did not come under state control.

For the Catholics, the issue is the existence of two parallel hierarchies, one loyal to Rome and the Pope, the other to Beijing and the CCP. Unilateral consecrations of bishops by either side have led to periodic flashes of tension, although the reality on the ground is quite complex. While in some places, members of the official and unofficial Catholic churches boycott each other, leading some to speak of a "schism," in other places official and unofficial clergy informally divide territories between themselves to avoid conflict, or even jointly minister to the same community. The issue of authority within the Church — the CCP willing to grant the Pope a spiritual authority, but no institutional power — is compounded by the question of diplomatic recogni-tion, the Vatican remaining as one of the few states in the world to recognize the Republic of China on Taiwan rather than the PRC. Both governments are divided between hard-line and accommodationist factions, and overtures are consistently torpedoed by provocative actions, typically the unilateral appointment of bishops by either side. (Lozada, 2001; Liu and Leung, 2002; Leung, 1998).

For Protestants, the issue is not one of two parallel hierarchies, but an asymmetrical relationship between a centralized, state-sponsored institution and a diffused galaxy of thousands of independent congregations ranging in size from prayer groups in homes to national networks of hundreds of thou-sands of believers, which have their own printing presses, retreats, and training systems. While the official churches control most buildings and assets in the large cities, this has not stopped the growth of house churches among urban residents, while in the rural areas and in the hinterland some unofficial groups have become so large that they often move out of the "houses" and build large church structures which can seat thousands.

Indigenous networks such as the Fangcheng Fellowship, the China Gospel Fellowship, and the Born-Again Movement send evangelists to all parts of China, converting millions. These networks practice charismatic and Pentecostal forms of worship. Healing, speaking in tongues, and prophecy are integral to their practices of worship; morality and repentance are central to their spirituality. Many churches have become so colored with local culture that they increasingly resemble the sectarian cults and salvationist movements of Chinese religion, with charismatic preachers leading their followers to turn to Christ for healing and exorcism (Hunter and Chan, 1992, p. 178; Yip, 1999; Bays, 2003, pp. 496–497).

While Catholicism continues to grow at the same rate as China's population, Protestantism has witnessed a phenomenal expansion — from one million in 1949 to at least 30 million by the end of the century — a thirty-fold increase. While such a figure still represents only 2% of the population, the rate of growth is so rapid that, if sustained over several decades in the 21st century, many Christians hope to eventually convert a significant proportion of the population. Already, some entire ethnic localities in the Southwest have become Christian — with the support of local authorities delighted at their accomplishments in curbing drug trafficking and crime — and several house churches dream of, and have begun preparations for, the goal of sending thousands of Chinese missionaries to convert the Muslims of the Middle East, as the last stage in a movement "back to Jerusalem" in expectation of the Second Coming (Aikman, 2003, pp. 193–205).

Although observers in the 1990's described the growth of Christianity as occurring primarily among elder, poorly-educated rural residents, it was clear by the late 1990's, that Christianity also held a strong appeal among educated urbanites and affluent entrepreneurs. In the city of Wenzhou, one of China's richest coastal cities with a large number of Christians (estimated at around 10% of the population), a new breed of "boss Christians" has appeared. These business owners, who are also zealous believers and leaders in congregations, preach a prosperity gospel and compete to build ever-larger and more dynamic churches. They consciously try to refashion Chinese Christianity into a more modern and sophisticated lifestyle that can satisfy the aspirations of people living in a market-oriented culture (Cao, 2011).

The growth of Christianity in the cities is largely extra-institutional: while official churches are simply unable to respond to demand, McDonald's restaurants have become as likely a place to conduct Bible study sessions as private apartments. For these urban believers, Christianity is part of the cosmopolitan, Western-inspired culture they aspire to — but also reaffirms moral values in continuity with traditional ethics (F. Yang, 2005).

It is too early to assess to what extent Christianity may affect public life in China in the future. The theological orientation of most Chinese churches leads them away from this-worldly concerns. But there are many Christians among a movement of lawyers and activists who are willing to defend the rights of farmers, workers, and religious believers in the Chinese courts, at great risk to their careers and lives. For these activists, religious faith translates into an active engagement to protect individual rights within the framework of what the Chinese state claims to be an emerging rule of law.

Conclusion

China in the early 21st century has become a laboratory for religious change and innovation. Unlike most countries, China has no dominant religious orthodoxy, and all forms of religion are expanding. State policy has kept religious institutions weak, but the hegemony of a secularist and anti-religious ideology, which was dominant over most of the 20th century, is on the wane as well. The spiritual and religious yearnings and aspirations of Chinese people are finding ever more diverse outlets for expression, even as official policy, more open to religion but still anchored to a framework inherited from the 1950s, is at pains to adapt to an ever-shifting reality. While the 1980s and 90s could be characterized as decades of restoration and revival following the traumas of the Maoist period, in the 21st century, the dynamic is moving toward innovation and diversification of religious practices and pathways.

References

Aikman, D. (2003) *Jesus in Beijing. How Christianity is transforming China and changing the global balance of power*. Washington, D.C.: Regnery Pub.

Bays, D. H. (2003) Chinese Protestant Christianity today. *The China Quarterly*, 174, 488–504.

Billioud, S. and J. Thoraval (2007) Jiaohua: The Confucian revival in China as an educative project. *China Perspectives*, 4, 4–21.

Billioud, S. and J. Thoraval (2008) The contemporary revival of Confucianism: *Anshen liming* or the religious dimension of Confucianism. *China Perspectives*, 3, 88–106.

Billioud, S. and J. Thoraval (2009) *Lijiao*. The return of ceremonies honouring Confucius in modern China. *China Perspectives*, 4, 82–100.

Cao, N. (2011) *Constructing China's Jerusalem: Christians, power, and place in contemporary Wenzhou*. Stanford, CA: Stanford University Press.

Castets, R. (2003) The Uyghurs in Xinjiang — The malaise grows. *China Perspectives*, 49, 34–49.

Chan, K. K. and E. C. Carlson (2005) *Religious freedom in China: Policy, administration and regulation. A research handbook*. Santa Barbara, CA, Institute for the Study of American Religion/Hong Kong, Hong Kong Institute for Culture, Commerce and Religion.

Chan, S. and G. Lang (2011) Temples as enterprises. In A. Y. Chau (Ed.), *Religion in contemporary China: Revitalization and innovation*. Abington, Oxon: Routledge, pp. 133–153.

Chau, A. Y. (2005a) The politics of legitimation and the revival of popular religion in Shaanbei, North-Central China. *Modern China*, 31(2), 236–278.

Chau, A. Y. (2005b) *Miraculous response: Doing popular religion in contemporary China*. Stanford, CA: Stanford University Press.

Chau, A. Y. (2006) "Superstition specialist households?" The household idiom in Chinese religious practices. *Minsu quyi/Journal of Chinese Ritual, Theatre and Folklore*, 153, 157–202.

Dean, K. (2001) China's second government: Regional ritual systems in Southeast China. In C.-K. Wang, Y. Zhuang and Z. Chen (Eds.), *Shehui, minzu yu wenhua zhanyan guoji yantaohui lunwenji*. Taipei: Hanxue yanjiu zhongxin, pp. 77–109.

Dean, K. (1993) *Taoist ritual and popular cults of south-east China*. Princeton: Princeton University Press.

Dean, K. (2011) Daoism, local religious movements, and transnational Chinese society: The circulation of Daoist priests, Three-in-One self-cultivators, and spirit-mediums between Fujian and Southeast Asia. In D. A. Palmer and X. Liu (Eds.), *Daoism in the 20th century: Between eternity and modernity*. Berkeley, CA: University of California Press.

DuBois, T. D. (2005) *The sacred village: Social change and religious life in rural North China*. Honolulu: University of Hawai'i Press.

Dunch, R. (2008) Christianity and adaptation to socialism. In M. Yang (Ed.), *Chinese religiosities: The vicissitudes of modernity and state formation*. Berkeley, CA: University of California Press.

Dunn, E. C. (2009) 'Cult,' church, and the CCP: Introducing Eastern Lightning. *Modern China*, 35(1), 96–119.

Dutournier, G. and Z. Ji (2009) Social experimentation and "popular Confucianism": The case of the Lujiang Cultural Education Centre. *China Perspectives*, 4, 67–81.

Fan, L. and J. Whitehead (2011) Spirituality in a modern Chinese metropolis. In D. A. Palmer, G. Shive and P. Wickeri (Eds.), *Chinese religious life*. New York: Oxford University Press.

Fisher, G. (2011) Morality books and the regrowth of lay Buddhism in China. In A. Y. Chau (Ed.), *Religion in contemporary China: Revitalization and innovation*, pp. 53–80. Abington, Oxon: Routledge.

Fuller, G. and J. Lipman (2004) Islam in Xinjiang. In F. Starr (Ed.), *Xinjiang: China's Muslim borderland*. Armonk, New York: M. E. Sharpe.

Gillette, M. B. (2000) *Between Mecca and Beijing. Modernization and consumption among urban Chinese Muslims*. Stanford, CA: Stanford University Press.

Gladney, D. C. (1996) *Muslim Chinese: Ethnic nationalism in the People's Republic.* Cambridge, Mass.: Council on East Asian Studies, Harvard University.

Gladney, D. C. (1999) The Salafiyya movement in Northwest China: Islamic fundamentalism among the Muslim Chinese?" In Manger L. (Ed.), *Muslim diversity: Local Islam in global contexts*, pp. 102–149. Surrey: Curzon Press.

Goldstein, M. and M. T. Kapstein (Eds.) (1998) *Buddhism in contemporary Tibet: Religious revival and cultural identity*. Berkeley: University of California Press.

Goossaert, V. and L. Fang (2009) Temples and Daoists in Urban China since 1980. *China Perspectives*, 4, 32–41.

Goossaert, V. (2011) The social organization of religious communities in the 20th century. In D. A. Palmer, G. Shive and P. Wickeri (Eds.), *Chinese religious life*. New York: Oxford University Press.

Goossaert, V. and D. A. Palmer (2011) *The religious question in modern China*. Chicago: University of Chicago Press.

Herrou, A. (2011) Networks and the 'cloudlike wandering' of Daoist monks in China today. In A. Y. Chau (Ed.), *Religion in contemporary China: Revitalization and innovation*, pp. 108–131. Abington, Oxon: Routledge.

Huang, C. J. (2008) *Charisma and compassion: Cheng Yen and the Buddhist Tzu Chi movement*. Cambridge: Harvard University Press.

Hunter, A. and K.-K. Chan (1993) *Protestantism in contemporary China*. Cambridge: Cambridge University Press.

Lai, C.-T. (2003) Daoism in China today, 1980–2002. *The China Quarterly*, 174, pp. 413–427.

Ji, Z. (2011) Buddhism in the reform era: A secularized revival? In A. Y. Chau (Ed.), *Religion in contemporary China: Revitalization and innovation*, pp. 32–52. Abington, Oxon: Routledge.

Johnson, D. (2010) *Spectacle and sacrifice: The ritual foundations of village life in North China*. Cambridge, MA: Harvard East Asian Monographs.

Jones, S. (2010) *In search of the folk Daoists of North China*. Aldershot: Ashgate.

Jones, S. (2011) Revival in crisis: Amateur ritual associations in Hebei. In A. Y. Chau (Ed.), *Religion in contemporary China: Revitalization and innovation*, pp. 154–181. Abington, Oxon: Routledge.

Kuah, K. E. (2000) *Rebuilding the ancestral village: Singaporeans in China*. London: Ashgate.

Kung, L.-Y. (2006) National identity and ethno-religious identity: A critical inquiry into Chinese religious policy, with reference to the Uighurs in Xinjiang. *Religion, State and Society*, 34(4), 375–391.

Lagerwey, J. (2010) *China: A religious state*. Hong Kong: Hong Kong University Press.

Laliberté, A. (2011). Contemporary issues in state-religion relations. In D. A. Palmer, G. Shive and P. Wickeri (Eds.), *Chinese religious life*. New York: Oxford University Press.

Laliberté, A., D. A. Palmer and K. Wu (2011) Religious philanthropy and Chinese civil society. In D. A. Palmer, G. Shive and P. Wickeri (Eds.), *Chinese religious life*. New York: Oxford University Press.

Leung, B. (1998) The Sino-Vatican negotiations: Old problems in a new context. *The China Quarterly*, 153, 128–140.

Liu, W. T. and Leung, B. (2002) Organizational revivalism: Explaining metamorphosis of China's Catholic church. *Journal for the Scientific Study of Religion*, 41(1), 121–139.

Lozada, E. P., Jr. (2001) *God aboveground: Catholic church, postsocialist state, and transnational processes in a Chinese village*. Stanford, CA: Stanford University Press.

MacInnis, D. E. (1989) *Religion in China today: policy and practice*. Maryknoll: Orbis.

Madsen, R. (1998) *China's Catholics: Tragedy and hope in an emerging civil society*. Berkeley: University of California Press.

Madsen, R. (2007) *Democracy's Dharma: Religious renaissance and political development in Taiwan*. Berkeley: University of California Press.

Madsen, R. and J. Tong, (Eds.) (2000) *Local religious policy in China, 1980–1997*. *Chinese Law and Government*, 33(3).

Makeham, J. (2008) *Lost soul. "Confucianism" in contemporary Chinese academic discourse*. Cambridge, MA: Harvard University Asia Center.

Makley, C. E. (2007) *The violence of liberation: Gender and Tibetan Buddhist revival in post-Mao China*. Berkeley, CA: University of California Press.

Nedostup, R. A. (2009) *Superstitious regimes: Religion and the politics of Chinese modernity*. Cambridge, MA: Harvard University Press.

Overmyer, D. L. (2001) From "feudal superstition" to "popular beliefs": New directions in Mainland Chinese studies of Chinese popular religion. *Cahiers d'Extrême-Asie*, 12, 103–126.

Ownby, D. (2008) *Falun Gong and the future of China*. Oxford: Oxford University Press.

Ownby, D. (2009) Kang Xiaoguang: Social science, civil society, and Confucian religion. *China Perspectives*, 4, 101–111.

Palmer, D. A. (2007) *Qigong fever: Body, science and utopia in China*. New York: Columbia University Press.

Palmer, D. A. (2008) Heretical doctrines, reactionary secret societies, evil cults: Labelling heterodoxy in 20th century China. In M. Yang (Ed.), *Chinese religiosities: The vicissitudes of modernity and state formation*, pp. 113–134. Berkeley, CA: University of California Press.

Palmer, D. A. (2009) China's religious *danwei*: Institutionalizing religion in the Peoples' Republic. *China Perspectives*, 4, 17–31.

Palmer, D. A. (2011) Chinese redemptive societies and salvationist religion: Historical phenomenon or sociological category? *Journal of Chinese Theatre, Ritual and Folklore / Minsu Quyi*, 172, 1–52.

Penny, B. [forthcoming] *The religion of the Falun Gong*. Chicago, IL: University of Chicago Press.

Siegler, E. (2011) Daoism beyond modernity: The "Healing Tao" as postmodern movement. In D. A. Palmer and X. Liu (Eds.), *Daoism in the 20th century: Between eternity and modernity*. Berkeley, CA: University of California Press.

Siegler, E. and D. A. Palmer [forthcoming] *Dream Trippers: Global Daoism and the predicament of modern spirituality*.

Tam, W. L. (2011) Communal worship and festivals in Chinese villages. In D. A. Palmer, G. Shive and P. L. Wickeri (Eds.), *Chinese religious life*. New York: Oxford University Press.

Tong, J. W. (2009) *Revenge of the Forbidden City: The suppression of the Falungong in China, 1999–2005*. New York, NY: Oxford University Press.

Tsai, L. L. (2007) *Accountability without democracy: Solidary groups and public goods provision in rural China*. Cambridge, MA: Cambridge University Press.

Vala, C. (2009) Pathways to the pulpit: Leadership training in 'patriotic' and unregistered Chinese protestant churches. In Y. Ashiwa and D. L. Wang (Eds.), *Making religion, making the state: The politics of religion in contemporary China*, pp. 96–125. Stanford, CA: Stanford University Press.

Vermander, B. (2009) Religions revival and exit from religion in contemporary China. *China perspectives*, 4, 4–15.

Welch, H. (1972) *Buddhism under Mao*. Cambridge, MA: Harvard University Press.

Yang, C. K. (1960) *Religion in Chinese society. A study of contemporary social functions of religion and some of their historical factors*. Berkeley and Los Angeles, CA: University of California Press.

Yang, D.-R. (2005) The changing economy of temple Daoism in Shanghai. In F. Yang and J. Tamney (Eds.), *State, Market, and religions in Chinese societies*. pp. 113–148. Leiden: Brill.

Yang, D.-R. (2011) Revolution of temporality: The modern schooling of Daoist Priests in Shanghai at the turn of the 21st century. In D. A. Palmer and X. Liu

(Eds.), *Daoism in the 20th century: Between eternity and modernity*. Berkeley, CA: University of California Press.

Yang, F., A. Hu., F. Jiang., R. Leamaster, J. Lu and Z. Tang (2010). Quantifying religions in China. In *Proceedings of the 7th annual conference of social science of religion in China: The present and future of religion in China*. Renmin University, July 26–27, 3, 1210–1212.

Yang, F. (2005) Lost in the market, saved at McDonald's: Conversion to Christianity in urban China. *Journal for the Scientific Study of Religion*, 44(4), 423–441.

Yang, F. (2006) The red, black, and gray markets of religion in China. *Sociological Quarterly*, 47, 93–122.

Yang, F. (2010) The state of religion in China: The first glimpse through a survey. In *Newsletter of the Center on Religion and Chinese Society, Purdue University*. 3(2), 1.

Yang, M. (2004) Goddess across the Taiwan strait: Matrifocal ritual space, nation-state, and satellite television footprints. *Public Culture*, 16(2), 209–238.

Yang, M. (2000) Putting global capitalism in its place. Economic hybridity, Bataille, and ritual expenditure. *Current Anthropology*, 41(4), 477–509.

Yip, C.-W. (1999) Protestant Christianity and popular religion in China: A case of syncretism? *Ching Feng*, 42(3–4), 130–175.

12

LITERATURE

Ling Tun Ngai

Abstract

The end of the Maoist rule following Mao Zedong's death in 1976 marked the new beginning of Chinese literature. In the decades that followed, especially in the 1980s, literature flourished in an unprecedented way. The 1980s witnessed the ebb and flow of various literary schools and trends as well as the emergence of many new talents. In the realm of fiction alone, Roots-Seeking Literature, Experimental Fiction, Neo-Realist Fiction, Hooligan Literature and Women's Writing yielded remarkable results. New writers who found fame in this decade include Mo Yan, Yu Hua, Liu Zhenyun, Wang Shuo and Wang Anyi, to name the most recognized few. Poetry also fared well in the 1980s. Bei Dao, Gu Cheng, Yang Lian, Yu Jian, Han Dong and Xi Chuan and many more rank among the best poets the People's Republic has ever produced. Drama may pale by comparison with fiction and poetry, yet one of the pioneering avant-garde playwrights of this decade, who is also a fiction writer, went on to win the Nobel Prize for Literature in 2000. The writer's name is Gao Xingjian. If the 1980s was the heyday of elite literature, the next two decades were the era of mass media, popular culture and entertainment. After the June 4 Massacre of 1989, literary creativity sagged, and literature began to lose a large number of its audience to popular culture and entertainment. The situation was further aggravated when economic reforms accelerated in 1992, prompting a drastic change in lifestyles and social values. The overall influence of literature on the nation diminished considerably since then, regardless of the fact that good literature has never ceased to exist.

Keywords: Post-socialist; scar literature; literature of reflections; roots-seeking literature; experimental fiction; neo-realist fiction; hooligan literature; women's writing; obscure poetry; post-obscure poetry; social problem plays; realist plays; exploration plays; nobel prize for literature; Gao Xingjian

Introduction

Chairman Mao (Mao Zedong, 1893–1976) died in 1976. Within days, Madame Mao and three other high-ranking officials — later dubbed "The Gang of Four" by the new leadership — were arrested in a palace coup. In retrospect, these events are undoubtedly a watershed in modern Chinese history. It marks the end of the Cultural Revolution (1966–1976), the reign of ultraleftism and the beginning of the post-socialist era. Although the full impact of the downfall of the Maoist rule is yet to be measured, its salutary effects on Chinese literature and art alone have been apparent.

When Deng Xiaoping (1904–1997) and his supporters seized power in the Third Plenum of the Eleventh Central Committee of the Chinese Communist Party in December 1978, they called for reform and "emancipation of the mind within the framework of Marxism-Leninism and Mao Zedong thought." On the occasion of the Third National Congress of the Writers Union in 1979, which was convened simultaneously with the Fourth National Congress of the Pan-China Federation of Workers in Literature and Art, Deng issued an edict of freedom of speech for Chinese writers and artists: "In the areas of artistic and literary creation and criticism, administrative directives (from the Party) will be abolished. . . . With regard to the question of what to write, this shall remain the decision of literary and artistic workers: they alone will provide the solutions as they explore and practice their craft." In the years that followed, Chinese writers did enjoy a comparatively greater degree of freedom of speech, though from time to time it was set back by political campaigns caused by intra-Party factional strife.

Many positive factors have contributed to the vitality of post-1976 literature. In 1978, the students who were sent "up to the mountains and down to the countryside" during the Cultural Revolution returned to the cities. Some of them enrolled in the university and put pen to writing about their experiences, now known as "Literature of the Sent-down Youth." In 1979, the new leadership annulled an official document of 1966 entitled "Minutes of the Liberation Army's Forum on Literature and Art," which had restrained the development of literature and art. Most writers who were once blacklisted as "rightists" were now rehabilitated. When these veteran writers resumed their normal civilian status, they started writing again and their output was massive. On top of that, writers were now entitled to receive a fairly handsome amount of money for their published works. Thus, some writers were able to quit their jobs and devote themselves fulltime to creative writing. What is most important is perhaps the mushrooming of literary journals across the country, which provided writers with ample opportunities for publication. Major official literary gazettes and magazines such as *Literature and Gazette* resumed publication in 1978. New literary journals like *Mount Zhong* and *October*, which later became prestigious, were also brought out in that year. In the years that followed, a plethora of literary magazines inundated the market. China had not witnessed such a boom in the production of literary journals since the May Fourth Movement in 1919.

The introduction of Western Modernism, Latin American Magical Realism and many more literary schools in the 1980s also helped to breath new imaginative life into Chinese literature. After thirty years of intellectual incarceration, Chinese men of letters were drawn to all kinds of literary ideas and techniques that were different from the predominant dogma of Socialist Realism. The craze for foreign literature began in the late 1970s and lasted throughout the 1980s. Literary translations and critical studies multiplied, conferences were held, and new journals on foreign literature were founded.

It was against such a background that the "post-1976 euphoria" in the literary circles continued to spread, even in 1983 and 1984, in total disregard of the anxiety caused by the political campaign against "Spiritual Pollution." A large number of literary salons of diverse persuasions were organized by writers, aficionados and critics in one city after another. Chinese writers were somehow convinced that a breakthrough in literature was on the horizon. An account given by a friend of the critic Li Tuo (b. Kuku Batu, alias Meng Keqin, 1939) captures the spirited enthusiasm of the time: upon finishing a new poem, a poet in Chengdu caught an overnight train to another city just to discuss it face to face with his friends. This anonymous poet certainly deserves a mention in "The Free and Unrestrained" section, if a modern version of *A New Account of Tales of the World* (432–444) were to be written.

Agitation for achievement and breakthrough was not confined to writers. Scholars were equally affected by the intellectual ardor, though they were more interested in reexamining China's cultural past. In June 1982 the first conference on Chinese cultural history was convened in post-Mao China, followed by another in December. The impact of these two conferences was enormous and far-reaching. They entailed fervent debates that went on for some time, bringing up more imperative topics such as contemporary cultural phenomena and the future of traditional Chinese values. In their wake, conferences on contemporary Chinese culture were held in 1984 and 1985. Among the many topics, comparisons between traditional and modern ideas and between Chinese and Western cultures were the most popular. When the campaign against "Spiritual Pollution" began to falter in 1984, an informal conference was held in Hangzhou by *Shanghai Literature* and the Writers' Association of Zhejiang Province in response to the "Culture Fever." The participants were exclusively writers and critics of a younger generation, eager to explore regional and marginal cultures in their literary works.

All these developments added to the momentum for a literary and artistic breakthrough in 1985. In retrospect, the year 1985 is indeed an *annus mirabilis* for literature and art of the People's Republic. It was a year when Chinese writers, painters and film directors of a younger generation turned their back on the directives of Socialist Realism, asserted aesthetic autonomy, reaped great success and gained international recognition. In Li Tuo's opinion, that year is particularly important for Chinese fiction, because the young writers not only made an impressive debut but also brought an end to the era of "Literature for Workers, Peasants, and Soldiers." After 1985, literature and art continued to thrive in a dazzling way, until the bloody crackdown of the students' democratic movement on June 4, 1989, which turned the collective sense of euphoria into despair, cynicism and nihilism.

If the 1980s was the heyday of elite literature, the 1990s witnessed the birth of Chinese mass media, popular culture and entertainment. After the June 4 Massacre, literary creativity sagged, and literature began to lose a large number of its readers to the emerging popular culture and entertainment, spearheaded by TV programs such as *Yearning*, a fifty-episode melodrama about the fate of two families caught in the turmoil of the Cultural Revolution. When the program was aired in 1990, it made an instant success. It was reported that the show actually emptied the streets in some major cities. Despite the spectacular popularity of *Yearning*, literary critics were both amazed and repelled by the program's vulgar style, cheap sentimentality, negative portrayal of intellectuals and, worst of all, unabashed promotion of conservative values at the expense of budding individualism. *Yearning* was soon followed by *The Story of an Editorial Office* in 1992, another milestone in TV entertainment. In retrospect, it is hardly surprising that Wang Shuo (b. 1958) was on the script team of both programs. Wang is not only the forefather of Hooligan Literature, but also the first best-selling writer in the People's Republic to reap handsome pecuniary rewards. The production of *Yearning* and emergence of Wang Shuo portended the advent of market-oriented popular culture, the diminishing of high culture's influence on the general public and the gradual phasing out of the residual utopian ideal-ism of the 1980s. After 1992, with the blessing of Deng Xiaoping, Chinese economic reforms began to accelerate at an unprecedented pace, and capitalism, behind the veneer of "Socialism with Chinese characteristics," returned to China with a vengeance. Within a few years, the entire nation was thrown into the frenzy in pursuit of wealth and prestige, as if engaged in a collective ritual to exorcise the lingering phantom of Communist Revolution. It is against this background that a discussion about the absence of "the spirit of humanism" took place, primarily between 1993 and 1998, among some leading intellectuals in China who were gravely concerned with the cultural crisis triggered by the disillusion with socialism and the advent of capitalism. Despite the momentous changes in Chinese society and cul-ture, literature and art revived a few years after the 1989 Massacre, and lingered on into the twenty-first century, with their overall influence on the nation on the wane.

Needless to say, any attempt at a survey of Chinese literature in the last three decades is rather difficult, if not altogether impossible. The sketchiness of this survey is inevitable. However, it is hoped that this brief outline will offer vital clues to readers interested in contemporary Chinese literature. Due to its limited space, this report will focus on new writers who exploded onto the literary scene and shaped the literary landscape of the "New Era," while acknowledging tacitly the contribution of the first and second generations of writers who remained active and productive during this period. For the same reason, this survey covers only three major genres, namely fiction, poetry and drama, with a focus on fiction, the most vibrant of the trio. Although prose is not covered in this survey, the endeavors of writers in this genre are not to be overlooked. Potentially good candidates as essayists, if included in this report, include Ba Jin (1904–2005), Zhang Zhongxing (b. Zhang Xuan, 1909–2006), Yang Jiang (b. 1911), Ji Xianlin (1911–2009), Jin Kemu (1912–2000), Sun Li (b. Sun Shuxun, 1913–2002), Yu Qiuyu (b. 1946), Zhang Chengzhi (b. 1948), Shi Tiesheng (b. 1951), Wang Xiaobo (1952–1997) and Han Shaogong (b. 1953), to name just a notable few.

Fiction

Scar Literature

In the summer of 1977, when Liu Xinwu (b. 1942) penned his most famous story "The Class Teacher," he did it not without qualms. To make sure that he was toeing the party line, he re-read Chairman Mao's *Talks at the Yan'an*

Conference on Arts and Literature (1943) twice. His submission of the story to the *People's Literature* rocked its editorial office. It was reported that the first editor who read the story was deeply moved and "broke down and wept." Other sober editors went through the story, and they were unnerved by its exposure of the aftermath of the Cultural Revolution and its criticism of the ultraleftist mindset. The editor-in-chief called a meeting to review the story, and they eventually decided to have it published on the condition that Liu revised it according to their suggestions.

"The Class Teacher" came out in the November issue and became an immediate success. Readers from all over China reacted enthusiastically by writing to the editors, and seminars were held in Beijing to discuss the story's significance. Soon Liu's effort was officially endorsed. In 1978, he won the first prize of National Best Short Stories Awards by this story, thus inaugurating what Chinese literary historians call the "New Era" of Chinese literature. Though artistically naïve, the story is historically important for being the first attempt of Chinese writers to measure, however inadequately, the aftermath of the Cultural Revolution. In the story, a high-school teacher by the name of Zhang is given the unenviable task of educating two recalcitrant students. One is a follower of political hardliners, the other a delinquent. In Liu's view, both are unfortunate victims of the ideologies perpetuated by the "Gang of Four." As a teacher devoted to his job and his country, Zhang determines to "save the children," invoking the most famous lines of Lu Xun (1881–1936). Although Zhang is too preoccupied with his high-flown thoughts to do anything substantial to "save" his students, his courage to reveal the harm caused by a political faction on the Chinese people inspired emulators, who were equally eager to expose the injustice and injuries inflicted on the nation by the Cultural Revolution.

Another piece of short story that quickly caught national attention was "The Scar." It was written by Lu Xinhua (b. 1954), a freshman at Fudan University. In comparison with "The Class Teacher," this tear-jerking story published in 1978 is ideologically less rigid, and artistically less contrived. But its simple plot of the destruction of human bonding by political persecution touched the heart of millions. At the height of the Cultural Revolution, a teenage girl by the name of Xiaohua is appalled to learn that her mother is branded by the government as traitor. To show her loyalty to the country, she cuts herself off from all contact with her mother and leaves to work in a state farm in the countryside, in a desperate attempt to redeem herself from her mother's political sin. When the Cultural Revolution ends nine years later, she is once again shaken by the news that her mother has all along been wrongly accused. She rushes home to Shanghai, only to find that her mother has passed away. Devastated, Xiaohua vents all her grief and rage at the "Gang of Four," vowing never to forgive those "who inflicted those wounds on our hearts." Before the story ends, a ship sounds its siren, as if signaling a new beginning and hope. Upon hearing this, Xiaohua holds her boyfriend by the arm, and together they march triumphantly towards "the brightly-lit Nanjing Road."

In the wake of these two pieces of pioneering works, stories disclosing the atrocities of the Cultural Revolution and personal tribulations began to surface. Despite their apparent lack of artistic sophistication, these literary works were eagerly read and discussed by readers throughout China. It is as if the whole nation was engaged in a collective act of mourning and catharsis. The impact created by "The Scar" has given rise to the term "Scar Literature" or "Wound Literature," referring to the fiction written primarily between 1977 and 1979, with a focus on the trauma caused by the Cultural Revolution on ordinary people. Other works of fiction that have made an impact upon Chinese readers include "Maples" by Zheng Yi (b. Zheng Guangzhao, 1947), "Corner Left Unnoticed by Love" by Zhang Xian (b. Zhang Xinhua, 1934), "Sacred Duty" by Wang Yaping, "The Noble Pine" by Wang Zonghan, "Red Magnolias Beneath the Walls" by Cong Weixi (b. 1933) and *Xu Mao and His Daughter* by Zhou Keqin (b. 1937–1990). "Maples," "Corner Left Unnoticed by Love" and *Xu Mao and His Daughter* were later adapted into feature films bearing the same titles, reaching an even larger audience in China.

Literature of Reflections

Both writers and readers realized that the "Gang of Four" was only the tip of the iceberg that sank the Titanic of socialism. To understand the provenance of Cultural Revolution, one has to review the history of the People's Republic, or at least the incessant political campaigns and social events that have affected the daily life of the entire nation since the 1950s. In the retrospective and at times introspective narratives called "Literature of Reflections," the following historic dates feature prominently — 1949 (the year the People's Republic was founded), 1957 (when the Anti-Rightist Campaign was launched, followed by the Great Leap Forward in 1958, and the famine and economic crisis of the early 1960s), 1966 (when Cultural Revolution broke out), and 1976 (when Cultural Revolution came to an end). The subjects covered by Literature of Reflections are indeed extensive. The hardships endured by people from various sectors of society over a span of three decades are earnestly portrayed.

Among the well-liked works of this trend, "Li Shunda Builds a House" by Gao Xiaosheng (b. 1928) and "Butterfly" by Wang Meng (b. 1934) stood out. Gao is a peasant writer, who was labeled a "rightist" in 1957 and as a result banned from creative writing for the next two decades. When he resumed writing in 1979, he created two peasant characters, Li Shunda and Chen Huansheng, which became household names. "Li Shunda Builds a House" is a wry account of Li's monumental effort, since the founding of the People's Republic, to build a brick house for his family against all political vagaries. His hope is dashed thrice: first in 1957, when his hard-earned building materials are confiscated for collective use, and then in 1966, when his savings are cheated by a Red Guard and he himself is thrown into jail for his unfavorable comments on socialism, and finally, in the early 1970s, when he has once again saved enough money but is unable to purchase any building materials which are in severe shortage. He has to wait until the end of Cultural Revolution to realize his dream, partly by resorting to bribery. It has taken him almost three decades to see his perseverance pay off. Gao Xiaosheng's sarcasm of the absurdity of Chinese reality is best captured in the episode of Li's imprisonment. For the first time in his life, Li finds himself inside an unusually solid building, unlike any hut or dungeon he has ever seen before. Thanks to proletarian dictatorship, Li is given the invaluable chance of learning his first lesson on architecture in a prison.

If Gao Xiaosheng speaks on behalf of the peasantry who has the slightest idea of ideological changes, Wang Meng penetrates the mindscape of the architects of political campaigns. "Butterfly" is a novella recounting the story of Zhang Siyuan, a high-ranking Communist cadre who joins the Communist Party in the 1930s, rises to power after the founding of the People's Republic, falls into political disgrace during the Cultural Revolution, and eventually resumes power as a Deputy Minister in Beijing in 1979. The narrative of his professional ups and downs is interwoven with that of his private life, particularly his romance with three women and his love-hate relationship with his son, sprinkled with his reverie and introspection about his life and his nation. The title is an allusion to the philosophical anecdote of Zhuangzi, in which a philosopher wakes up from a butterfly dream, wondering whether he has dreamed about the butterfly or he is just a figment of the butterfly's dream. However, Zhang's rumination is not as metaphysical as the title of the novella suggests. It is simply a metaphor for his identity crisis triggered by his political downfall. He keeps on asking himself: Is he a revolutionary or a counterrevolutionary? Is he a conscientious cadre serving the people, or a corrupt bureaucrat served by the people?

Zhang's bewilderment does not bother him long, for he redeems himself ideologically by earning the respect and support of the farmers with whom he works during the years of his demotion. Eventually, he is not only rehabilitated but also gets promoted by the Party, confirming his revolutionary status. Although Zhang has done some soul-searching in difficult times, his position as a high-ranking official of the Communist government prevents him from genuinely reflecting on his blindness and complicity in executing the Party's irrational directives. In the end the novella turns out to be not so much a reflection on the Party's misdeeds as a panegyric of the Party's infallibility.

In sharp contrast to Gao Xiaosheng's plain and casual style, Wang Meng's language is complex and embellished. While Gao's narration follows the chronological order, Wang's spatio-temporal frame is constantly shifting, as if guided by the inner thoughts of the protagonist. In the early 1980s, Wang's attempt to break away from the conventions of realism and socialist realism is manifested not only in this novella, but also in a series of short stories that focus on the inner life of their main characters, such as "Bolshevik Salute," "Voices of Spring" and "Eyes of the Night." Some critics regard these works as Wang's experimentation with "stream-of-consciousness," one of the main features of twentieth-century literary modernism. Wang Meng's endeavor was applauded by Gao Xingjian (b. 1940), then an obscure translator and writer who had started publishing on the art of modern fiction and literary modernism since the late 1970s. Wang's conspicuous inward turn and occasional use of second-person narration in his third-person narratives were noticed by Gao, for the techniques of "stream-of-consciousness" and "alternation of person" featured prominently in Gao's theorization of modern narrative art. In 1981, these articles were included in Gao's book entitled *A Preliminary Exploration of the Techniques of Fiction*, which caught the attention of writers immediately. His espousal and exposition of modernist techniques was met with acclaim and criticism. Wang Meng and Feng Cicai (b. 1942) wrote favorable reviews, while Gao's detractors accused him of deviating from the norms of realism and socialist realism. And the issue of modernism would keep on coming back to haunt the Chinese literary circle throughout the 1980s.

Other influential works of fiction that relate to Literature of Reflections, mainly published between 1979 and 1983, include the following: "A Story out of Sequence" by Ru Zhijuan (1925–1998), "Who Am I" by Zongpu (b. 1928), "Legend of Mount Tianyun" by Lu Yanzhou (1928–2006), "Lunar Eclipse" by Li Guowen (b. 1930), "Story of the Criminal Li Tongzhong" by Zhang Yigong (b. 1934), "Bolshevik Salute" by Wang Meng, "At Middle Age" by Shen Rong (b. Shen Derong, 1936), "Mimosa" and "Half of Man Is Woman" by Zhang Xianliang (b. 1936), and *Hibiscus Town* by Gu Hua (b. Luo Hongyu, 1942). "Legend of Mount Tianyun" was adapted into a major feature film by the veteran director Xie Jin (1923–2008), bearing the same title. In 1981, the adapted film won the Best Feature Film Prize and other prizes at the First Golden Rooster Awards, and the Best Feature Film Prize at the Fourth Hundred Flowers Awards. Gu Hua's novel *Hibiscus Town* was also made into a feature film by Xie Jin. In 1987, *Hibiscus Town* won the Best Feature Film Prize and other prizes at both the Seventh Golden Rooster Awards and the Tenth Hundred Flowers Awards, and the Grand Prix at the 26th Karlovy Vary International Film Festival in Czechoslovakia in 1988.

Roots-Seeking Literature

Right after the Hangzhou conference of 1984, Han Shaogong (b. 1953) published an article entitled "The Roots of Literature" in 1985. Han's appeal to infuse cultural elements into literary creation so as to revitalize Chinese literature sparked enthusiastic responses from many writers of his generation, most of whom had attended the conference. In a few months, the issue of "cultural roots-seeking" caught the imagination of Chinese writers, and quite a number of remarkable short stories and novellas written in this vein got into print. As a result of this collective effort, the year 1985 witnessed the first cornucopia of high literature in post-socialist China. As a matter of fact, some critics were so galvanized that they were prompted to assert that modern Chinese fiction actually came into being in 1985.

In Han's programmatic article, he contends that the Chinese mode of thinking is basically intuitive and pictographic, and as a result of which, Chinese literature excels in subjective expression. In his opinion, such cognitive and aesthetic characteristics are best exemplified by the culture of Chu (in southwestern region of China), which culminated in the *Songs of Chu* (3 B.C. — 2 A.D.). Han bemoans the long absence in Chinese culture of "mystic, sumptuous, uninhibited and indignant" qualities essential to Chu culture, and appeals for their revival in literary writing. Han believes that the unrestrained imagination and vitality of Chu culture has not vanished; it must have been conserved in the customs of ethnic tribes residing in the remote areas bordering Hunan and Guangxi provinces, and Chinese writers should leave no stones unturned in order to find it. To revitalize Chinese literature, Han argues, one has to return to the potencies of the cultural traditions of Chu for inspiration. Only when the unique cultural essence of China is represented can Chinese literature fashion an identity of its own and go on to hold a genuine dialogue with world literature. In

short, the "roots" of modern Chinese literature with distinctive characteristics lie in marginal cultures.

Li Hangyu (b. 1957) echoed Han's views in several of his articles, the
most important of which bears the title "Sort out our 'Roots.'" Li suggests
that writers find their muse in folk culture and cultures of ethnic tribes, and
cast aside "Culture of the Central Plains," which has been dominated by
Confucianism. Li's disillusion with Confucianism is totalistic and bitter, holding its pragmatic and ethical orientations responsible for the pauperization
of Chinese imagination. Like Han, Li believes that the quintessence of
Chinese culture is well maintained in marginal cultures, and writers should
turn to these "roots" from time to time for literary innovations.

A Cheng's (b. Zhong Acheng, 1949) explication of the term "culture"
and his understanding of the "roots" of literature differ from those of Han
and Li. In an article entitled "Human Beings Conditioned by Cultural
Factors," he argues that literature is a means of representing and comprehending humanity, yet humanity is less an innate quality than an acquired
consciousness shaped by the linguistic and value systems of the community.
When a writer sets himself the task of portraying humanity, he will find himself constrained by his own culture. The more he understands the systems in
and by which he operates, the more successful his depiction is likely to be.
Unlike Li Hangyu, A Cheng does not distrust traditional culture. He also differs from Han Shaogong in that he is not particularly interested in regional
sub-cultures.

Immediately following the appearance of his controversial article, "The
Roots of Literature," Han Shaogong published several stories in the spirit
of "cultural roots-seeking." "Papa-pa" stands out as his outlandish *tour de
force* and has been widely discussed, both at home and abroad. It is a
novella about the fate of a moribund tribe living in Chicken Head village,
located somewhere in the remote backland. The plot develops around
Little Bing, the idiotic son of a country midwife by a shady father.
Linguistically handicapped, Bing is constantly bullied by his fellow tribesmen. However, when a famine caused by a crop failure befalls the tribe, the
tribesmen, out of despair and ignorance, turn to Little Bing for help,
resorting to his unconscious utterances — "papa-pa" and "mama" — for
divination. Convinced by the superstitious gossip that Mount Chicken has
"eaten up" all the crops and fertilized the Chicken Tail village, the
Chicken Head Village decides to blow up the "head" of Mount Chicken.
Upon hearing the news, the villagers living in the Chicken Tail Village,
who are equally superstitious, are infuriated and vow to protect the
"chicken head." Feuds ensue, and end in violence. Despite Bing's

auspicious premonition in the form of uttering "papa-pa," the Chicken Head Village turns out to be the loser in the conflict. With no more food to feed the survivors, the young and strong of the Chicken Head Village set on a migration journey to find a new place to settle down, while leaving the old and sick behind to commit suicide. To the horror of many literary critics, Little Bing, who is abandoned by the tribe and fed with the most virulent of poisons, survives.

The obscure spatio-temporal frame and well-structured symbolism of this story render it susceptible to allegorical readings. In general, critics tend to read the story as a disconcerting depiction of the Chinese civilization in decline. The monstrous character of Little Bing has also attracted much of critical attention, deemed by many readers as a symbol of the crudity of revolutionary logic prevalent during the Cultural Revolution. The critic Liu Zaifu (b. 1941) recalled in agony how accustomed he was to such a simplistic mode of dichotomous thinking, aptly captured by Han Shaogong in Little Bing's *yin* and *yang* predictions. After reading "Papa-pa," the veteran writer Yan Wenjing (Yan Wenjin, 1915–2005) was so unnerved by the story that he was prompted to ask: "Am I not an aged Bing?"

If Han is considered a vanguard from the south, A Cheng is hailed as a representative from the North. "The Chess Master," published a year before Han's "The Roots of Literature" and "Papa-pa," is applauded by critics as a precursor to the roots-seeking movement as well as a major contribution to its success. Unlike Han Shaogong and Li Hangyu, Ah Cheng is particularly concerned with his generation's lack of formal education and insufficient knowledge of traditional Chinese culture. He also shares his fellow writers' conviction that a deep understanding of culture is the prerequisite of good literature. However, in view of the massive destruction of traditional elite culture on the Chinese mainland, writers can only resort to informal culture preserved by the common folks for literary inspiration. Nevertheless, skeptical as he is about the continuity of the Chinese cultural tradition, Ah Cheng has tried to steer away from cynicism and pessimism in his fiction. His faith in cultural populism explains in part why in "The Chess Master," the "way of chess" is kept in the hands of a young man of humble origin.

"The Chess Master" is deceptively simple, relayed in the most traditional way. As the story begins, Wang Yisheng, an aficionado of Chinese chess from a poor family, chooses to leave the city where he has been living during the Cultural Revolution and work in a state farm. The hardships of daily life do not seem to bother him at all, for he is single-mindedly obsessed with chess. The story begins to get interesting as well as symbolic when Wang beats Ni Bin in a chess game. Ni is the best chess player from another farm and a descendant of a notable family. His ancestor is none other than Ni Zan (1301–1374), the famous painter, calligrapher and poet of the Yuan Dynasty. Moreover, according to Ni Bin, Ni Zan was also a great chess player, and there is a long tradition of chess playing in his family. In sharp contrast to Ni, Wang is an orphan, who learns chess from an old garbage collector who happens to own an ancient chess anthology of a very obscure origin.

Awed by Wang's talent as a chess player, Ni Bin introduces him, about six months later, to the runners-up of a regional tournament and challenges them to play against Wang. As the news gets out, more players volunteer to play against Wang, including the champion. In the end Wang has to play a multiple game blind, against nine contestants at the same time. This is indeed the most captivating episode in the story, when Wang concentrates on the grueling marathon in a state of utmost tranquility that only a master of Daoism can emulate. Wang defeats his opponents one by one, until the last one, namely the regional champion, shows up in person and asks for a draw. He turns out to be a suave and sophisticated old man from a respectable family. To save the gentleman's face, Wang gracefully agrees.

As the story draws to a close after Wang's great victory, he begins to understand dimly the larger implication of the game of chess hitherto unknown to him. Now he can appreciate its value as a simple means for an ordinary man to achieving a truly meaningful life, though he is unable to articulate it. Wang Yisheng's peculiar image and his mysterious "way of chess" have given rise to many interpretations. One critic holds that chess represents the primacy of spiritual sustenance in a truly human life, and such sustenance comes from the cherished values of traditional culture, which are passed down from the old man to Wang. Wang's final victory affirms not only the necessity of abstract values in general, but also the imperative of transmitting the true spiritual heritage of traditional China in particular. The other critic sees Wang's immersion in the art of chess as a backhanded act of defiance, a subtle challenge to the daily politics of the Chinese state. The metaphysical aura of chess, as invoked in the final scene depicting Wang's trance-like conditions, further enhances the game's transcendent value as a counterpoint to the dreary and dreadful political environment.

In 1985, Wang Anyi (b. 1954) came up with an intriguing novella that also deals with the theme of "cultural roots-seeking." In "The Bao Village," she spins a yarn about a seven-year-old boy by the nickname of Laoza. In a style typical of Wang's fiction, the story is dense in description, complex in narration, and vivid in its representation of regional dialects. However, in spite of Wang's technical dexterity, the story is somewhat flawed by her overt characterization of Laoza as a paragon of residual Confucian virtue.

Throughout the story the little boy is repeatedly praised by other characters as "humane" and "righteous," on top of the narrator's untiring account of his altruistic deeds, which culminate, rather dramatically, in a purported act of heroic self-sacrifice in a deluge of biblical proportion that wipes out the entire Bao Village. As the little boy's story travels from town to town, it attracts the regional government's attention. Soon this story is appropriated by the government and rewritten into a hagiography of a little Communist saint. Laoza's altruism and self-sacrifice are now re-interpreted from the angle of official ideology; his devotion to his relatives following the Confucian ethic imperatives is now extolled out of context as a model for proletarian comradeship. There is indeed nothing more ironic than such an unexpected twist in the plot, for the tacit agenda of the roots-seeking movement, according to informed critics, is the implicit challenge of traditional culture to Communist ideologies.

Another important writer who was marginally involved in the roots-seeking movement is Mo Yan (b. Guan Moye, 1956), whose publication of the Red Sorghum series since 1985 immediately put him in the national spotlight. Attracted by Mo Yan's stylistic ebullience, Zhang Yimou (b. 1951) adapted two of these stories for his directorial debut, *Red Sorghum*, in 1987. This feature film garnered national and international acclaim, and won the Golden Bear award at the 1988 Berlin International Film Festival. Partly because of the huge success of the movie, Mo Yan's gift as a storyteller quickly gained international recognition.

In the 1930s, red sorghum is a symbol of the Chinese resistance to the Japanese invasion. During the Resistance War (1937–1945), the sorghum fields were the hideout for guerrillas in Northeast China. In this regard, the composer Xian Xinghai (1905–1945) and the lyricist Guang Weiran (b. Zhang Guangnian, 1913–2002) were Mo Yan's forerunners. In their famous *Yellow River Cantata* (1939), a song named "Defending the Yellow River" is at once a call to arms and a celebration of the exploits of resistant guerrillas in the sorghum fields. The cantata was so successful in invoking patriotism and nationalism that it was later assimilated by the People's Republic into official ideology to define modern Chinese identity. Mo Yan's Red Sorghum series were also anticipated by Xiao Jun's (b. Liu Honglin, 1907–1988) *Village in August* (1935), the first successful novel to embody the theme of anti-Japanese resistance.

However, Mo Yan's Red Sorghum series, later collected in a book entitled *Red Sorghum*, are not so much a eulogy of patriotism as a celebration of passion and valor. Mo Yan is more interested in depicting the extraordinary drama of love, courage and death of ordinary people when they are caught in a time of social unrest and military conflicts. The episode recounting the villager's waylaying of a Japanese division is but one movement in Mo Yan's complex symphony of the love and hate affairs of the narrator's forebears and the contest for military dominance among Communists, the local government, and bandits.

An idiosyncratic writer of farming stock, Mo Yan's Red Sorghum saga is unlike anything Chinese readers have read before. His potently "rustic" preference for grotesque realism, carnivalesque outlook, gallous humor, excessive narration, scatological pranks, fantastic plots, sensory impressionism and heterogenous registers is indeed phenomenal and unprecedented, sometimes quite hard for critics and readers of conventional taste to swallow. As a peasant writer, his ambivalent attachment to regional culture and peasantry is also obvious, setting him drastically apart from Han Shaogong, A Cheng and Wang Anyi, who tend to view regional cultures from an elitist point of view. Mo Yan's ambivalence towards his cultural "roots" is best captured by the words of the narrator of the Red Sorghum series: "Northeast Gaomi Township is easily the most beautiful and most repulsive, most unusual and most common, most sacred and most corrupt, most heroic and most bastardly, hardest-drinking and hardest-loving place in the world."

However, the brave old world of the Gaomi County is but an imaginary reference point created by Mo Yan to judge the present. According to the narrator, who is an offspring of the Red Sorghum Family, his family has suffered from a "racial degeneration" as a result of social "progress." If the forebears of the family embrace life with pride, passion and prowess, their descendants preserve life through hypocrisy and calculation. While the strengths of the ancestors are said to be nourished by the rural environment, the weaknesses of the offspring are attributed to the erosion by urban civilization. In this regard, Mo Yan's elegiac tone seems to echo that of Han Shaogong's "Papa-pa."

Other writers who enjoyed the spotlight in this roots-seeking movement include Wang Zengqi (1920–1997), Zheng Wanlong (1944), Li Rui (b. 1949), Jia Pingwa (b. 1952), He Liwei (b. 1954), Li Hangyu (b. 1957) and Zhaxi Dawa (b. 1959). Wang Zengqi is a veteran writer, who began publishing his stories in the 1940s. His representative works of fiction in the "New Era" include two remarkable tales, "Buddhist Initiation" and "A Tale of Big Nur," both highly acclaimed as masterpieces of storytelling which capture the flavor of the traditional way of life. Zheng Wanlong, Li Hangyu, Li Rui and Jia Pingwa excel in their depiction of regional cultures. Zheng Wanglong's "The Tavern," Li Hangyu's "The Last Fisherman" and Li Rui's collection of short stories *Deep Earth* rank among the best short stories representing the achievement of this movement. Jia Pingwa is known for his essays and stories with a focus on the culture of Shangzhou.

The writers who emerged during the roots-seeking movement continued to make an impact on Chinese literature in the following decades by going beyond their preoccupation with the issue of culture. Ah Cheng's next two acclaimed stories, "The Tree Master" and "The Children's Master," were published in 1985. Han Shaogong's major novel *A Dictionary of Maqiao* was released in 1996, now regarded as one of the classics of twentieth-century Chinese fiction. Mo Yan's unbridled literary imagination continued to impress domestic and international readers with his landmark novels such as *Big Breasts and Wide Hips* (1996), *The Sandalwood Torture* (2001) and *Life and Death Are Wearing Me Out* (2006). Wang Anyi's endless cascade of words emerged from her pen since 1985, crystallizing in her carefully crafted *Realism and Fabrication* (1993) and *The Song of Everlasting Sorrow* (1995). Jia Pingwa rose to fame with the publication of his representative novels including *Turbulence: A Novel* (1988), *Defunct Capital* (1993) and *Qin Melody* (2005). Li Rui's consistent literary achievement in novels since the mid-1980s is also highly admired, as vindicated by *Silver City* (1993), *Trees without Wind* (1996), *No Clouds for Ten Thousand Miles* (1998) and *A Tale of Silver City* (2002).

Experimental Fiction

Another main trend in creative writing that became apparent in the mid-1980s was Experimental Fiction, or Avant-garde Fiction. In 1985, Liu Suola (b. 1955) published "You Have No Other Choice," followed by Xu Xing's (b. 1956) "A Variation without a Theme," both regarded by literary historians as portents of Experimental Fiction. In all fairness, these two stories are not so much "experimental" as realist fiction, although they do remarkably well in capturing the urban youths' sense of ennui and skepticism by their loose plot and playful tone.

The writers who introduced new techniques and ideas for Experimental Fiction are Ma Yuan (b. 1953) and Can Xue (b. Deng Xiaohua, 1953). Ma Yuan's publication of "Goddess of the River Lhasa" in 1984 was regarded by critics as the seminal text that brought about the narrative revolution of the 1980s. In 1985 and 1986 respectively, Ma Yuan went on with his narrative experimentation in "The Attraction of the Ganges" and "Fabrication." Also in 1985 and 1986, Can Xue's "A Cabin on the Mountain" and *Yellow Mud Street* saw print respectively, causing quite a stir with her unconventional plot and quirky images.

Ma Yuan's stories are often marked by the distinct presence of a flippant narrator, who constantly reminds his readers of the glaring fact that what they are reading is nothing other than sheer fiction, depending on his whims. As if to mock his readers' reading habit, Ma sometimes deliberately fashions his narrator from his own image, or even names him "Ma Yuan" as he does in "Fabrication," thus invoking a false sense of verisimilitude in an otherwise purely fictional literary text. Ma also employs the metafictional technique of metalapsis (the intrusion of the extradiegetic narrator into the diegetic world of characters or the inverse) to tease his readers and impress critics who are unfamiliar with this popular gimmick of postmodernism. For instance, in "A Wall Painted with Strange Patterns," a female character keeps on talking about a certain "Ma Yuan," who is very likely the narrator, who does not take part in the story, or even Ma Yuan himself. Furthermore, Ma is fond of assembling several tales to form a loosely coherent narrative, such as what he does in "The Attraction of the Ganges," challenging his readers to make sense of the whole story by themselves.

In general, Ma Yuan is a novelist engrossed in the art of narration rather than the stories themselves. However, since his stories are primarily set in Tibet, they have an exotic air rarely seen in contemporary Chinese fiction. His subject matters range from the scandalous to the mundane, also limited to Tibetan legends and everyday life. He may make up a sensational story of a Chinese man's sexual encounter with a Tibetan leper on the one hand as in "Fabrication," and give a matter-of-fact description of an ordinary picnic that takes place by the Lhasa River on the other hand. Unlike the writers of the roots-seeking school, Ma Yuan shows little interest in the significance of Tibetan culture that he is writing about. To him, fiction is a playground in which a writer indulges in language games and narrative possibilities. In this sense, Ma Yuan is indeed the first experimental writer in post-socialist China.

In comparison, Can Xue's fiction is chillingly grim. Can Xue distinguishes herself as an avant-garde writer by her uncompromisingly gloomy and grotesque rendition of humanity and society. Her fiction abounds with sub-human characters who barely survive in an apocalyptic world that exists somewhere between reality and nightmare. Their life is haunted by their own strange hallucinations and the inexplicable behavior of others, only to be interrupted once in a while by ludicrous dialogues and loquacious officialese. The provenance of such a fictional world can be traced to the social-political events that have severely distorted the life and mind of the Chinese people, as illustrated in one of her representative works, *Yellow Mud Street*. Although the novel is meant to be historically unspecific, the sprinkling of political slogans and Maospeak in the daily conversation of the characters betrays its close relationship with the Cultural Revolution. If one follows the storyline closely, one will notice a recurrent motif of a secret investigation, which is very likely an insinuation of the incessant hunts for class enemies and dissidents since the founding of the People's Republic. Throughout the story, residents of the dilapidated and plague-stricken Yellow Mud Street are perturbed by a rumor that someone heavily disguised or something entirely alien is coming to the community to trace the sources of the plague. Nothing is known for sure about the identity of the investigator, nor his real mission. The community is kept in the dark and in suspense throughout. Although the inner commotion of the community is depicted in the most absurd way, one can still detect traces of the social practices prevalent during the Cultural Revolution, such as mutual surveillance and political gatherings. Most interesting of all, the existence of Yellow Mud Street is denied toward the end of the novel by everyone except the narrator, who refuses to forget such a nightmare of the past. Undoubtedly, the denouement is Can Xue's tacit comment on the nation's negation of the collective trauma caused by reckless socialism.

"The Cabin on a Mountain" is not only the most critically acclaimed story by Can Xue, but also arguably one of the classics of "New Era Literature" that reveals the harm inflicted by society and family on individuals under abnormal circumstances. The story is told in the first person, in which the unreliable narrator (gender unspecified) gives a conflicting account of the existence of a cabin on a mountain at the back of the narrator's house. At the beginning of the story, the cabin seems to exist; but at the end of the story, its existence is flatly denied. Whether the cabin exists or not is probably beside the point, for it seems to be a projection of the anxiety and desperation of the narrator, who, suffering from insomnia, claims to hear at night that a person (gender unspecified) locked up inside that cabin bang at the door, trying to get out. This projection of self-image is a reflection of the narrator's predicament at home, where the insensible family seems to scheme against each other. Every night Father transforms himself into a howling wolf, running around the house, while others rummage through the narrator's cabinet during his or her absence. Worse still, threats also come from outside. Thieves gather around their house at night; some even poke holes on their windows, as if trying to break in. The sense of insecurity and anxiety is so intense that the story resembles the babble of a paranoid.

Characteristically, this story also abounds with Can Xue's unusual images. While the narrator collects dead moths and dragonflies as a hobby, Father is forever pestered by the thought of his lost scissors. Sister's left eye would turn green when she talks to the narrator, and Mother's intense gaze could cause a bump on the narrator's head.

Immediately following Ma Yuan's and Can Xue's success, Yu Hua (b. 1960) and Ge Fei (b. Liu Yong, 1964), two of the most gifted writers of China, burst onto the literary scene with their unique experimentation with innovative styles and exploration of new subjects. Yu Hua specializes in clinical anatomy of human brutality, while Gu Fei is obsessed with the dizzying effects of narrative labyrinths. Yu Hua made his debut in 1987 with "Travelling at the Age of Eighteen," a short story about an eighteen-year-old boy's shocking encounter with human irrationality and brutality on his first trip. This was soon followed by his gory masterpieces, "Nineteen Eighty Six," "One Kind of Reality" and "Classical Love." "Nineteen Eighty Six" confronts its readers head-on with the sudden outburst of cruelty latent in Chinese culture. A history teacher well-versed in ancient Chinese capital punishments loses his mind during the turbulent years of Cultural Revolution. In 1986, when this utterly deranged man returns to his hometown, now peaceful and prosperous in the "New Era" of economic reforms, he begins to mete out cheerfully in public his imagined penalties to himself, much to the horror of onlookers. First he uses a saw to cut out his nose, and then his legs. After resting for a while, he musters all his strength and lifts a stone to smash his penis and testicles. No one dares to interfere with his relentlessly masochistic self-torture. Despite the excruciating pain, he manages to brandish a chopper and slices up himself. Eventually the onlookers cannot take it anymore and join hands to subdue him. While struggling to free himself, the history teacher has the illusion that he is undergoing the capital punishment of dismemberment by five chariots pulling in different directions. This gruesome story is told from two perspectives: the teacher's limited point of view and the narrator's omniscience, offering a poignant contrast between personal suffering and collective oblivion. While the teacher is lost in his traumatic experience of the recent past and the terrible tortures invented by ancient Chinese culture, the people in his hometown, including his ex-wife and daughter, who have failed to recognize him, seem to have forgotten the atrocities of the Cultural Revolution and live on merrily as if nothing significant ever happened. By juxtaposing two contrastive points of view, Yu Hua seems to remind his readers that the specter of historical violence is still lingering, behind the veneer of material well-being and burgeoning consumerism of the mid-1980s, ready to emerge at any moment. Unfortunately, Yu's sense of apprehension was vindicated by the tragedy of June 4, 1989.

"One Kind of Reality" is a drastic drama of family feud, enacted in a cycle of revenge. The narrator's indifferent tone of narration and the characters' lack of conscience make this story particularly disturbing. Two brothers, Shangang and Shanfeng, and their families live in the same house. One day Shangang's four-year-old son Pipi discovers the joy of making his baby cousin cry, so he begins to slap and strangle the baby alternatively in order to extract halting yet "luscious" sobbing from it. After a while, Pipi stops torturing the baby and carries it in his arms. However, he gets tired soon, and drops the baby by accident. The baby is killed instantly. Shanfeng's wife is so upset with the accident that she asks Shanfeng to avenge their child's death. Despite Shangang's repeated effort to stop Shanfeng from killing Pipi, Shanfeng still succeeds in murdering him. Shangang retaliates by killing Shanfeng. He is later arrested by the police and indicted for murder. Immediately after Shangang's execution, his body is sent to a hospital for organ transplant, for Shanfeng's wife has disguised herself as Shangang's spouse and donated Shangang's body to the authorities for medical use. The story ends with a detailed description of Shangang's dismemberment. The moral imperative of vengeance upheld by traditional narratives is pushed to an absurd extreme, so much so that the characters caught by this logic are reduced to sheer agency of violence with very little human traits.

In Yu Hua's fictional world, violence takes many forms. In "Classical Love," its presence is felt in the inscrutable fate befalling the female protagonist by the name of Hui. When the story begins, a young scholar named Liu travels to the capital for a qualifying examination and meets by chance the beautiful Hui in her garden. As expected, they fall in love at first sight and spend a night together in her boudoir. However, Liu, unlike the handsome talents in traditional stories, fails ungracefully in the examination and returns crestfallen. On his way home, he pays a visit to Hui. To his dismay, he finds Hui's magnificent house in ruins, and his lover nowhere to be found. No explanation is given about the destruction of Hui's family, nor what has happened to Hui. Three years later, during a famine, Liu sets off again for the capital. Once again he meets Hui by chance, in a countryside tavern, where she is kept in the kitchen, ready to be butchered, with one leg already chopped off. The brutal insertion of cannibalism into a romantic story is indeed profoundly disturbing. Yu Hua's fascination with unpredictable violence is so intense that he can no longer hold it within the confines of the story, and has to violate the conventions of talent-and-beauty fiction in order to drive his point home. To Yu Hua, there is nothing more real in life than violence, whether it is caused by human, historical, or cosmic forces.

To understand the perennial sense of being lost which is characteristic of Ge Fei's fiction, one may begin with "The Lost Boat," which was published in 1987. This story is set against the background of the Chinese civil war of 1928. When the forces of the Northern Expeditionary Army approach Qishan, War-lord Sun Chuanfang deploys his crack divisions to defend the town. One night, Xiao, the commander of the 32 brigade of Sun's forces, accompanied by his bodyguard, slips into a little village on the bank opposite Qishan to gather military information. As a battle is imminent, a military drama of epic scale seems about to unfold. However, this is not what Ge Fei, or his protagonist, has in mind. When Xiao ascends a mountain that afternoon to inspect the situation, he is suddenly seized by an urge to write poetry. Xiao's lyrical impulse sets the tone for the remainder of the story regardless of the epic momentum gathered at the beginning. It is later disclosed in the story that Xiao has an agenda of his own — to attend his father's funeral in the little village, where his parents reside. Xiao's military mission is further compromised when he runs into Xing (meaning "apricot," yet homonymous with "sex"), his beautiful cousin on whom he has a huge crush. Although married, Xing betrays her husband and sees Xiao. Xiao's trysts with Xing arouse his bodyguard's suspicion and infuriates Xing's husband. Xing's husband succeeds in ambushing Xiao, but later decides to spare his life. When Xiao returns to his parents' house, he is executed right away by his bodyguard, who has been suspecting him of treason. Caught in a lyrical mood and driven by his libidinal desires, Xiao is hopelessly lost in the village he is most familiar with. His deviation from the logic of war is eventually punished, for his sexual escapades are completely lost on his young, rigid and unperceptive company.

The main character in "Green Yellow" is a university lecturer, whose intellectual curiosity about a historical term "Green Yellow" leads him into the labyrinth of polysemy and reality. Skeptical of a highly improbable explanation of the term as a reference to a group of prostitutes in Mai Village, the protagonist travels to Mai Village for field investigation. Ironically, the more people he interviews and the more questions he asks, the more problems he has to face and the more confused he gets. As time goes by, the investigation begins to deviate from its original course and bifurcates into endless possibilities. At this moment, the protagonist's memory about an encounter with an old man at Mai Village many years ago rushes back to him. Once again he is absorbed in the old man's strange behavior that has puzzled him for a long time. The two storylines linger on, side by side, keeping the reader in nail-biting suspense. Before the story draws to a close, the protagonist suddenly runs into two more usages of "Green Yellow," which are irrelevant to his investigation — the name of a dog and of a plant respectively. Ge Fei's simultaneous employment and rejection of the hermeneutic code of storytelling is not only a challenge to the conventional mode of thinking, but also a demonstration of his radical epistemological openness. Ge Fei seems to tell his readers that only when the limitation of rational faculty and discursive practice is reckoned with can one arrive at a better understanding of the mystery of reality.

"Whistling" is arguably one of the most arcane works of fiction written by Ge Fei. On the one hand, the reader has to know its literary pretext, namely, its allusion to Chinese history and culture, in order to get a preliminary understanding of the inaction of the main character, Sun Deng. On the other hand, the reader is required to read the text attentively, for Ge Fei indicates the passage of time by means of minuscule and subtle changes in his description of the environment, as they were perceived, however subliminally and unreliably, by the old man Sun Deng himself. As many critics have pointed out, the protagonist bears the same name as the historical figure Sun Deng (c. 220–280), an eminent Daoist hermit of the tumultuous Wei-Jin period. Sun Deng was well-known for his eccentric behavior of maintaining absolute silence whenever he was approached by knowledgeable admirers seeking his advice. If Sun had anything to say, he would bypass language and conveyed his message by prolonged whistling, which was considered a high-minded way of self-expression and communication among the literati of the third century. Yet in Ge Fei's rendition, Sun Deng's transcendental subjectivity is reduced to the insipid existence of an emaciated old man, who has lost not only some of his mental faculties but also his physical ability to whistle. Sun Deng idles the days away, entirely lost in his fading consciousness, which alternates between perception and reverie. Written at a time when the tide of cultural roots-seeking had just ebbed, "Whistling" is not only an experimentalist's serious questioning of the validity of such an attempt, but also a mockery of the powerlessness felt by Chinese intellectuals in the face of reality. Incidentally, "Whistling" was published in Hong Kong in the fateful year of 1989.

Other important avant-garde writers who emerged during the mid-1980s include Sun Ganlu (b. 1959), Zhaxi Dawa (b. 1959), Hong Feng (b. 1959) and Su Tong (b. Tong Zhonggui, 1963). Sun Ganlu's short stories such as "I Am a Young Drunkard," "Visiting a Dreamscape," "Letter of a Courier" and "Riddles for Women" are his most famous. Zhaxi Dawa's "Souls Tied to the Knots on a Leather Cord" and "The Hidden Life in Tibet," Hong Feng's "Funeral" and "The Prairie," and Su Tong's Maple Tree series of short stories are regarded as pioneering works of experimental fiction. Su Tong prospered in the 1990s as one of the most popular writers in China. Yu Hua's style changed dramatically in the 1990s, when he revived the long-cherished tradition of realism to general acclaim in *To Live* (1992) and *Chronicle of a Blood Merchant* (1995). The former novel was adapted for film by Zhang

Yimou in 1994. In 2005 and 2006, *Brothers*, the most ambitious social novel written by Yu Hua so far, was released in two volumes. It sold extremely well, yet its blend of sentimentalism, satire, comedy and social polemic also evoked virulent criticism from professional readers. The most recent works of fiction by Ge Fei are *Human Faces and Peach Blossoms* (2004) and *Dreaming of Mountains and Rivers* (2007), the first two volumes of his utopian trilogy which represents an in-depth reflection upon the history of Chinese revolutions and social events of the twentieth century.

Neo-Realist Fiction

The term "neo-realism" was coined by editors and critics in the late 1980s to designate the resurgence of interest in critical realism in contemporary fiction. The prefix "neo" refers not so much to new aesthetics as a return to the plain yet honest style of representing the life of ordinary people, which was once denied by socialist realism. The year 1987 witnessed the publication of Chi Li's (b. 1957) "Vexing Life" and Fang Fang's (b. 1955) "Landscapes," both lauded by critics for their candid portrayals of workers and lumpen proletarians, which were quite unimaginable in the previous years. Other writers were inspired and followed their footsteps, the most notable among them being Liu Heng (b. Liu Guanjun, 1954) and Liu Zhenyun (b. 1958), who published, respectively, "Fuxi Fuxi" in 1988 and "A Place Covered with Chicken Feathers" in 1991.

Chi Li's "Vexing Life" zooms in on the daily routine of Yin Jiahou, a poverty-stricken factory worker in his mid-thirties, in a single day. The story begins and ends at midnight, recounting the frustrations, minor or critical, he has to face at home, at work and during commuting. Chi Li spilled much ink on his haplessness and sentimentalism, showing sympathy for his financial predicament and impending crisis of being evacuated from his dormitory. Yin resigns himself to his fate, treating his wife, his son and himself rather ambivalently. Even his admirer, a female worker in her twenties, can hardly stir his romantic imagination. In sharp contrast to the harsh daily life in post-socialist China, life during Cultural Revolution in the countryside seems idyllic and idealistic. From time to time Yin seeks solace in his nostalgic reminiscence of bygone days and his first love that he has lost. Although the story ends with Yin's determination to better his life, it remains one of the bleakest neo-realist stories that depict the difficult life of urban proletarians.

If Chi Li's realism is tinged with sentimentalism, Liu Zhenyun's rendition of the unbearable mundane existence of a young couple smacks of cynicism. The title of Liu's story is an idiomatic expression meaning trifles. In Liu's vision, life in China is studded with maddening irritants, such as bickering with the housemaid, applying for job transference, seeking for children's admission to the kindergarten and seeing a doctor at an exorbitant fee. In a world ridden with nepotism and backdoorism, the only way out for the young couple, both honest employees of state enterprises with meager incomes, seems to be earning quick money by moonlighting on the free market as well as resorting to bribery. Liu's language is poignantly witty and sarcastic, probably at its best when he uses Maospeak out of its socialist and idealistic contexts for self-mockery, a stylistic feature which gained in popularity in the literary works of the 1990s.

Fang Fang's "Landscapes" tells the tale of a lumpen proletarian family, covering a span of several decades. Though primarily realist in style, the story sounds unusually eerie because of its unlikely narrator, who is the youngest son of the family, already dead before the beginning of the narration. Now resting in peace, he observes and reports in utter detachment the tribulations of each of his family members. This is indeed an indigent and dysfunctional family, dominated by a violent father, who is a brainless gangster, and an uncaring mother, who cannot help flirting with men in spite of her husband's jealousy and repeated beatings. The behavior of the two sisters in the family is also morally questionable and at times potentially masochistic. While growing up, they seem to have a good time setting up their younger brothers and watching them suffer. Little is mentioned about Fifth Brother and Sixth Brother, except their raping of a young girl. These two brothers grow up to be wealthy hawkers, benefited from the laissez-fair economic policy of the late 1980s. Big Brother, Second Brother, Third Brother and Fourth Brother are portrayed in relatively positive light. Big Brother is a reticent man, who bears the economic burden of the family rather early in his life and is the only person strong enough in the family to put up a good fight with his father. Second Brother is a hopeless romantic who aspires for a better life. He commits suicide for his lover, a girl from a respectable family who does not seem to care about him. Devastated by Second Brother's suicide, Third Brother turns into a misogynist. The speech-impaired Fourth Brother is the only child in the family who has never been brutally treated by his father. He grows up to be a worker, marries a blind girl and lives happily ever after.

The fate of Seventh Brother is a wry bildungsroman of a lumpen proletarian in post-socialist China. Maltreated by most family members throughout his childhood, Seventh Brother volunteers to go to work in the countryside during the Cultural Revolution so as to flee from his family. His decision is mistaken by the cadres as an act of political loyalty, committed to the course of Communist revolution. After spending several peaceful years in the countryside, Seventh Brother is recommended by the officials for admission to Peking University, the most prestigious institution of high learning in China. The only thing that Seventh Brother learns from his college education, or rather, from one of his classmates, is the twisted spirit of "the end justifies the means." He is convinced that a person's aim for greater personal good makes all the evils he has done to others right. After his graduation, he dumps his girl friend and courts a woman who is the daughter of a high-ranking official in order to advance his political career. Towards the end of the story, he seems to be making rapid progress in his career and having a good time enjoying his life. The narrator of the story refrains from passing judgments on Seventh Brother's belief and deeds, only commenting in passing that Seventh Brother is as naïve and superficial as his siblings. Fang Fang's remarks are ambivalently vague. As a realist writer, she is more than ready to show Seventh Brother in his true colors; yet as a citizen of the People's Republic, who was brought up in a culture that claims to promote socialism and favor altruism, she was unsettled by Seventh Brother's unabashed pursuit of self-interest — at least for a while during the 1980s.

Liu Heng's "Fuxi Fuxi" is regarded by some critics as a representative work of "neo-realist" fiction, although its action takes place between 1944 and 1968 within rustic settings. This is a chilling story of adultery and incest, committed by two young members of the Yang family. Yang Jinshan is a wealthy peasant in his late forties. When his wife dies, he remarries a young woman by the name of Wang Judou in order to produce an heir. As time goes by, Jinshan realizes his impotence and vents his frustration at Judou by torturing her, which arouses the sympathy of Tianqing, who is Jinshan's adopted son by his younger brother. The more Jinshan maltreats Judou, the more Tianqing is drawn towards her. Judou and Tianqing eventually commit adultery and Judou becomes pregnant, much to the joy of the unsuspicious Jinshan. The fact is not revealed to Jinshan until he has a massive stroke and loses his speech and mobility. Judou and Tianqing revel in their newfound freedom, unaware of the grim prospect that their son Tianbai will eventually regard Jinshan as his father, much to Jinshan's delight and Tianqing's dismay. After Jinshan dies, Tianbai grows up to be a stubborn adolescent determined to protect the name of his "father" at whatever cost. Under the watchful eye of Tianbai and the villagers, Judou and Tianqing still manage to see each other and try out various means of contraception. When their primitive contraceptive measures fail again, Tianqing becomes so distressed that he kills himself. Judou later gives birth to her second child in secret and returns to her hometown for the rest of her life. The story was hailed by critics for its candid depiction of human emotions and the miseries caused by conservative cultural traditions. The story attracted the attention of Zhang Yimou, who adapted it into a major feature film in 1990 that garnered a number of prestigious international accolades.

Other representative "neo-realist" works of fiction published in the late 1980s and early 1990s include Chi Li's "Don't Speak of Love," "Sun Coming into the World," and "No Matter Whether It's Hot or Cold, Living Is Good," Fang Fang's "Grandfather as Remembered by Father," Liu Heng's "Fucking Food," and Liu Zhenyun's "The Unit," "Officialdom," and "Officials." Liu Xinglong's (b. 1957) "The Tipsy Wind of Autumn" (1992), "Phoenix Zither" (1992) and "Sharing Difficulties" (1996) also belong to this category. The former two stories were adapted for film, released as *Back to Back, Face to Face* and *Country Teacher* respectively in 1994. Yan Lianke's (b. 1958) famous works of fiction such as *Enjoyment* (2003) and *Dream of Ding Village* (2006), Liu Qingbang's (b. 1951) *Songs on the Plain* (2004) and *Red Coal* (2006), Tie Ning's (b. 1957) *Benhua Village* (2006) and Liu Zhenyun's *My Name Is Liu Yuejin* (2007) may also be included in this category.

Hooligan Literature

Wang Shuo (b. 1958) began publishing in 1986 and rose to fame in 1988, a year in which at least four of his stories were made into feature films. Known for his farcical travesty of the state and intellectuals, Wang became perhaps the closest thing that China had in the post-socialist era to a counter-culture icon. His fiction, imbued with irreverence and cynicism, became so popular among readers in North China that some critics consider him the first best-selling writer in post-Mao China, though much to the dismay of stern literary critics. What makes Wang's works of fiction and later his television and cinematic productions so popular is not so much their artistic merits as their propensity to give full vent to dystopian sentiments in a jocular way that strikes a chord with the general public.

Wang's fiction mainly portrays the subculture of a gang of often garrulous urban youths, who have neither formal education nor regular employment — thanks to the Cultural Revolution and economic reforms — yet are able to earn a living by wheeling and dealing in the free market. In short, what Wang Shuo describes in his fiction is the emerging self-employed entrepreneurs who have lost faith in the socialist system, yet still strive to lead a decent life by making money in the burgeoning capitalist market. The term "hooligan" actually refers to this type of characters in Wang's fiction. Wang's representative works of fiction are legion; suffice it to mention the most notable ones: "Master of Mischief" (1987), "An Attitude" (1989), "Please Don't Call Me Human" (1989) and "Wild Beast" (1991). In 1988, "Master of Mischief" was adapted into a feature film entitled *The Troubleshooters* by director Mi Jiashan (b. 1947). In 1994, Jiang Wen (b. 1963), the lead actor in Zhang Yimou's *Red Sorghum*, adapted Wang Shuo's "Wild Beast" into his debut film *In the Heat of the Sun*. It won the Venice International Film Festival's Best Actor prize for its young lead actor Xia Yu (b. 1976) as well as the Golden Horse Film Awards for Best Picture, Best Director and Best Actor. It was the first mainland Chinese film to win the Best Picture in the Golden Horse Film Awards of Taiwan.

Wang Shuo's cynical and sarcastic style was later picked up and refined by Xu Kun (b. 1965), who began to publish in the early 1990s and quickly earned the acclaim of critics. As a scholar specialized in contemporary Chinese literature, Xu's observation of the shortcomings of certain types of Chinese men of letters, artists and the culture industry is particularly keen, and her exuberantly disrespectful treatment of these people and institutions is absolutely hilarious. "Avant-Gardism" (1994) mocks the immaturity and pomposity of *soidisant* artists of the 1980s. "Buddhist Songs" (1994) revels in exposing the vulgar commercialization of all sectors of life, including religion and scholarship, which is further aggravated by the philistinism of the mass media. Although "Tender as the Flowing River" (1997) laments the passage of time, especially the idealistic 1980s, it also creates a devastating caricature of the corruption and mediocrity of the literary circles of this period.

Wang Shuo's "hooligan" style has infected other writers of his generation, such as Han Dong (b. 1961) and Zhu Wen (b. 1967), both are published poets of repute. Han Dong's "A New Travelogue of the Yellow Mountain" (1994) and "Hindrance" (1994), and Zhu Wen's "I Love US Dollars" (1994) are remarkably trenchant works written in the "hooligan" style. Other notable pieces include He Dun's (b. He Bin, 1958) "To Live Is Not Guilty" (1993) and "Yo, Brother" (1993). Wang Xiaobo's (1952–1997) fiction, famous for his witticism, playfulness and social criticism, can be regarded as a variant of Hooligan Literature. Wang's most influential works of fiction, published posthumously in the late 1990s, include *Golden Times*, *Silver Times* and *Bronze Times*, also known as "The Trilogy of Our Times."

Women's Writing

In terms of both quantity and quality, women writers have made considerable contribution to the flourishing of post-socialist literature. Apart from Wang Anyi, Liu Suola, Can Xue, Fang Fang, Chi Li and Xu Kun, there are other equally creative and productive female authors such as Zong Pu (b. Feng Zongpu, 1928), Shen Rong (b. Shen Derong, 1936), Zhang Jie (b. 1937), Dai Houying (1938–1996), Lu Xing'er (b. 1949–2004), Zhang Kangkang (b. Zhang Kangmei, 1950), Bi Shumin (b. 1952), Zhang Xinxin (b. 1953), Jiang Zidan (b. 1954), Zhao Mei (b. 1954), Tie Ning (b. 1957), Xu Xiaobin (b. 1958), Chi Zijian (b. 1964), Xu Lan (b. 1969), and many more. In the 1980s, women writers' works of fiction were rarely singled out as a unique category for critical attention. They were generally considered individually, and evaluated according to their own literary merits.

However, according to Xu Kun, things began to change in the late 1980s, when scholars influenced by Western feminism such as Li Xiaojiang, Meng Yue and Daijinhua published on feminist aesthetics and women writers of the Republican period. The convocation of the Fourth International Women's Congress in Beijing in 1995 marked the beginning of a new age of women's writing. More than four series of women's literature were launched in Beijing, Sichuan, Hebei and Yunnan. In 1995 alone, nine scholarly monographs relating to women's literature, one introductory book on Western feminism and an anthology of Western feminist literary theories were published. Conferences on individual women writers such as Wang Anyi, Zhang Kangkang, Zhao Mei, Xu Xiaobin, Lin Bai (b. Lin Baiwei, 1958) and Chen Ran (b. 1962) were organized in different cities. The relatively loose concept of "women's literature" referring to the literary works produced by female writers was now replaced by a more rigorous and complex notion of women's writing, which addresses the interrelated issues of writing, subjectivity and femininity. Two of the young and talented women writers were spotlighted in this collective effort to articulate this novel notion of *écriture feminine* — Lin Bai and Chen Ran.

Lin Bai's roundabout style in invoking femininity is best exemplified by her short story "A Chair on the Sinuous Corridor" (1993). A young female narrator stumbles upon an old and magnificent mansion during a trip to the Southwest region of China. An old lady who lives there confides to her the past of the mansion and the fate of its owner. It is a story about the Communists' suppression of her master's armed revolt in the early days of the People's Republic. However, the gist of the short story lies elsewhere. Against this gruesome background of men's mutual slaughtering, there is an elegantly serene and suggestive sororial relationship between the master's second concubine and her maid, who turns out to be the old lady now keeping the house. Lin Bai's ability to create the young concubine's enigmatic aura and melancholic exquisiteness is simply peerless. Although the concubine is a modern woman who has received good education, she has for some unknown reasons remained reticent throughout her life and stayed away from men's world. Even her husband, the master of the house, does not have a clue about what she is thinking. The mysterious fragrance that exudes from her siesta seems to suggest her rejection of the squalor and bloodshed of men's history, as symbolized by the boisterous scene of men butchering a pig in the court-yard. After the execution of her husband, the concubine disappears and no one has since seen her again. The concubine seems to have escaped from his-tory, leaving behind only the maid, her loyal confidante, as if she were her shadow in time. If the concubine is a figure of Lin Bai's ideal woman, her notion of femininity is characterized by elusiveness, inexplicability, serenity and ethereality, all vividly captured in her mellow prose.

Chen Ran's depiction of female sensibility is direct and descriptive, as evidenced by "Nowhere to Hide" (1991). The lonely, lethargic and some-what dour heroine of the story is a lecturer in Philosophy by the name of Dai Er, who is reminiscent of the frail and forlorn figure of Lin Daiyu, the major female character of *Dream of the Red Chamber*. Dai Er constantly finds her-self alienated from normal life, either in China or in the United States. She has a hard time coping with the fact that all her best friends are married. She does not get along well with her caring ex-boyfriend, who has married one of her best friends, and she finds herself reduced to a somatic existence by her sexually active American boyfriend. Moreover, her mother's attentive-ness to her daily needs suffocates her. It is apparent that Dai Er is not particularly interested in heterosexual relationship, neither is she comfort-able with homosexual intimacy. Worst of all, philosophy has never come to her rescue. Even the thought of committing suicide cannot ease her existen-tial angst. In short, Chen Ran's portrayal of women's life tends to be realistic and agoraphobic, while Lin Bai eschews realistic conventions in order to find a possible route of escape for her favorite female characters. Against the urban and global background in Chen Ran's story, Dai Er seems to be too typical a traditional figure to overcome the constraints of modern society. In contrast, the rural and exotic setting in Lin Bai's fiction is less confined as it appears to be, and offers a mysterious way out to the heroine who rejects history.

Other major works of women's writing of the 1990s include the follow-ing: Wang Anyi's *Realism and Fabrication* (1993) and *The Song of Everlasting Sorrow* (1995), Lin Bai's *A Person's Warfare* (1994), *Guarding Hollow Times* (1996) and *Speak Up, My Room* (1997), Jiang Zidan's *Left Hand* (1996), Chen Ran's *Dangerous Destinations* and *Forbidden Return* (1996), Xu Xiaobin's "Secrete Garden," "Pisces" (1995), "Ruo Mu" (1997) and *Feathered Snake* (1998).

Poetry

Obscure Poetry

In the snowy winter of 1978, a group of young men gathered in a small apartment in Beijing. They worked around the clock, all excited by the idea of seeing their underground journal of poetry published. When the inaugural issue finally came out, it was time to post it on the Democratic Wall. However, they balked. No one was sure whether it was safe for them to express their poetic aspirations in public. Three volunteered to take the risk and post the samizdat. Before leaving the apartment, these young men cried, unsure of the fate awaiting them. The samizdat was eventually posted, and fortunately no one was arrested. This is the birth of the renowned literary journal *Today*, forecasting the flow of a new tide of Obscure Poetry. Although the term "obscure" was first used by unsympathetic critics to disparage the individualist styles of new poets, it later gained popularity among readers and critics and took on a positive meaning.

Bei Dao (b. Zhao Zhenkai, 1949), one of the volunteers, proved himself not only a person of valor but a poet with a distinctive voice. His debut poem, "The Answer," which first appeared in the inaugural issue of *Today* and then republished in the official journal *Poetry* in 1979, is now regarded as one of his representative works and a classic of contemporary Chinese poetry. What distinguishes Bei Dao from his peers is his poetic persona, which is represented as morally upright and tragically heroic. In "The Answer," one can see the figure of a lone martyr who stands up fearlessly against social injustice and political oppression: "Listen. *I don't believe!*/OK. You've trampled/a thousand enemies underfoot. Call me/a thousand and one." The martyr knows well what lies ahead for him, yet he is willing to accept it, for this is the only option left for him to prove his moral integrity in a world of corruption: "The scoundrel carries his baseness around like an ID card./The honest man bears his honor like an epitaph" (Barnstone, 45). As this poem was conceived in April 1976, it would not be too far-fetched to speculate that it was written in the spirit of commemorating the Tiananmen Square demonstration of April 5, 1976, the first open exhibit of popular consciousness in defiance of the oppressive state since the founding of the People's Republic.

"Declaration" is another memorable verse written by Bei Dao. It was dedicated to Yu Luoke (1942–1970), a writer who was executed by the Chinese authorities in 1970 for his open questioning of the orthodox view that class consciousness is inheritable. Yu's last thoughts before the execution represent a generation's solemn determination to pursue justice and liberty: "The still horizon/Divides the ranks of the living and the dead/I can only choose the sky/I will not kneel on the ground/Allowing the executioners to look tall/The better to obstruct the wind of freedom." Bei Dao declares that martyrs will never die in vain; their sacrifices will bring about changes: "From star-like bullet holes shall flow/A blood-red dawn" (Barnstone, 44–45). Another good example of Bei Dao's eulogy to self-sacrifice in the face of political persecution can be found in "Rainy Night": "If even by tomorrow morning/The gun muzzle and bloody clouds of dawn/Force me to give up freedom, youth, and pen/I will never give up this evening/I will never give you up/Let walls barricade my mouth/Let iron bars partition my sky/A tide of blood will go on as long as my heart beats/Your smile will be engraved on the scarlet moon/As it rises each night at my small window/To awaken all my memories" (Morin, 80).

When Bei Dao turns his gaze away from heroic figures and focuses on the stage where the drama of history unfolds, the image of a spiritual wasteland begins to take shape. In "Red Sailing Boat," the perplexed poet inquires: "Crumbling walls and dilapidated houses are everywhere/How can a road stretch under my feet?" "An Old Temple" gives a detailed depiction of a derelict temple, which is arguably an allusion to the cultural barrenness of China, seen from the perspective of the survivors of the Cultural Revolution. The temple, abandoned by monks, worshipers and legendary creatures, perishes in absolute silence. Nothing about its glorious past is traceable, unless the stone tortoises that bear the tombstones were resurrected to impart the secrets. The overwhelming sense of devastation invoked by this poem suggests that Bei Dao also mourns the downfall of the Chinese civilization.

Together with Bei Dao, another poet in the ascendant is Gu Cheng (1956–1993). His poetic vision of Chinese landscape after the Cultural Revolution is even bleaker, as manifested in his controversial "Ending," a poem overshadowed by decay and death:

> Then the avalanche
> Stopped.
> The riverside is piled high with giant's head.
>
> Junks draped in mourning
> slowly pass,
> their saffron shrouds unfurled.
>
> Green tress gracefully
> twisted in pain
> weep over the heroes.

The splintered moon
is God-hid in fog.
All is finished (Crippen, 22).

Hailed by many critics as a "fairy-tale poet," Gu Cheng has the unique gift of transforming platitude into poetry and turning despair into hope in his writings, as demonstrated by his impressionistic masterpiece, "Feeling." Hope is suggested through a subtle juxtaposition of people and the backdrop and a sharp contrast between vivid and dull colors: "The sky is gray/the road is gray/the buildings are gray/the rain is gray"; "through an expanse of dead gray/two children pass/one bright red/one pale green" (Crippen, 50). Writing at a time when the nation had just woken up from the nightmare of the ultraleft reign and in need of a new direction, Gu Cheng pulled off his poetic feat of converting despair into hope in "A Generation." This short poem struck a chord with millions of readers and became one of the most-quoted poems of the 1980s. Critics lauded it as a gem of contemporary Chinese poetry, for it expresses the stoic optimism of a nation: "the black night gave me black eyes/still I use them to seek the light" (Crippen, 22).

Unlike Bei Dao and Gu Cheng, Shu Ting (b. 1952) attracted the attention of the reading public by her romantic theme and lyrical style. Two of her most widely-read poems, "To the Oak Tree" and "Two-Masted Ship," deal with the subject of two independent individuals involving in an intimate yet subtly detached relationship. As a woman poet of the "New Era," Shu Ting stresses the importance of women's independence and their role as an equal partner in a romantic relationship. In "To the Oak Tree," Shu Ting's poetic persona speaks in the first person, describing herself as "a kapok tree" that stands by her lover, "the oak tree." If her lover has "bronze boughs and iron trunk/Like knives and swords," she declares herself a fighter of equal status, albeit a little melancholic in temperament: "I have my red flowers/Like heavy sighs,/Also like heroic torches." As lovers, she stands by her lover's side in solidarity, yet comfortably apart to maintain her individuality: "We share cold waves, storms and thunderbolts;/Together we savor fog, haze and rainbows./We seem to always live apart,/But actually depend upon each other forever" (Morin, 102).

In "Two-Masted Ship," the poet's persona compares herself to a sailing ship, forever caught in the romance of seeing the shore and parting with it. In sharp contrast to the traditional image of a woman waiting and pining for her lover's return from a voyage, Shu Ting's heroine sets off on an odyssey of her own, yet maintaining a delicate relationship with her lover: "Remember the storm, the lighthouse/That brought us together/Another storm, a different light/Drove us asunder again/Even though morning or evening/Sky and ocean stand between us/You are always on my voyage/I am always in your sight" (Morin, 101).

The poetry of Jiang He (b. Yu Youze, 1949) and Yang Lian (b. 1955) is characterized by their engagement with cultural archetypes. Jiang He draws inspiration from ancient Chinese myths and devotes some of his early shorter poems to mythical figures, while Yang Lian resorts to Chinese classics such as *Book of Changes* for poetic images and philosophical enlightenment. However, Jiang He's most memorable cycle poems have nothing to do with ancient Chinese civilization, but with modern barbarity. Take "An Unfinished Poem" for example. It was written in memory of Zhang Zhixin (1930–1975), a Communist martyr who was executed during the Cultural Revolution for her open criticism of the Cult of Mao. The most chilling part of Zhang's fate is neither her incarceration between 1969 and 1975 nor the execution itself, but the authorities' atrocious act of cutting her vocal chords before the execution. The precise images of the first poem, "An Ancient Tale," suggests the Chinese Prometheus' acute pangs of pain caused by torture, yet at the same time celebrates her fortitude: "I am nailed to the prison wall/Gathering black time — flocks of crows/From every corner of the world, every night in history/Peck at heroes one after another on this wall." Towards the end of this poem, the heroine's excruciating agony and death are transformed into a furious call to arms, echoed by her soul-mates: "Once again I am here/To resist and forestall slavery/To shake the mud off the wall with my fierce death//To make those who die in silence get up and shout."

In the fourth poem, "On the Way to Execution," Zhang's execution is described as a personal choice, motivated by self-fulfillment and altruism, rather than a punishment inflicted by the state. "A slaughter was going on/I could not hide in the house/My blood would not let me/The children of the morning would not let me"; "I walked to the execution ground, glancing contemptuously/At this night in history, this corner of the world/There is no other choice — I have chosen the sky/The sky will not rot/I must be executed, or darkness would have no place to hide/I must be born in darkness to create light/I must be executed, or lies would be smashed/I object to everything that light does not tolerate — including silence." Only through self-sacrifice can justice and truth prevail: "I am nailed to the wall/My lapel sways/Like a rising banner" (Yeh, 175–78).

Yang Lian is famed for his ambitious attempts at composing complex cycle poems that reach out for the sublime, as amply demonstrated in *Banbo*, *Dunhuang* and *Nuorilang*. One can get a sense of Yang's idea of the aesthetic sublime by the following two stanzas from "Solar Tide," in which the magnificent yet desolate highland in southwest China is portrayed with dazzling images: "The high plateau like a violent tiger is burning brightly on the shore of the angry tide./O, light is everything, a round setting sun floods toward you and the earth hangs in the air." "Now what lost white scarf of cloud will you grieve for,/enduring the ondriven dusk, here under time's heel./On the desert horizon thousands of tombstones are anchored like castaway plows./Forsaking each other, they are forsaken forever: let copper return to the earth and let blood turn to rust./Will you still weep with every storm?" (Barnstone, 55).

In Yang Lian's extended meditation on nature, culture and history, there are hesitant moments, as expressed in the interior monologue of an apsara in "A Flying Apsara." An apsara is a fairy who entertains the Buddha with music while sprinkling flowers from her sleeves. Wall paintings of apsaras gliding in the sky are found in the stone caves of Dunhuang in northwestern China. The image of an apsara suspended in the air very well captures the sense of uncertainty felt by the poet, or perhaps by a generation of Chinese, in the post-socialist age of sea change: "My body trapped in a certain moment, a certain spot/Am I flying, or am I motionless?/Am I transcending life or struggling on the brink of death,/Rising or falling (in the same elegant posture),/Heading toward millennia to come or millennia past?" The poem ends with an ambivalent note of hope and despair: "I long to fly in no direction, therefore all directions;/I long to fly around yet retreat to the heartless stillness./Drifting/In the millennia to come, the millennia past,/I fly like a bird, beyond vision and hearing./I fall like a fish, with an open mouth yet without a sound" (Yeh, 218–219).

Gu Cheng left China in 1988, Bei Dao and Yang Lian in 1989. Among the Obscure poets, Bei Dao and Yang Lian are the most prolific, who continued publishing their poetry overseas, and their poetry has been widely translated. Bei Dao's achievements in poetry have been internationally recognized, and he has been repeatedly nominated for the Nobel Prize for literature.

Post-Obscure Poetry

In the heyday of Obscure Poetry, there were already dissenting voices from many emerging poets of various literary persuasions. These up-and-coming poets, whom Chinese literary historians have variously termed as "Newborn Generation," "Third-Generation" or "Post-Obscure" poets, did not share their predecessors' poetic tenets and sensibility. To be precise, they found their heroic sentiments, obsession with China, predilection for imagism and pursuit of the sublime repugnant. The poems written by post-Obscure poets, such as those by Han Dong (b. 1961) and Yu Jian (b. 1954), were characterized by their deliberate insouciance, anti-idealistic deflations and unobtrusive colloquialism.

In contradistinction to Yang Lian's celebration of the Dayan Pagoda (1980) as a symbol of Chinese culture and history in his poetry, Han Dong's depiction of the Dayan Pagoda in "About Da Yan Pagoda" (1983) carefully refrains from emotional gestures and opinion-mongering. Han's poem is so fundamentally pedestrian yet profoundly shocking that it has become a classic in its own right. Here is the first stanza: "About Da Yan Pagoda/What more to know?/The people come far/To climb it, to be/Heroes for once, or even a second time/Some of them, or perhaps more./The unhappy ones, and also ones/Ample in the flesh of their leisure./These, whole gangs of them, climb together,/Becoming heroes for once,/And then climb down,/Disappearing instantly almost/Into the streets and crowds below./There are also those, a very few,/The seed people who, leaping from the stairs,/Burst into scarlet flowers./These are the true heroes, yes,/Heroes for our time." And the second stanza brings the poem to an abrupt end with an anti-climax: "Of Da Yan Pagoda/What more to know?/We climb into the view,/Then hurry down" (Zhang and Chen, 69).

Another representative short poem called "You've Seen the Sea" (1984) by Han Dong also seems prosaic, yet its artfully modulated repetition of simple phrases creates a rhythm unavailable to conventional poeticisms: "so you've seen the sea/you've imagined/the sea/you've first imagined the sea/and then seen it/that's just how it is/so you have actually seen the sea/and imagined it too/but you're not a sailor/that's just how it is/so you've imagined the sea/you've seen the sea/maybe you even like the sea/that's how it is — at the most/so you've seen the sea/and you've imagined the sea/you're not willing/to drown in the water of the sea/that's just how it is/that's how everyone is" (Van Crevel, 1996: 84).

In comparison with Han Dong, Yu Jian's poetry is less belligerent in tone. His subject is mainly the appeal of banal events of everyday life. His narration is reader-friendly, often displaying a dilly-dally attitude. "No. 6, Shangyi Street" (1986) stamped its author as one above the ordinary, and it is lauded as a landmark in contemporary Chinese poetry. Since this poem is too long for this small survey, suffice it to mention instead another short poem of his, "Opus 39" (1983), which is similar in mood and tone, for a glimpse of his carefree poetics. In the first stanza, the poet is lost in thought, missing his pal who lives in a faraway province: "During the years crowds jammed the streets/You lit off by yourself for Xinjiang/Maybe it's not so bad out there in the boonies/You really looked outlandish in a crowd/Try on those jeans and see/How well they've lasted/Only three and a half years wear and still like new/Remember the time/You and I got into that heaving rapping/That made everybody around clam up/You never went in for banging my ears/How well you know in your heart/That we struggle all our lives/Just to put on a front of being human/Always at a loss what to do/When we're around good looking women/We're too dumb to even know how dumb we are/One of those women looked me up once/Said what a shame with your swell voice/You could have made it as a baritone/Sometimes I think of you borrowing my money/I would stand at my gate/Trying to spot you among the scruffy men/I know you're going to come back here some day/Three short novels and a bottle of booze in your arm." The poem ends with the poet's reverie of having his friend's company in the second stanza: "Sitting in that rattan chair from Sichuan/Speaking for a couple of hours/As if the whole world were your audience/Now and again you'll glimpse yourself in the mirror/Heart brimming with sudden rushes of joy/Afterward you'll watch me a while in dead silence/Then go home with the empty bottle under your arm" (Morin, 123–24).

In 1994, Yu Jian published "File No. 0," his most unconventional work of poetry so far. It is a conglomeration of narrative, resume, inventory, confession, poetry and medical report, in which the identity of an ordinary citizen of the People' Republic is defined. This exceptional poem of protest against modern surveillance of individuals marks another milestone for Chinese experimental poetry. In the same year, it was staged in a theatre, directed by Mu Sen (b. 1963), as an avant-garde play.

There are so many schools and societies of poetry that mushroomed since the mid-1980s that it is impossible to list all of them here. The most influential group of poets gathered around the literary journal *They* (1985–1995), founded by Han Dong. These poets, who made a considerable impact on the development of contemporary Chinese poetry, include Yu Jian, Chen Dongdong (b. 1961), Lü De'an (b. 1960), Wang Yin (b. 1962), Lu Yimin (b. 1962), Ding Dang (b. 1962), Zhu Wen (b. 1967), Li Feng (b. 1968) and Lu Yang (b. 1963), to name the notable few. A rival faction of poetry was led by Zhou Lunyou (b. 1952), Lan Ma (b. 1956) and Yang Li (b. 1962). They published a literary journal by the title of *Feifei*, which can be roughly translated into English as "non non," implying the journal founders' "non-sublime" and "non-rational" approaches to poetic writing. Distinguished poets of this faction are He Xiaozu (b. 1963), Li Yawei (b. 1963), Jimulangge (b. 1963), Nan Ye (b. Wu Yi, 1955) and Liang Xiaoming. Women's poetry voicing feminist aspirations also thrived during the 1980s, pioneered by

Zhai Yongming's (b. 1955) cycle poem *Woman* (1984), followed by Lu Yimin's (b. 1962) "An American Women's Magazine," Yi Lei's (b. Sun Guizheng, 1951) cycle poem *The Bedroom of a Celibate Woman*, and Chen Yu's *Dreams Basking in the Sun* (2003).

In the late 1980s, a group of poets became gravely concerned with the popular trend of making extensive use of everyday and colloquial language in portraying mundane subjects in poetry. They called for an "intellectual writing" which upholds independent thinking, critical skepticism and moral motivation as the backbone of creative poetry, the mission of which is nothing other than confronting major issues of the times they live in. Poets who are sympathetic to or follow this basic tenet of poetry are legion, including Xi Chuan (b. Liu Jun, 1963), Ouyang Jianghe (b. 1956), Wang Jiaxin (b. 1957), Zang Di (b. 1964), Sun Wenbo (b. 1959), Zhang Shuguang (b. 1956), Chen Dongdong, Xiao Kaiyu (b. 1960), Zhai Yongming, Wang Yin, Meng Lang (b. 1961), Bai Hua (b. 1956), Lü De'an, Zhang Zao (1962–2010) and Sang Ke (b. Li Shuquan, 1967). In 1997, Xi Chuan published *Roughly Speaking*. It includes an experimental series of stylistically complex poems under the title "Misfortune," which is now regarded as a major breakthrough of the 1990s poetry.

The popular trend of poetry continued to flourish in the 1990s, culminating in Lower Body Poetry in 2000, which was promulgated and led by Shen Haobo (b. 1976), followed by Yin Lichuan (b. 1973), Sheng Xing (b. 1978), Ma Fei, Li Hongqi, Duo Yu (b. Gao Zhaoliang, 1973), Zhu Jian, Nan Ren, Song Lieyi and many more. Lower Body Poetry is basically anti-intellectual in orientation. It defies the upper body, which signifies culture and reason, and celebrates the *joie de vivre* offered by the lower body stratum in all its splendor and excess. Due to their resistance to highbrow culture and fixation on the flesh, some critics find their poetry one-dimensional and shallow, lacking in both linguistic and philosophical sophistication. Nevertheless, a closer look at their poetry reveals not only their penchant for hedonism but also their recalcitrance and cynicism typical of Hooligan Literature. If the martyr in Jiang He's poem is nailed to the prison wall and howls in protest, the hedonist in Yin Lichuan's poem, which is entitled "Why Not Make It Feel Even Better" (2000), screams out loudly and impishly, imploring for more and harder hammering: "ah a little higher a little lower a little to the left a little to the right/this is not making love this is hammering nails/oh a little faster a little slower a little looser a little tighter/this is not making love this is anti-porn campaigning or tying your shoes/ooh a little more a little less a little lighter a little heavier/this is not making love this is massage writing a poem washing your hair or your feet."

Even in the heat of the moment, the hedonist has not forgotten to mock current aesthetic tenets of poetry: "why not make it feel even better huh make it feel even better/a little gentler a little ruder a little more intellectual a little more popular." Yin Lichuan ends this poem with a very short stanza, pronouncing the ultimate purpose of Lower Body Poetry: "why not make it feel even better" (Van Crevel, 2008: 179).

Publication of poetry dwindled significantly in the first decade of the twenty-first century, due to the rapid commercialization of the publishing industry and marginalization of poetry in Chinese society. Poets turned to the internet and non-official journals for publication and circulation of their poems. Even though the eventful 2005 was regarded by some critics as the year of "Poetry Fever," clear-headed critics and poets such as Xu Jingya (b. 1949) and Tang Danhong (b. 1965) thought otherwise. In their opinion, poetry had lost almost all relevance to contemporary life; poets lingered on merely as a prop or a setting in the greatest show of commercialization ever since the founding of the People's Republic.

Drama

Social Problem Plays

Modern Chinese spoken drama revived soon after the downfall of the "Gang of Four." It is not surprising that the plays written and performed during the late 1970s were marked by their preoccupation with the socio-political events of the Cultural Revolution, focusing on idealistic young men and women's resistance to ultraleftism and Communist veterans' grievances against unfounded political persecutions. Their thematic resemblance to the representative works of Scar Literature is obvious. Though spurred by the realist intent to reveal the seamy side of life under the reign of the "Gang of Four," the playwrights, being unsure of the political climate, hesitated about staging their plays. For instance, the mixed feeling of excitement and fear gave Wang Jingyu (b. 1936) and Jin Zhenjia (b. 1927) palpitations after they finished their script of *When Maple Leaves Turn Red* in 1977. They discussed it at length with their colleagues at the Theater of Chinese Young Artists, but neither they themselves nor their first readers knew for sure whether their play was politically permissible, until it was approved by the Ministry of Culture. The play was an immediate success, ushering in the new trend of what drama critics describe as "social problem plays," in which the evils of the "Gang and Four" and the damages caused by the Cultural Revolution were portrayed according to the new leadership's political and literary directives.

However, it was the staging of Zong Fuxian's (b. 1947) *In the Land of Silence* in 1978 that shook the Chinese theater. The action of the play takes place in Shanghai, right after the Tiananmen Square demonstration of April 5, 1976 when Beijing residents gathered to commemorate the death of Premier Zhou Enlai, who was regarded by many as an upright political leader who stood up to the "Gang of Four." When the story begins, a young man by the name of Ouyang Ping, after disappearing for almost a decade during the Cultural Revolution, returns to Shanghai, accompanied by his ailing mother, to pay his girlfriend He Yun and her family a visit. At the same time, He Yun's father, a junior ranking official at the Foreign Trade Bureau, is arranging a date for He Yun with Tang Youcai, who is a rising political star of the "Gang of Four" faction, for the purpose of advancing his own career. Tormented by Ouyang's long absence, He Yun, now a police officer by profession, is only too happy to see him back, unaware that he is the most wanted fugitive in China, being accused of distributing the elegiac verses recited by young poets in memory of Zhou Enlai in the April Fifth demonstration. As the story unfolds, He Yun is stunned to learn that her father is not only a follower of the "Gang of Four," ready to turn in her lover, but also an accomplice involved in the political frame-up of Ouyang's mother, a Communist veteran, about nine years ago, despite the fact that she has once risked her life to save him. Towards the end of the play, when the He residence is finally surrounded by Tang's militia and Ouyang's arrest is imminent, He Yun, her guilt-ridden mother and cynical brother turn against the father and vow to follow Ouyang's example in fighting against the "Gang of Four" and their followers until they are overcome by the people.

Although the play primarily follows the realist form and convention, its depiction of the major characters betrays its consanguinity with socialist realism. The contrast between stereotypical heroes and villains could not be more rigid and obvious. While Ouyang Ping and his mother embody the positive qualities desirable in an ideal Communist, such as moral integrity, unwavering loyalty, remarkable resilience and perpetual optimism in the face of hardship, He Yun's father and Tang Youcai are cast in a negative light. As a Communist cadre, He Yun's father lacks political sagacity; as an ordinary man, he has committed the unforgivable sin of betraying his benefactor twice. In comparison, Tang's sins seem venial, for he is simply an unintelligent fanatic who takes great pleasure in defending the proletarian dictatorship as instructed.

Other social problem plays that are closely related to Chinese reality at that time include Cui Dezhi's (b. 1927) *Flowers Announcing the Arrival of*

Spring, which challenges the ultraleftist notion of class determinism, Zhao Guoqing's *Save Her*, a play about the new life of a young delinquent, Zong Fuxian (b. 1947) and He Guofu's *Blood Is always Warm*, a play about industrial reform, and Sha Yexin's (b. 1937) *If I Were Real*, a famous play about the misdeeds of an imposter. Although these plays were rated highly by the audience, critics found them wanting, in terms of dramaturgy or social vision. The Chinese audience had to wait until the mid-1980s to witness the return of mature realist plays.

Realist Plays

Realist drama had played an important role in modern spoken drama since its introduction to China in the early twentieth century. But after being discredited for about three decades, the attraction and influence of realist plays seemed to have faded, and high-quality realist plays were rather hard to come by in the post-socialist years.

Yang Limin's (b. 1947) *Black Stones* was first staged in 1987. It is a story about a team of drillers in the petroleum industry stationed in a prairie in northeastern China. Unlike the well-known socialist realist film *Starting Our Own Petroleum Industry* of 1974, Yang has no interest in extolling workers' heroism or patriotism. Rather, he focuses on the prosaic and perhaps dreary aspects of their lives. It is a drama not so much about conflict and resolution as about characterization and humanity. The play was met with acclaim, and highly praised by practitioners of drama including Cao Yu (1910–1996), the doyen of modern Chinese spoken drama.

Number One Restaurant in the World, written by He Jiping (b. 1951), made a resounding success when it was staged in Beijing in 1988. It is sated with so much distinctive old Peking flavor, which is especially evident in its lively representation of speech, mannerism and culinary culture, that critics recognized it right away as a rare and direct descendent of Lao She's (1899–1966) literary style, as represented by his masterpiece *Tea House* (1956–1957). Although He's story is set in the Republican era, its urgent message about business reform and effective management is meant for the up-and-coming entrepreneurs of the post-socialist era. When the curtain goes up, Fu Ju De, the renowned restaurant serving the best roast duck in Peking, is on the verge of bankruptcy. While the proprietor Tang Deyuan is too old and ill to take good care of business, his two sons squander their time and money by dabbling in opera and martial arts. A professional executive by the name of Lu Mengshi is thus hired by Tang Deyuan, in the hope of resuscitating business. The main action of the play focuses on Lu's charismatic leadership and management skills, actualized in various entertaining scenes of dramatic conflict. Under Lu's direction, Ju Fu De not only survives the crisis, but also thrives. However, Lu's tremendous success in running the restaurant arouses jealousy and anxiety among Tang's sons. After Tang dies, they decide to fire Lu and run the business on their own. Although the fate of the restaurant seems to remain uncertain when the curtain falls, what Lu has in mind is in fact a premonition of its eventual downfall, predictably brought about by the Tang brothers' inept management. Lu's warning to the Tang brothers is both tactful and sinister. When they take over the restaurant, Lu sends them an antithetical couplet, which is inscribed by Chinese calligraphy on two vertical wooden planks, as a gift. What is left unsaid, as is sometimes indicated by the horizontal streamer that accompanies the couplet, is correctly guessed by a gourmet — "All good things must come to an end" (literally "there is no banquet which does not end"). Undoubtedly, Lu's warning was meant for the first generation of private businessmen in the People's Republic, who were learning and learning fast the art of management in a rapidly modernizing society.

In contrast to He Jiping's successful portrayal of businessmen, Guo Shixing (b. 1952) made a name for himself with his "Idler Trilogy" in the mid-1990s. The trilogy consists of *Birdmen* (1993), *Chess Players* (1995) and *Angler* (1997). Of these three plays, *Chess Players* has attracted considerable critical attention. He Yunqing, the protagonist, is a master of *go*. At 60, he realizes that he has idled away the past 50 years on the chessboard, and regrets that life and love have passed him by. His decision to quit playing chess altogether shocks his friends, who respect his talent and enjoy playing chess with him. However, one of his chess mates, who is a doctor, asks him to do a favor for a young patient of his by playing chess with him. According to the doctor's explanation, his patient, whose name is Si Yan, requires a special therapy. As Si Yan is too intelligent to remain mentally idle, the only way to keep him from breaking down is to engage him constantly in the chess game. Unfortunately, Si Yan has never met a real opponent, for his mother prohibits him from playing chess. It turns out that his mother is none other than He Yunqing's ex-lover, who cannot bear his preoccupation with chess.

He Yunqing agrees to meet the young man. Deeply impressed by his knowledge of *go*, He decides to play against him. One night He is drunk and finds himself facing the ghost of Si Yan's father, who implores him to discourage his son from playing chess, for the odd reason that Si Yan's mother needs his full attention. When He becomes completely sober the next morning, Si Yan's mother shows up and makes the same plea, while pouring out her old and new grievances against him. Although He is sympathetic with

Si Yan, he accedes to his parents' rather selfish request. He promises Si Yan's mother that he will make a deal with Si Yan. If Si Yan loses the match, he will have to quit chess altogether. Si Yan accepts the challenge, plays the game, and is defeated. Soon after the match Si Yan dies. However, before departing for the netherworld, his ghost pays He Yunqing a visit, asking him to go over the game with him. This time Si Yan makes a different move at a critical juncture and wins the game. The outcome surprises He Yunqing and pleases Si Yan. As a victor, Si Yan's soul leaves in peace.

Although the plot of *Chess Players* may seem gripping, a closer reading of the play reveals some of its inadequacies. The characters are flat, and their relationships are conceived in a rather simplistic way. Most detrimental to the play is perhaps its major characters' sententious reflections on the art of chess and the significance of a player's lifelong devotion to it. Given the top-class performance of Ah Cheng in "The Chess Master," one has every reason to expect He Jiping to challenge his precursor, if not to surpass him, in terms of narrative sophistication and philosophical outlook. Apparently *Chess Players* has underachieved in both areas.

Shen Hongguang's (b. 1948) *In the Same Boat* (1995) is a modest attempt at tackling the intricate issue of human bonding. It zooms in on the daily life of two families sharing an apartment. A young couple, Liu Qiang and his wife Mi Ling, live in one room, while Miss Fang, a retired, introvert and single teacher in her early sixties, lives in another. The two families are not on good terms. The plot develops along two storylines: first, the young couple's prank of placing a dating advertisement on behalf of Fang, which leads to the visit of Captain Gao, who immediately falls for Fang, which deeply disconcerts her; second, Mi Ling's desire to earn a better living prompts her to work for her ex-boyfriend's company, thus giving rise to intense bickering at home. When Liu and Mi's marriage runs into trouble, a local television finds the dating advertisement of Fang fascinating and decided to do a short documentary on her romance. And starting from here, things begin to get out of hand.

Apart from her dexterity in storytelling, Shen Hongguan excels in bringing her characters to life by engaging them in humorous, sarcastic or bitter dialogues. There are moments when these characters express their personalities vividly through their speeches — surely a feat indispensable for a playwright of spoken drama. The most touching — and chilling — moment of revelation about human relationship comes when Gao talks about his divorce in his younger days, as a parable for the young couple, soon after he finds out that he has been set up by them and rejected by Fang. According to Gao, when he realized that his wife had cheated on him, he tracked down her lover, offered to help him find a wife and paid for his wedding expenses. Making sure that this man had properly married, Gao returned home and divorced his wife. As time went by, Gao began to realize, with deep regret, that his revenge on her was actually driven by his strong attachment to her. However, what had been done could not be undone; his ex-wife refused to see him for the rest of her life. Gao's personal story touches the young couple, but not Fang. A few weeks later, the young couple manages out of good will to arrange another rendezvous for Gao and Fang. But it is already too late, for Gao has passed away on his voyage home. Even if Fang changes her mind now, she has forever missed the opportunity to travel with him "in the same boat."

In comparison, Yang Limin (b. 1947) set himself a much grander task in *Geologists* (1997), which was widely anthologized as one of the representative realist plays of the 1990s. The play traces the fortunes of a group of university graduates, who are specialized in geology, from 1961 to 1994, focusing on Luo Dasheng, Luo Ming and Lu Jing. Upon graduation in 1961, Lu Jing is assigned a teaching position on campus, since she is the first girl in class. Luo Dasheng and Luo Ming are sent to the wilderness in northeastern China, together with other classmates, to prospect for oil. Luo Dasheng and Luo Ming are good friends, and they both have a crush on Lu Jing, who treats them as comrades, while being vaguely attracted to Luo Ming. Despite Luo Ming's outstanding expertise, he is deprived of the right to publish his research papers because of his overseas' connections. An optimist, Luo Ming publishes his research under Luo Dasheng's name. As a result, Luo Dasheng gets promoted quickly and is soon transferred back to Beijing. For some reasons Luo Ming is demoted and assigned menial tasks. From here onward the reader or audience begins to feel a strong sense of déjà-vu, for the author's portrayal of Luo Ming begins to takes on the traits of model workers, patriotic peasants or PLA soldiers typical of the literature of the Cultural Revolution era.

After spending more than a decade in one of the harshest environments in China, Luo Ming's masochistic self-sacrifice finally ruins his health. In 1977, with the assistance of Luo Dasheng and Lu Jing, who are now married, he returns to Beijing, accompanied by his wife, for medical treatment and political rehabilitation. When the next act begins, it is already 1994. Now an overachieved professional geologist, Luo Ming possesses the essential attributes of model intellectuals of the "New Era," as exemplified by the mathematician Chen Jingrun (1933–1996), whose achievements were widely reported and extolled in reportage literature and official newspapers during the late 1970s. Luo Ming's glory contrasts sharply with Luo Dasheng's underachievement. Since his transference to Beijing in the 1960s, Luo Dasheng has been promoted in the bureaucratic system and lost his incentive to do research. And now he is turning 60. Nevertheless, the play manages to end with a crescendo, when Luo Ming pays Luo Dasheng and Lu Jing a visit and encourages them to join him in a large national project of petroleum exploration. Inspired by Luo Ming's enthusiasm, Luo Dasheng makes up his mind to begin working on his monograph that he conceived some 30 years ago.

The play is meant to pay homage to Chinese geologists who have dedicated their life and work to the Chinese petroleum industry. Despite its honorable intention, the play's representation of dedicated intellectuals is rather naïve. Most characters in this play are one-dimensional and shallow. This is particularly obvious in the reputed "romance" between Lu Jing and her two best friends, Luo Ming and Luo Dasheng. Throughout the play, their relationship is awkwardly portrayed, and there is hardly any attempt on the part of the playwright to probe the heroine's subjectivity, much less her delicate and mixed feeling about the two admirers. When she marries Dasheng, it simply happens as if Luo Ming has never existed. Furthermore, when Luo Ming's girl friend tells Lu Jing in a joyful tone that Luo Ming has written a pile of unposted letters to her, Lu Jing remains totally unmoved. Apparently, at such a moment of heart-to-heart chat, considerations for comradeship override self-interest.

Other illustrative examples of realist plays include *Xiaojing Alley* (1981) by Li Longyun (b. 1948), *Old Friends* (1983) by Bai Fengxi, *Weddings and Funerals* (1984) by Wei Min *et al.*, *In Search of a Real Man* (1986) by Sha Yexin (b. 1939), *There Is A Sacred Fire Beyond* (1990) by Zheng Zhenhuan (b. 1942), *Old House* by Shi Ling (b. 1949), *Beijing Master* (1995) by Zhong Jieying (b. 1934), the blockbusting *Public Toilet* (2004) by Guo Shixing, *White Deer Plain* (2006) directed by Lin Zhaohua (b. 1936) and *We Walk on the Road* (2006) by Huang Jisu.

Exploration Plays

In 1982, the Chinese audience witnessed the first breakthrough in spoken drama in the post-socialist era. The staging of *Alarm Signal*, which was co-authored by Gao Xingjian (b. 1940) and Liu Huiyuan, signaled the arrival of exploration plays. The play was first shown to a limited audience, and later to the general public after obtaining the approval of authorities. It is a play about an aborted train robbery, yet throws light on the plight of Chinese young people who live off odd jobs. What was most striking about this play was its deliberate deviation from realist dramaturgy. For instance, the play focuses mainly on the characters' mental activities rather than their physical actions. From time to time, the characters would show their thoughts through interior monologue, lose themselves in reminiscence, or let their imagination run away. What they reminisce or imagine are no longer represented by speech, as is often the case with Chinese spoken drama, but actualized on stage by the actors' performance. The shift in space and time is indicated by the alternation of lighting, sound effect and the actors' positions on stage, as well as their styles of performance. To foreground the actors' subtle performance and to stimulate the audience's imagination, the set is kept to a minimum, with its realist details significantly reduced. As the play was performed in a small theater, the blurring of the boundary between the stage and the auditorium on the one hand, and the increased proximity between actors and the audience on the other, gave rise to an intimately interactive performing and viewing experience unavailable in large theaters. The success of *Alarm Signal* inspired many directors to tap the potentials of the small theater further in the following two decades.

Gao Xingjian wrote *The Bus Stop* a year before *Alarm Signal*. Yet the play was not staged right away, for Gao's immediate superiors at the Beijing People's Art Theater thought it would be politically prudent if Gao made his debut with a play which is not experimental in nature. Following the success of *Absolute Signal*, *The Bus Stop* was performed to a limited audience in 1983, with the moral support of Cao Yu. Despite being applauded by drama aficionados, the play was later banned by the authorities. Apparently, Gao's criticism of Cultural Revolution and exposure of current social ills, in an unprecedented absurdist style redolent of Samuel Beckett's *Waiting for Godot*, made the authorities bristle with rage. It was rumored that He Jingzhi (b. 1924), the deputy minister of the Publicity Department of the Central Committee of Chinese Communist Party and a playwright renowned for his revolutionary play *White-Haired Girl*, was so offended by Gao's play that he condemned it as the most "pernicious" drama since the founding of the People's Republic. When the political campaign to purge "spiritual pollution" was brewing, the Publicity Department ordered a short re-run of *Bus Stop* for the purpose of orchestrating a public denunciation of the play. As the political pressure was mounting and Gao was misdiagnosed with lung cancer, he decided to flee from Beijing and spent five months roaming in the backland of southwestern China in search of peace of mind. Gao's flight from the impending political persecution yielded unexpected results. During his wandering in the south, the ideas of writing *The Wild Man*, which was the third of his exploration plays, and *Soul Mountain*, his major work of fiction which would eventually put modern Chinese literature on the map of world literature, began to take shape.

The Bus Stop, as any other Gao's plays, is characterized by its formal experimentation. To highlight its formal features, Gao keeps the plot of this play simple and easy to understand. It is a story about a group of people waiting at a suburban bus stop for a city-bound bus, which seems to have been unreasonably late. Among them, Silent Man is the only character who decides not to wait anymore and takes the resolute action of leaving for the city on foot. Others keep on waiting, and dally for ten years. When the story draws to a close, those who remain waiting suddenly discover that the bus stop has long been abandoned and realize to their dismay that the bus has changed its route without giving any prior notice. Before the curtain falls, they decide to leave, yet remain motionless.

Four things stand out in Gao's conception of this play. First, there is a consistent use of a musical score to represent Silent Man, who for the most part is absent from the stage. However, even Silent Man exits early in the play, the impact of his action is felt throughout the performance. The musical theme signifying his determination recurs at several important junctures, as if mocking the inaction of others. Second, in sharp contrast to Silent Man, the other characters are marked by their loquacity, either in dialogue or in monologue. There are moments when their respective dialogues (or monologues, or both) overlap, in multifarious ways, creating a sound effect rarely encountered in spoken drama, which Gao terms "multivocality." Third, the characters in the play often turn towards the audience and address them as if they were taking part in the drama. According to Gao, the impact of such an attempt to establish direct contact between the actor and the audience, especially in a small theater, is tremendous. Gao considers it a vital means to establish "theatricality," meaning the involvement of the audience in the actualization of a play. Fourth, towards the end of the play, the actors momentarily disengage themselves from the performance and speak in their own voice, commenting on the characters they play and reflecting on the nature of the drama. To Gao, such a defamiliarizing attempt on the part of actors serves two related purposes. On the one hand, it dispels the illusion of verisimilitude required by realism, which has dominated the spoken drama since the early twentieth century. On the other hand, it prompts the audience to rethink the nature of theatrical performance, which, according to Gao, is nothing other than an art of "suppositionality," namely the art of bringing unreality to life through subjective imagination and calculated representation in the theater.

Gao Xingjian returned to Beijing when the political campaign against "spiritual pollution" subsided in mid-1984. In November, he completed a new play called *Wild Man*, which ponders over the ecological disaster and cultural dispossession in southwest China, making full use of the unusual material he collected during his self-exile. This is his first attempt at what he calls "total theater," a notion of theatrical performance which departs considerably from the tradition of modern spoken drama. According to Gao, the play is thematically "polyphonic," dealing with multiple subjects simultaneously. It depicts the failed marriage of an ecologist and his research trip in southwestern China, dwells on the issue of deforestation, the predicament of endangered species and the vanishing shaman tradition, and ruminates over the fate of women and the legend of wild man.

In terms of performance, the play is also polyphonic in nature. On top of conventional and multivocal dialogues, Gao calls to his aid recitation, singing and dancing. Moreover, narrators are unobtrusively introduced. Gao drew extensively on exotic regional cultural traditions and appropriated their epic of genesis, ritual songs and sacrificial dances, making the play a theatrical pageantry in front of a large audience at the Capital Theater in 1985. In this play, the "suppositionality" of theatrical performance is also stressed by resort to metatextual devices. For instance, one male actor is required to play two roles in one scene, and he has to perform the role shift in front of the audience, while several others alternate between immersing in their roles and resuming their own identity as an actor to pass their comments on their roles and the play.

If Gao Xingjian's *Alarm Signal*, *Bus Stop* and *Wild Man* are regarded by critics as the pioneers of exploration plays, Jin Yun's (b. Liu Jinyun, 1938) *Uncle Doggie's Nirvana* (1986) and Chen Zidu (b. 1952) *et al.*'s *Sangshuping Chronicles* (1988) are generally accepted as the representative exploration plays of the 1980s. *Uncle Doggie's Nirvana* recounts the traumatic story of a peasant by the name of Chen Hexiang, also nicknamed "Uncle Doggie," from the early years of the People's Republic to the post-socialist era, with a focus on his obsession with land and cattle, which results in his eventual breakdown. As a young man, Chen dreams about having his own lands and cattle, which cannot be realized until the Communist seizes power and re-allocates landlord Qi Yongnian' properties and lands to the peasantry. But Chen's happy days are short. His lands and cattle are confiscated soon in a political campaign to promote collectivization. Unwilling to accept the drastic change in his fortunes, Chen loses his mind, and his wife remarries. Twenty years has gone by before the state changes its policy again. In the post-socialist era, Chen is given back his lands and cattle. Throughout these years, what Chen treasures most, apart from lands and cattle, is the gate tower allocated to him. It represents not only Qi's wealth and power that he envies, but also his shameful past — he was once tied up there and beaten up by the landlord. However, time has changed, and this monument of power and wealth is to be torn down by his son, to make room for a marble factory that he is building. Once again Chen refuses to surrender his prized possession, he decides to set fire on the gate and let it burn down to ashes.

In a way, this play echoes the theme of Gao Xiaosheng's "Li Shunda Build a House," in which a peasant struggles to adjust to the whimsical policy changes over the years. However, the literary techniques of this play are more complex. The play alternates seamlessly between the past and present, defying the spatio-temporal conventions of realism. In scene 2, characters existing in different time zones appear synchronically on stage. When the young Chen murmurs to himself about farming, Qi's ghost and Chen's son, both from the future, show up on stage and pass comments on what he is saying. What is most intriguing about this scene is its improbable merging of different temporal frames. For Chen, the moment of enunciation is the present. But for Qi's apparition, Chen's enunciation took place in the past. As for Chen's son, Chen's rambling is twice removed from his present; it is actually Chen's account of his past, as remembered by Chen's son. Scene 11 is also interesting. When Chen sees Qi's ghost in the broad day light, they begin to chat. After a while, Chen's son approaches with his wife — who is incidentally Qi's daughter — and they start up another conversation with Chen. At that moment, Chen is caught between two worlds — the world of the dead on the one hand and the world of the living on the other.

Sangshuping Chronicles presents a cross-section of life in Chinese countryside during the late 1960s. Its approach to reality is critically realistic, yet its performance is formally innovative. The play has been hailed by critics as a milestone of contemporary drama. A typical tale about poverty and injustice in the Chinese backland, it aims to expose both the misrule of the Communist regime and the backwardness of its Chinese subjects. In a way, this play is reminiscent of Chen Kaige's harrowing film *Yellow Earth* (1984) and Han Shaogong's bleak story "Papa-pa" (1985) in its poignant portrayal of the unenlightened rural masses. The story revolves around Li Jindou, the production team leader of Sangshuping. He seems to be a responsible and courageous man when he stands up against more senior state officials and protect the livelihood of his clan. But on the other hand, he is a stubborn, calculating and mean patriarch. He bullies the only family in the village which does not bear the surname Li. He also tries to coerce his widowed daughter-in-law to re-marry his second son, who suffers from Kaschin-Beck disease, though to no avail. He advises a family to trade their daughter for a wife for their only son, who is mentally deranged, resulting in an unhappy marriage. In short, Li Jindou is a character that embodies the unenlightened aspects of Chinese rural culture, despite his leadership and kindness to the villagers.

What makes this thematically depressing play enjoyable is its creative performance. A chorus is introduced in this play, mainly at the beginning and ending of each act. Unlike the chorus in Gao Xingjian's *Wild Man*, which is critical in nature, the chorus in *Sangshuping Chronicles* serves the purpose of narrating. Apart from the chorus, there are moments in the play when individual characters sing their own themes, and dancers dance in the background to indicate the change of moods. Cinematic montage is also employed. For instance, in Act 1, Scene 6, the three stages of Cai Fang and Yu Wa's love affair are indicated by the changes in lighting, while the actors remain in the same spots on stage and act out different scenarios. A ghost also features in this play. In Act 3, Scene 2, when Wang Zhike is forced to leave the village, he comes to his wife's tomb to pay his last tribute to her. While talking to his wife's ghost, he also converses with Li Jindou. Once again we have this curious scene in which a character speaks to the denizens of two different worlds simultaneously. The return of the dead is indeed a recurrent motif of many exploration plays of the post-socialist era.

If two of the highly-regarded exploration plays of the 1980s are concerned about rural life as well as the backwardness of China, the avant-garde exploration plays of the 1990s focus on urban life with a keen global awareness. Take *I Love XXX* (1994) by Meng Jinghui (b. 1964) for example. This is hardly a play, but more likely a four-part poetry recitation, with the exception of Part 2, which is not meant to be read but projected onto the stage as silent subtitles. According to the script, there is no character, no description of the setting, and there is only one short passage of stage instruction, which appears, rather late and oddly, in Part 3 as a short essay. The main body of the script consists of parallel sentences, all uttered in the first person, which run throughout the four parts of the play non-stop. The recitation begins with the description of a bell tolling, ushering in the year 1900, hence the twentieth century and the significant events that are taking place in different parts of the world. Imbued with a Whitmanian passion, the play seems to embrace everything that belongs to the twentieth century. However, there are certain incidents in world history that are perhaps too repulsive to poetic imagination that they have to be erased the moment they are about to be enumerated: "I love all these that have never happened."

While Part 1 and Part 2 draw up inventories of global events, Part 3 goes over contemporary Chinese history, the first-person narrator's experiences of growing up in China, and, finally, his love and lust. Apparently the playwright feels very much at home in Part 3, for the sentences here are sprinkled with amusing parodies of cultural and political references. Part 4 is primarily meta-textual in nature, reflecting upon the ongoing theatrical performance. When the play begins, the I-you relationship in the recitation is meant to involve the audience in the play, through their imagination or theatrical "suppositional-ity": "I love light/I love, therefore there is light/I love you/I love, therefore there is you/I love myself/I love, therefore here I am." When the play comes to an end, it is time for the performers and the audience to declare their mutual passion for the theatre, even though the play has come to an end. Hence the recitation: "I love the stage/I love, therefore there is a stage/I love to leave/I love, therefore I leave."

A Rhinoceros in Love (1999) by Liao Yimei is also highly conscious of the passage of time. In Act 1, people are busy building an enormous bell on a square in a city to mark the arrival of the twenty-first century, and the merry melody of the chorus is suffused with hope, optimism and determination. Yet there lurks a motif of despair in the background, regardless of the over-whelming sense of rejuvenation at the turn of the century: "Love is so beautiful, yet it will collapse at the first blow." As the title of the play suggests, this is a story about love and courtship, especially about unrequited love, at the dawn of the new millennium. Ma Lu, a rhinoceros keeper, is enamored with Ming Ming, a secretary who fancies an artist. No matter what Ma Lu does, even after he has won the first lottery of the twenty-first century, Ming Ming remains indifferent to his advances. She is simply not interested in him. At the same time, Ming Ming is rejected by the artist. In the end, Ma Lu takes a desperate move and kidnaps Ming Ming. He blindfolds her, ties her onto a chair and pours out his heart to her. Still, Ming Ming remained unmoved. The play begins with Ma Lu's humorously plaintive monologue and ends with it. Despite the good-humored and at times absurdist tone, the play bemoans the absence of mutual love in the new millenium. Ma Lu is as lonely as the single rhinoceros he is taking care of. Unlike the highly experi-mental play *I Love XXX*, this is an entertaining and melancholic exploration play that caters to the taste of the general audience as well as theater afi-cionados. When it was staged in 1999, the play was very successful.

Other notable exploration plays include *There Are Warm Currents Out There* (1980) by Ma Zhongjun, *et al.*, *An Investigation of Fifteen Cases of Divorce* (1983) and *Interviews with the Witnesses by the Deceased* (1985) by Liu Shugang (b. 1940), *Magic Cube* (1985) by Tao Jun, *Pan Jinlian* (1985) by

Wei Minglun (b. 1941), *The Runner or No Where to Hide* (1991) and *Wind, Rain, and Pavel Korchagin* (1995) by Diao Yinan (b. 1969), *Stirrings of Love* (1992) by Meng Jinghui (b. 1964), *Comrade Ah Q* (1996) by Huang Jingang, and Meng Jinghui's two highly experimental plays, *Flowers in the Mirror and the Reflection of the Moon in Water* (2006) and *Comments on Life by Two Dogs* (2007).

The Nobel Prize for Literature, 2000

In 1983, when Gao Xingjian's *Bus Station* was banned and he was very likely to become the target of a political campaign, he left Beijing and went into self-exile in southwest China. While he travelled along the Yangtze River, Gao came across a wealth of anthropological material that he would eventually used in his play *Wild Man* and his *tour de force, Soul Mountain,* which took him about seven years to finish. Gao's literary endeavors in the 1980s caught the attention of Göran Malmqvist, a renowned Swedish linguist, sinologist and translator, who was admitted to the Swedish Academy in 1985. Malmqvist began translating Gao's works into Swedish, which is pivotal in making Gao's works fully accessible to other members of the Swedish Academy who do not read Chinese.

When Gao Xingjian won the Nobel Prize for Literature in 2000, he was lauded for his achievements in both fiction and drama. Although he is praised for his "oeuvre of universal validity, bitter insights and linguistic ingenuity," it is his portrayal of an individual's protest against the oppression of the masses in China, and his detailed depiction of the exuberant cultures at the fringe of Chinese civilization that have fascinated and impressed the Nobel Committee. In the opinion of the Nobel Committee, what is most artistically intriguing about Gao Xinjian's literary works is his "unrestrained use of personal pronouns," by which he "creates lightning shifts of perspective and compels the reader to question all confidences." Gao's experiments on "alternation of persons" began rather early, especially in his short stories collected in *Buying a Fishing Rod for My Grandfather* (1989). In *Soul Mountain* (1990), three personal pronouns are employed to refer to the main character in three different narratives. The first-person narrative is the protagonist's self-account of his peregrination in southwest China, while the unusual second-person narrative recounts his imaginary journey in search of the Soul Mountain, in which the protagonist visualizes himself as an intimate friend and talks to himself in the second person. For the most part of *Soul Mountain,* the two narratives alternate regularly. The third-person narrative is seldom used, and mainly for the purpose of self-reflection. In the third-person narrative, the protagonist refers to himself as another person, defending on aesthetic grounds his composition of *Soul Mountain* on the one hand, questioning in philosophical terms the possibility of spiritual transcendence as envisioned in the second-person narrative on the other. Simply put, Gao's *magnum opus* is a traveler's diary, in which the author not only records his actual and imagined experiences, but also reflects upon his desire to transcend reality and his very act of writing.

"Alternation of persons" is also used in *One Man's Bible* (1999), though to a different effect. *One Man's Bible* is comprised of second-person narrative and third-person narrative, with both personal pronouns denoting the male protagonist. The third-person narrative recounts the protagonist's involvement in the Cultural Revolution, while the second-person narrative tells about his present experiences abroad. By using two personal pronouns to refer to the same character, Gao divides the character's life into two discontinuous parts. The monstrous self of the protagonist is cast in the third person as if to keep it at a distance, providing a sharp contrast to the more amiable self, which is addressed intimately in the second person.

Gao Xingjian's experimental use of personal pronouns is also evident in his drama, although in a way quite different from his fiction. In *Between Life and Death* (1991), the female actor keeps on telling the tale and reporting the speech of the heroine whom she is playing in the third person, creating a very strong sense of self-alienation on stage. In the third act of *Nocturnal Wanderer* (1999), the actors are required to perform in a similarly self-alienating fashion. They do not say their lines, rather they report the speeches of the characters they play. An eerie sense of breakdown of human communication is thus achieved on stage. Although these characters are having a conversation, they are not really talking to each other — a character refers to himself in the second person, as if he is murmuring to himself, while the others refer to themselves in the third person, as if they are not related to themselves at all. Gao Xingjian's experimentation with personal pronouns in both fiction and drama is indeed phenomenal, rarely seen in contemporary literature written in Chinese.

Since Gao Xingjian left China in 1987 and settled down in France after the June 4 Massacre in 1989, his Nobel Prize sparked drastically different reactions from readers in China and the Chinese community overseas. While Gao's success was cheered by overseas Chinese, readers in China tended to question Gao's legitimacy as a representative of China and Chinese literature — despite the obvious fact that the Nobel Prize was meant to be an award to an individual for his literary achievements rather than a token recognition of a national literature. Liu Zaifu (b. 1941), the eminent Chinese literary critic in exile, regarded Gao's prize as an appreciation of his unique sensibility and the beauty of literature in Chinese. Yang Lian, the Obscure poet in exile, hailed the award as "the victory of exile." Qian Liqun, a retired Professor of Chinese Literature at the Peking University, considered Gao's Nobel as an international affirmation of creative writing in Chinese, which, in his opinion, had already flourished overseas and become an integral part of world literature. Despite the ambivalence of Gao's literary identity as a French writer publishing mainly in Chinese, Gao's achievements in fiction and drama have testified — to a considerable extent — to the creativity and vibrancy of post-socialist Chinese literature. Indeed, it is quite difficult to imagine the emergence of Gao Xingjian without the exuberant cultural ambience of the 1980s, in spite of the fact that Gao is a lone wolf, who had already left China when literature of the "New Era' was in full swing.

References

Barnstone, T. (Ed.) (1993) *Out of the howling storm: The new Chinese poetry.* Hanover: Wesleyan University Press.

Crippen, A. (2005) *Nameless flowers: Selected poems of Gu Cheng.* New York: George Braziller Inc.

Morin, E. (Ed.) (1990) *The red azalea: Chinese poetry since the cultural revolution.* Honolulu: University of Hawaii Press.

Van Crevel, Maghiel. (1996) *Language shattered: Contemporary Chinese poetry and Duoduo.* Leiden, the Netherlands: Research School CNWS.

————. (2008) "Lower body poetry and its lineage: Disbelief, bad behavior and social concern." In J. Lu (Ed.), *China's literary and cultural scenes at the turn of the 21st century*, pp. 179–205. London and New York: Routledge.

Yeh, M. (Ed.) (1992) and trans. *Anthology of modern Chinese poetry.* New Haven and London: Yale University Press.

Zhang, E. and D. Chen (Eds.) (2007) *Another kind of nation: An anthology of contemporary Chinese poetry.* Jersey City, New Jersey: Talisman House Publishers.

13

CINEMA

Rui Zhang

Central Academy of Arts

Abstract

In the past three decades, Chinese cinema has undergone dramatic changes. Due to the ever-growing development of Chinese economy, Chinese cinema has been gradually transformed from a fully-controlled propaganda tool to an industry with an overt intention of profit-making. The result is the transformation of a political machine into a money machine, though still under the close monitoring of the Communist Party. The 1980s witnessed the emergence of the Fifth Generation directors, who demonstrated a changing face of Chinese cinema to both domestic and foreign audiences. Since then they have been major players in the arena of Chinese cinema. In the 1990s, when the Communist Party implemented aggressively a series of economic reforms, entertainment films represented by Feng Xiaogang's movies became popular and generated high box-office returns. Towards the end of the century, four modes of productions — government-sponsored, private, co-production, and underground cinemas — formed a mosaic of Chinese cinema. In the new millennium, due to the pressure of profit-making, all these different modes of production have been merging into a mainstream of a highly commercialized yet still politically-correct cinema.

Keywords: Chinese cinema; censorship; commercialization; Zhang Yimou; Chen Kaige; Feng Xiaogang; Fifth Generation; Sixth Generation.

Part One: Introduction

Since the Communist Party came to power in 1949, Chinese cinema functioned mostly as a propaganda tool. As a result, for several decades, the Party
was in control of the film industry through a full ownership of the industry's
infrastructure — studios, movie theaters, and distribution companies.
Although some national film studios in recent years have been transformed
into listing companies at Chinese stock market, the Party is still the most
important stockholder of these "public companies."

As political correctness has been the indisputable criterion for the Party
to decide whether a film could be screened, Chinese films' priority since
1949 is the subservience to communist ideology. Under different political
atmosphere and social background, different generations of filmmakers
took various approaches in complying with the party's needs. In the past
three decades, as the scope and depth of economic reform became broader
and deeper, a market economy was adopted, and the film industry followed suit. For popular films, the force of market has become increasingly
important, sometimes as crucial as political correctness, but never strong
enough to challenge the party line. Therefore, the most important Chinese
filmmakers in the past thirty years are not those who produced large number of films or those praised by the film authorities, but those who
represented major cinematic trends or exerted influence on the films of
their contemporaries and later followers. In this regard, Xie Jin's films epit-
omize the essence of Socialist Realist cinema and "Scar" films; Chen Kaige
and Zhang Yimou are the most important figures in the 1980s; and Feng
Xiaogang is the most successful filmmaker at the turn of the century. Their
compromise, resistance, and success can be seen as a barometer of the
political climate in China.

Art Policy — Perpetuation of Yan'an Talks

To better understand the path of Chinese cinema under the control of
Communist party, it is imperative to take a glance at the origin and implementation of the party's art policy.

Communist China's art policy is based on talks given by Mao Zedong at
the Forum of Art and Literature in 1942 in Yan'an, the center of the
Communist-controlled area during the Anti-Japanese War. In these talks,
Mao defines the duties of intellectuals, stating that artists should consider
themselves part of the revolutionary force and that the audience for literature
and art should be workers, peasants, and soldiers. The idea of "art for art's

sake" is also denounced in these talks. Mao stresses that "the fundamental task of all revolutionary artists and writers is to expose all dark forces which endanger the people and to extol all the revolutionary struggles of the people"; and that "writers and artists who cling to their individualist petty-bourgeois standpoint cannot truly serve the masses of revolutionary workers, peasants, and soldiers." It is very clear that in the new country imagined by Mao there would be no unlimited freedom of artistic expression, especially from the "petty-bourgeois standpoint." Instead, Chinese artists' major task would be to glorify and idealize the new world and the new people. If they wanted to criticize, the target of their criticism had to be the old society and counter-revolutionaries. Contemporaneous social and political issues could not be the subject of the criticism. The essence is summarized as "serving the people and serving socialism," and sometimes shortened as "Two Serves" (*erwei*).

The doctrines derived from Mao's "Yan'an Talks" — particularly the idea that art should serve politics and socialism — have remained forceful in the creation of a cinema that has, in many ways, withstood the many changes in Chinese society over the last decades. Nonetheless, as China has gone through great social, technological, political and economical transformations in the past three decades, other forces such as commercial investments and independent film productions have gradually emerged.

Censorship — The Control System of Chinese Cinema

During the socialist era, all Chinese film studios had editorial departments responsible for censoring film scripts as well as final versions of films. But the Party leadership always had the priority to override any decisions made by the studio. Since most leaders of these film studios were Party members, they performed a double duty as both filmmakers and Party cadres. Hence, the boundary between government censorship and industry self-censorship became indistinct.

In terms of content, two major issues always cause special attention among Chinese censors — morality and politics. The Tenth Clause of the *Dianying shencha tiaoli* (Regulations of Film Censorship) issued in 1997 specifies that plots containing obscene and vulgar content such as sex, extra-marital affairs, violence, superstition, or any other content that is "abhorrent to morality and virtue would need to be deleted and modified" (Ministry of Radio, Film, and TV, 1997). Besides these common concerns, Chinese censors also pay particular attention to the political and ideological rectitude of films.

In the early years of the PRC, total banning of films deemed inappropriate and the oppression of filmmakers were common. In the 1980s, authorities began to resort to legislation to regulate films. In 1989, on the basis of a request from the State Council of the PRC, the Ministry of Radio, Film, and Television issued an announcement promoting the special category of "Not Appropriate for Children" (shaoer buyi), to be applied in film distribution and exhibition. This "Announcement of the Implementation of Film Censorship and Exhibition Rating System" (Guanyu shixing dianying shencha, fangying fenji zhidu de tongzhi) indicates that the rating is applicable to both domestic and imported films:

1. with rape, theft, drug abuse, drug traffic and prostitution;
2. with violence, murder, or action that can easily cause children to be afraid;
3. depicting sex and sexual behavior;
4. depicting abnormal phenomena in society.

The announcement also requires not only that a rating of "Not Appropriate for Children" be printed on each copy of the film and shown before the appearance of the title, but also that the rating should be indicated on movie posters and other promotional materials. In November 1989, the Chinese Film Distribution and Exhibition Company, a subsidiary company of the MRFT, issued a similar regulation designed to implement the policy: "Regulation for Exhibiting Films Rated 'Not Appropriate for Children'" (fangyin shaoer buyi yingpian de guanli banfa). Although the motivation behind these regulations was to regulate entertainment films and protect children under the age of 16 by specifying which films were inappropriate for certain audiences, the institution of the category of "Not Appropriate for Children" actually allowed some filmmakers and distributors to exploit particular audiences and generate more revenue. Starting from this not so successful attempt, a series of censorship laws were implemented in later years. "Regulations of Film Censorship" (dianying shencha tiaoli) was issued in the 1990s and then revised. Motions of film ranking were frequently initiated by film industry experts at the Party Congress. Nonetheless, every now and then, films with "inappropriate" content still fell victim to arbitrary banning with or without explicit explanations of reasons from the film authorities. Zhang Yimou's *To Live*, Jiang Wen's *Devils at Doorstep* and Lou Ye's *Summer Palace* are well-known examples.

Part Two: Chinese Cinema of the 1980s — The Fourth and Fifth Generations and the Rise of Entertainment Films

Chinese cinema at the end of the 1980s was surprisingly similar to that at the turn of the 21st century. In both periods, a relaxed political and social context allowed film leaders to encourage a cinema with diversified subject matter. As a result, the Fifth Generation cinema began to attract attention at foreign film festivals and surprised Chinese film critics with unorthodox styles and cinematic languages. Meanwhile, entertainment films — martial arts, suspense, and comedy — became very popular at the movie theaters. These two trends and their fortunes illustrate a recurring theme in the film history of the PRC: the party's indecision about how to view the medium of cinema, whether as a powerful tool of propaganda under the full control of the party, or as a medium that should meet the demands of the audiences. Consequently there developed a continuous struggle between Party control and the desire for "free" expressions.

The Fourth and Fifth Generations

Chinese filmmakers were traditionally divided into generations. The first generation was the pioneers in the early 20th century who first experimented with the new medium of cinema. The second generation began a golden age of Chinese cinema in the 1930s and 40s. The third generation filmmakers were those who started their career after 1949 and made films that were considered the quintessential socialist realist cinema. Xie Jin's films are such examples. The fourth generation filmmakers, such as Wu Yigong, Xie Fei, Zhang Nuanxin, and Huang Jianzhong, gained their professional trainings in the 1960s, but it was not until the end of Cultural Revolution in the late 1970s that these filmmakers began to make their own films. The Fifth Generation filmmakers were mainly the students admitted to Beijing Film Academy after the Cultural Revolution in 1978 and made their first films in the early 1980s. Among them, Chen Kaige, Zhang Yimou, and Tian Zhuangzhuang are the most prominent. Although the influences of previous generations of directors could still be seen in the late 1970s and early 1980s in films such as *Legend of Mt. Tianyun* (Tianyun shan chuanqi, dir. Xie Jin, 1980), the Fourth and Fifth Generations were the major players of Chinese cinema from 1979 to 1989.

Deviations from Socialist Realism can already be seen in the films of the Fourth Generation. In films such as *The Little Flower* (Xiao hua, dir. Huang

Jianzhong, 1979), *Troubled Laughter* (Kunao ren de xiao, dir. Yang Yanjin, 1979), *Seagulls* (Sha ou, dir. Zhang Nuanxin, 1982) and *The Sacrificed Youth* (Qingchun ji, dir. Zhang Nuanxin, 1985), more humane approaches to typical socialist subjects are evident. In *The Little Flower*, the heroism of a PLA soldier becomes the backdrop of his journey to find his lost sister, creating suspense and sentimentality in an otherwise typical glorification of the hero's bravery. Similar to the unprecedented image of a war hero depicted as a caring and sensitive brother in *Little Flower*, in *Seagulls*, the image of the self-sacrificing female volleyball player who dedicated her life, love and health to defending China's national pride in championship games is portrayed as a fallen hero who experiences disillusion, frustration and displacement. The previous idealized revolutionary heroes and diligent socialist workers are replaced by protagonists who are either not perfect or have feelings just as ordinary people do. Another difference of the Fourth Generation cinema is its self-conscious cinematic language, a clear departure from the standard aesthetics of "red, shiny, and bright" in socialist cinema during the Cultural Revolution. Wu Yigong's *My Memories of Old Beijing* (Chengnan jiushi, 1982) for example, tells a nostalgic story from a little girl's perspective about her family life in Beijing during the Republican era; the film impresses both critics and audiences with its gracefully moving camera, subdued tone in *mise-en-scène*, and emphasis on ordinary people's happiness and suffering. Xie Fei's *A Girl From Hunan* (Xiangnü Xiaoxiao, 1984), adapted from Shen Congwen's famous novella, is also void of political rhetoric, but filled with delicate depiction of the life of a young girl who is trapped in an arranged marriage to a little boy but becomes pregnant with another man.

What finally brought Chinese cinema into international attention in the 1980s was the rise of the Fifth Generation cinema. The emergence of this generation in the late 70s and early 80s was the result of a series of complex social and cultural factors. These filmmakers, Zhang Yimou, Chen Kaige, Tian Zhuangzhuang, Zhang Junzhao and others, were the first students admitted to Beijing Film Academy after its decade-long closure during the Cultural Revolution. When they entered the academy, they were already in their late twenties or even early thirties and had endured the turmoil and devastations of the Cultural Revolution. Chen Kaige's father, Chen Huaikai, former Director of Beijing Film Studio, was condemned as a traitor and counter-revolutionary and had to face public humiliation initiated by his own son. And Chen Kaige himself was sent to a remote province to accept "re-education" from local peasants. Zhang Yimou worked as a country teacher and had to sell his own blood in order to purchase his first camera. After the Cultural Revolution, when they came to the film academy, they were mature enough to interrogate the underlying historical and political reasons that caused their personal as well national sufferings. The late 70s and early 80s also marked an end to the previously well-established official Maoist rhetoric. In Beijing Film Academy, when viewing a socialist film at class, students hooted with laughter at the scenes that were clichés of socialist-realist formulas. When they got their first chance to make their own films after graduation, idealized heroism, nationalist monumentality, and party rhetoric of Chinese history were the last things they would put into their own works. The first films with an astonishingly different cinematic aesthetics of the Fifth Generation cinema were *One and Eight* (Yiige he bage, dir. Zhang Junzhao, 1983) and *Yellow Earth* (Huang tudi, dir. Chen Kaige, 1984). *One and Eight* tells the story of how a communist soldier who is persecuted as a counter-revolutionary counters Japanese attacks with eight other prisoners when they are on their way of relocation. *Yellow Earth* depicts the story of a communist soldier who collects folk songs in China's rural area; staying with a peasant family, he witnesses the rural hardship and the suffering of peasants. Zhang Yimou, the leading figure of the Fifth Generation, worked as assistant cinematographer and chief cinematographer in the two films while Chen Kaige directed *Yellow Earth*. With asymmetrical composition of shots, subdued tone of settings and costumes, prolonged empty and silent shots of rural landscape, these two films signify a new cinematic mode that emphasizes visuality and an alternative approach to Chinese history. These two films are the first collaborative projects that explicitly demonstrate a radical break with well-established socialist cinematic dogma. Zhang Yimou's *Red Sorghum* (Hong gaoliang, 1987), which is the first Golden Bear winner from PRC at the Berlin Film Festival, went on to surprise international film audienes with a new face of Chinese cinema. The story of *Red Sorghum* is still a traditional subject of Chinese people's bravery in the resistance against Japanese invasion. Its presentation, however, has been controversial. It uses extensively bright colors of red, yellow, and blue, and features a merciless realism that exposes a barbarism and vulgarity in ordinary people's life. Another leading figure of the Fifth Generation, Chen Kaige, also arrives at the peak of his career around this time. And in 1993, his *Farewell My Concubine* garnered a series of major international film awards, including the Palme d'Or from Cannes.

Rise of Entertainment Films

The end of the 1970s and the beginning of the 1980s witnessed a great increase in film attendance. In 1979, the number of moviegoers was as high as 29.3 billion, which means that an average of 30 films were seen per person in one year. In 1980, the number of moviegoers was 23.4 billion, for an average of 29 films per person. Nonethless, the prosperity of Chinese cinema in the post-Cultural Revolution era was short-lived. Beginning in 1980, the number of attendees declined by one billion person-times annually. In the mid-1980s, the situation worsened. The cost of making a film increased from around forty to fifty thousand RMB in 1985 to eighty thousand per film in 1988, while the earnings from selling the rights of distribution declined to half of that in 1983. Out of 142 films made in 1987, only 34 were able to break even or make a profit.

It was against this background that entertainment films that were non-political began to show their potential for resurrecting Chinese cinema in the second half of the 1980s; by the end of the 1980s they occupied a predominant position in Chinese cinema. The first popular entertainment films were mostly martial art, crime, and suspense genres. Examples include *Mysterious Buddha* (Shenmi de dafuo; dir. Zhang Huaxin, 1980), *Shaolin Temple* (Shaolin si; dir. Zhang Xinyan, 1982), *Murder Case No. 405* (Siling wu mousha an; dir. Shen Yaoting, 1981), and *Wu Dang* (Wu dang; dir. Sun Sha, 1983). This trend culminated in 1988 when China's major studios were vying to produce as many entertainment films as possible. Beijing Film Studio made *Huang Tianba* (Jingbiao Huangtian ba; dir. Li Wenhua, 1987), *The Mahjong Incident* (Feicui majiang; dir. Yu Xiaoyang, 1987), *The Case of Silver Snake* (Yinshe mousha'an; dir. Li Shaohong, 1988); Xi'an Film Studio made *Desperation* (Zuihou de fengkuang; dir. Zhou Xiaowen, 1987), *Great Swordsman of the Yellow River* (Huanghe da xia; dir. Zhang Xinyan and Zhang Zien, 1987), *The Grave Robbers* (Dongling da dao; dir. Li Yundong, five parts, 1984–1998); Shanghai Film Studio made *The Tribulations of A Young Master* (Shaoye de monan; dir. Wu Yigong and Zhang Jianya, 1987); E'mei Film Studio made *Soccer Heroes* (Jingdu qiu xia; dir. Xie Hong, 1987). Among 158 films produced in 1988, 80 were martial arts, suspense, crime, or musical genres (Zhong, 1991).

The rise of entertainment films was accompanied by the emergence of an urban cinema, which formed a new trend in the late 1980s. The year of 1988, labeled by some film critics as the "Year of Wang Shuo," witnessed the adaptation of four of his works into films — *Samsara* (Lun hui, 1988, dir. Huang Jianxin, adapted from *Emerging from the Sea* [Fuchu haimian]), *Troubleshooter* (Wan zhu; dir. Mi Jiashan, 1988, adapted from the short story of the same title), *Deep Gasping* (Da chuanqi; dir. Ye Daying, 1988, adapted from *Rubber Man*, [Xiangpi ren]), and *Half Sea, Half Flame* (Yiban shi haishui, yiban shi huoyan; dir. Xia Gang, 1988, adapted from the short story of the same title). These films display in full the sense of cynicism and disillusionment common among urban youth in the late 1980s. The emergence of these sentiments caused heated debates among film officials with some viewing these films as a morbid reflection of society, while others seeing this as a tendency that would enrich Chinese cinema. Although this so-called "Wang Shuo Fever" was later denounced by film authorities due to the Tian'anmen Incident, its influence on Chinese cinema of the 1990s was far-reaching. These films playfully subvert the hegemony of Maoist ideology by combining absurdity, profanity, and even obscenity. The Wang Shuo Fever also implicitly challenged official rhetoric of the postsocialist regime without hinting at any other alternatives (Yao, 1995). In Chinese urban cinema of the 1990s, this ideological ambivalence was perpetuated in films such as Huang Jianxin's *Back to Back, Face to Face* (Liang kao liang, bei dui bei, 1994), *Signal Right, Turn Left* (Hongdeng ting, ludeng xing, 1996), and *Surveillance* (Maifu, 1996), which paradoxically questioned the hegemony of official ideology and supported, somewhat reluctantly, the *status quo*.

Beginning in the second half of the 1980s, reforms of Chinese film industry targeting the monopolies in film distribution and ticket pricing were initiated. Before the reform, the only legitimate film distributor in China was the state-owned China's Film Corporation (CFC). It purchased films outright from studios at a flat rate usually based on the length of the film. The film studio would neither be held responsible for the financial failure of a film, nor could it make money from a successful one. Therefore, in the first three decades of the PRC, following the guidance of the film administration and relying completely on government financial support, the film production sector was indifferent to the film market. However, this situation began to change in the 1980s as the government began to initiate economic reforms that challenged the insufficiencies of the planned economy and promoted a "planned market economic system." Beginning in the 1980s, some studios began to demand more autonomy from the CFC in terms of film distribution and the right to share profit. Partially emancipated from the distribution monopoly of the CFC and stimulated by the profit-sharing potential, the film studios began to show enthusiasm for films that they felt would be most profitable.

Besides the industry reform, a cultural and political liberalization in the 1980s also contributed to the rise of non-political entertainment films. In December 1988, the Vice President of MRFT, Chen Haosu, delivered a talk "On the Dominance of Entertainment Film," in which he stated that cinema functions on three levels: At the most fundamental level is the function of entertainment; and with this as basis, it can be further developed into the artistic and the pedagogical. Different from the fate of the first two waves of entertainment films in the early 1950s and 1960s, which either provoked administrative intervention or were suppressed by film authorities through political campaigns, the new round of entertainment films was initiated and encouraged by leaders among the film authorities.

The emergence of the Fifth Generation cinema and the popularity of entertainment films in the 1980s reflect a relative relaxation in film policies and administration. Although these tendencies stagnated in 1989 after the Tian'anmen Incident, they resumed in the mid-90s and signaled a more thorough transformation of Chinese film industry.

Part Three: Chinese Cinema in the 1990s: Stagnation, Hollywood Imports and Commercialization

Main Melody Films

According to Communist Party Press, the Tian'anmen Incident was a by-product of the influences of Western culture, including popular songs from Taiwan, action and martial arts films from Hong Kong and Hollywood, and Chinese avant-garde art. As a result, while denouncing cinema's function as a medium for entertainment, the film authorities gave the so-called Main Melody (zhu xuan lü) film the mission of helping the Party to advocate its policies. Throughout the 1990s, these films became the primary weapon through which the Party held on to and voiced its political message to the mass audiences.

Even though the notion of Main Melody films was first promoted by some film leaders at the end of the 1980s, it was not until the end of the 1989 that it became an officially sanctioned category of film. In 1988, 60 percent of the annual film production consisted of martial arts, suspense, and musical genres (Zhong, 1991), while the end of 1989 witnessed an unexpected rise in the production of historical epics such as *Founding of the Nation* (Kaiguo dadian; dir. Li Qiankuan and Xiao Guiyun, 1989), a portrayal of the days leading to the establishment of the PRC, and *Baise Rebellion* (Baise qiyi; dir. Chen Jialin, 1989), a biographical picture about an uprising lead by Deng Xiaoping in his twenties. The year of 1991, later labeled the "Year of Revolutionary History Films with Significant Subjects" (*zhongda geming lishi ticai nian*), saw the culmination of Main Melody films with the appearances in films top leaders and key events of China's revolution. For example, *Decisive Engagements* (Da juezhan; dir. Cai Jiwei, Yang Guangyuan and Wei Lian, 1991), a ten-hour epic with three parts depicting the three major military campaigns between the Communist and Nationalist armies during the

Civil War (1945–1949). The story of *Creation of the World* (Kaitian pidi; dir. Li Xiepu, 1991) goes back to the end of the 1910s, when Marxism was first introduced to China. *Mao Zedong and His Son* (Mao Zedong he tade erzi; dir. Zhang Jinbiao, 1991) tries to portray Mao from a more human and senti- mental perspective, focusing on Mao's selflessness in sending his son to the front in the Korean War, and his fatherly sorrow when he learns that his son died in an air raid. Main Melody films also portray subjects such as socialist construction and model workers' or party cadres' dedication to the Party. For example, *Sun on the Roof of the World* (Shijie wuji de tai yang; dir. Wang Ping, 1991) deals with the industrialization of Tibet; *The Nanpu Bridge* (Qingsa pujiang; dir. Shi Xiaohua, 1991) focuses on the construction of the Nanpu Bridge in Shanghai; and *Her Smile Through the Candlelight* (Zhuguang li de weixiao; dir. Wu Tianren, 1991) shows a loving school teacher's selfless dedication to her students. At this stage of their development, Main Melody films were largely a continuation of the socialist realist film ideology of the early 1950s, demonstrating an unapologetic emphasis on party leaders, his- torical events, and victory of the Party.

The makers of these films were mostly trained in state film schools in the 1960s, and entered the film world in the 1960s or 1970s. For example, Cai Jiwei, the director of the *Decisive Engagements* trilogy, started to make films as a cameraman in *A Sparkling Star* (Shanshan de hongxing, 1974), a quintes- sential socialist-realist film of the Cultural Revolution period, and had made two other war films before *Decisive Engagements*. These filmmakers were not influ- enced by Republican-era cinema, which included films of realism with social criticism produced by private studios in Shanghai. Instead, these directors were more familiar with the glossy and non-naturalistic style of socialist-realist cin- ema, and with subjects that supported Party rhetoric. Filmmakers who either grew up in the tradition of Republican-era cinema, such as Xie Jin, or worked outside of the official moviemaking system, such as Feng Xiaogang, Zhang Yimou, were rarely granted opportunities to work on these films.

Although the Main Melody films have become an established genre in the development of Chinese cinema since 1990, their "triumph" was only nomi- nal. These films did not succeed in re-constructing a cinema of heroic images and didactic messages that dominated in the first three decades of the PRC. Meanwhile, because of the extravagant cost of production, Main Melody films drained the industry of already limited state-sponsorship in production and brought the state-owned studios more financial troubles. For example, *Pingjin Campaign*, costing 20 million RMB to make, made only 5.4 million RMB at the box office, leaving a deficit of over 15 million RMB. *Sun on the Roof of the World* and *Qingsa Pu River* also incurred large losses. *Sun on the*

Roof of the World spent 1.9 million RMB in production, but collected only 460 thousand RMB.

Although the basic doctrine of these films continued unchanged through the 1990s, Main Melody films in the mid-1990s began to undergo a transformation. Some changes can be seen in characters, subject matters, and style. First, the clichés in portraying characters and events were replaced by more realistic and not too idealized depictions. For instance, *Choice Between Life and Death* (Shengsi jueze; dir. Yu Benzheng and Zhang Ping, 2000) features a city mayor who is not only a loyal and virtuous Party cadre, but also a "family man" — a loving husband and father. The movie tells the story of his decisive struggle in a case of official corruption that involves his wife. *Postman in the Mountains* (Nasha, naren, nagou; dir. Huo Jianqi, 1998) is about an old postman's last trip to deliver mail to villages in a desolate mountain area. While still consistent with Party propaganda, these films do not directly glorify the Party and its leaders, but promote general virtues such as patriotism, self-sacrifice, and loyalty in ordinary Chinese people. For example, *The Accused Uncle Shan Gang* (Beigao Shangang ye; dir. Fan Yuan, 1995), features a case of whether an old Party secretary in the village should be held responsible for the death of a woman who commits suicide after being ordered by the secretary to submit to public humiliation as punishment for her mistreatment of her mother-in-law. This film was highly praised by film officials as an example of Main Melody films of the mid-1990s. In style, Main Melody films abandoned their emphasis on theatrical qualities such as frontality, stationary camera work, and long takes, and began to borrow devices such as fast-pace editing and multi-line narrative. Moreover, cinematic novelties such as three-dimensional animation and special effects were also incorporated into Main Melody films. However, despite these changes, Main Melody films continued to rely heavily on government support for distribution and promotion. Although still functioning as mouthpieces of the government and propagating the government's new policies and heroic models, or simply legitimizing the *status quo*, the changing face of Main Melody films suggests a concurrent transformation in the Party art policy, specifically, a switch from the glorification of Party and state leaders to broader themes stressing common virtues such as patriotism, self-sacrifice, and loyalty.

Another interesting trend in the 1990s is that non-political entertainment films, including the art films of Fifth Generation directors, began to toe the party line. The earlier attitudes of criticism and cynicism towards social issues were less pronounced, while the messages conveyed became more supportive of official policy.

Entertainment Films

Unlike Main Melody films that enjoyed tremendous support from the government but received only lukewarm welcome among audiences, entertainment films were frequently treated with indifference by film officials, but enjoyed great popularity among audiences. Many popular cinematic trends of the 1980s, such as the adaptations of Wang Shuo's works, were viewed by many film officials as products of the "bourgeois liberalization" of the mid-1980s. Consequently, in the post-1989 socio-political milieu, these officials felt an urgent need to "purify" Chinese cinema and save it from the damages of "bourgeois liberalization." The more liberal vice-minister of the MRFT, Chen Haosu, who enthusiastically promoted "entertainment films" in the 1980s, was dismissed from his position. The film policy that he had supported also underwent a dramatic change. The orthodox Communist art and literature agenda of the "Two Serves" (*er wei*) — meaning that literature and art should serve the people and socialism — was reinforced as the fundamental film policy. Declaring that cinema should serve socialism, film officials returned to the former orthodoxy concerning the function of cinema, while the previously promoted entertaining function fell into disfavor. In the aftermath of the 1989 Tian'anmen Incident, the debate in the mid-1980s over entertainment films finally came to an end, and the Party's emphasis on Main Melody film signaled the return of a conservative ideological atmosphere.

In the 1990s, a new round of economic reforms, which placed market demand in the foreground, also had its influence on Chinese cinema. In the film industry, this reform, like the one in the mid-1980s, first affected the distribution system and ticket pricing. Although the 1987 reform was intended to free studios from the CFC monopoly by allowing provincial or local distributors to participate in film distribution, it, unfortunately, complicated the situation of film distribution for the studios. Whereas they had previously needed only to deal with CFC, now they had to negotiate with more than thirty distributors for a film that was to be distributed nationwide. Moreover, as the whole industry was pushed into the forefront of a market economy, government involvement in the form of financial support was reduced dramatically. Once fully supported by the government, the film industry now received less than 50 million RMB annually, only enough to produce 30 films at an average budget of 1 million to 1.5 million RMB. Facing a film production target of 100 films a year, state-owned studios had to rely on non-governmental investments to make around sixty films. Given these circumstances, although the film authority strove to keep film ideology under its control, it could hardly refuse investments from non-state institutions. As a result, investments from private domestic and foreign film companies, including many from Taiwan and Hong Kong, were involved in China's domestic film production under the name of "co-production" with state film studios. In this sort of co-production, state studios only nominally participated in the process of production by collecting licensing fees, while the non-state companies were responsible for the majority of film production. Therefore, despite the burgeoning of Main Melody film and revival of the conservative view toward cinema among film officials, non-political entertainment films remained an essential category in the Chinese film industry. Among 151 films produced by the sixteen state film studios in 1992, only three, *Pingjin Campaign*, *The Story of Mao Zedong*, and *Liu Shaoqi's 44 Days*, could be described as "Revolutionary History Films with Significant Subjects." At the same time, out of 22 films bearing licenses from the Beijing Film Studio, two-thirds were co-productions.

Throughout the 1990s, entertainment films thrived in an awkward situation. In spite of the vital role they played in supporting the Chinese film market, their importance was not recognized by either art officials or film critics. In the talks by and documents of film officials, it was still Main Melody films that attracted most attention, while entertainment films were considered only a useful source for subsidizing film production. They were perceived as the "milk cows" for the operation of state film studios and official film institutions, but always suspected as the potentially dangerous outsider that received marginal treatment in official rhetoric.

The Fifth Generation

In the second half of the 1990s, filmmakers who were not financially supported by the state sought alternative modes of production. However, the fact that their funding came from various non-governmental sources did not prevent these films from becoming more entertaining and less politically critical. This trend can be seen clearly in the films of the Fifth Generation directors, whose film productions relied primarily on foreign capital. As Hollywood began to export its films to the domestic Chinese market, it also began to be involved in Chinese film productions. Their first bankable assets in China were the by then internationally famous Fifth Generation directors. Zhang Yimou's *Hero* (Yingxiong, 2002) was produced by Miramax; Chen Kaige's *Temptress of Moon* (Feng yue, 1996) was financed by a Hong Kong company; and *Together* (He ni zai yiqi, 2003) received investment from Sony. Although these films had adequate financial support and advanced filmmaking equipment, the demands for maximization of profit meant that they were inevitably designed as profit-generating tools. As a result, the center of the filmmaking process became the producer, rather than the director. The producer, representing investors and foreign studios, supervised every aspect of filmmaking from shooting to editing, and retained authority over the final cut. Under the impact of this mode of production, films of the Fifth Generation began to become less political and more commercialized. Priority was placed on pleasing audiences and meeting market demands, while the filmmakers' own intentions had to be compromised if they might impair box-office revenue. Chen Kaige had to re-edit *The Emperor and the Assassin* (Ci qing, 1999) after the initial viewing by critics and the press because many felt that the structure and narrative of the film were incomprehensible. When promoting the film *Hero* (2003) in an interview with CCTV (China Central Television), Zhang Yimou commented that the version of his final cut of the film was around 120 minutes, but because of the demands of the producer from Miramax, who pointed out that an American audience's interest in foreign language subtitled films usually lasted no more than 90 minutes, Zhang had to cut 30 minutes from the original version. In addition to changes in structure and length, many of these filmmakers abandoned the politically critical stance that had characterized their earlier films. The adoption of a critical political stance was very likely to cause troubles with the censors and thus posed the risk that the films might not reach the market. Therefore, films by Fifth Generation directors in the second half of the 1990s began to share with other films a similar ambition to achieve good market performance and avoidance of controversy. For example, after making *Farewell My Concubine* in 1993, whose retrospection of the Chinese people's painful experiences during the previous decades of social flux and political campaigns had caused censorship delays, Chen Kaige's next four films — *The Emperor and The Assassin*, *Temptress Moon* (Feng yue, 1996), *Killing Me Softly* (2002), and *Together* (He ni zai yiqi, 2002) — steered clear of overt criticism and retrospection. Rather, they featured thrilling suspense (*Killing Me Softly*), a story of a father's self sacrifice for his talented son (*Together*), and themes of love and betrayal (*Temptress Moon*). As the Fifth Generation's films became less political, they became increasingly commercialized throughout the early 2000s.

Private Film Companies

In the 1990s, the semi-independent or co-dependent cinema, which consisted primarily of films produced by private film production companies and distributed by state-owned sectors, also began to explore ways of making films that were attractive to film audiences and inoffensive to film authorities.

Though privately produced, these films still required approval for exhibition from the censors, and a license from a state-owned studio in order to enter distribution channels. Unlike state-sponsored films, these films had a diversity in their subject matters. However, because they relied on state film studios for distribution, they remained under the surveillance of film censorship. Therefore, any explicit criticism of sensitive issues could cause troubles with censorship and thus a loss at the box-office. This issue was of considerably more importance for these private filmmakers than it was for Fifth Generation filmmakers who enjoyed adequate financial support from foreign investors and access to overseas markets. Films by private companies had to rely on a relatively restricted budget during production and a limited domestic film market.

Although these films were mostly in the genres of non-political subjects such as comedy, romance, and urban melodrama, it was inevitable that they merged with the genres once identified most strongly with Main Melody films. Ye Daying's films, *Red Cherry* (Hong yingtao, 1995) and *Once Upon A Time in China* (Hongse liangren, 1998), made by his own production company and relatively successful at the box-office, are good examples of this merger. *Red Cherry*, a story of two children's experiences during World War Two, takes a humane approach to the question of individual suffering during the war. But these children's unusual backgrounds — both have parents who are high-ranking Chinese communist officials who died during the civil war — and their constant recounting of their parents' heroic acts emphasize the dedication of elite Chinese communists to the Chinese revolution, a hallmark of many Main Melody films. In *Once Upon A Time In China* (Hongse lianren), a young college student, the daughter of an officer in the secret police, is in love with an underground Communist and wants to help him to escape her father's persecution. Beneath the main storyline of doomed love, the story also draws attention to the trials and sacrifices endured by lovers for the sake of revolution. A similar mode of setting sentimental stories against the background of China's revolution, and combining ordinary people's personal experiences with grand themes such as patriotism, self-sacrifice, and collectivism can also be found in films such as *Days Without Lei Feng* (Likai leifeng de rizi; dir. Lei Xianhe, 1997), *Red River Valley* (Hong hegu; dir. Feng Xiaoning, 1997) and *Love Story By the Yellow River* (Huanghe juelian; dir. Feng Xiaoning, 1999). Most of the films follow the official rhetoric about China's current situation, revolution, history, and the Party. Feng Xiaogang's New Year Films are also good examples of this kind of film. His New Year Films — *Party A, Party B* (Jianfang yifang, 1997), *Be There Or Be Square* (Bujian busan, 1998), *Sorry Baby!* (Meiwan meiliao, 1999), *Big Shot's Funeral* (Da wan, 2002) and others such as *Sigh* (Yi sheng tanxi, 2000), *Cell Phone* (Shou ji, 2003), *A World Without Thieves* (Tianxia wuzei, 2004), *The Banquet* (Ye yan, 2006), *Assembly* (Jijie hao, 2007), *If You Are the One* (Feicheng wurao, 2008), and *Aftershock* (Tangshan da dizhen, 2010) — have consistently achieved box-office success. These films not only reflect the changing social-political contexts of Chinese cinema since the mid-1990s, but also demonstrate the nation-wide growth of popular cinema, a cinema that meets the needs of domestic audiences instead of serving as political propaganda or catering to the demands of international film festivals.

Hollywood Imports

In 1994, the Chinese Film Import and Export Corporation signed a contract with major Hollywood studios to import ten Hollywood films each year with a promise to raise the quota gradually until China's entry into the World Trade Organization, after which Hollywood would be allowed to export films to China without any restrictions or quotas. In 1995, ten Hollywood block-busters, including *True Lies* and *The Fugitive*, entered Chinese movie theaters, bringing with them both hope and danger for Chinese cinema. These blockbuster films attracted audiences back to movie theaters, thus play-ing a driving force in the rejuvenation of a weak film market. Attendance had waned since the early 1990s and had shown a significant decline of 60% in 1993, but the box-office revenue of the Hollywood films showed a resur-gence of audience interest. *True Lies* had revenues of 8 million RMB in Beijing and 13 million in Shanghai; Jackie Chan's *Rumble in the Bronx* broke a record with revenues of 3 million RMB in Guangzhou. Although these Hollywood films lured audiences back to the movies, most domestic films, with meager production budgets averaging only about fifty thousand dollars per film, had little hope of competing successfully with the multi-million dol-lar American productions. Therefore, although several domestic films met with success in 1995, most domestic films became increasingly unappealing to audiences who gradually became accustomed to the high production qua-lity of Hollywood blockbusters. The annual domestic film production of 1995 and 1996 was around 100 films per year; however, these films received only 30% of box office revenues, while the other 70% went to the ten Hollywood imports. And during the 45 days that *Titanic* was screened in Beijing, it earned amazingly four million US dollars at the box office, equivalent to 30% of Beijing's film market revenue that year. In the late 1990s, an underground mar-ket of cheap pirated versions of Hollywood films at an average price of 7 or 8 RMB per film resulted in the flooding of many more Hollywood films throughout China. Given all this, the Hollywood invasion generated both enthusiasm and alarm in Chinese cinema; its attractions seemed at once irresistible and disturbing.

The Sixth Generation and Underground Cinema

The underground cinema, sometimes labeled Sixth Generation, was nearly invisible on the landscape of Chinese cinema in the 1990s. The obscurity resulted from an absence of opportunity or desire to make films within the official film production system. Most of the film academy graduates of this group made films that did not rely on any official filmmaking entities. As a result, these films were inaccessible to ordinary Chinese audiences. However, in the early 2000s, these works began to attract the attention of foreign film critics at international film festivals. Lou Ye's *Suzhou River* won the Tiger Award at the 2000 Rotterdam International Film Festival and Wang Xiaoshuai's *Beijing Bicycle* won the Silver Bear at the Berlin International Film Festival in 2003. Also in the early 2000s, when there was relaxation in the Chinese political scene, these filmmakers surfaced from the underground, joined mainstream filmmaking, and began to be noticed by domestic audiences. Although the influence of these filmmakers on Chinese cinema of the 1990s was relatively insignificant, they demonstrate the promising potential for Chinese film in the 2000s.

This group of filmmakers' cinematic styles took form in the 1990s. In *Xiaoshan Returns Home* (Xiaoshan huijia, ca. 1996) and *Xiaowu* (Xiaowu, 1997), Jia Zhangke developed his own cinematic style characterized by the use of non-professional actors filmed by hand-held camera and stories of people living in urbanized rural areas rapidly marginalized by a transforming society. Wang Xiaoshuai's films, such as *The Days* (Dongchun de gushi, 1993) and *Frozen* (Jidu hanleng, 1996), though far more traditional in filmmaking — steady camera, well-framed composition, and professional acting — express his concerns for a reality that provides people with more illusory than real benefits. Although the production value of these films could not compete with that of the state or commercial production companies, they willingly did what mainstream filmmakers were unable to do, especially in terms of addressing the dark side of the society. Their films criticized social problems such as poverty and class discrepancy and drew attention to people from the lower levels of society. However, starting at the end of the 1990s, more and more independent filmmakers have been able to move out of the peripheries toward the center and began to make films with the commercial filmmaking system. In some cases, making a successful independent film has become a passport for entry into the mainstream. In the early 2000s, some Sixth Generation filmmakers, such as Luo Ye, Zhang Yuan, Jia Zhangke, and Wang Xiaoshuai, began to work with commercial production companies to make films.

Part Four: Chinese Cinema in the New Millenium

The WTO and "the Corporate Era" of Chinese Film Industry

On December 11, 2001, after lengthy negotiations beginning in 1986, China officially became the 143rd member of the World Trade Organization (WTO). China's long delayed entrance into the WTO was due to debates regarding the impact this entry would have on the global economy. On the one hand, as the most populous country in the world, China is the world's largest market. Its market of over 1.3 billion people provides corporations with opportunities for rapid growth in product sales. On the other hand, the cheap labor, inexpensive industrial land, and educated workforce that make China an ideal manufacturing center also threaten other established centers. Not only would developing countries that had historically offered cheap labor suffer from Chinese competition, developed countries, such as the US, were also threatened with the loss of thousands of manufacturing jobs. But attitudes toward China's entry into the WTO varied in different industries, depending on the expected benefits or losses that would result. Businessmen who favored China's accession to the WTO included Hollywood moguls, who envisioned great potential benefits for Hollywood. According to Jack Valenti, the chairman and Chief Executive Officer of the Motion Picture Association of America, China promised the Hollywood film industry that the following benefits would be given to Hollywood upon China's entry into the WTO (Valenti, 2000):

- China will double the quota of "revenue sharing" films from 10 to 20. (Revenue sharing means that China splits the box office receipts on a 50–50 basis). China will also allow an additional 20 foreign films per year on flat fee licensing terms. By the third year, the combined film quota will be increased from 40 to 50 films.
- China will, for the first time, permit foreign investment in joint ventures engaged in the distribution of videos.
- China will lift its investment ban on cinema ownership. U.S. investors will be allowed to own up to 49% of companies that build, own, and operate cinemas.

- China will reduce tariffs on films from the current level of 9% of the value of the film to 5%. Tariffs on home videos will drop from 15% to 10%.
- China will also assume full obligations to protect intellectual property, as required by the WTO's Agreement on Trade Related Intellectual Property.

All these measures, which seemed to offer few reciprocal benefits for China, if fully implemented, would lift almost all the major barriers to the entrance of Hollywood films into Chinese market. The potential gain for Hollywood was huge. Valenti estimated in a talk delivered in 1999 that "if the barriers to film distribution were lifted, and if a legitimate video sales and rentals market captured the market now lost to piracy, an increase in US revenues in China in excess of $200 million is achievable" (Valenti, 1999). The rosy future of Hollywood in China means that domestic Chinese cinema would eventually face an expansion of the menace that had been hanging over the Chinese market even before Valenti's optimistic talk. Starting in 2003, as part of its obligations as a member of the WTO, China raised the quota of imported films to 20 per year. Although the box-office revenues of these films did not match the impressive amounts recorded by Hollywood imports in the 1990s (mainly the result of pervasive cheap pirated versions and inadequate show times due to a limited number of screens and first-class movie theaters), their potential should not be underestimated. In 2003, the total box-office revenue of the top ten among the twenty imported films, all from Hollywood, was 299 million US dollars, which is much more than the 200 million estimated by Valenti. It was not until 2004 that the total box office revenue of domestic films exceeded that of the imports, with 10% more income than imported films. But a closer examination of this figure shows that the success is somewhat misleading. The total revenue of Chinese films was generated by 212 domestic films, while only around 20 imported films took 45% of total box-office revenue. In recent years, when the number of imported films doubled, domestic films struggled to maintain such a record.

Facing pressure from Hollywood imports, a new round of industry reform on an even more dramatic scale was implemented in the early 2000s. Beginning in 1999, some state-owned studios began to be either reconstructed as joint-venture companies or incorporated into large entertainment-related enterprises. Next, as the three sectors of production, distribution, and exhibition were opened to private companies, many local and international investors got involved in the moviemaking industry. Films made by these local, non-state production companies gradually became a vital force in Chinese cinema. The beginning of these reforms started in the state-owned film studios. Beijing Film Studio, the most prolific filmmaking center in the 1990s, and other filmmaking-related institutions in Beijing, including Beijing Film Printing and Recording Factory, China Film Equipment Company, China Film Co-Production Corporation, and the Movie Channel of China Central TV station, were merged into a large enterprise called China Film Group (CFG). This merger in 1999 represented the first stage of reform — the transformation of state-owned studios into media empires consisting of all vertical sections of the film industry. In 2004, another major move regarding the ownership of the supposedly state-owned enterprises was taken by CFG. After several international media companies became shareholders in some of CFG's subsidiary companies, the group was changed from a property of the state to a Chinese-foreign joint-venture enterprise. In November 2004, Sony Picture Television Group and China Film Group co-organized a company, Huasuo TV and Film Digital Production, which was to focus on digital TV and film production, with CFG holding 51% of the company shares and Sony 49%. At around the same time, another of CFG's subsidiary production companies, a company specializing in co-productions with foreign companies, Zhongying Hua'an Hengdian Film and TV Corporation Ltd., was founded through investments from CFG, the Hengdian Group (a private enterprise whose business encompasses electronics, pharmaceutical and chemical production, film and entertainment, and property investment), and Time Warner Inc. The previously state-owned Beijing Film Studio, after merging all its assets with the CFG, not only became one of the subsidiary branches of the parent company CFG, but was also physically removed from its site in a busy area in the northwestern part of the city and relocated to the northeastern outskirts of the city where a huge complex consisting of 20 shooting stages, a public square, and movie theaters was constructed. The director of BFS, Han Sanping, though optimistic about the capacity for filmmaking at the new site and the possibility of meeting BFS's target of producing 10 films annually after its merger with the CGF, remained concerned that BFS would become merely a production unit of one of CFG's subsidiary companies. As a result, the previously preeminent and self-contained Beijing Film Studio was almost history.

Another mode of reform, the acquisition of state-owned film studios by groups or enterprises whose own businesses were not related to film production, is represented by the reconstruction of the Changchun Film Studio (CFS), one of the earliest Communist filmmaking centers. In 2000, Changchun Film Studio announced its intent to reorganize the studio into a joint-stock company with Guoxin Investment Group. Guoxin, a provincial investment enterprise engaging in real estate construction and management, was to invest 13.5 million RMB in the project. If the re-organization of the Beijing Film Studio provided certain possibilities for the strengthening of the studio, the deal between CFS and Guoxin was more of an exploitation of the assets and properties of the state-owned studio. Since the end of the 1990s, in the name of co-development, Guoxin's newly constructed real estate projects have occupied the majority of the land where CFS's production studios were once located. Accused of selling out state-properties, the director of the CFS, Zhao Guoguang (also a major shareholder in Guoxin), promised to use 3 billion RMB earned from selling CFS's land to Guoxin plus bank loans to build a theme-park/movie theater equivalent to Universal Studios in Los Angeles. This project, consisting of technologically advanced movie theaters and other film-related adventure projects, would be located in the outskirts of the city of Changchun.

In both cases, after the selling of the studios' physical facilities, new production centers remained only in the planning stages and the film production of both studios declined dramatically. Most "productions" of these two state-owned studios in recent years have been only nominally linked to the studios. The studios have merely outsourced their equipment or staff and casts to film projects undertaken by private or foreign companies, rather than truly participating in the whole process of moviemaking. In 2004, CFS produced 13 films, but none were made independently by the studio. In 2005, one of the major feature films on the production list of CFS was a Sino-American co-production, *Smile* (Weixiao; dir. Jeffery Kramer, 2005). In this film, investment from CFS was only 10% of the total production budget, and none of the scriptwriters, directors, or cast members came from CFS.

The "corporate era" of Chinese cinema brought some significant changes that were unthinkable in the decades when the cinema was fully controlled by the Party as a propaganda tool. Most importantly, the involvement of foreign capital in all sectors of the film industry undermined the very ideological foundations of Chinese cinema. Previously regarded as a didactic tool to support Party policy, Chinese cinema increasingly had to answer to the demands of domestic and foreign investors for profits. As a result, Party film policy had to change in order to both legitimize the Party-approved industry reforms and to lift barriers that had served as impediments to the progress of reform. The drive for profit and commercialization in every possible way became a major preoccupation of the Chinese filmmaking industry in the early 2000s.

Domestic Turn of the Fifth Generation Cinema

If the second half of the 1990s featured four different modes of production, the early years of the new Millennium witnessed a ubiquitous compliance with the mainstream tendency toward commercialization, as filmmakers from all backgrounds — Fifth or Sixth Generation filmmakers, specialists in Main Melody or commercial films — were driven by the pervasive profit imperatives. This tendency was strengthened by the involvement of foreign film companies, especially from Hollywood, which excels in turning 90–120 minute films into money-making machines, and in turning almost every aspect of moviemaking into a lucrative business. The model of these foreign companies proved tantalizing to Chinese state and private film companies. Furthermore, the success of Feng Xiaogang's films at the domestic box-office in the late 1990s drew the attention of Chinese and foreign filmmakers to the potential of domestic filmmakers and films with localized subject matters. Therefore, the feverish commercialization of cinema has been accompanied by a domestic turn: the targeting of domestic audiences with the unmistakable goal of making profits. Not only have well-established Fifth Generation directors, such as Zhang Yimou and Chen Kaige, abandoned their elitist *auteur* pretensions and begun to make films meant to appeal to the general domestic audience, the previously subversive Sixth Generation directors, including Zhang Yuan, Jia Zhangke, and Lou Ye, have given up their positions as dissidents and begun to be absorbed into commercial film production.

Starting in the new millennium, Fifth Generation directors have shown an unapologetic attitude toward the making of pure entertainment films. Zhang Yimou's collaboration with Zhang Weiping, the founder of Beijing New Picture Distribution Company (Beijing xin huamian yingye youxian gongsi), in 1996, signaled a turning point in his film career. Zhang Yimou's six films made after 1996, *Be Cool* (You hua haohao shuo, 1997), *The Road Home* (Wo de fuqin muqin, 1999), *Not One Less* (Yige dou bu neng shao, 1999), *Happy Times* (Xingfu shiguang, 2000), *Hero* (Yingxiong, 2002), *House of Flying Daggers* (Shimian maifu, 2004), *Riding Alone for Thousand Miles* (Qianli zou daqi, 2005), *Curse of the Golden Flowers* (Mancheng jin dai huangjin jia, 2006) and *A Woman, A Gun and A Noodle Shop* (Sanqiang paian jingqi, 2009) were all sponsored by the New Picture Company with market orientations.

In comparison with the films Zhang made before 1996, such as *To Live* (Huozhe, 1994), *Raise the Red Lantern* (Da hong denglong gaogao gua, 1991), and *Judou* (Ju dou, 1990), there are both similarities and differences with his more recent films. While Zhang has totally given up iconoclastic targeting of decadence and depravity in the Chinese political system (*To Live*), Chinese culture (*Raise the Red Lantern*), and humanity (*Judou*), he has continued to strive to produce films that are appreciated by film critics as well as the domestic film market. However, his attempts so far have failed to satisfy either side. For instance, in 2000, encouraged by the success of Feng Xiaogang's New Year films, he followed suit with the film *Happy Times*, targeting the New Year audience. The film tells the story of Zhao, an aging bachelor and an unemployed factory worker, who woos an obese woman by claiming that he is a manager of a hotel. Taking advantage of his love and "wealth," his new girlfriend shirks her responsibility for raising her blind step-daughter and lets the man take care of her. Zhao and his former colleagues, all unemployed workers, devise one ploy after another to fool the girl into believing his lies. In the process, a tender friendship develops. In an interview, Zhang explains that *Happy Times* is a tragi-comedy (*beixiju*), through which he wants to provide a touching story about honest human relationships in a materialistic world. However, this intention appears not to have reached his audiences. The film was first released in January 2001 in Dalian, the northeast port-city where the film was shot. According to an article published in *Yangcheng Wanbao* (Yangcheng evening news) on March 15, 2001, the film's open ending, which does not provide any clear resolutions for the blind girl's fate nor of Zhao's plot to cover up his lies, disappointed not only early audiences in Dalian and Beijing but also potential foreign distributors. In order to save the film from a box-office disaster, Zhang recalled the whole cast and crew and re-shot the entire ending. Re-released in Shanghai and Guangzhou in March, the new version, which is now circulated in the overseas market, ends with the girl knowing all Zhao's plots and leaving him to find her father in the South; Zhao is killed in a car accident while looking for her. This ending still did not manage to rescue the film at the box-office. The tragic ending was totally out-of-sync with the traditional happy celebration of the Chinese New Year. In the first Saturday of the film's initial release in Shanghai, one of the first-run theaters sold only sixteen tickets. In Huanyi Theater, another first-run movie theater, the total income of the first week of exhibition was only 16,000 RMB, while another much less known domestic film, *Gua Sha Treatment* (Gua sha; dir. Zheng Xiaolong, 2001) earned 60,000 RMB (Cai, 2001). The box-office failure of *Happy Times* was not offset by positive film reviews. Harsh reviews criticizing flaws in the plot and narrative, the altered ending, Zhang's inability to deal with contemporary subjects, and the methods used in casting the film (Zhang used a national campaign to recruit the leading characters), appeared in almost all major newspapers in China.

Zhang's attempt to cater to the tastes of a popular audience by altering the ending after the film was already released resulted in miserable total box-office revenues of only around 8 million RMB nationwide, almost four times less than the income of Feng Xiaogang's *Big Shot's Funeral*, released at the end of the same year.

Apparently having learnt his lesson from his failed attempt at New Year films, Zhang's later films, mostly set in ancient China, began to follow another trend that seemed more promising not only domestically, but also internationally. In 2000, Taiwan-American film director Ang Lee's *Crouching Tiger, Hidden Dragon* (Wohu canglong), collected four Oscars at the 73rd Annual Academy Awards. Whereas Chinese fans of martial arts films, who are accustomed to the astonishing high-flying fights common in Hong Kong cinema, giggled with disdain over the artificial special effects and naïve plots of *Crouching Tiger*, American audiences found it poetic and attractive (Mitchel, 2000). In China, the unexpected awards and acclaim the film received from the US inspired many Chinese filmmakers to explore the potential of this genre. He Ping made *Warriors of Heaven and Earth* (Tiandi yingxiong, 2003), a Tang Dynasty (7th AD–10th AD) story of two warriors' endeavor to protect a princess on an adventure trip, while Chen Kaige's blockbuster *Promise* (Wu ji), a mixture of action, mystery, fantasy, and romance, was shown in 2004.

In the early 2000s, Zhang Yimou made two martial arts films. *Hero* provides a new take on the millennia-old tale of the assassination of the King of Qin. Narratively similar to Akiro Kurosawa's film *Rashomon* (1950), in which four witnesses to a murder have strikingly contradictory accounts of the event, *Hero* tells the story of the assassination from different characters' perspectives. However, dwarfed by its exquisite computer-generated visual effects, the contradictory accounts of stories and counter-stories in *Hero* do not succeed in creating an equally exquisite sense of narrative complexity. Instead, audiences were frequently distracted by the beautiful but excessively poetic renditions of fights and war scenes, and the constantly shifting perspectives created more confusion than suspense. And anachronisms of many contemporary expressions such as "one-night stand" (*yi ye qing*) and "peace" (*he ping*) in the dialogues between swordsmen and kings from the Third Century BC caused much laughter and giggling at the theater. Like *Hero*, *House of Flying Daggers* features beautifully crafted visual effects, but has fatal flaws in the narrative. Set in the Tang Dynasty, the film is an action/suspense/love story between a local captain and a member of an anti-government organization. In addition to several less than compelling plots, the most prominent flaw is the unusual "deaths" of the female protagonist in the second half of the film. After her "death," she is brought back to life on four occasions to save her lover.

These two films distinguish themselves from Zhang's films in the early 1990s by their clear profitmaking intention. They feature an international cast of bankable Asian stars from Mainland China, Hong Kong, Japan, and Taiwan and deploy extensively Zhang's hallmarks of visuality in order to attract audiences in Asia and the world. They were also promoted with an unmistakable concern for maximizing profits. *Hero* became the first non-Main Melody film to be advertised in official Party organs. Its trailer was shown on stations of China Central TV as well as other local stations; even the most influential prime time news show of CCTV, *Xinwen Lianbo*, a hard-line promoter of the Party's domestic and international policies, devoted two minutes to its opening. The Ministry of Culture even issued an official document requesting local film authorities to prevent and confiscate pirated versions of *Hero*. Although pirated DVDs and VCDs have been extremely pervasive in China for almost a decade, the Ministry of Culture has only issued two official documents urging its local departments to take measures against piracy. The administrative document regarding *Hero* is the only one specifically related to a domestic Chinese film.

Product Placement in Film

Although some popular films in the 1990s contained some criticism of the expansion of consumerism and commercialization, they became much less cynical and pointed in the early 2000s. With the sponsorship of brand name companies and the pressures of profit making, popular cinema, represented by Feng Xiaogang's films, have inevitably collaborated with the menacing power of consumerism.

In a talk delivered at China's Communication University after the 2004 release of *A World Without Thieves*, Feng admitted that several plots of the films were deliberately designed to attract the audiences and thus to ensure good box-office revenue. According to him, the sentimental ending where the husband, played by Hong Kong popular movie star Andy Lau, is killed ruthlessly by Uncle Li, was specifically designed to for its tear-jerking effect (Zhao, 2004). He said that in order to appeal to the audience's expectation for funny dialogues and humorous lines, the hallmarks of his early films, he had to sacrifice the stylistic consistency of his tragic films by adding some farcical scenes. One such scene was a robbery that was rendered more like a hilarious and playful prank than a frightening and dangerous act. Feng conceded that this scene was totally at odds with the style of the film, but "as long as the audiences like it, my style has to be sacrificed" (Zhao, 2004).

In addition to the pressure from profit making, Feng also has to deal with his investors' needs. Feng's production company and the backer of almost all his recent films, Huayi Brother TV and Film Investment Company, attracts investors by allocating slots for appearances of commercial logos and products in the films. In this fashion, instead of relying solely on the production company's own money, the financial pressures of film production are shared by sponsors who are promoting their products in a popular film. However, this arrangement increases pressure on the film director, as he has to find appropriate ways to present the sponsors' products or logos in the films. Furthermore, the greater the investments a film attracts, the more ads a film has to bear. As a result, if a film is financed by many companies from different industries, the film has to function as a lengthy series of exquisite and sophisticated commercials by placing as many products as possible. Often these promotions are too overt. For example, in *Sigh* (2000), the story of an intimate family affair, signs of commercial ads, brand names, and product slogans are everywhere: Ikea furniture fills the protagonist's newly decorated apartment; his secret meetings with his lover take place in one of Beijing's Starbucks; one of the subplots in the film concerns the scriptwriter's search for a new apartment in which his wife constantly mentions a real estate project, even giving specific information of its location, prices and quality. Not surprisingly, all these brand names can be found in the film's list of sponsors in the final credits.

At a press conference held by the Huayi Brother investment company before the shooting of *Cell Phone* (2003), the president and CEO of Huayi, Wang Zhongjun, announced that the company had already signed investment and advertisement contracts with four companies — Motorola, BMW, China Mobile, and Mtone Wireless — whose investments in the film comprised almost half of the total budget. What the four companies got in return was numerous placements of their products in the film. A film about cell phones certainly provided an ideal platform for advertisements of cell phones. From beginning to end, the audience was introduced to (or, bombarded with) the many special functions of the various models of Motorola cell phones used by every character in the film. The newest model of the year, MotoA70, was officially launched in the Chinese market through this film. Commercials for a wireless service provider, China Mobile, appeared many times in the film; and other brand names or products, such as BMW and a text message company, also appeared frequently. An upscale steakhouse owned by one of the sponsors of the film was not only mentioned by the main character verbally, but also became the location for the crucial scene of the first confrontation between his wife and his lover.

This practice of production promotion went into high gear with *If You Are the One*, which was released in December, 2008 in anticipation of the 2009 Chinese New Year. The film could easily be described as a series of ads strung together by a plot. But the film grossed more than 300 million RMB within a month. Following the venerable Hollywood tradition, a sequel was marketed before Christmas in 2010.

Part Five: Conclusion

During the first two decades after the Cultural Revolution, the emphasis on cinema's didactic and political functions had been the major concern of China's film authorities. Film companies not owned by the state consequently encountered more difficulties in gaining access to official channels of distribution and exhibition. Films of social criticism were always discouraged by film censorship. But entertainment films such as comedy and action films that did not challenge official Party rhetoric faced no such interference. If certain social commentary was necessary, it had to be carefully conducted beneath seemingly non-political scenes and plots, and addressed only to sophisticated audiences.

At the turn of the century, loosened ideological control and large scale industry reform intended to emancipate the industry from state monopolies in production, distribution, and exhibition gradually transformed a state-controlled and ideologically censored institution for the masses into a director/writer-centered and studio-owned popular medium for an urban audience. As a result, the early 2000s finally witnessed the prosperity of a popular cinema that not only proved irresistible to filmmakers from diverse backgrounds, but also gained a certain degree of support from film officials through new film policies and legislation. Meanwhile, the more open atmosphere also allowed more freedom for filmmakers in choosing the subjects of their films. The return of some social criticism in a few films would not have been possible without such changes in the film industry and ideology. However, as participants in a highly materialistic environment, Chinese filmmakers inevitably fell victim to the drive for profits. Although pressure from film officials regarding political correctness was lessened, the demand to maximize profits forced Chinese filmmakers to consider the box-office returns most seriously. Filmmaking has thus become a new and delicate act of balancing.

References

Cai, Y. (2001, April 21) Piaofang shouru jin shi ji wan, Zhang Yimou Shanghai zaoyu Huatielu (Only 10,000 at box office, Zhang Yimou's Waterloo in Shanghai), *Shanghai Qingnian Bao.*

Ministry of Radio, Film, and TV. (1997) *Dianying shencha tiaoli* (Regulations of film censorship). Beijing, China.

Mitchel, E. (2000, October 9) Action fans: Be prepared for heart and feminism. *New York Times.*

Valenti, J. (1999, June 8) Statement of Jack Valenti, Chairman and Chief Executive Officer, Motion Picture Association, before the Committee on ways and means subcommittee on trade, regarding US-China trade relations and the possible accession of China to the World Trade Organization. *Official Website of Motion Pictures Association of American.* Retrieved from http://www.mpaa.org/jack/99/99_6_8a.htm

Valenti, J. (2000, April 11) Valenti urged senate to grant PNRT to China. *Official Website of Motion Pictures Association of American.* Retrieved from http://www.mpaa.org/jack/2000/00_04_11a.htm

Yao, E. (1995) International fantasy and the "New Chinese cinema." *Quarterly Review of Film and Video*, 14(3), 100–105.

Zhao, N. (2004, December 27) Feng Xiaogang jiantao *Tianxia wuzei* (Feng Xiaogang criticizes *A World Without Thieves*). *Jinghua shibao.*

Zhong, C. (1991) 1988 Zhongguo yingtan de liang ge remen huati — "yule pian" yu "zhuxuan lu" zhi wo jian (1988: Two hot topics in Chinese cinema — My opinions on "entertainment films" and "Main Melody film"), *Zhongguo dianying nianjian 1991*. Beijing: Dianying chubanshe.

14

CONSUMPTION AND LEISURE

Kevin Latham

SOAS, University of London

Abstract

Leisure and consumption have become key features of post-Mao China being associated with economic reform, political change and stability, the legitimacy of the Communist Party and notions of modernity and post-modernity in China. This chapter offers an overview of the key characteristics of leisure and consumption in contemporary China with important historical contextualization. It identifies and introduces some of the most common analyses and understandings of consumption in China showing how they are often linked together. The chapter suggests that we need to treat the notion of consumption in China with caution to avoid oversimplification and neglect of the increasing complexity and diversification of Chinese leisure and consumption practices.

Keywords: Consumption; leisure; media; technology; modernity; politics

Introduction

The post-Mao era in China has become known as the "reform era" due to the fundamental importance of Deng Xiaoping's economic reforms in transforming so many aspects of everyday social life and interaction in China, not to mention all kinds of economic and cultural production, education, industry, agriculture, technology and communications. It is partly due to the economic nature of these reforms that this period of recent Chinese history has also been widely associated with a rapid rise in consumption and consumerism. The reforms were primarily focused on shifting production away from the

411

state and increasingly into private hands, but their emphasis on individual and household responsibility, individual skills and earning power as well as self-reliance and personal decision making at a time when personal disposable income was rising and the range of consumer goods available to Chinese people was dramatically diversifying, led inexorably towards greater consumption and the emergence of new consumer attitudes, values and expectations (Latham, 2006a; Davis, 2000; Link *et al.*, 1989, 2002; Davis and Vogel, 1990; Davis and Harrell, 1993; Li, 1998; Huot, 2000; Chen *et al.*, 2001).

Importantly, this period also saw a dramatic shift in the nature and quantity of leisure time that Chinese people, particularly in the cities, could enjoy with a shift from highly structured and often politicised periods of limited non-working time in the Mao period making way for shorter working hours, less work-unit organization of leisure activities, fewer political meetings and greater individual freedom in the post-Mao period (Wang, 1995). Consequently the issues of leisure and consumption in post-Mao China are closely interrelated. Much of people's extra leisure time has been passed spending their greater disposable income on eating, drinking, entertainment, on purchasing electronic consumer goods, paying for home improvements and more recently acquiring communications equipment of various kinds (principally mobile phones and computers). Consumption has also contributed to the dramatic transformation of social space in China, particularly in the cities where many domestic spaces have been transformed from dimly lit concrete-floored and simply-furnished apartment dwellings into well-illuminated, modern homes with parquet floors, air conditioning, European-designed flat-pack furniture, contemporary lighting and stylish kitchens (Davis, 1989, 2002). Meanwhile public spaces now include a range of shopping environments from street markets and the cheaper, densely packed and lively indoor market-style shopping malls popular with ordinary urban and suburban consumers to the shiny luxury malls housing international designer brand stores catering to China's elites and *nouveaux riches* (Thornton, 2010; Wang and Guo, 2007).

In the Mao period many basic necessities such as rice, flour and oil were rationed and distributed by the state while the availability of other consumer goods was often extremely limited. Consequently, it is easy to see why the reform period has also often been referred to in terms of China's "consumer revolution" (see e.g., Davis *et al.*, 2000; Chao and Myers, 1998; Li, 1998; Wu, 1999).[1] The

---

[1] Such a depiction clearly points to the scale of the changes that have occurred in terms of consumption in China over the last three decades, but, as I have pointed out elsewhere, it also runs the risk of distracting attention away from other important features of China's contemporary social landscape (see Latham, 2002, 2006).

emergence of widespread consumption and consumerism has undoubtedly been one of the most eye-catching features of China's rapidly changing social and economic landscape.

Scholarship on consumption in China over the last couple of decades has broadly speaking attempted to achieve two things with clear overlap and inter-action between the two. The first is to detail the practices and phenomena of consumption itself, largely as elements of ethnographic and historical interest in themselves. The second is to offer a more analytical consideration of how con-sumption figures within broader social, political and historical changes and transformations taking place in the country. These include for instance, debates about the political significance of consumption and consumerism for main-taining party legitimacy (Ci, 1994; Latham, 2002; Whyte, 2010), whether con-sumption constitutes a shift from modernity to postmodernity in contemporary China (Dirlik and Zhang, 1997; Tang, 1996; Liu, 1997) or the role that con-sumption plays in the emergence of China's much-discussed middle class (see e.g., Anagnost, 2008; Zhang, 2008; Tomba, 2004). These issues will be dis-cussed further below. However, within this literature we can also detect a movement towards more subtle and nuanced understandings of consumer prac-tices in China that pay greater attention to different contexts of consumption, the significance of diverse social backgrounds and the need to differentiate between urban and rural, large and smaller cities or eastern and western China. Indeed, it is important neither to over-homogenise the experiences and atti-tudes of Chinese consumers nor to oversimplify the significance of consumption and consumerism for understandings of contemporary China. Chinese con-sumption is not one unified set of social practices but a massively diverse array of behaviors that increasingly need to be considered in their own right rather than subsumed under one broader general category. With China undergoing massive and rapid social and economic transformations in recent decades it is also important to situate these diverse practices in their appropriate historical contexts.

In fact, even over the relatively short period of the post-Mao reform era, it is important to chart historical changes in Chinese consumption (see also Latham, 2007, pp. 239–245). The 1980s saw the depoliticization of con-sumption as well as the emergence of new consumption contexts, from private restaurants to street markets, and the expansion of the range of goods and services available to Chinese consumers. At this time there was a great sense of novelty and experimentation that characterised people's leisure activ-ities and consumption habits. People found themselves taking part in activities that just a few years earlier they would never have dreamed possible even if these activities, like shopping in a supermarket, going to a disco or a karaoke bar, might have been considered mundane or normal everyday activities in other parts of the world.

In the 1990s China's consumers started to mature considerably. They increasingly knew what they wanted, they became more selective about what they bought and they had a better understanding of consumer issues and consumer rights. Consumption became less novel in itself and the sense of experimentation moved away from the consumption *per se* to the exploration of new areas of consumption of which many emerged in this decade. For example, many foreign companies arrived in China bringing fast food chains like McDonalds and Kentucky Fried Chicken (Yan, 1999; Watson, 1999) and Hong Kong and Taiwanese businesses increasingly invested in theme parks, cinemas, restaurants, bowling alleys and many other leisure and entertainment enterprises. In terms of media consumption, the 1990s also saw important developments, most notably the expansion of cable and satellite television services, the shift from VHS video tapes to VCDs (video compact discs) and the increasing availability of both domestic and public telephony. In the 1990s the Chinese government also started actively promoting consumption as a means of driving and maintaining economic growth while also boosting the opportunities for Chinese companies in the domestic market. In 1995 the government promoted a two-day weekend for most Chinese workers and two years later two major national holidays — May 1 (labor day) and October 1 (National Day) — were both extended to one full week. Moreover, these holidays were soon accompanied by media stories explicitly linking this extended leisure time to consumption opportunities such as travel, the purchase of flats, home improvements or spending on electronic consumer goods (Pun, 2003, p. 471). This association of lengthy national holidays with consumption has since become an established feature of Chinese media reporting and given consumer-related stories several fixed slots in the Chinese media calendar.

These trends continued into the 2000s as leisure opportunities continued to proliferate. Golf courses appeared in the wealthier parts of the country (Giroir, 2007) and luxury consumption became increasingly widely available, from Ferraris, Rolls Royces and luxury villas through to designer luggage, clothing and connoisseur dining. Luxury consumption is still not mainstream and remains largely the prerogative of the very wealthy elite, but it has also increasingly found its way into ordinary consumers' everyday lives through media representations, from advertising to newspaper articles to television dramas. Consumption has now also developed in new directions with a focus on services as much as on goods. Chinese people are increasingly buying insurance, personal and professional training, value-added services for their mobile phones, language classes, tourist trips, holidays and much more.

Indeed, one of the most popular emerging forms of consumption — either actual or aspirational — in the 2000s has been of education (Pun, 2003, p. 483; Kipnis, 2010; Lin, 2006).

The 2000s also saw an increasing internationalization of Chinese leisure and consumption with overseas tourism becoming increasingly popular, especially with the burgeoning middle classes, with ever more international investment in China's leisure industries and the staging of international sporting events from golf and tennis tournaments to the first Formula 1 grand prix in Shanghai's specially built circuit in 2004. This trend culminated in the Beijing Olympics in 2008 and the Guangzhou Asian Games in 2010. Meanwhile technological developments have continued apace over the last decade with the rapid rise of Internet and mobile phone use dramatically transforming the Chinese popular cultural landscape.

Recent market surveys have suggested that Chinese consumers in 2010 have become far more pragmatic, with a keen eye on both value for money and the bottom line. They often look to "trade up" to better quality products that are important to them, but in order to do so will reduce expenditure on what they regard as less important items. They are strongly driven by branding, but are reluctant to pay excessive prices even for the best known names. Importantly they also take personal market research very seriously and often conduct Internet searches for information on products before purchase (Atsomon, Dixit, Magni and St. Maurice, 2010).

Given the complexities of these changes it is difficult to offer a comprehensive overview of consumption and leisure in China. Consequently, in what follows I look to identify four broad areas of interest that are important for understanding consumption in contemporary China. First, because in many ways it relates to the mediation of all the others, I will consider briefly key developments in media and technology and how they have shaped consumer possibilities in the country. I will then discuss the relationship between consumption and leisure, modernity and postmodernity with a particular emphasis on urban contexts. These urban contexts have also become primary locations for the consumption of social class, particularly the middle class, in China and this will be the focus of the following section. Finally, we will consider how all of these developments may relate to questions of political legitimacy in China as it undergoes dramatic social and economic change.

Media, Technology, Leisure and Consumption

Leisure and consumption in China are highly mediated and the role of media in Chinese consumption has expanded dramatically over the last two decades.

In the early reform era, the media's principal consumption-related role was through the advertising that it carried. In the 1980s editorial content on television, radio and in newspapers was still relatively politicised but the amount of advertising increased rapidly promoting consumption of everything from television sets to restaurants (Zhao, 1998; Latham, 2001). However, over the following decade the transformation of China's media landscape saw the media's role in promoting and facilitating consumption and leisure practices expand and diversify considerably. Consumption in itself became a focus of media content (see e.g., Latham, 2006b) with television and radio programmes offering consumer information and advice and newspapers regularly carrying articles on and printing special supplements related to cars, housing, home furnishings, fashion, electronic goods and leisure and entertainment services. At the same time, as the number of television channels proliferated there emerged a new consumer space on television in the form of shopping channels and programming.

However, the role of the media in consumption is not simply to promote awareness of consumer goods. The media and new technologies now have a more complex relationship to consumption. To begin with, the media are themselves also objects of consumption and constitute some of China's most popular leisure activities. Television viewing in particular is the country's favourite national pastime with more than a billion people watching television on a regular basis. Official figures put the size of the national audience at around 1.16 billion, that is around 96% of the population enjoy television coverage (SARFT, 2008). Newspapers, magazines and books are also very popular. Chinese people are avid newspaper readers with more than a quarter of the World Association of Newspapers and Journalists' Association's top 100 list of the world's daily newspapers in 2010 being Chinese with the *Reference News (cankao xiaoxi)* ranked sixth and the official *People's Daily* ranked tenth globally, even if the latter is not a good indication of popular reading.[2] Around 100 million newspapers are sold daily in China, with most of those being local

---

[2] *The People's Daily* has for decades been seen as the official voice of the Chinese government and is perhaps the best known Chinese newspaper overseas. However, its high circulation figures in China reflect compulsory institutional subscriptions rather than individual purchases. Indeed, it is virtually impossible to buy the newspaper on the streets of most Chinese cities. It is the first choice newspaper of very few Chinese readers. It is also worth noting that the Chinese newspaper market is highly localised with few titles finding popularity outside their region of publication. That has not stopped some more progressive titles, largely from Guangdong Province, becoming household names around the country (e.g., the *Southern Weekend, Southern Metropolitan News, Beijing Youth News* etc.).

newspapers. Media technologies also constitute another important area of consumption, with television sets, radios, DVD players, mobile phones and computers all among the best selling consumer items in China today.

In recent years, however, new media technologies have transformed consumption in China in other ways. The Internet has opened up new worlds of consumption with online gaming, for instance, a multi-billion dollar industry in China. E-commerce is becoming an increasingly important sector. Official figures from the China Internet Network Information Centre (CNNIC) put the number of Internet users in China at the end of June 2010 as 420 million of whom 142 million, or 33.8%, engage or have engaged in online commerce of some kind (CNNIC, 2010). According to the CNNIC 30.5% of Internet users paid for goods online over the first half of 2010, representing a strong growth in confidence in the Internet as a mode of consumption. What is more, the Internet has become an increasingly important source of consumer information. A recent business report on Chinese consumer habits found that on average 25% of mainland Chinese shoppers said that they never bought a product without first checking the Internet and for expensive items this figure could rise to as much as 45% (Atsmon, Dixit, Magni and St-Maurice, 2010). Levels of trust of the Internet as a source of consumer information are also relatively high compared to other countries.

However, the Internet is not the only new technology that has facilitated the transformation of Chinese consumption. In 2010, there were more than 700 million mobile phone users in China making them far more widely used than computers. Indeed, there were 277 million Internet users accessing the web using their mobile phones (CNNIC, 2010) thus further facilitating access to online consumer information and enabling online purchases while on the move. Mobile phone users regularly receive text message advertising for a wide range of goods and services from restaurants to housing developments and they have transformed social habits in relation to food and entertainment consumption over the last decade. As in other parts of the world, arrangements to meet in restaurants, bars, discos or cinemas are now invariably made using mobile phones — texting in particular — rather than more traditional face-to-face modes of communication.

The digital age has also seen the arrival of public space television in shopping malls, lift lobbies, in taxis, buses, trains and on large screen displays in streets and squares in China's large cities. This has opened up new possibilities for both television consumption — with special short item programming being developed for underground train systems and buses for instance — and advertisers, while also transforming the experience of urban spaces. Media accompany people everywhere in China's cities and have become an inextricable feature of leisure and consumption practices. Media also play key roles in linking Chinese consumption to notions of modernity and postmodernity as we shall see below (Wong and McDonogh, 2001).

Urban Leisure, Consumption, Modernity and Postmodernity

Since at least the first half of the twentieth century, consumption in China has been associated with notions of modernity. At that time it was often foreign imported products and technologies that became markers of modernity, particularly in cities like Shanghai and the other Treaty Ports where the foreign presence and influence was strong. In Shanghai, considered China's most modern city in the early twentieth century, the consumption of everyday items such as calendars or magazines could become indicators of Chinese modernities. Calendars, for instance, started to display both the conventional Chinese lunar calendar and the western solar calendar together, indicating the shifting standards of measurement of time in modern Shanghai (Lee, 1999, 2000). Similarly, going to the cinema could be a way of not only being entertained but actually living a sense of modernity through the spaces of Shanghai's sometimes highly luxurious and architecturally exuberant cinema spaces (Zhang, 2004) or as part of the spectacle of visual consumption itself (Pang, 2007, see also Dong and Goldstein, 2006).

However, cities were not only considered the epitome of the modern in the early twentieth century. Such associations have continued to the present day in one form or another, even if during the Mao period political philosophy also designated the countryside as a key site of modernising potential (Tang, 1996; Ma and Hanten, 1986).[3] In contemporary China, the cities link leisure, consumption and modernity in key ways. Cities are the primary sites of leisure and consumption — they are where the latest consumer goods arrive first and where people from the countryside look to see what the latest technologies, fashions and trends are and where Chinese people find the greatest choice of leisure and entertainment opportunities from bowling alleys (Wang, 2000) and golf driving ranges to night clubs, karaoke centres

---

[3] In the case of the Great Leap Forward starting in 1959, this was with some disastrous consequences. Farmers, distracted by the political imperatives of the time, neglected their agricultural tasks in order to build ad hoc iron foundries that often produced iron that was unusable, while also denuding the local forests and hillsides for fuel to fire the furnaces. These moves contributed greatly to the devastating famines that took the lives of tens of millions of Chinese in the early 1960s.

and restaurants offering a large selection of both foreign and diverse regional Chinese cuisines (Klein, 2006). With generally wealthier populations and a massive array of consumption possibilities China's cities have become the most evident and up-to-date places for consumerism of all kinds to thrive. The association of cities with the consumption of the latest goods and services also links those locations to modernity. By buying the latest electronic goods and gadgets, the latest home furnishings, the most recent fashions or the newest model of car, Chinese consumers, in a time-honoured fashion, establish themselves in one or other of China's contemporary modernitities.[4]

Consumption has also therefore played a part in redefining scholarly understandings of Chinese modernities. Until relatively recently, modernity in China scholarship was principally associated with the large political movements that shaped Chinese history in the late nineteenth and then twentieth Centuries. These have importantly included the ideas of the late nineteenth Century reformers such as Liang Qichao who sought to modernise the Chinese imperial system, Sun Yatsen's revolutionary visions for a Chinese republic and the nationalist movements that evolved from them, the May 4 Movement and its efforts at cultural reform and modernization, Chinese communism, Mao's utopianism or Deng Xiaoping's economic reform with the so-called four modernizations.[5] All of these are vital for understanding China's relationship with emerging modernities and their associated visions over the last century, but more recent interest in consumption has actually shifted the focus of some of the debate onto everyday practices and the way that notions of modernity are lived through the often rather mundane encounters and experiences of ordinary people in their everyday lives.

For instance, Leo Ou-fan Lee (1999, 2000), although principally writing of the 1930s in Shanghai, has nonetheless suggested an approach to modernity that resonates with the emphasis on the everyday in more contemporarily focused scholarship (e.g., Tang, 1996; Dutton, 1998; Dong and Goldstein, 2006; Rofel, 1990; Martin and Heinrich, 2006). Lee sees modernity as a product of the commodified culture of consumption that changed the semiotics of everyday practices at the popular level. He attempts to set out an alternative to the conventional approaches to Chinese modernity that have forefronted the importance of the communist party, by focusing on business,

---

[4] In a country as large and diverse as China with countless divergent contemporary social realities and personal histories of modernity, it is more appropriate to talk of Chinese "modernities" rather than any singular modernity (see e.g., Rofel, 1990).

[5] The four modernizations pointed to the modernization of the four key sectors of the economy, industry, the military and science and technology.

rather than politics, on ordinary people's desires for a good life rather than a just society and focusing on the transformative capacity of private enterprise rather than collective action. As Yeh Wen-Hsin summarises this approach, "modernity came into being not by the committed break with the past effected by a handful of the awakened mobilizing themselves for revolutionary politics, but as the sum total of the daily practices by ordinary people going about their business as publishers, readers, advertisers, consumers, innovators, entrepreneurs etc." (Yeh, 2000, p. 7) Of course both of these approaches — that focused on grand politics and that focused on the everyday practices of ordinary people — are important and have their role to play in our understandings of Chinese modernities. However, what is significant here is the way that such alternative approaches refocus attention on practices of leisure and consumption in people's everyday lives as a way to understand not just how modernity has been conceptualised and ideologised, but also how it has been lived and experienced at a more mundane, though equally important level.

However, over the last couple of decades the focus on modernity in China has also been accompanied by debates over whether or not China should be considered not so much modern as postmodern (see e.g., Dirlik and Zhang, 1997; Jameson, 1994; Liu, 1997) and within these debates it is practices of leisure and consumption that often come to the fore as ways in which such a postmodern condition may be identified. Some scholars have argued that China is only just entering modernity and still has many parts of the countryside that have yet to arrive even there. Consequently, they argue, to talk of postmodernity, assuming it has to follow modernity, is folly (e.g., Zhao, 1995; Xu, 1995). However, on the other side of the argument there are broadly speaking two ways that the proposition can be argued. One is to look for evidence in China of what have been taken as markers of postmodernity elsewhere such as pastiche, nostalgia, simulacra or hyperreality and the collapse of grand narratives (see e.g., Jameson, 1991; Harvey, 1990; Lyotard, 1984; Poster, 1988). Leisure and consumption provide a range of such examples, from nostalgic Cultural Revolution-themed restaurants also conceivable as simulacra, through the reinvention of Confucius and the collapse of Maoism to the Chairman's reinvention as a cultural icon for mass consumption (see e.g., Barme, 1999). However, giving credit to both sides of the argument, Dirlik and Zhang (1997) prefer an alternative way to consider China postmodern. That is through the radical nature of the disjunctures and contradictions that constitute contemporary Chinese society with highly mobile, electronically connected youths in the cities, for instance, contrasting with almost medieval poverty in the poorer and more remote parts of the countryside. For Dirlik and Zhang it is the very juxtaposition of elements of unchanging traditionality alongside examples of the modern or what some would call postmodern that for them is evidence of China's condition of post-modernity.

This understanding of postmodernity also shifts attention onto the diverse and fragmentary nature of China's contemporary social realities, with huge disparities of outlook, experience and status evident everywhere on the basis of age, gender, wealth, geographical location, household registration (urban or rural), education, class and much more. Consumption, as we consider next, is a major marker of many of these differences (see also e.g., Latham, 2006a; Evans, 2006).

Consumption, Class and China's New Social Realities

Since the early days of economic reform in the 1980s when Chinese people first found themselves with access to a widening range of consumer goods, consumption has operated as a marker of social status. Consumer items also played a role in supporting gender divisions (Robinson, 1985). In those days, young people's marriage prospects could be significantly influenced by their ability to offer into the marriage deal bicycles, washing machines, furniture, television sets and other household items. Over the subsequent decades the range of desirable products has expanded enormously to include among other items, VHS and then VCD and DVD players, mobile phones, computers, motorbikes and later in the 2000s even cars or houses. However, in the early years of reform, the aspiration to own prestigious consumer items was relatively homogenous reflecting the still relatively small degrees of social differentiation by wealth at the time. The very notion of the nationally recognised "four goods" — that is a color television set, a stereo cassette player, a washing machine and a refrigerator — which Chinese people aspired to own in the 1980s, is a clear illustration of this relative homogeneity. However, over the last decade China has seen consumption take on new forms of social significance and become one of the key markers of social stratification in contemporary China as the range of goods and services available has grown to such an extent while the levels of social inequality have increased enormously.

There are huge differences in the lifestyle, attitudes and experiences of Chinese people of different ages and generations, from the countryside or the cities, from the economically developed or less developed parts of the country, from the east or the west of the country and for men and women. In addition to all of these differences Chinese society has also become more highly stratified ranging from the poorest peasants or manual migrant workers at one end of the scale through to the multi-billionaire business people at the other end with a wide spread of people in between. Such wealth differentials are clearly marked by consumer habits and capabilities with consumption having become widely associated with the country's middle classes on the one hand and the super rich on the other. The wider range of products available and the ever widening gaps between both the cheapest and most expensive of these products along with changing relative incomes and wealth have all contributed to making consumption an ever more visible and widely recognized indication of social status. Most notably, consumption is linked to the identification of China's burgeoning middle class (see e.g., Zhang, 2008; Anagnost, 2008; Hanser, 2008; Lin, 2006).[6] Li Zhang (2008) has investigated the emergence of China's middle class in Kunming in southwest China where she found a host of ambiguities and uncertainties about just what constituted being middle class. Luigi Tomba (2004) echoes this observation in his own investigation of the relationship between housing and class in Beijing. Noting that "class" no longer carries the political certainties that it once had (see also Anagnost, 2008; Zhang, 2008), he argues that:

> Although these groups [the salaried middle classes] might appear amorphous and lack the cohesiveness required by the traditional definitions of class, they appear increasingly to shape their status around a new set of collective interests, especially in their modes of consumption and access to resources. (Tomba, 2004, p. 4)

China's strata of middle-income households comprises a diverse range of people ranging from wealthy peasants through to university professors or entrepreneurs. These people may have very little in common in terms of social backgrounds and outlooks, but as public discussion of the middle classes has burgeoned, so too has the desire among such people to be designated part of them. In such a context Zhang identifies consumption — which ranges from the purchase of apartments through to clothes, food and leisure or educational services — as one of the clearest ways that people could identify themselves with notions of middle-classness:

---

[6] In Chinese the term used for "class" in this instance is *jieceng*, or "strata", to differentiate it from *jieji*, class, which brings with it heavy historical and political baggage in China (see Anagnost, 2008; Zhang, 2008). I use the term "middle class" here due to its relative familiarity to readers and the fact that in this particular discussion the distinction between "class" and "strata" is not of great relevance.

"The ability to consume the right kinds of things is taken not only as the measure of one's prestige (*zunrong*) and "face" (*mianzi*) but also as an indication of whether one deserves membership in a particular community. If one's consumption practices are not compatible with the kind of housing or community in which one lives, one would be seen as "out of place". Such social pressure... is embedded in the everyday cultural milieu." (2008, p. 35)

In this sense consumption becomes performative in two ways. First, it is through the act of consumption itself, that Chinese people identify themselves with particular social groupings.[7] Anagnost also attributes such performativity to the scholarly and journalistic writing about consumption and class in contemporary China "as if mapping out the emerging categories of social difference could produce their emergence in fact" (2008, p. 508). China's middle classes are in a state of becoming in which actions are as important as labels (Zhang, 2008). Consequently, however, these acts of consumption are also performative in the sense that they are very often intended to be seen by others (cf. Goffman, 1959) — such consumption is often more conspicuous than discreet — while the media play a crucial role in identifying and promulgating ideas of what should be consumed in this process. As Anagnost put it: "mass-mediated forms of representation are anticipatory in the sense of a certain incitement to subjectivity." (2008, p. 507). The media — through journalism, television dramas, advertisements and much more — posit a range of socially stratified subjectivities with which Chinese people then identify themselves.

However, Chinese people find themselves differently placed in relation to these structures of identification through consumption. The media tend to highlight middle class and affluent consumption, but as Pun Ngai points out in relation to migrant women workers in Shenzhen, they too aspire to leisure consumption even if their primary relationship to the economy is through production (see also Yan Hairong, 2003, 2008; Sun, 2009). Pun explains that "rural migrants too display an eager desire to elevate their social status through the process of consumption" (2003, p. 484; see also Schein, 2001; Yan Yunxiang, 2000). Here she is making two points that require us to problematise the dominant representations of consumption that focus on the middle classes to the exclusion of others. First, she is pointing out that those of lower social strata are also both active and aspiring consumers (see also

---

[7] We might think of how we may do things with words as noted in speech act theory (cf. Austin, 1959) or performative notions of theatre and knowledge production (Ward, 1979; Fabian, 1990).

below) and they too are drawn into the public discourses of social distinction via consumption both of goods and leisure activities. Second, at the same time, however, Pun points out how strong these dominant discourses are in China in defining who is publicly deemed to be a "qualified consumer" (2003, p. 485). She tells an anecdote of some migrant workers (*dagongmei*) going to a theme park on their day off and being discriminated against because, despite their efforts to the contrary, they were still visibly distinguishable from the majority of wealthier, urban, middle class tourists at the park: "One's social location determines who is qualified to consume and who is not. Although the dagongmei are ready and eager to consume, they nonetheless encounter exclusion and humiliation in a myriad of little dramas occurring daily at newspaper stands, hair salons and on public buses" (2003, p. 485). Taking aim at those who have argued that consumption may be a "democratizing" force in contemporary China (see e.g., Davis, 2000), Pun therefore suggests that given such discrimination, any such democratization can only be seen as hallucinatory.

These examples only start to introduce some of the main ways that consumption and leisure activities relate to the demarcation and maintenance of social distinctions in China. There are many more that cannot be covered here. However, what these examples show is that there is more to this relationship than may at first meet the eye. In all cases, there are complexities and intricate details that demand recognition and attention — the middle classes consume to demonstrate their status, but just what that status — what we might call "middle-classness" — is may be ambiguous; or migrant workers may also consume even if the dominant discourses of the day exclude them from doing so in a way that undermines their own efforts at status display through consumption. We are also reminded that China's social fabric is increasingly complex, fragmentary and differentiated, something that as shall see in the next section has raised questions about the relationship between consumption, social stability and political legitimacy.

Consumption, Political Legitimacy and Time

Martin King Whyte recently argued that the notion of a "social volcano" in China, ready to erupt at any moment due to rising social and economic inequalities in the country, should be considered a "myth." Following a systematic nationwide survey of Chinese public attitudes towards social inequalities and distributive injustice, Whyte concludes that these arguments and expectations — that widespread social unrest could be just around the corner — are misplaced. He argues that among other factors, rising standards of living play a particularly important role in maintaining high levels of social satisfaction and political compliance, despite rising levels of social inequity. Indeed, Whyte concludes that "Chinese attitudes about current inequalities probably are more conducive to political stability than to instability" (Whyte, 2010, p. 197). These conclusions are reminiscent of other longer-running arguments in commentary on China — both scholarly and popular — that have linked consumption to political stability and the legitimacy of the Chinese Communist Party (CCP).

As consumption became an increasingly prominent feature of post-Mao China, and an ever more common focus of attention for China commentators, it also became embroiled ever more often in debates about the political legitimacy of the CCP. For instance, Ci Jiwei (1994) put forward the argument in the 1990s that the "hedonism" of consumption in the reform era should be contrasted with the utopianism of the Mao period. Yet, importantly, he sees these two characteristics of the two periods as inextricably linked. Ci suggested that hedonistic consumption in the post-Mao era helped fill the ideological void that accompanied the collapse of Maoism and all the political certainties that it appeared to offer — the fundamental defining importance of class struggle for all understandings of society and politics and the gradual progression towards a socialist utopia. Importantly, Ci argues that what we see with post-Mao hedonism, however, is the short-circuiting of the Maoist utopian timeline which had always promised the universal satisfaction of material needs some time in the more or less distant future. By contrast, the post-Mao reforms aimed at achieving such satisfaction in the here and now of contemporary China. This kind of argument contributes to an understanding of consumption as a "social palliative" (Latham, 2002). On such an understanding, Chinese consumption plays a key role in maintaining the legitimacy of the CCP since the ever greater satisfaction of material needs keeps Chinese peoples' minds away from questions of politics (see also e.g., Liu, 1997; Ci, 1994; Croll, 1994). As Tang Xiaobing has put it, "a direct function of the rising consumerism is to contain and dissolve the anxiety of everyday life, to translate collective concerns into consumer desires (Tang, 1996, p. 113). Liu Kang (1997) has put forward a similar argument that as the rhetorics and imagery of Maoist utopianism became ever more distanced from the everyday experiences of Chinese citizens, such that they "failed to provide a stabilizing and enduring point of reference" (1997, p. 120) for them to hold onto. For Liu, then, the social relevance of everyday life has come to be affirmed through the contemporary culture industries and the rise of commercial popular culture (Liu, 1997, p. 120).

More recent versions of such arguments also appeared with the global economic crisis which saw many commentators in 2008 asking whether the effects of the global economic downturn for the Chinese economy would be greater unemployment, financial hardship, greater social unrest and a questioning of the legitimacy of the CCP (see e.g., Bristow, 2008). Certainly, economic development and the improvement in lifestyles that this has brought for hundreds of millions of Chinese people over the last three decades has played an important role in nurturing support — even if sometimes reluctant — for the CCP. Many Chinese people do look at their "freedom to consume" (McGregor, 2010) and their increasing ability to do so over the last thirty years, as important reasons for accepting the current political regime. With Chinese modern history littered with extended periods of great social and political turmoil, social unrest, warfare, famine, uncertainty and tragedy it is not surprising that the legitimacy of the regime that has managed to bring about three decades of general social stability, unerring economic growth and increasing living standards has not been widely questioned by the general populace. However, it is important not to oversimplify the situation by equating consumption with political legitimacy. The two are connected, but there are many other factors in play that should not be overlooked.

First of all, although consumption, particularly conspicuous consumption, is the more eye-catching and visible feature of economic prosperity that people see, it should not be detached from that economic prosperity as a whole. It is not only the consumption itself that brings individuals and families satisfaction and peace of mind, it is also their greater earning power, their better jobs, their rising disposable income and their ability to see a horizon populated with all kinds of possibilities that simply did not exist a relatively short time ago in China. Widespread consumption is not possible without broader economic wealth and stability. However, what is important in maintaining party legitimacy is not only the ability to satisfy material needs increasingly comfortably, but also a range of historical and political factors that encourage political tolerance and compliance and discourage dissidence and unrest.[8] As Whyte points out, "Chinese socialism in the 1960s and 1970s produced a social order that was highly inequitable, in that individuals who acquired more training, worked harder, produced more output, and more innovations were not rewarded for their contributions, even while those most deft at demonstrating political loyalty might earn promotions" (Whyte, 2010,

---

[8] Although it is not the most important factor, this range if factors must also include the threat of violence, imprisonment and other state sanction on people who stand up against a regime that has clear and widely recognised limits to its toleration of political dissent.

pp. 193–4; see also, Shark, 1984). Whyte's contention based on his survey results is then that even if economic inequalities are greater today then they were in the past, they are somehow viewed as fairer because the benefits of the new system are seen to be more equitably available to all (2010, p. 194).

This reminds us of the important role that ideological factors play in maintaining party hegemony. Given the Communist Party's only limited tolerance of political dissidence and freedom of speech, the threat of state violence is always going to be a factor in maintaining its political control. However, it is not sufficient to focus simply on either state violence or material satisfaction as the props of party legitimacy. There is also a range of rhetorical and ideological devices through which the Party has maintained hegemonic dominance in an increasingly divided society. Indeed, the Party has turned social difference to its advantage in several ways. For instance, the important discourse of *suzhi* or human "quality", in contemporary China maintains an understanding of inequality that legitimizes Party intervention for the weaker in society (Anagnost, 1998).[9] Those without *suzhi* — usually the poor, rural-urban migrants and manual workers — are portrayed as both vulnerable (and in need of the Party's education and care) but also dangerous (and therefore in need of the Party's control). I have argued elsewhere (Latham, 2002) that the fear of chaos has also worked to support party legitimacy. The backdrop of social unrest and political violence of many kinds that constitutes China's twentieth century history is enough to make anyone think twice about pushing for the forceful overthrow of the regime and the CCP has used this sentiment to good political effect.

Consequently we can see that it is over-simplistic to say that Party legitimacy is due to the feel-good factor that derives from materialistic consumption. Rather, consumption and consumerism are if anything indexes of a broader economic wellbeing that should not be reduced to the ability and propensity to consume. Indeed, understanding the dynamics of Chinese consumerism and its relation to poltical legitimacy requires also appreciating the importance of aspiring consumers — those who may have limited ability to consume but nonetheless show the desire to do so — parsimonious consumers — some of the older generation who have lived through times of great scarcity or savers and investors for instance — and those whose primary relationship to the economy and consumer goods may be through production rather than consumption — the hundreds of millions of factory workers

---

[9] *Suzhi* is literally "quality" — the term covers a range of complex factors and is also used in various different ways beyond the scope of this discussion, but in brief it points to the educational level and social capital that people are able to command.

driving China's export-driven economic boom for instance. Let us consider each of these examples briefly in turn.

The aspiration to consume — the desire, one day, to have a car, an iPhone or a house for instance — does reflect a degree of confidence in both present and future stability, but as Ci Jiwei (1994) reminds us, such aspirations were actually at the heart of the Maoist utopian project and reflect continuity as much as change between the Maoist and post-Mao periods. What may be different in the reform era, compared to the late Mao period, is not so much the aspiration itself as the faith that the system will eventually be able to deliver. Importantly, however, here we see the inextricable relationship between consumption, political legitimacy and time. Mao's utopian vision and the aspirations of contemporary consumers both defer consumption into the future, highlighting the importance of understanding consumption not simply as hedonistic satisfaction in the present, but something micro-managed by individuals and families over extended periods of time.

An oversimplistic emphasis on rampant consumerism also overlooks the fact that many Chinese people actually have a greater propensity to save or to invest rather than to spend their new found wealth. In fact, investment is perhaps a stronger master trope for understanding Chinese people's attitudes towards money than that of conspicuous consumption. At various junctures from the late 1990s on, for instance, the Chinese authorities have actually had to find ways to stimulate consumption, not because people did not have the money to spend, but because they often envisaged greater benefits for themselves and their families if spending were somehow deferred into the future. Much Chinese spending by families and individuals should also be understood with reference to investment rather than consumption. Consider, for instance, the massive boom in spending on education in recent years (see e.g., Lin, 2006; Kipnis, 2008). Both rural and urban families across both poorer and middle strata in society often consider expenditure on their children's education to be money invested in the future both of the child in question and of the family as a whole. In recent years, in the large cities, there has also been a boom in expenditure on an array of training and self-improvement opportunities ranging from language learning to neuro-linguistic programming (NLP). These forms of consumption again involve appreciation of a longer timescale and cycle of expenditure and return that defy simplistic understandings of material satisfaction.

Not everyone in China commands great spending power, however. Indeed, there are many workers in Chinese factories who spend the vast majority of their waking hours involved in production rather than consumption. Rural to urban migrant factory workers for example are likely to be saving to send money back to the countryside or to invest in future consumption back home — eventually building a village house for instance. Many factory workers live in dormitories provided by their employers, eat food from a works canteen and possibly even wear work overalls for much of their time. For these workers, even if they are also occasional consumers, their primary relation to the economy and to consumer goods is through production (cf. McRobbie, 1997). These kinds of factory workers also span the three groups we are discussing here: as well as playing a key role in production, they are often aspiring consumers trying to save for some kind of consumption in the future — such as a house — which will also be seen as an investment.

These examples are not intended to represent iron-clad categories of consumers. Nor are they in any way a comprehensive summary of Chinese consumer types. In fact, most consumers will demonstrate a range of different relationships to consumption as they go through their daily lives. However, what these examples do show is the need to treat consumption not as a single category of economic practice, but rather as a complex array of diverse and even contradictory or overlapping practices with important social and political as well as economic implications. They warn us about oversimplifying the relationship between consumption and political legitimacy and draw our attention to the importance of time in understanding these complex consumer practices.

Conclusion: The Future of Leisure and Consumption in China

China's leisure and consumption sectors have matured enormously over the last three decades. The country has seen its consumers move from their first excited but tentative steps into a state-capitalist consumer society thirty years ago, to being increasingly wise, discriminating, astute and calculating consumers as they enter the second decade of the third millennium. From this vantage point it is clear that the certainty that is China's consumer society is here for the long term. It is not going to disappear or retreat in the foreseeable future. On the contrary in fact, the expectation now must be that the sophistication of urban consumption in the most developed cities will increasingly find its way into the more remote and economically less developed parts of the country even if the gap between the two does not look likely to reduce in the near future and urban consumption will continue to develop at a considerable rate. However, Chinese consumers everywhere are likely to become increasingly sophisticated in their choices, their planning and the personal management of their consumption and leisure activities.

Apart from general economic growth some of the key factors that will drive further consumption include: the effects of new technologies, the development of personal banking and credit facilities, the ratio between rising incomes and rising prices, and the expansion of retail networks ever further into the Chinese countryside and lower level towns or cities. Technologies are fundamental not only for providing new consumer goods for people to buy, but also for the way that they facilitate consumption and open up new consumer possibilities. The Internet is becoming an increasingly important site for many kinds of consumption from book purchases to online gaming and the acquisition of virtual goods. However, mobile phone technologies will be even more important once mobile shopping platforms are better developed and more widely accessible through third generation (3G) mobile networks. Related to technologies are also banking services. As credit and debit cards become increasingly popular and available across China, so consumption will become easier for ordinary people. Online payment has grown rapidly in popularity over recent years, displacing payment on delivery as the most popular form of payment for goods purchased online. With the majority of consumer purchases in China still made in cash, the future for Chinese consumers will increasingly involve banks, banking and credit facilities.

With the economy continuing to grow at around 8% per annum, even in times of global economic crisis, it is a fair assumption that household incomes in China will continue to rise. However, the degree to which this stimulates even more consumption will depend at least in part on how fast prices may rise at the same time. In recent years there has been a lot of pressure on key food staples such as grains and oil pushing up commodity prices worldwide. China is not immune to these pressures. Meanwhile the cost of many other raw materials has also been rising while Chinese workers are demanding ever better working and living conditions while they work to supply global consumer markets. This combination, especially while global economic uncertainty continues, is likely to make Chinese consumers more cautious over the coming years. As we have seen, more disposable income does not necessarily lead to greater leisure consumption or the purchase of consumer items. In fact, as Chinese people become wealthier, they are likely to spend more on various kinds of investments for the future for themselves and their families including education, training, savings, property and status display. Two things, however, are certain: China will remain and continue to develop as the world's largest consumer society; and scholarly understanding of how this is happening will have to become increasingly nuanced and sophisticated to keep pace with the increasing nuance and sophistication of Chinese consumers themselves.

References

Anagnost, A. (2008) From "class" to "social strata": Grasping the social totality in reform era China. *Third World Quarterly*, 29(3), 497–519.

Atsomon, D., M. and St. Maurice (2010) China's new pragmatic consumers. *McKinsey Quarterly*, October 2010. Retrieved from http://www.mckinseyquarterly.com/Marketing/Sales_Distribution/Chinas_new_pragmatic_consumers_2683?gp=1

Barme, G. R. (1999) *In the red: On contemporary Chinese culture*. New York: Columbia University Press.

Bristow, M. (2008) China fears grow over job losses. Retrieved from http://news.bbc.co.uk/2/hi/asia-pacific/7739245.stm

Chao, L. and R. H. Myers (1998) China's consumer revolution: The 1990s and beyond. *Journal of Contemporary China*, 7(18), 351–368.

Chen, N. N., C. D. Clark, S. Gottschang and L. Jeffrey (Eds.) (2001) *China urban*. Durham, NC: Duke University Press.

Ci J. (1994) *Dialectic of the Chinese revolution: From utopianism to hedonism*. Stanford, California.: Stanford University Press.

CNNIC (2010) *Zhongguo hulian wangluo fazhan zhuangkuang tongji baogao* (Report on the development and current situation of the internet in China, July 2010). Beijing: CNNIC.

Croll, E. (1994) *From heaven to earth: Images and experiences of development in China*. London: Routledge, 1994.

Davis, D. S. (1989) My mother's home. In P. Link, R. Madsen and P.G. Pickowicz (Eds.), *Unofficial China: Popular culture and thought in the People's Republic*. Boulder: Westview Press.

Davis, D. S. (2000) Introduction. In D. S. Davis (Ed.). *The consumer revolution in urban China*. Berkeley: University of California Press.

Davis, D. S. (2002) When a house becomes his home. In P. Link, R. P. Madsen and P. G. Pickowicz (Eds.), *Popular China: Unofficial culture in a globalizing society*. Lanham: Rowman & Littlefield Publishers, Inc.

Davis, D. S. (Ed.) (2000) *The consumer revolution in urban China*. Berkeley: University of California Press.

Davis, D. S. and S. Harrell (Eds.) (1993) *Chinese families in the post-Mao era*. Berkeley: University of California Press.

Davis, D. S., R. Kraus, B. Naughton and E. J. Perry (1995) *Urban spaces in contemporary China: The potential for autonomy and community in post-Mao China*. Woodrow Wilson Center Series. Cambridge: Cambridge University Press.

Davis, D. S. and E. Vogel (1990) *Chinese society on the eve of Tiananmen: The impact of reform*. Cambridge, MA: Harvard University Press.

Dirlik, A. and X. Zhang (1997) Introduction: Postmodernism and China. *Boundary 2*, 24(3), 1–18.

Dong, M. Y. and J. L. Goldstein (Eds.) (2006) *Everyday modernity in China*. Seattle: University of Washington Press.

Dutton, M. (1998) *Streetlife China*. Cambridge: Cambridge University Press.

Evans, H. (2006) Fashions and feminine consumption. In K. Latham, S. Thompson, and J. Klein (Eds.), *Consuming China: Approaches to cultural change in contemporary China*. London: RoutledgeCurzon.

Giroir, G. (2007) Spaces of leisure: gated golf communities in China. In F. Wu (Ed.), *China's emerging cities: The making of new urbanism*. London: Routledge.

Goffman, E. (1959) *The presentation of self in everyday life*. London: Penguin.

Hanser, A. (2008) *Service encounters: Class, gender, and the market for social distinction in urban China*. Stanford: Stanford University Press.

Harvey, D. (1990) *The condition of postmodernity: An enquiry into the origins of cultural change*. Oxford: Blackwell.

Huot, C. (2000) *China's new cultural scene: A handbook of changes*. Durham and London: Duke University Press.

Jameson, F. (1991) *Postmodernism: Or, the cultural logic of late capitalism*. London: Verso.

Jameson, F. (1994) Remapping Taipei. In N. Browne, P. G. Pickowicz, V. Sobchack (Eds.), *New Chinese cinemas: Forms, identities, politics*. Cambridge: Cambridge University Press.

Kipnis, A. (2006) Suzhi: A keywords approach. *The China Quarterly*, 186, 295–313.

Kipnis, A. (2007) Neoliberalism Reified: *Suzhi* discourse and tropes of neoliberalism in the People's Republic of China. *The Journal of the Royal Anthropological Institute*, 13(2), 383–400.

Kipnis, A. (2001) The distrubing educational discipline of "peasants". *The China Journal*, 46, 1–24.

Klein, J. (2006) Changing tastes in Guangzhou: Restaurant writings in the late 1990s. In K. Latham, S. Thompson and J. Klein (Eds.), *Consuming China: Approaches to cultural change in contemporary China*. London: RoutledgeCurzon.

Latham, K. (2001) Between markets and Mandarins: Journalists and the rhetorics of transition in southern China. In B. Moeran (Ed.), *Asian media productions* London: Curzon/ConsumAsian.

Latham, K. (2002) Rethinking Chinese consumption: Social palliatives and the rhetorics of transition in postsocialist China. In C. M. Hann (Ed.), *Postsocialism: Ideals, ideologies and practices in Eurasia*. London: Routledge.

Latham, K. (2006a) Introduction: Consumption and cultural change in contemporary China. In K. Latham, S. Thompson and J. Klein (Eds.), *Consuming*

China: Approaches to cultural change in contemporary China. London: RoutledgeCurzon.

Latham, K. (2006b) Powers of imagination: The role of the consumer in China's silent media revolution. In K. Latham, S. Thompson and J. Klein (Eds.), *Consuming China: Approaches to cultural change in contemporary China.* London: RoutledgeCurzon.

Latham, K. (2007) *Pop culture! China: Media, arts and lifestyle.* Santa Barbara, CA: ABC-Clio.

Lee, L. O.-F. (1999) Shanghai modern: Reflections on urban culture in China in the 1930s. *Public Culture*, 11(1), 75–108.

Lee, L. O.-F. (2000) *Shanghai modern: The flowering of a new urban culture in China, 1930–1945.* Cambridge, MA: Harvard University Press.

Li, C. (1998) *China: The consumer revolution.* Singapore: John Wiley and Sons.

Lin, J. (2006) Educational stratification and the new middle class. In G. A. Postiglione (Ed.), *Education and social change in China: Inequality in a market economy.* Armonk, New York: ME Sharpe.

Liu, K. (1997) Popular culture and the culture of the masses in contemporary China. *Boundary 2*, 24(3), 1–18.

Lyotard, J.-F. (1984) *The postmodern condition: A report on knowledge.* Trans. G. Bennington and B. Massumi, foreword by F. Jameson. Manchester: Manchester University Press.

Ma, L. and E. Hanten (1986) Introduction. In L. Ma and E. Hanten (Eds.), *Urban development in modern China.* Boulder: Westveiw Press.

Martin, F. and L. Heinrich (eds.) (2006) *Embodied modernities: Corporeality, representation and Chinese cultures.* Honolulu: University of Hawai'i Press.

McGregor, R. (2010) The politics of Chinese consumption. Retrieved from http://blogs.ft.com/beyond-brics/2010/08/26/hey-bric-spender-the-politics-of-consumption-in-china/?utm_source=ft.com%Fbeyondbrics&utm_medium=twitter

McRobbie (1997) Bridging the gap: Feminism, fashion and consumption. *Feminist Review*, Consuming Cultures Special Issue 55, 73–89.

Murphy, R. (2004) Turning peasants into modern Chinese citizens: "Population quality", discourse, demographic transition and primary education. *The China Quarterly*, 177, 1–20.

Pang, L. (2007) *The distorting mirror: Visual modernity in China.* Honolulu: University of Hawaii Press.

Poster, M. (Ed.) (1988) *Jean Baudrillard: Selected writings.* Trans. M. Maclean, Oxford: Polity.

Pun, N. (2003) Subsumption or consumption? The phantom of consumer revolution in "globalizing" China. *Cultural Anthropology*, 18(4), 469–492.

Robinson, J. (1985) Of women and washing machines: Employment, housework and the reproduction of motherhood in socialist China. *China Quarterly*, 101, 32–57.

Rofel, L. (1999) *Other modernities: Gendered yearnings in China after socialism.* Berkeley: University of California Press.

State Administration for Radio Film and Television (SARFT) (2008) *Quanguo guangbo dianshi fugai qingkuang.* Retrieved from http://www.sarft.gov.cn/articles/2008/04/30/20080430174159330771.html

Schein, L. (2001) Urbanity, cosmopolitanism, consumption. In N. N. Chen, C. D. Clark, S. Gottscheng and L. Jeffrey (Eds.), *China urban.* Durham, NC: Duke University Press.

Sun, W. (2009). *Maid in China.* London: Routledge.

Tang, X. (1996) New urban culture and everyday-life anxiety in China. In X. Tang, and S. Stephen (Eds.), *In pursuit of contemporary East Asian culture.* Boulder: Westview Press.

Thornton, P. M. (2010) From liberating production to unleashing consumption: Mapping landscapes of power in Beijing. *Political Geography*, 29(2010), 302–310.

Tomba, L. (2004) Creating an urban middle class: Social engineering in Beijing. *The China Journal*, 51, 1–26.

Wang, G. (2000) Cultivating friendship through bowling in Shenzhen. In D. S. Davis (Ed.), *The consumer revolution in urban China.* Berkeley: University of California Press.

Wang, S. (1995) The politics of private time: Changing leisure patterns in urban China, In D. S. Davis, R. Kraus, B. Naughton and E. J. Perry (Eds.), *Urban spaces in contemporary China: The potential for autonomy and community in post-Mao China.* Cambridge: Cambridge University Press.

Wang, S. and C. Guo (2007) A tale of two cities: Restructuring of retail capital and production of new consumption spaces in Beijing and Shanghai. In W. Fulong (Ed.), *China's emerging cities: The making of new urbanism.* London: Routledge.

Watson, J. L. (Ed.) (1999) *Golden arches East: McDonald's in East Asia.* Stanford: Stanford University Press.

Whyte, M. K. (2010) *Myth of the social volcano: Perceptions of inequality and distributive injustice in contemporary China.* Stanford: Stanford University Press.

Wong, C. H. Y. and G. W. McDonogh (2001) The mediated metropolis: anthropological issues in cities and mass communication. *American Anthropologist*, 103(1), 96–111.

Wu, Y. (1999) *China's consumer revolution: The emerging patterns of wealth and expenditure.* Cheltenham: Edward Elgar Publishing Ltd.

Xu, B. (1995) Disan shijie piping zai dangjin zhongguo de chujing. (The situation of third world criticism in contemporary China) *Ershiyi shiji* (Twenty-First Century), 16–27.

Yan, H. (2003) Spectralization of the rural: Reinterpreting the labor mobility of rural young women in post-Mao China. *American Ethnologist*, 30(4), 578–596.

Yan, H. (2008) *New masters, new servants: Migration, development and women workers in China*. Durham, NC: Duke University Press.

Yan, Y. (1997) McDonald's in Beijing: The localization of Americana. In J. Watson (Ed.), *Golden arches east: McDonalds in East Asia*. Stanford, CA: University of Stanford Press.

Yan, Y. (2000) Of Hamburger and social space: Consuming McDonald's in Beijing. In D. S. Davis (Ed.), *The consumer revolution in urban China*. Berkeley: University of California Press.

Yeh, W. (Ed.) (2000) *Becoming Chinese: Passages to modernity and beyond*. Berkeley: University of California Press, 2000.

Zhang, L. (2008) Private homes, distinct lifestyles: Performing a new middle class. In L. Zhang, and A. Ong (Eds.), *Privatizing China: Socialism from afar*. Ithaca/London: Cornell University Press.

Zhao, Y. (Henry) (1995) "Houxue" yu Zhongguo xin baoshou zhuyi. ("Post-ism" and Chinese neoconservatism) *Ershiyi shiji* (Twenty-First Century), 4–15.

Zhang, Y. (2004) *Chinese national cinema*. London: Routledge.

Zhao, Y. (1998) *Media, market, and democracy in China: Between the party line and the bottom line*. Urbana/Chicago: University of Illinois Press.

15

INTERNET AND CIVIL SOCIETY

Guobin Yang

Barnard College, Columbia University

Abstract

In two articles published in 2003, I developed a preliminary assessment of the relationship between the internet and civil society in China. On the basis of analyses of data from the mid-1990s to the early 2000s, I made the following propositions:

- The internet influences civil society development by fostering public debate, enhancing civic organizing, and facilitating popular protest (Yang, 2003a).
- Civil society facilitates the development of the internet by providing the necessary social basis for communication and interaction (Yang, 2003a).
- The internet and civil society have an interdependent relationship and shape each other in a co-evolutionary trajectory (Yang, 2003b).

Almost ten years have passed. What has changed and what has not? In this chapter, I reassess the development of the internet and civil society in China in light of new developments since 2003. I argue that the internet and civil society have continued to follow their co-evolutionary path and that despite setbacks, both the internet and civil society have expanded and their influences have grown. Paradoxically, because of their growing social impact, both are also subject to new forms of political control and commercial manipulation.

Keywords: Internet; microblogging; civil society; commercialization.

The Internet Since 2003

The internet has continued to develop rapidly since 2003. In June 2003, there were 68 million internet users in China. This number jumped to 420 million in June 2010, meaning that close to one third of the Chinese population is now online. Of this 420 million, 73% are urban and 27% rural. Chinese internet users spent an average of 13 hours a week online in 2003. By 2010, they are spending about 20 hours a week. Figure 1 shows the growing numbers of internet users since 1997.

In 2003, the Chinese blogosphere was in its infancy. Although there were already many blog writers (about 230,000 in 2002), it was still a small percent of the internet users. By June 2009, 181 million internet users have blogs and about 63% of them report that they update their blogs often. Table 1 shows the growth of blogs in China.

Another important new development is the use of mobile telephony to access the internet. In December 2007, 50 million internet users in China (or 24% of the total number) went online via mobile phones. As of December 2009, 233 million, or 61% of the total, did so. In general, a higher percentage of the rural mobile phone users access the internet via mobile phones than urban mobile phone users, suggesting the importance of mobile telephony in bridging the digital divide.

Microblogging

The most important new development in recent years is undoubtedly microblogging. Although there were clones of Twitter in China such as

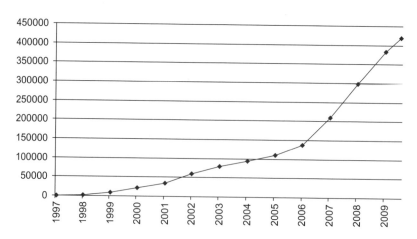

Figure 1. Internet users in China, 1997–2010, (in thousands)

Source: Author compilation based on CNNIC surveys. www.cnnic.net.cn

Table 1. Number of blogs, 2002–2009

	Total # of blogs	Active blogs
2002	510,000	230,000
2003	1,590,00	750,000
2004	4,590,00	1,840,000
2005	13,060,000	4,310,000
2006	34,220,000	9,240,000
2007	47,000,000	17,010,000
2008	162,000,000	87,320,000
2009	181,000,000	113,480,000

Source: CNNIC, 2008–2009 Research Report on the Blog Market and Blogging Behavior in China, July 2009.

Fanfou.com, which opened in May 2007 and was closed by the Chinese government two years later, it was not until Sina launched its microblogging service in August 2009 that microblogging began to catch on. Major commercial portal sites like Sohu, Netease, and Tencent, and the official People.com.cn all launched microblogging services one after another. One year after its launching, Sina's microblog had registered nine million users.

Microblogging limits the posting to 140 characters. It has sophisticated social networking functions. These technical features enable rapid real-time communication as well as strong networking. They enhance citizens' capacity to mobilize, organize, and publicize. Like other domestic internet services, microblogging services in China are censored for subversive political contents.[1] This limits the amount of critical political communication on Chinese microblogging sites, but cannot prevent it. A government regulation issued on September 25, 2005 prohibits the posting of eleven types of information online. They include standard items such as circulating information that violates laws or the constitution. They also include ambiguous types such as the spreading of rumors and "information that damages the credibility of state organs" and "information inciting illegal assemblies, association, demonstrations, protests, and gatherings that disturb social order."[2] These prohibitions apply to Chinese microblogs as well. Consequently, tweets that directly challenge the legitimacy of the party-state are censored. Nevertheless, protests and other contentious activities are still common on the microblogging sites.

---

[1] For a story on tightening control of micro-blogs in China, see Jonathan Ansfield, China tests new controls on Twitter-style services. *The New York Times*, July 16, 2010.

[2] www.cnnic.net.cn

An influential case concerns Fang Zhouzi's exposure of former Microsoft China executive Tang Jun. Tang claims in his autobiography that he had a PhD degree from the prestigious California Institute of Technology. In July 2010, Fang contended on his Sina microblog that Tang's degree was not from CalTech, but a Pacific Western University, which was basically a diploma mill selling academic credentials. Tang initially dismissed Fang's accusation but eventually backed down as Fang widened his accusations by exposing other false or dishonest information in Tang's published autobiography. The case made national news, bringing to national limelight the crisis of trust in Chinese society.[3]

Although Twitter is blocked in China, it has tens of thousands of active users inside China, who access it via circumvention technologies. Numerous Chinese "rights-defense" activists are on Twitter, forming a close activist network through Twitter's following-follower function. Popular names have followings in the tens of thousands. This network also includes many exiled and diasporic democracy activists, as well as other activists from Taiwan, Hong Kong, and other world regions. Although it already existed before the advent of micro-blogging services, the social networking functions of micro-blogging have given it unprecedented stickiness and salience. This large transborder[4] activist network generates an incessant slew of critical political discourse. Characterized by political opposition and subversion and the explicit goal of replacing the current one-party rule with a multi-party democratic political system, this radical discourse dominates the Chinese twittersphere.

Chinese Twitterers have mobilized several notable protests. In one case in July 2009, an anonymous and rather mystifying message titled "Jia Junpeng, your mother wants you to go home to eat" went viral in China's biggest online gaming community,[5] Baidu's "post bar" (tie ba) for World of Warcraft fans.[6] With just a title and no other content, this curious phrase

---

[3] As I discussed, Fang, the relentless muckraking writer and blogger, has been doing this for many years. On August 30, 2010, when he was on his way to his Beijing home, two men ambushed and attacked him, causing him slight injuries. His wife issued a statement on her micro-blog that Fang Zhouzi is never scared of exposing social evils.

[4] It is transborder in double senses. Activists in the network not only span geographical and territorial borders, but also cross the virtual borders of internet censorship erected through the Great Fire Wall by "scaling the wall."

[5] For my analysis of this case, see Guobin Yang, "The curious case of Jia Junpeng, or the power of symbolic appropriation in Chinese cyberspace." The China Beat Blog, October 20, 2009.

[6] "post bar" is Baidu's name for its online bulletin boards. Through this function, Baidu built a gigantic, multi-layered online community that becomes an important consumer base for its search engine. This online community is a contributing factor to the huge success of Baidu's search engine.

became a popular internet meme in Chinese cyberspace, which was then appropriated for political activism. Just one day before the Jia Junpeng posting appeared, blogger Guo Baofeng was detained by local police in the town of Mawei in Fujian province under the charge that he had used his blog to spread rumors about local police. At the police station, he secretly sent a Twitter message asking for urgent help: "I have been arrested by Mawei police, SOS." Upon receiving his tweet, his friends started campaigning for his release. Inspired by the Jia Junpeng posting, one blogger called on people to send postcards with the phrase "Guo Baofeng, your mother wants you to go home to eat" to the police station where Guo was detained. The address of the police station was posted online. This created a "postcard movement," which Guo himself believed led to his release.[7]

Despite its instant popularity, microblogging has not replaced other established internet services. The good old bulletin board systems (BBS) remain as popular as ever and still provide the most important platform for online protest. The majority of the new cases still happened in online communities supported by bulletin board systems. This is because BBS forums are more interactive and anonymous, whereas more and more bloggers and microbloggers are choosing to use their real names. In environments of anonymous interaction, users have a screen of protection from cyber police and hostile and militant fellow community members. More importantly, it is only when there are interactions, when users respond to and debate about postings, that the issue under discussion has a chance of becoming a contentious event. Another reason why BBS forums continue to ferment protest is history. If popular online communities have routinely generated protest and are known as places for such activities, then when people have concerns to bring to public attention, their first thought would be to go to these communities.[8] Habits once formed are hard to change.

Microblogging is thus not a replacement for other internet services. The trend is clearly the interfacing of multiple services, so that users may choose different ones for different purposes. The various application programming interfaces (API) easily link together different services, as for example, people can easily bundle their blogs on Sina.com with their microblog accounts so that each time a blog entry is posted, it is automatically announced on their microblog.

---

[7] Baofeng, G. (2009) How did I break out of the jail? August 11. Retrieved from http://amoiist. blogspot.com/2009/08/how-i-broke-jail.html

[8] Interview with a marketing executive of a major online community, July 9, 2010, Beijing.

Civil Society Since 2003

Civil society has experienced some ups and downs in this period due to changing political conditions, but growth is the general trend. The number and impact of civic associations continue to grow. Take environmental NGOs for example. In April 2001, there were about 184 student environmental organizations in China. In 2002, there were fewer than 100 non-student ENGOs (or about 73 according to one estimate, see Yang, 2005). By 2005, the number of grassroots ENGOs had doubled to more than 200 while student environmental associations exceeded 1,000 (All-China Environmental Protection Federation, 2006).

The space for public communication and discussion has expanded. Again, take environmental issues as an example. Public discussions about environmental issues have become more extensive and contentious, as evidenced in the debates surrounding dam-building on the Nu River and the "Respect Nature" debate in 2005. Debates about all sorts of other critical social issues not only fill cyberspace, but have also become important sources of information for mainstream mass media and government leaders. Communication scholar Min Jiang's work on authoritarian deliberation illuminates the diverse online spaces by differentiating four different types, which she calls central propaganda spaces, government-regulated commercial spaces, emergent civic spaces, and international deliberative spaces respectively (Jiang, 2010).

Third, related to the expansion of public space for communication, a citizens' rights protection movement has gained momentum (Kelly, 2006). All forms of citizen action, radical or moderate, has been happening, involving migrants, peasants, workers, and homeowners (see respectively Qiu, 2009; O'Brien and Li, 2006; Lee, 2007; Hsing, 2010; and Zhang, 2010). The struggles for citizen rights already started in the 1980s, but they have taken on new forms in the recent decade. This prompted the Chinese scholar Fan Yafeng (2005) to suggest that after 2003, citizenship struggles "went social." They became a general social phenomenon instead of being limited to small intellectual and activist circles.

Finally, related to the above development is the mainstreaming of a Chinese discourse on civil society. There were already intellectual discussions about civil society in China as early as in 1986 and this discourse became stronger in the late 1980s (Ma, 1994). In the aftermath of the suppression of the student movement, this discourse weakened until it began to resurface in the mid-1990s. Yet it is not until very recent years that civil society becomes a public discourse, as opposed to an intellectual discourse confined to scholarly debates. At the end of 2009, for example, several mainstream media channels published lists of "top ten" national news stories of the year related to civil society developments. This included the magazine Ban Yue Tan (Biweekly Review), sponsored by the Propaganda Department of the Chinese Communist Party, which included in its top ten stories the retraction of the policy about the installation of the Green Dam software due to the pressure of public opinion.[9]

The interactions between the internet and civil society have been sustained for well over a decade. The two are increasingly interfaced. It is no long possible to imagine Chinese citizens and civic groups expressing their opinions or organizing for action without using the internet. This suggests that a digital civil society is on the rise. In my earlier study of the internet and civil society, I identified three components of civil society, namely, civic organizations, popular resistance, and public spaces for communication (Yang, 2003a). To the extent that a digital civil society is in the making, it encompasses the large numbers of online communities, web-based social networks and loose organizations, as well as the active online presence of offline civic associations. In terms of civic spaces of communication, it consists of numerous BBS forums, blogs, microblogs, and online magazines. Internet-based protest is the third element.

Internet Events and National Crises

Earlier, I have emphasized their interactions in the context of political control and the development of an information technology industry, as well as how internet users creatively negotiate control (Yang, 2003a, 2003b). Developments since 2003 have brought to relief the significant impact of internet events and national crises in shaping the interactions between the internet and civil society.

Internet events, or *wangluo shijian* in Chinese, are contentious events linked to the use of the internet. They may be protest activities that happen mainly or purely online, often in response to offline events. Before 2003, there were already a number of influential internet events, such as nationalist protests in 1999 that happened on the "Strengthening the Nation Forum" and protests surrounding the death of a student in Peking University in 2000 (Yang, 2007). The role of these events in shaping civil society and online participation was evident in the earlier period. Yet in recent years, their frequency and impact have dramatically increased. Table 2 shows an abbreviated annotated list of major cases since 2003.

---

[9] See below for more discussions of the "Green Dam" case.

Table 2.   Selected internet events in China, 2004–2010

Year	Event
2004	Online petition to oppose Japan's bid for UN security council permanent member seat.
2004	Online protest against light sentencing of BMW driver who killed a farmer.
2004	Media campaign to oppose Nu River dam project.
2005	Online and offline anti-Japanese demonstrations.
2005	Online protest about Songhua River pollution.
2006	Online protest against closure of YTHT BBS of Beijing University.
2007	Online protest concerning use of abducted child labor in "black kilns" in Shanxi.
2007	Online mobilization of environmental demonstration against chemical factory project in the city of Xiamen.
2007	Zhou Zhenglong, a farmer in Shaanxi, claimed he sighted a South China tiger in the mountains of his hometown and local government agencies released photos of the tiger supposedly taken by Zhou. After an extended and intense debate, the tiger photos were exposed by netizens as forgeries.
2008	Anti-CNN campaign to expose Western media bias in coverage of Tibetan riots.
2009	Viral dissemination of internet meme and image "grass-mud horse" as parody of government control of internet.
2009	Deng Yujiao was hailed as a heroine as she stabbed to death an official who attempted to solicit sex.
2009	Ministry of Industry and Information Technology suspended filtering software project "Green Dam-Youth Escort" in response to online protest and international pressure.
2009	A mysterious posting "Jia Junpeng, you mother wants you to go home to eat" went viral. Jia Junpeng was appropriated as a political symbol by microbloggers.
2010	Google withdrawal from China triggered online protest about internet control in China.
2010	Workers made use of SMS and BBS in labor strikes.
2010	Fang Zhouzi exposed fake diplomas on his microblog, triggering national debates. Fang was physically attacked by two unknown men.

Source: Author's own compilation.

National crises refer to crisis situations caused by human intervention or natural disasters. In 2008, the hijacking of the Olympics torch relay in several countries in the buildup to the Beijing Olympics created moments of crisis and national anxiety. The disastrous earthquakes in Sichuan on May 12, 2008, which claimed nearly 70,000 lives, were another national crisis.

The Sichuan earthquakes were particularly notable for the use of the internet in citizen communication. A survey conducted by researchers at

Tsinghua University shows that in terms of information seeking for citizens, the internet was the most important channel during the earthquake, with television trailing behind as the second most important. With respect to *communication* among citizens, the instantaneous and interactive functions of internet network services such as online chatting and internet forums were the most important channels, while telephone ranks below these internet functions as the third most important channel.[10]

The internet also proved effective for mobilizing citizen action. On the day of the earthquake, Tianya.cn, a popular online community, launched an online fundraising project in partnership with four other portal sites and Jet Li's One Foundation. By noon, May 15, the project had raised RMB 24 million (US$3.5 million) for disaster relief, mostly from online individual donations. The day after the earthquake, several environmental and educational NGOs in Beijing initiated a "Green Ribbon" campaign, with members and volunteers fanning out in the streets for fundraising and blood drives. On the same day, 57 civic groups issued a joint statement calling for concerted disaster relief efforts among all NGOs. Fifty-one other groups jointly established an office in Chengdu to coordinate NGO relief activities.

Much of the civic organizing was done through web sites, mailing lists, blogs and online communities. For example, ngocn.org, a major information hub for Chinese NGOs, set up a special bulletin board for the NGO relief office in Chengdu to post announcements. The internet proved crucial for timely, extensive, and in-depth coverage. Large websites, both commercial and government-owned, set up special earthquake sections. Professional reporters and common citizens alike posted witness accounts in multimedia formats, with personal stories, images, digital videos of relief efforts filling cyberspace.

Internet events and national crises have shaped the co-evolution of the internet and civil society in many ways. They affirm the power of netizens and online public opinion by demonstrating it. They create new symbolic forms, new organizations, and new forms of collective action. For instance, citizen mobilization in the wake of the Sichuan earthquakes led to the establishment of civil society coalitions for disaster relief. The appropriation of the Jia Junpeng incident, which I discussed above, invented a "postcard" movement as a new form of collective action. Because of the "South China tiger event" involving a farmer named Zhou Zhenglong and his forged tiger photos, netizens created the new proverb "Zhenglong shooting a tiger" to refer to people who try to gain fame or profit by deception. The most ingenious invention is the symbol of the grass-mud horse, a mythical animal and a pun on a dirty

---

[10] http://academic.mediachina.net/article.php?id=5726

Chinese word, which netizens use to mock internet censorship in China. The image of the mythical horse has morphed into numerous versions, easily found online, and is often shown in an epic battle with river crabs, another pun and a symbol of internet censorship.[11] These new internet memes and symbols have not only become part of the cultural tool-kit for internet activists, but have entered daily language, a sign of their impact on contemporary culture more broadly.

Finally, internet events and national crises have enhanced the legitimacy of online protest and online public opinion. The establishment in 2008 of an "Media Opinion Monitoring Office" by People's Daily Online clearly recognizes that the internet can generate influential public opinion. Since July 2009, this office has published quarterly reports on local governments' capacity to respond to "internet mass incidents," an official euphemism for online protest. The first report lists ten incidents in the first half of 2009 and ranks local governments according to how well they responded to them. The rankings are based on six parameters: government responsiveness, transparency of information, government credibility, restoration of social order, dynamic responsiveness, and accountability of government officials. Based on the total points on the six parameters, the report assigns four color-coded rankings to the local governments. Blue means "response is appropriate," yellow means "needs improvement," orange indicates "clearly problematic," and red sounds a loud alarm meaning "serious and major problem." The municipal government of Shishou of Hubei province earned a "Red" warning for its poor handling of a riot in June 2009, which caused lots of negative publicity online.

Besides the rankings, the report contains expert analyses of the cases and ends with ten policy recommendations. These recommendations provide additional evidence of the government's recognition that internet protests have some degree of legitimacy and must be treated seriously. The report states that the large numbers of netizens have formed a new "pressure group" in China and that with multiple online channels, it is impossible not to let them talk. Therefore it is essential for government officials to be responsive to online opinion and handle it in a way that will not intensify social conflict or damage the image of the government. Publicizing information is a better approach than damming it.[12]

---

[11] Michael Wines, A dirty pun tweaks China's online censors. *The New York Times*, March 11, 2009.

[12] Media opinion monitoring office of People's Daily Online, "Rankings of Local Governments' Capacity to Respond to Internet Public Opinion in the First Half of 2009," July 23, 2009. http://yq.people.com.cn/zt/dz3/

The Evolution of the State's Internet Strategy

As the internet and Chinese civil society develop in their co-evolutionary trajectory, the state has not relaxed its control. The state has attempted both to tighten control and to adapt to the power of an incipient digital civil society. It has adopted a more proactive approach to the management of this contentious terrain.

The evolution of China's internet-control regime has spanned three stages (Yang, 2009). The first stage, from 1994 to 1999, focused on the regulation of network security, Internet service provision, and institutional restructuring. The second stage, from 2000 to 2002, was characterized by the expansion and refinement of control.

The third stage, from 2003 to the present, is the most proactive stage. In this period, guided by the 2004 CCP resolution on improving governance, the internet-control regime developed a comprehensive and coherent strategy for what it calls the "administration" of the internet. This strategy is described as a Chinese model of internet administration in the white paper on "The Internet in China" issued by the Information Office of the State Council on June 8, 2010: "China adheres to scientific and effective Internet administration by law, strives to improve an Internet administration system combining laws and regulations, administrative supervision, self-regulation, technical protection, public supervision and social education."[13] This is a policy translation of the principles set out in the CCP resolution on governance. Despite some of its controversial claims,[14] the white paper affords legitimacy to online public opinion by stating, "The authorities attach great importance to social conditions and public opinion as reflected on the Internet, which has become a bridge facilitating direct communication between the government and the public."[15]

This model supports a more proactive and more sophisticated approach to internet censorship and control. Aligned with China's soft power strategy

---

[13] http://www.china.org.cn/government/whitepaper/node_7093508.htm

[14] For two responses to the document, see Rebecca MacKinnon. China's internet white paper: Networked authoritarianism in action. RConversation, July 15, 2010. http://rconversation. blogs.com/rconversation/2010/06/chinas-internet-white-paper-networked-authoritarianism.html; and Monroe Price. The battle over Internet regulatory paradigms: An intensifying area for public diplomacy. Center for Public Diplomacy, August 3, 2010. http://uscpublicdiplomacy.org/index.php/newswire/cpdblog_detail/the_battle_over_internet_regulatory_paradigms_an_intensifying_area_for/

[15] *Ibid.*

in the international arena,[16] this internet strategy is now in full swing. One major new initiative is to stimulate the growth of official news web portals through the market mechanism. This is based on the understanding that a strong web presence of official news media will enhance the positive influence of party media. Although the Chinese government has all along encouraged official news media to go online, until recently, it has forbidden official news web sites to be listed in the stock market. The web sites of large news agencies like *People's Daily* and China Central Television (CCTV) are appendages of their parent media, with limited financial resources. There is no way they can rival the popularity and successes of commercial portal sites.[17] In May 2010, however, ten official news web sites, including those of *People's Daily* and CCTV, were reportedly approved for listing in the A-share market, marking the beginning of the marketization of official news portals.[18]

Meanwhile, other new initiatives have been launched to strengthen control. In one abortive attempt, the Ministry of Industry and Information Technology (MIIT) issued a directive on May 19, 2009 stating that beginning on July 1, all computers sold in China must be pre-installed with a filtering software called Green Dam-Youth Escort. The policy was supposedly designed to protect minors from pornography, yet it immediately set off fears and protests about broadening Internet surveillance. These fears were proven to be well founded, when computer experts cracked the code of the software and found that it was also programmed to filter politically sensitive terms.

Although MIIT suspended this initiative under domestic and international pressure, it was only a tactical concession. MIIT continued to roll out more policies aimed at strengthening control. In February 2010, it issued a directive requiring domain name service providers to verify domain name applicants' personal information and keep records of their ID cards.[19] This is consistent with the steps being taken to institute a real-name registration system for news web sites and major commercial portals.[20] If put in place, the real-name registration system will be another major initiative with adverse

[16] Zhang, X. (2009). From "foreign propaganda" to "international communication": China's promotion of soft power in the age of information and communication technologies. In Zhang, X. and Y. Zheng (Eds.) *China's Information and Communication Technology Revolution: Social Changes and State Responses*, pp. 103–120. London: Routledge.

[17] Internet with former chief editor of major official news web site, July 10, 2007.

[18] http://www.cb-h.com/news/wh/2010/63/106337HGI4FC2I6J29804.html

[19] http://www.cnnic.net.cn/html/Dir/2010/02/23/5785.htm

[20] Peter Foster. China to force internet users to register real names. Telegraph.co.uk. May 5, 2010. http://www.telegraph.co.uk/news/worldnews/asia/china/7681709/China-to-force-internet-users-to-register-real-names.html

effects on online political participation because of the loss of the protection of anonymity for Chinese netizens.

The proactive approach to internet control encourages practices that not only curtail online expression, but actively promote views in line with party policy. An example is the practice of "internet commentators" (*wangluo pinglun yuan*), which was introduced in 2004 to guide and influence online public opinion. Hired as volunteers or paid staff, internet commentators intervene in online discussions by writing responses to postings and joining the debates. Their mission is to covertly guide the direction of the debates in accordance with the principles laid down by the propaganda departments of the party. The guidance is covert because internet commentators do not sign into online forums as such. Rather, they post anonymously and supposedly earn fifty cents for each posting. Because of this deceptive role, they have earned themselves the derogatory name of "fifty-cent party."

The comprehensive internet strategy articulated in the white paper on "The Internet in China," if fully implemented, may affect Chinese digital civil society in two ways. On the surface, it offers more political opportunities for online activism because of its explicit acknowledgement of the legitimacy of online public opinion. Its emphasis on the strategic importance of the telecommunications industry for national economic development means that as a new industry, the internet will continue to grow. At the same time, the emphasis on a Chinese model of administration, on sovereignty and national security, and on law-based administration, means that the control of the internet will continue but in more subtle and sophisticated forms. There will be more efforts to generate "positive" public opinion by official news portals and more hidden ways of penetrating online spaces and activist networks. Together with the commercially motivated practices of "pushing hands," party-recruited internet commentators may neutralize the power of online activism by reducing the credibility of online information.

The Impact of Commercialization

In the early history of the internet in China, civil society use of the internet was ahead of commercial uses (Yang, 2003a). This is still the case today, although clearly, commercial uses have increased greatly. As Table 3 shows, many more people are shopping online than before 2003, even though use of the interactive functions has continued to increase as well.

The commercial use of the internet by consumers is a different matter from the profit-driven use of the internet by businesses. Internet businesses play a central role in promoting civic society use of the internet. The major

Table 3. Most frequently used network services in China (selected items, multiple options), June 2003–June 2010 (%)

	Total user	Email	BBS	Blogs	SNS	Online shopping
June 2003	68 m	91.8	22.6	N/A	N/A	11.7
December 2003	79.5 m	88.4	18.8	N/A	N/A	7.3
June 2008	253 m	62.6	38.8	42.3	N/A	25
December 2008	298 m	56.8	30.7	54.3	N/A	24.8
June 2009	338 m	55.4	30.4	53.8	N/A	26
December 2009	384 m	56.8	30.5	57.7	45.8	28.1
June 2010	420 m	56.4	31.5	55.1	50.1	33.8

Source: CNNIC survey reports: See <http://www.cnnic.net.cn>.

commercial portal sites like Sina, Netease, and Sohu all have large online communities that are alive with contentious activities. Some websites encourage contentious activities for the volumes of web traffic they bring. In this sense, these web sites are incubators of internet events (Yang, 2009).

In recent years, however, seeing the potentials of profit in internet events, some businesses have begun to use them for marketing purposes. A new commercial practice has appeared that specializes in manufacturing internet events. Known as "internet pushing hands" (wangluo tuishou), this practice may significantly harm the credibility of online information in the long run and thus undermine the power of the internet as a platform for citizen action.

Suppose a business company has a new product to market. It might hire an "internet pushing hand" agency to market it. The contractor will design a plan and hire internet users as "pushing hands." These people will write blogs or BBS postings crafted to provoke controversy in order to draw responses and enhance online interaction. Once the postings have generated enough attention online, mass media will cover the story. With mass media coverage, a public event is born and the pushing hands have successfully marketed the product.

There is money in this business. According to one report, each posting costs about fifty cents (similar to the amount paid to politically motivated "internet commentators"). If the posting is headlined in a major BBS forum, then the cost goes up to 600 to 1,000 RMB. Web traffic is crucial. If a posting gets 10,000 hits, it is a "hot posting" and it costs 100,000 RMB.[21] It is estimated that there are a thousand companies nationwide specializing in this business.[22]

---

[21] Ding Yiyi and Zhou Yuanying. Who is manipulating online public opinion?. *IT Weekly*, January 5, 2010.
[22] *Ibid.*

Business companies can also pay to block online information unfavorable to their image or their products. Baidu's entanglement in the tainted milk scandal at the end of 2008 is a case in point. In that year, it was discovered that the baby formula milk products manufactured by Sanlu were the likely cause of kidney damage in hundreds of children because harmful chemicals had been added into the formula to make it look more nutritious. The manufacturer Sanlu reportedly approached the Chinese search engine giant Baidu with a three million yuan (in RMB) price tag for Baidu to screen negative information about Sanlu.[23] Baidu refuted the allegations of any deals with Sanlu, but the case undoubtedly indicates the vulnerabilities of internet businesses to commercial interests.

Conclusion

This chapter has provided a reassessment of the development of the internet and civil society in China based on analyses of data since 2003. Evidence presented here suggests that the internet and civil society have followed the co-evolutionary trajectory that I initially described in 2003. Both have grown rapidly, with ever greater social and political impact. Yet the power of a wired citizenry and civil society has caused deeper concerns among the Chinese leadership. Consequently, the forms of governing and controlling the internet are refined. A more proactive internet strategy has been introduced, which also entails promoting the public appeal of the web sites of official news agencies. More invisible forms of control, such as the use of anonymous "internet commentators" to shape online opinion, have been devised.

In recent years, the commercial manipulation of the internet, as shown in my discussion of the commercial "pushing hands," is posing serious threats to the quality of online information. Commercially-motivated manipulation is no less serious a threat to the free and open use of the internet than political censorship. Indeed, it might be even more dangerous. News in the global media at least constantly reminds readers of new measures of political control. Yet commercial manipulation such as the practice of "pushing hands" often takes more hidden forms and is more deceptive.

The future of the internet thus appears more uncertain than before, as it becomes more intensely fought over by political power and commercial interests. Yet it would be too early to declare the end of the internet as we know it. If ordinary users have significantly shaped the forms of the internet

---

[23] Shai Oster and Loretta Chao. China arrests 2 in milk scandal as number of sick infants rises. *The Wall Street Journal*, September 16, 2008. http://online.wsj.com/article/SB12214706-1860735851.html

through their own participation, they will continue to do so. The logic of social production, where users play an important role as content producers, may function as a brake on pure manipulation. The practices of social inter-action, peer sharing, and distributed peer production have a mechanism of self-correction and knowledge aggregation. Most importantly, Chinese inter-net users are not passive consumers. From the very beginning, they have been actively engaged in debating and questioning the information they receive. They are both champions and critics of the internet. The future of the inter-net will also depend on whether and how they continue to participate in the making and remaking of the internet culture.

References

All-China Environmental Protection Federation (2006) Blue book on the conditions of environmental NGOs in China. Unpublished report.

Fan, Y. (2005) Weiquan zhengzhi lun [The politics of rights defence], *Zhongdao Forum* no. 4. Retrieved from http://www.blogchina.com/new/display/87613.html

Hsing, Y.-T. (2010) *The great urban transformation: Politics of land and property in China*. New York: Oxford University Press.

Jiang, M. (2010) Spaces of authoritarian deliberation: Online public deliberation in China. In J. Ethan Leib and H. Baogang (Eds.), *The search for deliberative democracy in China*, pp. 261–287. New York: Palgrave MacMillan.

Kelly, D. (2006) Citizen movements and China's public intellectuals in the hu-wen era. *Pacific Affairs*, 79(2), 183–204.

Lee, C. K. (2007) *Against the law: Labor protests in China's rustbelt and sunbelt*. Berkeley: University of California Press.

Ma, S.-Y. (1994) The Chinese discourse on civil society. *China Quarterly*, 137, 180–193.

O'Brien, K. and L. Lianjiang (2006) *Rightful resistance in rural China*. Cambridge, MA: Cambridge University Press.

Qiu, J. L. (2009) *Working-class network society: Communication technology and the information have-less in urban China*. Cambridge, MA: MIT Press.

Sun, L. (2003) *Duanlie: Ershishiji jiushi niandai yilai the Zhongguo shehui (Fractured: Chinese society since the 1990s)*. Beijing: *Shehui kexue wenxian chubanshe*.

Yang, G. (2002) Civil society in China: A dynamic field of study. *China Review International*, 9(1), 1–16.

Yang, G. (2003a) The internet and civil society in China: A preliminary assessment. *Journal of Contemporary China*, 12(36), 453–475.

Yang, G. (2003b) The co-evolution of the internet and civil society in China. *Asian Survey*, 43(3), 405–422.

Yang, G. (2003c) The internet and the rise of a transnational Chinese cultural sphere. *Media, Culture and Society,* 25(4), 469–490.

Yang, G. (2007) How do Chinese civic associations respond to the internet: Findings from a survey. *The China Quarterly,* 189, 122–143.

Yang, G. (2009) Of sympathy and play: Emotional mobilization in online collective action. *The Chinese Journal of Communication and Society,* 9, 39–66.

Yang, G. (2009) *The power of the internet in China: Citizen activism online.* New York: Columbia University Press.

Yang, G. (2009) The internet as cultural form: Technology and the human condition in China. *Knowledge, Technology and Policy,* Special Issue on Political Culture of Web 2.0 in Asia, 22(2), 109–115.

Zhang, L. (2010) *In search of paradise: Middle-class living in a Chinese metropolis.* Ithaca: Cornell University Press.

Zhao, Y. (2007) After mobile phones, what? Re-embedding the social in China's 'Digital Revolution.' *International Journal of Communication,* 1, 92–120.

INDEX